The Beginnings of

RUSSIAN

Industrialization

1800-1860

The Beginnings of
RUSSIAN
Industrialization
1800-1860

WILLIAM L. BLACKWELL

PRINCETON, NEW JERSEY
PRINCETON UNIVERSITY PRESS
1968

Acknowledgments

Research for this book has been done in libraries all over the world, and I would like to express my appreciation here to these institutions, which were at all times very cooperative: the New York Public Library; the Butler Library of Columbia University; the Library of Congress; the British Museum; the Bibliothèque Nationale, the libraries of the Institut d'Études slaves and of the École nationale des langues orientales vivantes in Paris; the Lenin State Library and the State Historical Library in Moscow; the Saltykov-Shchedrin Library in Leningrad; and the libraries and archives of the Pennsylvania Historical Society and the Maryland Historical Society. I am indebted to the last two organizations and to the Manuscript Division of the New York Public Library for permission to quote from unpublished materials in their collections; to Cyril E. Black for the use of unpublished articles and papers; and to the *Slavic Review* for allowing me to publish a version of my article, "The Old Believers and the Rise of Private Industrial Enterprise in Early Nineteenth-Century Moscow," which appeared in the September 1965, issue.

I also wish to acknowledge the support of New York University, which provided funds to pay for some of my research expenses. In addition I wish to express my thanks to my colleagues at New York University, Professors Edward Tannenbaum and Irwin Unger, for helpful criticism and discussion; to Mrs. Selma Chernigow Reiff for assistance with the notes; and to Mr. Nicholas Lupinin and Mr. Gennady Klimenko for help with the tables. This book and its author owe a particular debt to Professor Cyril E. Black of Princeton University, who first interested him, not only in Russian history, but in the history of modernization, to which this work may be considered a contribution.

A Glossary at the end of the book gives the meanings of many of the important Russian words which are italicized in the text. The Julian, or "old style" calendar, which was used in Russia until 1918, has been used throughout except in correspondence where both Gregorian and Julian dates were entered by the author. The transliteration system of the Library of Congress has been adhered to, by and large. Spellings of names which have passed into common English usage have been employed.

Contents

Part III. Private Industrial Enterprise

Part IV. Transportation

Contents

Part V. Technology

The Beginnings of
R U S S I A N
Industrialization

1800-1860

Introduction

The purpose of this book is to reconstruct a phase of Russian history which hitherto has received little attention from historians, particularly in Europe and the United States. Its subject is the earlier stages of industrial development in Russia during the first sixty years of the nineteenth century. The choice of this period of Russian industrial history for study does not imply a thesis about the periodization of Russian economic growth. No attempt will be made to place the "industrial revolution" in Russia at an earlier date than has generally been recognized, or to attribute previously unappreciated dynamic qualities to Russia's essentially agrarian economy or to the tsarist regime in the prereform era. Backwardness is as much the subject of this study as progress. An attempt will be made to explain why Russia failed to industrialize rapidly and comprehensively during the same period when many Western nations were undergoing their industrial revolutions. However, the most important aim of the book will be to explore the more immediate causes and the background of the rapid industrial growth which began in Russia during the late tsarist period. Many economists have noted that periods of quick and massive industrial development are usually preceded by longer periods of preparation, of slower, less dynamic, less comprehensive change. It has been observed that the preparatory processes "become manifest to the casual historical observer only when the pace of overt action changes."[1]

The present volume is intended as the first part of a larger study of Russia's economic growth and backwardness in the nineteenth century. It does not treat the process of modernization as a whole—the development of bureaucracy, science, education, political movements, and social as well as psychological phenomena.[2] Rather, it is more concerned with the economic aspects of modernization: transportation, private enterprise, state industrial policy, commerce, business institutions, and the growth of factory industry and technology. By this definition, the acceleration of Russian economic growth—the industrial revolution defined more broadly than in the classical or Soviet Marxian uses of the term—cannot be placed earlier than the last third

---

[1] E. E. Hagen, *On the Theory of Social Change* (Homewood, Illinois, 1962), p. 23. Part I and the appendices of Hagen's book summarize some of the theories of preparatory and beginning economic growth. See also my Conclusion. The terms "preparation," "precondition," or "beginning" are all, of course, not very concrete. Without proper qualification, they could be taken to embrace centuries of development, or for that matter, all history. The present study focuses primarily on the results of these deep-rooted processes, on how specifically they worked to activate industrialization, rather than on their ultimate derivation.

[2] See C. E. Black, *The Dynamics of Modernization* (New York, 1966).

· 3 ·

of the nineteenth century. Hence, the period of the Crimean War
and the beginning of the Great Reforms will be the terminal point of
this volume. This period marked the beginning of a new era, economically as well as politically.

To be sure, the roots of Russian industry can be traced back to the
reign of Peter the Great. The eighteenth century marked an important
stage in the industrial history of Russia, and I do not mean to deny
its significance. Indeed, it deserves treatment in a separate volume,
and some aspects of eighteenth-century development have been explored, not only in numerous Soviet monographs, but also recently by
scholars in France and the United States.[3] There is, however, no
equivalent study in the Western languages for the early nineteenth
century. For these reasons, the span of years extending roughly from
the end of the eighteenth century to the beginning of the 1860's has
been selected for the focus of this book. Chapter 1 summarizes the
most important recent literature on problems of economic development in eighteenth-century Russia by way of providing historical
background.

The scope of the work may be judged both too narrow and too
broad; some major areas of Russian social and economic history during the early nineteenth century have not been included. Such subjects
as the phenomenon of the serf entrepreneur, the emergence of capitalists and of a wage earning labor force from among the peasantry, as
well as the utilization and the living conditions of servile peasant
labor in factories have been examined, but the wider history of serfdom, of agrarian reforms, of the legislative precursors of the 1861
emancipation, of agricultural production and prices, and of peasant
industries and other transitional forms of manufacture, have *not* been
included. This broader context is important for a complete understanding of the transformation of Russia from an agricultural to an
industrial society, but an adequate treatment of these subjects would
require a separate volume. I have therefore excluded many aspects of
the purely agricultural history of Russia during the early nineteenth
century, without, however, eliminating those commercial and social
aspects of agrarian Russia that form the immediate background to
the emergence of factory industry.[4]

---

[3] Roger Portal, *L'Oural au XVIIIe siècle* (Paris, 1950); A. Kahan, "Entre-
preneurship in the Early Development of Iron Manufacturing in Russia,"
Economic Development and Cultural Change, vol. 10 (1962), 395-422; and
"Continuity in Economic Activity and Policy During the Post-Petrine Period in
Russia," *Journal of Economic History*, vol. 25 (1965), 61-85.

[4] A substantial part of Jerome Blum's *Lord and Peasant in Russia from the
Ninth to the Nineteenth Century* (Princeton, 1961) is devoted to general
agrarian problems during the early nineteenth century. Little has been written
on peasant industry during this period. There is a monograph by I. V.
Meshalin, *Tekstil'naia promyshlennost' krestian moskovskoi gubernii v XVIII i*

Introduction

The industrial development experienced by most of the non-Russian nationalities of the tsarist empire during this period also has been omitted. For some of these peoples, there was no industrial growth of any significance in the prereform era, particularly the nationalities in the southern and eastern parts of the empire. However, the Baltic provinces and most especially the Kingdom of Poland underwent some industrialization at an earlier time. Here again, the author has felt obliged to make omissions by excluding the histories of non-Russian societies and cultures whose distinctive values and patterns of behavior deserve extensive, individual analysis. He refers the reader to a literature that is developing on the early industrialization of the Baltic states and of the Kingdom of Poland, the rise of the German and Polish industrial middle classes of these areas, and related subjects.[5] The links of the economies of the nationalities to the industrialization of Russia proper are, of course, more pertinent, and will be discussed. Moreover, Belorussia and the Ukraine were more closely bound with the Russian economy, society, and administrative structure, and will be treated more extensively.

What might be called the disintegrative aspects of modernization—the political, intellectual, and psychological break up of the traditional society—will not be dealt with here as a separate and central problem. Still another book could be written about the alienation of the educated classes and the emergence of a revolutionary movement in response to the backwardness of early nineteenth-century Russia. Inevitably, these crucial subjects will be brought into the background of a number of the economic problems under discussion.

In view of the very large literature on the beginnings of Russian industrialization which comes largely from the Soviet Union (monographs, dissertations, articles, collective works, histories of individual industries, works on technology and social change), it may legitimately be asked whether a work on this general subject is justified. Such broad scope has been given to this book because no extended study of the subject exists in Western literature. What is being presented here is history that is practically unknown to historians reading Western languages; even specialists in the field of economic history know the subject only through scattered articles. Only a handful of the many scholars in Russian studies have turned to economic history, particularly of the pre-Soviet period, and this book, which is a

---

pervoi polovinie XIX veka (Moscow-Leningrad, 1950); and the collection of sources edited by V. N. Kasin and later by I. V. Meshalin, *Materialy po istorii krestianskoi promyshlennosti XVIII i pervoi poloviny XIX v.* (Moscow-Leningrad, 1935-1950), 2 vols.

[5] See the recent articles by E. Edlitskii, O. O. Karma, and G. A. Iesh in *Genezis kapitalizma v promyshlennosti, sbornik statei* (Moscow, 1963), and the bibliographical note on pp. 278-79.

synthesis based on a wide variety of obscure primary and secondary sources, brings together a large mass of pertinent material. It is intended as a preliminary kind of work, then, a mapping out of territory never before adequately surveyed.

Soviet scholars, in contrast to those of the West, have written extensively on this subject. They have tended almost exclusively, however, as individuals and more often as teams, to present their findings in the traditional Russian scholarly genre of the *ocherki*, or separate essays on related subjects. At worst, such an approach represents the binding together under one cover of a disconnected group of articles and fragments; at best, the results are uneven in quality and distorted in emphasis.[6] Surely, one individual cannot match the scholarship of several experts in thoroughness and grasp of materials, but he may give a sense of synthesis and unity not easily obtainable in a collective work.

The individual historian approaching such complex and broad subjects as economic growth and modernization must also inevitably take into account the methodology and findings of several disciplines. The present book, in its narrowest construction, deals with problems of sociology, technology, and economics, in addition to the more traditional historiographical concerns of state policy, bureaucracy, and institutional development. The newer fields of economic growth and measurement and of entrepreneurial history have developed techniques and reached conclusions that are of particular relevance to the subject and period studied here. The author, whose professional training is that of historian, cannot ask questions of some of his materials with the same methodological and terminological sophistication that trained specialists in these fields might bring to them. However, he can utilize new ideas that they have developed about Russia specifically, as well as adapt their broader generalizations to the Russian context. This I have tried to do, working with the older formulations of Weber and Sombart, and the more recent theoretical works of Rostow, Black, Gershenkron, Baykov, and Kuznets, among others.

In purpose and execution, however, this book remains essentially

---

[6] The recent symposium, *Genezis kapitalizma v promyshlennosti*, for example, includes some excellent studies on the early development of private industrial enterprise in the Russian empire, which constitutes half of the book; the remaining section attempts to cover the subject for the rest of the world with six articles on Holland, Saxony, Bulgaria, Yugoslavia, China, and Japan. *Ocherki ekonomicheskoi istorii Rossii, pervoi poloviny XIX veka* (Moscow, 1959), edited by M. K. Rozhkova, includes excellent syntheses by individual scholars of commerce, heavy and light industries, and urban development, with a superficial covering of the important subjects of state policy and transport. Similarly, *Voprosy genezisa kapitalizma v Rossii* (Leningrad, 1960), edited by V. V. Mavrodin, skips over large stretches of Russian social and economic history, from such limited subjects as the tariff of 1850 to broader surveys of entrepreneurship among the nobility in the seventeenth and eighteenth centuries.

within the realm of traditional economic history; and the audience for which it is primarily intended consists of scholars and students in the field of Russian history, particularly in the United States. Russian historiography in the United States has been dominated for two generations by a concern with intellectual and political history, particularly as these apply to the revolutionary movement. It is not the place of this Introduction to examine the numerous and justifiable causes for such concern, or to criticize it. Rather, the book as a whole proposes to enrich these areas of the study of Russian history by attempting to understand the social and economic background from which ideas and movements have emerged in Russia. Without such knowledge, the intellectual and political history of Russia frequently becomes isolated and unreal.

In terms of method, this book does not claim to be an original work in the sense of supplying new information extracted from previously unexamined or unpublished archival materials. It is rather an attempt to bring together the findings of a large body of books, monographs, and articles by prerevolutionary and postrevolutionary Russian historians, as well as some works by Western scholars. Many of these works are the product of archival research, but the archives of the Soviet Union were not available to the author when he began his research for this book. He tried unsuccessfully to gain access to them while in the Soviet Union. A decision then had to be made concerning access to Russian archives, and it was deemed realistic to proceed on the assumption that this would continue to be denied.

Fortunately, published primary sources pertinent to Russian industrialization are abundant, and the author has utilized these extensively, as well as a few valuable unpublished materials in American archives. Some of these published and unpublished documents, which have been untouched or utilized insufficiently by Western and Soviet scholars, have yielded some fresh information. Readers particularly interested in this material are directed first to Chapter 5, where the Mordvinov archives provided insight into the economic thought and the problems of development of early nineteenth-century Russia. In Chapter 7, the Miliutin and Hagemeister memoranda provide valuable insights into economic conditions in Russia during the Crimean War and the impact of this war on the thinking of the ruling elite. The police reports on the Moscow Old Believers constituted a valuable primary source for the business and industrial activities of these groups, which are discussed in Chapter 9. Soviet scholars have made an exhaustive collection of official reports on protests and rebellions of factory workers in Russia during the nineteenth century, which yielded important material for several parts of the book. In Chapters 12 and 13, the unpublished letters and papers of the American engineers engaged in locomotive and track construction for the

first major Russian railroad—Thomas and William Winans, George
W. Whistler, and Joseph Harrison—were consulted with profit in
archives in Baltimore, New York and Philadelphia. Also noteworthy
as an extensive and rich source for recapturing specific aspects of
Russian industrialization during the early nineteenth century and for
evoking the immediate substance of economic life were scores of European travel accounts, as well as numerous Russian autobiographies
and memoirs of engineers, scientists, businessmen, and officials.
These sources were of uneven value in matters of interpretation, but
all rich in the kind of fact that humanizes economic history. A more
complete analysis of the primary and secondary sources will be found
in the Bibliography at the end of the book.

There are many effective ways of presenting industrial history.
Much can be said for a purely chronological approach. Scholars are
increasingly turning to a statistical approach, which focuses on the
measurement of industrial growth. On the other hand, much industrial history has traditionally been presented in the form of analysis
of the developments of particular industries or regions. A topical approach has been selected for this book as most appropriate to the task
of describing the origins and dynamics of the process of industrialization in Russia as a whole. It is essentially a study of motive forces and
catalysts, how these acted and what they brought about. Part I gives
the background and the setting: it summarizes developments in the
eighteenth century, and discusses commerce and finance, investment,
and urbanization; it also sketches the general evolution of light and
heavy industries and the emergence of new industrial regions during
the prereform period.

The remaining chapters of the book consider agents and key problems in the early industrial growth of Russia. Part II discusses the
views, organization, capabilities, achievements, and failures of the
Russian state as an agent for industrialization in the early nineteenth
century. Part III traces the religious and social origins of the private
industrial entrepreneur in Russia and the beginnings of foreign industrial enterprise. Part IV deals with the crucial problem of geography and size, with the beginnings of modern canal and rail transportation in the Russian empire, and the relationship of this development to the growth of trade and industry. Part V considers the
evolution of industrial technology in the several decades before 1861,
the development of technical education, and the degree to which the
Russians were able to build the foundations for an indigenous
technology.

Part I

Industrial Russia Before 1860

The gilded domes of Lucknow—the pagodas of China—Byzantine churches—Grecian temples—palaces in the style of Versailles—heavy inexpressive German buildings—wooden country cottages —glaring American signs—boulevards, gardens, silent lanes, roaring streets, open markets, Turkish bazaars, French cafés, German beer cellars and Chinese tea houses—all are found here, not grouped exclusively into separate cantons, but mixed and jumbled together, until Europe and Asia, the past and present, the old world and the new, are so blended and confounded that it is impossible to say which predominates. . . . At its southern end, the muezzin calls to prayer from the roof of his mosque, while at the northern, the whistle of the locomotive announces the departure of the train for St. Petersburg.[1]

Thus did Bayard Taylor, a well-known American journalist, romanticize about the city of Moscow in the late 1850's. Nikolai Chernyshevskii, writing at about the same time, was more matter-of-fact about the transformation that Russia was beginning to experience, in the style of a leader of the new generation of "realists": "It is clear to everyone," he wrote in a review of Haxthausen's study of Russia,

> that since the conclusion of our last war Russia has begun to take a more active part in the general European economic evolution. Everyone can see the rapid intensification of our industrial activity. Our private capital, moral and material, is emerging from its lethargical idleness; foreign capital is beginning to find profitable and secure investments here. A part of it has already been transferred to our country in large sums; another part is ready to migrate to us shortly in yet more significant amounts. There can be no doubt about the consequences of such developments.[2]

The Russian nihilist and the American reporter were perceiving, each in his own way, the beginnings of the more rapid industrialization of Russia. At the same time, they were observing the culmination of less conspicuous historical processes, which provided a foundation for the industrial metamorphosis which followed. For several decades the social structure of agrarian Russia had been changing. New groups who could assume the various functions of an industrial

---

[1] Bayard Taylor, *Greece and Russia* (New York, 1859), p. 326.
[2] N. G. Chernyshevskii, *Polnoe Sobranie sochinenii* (Moscow, 1948), vol. IV, p. 303.

society were beginning to form out of the traditional classes. The predominantly religious and administrative nature of Russia's capital cities was giving way before trade and industry as early as the end of the eighteenth century. Soon after, in Moscow and Vladimir provinces, small factory towns were appearing where peasant villages had stood. The commercial patterns of old Russia began to change soon after 1800. Permanent urban markets replaced fairs in the northern and central provinces. Signs that a money economy was on the way were evident well before the emancipation of the serfs. Although banks were not important in Russia until the late nineteenth century, the appearance many decades before of insurance companies and commercial exchanges in the main cities of Russia heralded the modernization of trading and financial practices. New industries appeared in Russia from 1800 until 1860, and some of the older ones were renovated along modern technical and organizational lines.

The most remote origins of Russian industry, to be sure, antedate the economic awakening that Chernyshevskii observed on the eve of the Great Reforms by at least a century and a half. The history—or rather, the prehistory—of Russian industrialization in the seventeenth and eighteenth centuries forms the logical beginning for this book. Needless to say, this is an extensive, complex, and important subject, and Chapter 1 presents only a general background statement based on the most significant and recent literature.

Chapter 1

Russian Industry and Technology Prior to 1800

Capital Accumulation and the Origins of Industry in the
Seventeenth Century

The ultimate beginnings of Russian industry can be traced to the seventeenth century. Prior to this period, there were no large manufacturing establishments employing wage labor in the Muscovite or Kievan states. There were craftsmen and shops to build churches and to make bells and cannon. Agricultural, military, household and luxury implements were made in the villages and towns, all to supply local needs. A few primitive iron forges and salt works supplied the requirements of the larger estates and commercial towns. In those trading cities—Novgorod, Suzdal, Moscow, and others—which were engaged in an extensive regional and foreign commerce dealing in local raw materials, a wealthy merchant class came into being and some metallic currency appeared during the period of the Mongol rule. But none of this commercial capital was diverted into industry; the village, estate, and monastery remained self-sufficient; and hired labor was practically nonexistent among an agricultural laboring mass gradually drifting into bondage.

The basis for a primitive Russian industry was created in the seventeenth century. The Muscovite tsars had built a unified state, and with this came a national market and the acquisition of vast borderlands and colonies, wealthy in furs and other commercially valuable raw materials. By the middle of the century, the civil war and discord that had characterized the Time of Troubles were past wounds that had healed, and Russia's population was beginning the rapid growth which was to characterize the next three centuries. The amount of money in circulation continued to grow. There was little machinery, of course, at this time, beyond the most primitive types of hand equipment. Factory organization and modernized transportation were phenomena of the distant future. However, the seventeenth century witnessed the beginnings in Russia of the processes defined as the pre-industrial (or by Marxists, the "original") accumulation of capital, the setting of the social and economic stage for industrialization in the emergence, although limited in scope, of hired laborers, industrial entrepreneurs, and capital which could be diverted into investment in industry.[1] The two ultimate sources of this capital were commerce

---

[1] See the discussion in *Istoricheskie zapiski*, vol. 54 (1955); L. G. Beskrovnyi, ed., *K voprosu pervonachal'nom nakoplenii v Rossii (XVII-XVIII v.v.), sbornik statei* (Moscow, 1958); and F. Ia. Polianskii, *Pervonachal'noe nakoplenie kapitala v Rossii* (Moscow, 1958). For a criticism, A. Gershenkron, "Rosario Romeo and the Original Accumulation of Capital," *Economic Backwardness in*

and the state, although there were many others of lesser significance.

Considering the change to investment in new enterprise, we must look first to the area northwest of Moscow, extending south to Tula. Here were to be found at least a dozen small plants engaged in various stages of the processing of iron and copper ore, usually for military purposes. Iron and copper plants existed also in the north between lakes Ladoga and Onega, and in the Urals.[2] About twenty such establishments could be counted in the latter region by the end of the seventeenth century. Little more than blacksmith shops, they can be compared to their larger counterparts in the Moscow and Tula areas since they were established by an outside impulse coming from the state or from private entrepreneurs, and were not merely forges which had come into being to satisfy local needs.[3] Another industry of importance which developed in the century preceding the reign of Peter the Great involved the manufacture of potash. Here, there was a high degree of concentration of production in a few dozen enterprises controlled by an even smaller number of industrialists. The production of Russian potash, some of which was exported, centered in the area of Nizhnii-Novgorod, where leather and linen were also produced in small factories. Salt was another big item in seventeenth-century Russian industry, the main center of its production being located in estate plants near the Kama River. Distilleries were established on some estates.

It can be seen that such industry as existed in Russia in the seventeenth century, beyond the traditional local crafts, was engaged in the making of products for military use or for public need, such as iron weapons, gunpowder, liquor, and salt, as well as a few luxury items for the court and aristocracy, such as glass. Industry, however, did produce a few materials for export, and most important among them was potash. Such industry naturally clustered around the national political capital and major commercial city of Moscow to cater to its needs, although some important industries were founded on private estates and monasteries far to the east of Moscow. At the same time, the future Urals industrial complex of the eighteenth century experienced a modest, but genuine beginning with the establishment of small iron plants.[4]

The state was obviously a very important source of capital for these early Russian industries, either through direct control of fac-

---

Historical Perspective (New York, 1965), pp. 90-118. See also my Conclusion.

[2] P. I. Liashchenko, *History of the National Economy of Russia to the 1917 Revolution* (New York, 1949), pp. 212-13 and map facing p. 215; also A. Kahan, "Entrepreneurship in the Early Development of Iron Manufacturing in Russia," *Economic Development and Cultural Change*, vol. X (1962), 395.

[3] Roger Portal, *L'Oural au XVIIIᵉ siècle* (Paris, 1950), pp. 20-21.

[4] The best summary is in Liashchenko, *National Economy of Russia*, pp. 211-15, including the map.

tories, the management usually being handed over to foreign specialists, or through the granting of monopolies and leases. Wealthy noblemen might also become important industrialists in the seventeenth century. Perhaps the most interesting of the large-scale nobiliary industrialists of this period were the great landowning family, the Morozovs, who practically controlled the production of potash, but also were involved in several other industries, in moneylending, and rather extensively in foreign and domestic trade. Monasteries also engaged in industry in the 1600's: we have the example of Voskresenskii monastery, which operated salt works employing hired labor. Other monasteries, like the Kirillo-Belozerskii at the beginning of the seventeenth century, had enough capital to engage in extensive moneylending operations.[5]

A novel and important form of industrial capital in the seventeenth century was derived from Russian merchants. The Muscovite trader was coming into a prominence and wealth which some families traced back to the reign of Ivan the Terrible. Great commercial fortunes were being built as a result of an expanding foreign and domestic trade. We have the example of one sixteenth-century merchant whose property and cash on hand amounted to about one million rubles, a fabulous sum for those days. One significant indication of the strengthening of a national market and the growing significance of domestic commerce on a far-ranging scale in seventeenth-century Muscovy was the establishment of fairs which served merchants from distant parts of the realm. In 1624, for example, the great Makarevskaia *iarmarka* (later moved to nearby Nizhnii-Novgorod) was formed. It was soon to become Russia's most important national fair. Also of significance to the national commerce and the accumulation of wealth by merchants and by the state was the conquest and exploitation of Siberia, which took place in the late sixteenth and seventeenth centuries. Most of the great commercial families of Moscow in the seventeenth century were involved in the Siberian trade.[6]

The classic example of Russian merchants who piled up a fortune from the development of Muscovy's eastern borderlands were, of course, the Stroganovs. Of peasant origin, the Stroganovs, in cooperation with the crown, had built a vast private domain in the east by the end of the sixteenth century. The original source of Stroganov wealth was the family's extensive commercial operations in many parts of Russia. They added to their treasure by moneylending, both to peasants and to tsars. Much of this capital was invested in salt min-

[5] Beskrovnyi, ed., *K voprosu pervonachal'nom nakoplenii v Rossii*, introductory essay, p. 26; and particularly the article by S. Ia. Borovoi, pp. 499-500, 504. On the Morozovs, see A. I. Iakovlev, ed., *Akty khoziaistva boyarin B. I. Morozova* (Moscow-Leningrad, 1940), 2 vols., and V. N. Iakovtsevskii, *Kupicheskii kapital v feodal'no-krepostnicheskoi Rossii* (Moscow, 1953), p. 23.

[6] Polianskii, *Pervonachal'noe nakoplenie kapitala v Rossii*, pp. 25, 35, 53.

ing, the main industrial occupation of the Stroganovs in the seventeenth century, although they also concerned themselves with silver, gold, and copper, built ships, established iron forges and leather-making shops, and sold fish. The Stroganov enterprises employed both serfs and hired labor, who worked with their hands in shops and peasant huts.[7]

Along with the beginning of manufacturing enterprises and an initial capital formation of various types, wage labor made its appearance in industry, commerce, and transportation in seventeenth-century Russia. Since the early 1920's, a number of specialized Soviet studies of hired labor in Russia in the immediate pre-Petrine period have appeared. Some have focused on the development of wage earners within the agrarian, servile context of the villages of large landowners and of monastery lands. Others have traced the appearance of hired workers in transport and fishing enterprises on the Volga River, in salt processing works of the Urals region, and in seventeenth-century trading and manufacturing centers, such as the town of Ustiug-Velikii.[8]

The extent and significance of these pre-Petrine phenomena can easily be overrated and have been somewhat inflated by Soviet historians. Historians are certainly concerned with origins, however obscure, and the remote origins of the Russian industrial mammoth of the present day must be traced ultimately to the seventeenth century. Russian historians, working with the raw materials of their craft, in the archives of monasteries, estates, and various localities, have amply demonstrated this. Origins of this kind, however, do not necessarily indicate a fundamental change in a society or an acceleration of economic growth. The materials we have on factories, entrepreneurs, capital, and labor in seventeenth-century Russia form the earliest kind of prehistory of Russian industrialization, an "original accumulation of capital," which was not, however, always a preindustrial one.

Russia had millionaire industrialists, to be sure, during this early period, but most of them were, in terms of their origins and the primary use of their wealth, landowners and agriculturalists. The great funds of capital which many of them accumulated were not channeled

---

[7] On the commercial, moneylending and industrial activities of the Stroganovs in the sixteenth and seventeenth centuries, see A. A. Vvedenskii, *Dom Stroganovykh v XVI-XVII vekakh* (Moscow, 1962), especially pp. 177-79, 213-14, 300-02.

[8] See the articles by A. A. Preobrazhenskii, K. N. Shepetov, Iu. A. Tikhonov, Z. A. Ogrizko, and N. A. Baklanov in Beskrovnyi, *K voprosu pervonachal'nom nakoplenii v Rossii*, pp. 38-144; also, the review of pertinent literature in the Baklanov article, pp. 117-19, and in the introduction to the book; and I. V. Stepanov, "Rabotnye liudi povolzh'ia v XVII v," in the collection *Voprosy genezisa kapitalizma v Rossii* (Leningrad, 1960), pp. 90-109.

in any comprehensive way into industrial enterprise. Industry remained a secondary occupation. The ultimate goal and achievement of their economic power was nobiliary status within the traditional social order. Seventeenth-century Russia had no real industrial entrepreneurial class per se.

Russia in the several decades prior to Peter the Great witnessed the building of its first factories, but these were little more than overgrown craftsmen's shops or loose agglomerations of individual workers in specific localities. There were no machines; Russian technology was primitive at best. Beyond some use of water power for mills, it was almost totally nonindustrial in its application, the work of occasional, dexterous hands in the employ of the church, the army, or the court. Science was nonexistent in a rigid, antirational religious environment, obscurantist and hostile to any innovation that smacked of the West.

A wide variety of industrial products was nevertheless produced in Russia in the seventeenth century, but no mass market existed: the state was the primary buyer. A few items, for the most part luxuries, were produced for consumption abroad or at home by the nobility. Russian domestic and foreign commerce increased during this period, and although goods were moved considerable distances from numerous, widely dispersed parts of the realm, the true binding of the nation's industries and markets, which could only come from the modernization, acceleration, and lowering of costs of transportation, was something that was far in the future. The Muscovite merchants of the seventeenth century inched their way across the vastness of Russia on the roads that nature had provided. The rivers, when navigable, were the primary arteries of commerce; and no highways or canals had been built.

Servile labor provided the motive power for the Russian economy in the 1600's, almost all of it devoted to agriculture. Hired laborers formed a small minority of those used in Russian industry, and the wage labor force, in the total of the population, was infinitesimal. The conclusions which Soviet historians have drawn or implied exaggerate the significance of a group which in many cases hardly exceeded the normal fraction of wage earners one would expect to see in the most traditional, unindustrialized society.

What this prehistory of Russian industry of the seventeenth century indicates are the ways by which Russia was to industrialize, but the society itself at that time was not yet changing as a whole. A more important and authentic initial phase in the history of Russian industrialization was to come with the Petrine reforms at the beginning of the eighteenth century. It is clear, however, that some of the characteristics of the Petrine and eighteenth-century Russian industrialization had already appeared in the preceding half-century.

Industrial Reforms of Peter the Great

Historians who have studied the economic development of Russia and who have maintained widely divergent general interpretations have been fairly unanimous in seeing the first really solid foundations of Russian industry in the reign of Peter the Great. They have been equally unanimous, however, in pointing out the failure of Petrine policies to effect any comprehensive transformation of Russian society from an agrarian to an industrial base.[9] Thus, Peter's reign becomes, in the eyes of its historians, like the seventeenth century, an early transitional phase, although far more significant than the preceding period. Owing not a little to developments which came before, it nevertheless constituted a kind of revolution, as did the other Petrine reforms, a setting into motion of forces which profoundly influenced the course of Russian industrial history for over a century to come.

Peter the Great was the first Russian tsar to develop an industrial policy, or, as the Soviet historian, Liashchenko has better put it, the first to take those elements of industry which had come into being before his time and mold them into a "developed system."[10] This does not mean, of course, that Peter evolved a "plan" for the industrialization of his country, that he intended to bring about the social and economic transformation of Russia from an agrarian to an industrial base, or that he was even conscious of such a possibility. Rather, it indicates that, under the guidance of the Petrine state, a large network (for its time) of heavy and light industry fully capable of supporting a modern war machine was established; new industrial areas were opened, with large concentrations of resources and workers in factory complexes; an entrepreneurial group was encouraged by the state to develop private industry; undertakings were financed and aided in various ways; finally, both the labor force and the market which could make large factories viable were provided.

In the abstract, this seems impressive, and must be qualified all the way down the line by an examination of the statistics and of the historical context of Petrine Russia. Peter's motives in building a Russian industry were primarily military. This is reflected in the type of industry which was established during his reign. Iron mills, arma-

[9] See Jerome Blum, *Lord and Peasant in Russia from the Ninth to the Nineteenth Centuries* (Princeton, 1961), p. 271; Liashchenko, *National Economy of Russia*, pp. 283-84; Portal, *L'Oural*, p. 51; E. I. Zaozerskaia, *Manufaktura pri Petra I* (Moscow-Leningrad, 1947); A. I. Pashkov, ed. and J. M. Latiche, transl., *A History of Russian Economic Thought: Ninth Through Nineteenth Centuries* (Berkeley, 1964), pp. 280-82; and N. I. Pavlenko, *Razvitie metallurgicheskoi promyshlennosti Rossii v pervoi polovine XVIII veka* (Moscow, 1953), p. 514.

[10] Liashchenko, *National Economy of Russia*, p. 283.

ments works, gunpowder plants, factories which could produce large quantities of army uniforms and sails—all of these were directed toward supplying the army and navy from Russian sources rather than foreign imports.[11] Although in the last half of Peter's reign, state industrial policy did develop more varied concerns and goals than simply those determined by war,[12] the military impulse remained dominant throughout. No program for Russia's modernization was implemented; moreover, we may agree with Portal that "there was nothing revolutionary in Peter the Great's work." What was done was accomplished "by necessity and not by conviction."[13] The social system was not changed; serfdom was preserved and even extended. An attempt was made to fuse it with Peter's industrial system.

The statistics indicate that Peter's industrial achievement was impressive. Russia had never before seen a productive establishment of such magnitude developed in such a short time. Several areas were improved, the most significant and extensive of the new ones being, of course, the Urals. A new type of large industrial complex, employing hundreds of workers became characteristic, particularly of the state factories of Peter's time. The nineteenth-century calculation, which attributed 233 industrial establishments to the period of Peter I, has been revised by Soviet scholars to about 200. Zaozerskaia in her monograph on Petrine manufacturing, lists 226 by the death of Peter, of which 21 date to the seventeenth century. The majority of these, including the largest factories, were engaged in metallurgy, and 43 percent of the total number of factories were owned by the government.[14] A typical factory of the time, according to Zaozerskaia, would employ between 200 and 300 workers, although there were a number of much larger complexes. The Nevianskii plant, largest of the Demidov enterprises, produced cast iron in four furnaces, amounting to a yearly quantity which ranged from 1,800 to 3,600 tons. One of the largest of the state concerns was the Moscow woolens factory which employed 593 skilled workers in a concentrated and specialized manufacturing operation during the last decade of Peter's reign. Elsewhere significant quantities of laboring people and craftsmen were physically concentrated in relatively large factory structures for the time: the state Ekaterinhof linen manufactory, located on the Neva, was by 1720 a two-story stone building with a dozen rooms, where 148 employees and supervisors worked a large number of looms.[15]

[11] Zaozerskaia, *Manufaktura pri Petra I*, p. 38.
[12] P. G. Liubomirov, *Ocherki po istorii russkoi promyshlennosti* (O.G.I.Z.: 1947), pp. 527-28.
[13] Portal, *L'Oural*, p. 51.
[14] Zaozerskaia, *Manufaktura pri Petra I*, pp. 9-10.
[15] Descriptions in Zaozerskaia, *Manufaktura pri Petra I*, pp. 17-18, 25, 32-33;

Prior to Peter the Great, almost all of the score or so of factories which Zaozerskaia itemizes for that period were controlled by the state or by foreigners—Marselius, Baldwin, Von Rosenbusch, Meyer, and others.[16] The majority of the factories established in Russia during the first half of the reign of Peter the Great were state enterprises. Peter needed foreign technicians, but he did not want his factories in foreign hands, and few foreigners were able to set themselves up in industry while he ruled. Among several cases, we have records of the petition of a foreign craftsman employed at a Voronezh tannery, one Rudolph Abel, who wished to establish his own factory and sought 600 rubles from the state treasury to do so. He was turned down.[17]

Those few Russians who had the capital were not inclined to channel it into the new enterprises. Many, apparently, were as suspicious of Peter's industrial experiments as they were of his other Westernizing innovations. In the first decade of the eighteenth century, the government relied only on factories owned by the state. After 1710, the tsar characteristically began to force Russians with capital to take over state manufacturing enterprises. The merchant class was a particular target of Peter's ambition to develop private industrial entrepreneurs in his country, and the state soon went all out to bring them into industry through the enticements of generous loans and tariff protection. This policy paid off in a limited way: by the end of Peter's reign, over half of Russia's factories, including some very large establishments, were privately owned. The light industries of Moscow were largely in private hands by 1725. The majority of the new industrial entrepreneurs of Russia were from the merchant class, and by the more stable period of the early 1720's, people from this group were far more able and willing to risk their resources in business undertakings, as evidenced by the relatively large number of private companies and factories which were established during this time.[18]

A few peasants were able to climb over the walls of poverty and privilege to enter the ranks of the industrial entrepreneurs during the reign of Peter the Great, but the number was of no significance compared to the peasant enterprise of the late eighteenth and early nineteenth centuries. The upper nobility remained aloof from industry during the early eighteenth century. A few of the intimates of the

see also, by the same author, *Razvitie legkoi promyshlennosti v Moskve v pervoi chetverti XVIII v.* (Moscow, 1953), pp. 154-68.

[16] Zaozerskaia, *Manufaktura pri Petra I*, chart, appendix, pp. 154-55.

[17] Zaozerskaia, *Manufaktura pri Petra I*, p. 52.

[18] Zaozerskaia, *Manufaktura pri Petra I*, pp. 55-56, 67; for an analysis of the social origins of the private industrialists, see Kahan, "Entrepreneurship in Russia," 403-06; for the distribution and magnitude of private ownership in the light industries of Moscow, see Zaozerskaia, *Razvitie legkoi promyshlennosti v Moskve*, particularly the charts, pp. 512-15.

tsar from among the highly placed, such as Shafirov, saw in the new factories opportunities to fill their pockets. Among the lesser gentry —low ranking army officers and petty bureaucrats—we find a few examples of industrial enterprise. A steward by the name of Khrushchev, to cite one instance, owned a small potash plant in the provinces in the early years of the eighteenth century.[19]

If Peter the Great had difficulties in nurturing a class of Russian industrialists, finding a factory working force presented even more complex problems, very nearly insurmountable ones within the framework of Russian society and culture during the early eighteenth century. With few exceptions, technical and managerial skills had to be imported from Europe. Some hired labor could be recruited from among Russian artisans and *obrok* serfs on furlough and available in the wintertime. Forced labor, however, almost from the beginning provided the main source for Peter's factory workers. Indeed, hired labor, which in some cases involved ten-year terms at negligible pay, was not always distinguishable from the various types of impressment that came to be used.[20] In the early years of the Petrine factories, such workers were scrounged from among the ranks of Swedish prisoners, soldiers and their children, convicts, and other such groups squarely under the thumb of the state. The numbers so provided were hardly adequate, and the government ultimately turned to its servile peasantry in an effort to end the factory labor shortage. State peasants were "assigned" to factories, and after 1721, industrialists of the merchant class were permitted to buy villages of serfs, who would then be attached to their factories. These "possessional" serfs became an industrial labor force on the condition that they remain permanently affixed to the factories. Through such unique methods, provided by a system of autocracy and serfdom that had been intensified and extended by Peter the Great, was Russia's first industrial working force, numbering in the tens of thousands, created.[21]

The Urals Industrial Area

The Urals factory complex was Peter's most significant and permanent industrial achievement. What Peter very rapidly developed into a major metal and armaments producing region became, by the 1750's, the center of Russian heavy industry. The large factories of the central and southern Urals by the last half of the eighteenth century constituted one of the major iron producing areas of the world, a top competitor in the international market and one of the principal sources for England's iron on the eve of the industrial revolution in

[19] Liubomirov, *Russkaia promyshlennost'*, p. 542.
[20] Zaozerskaia, *Manufaktura pri Petra I*, p. 113.
[21] Zaozerskaia, *Manufaktura pri Petra I*, pp. 131-33; Portal, *L'Oural*, p. 47.

that country. The Urals were in fact one of the first of the world's great industrial centers prior to the advent of steam-powered machinery.

Peter the Great founded twelve factories in this area, most of them after 1716. This impulse continued during the early and mid-eighteenth century: by 1762, when the Urals had reached a kind of maturity, both the central and southern regions were industrialized with a total of 97 factories. By 1790, there were 165. By the 1760's, the number of metallurgical enterprises in the Urals exceeded the total in European Russia and dwarfed the factories of the latter area in size and production. The Urals by 1763 produced two-thirds of Russia's iron in factories which exceeded the production of the largest in European Russia, in some cases by 50 percent. In one of the biggest plants in 1777, this meant a yearly production of over 9,200 tons of cast iron.[22] Although the state factory complex at Ekaterinburg was not the largest of the mid-eighteenth-century Urals enterprises, it was an important industrial and administrative center, from which the state mines of several eastern provinces were directed. The Ekaterinburg inventory, as detailed by Portal,[23] indicates the complexity and sophistication of the Urals industries by 1775: canals and dams, two blast furnaces and three large forges, a foundry, plants making cannon and anchors, several shops for various kinds of processing and repair, and numerous warehouses and private homes. Ekaterinburg employed 180 people, as well as a large government administrative staff and a military detachment with artillery. In addition, there was a school for the training of factory technicians, with a capacity for 100 students. To service this community of the frontier, there were stores, baths, a hotel, a tavern, a hospital, and a stone church.

Not all of these impressive achievements were the work of Peter the Great or strictly the product of impulses originally set in motion by him. There were other forces at work, during and after his reign, emanating both from the state and private sources and from abroad as well as from Russia. Peter brought a mining, metallurgical, and armaments industry into the frontier wilderness of the Urals to supply his war machine. The development of private enterprise and production for export were secondary motives at best. A predominantly state-financed and operated industry was established, together with a state bureau of mines, designed to aid and to buy from private entrepreneurs. All of this might easily have fallen into decay with the end of Peter's leadership, as did some of his other innovations, were it not for the talents and energies of the government administrators who were picked by the tsar for Urals service, and who continued his

[22] Portal, *L'Oural*, pp. 153-54, 169-71.
[23] Portal, *L'Oural*, pp. 223-25. Compare this with the sketch of the Nizhne-Tagil works a century later.

work through the 1720's and 1730's. Two of these officials, a German, Hennin, and a Russian, Tatishchev, were largely responsible for the consolidation and expansion of Peter's work. Hennin was particularly careful to develop industrial technology in the Urals and to systematize production. One notable achievement of Tatishchev in the 1730's was the absorption of the energies and diligence of the Old Believers of the area into the factory working force and as inspectors. Tatishchev was a modernizer in the Petrine tradition who believed in a state stimulated and regulated development of heavy and light industry, the introduction of industrial machinery, and in the establishment of technical schools. He was given considerable power over the Urals industrial complex.[24]

With the passing of Hennin and Tatishchev and the ascendency of intriguers and court favorites during the reign of the empresses in the 1730's and 1740's, the growth of state enterprise in the Urals was retarded. Foreigners, nobles, and courtiers managed to get their hands on factories which could be exploited as lucrative sinecures by people who had little interest in developing and improving Russian industry. However, by the mid-eighteenth century, more constructive private commercial interests began to invest in the Urals. What had been predominantly a state directed industrialization now became much more a private impulse. This coincided with the development of a laissez-faire attitude on the part of the government. With the pacification of hostile tribes in the southern Urals, an area which offered new opportunities for industrial exploitation was opened. Perhaps foremost as a factor in the mid-century industrial expansion of the Urals was the growing foreign demand for iron, particularly on the part of England. The Urals industrialists after 1750 were sending most of their iron abroad.

Although by the early 1760's, the Urals had reached a new peak of production and prosperity, the boom was short-lived. A marked decline set in during the mid-1760's, caused by a number of factors, the relative value of which scholars have debated. Portal has listed the inability of the primitive Russian economy to absorb the earlier rapid industrial expansion and construction of plants in the Urals, the backwardness of transport, wastefulness and mismanagement by factory owners, higher labor costs, and the exhaustion of mines—all of this aggravated by the Pugachev disturbances.[25] A partial revival oc-

[24] Sketches of the careers of Hennin and Tatishchev in Portal, *L'Oural*, pp. 60-67, 83-84, 94-99; and N. I. Pavlenko, *Razvitie metallurgicheskoi promyshlennosti Rossii*, pp. 145-58. On Tatishchev's views of industry, Pashkov, ed., *Russian Economic Thought*, pp. 362-64.

[25] Portal, *L'Oural*, pp. 306-15. The Soviet historian of eighteenth-century Russian metallurgy, N. I. Pavlenko, emphasizes depletion of resources, government policy, and a declining foreign market for Russian iron as factors in a

curred at the end of the century; however, by 1800, the Urals factories, having failed to modernize operations, were bypassed by the industrial revolutions of the West. Russia lost its world leadership in iron production and the Urals fell into stagnation.

Private enterprise came to dominate the Urals industrial scene in the late eighteenth century. Perhaps the most dramatic aspect of this development and, indeed, of the entire history of the Urals, can be seen in the story of the Demidov family and the industrial empire which they built. The origin of the Demidov fortune can properly be traced to the meeting of Peter the Great and a Tula arms-maker, Nikita Demidov, in the late 1690's. Contrary to the legend, Nikita was not a peasant or a simple blacksmith, whose skilfully wrought muskets impressed the tsar. He was a well-to-do manufacturer of weapons from the established Tula industrial community, an expert and an entrepreneur. Peter apparently believed that Demidov could produce implements of war of a quantity and quality sufficient to warrant generous state aid. This came in the form of land, tax exemptions, "assigned" labor, and other favors.[26] Nikita Demidov branched out from Tula and the central region of Russia to found factories in the Urals. By the end of the eighteenth century, he and his several sons and grandsons had founded over fifty, for the most part iron-manufacturing establishments, of which the family still controlled twenty-nine. Nikita's son, Akinfii, became a noble (as had his father in 1720) and a Major General in the army, holding a high civil service rank as well. He was able to study technology in Europe, and dressed in the latest French fashions.[27] By this time, tens of thousands of serfs labored for the Demidovs on their estates or attached to their factories. Kafengauz has estimated the Demidov estate in the mid-1740's at about a million rubles, the largest part of which consisted of industrial enterprises, although their agricultural holdings were substantial. In late nineteenth-century prices, according to the same author, the sale value of this property would amount to about twenty-five million rubles. In 1791, the yearly income of the Demidovs was well over 500,000 rubles, of which about half constituted pure profit.[28]

The management of this vast capital and the large-scale enterprises that produced it required by this time an elaborate administrative apparatus and the development of sophisticated accounting tech-

---

deceleration of the growth of Russian metallurgy. See N. I. Pavlenko, *Istoriia metallurgii v Rossii XVIII veka* (Moscow, 1962), pp. 535-36.

[26] B. B. Kafengauz, *Istoriia khoziaistva Demidovykh v XVIII-XIX vv* (Moscow-Leningrad, 1949), vol. I, pp. 82-85, 129, 167.

[27] Kafengauz, *Istoriia khoziaistva Demidovykh*, pp. 248, map facing 264-65, 259-60; Portal, *L'Oural*, pp. 56-58.

[28] Kafengauz, *Istoriia khoziaistva Demidovykh*, pp. 233, 477-79. Sixty years later, this income was the same.

niques. The labor force was immense, numbering over 30,000 by 1760. Although craftsmen, technicians, and various kinds of hired wage laborers were in evidence, the main source of factory hands remained seigneurial serfs from the Demidov estates and villages, and "assigned" peasants from the state.[29]

By the late eighteenth century, over half of the Demidov iron went abroad, about 80 percent of the total of exported goods going to England. However, almost a third was absorbed by the domestic market, where the Demidovs competed with other Russian manufacturers. The rest was purchased by the state. Most of the Demidov products were dragged through the many rivers and few canals of Russia by beasts and the teams of human draught horses called *burlaki*. Some goods inched their way between the river routes in cumbersome caravans. In any case, the journey from the Urals to Moscow and the Baltic area took months stretching into years and increased prices by as high as one-fifth. The transport of goods exported from Russia was monopolized by foreign shippers based in St. Petersburg.[30]

That the Demidovs were large-scale industrial capitalists could hardly be disputed. They dominated an entire industry, traded extensively with the outside world, managed huge enterprises with skill and sophistication, and could rally capital sufficient for a major expansion of their business. The Demidov industrial empire, as Kafengauz has pointed out, was no mere artificial creation of the Russian state or extension of European technology.[31] Nevertheless, Russia's first industrial moguls remained very much dependent on the agrarian and autocratic social and political order from which they had emerged and in the midst of which they thrived. The state no longer had to subsidize the Demidovs directly, or even provide a market for their products. Nevertheless, it continued to prop up their prosperity by tariff protection, tax exemption, land concessions, special patronage by the tsar, and above all, the provision—many times restricted and never fully adequate—of a servile laboring mass.[32] Beyond this, the Demidovs of the late eighteenth century—by then large-scale landowners—could derive impressive wealth as well as additional labor for their factories in the old seigneurial style, from numerous villages and estates which they had acquired. Primitive means of transport and a low level of technology further retarded the modernization of the Demidov enterprises and set the stage for a stagnation that was to characterize all but the biggest components of their industrial empire for much of the next century.

[29] Kafengauz, *Istoriia khoziaistva Demidovykh*, pp. 293-94, 338, 371, 489.
[30] Kafengauz, *Istoriia khoziaistva Demidovykh*, pp. 407, 455, 473-74, 490-91.
[31] Kafengauz, *Istoriia khoziaistva Demidovykh*, pp. 488-89.
[32] Portal, *L'Oural*, pp. 166-67; Pavlenko, *Razvitie metallurgicheskoi promyshlennosti Rossii*, p. 323.

Economic Development and Private Enterprise in the
Post-Petrine Period

Although they were the richest of the Russian iron magnates, the
Demidovs were atypical, or rather, representative of a small and declining group of industrialists who owed their fortunes originally to
the reforms of Peter the Great. During the last half of the eighteenth
century, a number of merchants bought or established metallurgical
enterprises in the Urals. If the career of Michael Gubin is representative, this group of entrepreneurs had accumulated considerable
wealth from their commercial activities, funds which permitted a
rather large-scale investment in industry. Gubin, originally a well-to-
do Moscow merchant, was able to buy six Uralian iron factories
and to build a seventh in the period from 1789 to 1798.[33] By 1800,
we find five wealthy families of middle class origin—most notably the
Iakovlevs—controlling fifty-six factories in the Urals. On a much
smaller scale, in the Moscow and Olonetz regions, forty-seven merchant families were associated with the iron industry during the eighteenth century. However, only eight of these entrepreneurs were still
in business by 1800.[34] Merchant capital thus played a not insignificant role in the growth of the metallurgical industry in Russia, particularly in the Urals, in the last part of the eighteenth century. Merchants also diverted their resources during the same period into most
of the infant consumer industries. They owned almost all of the few
dozen linen and silk manufactories, and distilled most of the liquor
sold in Russia, until in 1754, the making of liquor was declared a
monopoly of the nobility. In the last quarter of the eighteenth century, 337, or just over half of the number of new textile enterprises
founded in Russia belonged to merchants. The amount of commercial capital which was accumulating by this time was substantial. One
estimate for the year 1795 is 71,466,600 rubles.[35] This figure is necessarily a conservative one, since it is based on the amount of capital
declared by the merchants of Russia for tax purposes in that year.[36]

[33] M. Confino gives a detailed account of Gubin's career in his article,
"Maîtres de forges et ouvriers dans les usines métallurgiques de l'oural aux
XVIIIe-XIXe siècles," *Cahiers du monde Russe et Sovietique*, vol. I (1960),
239-41.

[34] Pavlenko, *Istoriia metallurgii v Rossii*, pp. 214, 271.

[35] Figures in V. N. Bernadskii, "Krepostnicheskoe i kapitalisticheskoe predprinimatel'stvo v tret'ei chetverti XVIII v.," V. V. Mavrodin, ed., *Voprosy
genezisa kapitalizma v Rossii* (Leningrad, 1960), pp. 115-16; and Polianskii,
Pervonachal'noe nakoplenie kapitala v Rossii, p. 66. On the capital of some of
the big merchant textile industrialists, which often exceeded 35,000 rubles and
in three instances surpassed 100,000 rubles, see the appendix to A. S. Lappo-
Danilevskii, *Russkaia promyshlennye i torgovye kompanii v pervoi polovine
XVIII stoletiia* (St. Petersburg, 1899), pp. 124-26.

[36] Confino, "Maîtres de forges de L'Oural," p. 241, shows that Gubin's capital
declaration in 1805 of 50,000 rubles was only a very small fraction of his
wealth.

Some of this capital was differentiated into industrial enterprise, as is clear from the evidence we have of the participation of merchants, in metallurgy, textiles, and distilling. Although it is difficult to determine precisely the extent of this participation, given the low level of technology and the scarcity of factory labor in late eighteenth-century Russia, it is very probable that only a small fraction of the available commercial capital was diverted into industry. Such a large fund indicates nonetheless, as the Soviet scholar Iakovtsevskii has emphasized, a significant development of commerce, markets, monetary wealth, and a mercantile class in the Russia of Catherine the Great, all important prerequisites for industrialization.[37]

Little capital was accumulated by the Russian peasantry during the eighteenth century, almost all of the nonagricultural earnings of peasants being derived from trade. A few peasants operated mills or were craftsmen, but most engaged in local commerce, which sometimes proved very lucrative. In one town at the end of the eighteenth century, there were 144 peasants occupied with trade, declaring an average capital of just over 1,600 rubles.[38] The Old Believers also derived great wealth in the same period from extensive commercial activities in the frontier regions of the empire.[39] A limited foundation of capital, skills, and incentives thus was built before 1800 among these two groups of lower class entrepreneurs, but another generation would have to pass before their business activities became important for the growth of Russian industry.

Another type of private entrepreneur was becoming prominent on the Russian industrial scene of the middle and late eighteenth century. This was the noble entrepreneur, a much more characteristic and significant phenomenon of the "golden age" of his class. Wealthy nobles, enriched by extensive landholdings or widespread commercial operations, established industries as early as the seventeenth century, as we have seen in the cases of the Stroganovs and Morozovs. Peter the Great awarded some of his prominent advisors—Tolstoi and Menshikov, among others—with factories. However, recent historians of the eighteenth-century Russian economy would locate a more significant and legitimate appearance of entrepreneurial activity among the gentry in the 1740's.[40] The nobility secured substantial control primarily in three industries during the ensuing several decades: liquor distilling, woolens manufacture, and metallurgy. Even

[37] V. N. Iakovtsevskii, *Kupicheskii kapital v feodal'no-krepostnicheskoi Rossii* (Moscow, 1953), p. 186.

[38] Polianskii, *Pervonachal'noe nakoplenie kapitala v Rossii*, pp. 82-84.

[39] See my Chapter 9.

[40] See Arcadius Kahan, "The Costs of 'Westernization' in Russia: The Gentry and the Economy in the Eighteenth Century," *Slavic Review*, vol. XXV (1966), 55; and N. I. Pavlenko, "K voprosu ob evoliutsii dvorianstva v XVII-XVIII vv.," in Mavrodin, ed., *Voprosy genezisa kapitalizma v Rossii*, pp. 61, 70.

before the government in 1754 made the distilling of liquor a gentry monopoly, landlords were producing in 1,925 registered distilleries over a fourth of the yearly national output of 12,863,967 gallons of alcohol. By 1769, nobles owned almost half of the seventy-three factories comprising the much smaller Russian woolens industry; and by the end of the century, nobles still operated twenty-three of seventy-one metallurgical plants founded by landlords or received from the state during the course of the eighteenth century.[41]

The Russian nobility became interested in industry in the eighteenth century fundamentally because they needed money. The traditional estate economy no longer provided an income sufficient to pay the bill for the amenities of the Westernized way of life that they had assumed as a result of the Petrine reforms.[42] At the same time, various forms of government assistance to some extent protected landlord entrepreneurs against losses, provided them with capital and labor, and insured profits. The existence on the estates of a servile labor force which could be diverted profitably into industrial activity further reduced the initial costs of establishing factories. The obligations of some serfs could be converted into cash payments and they could be furloughed to work in neighboring or distant factories, further increasing the funds which a landlord had at his disposal to buy European luxuries.

Liquor distilling was particularly attractive to landlords, both the petty and the great. A market was assured by state purchases, the raw materials were readily available on the estate, as was serf labor, and it required no great technical training, no sophisticated tools and equipment to build and operate stills. When the government in 1754 decreed distilling a nobiliary monoply, many nobles invested heavily in a form of enterprise that was now practically guaranteed against loss.[43] The manufacture of linen goods also attracted some nobles because it could be contained entirely within the estate economy. Aleksandr Ivanovich Polianskii, a retired colonel and wealthy landlord, who owned over 35,000 acres of land with a laboring force of 4,000 serfs, manufactured canvas and broadcloth for a growing market during the late eighteenth century. All of his raw materials and labor were derived from his estate. Although he paid cash wages to his factory workers at the beginning, even Polyanskii later dispensed with monetary arrangements and had serfs work off their *barshchina* obli-

[41] Pavlenko, "Dvorianstvo v XVII-XVIII vv.," pp. 62-63; *Istoriia metallurgii v Rossii*, pp. 383-84, 433-34.

[42] There is a full discussion of this problem in Kahan, "Costs of 'Westernization' in Russia," pp. 40-41, 55-60.

[43] Pavlenko, "Dvorianstvo v XVII-XVIII vv.," pp. 61-65. On the growth of the liquor industry in Russia during the late eighteenth century, see Appendix 2, Part 1, Table D.

gation at his looms.[44] The woolens industry presented greater technical problems than other eighteenth-century Russian manufacturing ventures, but the promise of state purchases and protection was enough to attract many nobles to it. Here, as in the liquor distilling business, we find the names of many titled aristocrats among the more prominent industrialists.

In the Urals, magnates, courtiers, generals, and important bureaucrats were not only encouraged and aided in entrepreneurial efforts by the government: they were given factories, together with serfs to work in them. Sometimes this was a matter of rewards and favoritism; at others, part of a policy of transferral of state enterprise into private hands with the idea of increasing production. Such gifts and transferrals proved a failure. Thirty-two factories were disposed of by the state in this manner, but not one of the new owners was able to hold on to his investment for very long. Whether this was because these landlords and military men lacked business skills, or because adventurers were perpetrating "open raids on the treasury" can be debated.[45] Other noble families of greater wealth and business experience, notably the Stroganovs, founded a larger number of metallurgical factories in the eighteenth century, and kept most of them.[46]

The increasing involvement of the Russian nobility in industrial enterprise in the eighteenth century was both a reflection of the powerful influence which they wielded over the monarchy in that period and a result of state policy favorable to the entrepreneurial development of that class. Although Catherine the Great looked with disfavor on the business activities of her gentry, she was obliged not only to help them in this endeavor but ultimately to formally recognize their right to do so. This right was granted in the Charter of the Nobility of 1785.[47] During the same period, Russia's merchants were increasingly restricted in the range of their industrial activities.

These constituted the basic changes in Russian state industrial policy after Peter the Great. Generally speaking, this policy in the last seventy-five years of the eighteenth century may be described as a continuation of the Petrine tradition under less forceful leadership. The traditional view that Russia's economic development was set back after Peter's reign because of a reaction in state policy which

[44] I. A. Bulygin, "Iz istorii votchinnoi manufaktury vo vtoroi polovine XVIII v.," *Voprosy sotsial'no-ekonomicheskoi istorii i istochnikovedeniia period feodalizma v Rossii, sbornik statei k 70-letiiu A. A. Novoselskogo* (Moscow, 1961), pp. 139-45. On the manufacture of woolens and linen cloth 1725-1815, see Appendix 2, Part 1, Tables B and C.

[45] Kahan presents the former view, "Cost of 'Westernization' in Russia," p. 56; Liashchenko, the latter, *National Economy of Russia,* p. 300.

[46] Pavlenko, *Istoriiu metallurgii v Rossii,* pp. 433-34.

[47] Pavlenko, "Dvorianstvo v XVII-XVIII vv.," p. 58.

withered the roots of industry that he had cultivated has been challenged by historians, both in the Soviet Union and the West.[48] To be sure, state industrial policy after Peter did not bear the reformer's vigorous personal signature. His essential policies were continued, however, if less forcefully—reflecting the political instability of the times—because such policies were necessary to maintain the Russian war machine.[49] The Petrine tradition, of course, remained strong wherever the reformer's assistants and protégés retained their positions. Under Tatishchev and Hennin, the state metallurgical enterprises of the Urals continued to grow; under M. I. Serdiukov, another personal appointment of Peter's, the Vyshnevolotsk canal system was maintained for a number of years.[50] Elsewhere, Peter's policies in the realms of trade, industrial taxation, labor, and the financing of enterprises remained in force, although as the century wore on, there was a trend toward greater industrial freedom: exemptions from taxes, the abolition of monopolies, lower tariffs, and the encouragement of private enterprise. These new trends did not mean that the state was relinquishing its very rigorous control of Russian industries in any significant way. It was exercising this control in different ways, rather than departing from its traditional mercantilism. The result during the remainder of the eighteenth century was a growth rather than decay of the Russian economy in general and Russian industry in particular. There was no dynamic mobilization of economic resources such as Peter had performed, and some of the more spectacular of his projects, such as the navy and the canal system, fell into ruins. Nevertheless, a foundation for most of Russia's metallurgical and textile industries was laid both in the Petrine and the post-Petrine periods.

Russian Technology in the Eighteenth Century

Some of the foundations for industrial technology in Russia were also built in the eighteenth century. Although there was almost no mechanization in Russian factories during this period, and techniques hardly more than primitive were employed in all but a few experimental enterprises, it nevertheless witnessed some of the advances in science and technology prerequisite to future industrial development. As with most other aspects of the modernization of Russia, the begin-

[48] See Arcadius Kahan, "Continuity in Economic Activity and Policy During the Post-Petrine Period in Russia," *Journal of Economic History*, vol. XXV (1965), 61-85; and F. Ia. Polianskii, "Promyshlennaia politika russkogo absoliutizma vo vtoroi chetverti XVIII veka (1725-1740 gg.)," I. V. Maievskii and F. Ia. Polianskii, eds., *Voprosy istorii narodnogo khoziaistva SSSR* (Moscow, 1957), pp. 85-137; Pavlenko, *Razvitie metallurgicheskoi promyshlennosti Rossii*. On iron production, see Appendix 2, Part 1, Table A.
[49] Polianskii, "Promyshlennaia politika russkogo absoliutizma," pp. 88, 91.
[50] V. S. Virginskii, *Tvortsy novoi tekhniki v krepostnoi Rossii* (Moscow, 1957), p. 23.

nings of a sophisticated and practical science and technology must be traced to the reforms of Peter the Great. Skilled craftsmen, to be sure, could be found in Russia long before Peter, as witnessed by the Tula arms shops and the massive cannon and church bells of Moscow of the sixteenth and seventeenth centuries. The latter required a considerable amount of mechanical and engineering knowledge to construct and move. In seventeenth-century Russia, chemists in the state *aptekarskii prikaz* consulted European works on their specialty. There was a primitive knowledge of mechanics and physics in late Muscovite times.[51]

It was not until Peter the Great, however, that the development of technology became a comprehensive state policy, not only for military, transport, and industrial needs, but also in the fields of education and basic scientific research. However, as with so many of Peter's reforms, the developments in science and technology during his reign were not spontaneous growths nourished by a receptive Russian cultural soil, but were artificial creations, stimulated into being by the will of the tsar and shaped by state decree. With the loss of Peter's leadership came a period of decay, although the post-Petrine period was not overly destructive of Russian science and technology. Peter's navy may have rotted, while the weeds grew high over his roads and canals, but it was not as easy to smother the few sparks of science that the reformer had carried to Russia. Something, however meager, accumulated to ignite genius, and the result was the appearance of Lomonosov, as well as several other outstanding but lesser known scientists and inventors. For the most part isolated and forgotten, these people kept alive the Petrine tradition in science and technology—although their work was not to bear fruit until the next century.

Peter the Great approached science from the point of view of a mercantilist ruler and a practicing technician: Russia was to appropriate Western scientific knowledge, which would be applied to the modernization of the Russian army and navy, the improvement of transport, and the development of industry. The tsar was advised by such eminent European philosophers as Leibnitz.[52] However, a tsar who himself was an accomplished carpenter and engineer, and who had designed several machines on his own did not have to be told of the practical value of science and of the uses to which it might be put by the Russian government.[53]

The simplest way for Peter to begin his scientific establishment was to send Russian students to Europe for a thorough education in

[51] *Istoriia Akademii Nauk SSSR* (Moscow, 1958), vol. I, pp. 16-17.

[52] A. Vucinich, *Science in Russian Culture: a History to 1860* (Stanford, 1963), pp. 46, 73-74.

[53] V. V. Danilevskii, *Russkaia tekhnika* (2nd edn., Leningrad, 1948), pp. 142-43.

Western languages, science, and technology, and conversely, to import European scientists, engineers, technologists, and educators. A more difficult but effective method of bringing science to Russia was through the establishment of elementary and secondary schools, a task hardly facilitated by the almost total illiteracy which then prevailed in Russia. Scientific and technical education required elementary schools which could provide people able to read, write, and calculate. At higher levels, an institution was needed for advanced basic research which would keep Russia abreast of progress in European science and technology. Such an institution could in addition pursue its own original research, engage in practical work for the government, and provide teachers for the lower schools.

Peter used all of these methods from the very beginning of his reign to build Russian science and technology, although it required almost two decades for most of his projects to take root. Russia's first technical school was set up in 1701. This was the School of Mathematics and Navigation in Moscow, which was later called the Naval Academy when it moved to St. Petersburg in 1715.[54] Its curriculum was designed to produce primarily military engineers and artillerymen, as well as navigators. Courses in elementary mathematics and geometry were offered: Russia's first mathematician of any importance, Leontii Magnitskii, taught at the School of Mathematics and Navigation during its initial period.[55]

The School of Mathematics and Navigation was followed by an artillery school. To provide a foundation for these, forty-two elementary schools were established in 1714. As with the higher schools, there was always the problem of finding not only qualified teachers who could speak Russian, but also the bare minimum of students. Many elementary schools closed almost immediately for lack of students; and others had to resort to importing from Europe both the listeners and the lecturers.[56]

Peter's interest in establishing a Russian center for scientific research and for the translation of foreign scientific treatises into Russian went back to the early years of his reign, and can be seen in his correspondence with Leibnitz and his visit in 1717 to Paris, when he was made a member of the French Academy. Nor was Peter unaware of the scientific achievements of other European academies. In 1725, the Russian Academy was established as a kind of hybrid scientific research center and university, a dual purpose which it retained until the end of the eighteenth century. A program in the basic natural sciences was developed, including more practical work in astronomy,

---

[54] See my Chapter 15 on its subsequent history.
[55] Vucinich, *Science in Russian Culture*, pp. 52, 55.
[56] Vucinich, *Science in Russian Culture*, p. 54; *Istoriia Akademii Nauk*, vol. I, pp. 20-21.

geography, navigation, and mechanics. In addition, the Academy was to concern itself with medical and legal subjects and with the liberal arts. In short, it was intended as a kind of intellectual center for the Russian empire. Despite the generality of its offerings, however, it experienced at the beginning the same difficulties as Peter's elementary schools in securing both students and faculty.[57]

The first Russian Academy consisted exclusively of foreigners. Many of the young men sent by Peter to study in Europe never became scientists or technicians. It was enough for many of them to master a foreign language, as witnessed by the fact that nearly half became government translators. They were certainly needed for this task, as were the foreign technicians and educators invited to Russia by Peter. All were encouraged to translate by the government. Farquharson, a Scot, who first headed the School of Mathematics and Navigation, translated many European scientific works into Russian. A few Russians began to write scientific textbooks and technical guidebooks. The first Russian arithmetic text, by Leontii Magnitskii of the School of Mathematics and Navigation, was published in 1703. In 1722, G. G. Skorniakov-Pisarev's *Statistical or Mechanical Science*, the first printed textbook on mechanics in the Russian language, appeared.[58]

Peter the Great was the first tsar to attempt to modernize the primitive transport system of his vast country, a reform indispensable for Russia's industry and military power. Land transport presented technical problems of construction which were insurmountable in Petrine times. A highway from St. Petersburg to Moscow was abandoned in the midst of the huge swamps that stood in its way. Canals to link the river systems between Asiatic and European Russia were less of a problem. Russian experience in canal construction preceded the eighteenth century, and could be combined with Dutch expertise to build the Vyshnevolotsk system. This system united the Caspian and Baltic seas for the first time by a series of canals, lakes, and rivers. A similar attempt to bind the Don and the Volga was abandoned. In solving hydrotechnical problems, Peter's assistants sometimes succeeded where European engineers had failed, as in the case of the Kalmuck engineer, M. I. Serdiukov. Serdiukov rebuilt, made navigable, and maintained the Vyshnevolotsk waterway for many years.[59] The Petrine élan eventually gave out, and for most of the eighteenth century, his canals were in disrepair. It was not until the reigns of

[57] Vucinich, *Science in Russian Culture*, pp. 67-68; *Istoriia Akademii Nauk*, vol. I, pp. 30-31, 33-36.

[58] Danilevskii, *Russkaia tekhnika*, pp. 137-39; *Istoriia Akademii Nauk*, vol. I, p. 21.

[59] See the sketch in V. S. Virginskii, *Tvortsy novoi tekhniki v krepostnoi Rossii* (2nd edn., Moscow, 1959), pp. 14-24.

Paul I and Alexander I, under the able guidance of Sievers and Rumiantsev, that the task pointed out by Peter the Great for the modernization of Russian waterways was in any way significantly furthered.[60]

Despite government indifference, bureaucratic interference, harassment by the church, and internal factionalism, the Academy of Sciences survived the intrigue and instability of the post-Petrine period.[61] The proof of its vitality was the appearance of Lomonosov by the mid-eighteenth century. By this time the Academy was becoming a Russian institution. In the conflict that had developed between the original German and the younger Russian faction, the Russians were winning the day by the 1740's. Russian scientists were capturing high positions in the Academy; Russian publications and translations of scientific works were appearing.

The Academy remained active during this period as a focal point for the development of Russian technology. Distinguished mechanics and inventors, such as Nartov, Leitman, and later under Catherine the Great, I. P. Kulibin, were brought into the Academy to maintain its laboratories and shops, to teach and to further their research. In 1728, the Academy began to publish the *Monthly Historical, Genealogical, and Geographical Notes* to its popular scientific journal, the *St. Petersburg Gazette*, which had been issued, first in German and then in Russian, since 1711. The *Notes* printed a number of articles written by academicians on technical as well as on other more abstract scientific subjects. Some of the more technically oriented articles dealt with such varied problems as metallurgy, oil, barometers, and thermometers. The Academy continued to publish textbooks during the immediate post-Petrine period, mostly translations from the German, on machines, mining, and other technical subjects. By the 1750's, public lectures on new inventions, electricity, and other popular technical subjects were being given and mining machinery was being built in the shops of the Academy.[62]

An important event in the history of Russian science and technology was the founding of Moscow University in 1755. The University was slow in getting started, but a physics laboratory was built as early as 1757 by Johann Schultz, a German teacher of mechanics. In the following year, another German, I. A. Rost, began reading courses in applied mathematics and gave the first instruction in mechanics. In the 1760's, Moscow University sent several of its students to study agriculture and mining sciences at Uppsala University. One of this group, Matvei Afonin, defended a dissertation before Linnaeus while in Sweden, and returned to Russia to teach natural history and agriculture at Moscow University, and later at the Mining

[60] See my Chapter 11.
[61] Summarized by Vucinich, *Science in Russian Culture,* pp. 80-88.
[62] *Istoriia Akademii Nauk,* vol. I, pp. 66-69, 134-37, 170-74.

Institute. One of Afonin's special interests was soil chemistry and conservation. By the 1780's, Moscow University was publishing some of Russia's first agricultural and scientific journals, the *Economic Magazine* (1780-1789), and the *Magazine of Natural History, Physics, and Chemistry* (1788-1790). In 1788, M. I. Pankevich of Moscow University published a dissertation on steam machines, the first such study to appear in Russia.[63]

The late eighteenth century witnessed the founding of the Mining Institute (1773), Russia's first advanced school for mining and metallurgical engineers, and the founding of Catherine the Great's system of provincial and district public schools. The twenty-five main or provincial schools included instruction in mechanics, physics, mathematics, and civil architecture.[64] The Free Economic Society, founded in 1765, was as much concerned with technology as with the improvement of agriculture and economic problems. In the founding statutes, members were urged to communicate information about mining and manufacturing developments, as well as of new inventions in the fields of mechanics and architecture. It was proposed that the society undertake the distribution of models for new tools.[65]

The first great scientist in Russia was Leonhard Euler, who came to the Academy in 1727 and, except for a long interlude in Berlin from 1741 until 1766, did much of his important work in Russia, where he died in 1783. A mathematician of international significance, Euler gave the Russian Academy prestige, and may be considered the founder of the mathematical tradition in Russia. Euler was very much interested in a wide range of scientific and technological problems. His research encompassed work in ballistics, the movements of ships in water, the utilization of machinery, and architecture. He was consulted by the government in technical matters, experimented with a sawmill in St. Petersburg, translated (into German) an English work on the principles of artillery, and in 1749 published a two-volume treatise in Latin on the construction and movement of ships.[66]

Lomonosov was in the tradition of the modernizers of Russia. His approach was universal, as befitted the "Leonardo da Vinci of Russia," the most genuine voice of the eighteenth-century Enlightenment in that country. All aspects of science, technology, society, and culture interested Lomonosov, and all related ultimately to his urgent

[63] P. A. Zaionchkovskii and A. N. Sokolov, eds., *Moskovskii universitet v vospominaniiakh sovremennikov* (Moscow, 1956), vol. I, p. 306; vol. II, pp. 370, 445; vol. III, pp. 230-32; *Istoriia moskovskogo universiteta* (Moscow, 1955), vol. I, pp. 56, 59, 62.

[64] Vucinich, *Science in Russian Culture*, p. 136; on the Mining Institute, see my Chapter 15.

[65] A. Khodnev, *Istoriia Imperatorskago Volnago Ekonomicheskago Obshchestva c 1765 do 1865 goda* (St. Petersburg, 1865), pp. 5-6.

[66] *Istoriia Akademii Nauk*, vol. I, pp. 91, 195; N. A. Figurovskii, ed., *Istoriia iestestvoznaniia v Rossii* (Moscow, 1957), vol. I, p. 281.

concern for eliminating the backwardness of Russia. Hence, the man who was a poet, historian, and philologist, whose most important work was in pure science in the fields of chemistry and physics, was also a man who was trained as a mining and metallurgical engineer, who experimented in the technology of colored glass and porcelain, who ran factories and invented new scientific instruments, founded universities, and formulated programs for the economic development of Russia.

Lomonosov's education was primarily a Russian one. His university training was obtained at the Academic University in St. Petersburg, Russia's only, and languishing, institution of higher learning at that time. An advanced education in chemistry and technology was acquired by Lomonosov in the Germanies, at Marburg and Freiberg. The latter city boasted one of the early mining and metallurgical schools in Europe, located in the heart of the Saxon mining region. Out of his experiences here came Lomonosov's first book, written in 1742 and published by the Academy of Sciences in 1763, *The First Principles of Metallurgy or the Art of Mining*. The book was actually a text for mining engineers: it dealt primarily with geology, the properties of metals, the organization of mining operations, mining machinery and tools, and the processing of iron and steel.[67]

The 1750's were a time of intense scientific and technological study for Lomonosov, both within the Academy of Sciences and outside of it. He conducted experiments with electricity, and in 1756 published his findings in *Theory of Electricity*. He organized a chemistry laboratory. In 1759, Lomonosov's dissertation, *On Greater Exactitude in Navigation*, appeared, the product of a long interest in navigation equipment and techniques. Lomonosov invented his own versions of lightning rods, compasses, thermometers, and other instruments of measurement, and was also active as a cartographer.[68]

During the 1750's, he also became interested in the manufacture of colored glass for mosaics. He conducted thousands of experiments before he was able to obtain satisfactory results. In 1753, Lomonosov was granted land to build a glass factory at Ust-Ruditsa, not far from St. Petersburg. Lomonosov made the machines for this factory, trained the workers, and established a mosaic craft shop for its glass in St. Petersburg. His aim was to produce an epic mosaic glorifying Peter the Great. Some of the completed parts of this grandiose project have been preserved. The factory also produced, in the fifteen years of its operation, numerous household utensils and glass curios.[69]

In 1761, some of Lomonosov's general ideas on Russian modern-

[67] An analysis of Lomonosov's activities in the field of metallurgy in Virginskii, *Tvortsy novoi tekhniki*, pp. 64-71.

[68] Lomonosov's various inventions and experiments are described in B. N. Menshutkin, *Russia's Lomonosov* (Princeton, 1952), pp. 86-91, 138-43.

[69] Menshutkin, *Russia's Lomonosov*, p. 98; Virginskii, *Tvortsy novoi tekhniki*, pp. 72-76.

ization were presented in a letter-essay to the Curator of Moscow University, I. I. Shuvalov. The letter bore the title: "On the Increase and Preservation of the Russian People." It concerned itself with state measures for raising the birth rate and lowering the death rate in Russia. Lomonosov proposed a number of purely administrative measures: the building of orphanages, changes in obsolete marriage customs, the regulation of monasticism, encouragement of immigration and discouragement of migration, the restriction of fasting and drunkenness, and cutting down of the crime of murder. The letter "On the Increase and Preservation of the Russian People" also urged a medical program whereby the state would take measures to fight diseases and plagues, particularly infant afflictions, and would provide against natural disasters. According to the introduction to this letter-essay, Lomonosov had collected notes for other essays dealing with education, agriculture, the arts, encouragement of the Russian merchant class, the state economy, and related topics.[70] In 1763, he did begin to develop a project for organizing a state college of farm management (*zemskoe domostroistvo*). He was influential in establishing Moscow University and worked for the founding of a St. Petersburg University independent of the Academy of Sciences. As a philologist, Lomonosov was very much concerned with the evolution of a modern Russian language and the development of scientific and technical terminology.[71]

If Russia could produce scientists of the first magnitude in the eighteenth century, she could also foster some rather remarkable inventors. These inventors were not isolated, self-taught peasant geniuses. They were of lower class origin, although they were not agricultural serfs. Most were born in an industrial environment, the sons of factory workers, of soldiers in industrial centers, or of petty merchants. Almost all received a substantial technical education at such state schools as the Ekaterinburg Mining School or the Navigation School of Peter the Great, or even abroad. All were given state support, which in some cases was quite substantial. Most were in communication with the most advanced technology of Europe through acquaintance with the publications of the Academy of Sciences on this subject.[72]

Perhaps the most famous of the eighteenth-century Russian inventors, at least in Soviet eyes, is I. I. Polzunov, who invented in

---

[70] Summarized by Menshutkin, *Russia's Lomonosov*, pp. 157-58; see also M. V. Lomonosov, *Sochinenie* (Moscow-Leningrad, 1961), pp. 466-79; on Lomonosov's views of the industrial development of Russia, see Pashkov, ed., *History of Russian Economic Thought*, pp. 373-76.

[71] Menshutkin, *Russia's Lomonosov*, pp. 159, 167-68; Virginskii, *Tvortsy novoi tekhniki*, pp. 82-83; *Istoriia Akademii Nauk*, vol. I, p. 164.

[72] This account is based on chapters 2, 4, 5, and 6, dealing with Nartov, Polzunov, Frolov, and Kulibin, in the most recent study by Virginskii, *Tvortsy novoi tekhniki*. Shorter analyses are in the older study by Danilevskii, *Russkaia tekhnika*.

1766 a 32-horsepower steam engine to pump water out of an Altaic mine. Polzunov's engine, thus, preceded that of James Watt by a few years, and represented an improvement on the earlier Newcomen machine. I. P. Kulibin was perhaps the most talented and sophisticated of the first Russian inventors. Employed as director of the workshops of the Academy of Sciences during the reign of Catherine the Great, Kulibin built telescopes, reflector lamps, electrostatic machines, and a number of other scientific instruments and devices. Perhaps his most ambitious project was the design of a single-arch wooden bridge to span the Neva River.[73]

The most practical of the eighteenth-century Russian inventors were Andrei Nartov and Kozma Frolov. Nartov, a protégé of Peter the Great, later placed in charge of the workshops of the Academy of Sciences, was the most important Russian machinist of the early eighteenth century. He was the only one of the Russian inventors we have discussed who received training in Europe, where he was sent early in his career at the behest of Peter the Great. Nartov started as a lathe master to the tsar, but soon was building government mint presses, canals and locks, and artillery pieces, including a gun with forty-four barrels. In the Altai mines during the late eighteenth century, another important inventor, Kozma Frolov, designed, built, and operated for many years elaborate and effective water-powered machines.

Nartov's and Frolov's inventions thus had a limited practical application. They were not, however, highly original or significant innovations, and were never adopted on any large scale. The more significant plans and inventions of Kulibin and Polzunov came to nothing. Kulibin's wooden bridge was turned down by the Academy of Sciences as impractical, although the plans were greatly admired. Polzunov's steam engine operated for only a short time after the inventor's death. It broke down, was never repaired and was quickly forgotten. Russian inventors of the eighteenth century, as important as one may rate their achievements, were operating in an economic void. These inventors were not out of touch with advancements in European technology, were not isolated from Russian scientists, and were not neglected by the Russian government. But there was simply no way for their machines to be used. A field of industrial and military application for new inventions would have to await the economic and technological developments of the next century.

The plight of the Russian inventors was similar to the general condition of the Russian industrial economy during the eighteenth cen-

[73] See the volume of documents with sketches, *Rukopisnye materialy I. P. Kulibina v arkhive Akademii nauk SSSR. Trudy arkhiva Akademii nauk SSSR*, vol. II (Moscow, 1953).

tury. Important changes had taken place. Patterns of militarism and state control, which would characterize Russian industrialization until the present day had been established. Peter the Great had provided a foundation for state and private industrial enterprise which could not be dismantled. The Petrine industrial tradition did not lapse in the immediate post-Petrine period. Russia's first great heavy industry complex in the Urals grew and prospered. Private industrial enterprise began among Russian merchants and nobles, and several great semicapitalistic fortunes were built. Although the statistics of the period are inaccurate and contradictory, it is safe to say that by the end of the eighteenth century there were hundreds of large factories and mines in Russia and thousands of small plants and shops.[74] Russian trade doubled in the late eighteenth century, and there was a phenomenal rise in population. From the end of the reign of Peter the Great to the end of that of Catherine II, the number of people in the Russian empire multiplied by over two and one-half times, from fourteen million to thirty-six million, an increase which reflected natural growth as much as the conquest of nations.[75]

With all this, by the end of the eighteenth century, craft shops and home industry accounted for most of the manufacturing in Russia. The number of factory workers by 1800 was less than 200,000. Many of these were serf or other types of forced laborers, rather than wage earners. The market for Russian industry was highly restricted. Domestically, no mass market for cheaply produced industrial goods existed. The state and the nobility remained the main purchasers of a limited output of military and luxury products, and the export market for such important items as iron and sailcloth was on the verge of ruinous European competition and a sharp decline. Distribution was confined largely to the antiquated, restricted, and costly fair system. Water and land transportation remained primitive, further pushing up prices. No modern industrial cities had replaced the traditional administrative, religious, and commercial centers. An industrial middle class had hardly begun to emerge from the ranks of the merchants, craftsmen, townsmen, peasants, and religious minorities. Although a fraction of the upper nobility and the dwindling remains of the Petrine industrialist class prospered from their highly protected factories, the bulk of their wealth remained in the land. Only a part of Russia's commercial capital was being diverted into industry. There was only one truly Russian university, where technical subjects were not yet taught, and a few languishing military engineering and technical schools. The masses were technically untutored and illiterate.

During the eighteenth century, Russia witnessed a superficial type

[74] See the discussion in Liashchenko, *National Economy of Russia*, 302-03.
[75] Jerome Blum, *Lord and Peasant in Russia From the Ninth to the Nineteenth Century* (Princeton, 1961), pp. 278-79.

of military industrialization of what remained an agrarian despotism—
the society as a whole did not change. There was neither the inner
social or intellectual forces to stimulate capitalism and technology,
nor did the impulse come from outside. The tsarist leadership had
no inkling of the significance for Russia of the economic developments in England in the last third of the eighteenth century: the first
important Russian statesman and writer to read the lessons of the industrial revolution, Admiral N. S. Mordvinov, was still serving at that
time as a young officer in the Black Sea fleet. Russia would not be
compelled to face the consequences of war with industrialized powers
for another half century. In 1800, she was still a respected contender
for the mastery of Europe. In relative terms, as Tarle maintained over
half a century ago, the Russia of Catherine the Great was not an economically backward country compared to the continental European
nations.[76] However, while these societies were on the verge of more
rapid economic growth, Russia was not equipped for such a rate of
change; and as Europe began to industrialize rapidly, Russia experienced a growing political and military crisis. Nevertheless, in
the several decades after 1800 not only the war machine, but the
Russian state as well as industry and society as a whole gradually
began to change.

[76] Ie. Tarle, "Byla li ekaterininskaia Rossiia ekonomichesku otstaloiu stranoiu?" *Sochineniia*, vol. IV (Moscow, 1958), pp. 443-68.

Chapter 2

Russian Industries in the Early Nineteenth Century

The most significant features of the statistical picture of Russian industrial growth from 1800 to 1860 have been established by numerous recent Soviet monographs and articles devoted to the histories of specific industries.[1] Important changes took place during this period. Some industries modernized and expanded. New industries developed. The most progressive of these was the cotton cloth industry, which experienced a remarkable growth in less than fifty years. Here, predominantly hired labor was used in mechanized factories organized along competitive capitalist lines. Other textile industries remained backward and even primitive. By the 1850's, more linen was produced than any other textile cloth in Russia, but for the most part, it continued to be homespun in millions of peasant huts to satisfy local requirements. By mid-century the far less significant Russian silk industry was little modernized. In the Russian woolens industry, however, we see a mixed picture. The traditional woolens industry, consisting of seigneurial enterprises, was heavily regulated by the state and nourished in backwardness through privilege and protection. However, after the Napoleonic wars, a new, technically modernized, capitalistic type of woolens industry came into being, located largely in the city of Moscow and its suburbs. By 1860, it easily constituted the most significant sector of Russian woolens cloth production. The manufacture of beet sugar, like cotton cloth a new industry to Russia in the early nineteenth century, also experienced rapid growth and mechanization, particularly in the 1840's and '50's. However, with few exceptions, the modernizers of this industry were not middle-class capitalists living in cities, but were landed aristocrats in the rural areas of the western Ukraine who were of Polish and Russian extraction. Religious outcasts played a smaller role worthy of

[1] The general summaries by P. A. Khromov, *Ekonomicheskoe razvitie Rossii v XIX-XX vekakh 1800-1917* (Akademiia Nauk, 1950), and more recently, M. K. Rozkhova, ed., *Ocherki ekonomicheskoi istorii Rossii, pervoi poloviny XIX veka* (Moscow, 1959), and the pertinent sections in *Genezis kapitalizma v promyshlennosti* (Moscow, 1963), and *Voprosy genezisa kapitalizma v Rossii* (Leningrad, 1960) with their notes and bibliographies, as well as my Bibliography, will give some indication of the massive amount of monographic work which has developed. Some of the more important studies of specific industries should be mentioned. For the textile industry, see K. A. Pazhitnov's two volumes on the woolens, cotton, linen, and silk industries, under the general title, *Ocherki istorii tekstil'noi promyshlennosti dorevoliutsionnoi Rossii* (Moscow, 1955 and 1958); for the iron industry, S. G. Strumilin, *Istoriia chernoi metallurgii v SSSR*, vol. I (Moscow, 1954). L. Tengoborskii's contemporary study, *Commentaries on the Productive Forces of Russia*, 2 vols. (London, 1855-56), is a work of sophistication and a mine of information.

note in the development of the Ukrainian beet sugar and woolens industries, just as they were important in the development of a capitalistic woolens industry in Moscow. In the Ukraine, this role was assumed by Jews; in Moscow, by Old Believers.[2]

In contrast to the consumer industries, heavy industry in Russia remained backward and stagnant for most of the early nineteenth century. Although iron production began to surpass eighteenth-century peaks by the 1840's, and a growing Russian market compensated for the loss of foreign buyers to European competition, the Russian iron industry, with the exception of the few very largest enterprises, remained technologically and organizationally unprogressive for most of the period. The traditional iron industries of the Urals languished behind a tariff wall and a barrier of distance which they were unable to overcome because of the failure to modernize their means of transport. They continued to rely on serf labor, and only the wealthiest enterprises were able to increase profits by diversifying into the production of copper and precious metals. The Russian gold industry experienced a Siberian boom in the 1840's which was soon overtaken on the world market by the California gold rush. The new Russian platinum industry was wrecked by state policy, and it passed from the hands of the Demidovs into those of foreigners. A Russian machine industry began to grow by the middle of the nineteenth century, centered for the most part in St. Petersburg. At the same time, we see the beginnings of a modern chemical industry. However, neither industry was adequate to meet the technical needs of various other Russian industries, which continued to rely primarily on European sources for chemicals and machinery.

Tengoborskii, writing in the mid-1850's, estimated the total annual industrial product of Russia at that time to be 375,000,000 rubles. This constituted, according to his calculations, 15½ percent of the gross national product, the remainder representing almost exclusively the agricultural wealth of Russia. Tengoborskii's definition of "industrial" implied, in his own words, "the widest signification of the term."[3] Even accepting such a definition, which for Tengoborskii meant practically everything not plucked from the ground and sold straightway, Russia in the middle of the nineteenth century was clearly an agricultural country just beginning, from the statistical point of view, to industrialize. Of course, Tengoborskii's broad definition cannot be accepted, since only part of the 15½ percent of the total product which he defined as "industrial" came from factories and machines. About 20 percent of Tengoborskii's figure for the total industrial product pertained, as he readily admitted, to the linen industry. This was for the most part a peasant industry, and

[2] For more detail, see my Chapter 9.
[3] Tengoborskii, *Commentaries*, vol. II, pp. 147-50.

most of its product was consumed locally. A similar situation prevailed with many other consumer industries which produced a significant part of the total value of Russian industry in the middle of the nineteenth century: silk and leather were perhaps the most prominent among them. Soviet scholars have identified a whole range of transitional types of production in the peasant industries of Russia during the eighteenth and nineteenth centuries. Many peasant craftsmen worked independently with their families in their own cottages; others worked elsewhere in the locality in cooperation with other peasant craftsmen; still others worked in the vicinity of cities and commercial centers on contract with merchants in their own homes or in lodgings rented from industrial entrepreneurs. This latter domestic system was widespread in all Russian industries in the early nineteenth century, even the most progressive ones.[4] The history of peasant industries in Russia, of course, is a vast subject in itself for which a substantial literature has developed in tsarist and Soviet times, including the disputes that go back to the days of Tugan-Baranovskii and the young Lenin.[5] If, for our more limited purposes here, we define industry as the employment of seasonal and full-time workers in factories, structures located usually but not always in cities, with varying degrees of technical improvement and new modes of power, the percentage of the industrial to the total product in early nineteenth-century Russia shrinks far below 15½ percent. The value of factory production as distinct from peasant industry is difficult to estimate, but we do have figures on the growth of the number of Russian factories and their labor force during the early nineteenth century. Here again, we encounter a problem of definition.

The official tsarist industrial statistics upon which we must rely employed the categories, "factories," and "plants" (*fabriki, zavodi*). The distinction between these terms never was made clear, nor was any definition provided as to size of a "factory" or a "plant," or the nature of the industry. A *fabrika* could mean a large iron mill employing thousands of workers or a tiny cubby hole where two or three men made cigars. The metallurgical industry was not included in the government statistics, since they were compiled by the Department of Manufactures and Domestic Trade, which had no jurisdiction over this industry. In a classic article published posthumously in 1946, the Soviet historian, Zlotnikov, pointed out these deficiencies and at-

[4] See the article by P. G. Ryndziunskii, "Melkaia promyshlennost," in Rozhkova, ed., *Ocherki ekonomicheskoi istorii Rossii*, p. 76.

[5] See a discussion of the historiography in I. V. Meshalin, *Tekstil'naia promyshlennost krest'ian moskovskoi gubernii v XVIII i pervoi polovine XIX veka* (Moscow-Leningrad, 1950), pp. 3-12. The Academy of Sciences of the U.S.S.R. has published two volumes of documents on the subject, under the editorship of V. N. Kasin and I. V. Mashalin, *Krest'ianskaia promyshlennost XVIII veka i pervaia polovina XIX veka* (Moscow-Leningrad, 1935 and 1950).

tempted to clarify the situation.[6] Zlotnikov first applied to the statistics Lenin's definition of a "factory," as consisting of not less than sixteen workers. The employment of sixteen or more workers presumably indicated a degree of diversification of function sufficient to distinguish an industrial enterprise from shops, artels, and other forms of craftsmen's and workmen's joint manufacturing efforts. Applying this criterion to the official figures, and adding data on the metallurgical industries, Zlotnikov concluded that there were about 1,200 factories in Russia in 1804, rather than 2,423; and in the 1850's, 2,818, rather than the official figure of 14,388. Zlotnikov's adjustments lowered the number of industrial enterprises, but he added most of the Russian metallurgical industry to the original figures, raising the count of workers in the middle of the nineteenth century substantially. By 1860, there were 859,950, about 40 percent of them serfs. Many factories, of course, remained very small at this time; others were huge, employing thousands of workers. By 1860, the average number of workers in cotton, woolens, and sugar factories, three of the most progressive Russian industries, was between 100 and 200.[7] We may conclude with the rough approximation that Russian factory industry more than doubled during the early nineteenth century, with a total product worth less than 10 percent of what Russia's basically agrarian economy was producing by the 1850's. To properly evaluate these figures, an analysis of the growth and stagnation of each of the most important industries, as well as the reasons for development and backwardness as the case may be, is necessary.[8]

Textiles

Similar to England and other countries which experienced early "industrial revolutions," the first modern forms of textile production in Russia appeared in the cotton industry. During the early nineteenth century, the spinning, weaving, and printing of cotton became a major business in Russia. By the early 1860's, the total yearly production of cotton cloth was valued at 77 million rubles. The Russian empire (including the Kingdom of Poland and the Grand Duchy of Finland) ranked fifth among the world's makers of cotton yarn by the mid-nineteenth century. By 1860, only England, France, Austria, and the United States had a larger number than Russia's two million spin-

[6] M. F. Zlotnikov, "Ot manufaktury k fabrike," *Voprosy istorii* (1946), nos. 11-12, pp. 31-48.

[7] For details on the factory labor force see my Chapter 4. See also Appendix 2, Part 2, Table A.

[8] The discussion here will be confined to basic industries, or those which were important for one reason or another, or unusual. It would be impossible to analyze in detail here the numerous traditional luxury, religious, handicraft, and agricultural industries—candles, beer, porcelain, paper, cigars, etc.—most of which were insignificant during the early nineteenth century.

dles.[9] The manufacture of cotton in Russia—at least the spinning and printing processes—constituted by the same year a large-scale, mechanized factory industry. The degree of concentration was unusual for the time, but characteristic of industrialization in tsarist Russia. Some of the biggest cotton spinning factories in the world—big family concerns or stock corporations—could be found in 1850 in St. Petersburg or Moscow. These factories dwarfed the largest competitors in New England or Philadelphia in this period.[10] Some of the larger Russian enterprises which combined the spinning and weaving processes of cotton cloth manufacture were beginning to mechanize in terms of steam power, mechanical spindles, and weaving looms by the middle of the nineteenth century. By 1861, in addition to the two million mechanical spindles in Russia, there were several thousand mechanical weaving looms. The cotton printing industry had begun large-scale mechanization with steam-propelled spinning cylinders by the end of the 1830's.[11]

Comparisons, thus, can be drawn between the Russian and English cotton industries in their early stages of modernization. Production vastly accelerated. A working force was concentrated in large, privately owned factories. Machinery was introduced into various stages of the manufacturing processes. Here the similarities end. The production and mechanization of the Russian cotton industry was small compared to the industry in England. Its drawbacks were many—conditions which England was spared. The circumstances which permitted it to develop were quite different than those operative for the growth of the English cotton industry. Its development might almost be considered exceptional. It was, however, to some extent dependent on the industrial revolution in England.

The most obvious contrast between the Russian and English cotton industries during the early nineteenth century was quantitative. As impressive as its development during this period may seem, Russian cotton manufacture constituted less than 10 percent of England's in terms of the total number of spindles and looms. Its goods were for the most part inferior in quality to those manufactured in Europe. There was no chance for Russia to seize parts of the European cotton market. A limited mass market for cheap cotton goods, to be sure, existed in Russia, but home consumption was insufficient to meet domestic production. One reason for this was the high price of Russian manufactured goods, shielded behind a protective tariff wall. Rus-

[9] A. Sherer, "Khlopchatobumazhnaia promyshlennost," *Obzor razlichnykh otraslei manufakturnoi promyshlennosti Rossii* (St. Petersburg, 1862-63), p. 455. See Appendix 2, Part 2, Table E.

[10] Sherer, "Khlopchatobumazhnaia promyshlennost," p. 462; see Victor S. Clark, *History of Manufactures in the United States* (New York, 1929), vol. I, pp. 547, 559.

[11] Khromov, *Ekonomicheskoe razvitie Rossii*, pp. 55-57.

sian cotton manufacturers, thus, were obliged to seek foreign markets. There was only one market which remained open to them, by virtue of its contiguity to the Russian empire and relative freedom from European competition—the Asian one, consisting primarily of the Middle East, Transcaucasus, Central Asia, and China.[12] Raw cotton of good quality was not grown in the Russian empire, and had to be imported during the early nineteenth century. Some cotton was imported from Asia through Astrakhan, but most of it came from Egypt and the American South, through England. Since Russia was not a naval power of any significance, such dependence of an industry caused it to remain in a precarious position.[13]

A number of exceptional circumstances favored the development of the Russian cotton industry. Of less importance in its development were: the Napoleonic wars and shifts of alliances which temporarily cut off English competition; the burning of Moscow, which stimulated the cotton printing industry of Vladimir; or state aid, particularly in the form of tariff protection after 1822. More essential than any of these factors in the development of the Russian cotton industry was its direct dependence on the industrial revolution in England. Without this, its growth certainly would have been stunted. It was the cheap yarn produced by England's improved spinning machines that Russians could weave and finish for a price low enough to reach a mass market. This permitted the growth of the cotton weaving and printing industries in Russia during the first quarter of the nineteenth century. The spinning industry began to expand in Russia in the 1830's, and grew even more rapidly in the following decade when the English ban on the exportation of spinning machinery was lifted. Without England, the Russian cotton industry would have been retarded for decades.

It was an industry which developed in reverse, the printing and finishing of woven cloth being modernized first, rather than the spinning of thread. Cotton cloth was dyed and printed by hand in late eighteenth-century Russia, for the most part by craftsmen from the southern and eastern parts of the empire. Europeans, however, had established a few modern cotton finishing factories in the suburbs of St. Petersburg.[14] At the beginning of the nineteenth century, Russian craftsmen who had been employed in these factories carried the secrets of the new processes to the central industrial region, to Ivanovo in Vladimir and to Moscow. These cities soon became the centers for the Russian cotton finishing industry. In 1801, there were 52 cotton

---

[12] On the Asian trade, see my Chapter 3.

[13] Pazhitnov, *Khlopchatobumazhnaia promyshlennost*, pp. 60-61; Tengoborskii, *Commentaries*, vol. II, p. 47.

[14] See the detailed account in N. N. Dmitriev, *Pervye russkie sitsenabivnye manufaktury XVIII veka* (Moscow-Leningrad, 1935).

DEVELOPMENT OF INDUSTRY AND TRANSPORTATION IN RUSSIA
1861

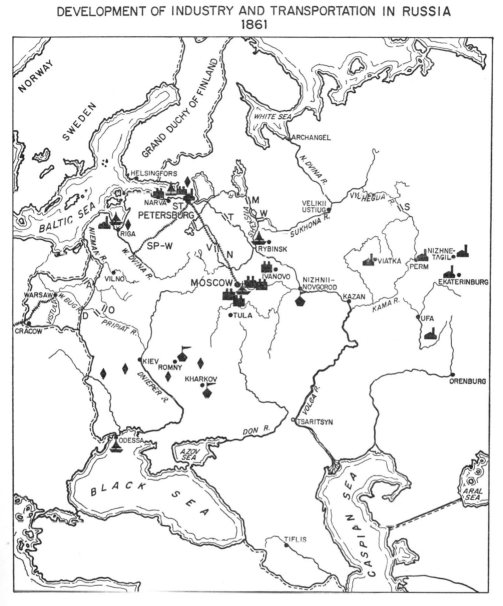

▦▦▦ Borders of Russian Empire	O	Oginski Canal System	▟	Center of Metallurgical and Machine Industries
▭▭ Canals	S	Severo-Ekaterinskii Canal		
▬▬▬ Railroads	SP-W	St. Petersburg-Warsaw RR	▟	Textile Industry Center
A Augustus Canal System	T	Tikhvinskii Canal System	◆	Sugar Industry Center
D Dnieper-Bug Canal System	V	Vyshnii-Volochok Canal System	⬟	Major Fair
M Mariinskii Canal System	W	Duke of Württemberg Canal	⚓	Major Port or Inland River Market
N Nicholas Railroad				

printing plants in Russia, most of them very small; in 1859, there were 320 such enterprises, some of them very substantial factories. Almost all were located in the central industrial region, with only 13 in St. Petersburg.[15]

At the beginning of the nineteenth century, the center for the Russian cotton weaving industry shifted to Moscow and Vladimir provinces, not from St. Petersburg, but from Astrakhan.[16] By the eve of the Great Reforms, almost all of this sector of the cotton industry was concentrated in the two central industrial provinces. There were few modernized cotton weaving factories in Russia before the late nineteenth century, however, and the number of mechanical looms constituted only a small fraction of the quantity of hand looms. By 1860, most of the Russian cotton cloth that was not being imported from England was being woven in peasant huts.[17]

The most progressive branch of the Russian cotton industry developed last. The spinning of cotton experienced a very rapid growth, beginning in the 1830's. The home of the new industry was St. Petersburg, where Russia's first spinning jenny had been installed by a Polish abbot turned industrialist in 1798. This plant was the forerunner of the state Aleksandrovsk works, which until the reign of Nicholas I was the largest cotton spinning factory in Russia. Here, new machinery for the industry was built and tested, Russian craftsmen were trained in modern techniques, and orphans were taught a trade.[18] Although Moscow developed its own cotton spinning industry during the early decades of the nineteenth century, and a few large plants were set up in Ivanovo, it was St. Petersburg where big capital was available in the 1830's to finance large-scale factory operations. Money came from the pockets of Russian and foreign merchants, bankers, and industrialists, as well as from wealthy aristocrats and high-ranking state functionaries.[19] It was in the St. Petersburg cotton spinning industry that some of the earliest Russian industrial stock companies were formed. Most famous of these was the Russian Cotton Spinning Company, founded in 1835 with a capital of 3½ million paper rubles. It had been preceded in 1833 by Baron Stieglitz's cotton spinning factory (later famous as the Neva factory), a large

[15] Pazhitnov, *Khlopchatobumazhnaia promyshlennost*, pp. 50, 57.

[16] Pazhitnov, *Khlopchatobumazhnaia promyshlennost*, p. 28.

[17] Khromov, *Ekonomicheskoe razvitie Rossii*, pp. 59-60.

[18] Details on the Aleksandrovsk factory in Ie. A. Tseitlein, "Iz istorii machinogo proizvodstva v Rossii; pervonachal'noe tekhnicheskoe oborudovanie Aleksandrovskoi manufaktury," Academy of Sciences, U.S.S.R., *Trudy Instituta Istorii, Nauki i Tekhniki*, 1st series, issue 3 (1934), pp. 263-72; V. K. Iatsunskii, "Rol otechestvennago mashinostroeniia v snabzhenii priadil'nym oborudovaniem russkikh fabrik v pervoi polovine xix v.," *Istoricheskie zapiski*, vol. 42 (1953), pp. 276-84.

[19] Count Nesselrode, for example. See Iatsunskii, in Rozhkova, ed. *Ocherki ekonomicheskoi istorii Rossii*, pp. 175-76.

modern establishment with the latest steam machinery and even steam heating.[20] For these and several other St. Petersburg cotton spinning factories established in the 1830's, the necessary capital was available, as well as the technological skill needed and a benevolent state policy. This enabled them to survive and flourish, and they launched the Russian cotton spinning industry. The government did its part through tariffs which kept out English thread. The price of St. Petersburg cotton cloth went up, but it was of a finer grade than that manufactured in the central industrial region and was designed for the Russian upper classes who could afford it. With English spinning machinery still impossible to obtain because of the export ban on it, the Russian spinners relied in the 1830's not only on French and Belgian machinery, but on machines manufactured in the state Aleksandrovsk works. However, these works were directed by an English machinist long in the Russian service, General Wilson.[21]

With the lifting of the export prohibition on English machinery, numerous entrepreneurs from that country descended on St. Petersburg to capitalize on their technical skill in the cotton spinning industry. Russian industrialists, with the German financial wizard Knoop as an intermediary, provided capital for modern mills using English machinery. Numerous large factories were founded in the 1840's and 1850's: the Petrovskii, Sampsonevskii, Spasskaia, Wright, and Shea mills, all with initial capital that ranged from 250,000 to 1,200,000 rubles.[22] From 1842 until 1860, the number of cotton spinning mills in Russia jumped from nineteen to fifty-seven. This involved 41,295 workers, concentrated not in small plants or peasant villages, but in large mechanized factories, usually located in the suburbs of big cities. Some of these factories were the largest in the world: by the early 1860's, the Stieglitz (Neva) factory employed 1,300 workers on 160,000 spindles.[23]

If the cotton industry can be considered the most progressive in Russia during the early nineteenth century, woolens cloth manufacture, or at least a large part of this much older industry (dating back to Peter the Great) must be considered stagnant. Although one sector of the industry began to modernize in several important respects after 1820, the most important impediments to progress were not cleared away until the late nineteenth century. The most comprehensive analysis of the weaknesses of the Russian woolens industry in the mid-1800's has been provided by its contemporary statistician, Ludwig Tengoborskii.[24] Tengoborskii emphasized backward technology

[20] On Stieglitz, see my Chapter 10.
[21] On General Wilson, see my Chapter 10.
[22] Iatsunskii, in *Genezis kapitalizma*, p. 132.
[23] Pazhitnov, *Khlopchatobumazhnaia promyshlennost*, pp. 16, 18-19.
[24] Tengoborskii, *Commentaries*, vol. II, pp. 7-11, 15-17.

and the use of servile labor as the two primary sources of the low productivity and high costs of the Russian woolens industry. Russian woolens manufacturers did not know how to sort and wash wool, and expensive middlemen pre-empted this function. Dyes were either costly or inferior. The industry was only beginning to mechanize: the machines and the men to run them had to be imported, raising both the initial and operating costs of production. Servile labor on private estates, where many Russian woolens factories continued to be located, was seasonal and generally less productive than wage labor. To the problems of labor and technology which Tengoborskii saw confronting this industry, one must add state policy, which tended to be more of a liability than an asset. The government, desperately in need of coarse woolens cloth for army uniforms, particularly during the period of the Napoleonic wars, subsidized, promoted, protected, and rigorously regulated the industry. For many woolens factories, it set quotas and prices and restricted the market to state orders. More often than not, the privileges accorded the woolens industry promoted its backwardness rather than its modernization; and regulation stifled rather than stimulated production.[25]

Recently, Soviet scholars have pointed to positive forces at work in the woolens industry, particularly after 1820. Pazhitnov, in line with contemporary tendencies in Soviet historiography, would term the second third of the nineteenth century a period of "preparation and beginning of the industrial revolution" in Russian woolens.[26] Even prior to this, the grip of the state on the industry had been somewhat relaxed. After 1816, a number of state-supported factories, formerly obliged to produce exclusively for military needs, could also sell their goods on the open market. The tariff of 1822 eliminated the foreign competition which had prevented some Russian woolens manufacturers from diversifying away from the manufacture of a coarse woolens product, or "soldiers' wool," as it was known (designed for military uniforms) to other types of woolens cloth which could be sold in the Russian consumer's market or exported to China. At the beginning of the nineteenth century, the government purchase of coarse woolen cloth exceeded private sales five times over. By the 1850's, this relationship had been reversed: soldiers' wool constituted only one-fifth of the total market.[27] The Asian market for Russian woolens grew significantly during the reign of Nicholas I, so that by 1850, Russia was exporting more woolen cloth than she was importing, accruing a balance of about 25 percent of the total average an-

[25] For details on state administration of woolens enterprises see my Chapter 6.

[26] Pazhitnov, *Sherstianaia promyshlennost*, p. 71.

[27] Pazhitnov, *Sherstianaia promyshlennost*, pp. 29, 71, 73; Iatsunskii, in Rozhkova, ed., *Ocherki ekonomicheskoi istorii Rossii*, p. 190.

nual export value (a 2,746,300 silver ruble yearly average, 1848-1850). Similarly, Russia in the same period had come to export by more than 10 percent the amount she was importing in woolens from the Kingdom of Poland, or a value of 2,747,000 silver rubles.[28] It is clear that Russia by the middle of the nineteenth century was still importing almost half of her woolen fabric from the Kingdom of Poland and from Europe. The reason for this dependence was the tardiness of Russian development in the manufacture of smooth woolen cloths. Such a process required a big investment in the most advanced technology, and it is not until the 1840's that we see this branch of the woolens industry appearing in Russia. It is interesting to note that the Guchkov brothers, scions of the elite of the Moscow Old Believers, had the necessary capital, derived from their communities, the European technical training, and the business foresight to be among the most significant pioneers in introducing the manufacture of worsteds in Russia. By mid-century, their industrial complex in the suburbs of Moscow brought in 1½ million rubles annually, and consisted of 22 stone and wooden buildings, 900 looms, a quarter of them of the most modern variety, and over 1,600 factory workers, with another thousand employed in homes in the vicinity. Tengoborskii makes note of what appears to have been a characteristic of the Moscow Old Believer industrial establishments: "The proprietors deserve the utmost credit both for their constant care to introduce the newest improvements and for their attention to the health of the work people and the instruction of the children."[29]

By 1850, there were 150 Russian worsteds enterprises with 16,244 workers, almost all concentrated in the city of Moscow and Moscow province.[30] The Guchkov establishment was the most progressive example of the most dynamic branch of the Russian woolens industry. For the rest of the industry, we see quite a contrasting picture. It is one not of technically modern, urban factories owned by middle-class industrialists and employing free wage labor, but rural estate industries, in the hands of the gentry, with more primitive methods of organization, little technical improvement, and primarily serf labor. According to Pazhitnov, the percentage of landlord entrepreneurs operating woolens factories on their estates actually increased from 1814 until the end of the 1820's, from 75 to about 80 percent. By the beginning of the 1860's, however, the percentage of estate factories had dropped to about one-fifth, or 145 out of 700 enterprises.[31] The seigneurial woolens enterprises employed about a

[28] Tengoborskii, *Commentaries*, vol. II, tables, on pp. 27-28.
[29] Tengoborskii, *Commentaries*, vol. II, pp. 24-25. For details on the Old Believer entrepreneurs of Moscow, see my Chapter 9.
[30] Pazhitnov, *Sherstianaia promyshlennost*, p. 79.
[31] Pazhitnov, *Sherstianaia promyshlennost*, pp. 33, 71, 85, 91.

third of the total number of workers (120,025) in the industry by the eve of the serf emancipation. The percentage of wage-earning workers in the woolens industry increased significantly during the early nineteenth century, from nine and seven-tenths percent in 1804 to 60 percent in 1861. This figure corresponds to that of the growth of urban, capitalistic woolens enterprises during this period, where most of the wage labor was employed. Servile labor continued to move the looms of most of the estate factories until the emancipation, although some big seigneurial woolens entrepreneurs took advantage of a law of 1840 which permitted the conversion of a special category of possessional serfs into wage laborers. This type of forced labor, established by Peter the Great, and which included perhaps 10,000 people in the woolens industry by 1840, had long since proved itself to be inefficient and unproductive.[32]

Apart from a few experimental ventures, wool was made very largely by hand in Russia until the 1820's. Some machinery was introduced as both urban and estate factories grew during the next two decades, but it was not until the 1840's and 1850's that any significant modernization of machine technology in Russian woolens began. It was the factories of Moscow that were mechanized during this period, the machinery being imported from Europe; and it was through the efforts of such foreign promoters as Ludwig Knoop that the financing of such plant modernization was facilitated for Russian woolens factory owners. This was similar to what was happening at about the same time in the cotton spinning industry.[33]

An advanced chemical technology, essential for the cheap production of high quality dyes for wool, did not appear in Russia during most of the early nineteenth century. Russian woolens manufacturers either had to raise their costs by importing expensive foreign dyes, or were obliged to depend on the dyes prepared by scientifically illiterate Russian craftsmen, and this reduced the quality of the product. This situation began to change by the late 1840's, with the improvement of chemical studies in the Russian universities, and the cooperation of Russian chemists with local industry. It was a Russian university chemist, Professor N. N. Zinin, who first made aniline from nitrobenzine, revolutionizing the world's dye industry. By the 1850's, some of the big woolens factories of Moscow maintained modern laboratories and chemical plants. Moscow University provided courses and a textbook on industrial chemistry. Production of

---

[32] Pazhitnov, *Sherstianaia promyshlennost*, pp. 33, 86, 90. See also the documents in "K likvidatsii possessionnykh fabrik," *Istoricheskii arkhiv*, vol. I (1936), pp. 259-90.

[33] Pazhitnov, *Sherstianaia promyshlennost*, table 20, p. 95, pp. 97, 103-04. On Knoop, see my Chapter 10.

Russian dye extracts began to expand; they reached an annual total of over 126,000 pounds by 1849.[34]

One might conclude that, by the middle of the nineteenth century, there were two woolens industries in Russia. The first, a new and progressive one, which emerged in Moscow after 1812, was a technically modernized capitalist industry producing for a consumer's market and using wage labor. In the case of the Old Believer factories, the biggest in the city, the labor force was composed more of permanent than seasonal workers. In the provincial areas—Tambov, Simbirsk, Voronezh, and also Moscow—wealthy landlords maintained, as they had since the eighteenth century, a woolens industry on the estates, relatively backward in technology and organization, using primarily serf labor, aided and protected by the government, and producing primarily woolen cloth for the armed forces. Although this sector of the Russian woolens industry grew slightly during the early nineteenth century, it was bypassed quickly by the new woolens enterprises of Moscow province in the 1840's and 1850's, and no longer dominated the industry as it had in the earlier part of the century. Of 703 woolens factories in Russia on the eve of the Great Reforms, only 145 were estate factories. This proportion corresponds roughly to the number of factories producing woolen cloth for state orders as compared to the number supplying the private market (in 1845). In 1861, according to Yatsunskii, there were 69,729 wage earners in the woolens industry and 59,562 serf workers.[35] In 1860, this industry produced wool products valued at 39,024,000 silver rubles, a growth of well over 50 percent since 1845. Coarse wool was still by far the main type of wool produced, but worsteds now constituted a third of the total value of production, whereas in 1845, they made up only about a sixth.[36]

The largest and most valuable of the Russian textile industries and at the same time the most backward during the early nineteenth century was the linen industry. The total value of its production by the 1850's exceeded that of cotton and wool combined. By the eve of the Great Reforms, however, for every one laborer working in a Russian factory, there were three or more peasants working in their huts—

[34] Figures from Tengoborskii, *Commentaries*, vol. II, p. 85. On university chemistry in Russia, see my Chapter 14.

[35] Iatsunskii, in Rozhkova, ed., *Ocherki ekonomicheskoi istorii Rossii*, p. 185. On state and private orders in 1845, see the official report edited by V. K. Iatsunskii, "Materialy o sostoianii sukonnoi promyshlennosti Rossii v 1845 g.," *Istoricheskii arkhiv* (1956), no. 4, pp. 82-126. Pazhitnov's educated guess on the number of possessional serfs in 1861 is about 11,000 lower than that of Iatsunskii—see Pazhitnov, *Sherstianaia promyshlennost*, p. 90. See Appendix 2, Part 2, Table G.

[36] Pazhitnov, *Sherstianaia promyshlennost*, table 24, p. 119, based on official reports.

spinning, weaving, and finishing linen products in the most primitive ways. Tengoborskii sets the number of Russian peasants engaged in linen and hemp production in the late 1850's variously at 2,812,500 and 4,500,000.[37] The largest part of the coarse linen produced in peasant cottages went to supply village and estate needs, although some types of rough canvas were processed by Russian manufacturers and shipped to the United States to be worn by slaves. The bottom fell out of this market by the middle of the nineteenth century, when the United States began producing its own "ravens-duck," as this coarse linen was called.[38] Similarly, finer types of linen and sailcloth, which were produced for upper-class consumption and export at the beginning of the nineteenth century in over 300 Russian manufacturing establishments which employed about 29,000 workers, lost both their domestic and foreign markets during the reign of Nicholas I.[39] The primary reason for this decline—which was not confined to the Russian linen industry alone—was the competition of cotton cloth. In addition, Russian linen manufacturers failed to modernize their technology. Flax was prepared in a primitive and wasteful way, it continued to be spun and woven by hand, and cloth was bleached by the sun. Chemical bleaching was practically unknown.[40] The resulting product was costly and inferior in quality, and could compete neither with foreign manufactured cloth nor with Russian homespun linen. Thus, it was not until the 1850's that a few businessmen, both Russian and foreign merchants and entrepreneurs, such as Alexander Stieglitz, set up modern factories for the processing of Russian linen. This made little difference: the Russian linen industry remained essentially a peasant one on the eve of the Great Reforms. Out of ninety-two linen manufacturing establishments reporting to the government in 1854, only twenty-five employed more than 100 workers and only six used steam-powered machinery. A similar situation prevailed in the hemp industry.[41]

The Russian silk industry, inherited from the eighteenth century, changed little in character or magnitude during the reigns of Alexander I and Nicholas I. As in the case of cotton and wool, the home base of this industry was Moscow province and the city of Moscow itself. The big silk factories of Russia were located in the old capital; 11 factories produced about a third of all the silk cloth in the empire

---

[37] Tengoborskii, *Commentaries*, vol. II, p. 147; Pazhitnov cites the lower figure from a later edition, *L'no-penkovaia promyshlennost*, p. 190.

[38] Iatsunskii, in Rozhkova, ed., *Ocherki ekonomicheskoi istorii Rossii*, p. 137; Tengoborskii, *Commentaries*, vol. I, pp. 521-23.

[39] Pazhitnov, *L'no-penkovaia promyshlennost*, pp. 172, 176.

[40] Tengoborskii, *Commentaries*, vol. I, pp. 513, 527.

[41] Pazhitnov, *L'no-penkovaia promyshlennost*, pp. 210-11; statistics from A. S. Nifontov, "Polotnianye manufaktury Rossii v 1854 g.," *Istoricheskie zapiski*, vol. 43 (1953), pp. 229, 234. See Appendix 2, Part 2, Table F.

(excluding the Kingdom of Poland) by the middle of the century.[42] The Russian silk industry as a whole, unlike many others, was controlled almost completely by merchants, townsmen, and peasants. In 1814, out of 158 silk manufacturing enterprises, only 6 were owned by nobles. At that early date, a high proportion—three-fourths—of the Russian silk workers were wage earners.[43]

The silk industry, notwithstanding, remained relatively insignificant in the Russian industrial economy as a whole during the early nineteenth century. The value of its product remained more or less stationary during the 1840's and 1850's, about 7 million rubles annually, and the number of workers never exceeded 15,000. Most of the preparation and weaving of Russian silk was done by village handicraftsmen. Most of the later stages of the processing did not produce a product of high quality, nor was Russian silk fiber, cultivated in the Caucasus, up to foreign standards. No attempts were made to mechanize the industry during the early nineteenth century, and its product was costly, although prices began to drop significantly by the 1840's and '50's.[44]

Beet Sugar Refining and Liquor Distilling

Of the few modernized and newly developed Russian industries which attained importance during the early nineteenth century, beet sugar must be placed next to cotton. The first beet sugar plant in Russia was founded in 1802, with government help, by a Tula landlord—Major-General E. Blankenhagel. The industry languished until the 1830's. In 1830, there were only thirty beet sugar plants in Russia. Most of these were owned by small landlords, using serf labor in technically primitive manufacturing establishments on their estates. By the 1840's, some of the great landlords of the Ukraine established beet sugar factories on their lands. Conditions were suitable in this area for large-scale cultivation of beets, and the big magnates had the necessary capital for major agricultural and industrial operations. Thus, by the eve of the Great Reforms, we see the titled families of Russian and Polish origin in the Ukrainian and central agricultural provinces—the Bobrinskiis, Potockis, Branickis, Poniatowskis, Vasilshchikovs, Golitsyns, Dolgorukiis, and others—establishing large-scale, modern beet sugar factories on their estates. Some families built factories on several of their estates, and by the 1850's were able to produce as much as 4,500 tons of sugar annually.[45] Only a

---

[42] Tengoborskii, *Commentaries*, vol. II, p. 42.

[43] Iatsunskii, in Rozhkova, ed., *Ocherki ekonomicheskoi istorii Rossii*, p. 135; Pazhitnov, *Shelkovaia promyshlennost*, pp. 313, 315.

[44] Tengoborskii, *Commentaries*, vol. II, pp. 40-41, 43; Pazhitnov, *Shelkovaia promyshlennost*, pp. 323-24.

[45] The families and production of their factories are indicated in B. V. Tikhonov, "Razvitie sveklosakharnoi promyshlennosti vo vtoroi polovine 40 kh

few nonnoble entrepreneurs were involved in this first spurt of the Russian beet sugar industry, usually enterprising peasants or Jews who leased land or factories from local magnates, or made some arrangement for financing and managing the new businesses with those who owned property. Israel Brodsky, founder of a late nineteenth-century sugar empire of twenty-two factories (the sales offices of which extended to Siberia and the Ottoman empire), started his operation in this way in 1844. By the early 1860's, the firm of Yakhnenko and Simirenko was one of the major sugar producing enterprises of the Ukraine; the owners were peasants of humble origin and little education who had gathered their initial capital in commercial activity. A modern industrial town—Gorodishchensk—was built on several hundred acres of land leased from Prince Vorontsov, and included a large seven-story refinery, an office building, a machine shop, a mill, and extensive housing for the workers.[46]

With such extensive capital, and with the aid and cooperation of such groups as the Committee of Sugar Manufacturers of the Moscow Agricultural Society,[47] the big beet sugar industrialists could systematically introduce into their factories productive techniques which used both imported and Russian steam machinery. By 1860, most of the industry had been modernized.[48] By 1847, there were 209 beet sugar plants in the Russian empire, 119 of them in the Ukraine. In the following year Russian manufacturers produced over 16,300 tons of beet sugar; this, however, was less than half of the cane sugar imported in that year (39,600 tons) from the new world. By 1860, with cane sugar imports of less than 18,000 tons, the end of the market for this product in tsarist Russia was in sight.[49]

Although improved technology cut down the costs of beet sugar production in Russia by the middle of the nineteenth century, government policy kept the prices up by the introduction of a domestic excise. The government, whose tariff protection originally and unwittingly had nurtured the Russian beet sugar industry, now wished to protect St. Petersburg cane sugar refiners from the competition of

---

i v 50-kh godakh XIX v. (K istorii nachala promyshlennogo perevorota)," *Istoricheskie zapiski,* vol. 62 (1958), pp. 150-51; and in Tengoborskii, *Commentaries,* vol. I, pp. 484-85. See Appendix 2, Part 2, Table B.

[46] Salo Baron, *The Russian Jew Under Tsars and Soviets* (New York, 1964), p. 107. See also my Chapter 9 on the Jewish entrepreneur. On the Ukrainian entrepreneur of peasant origin, see K. G. Voblyi, *Opyt istorii sveklo-sakharnoi promyshlennosti SSSR* (Moscow, 1928), vol. I, pp. 195-96.

[47] See Voblyi's appraisal, *Istorii sveklo-sakharnoi promyshlennosti SSSR,* pp. 67, 114-30.

[48] Tikhonov, "Razvitie sveklosakharnoi promyshlennosti," pp. 135, 169; Voblyi, *Istorii sveklo-sakharnoi promyshlennosti SSSR,* p. 146. See my Chapter 16.

[49] Tikhonov, "Razvitie sveklosakharnoi promyshlennosti," pp. 146-47; and Tengoborskii, *Commentaries,* vol. I, p. 463, for figures.

the provincial manufacturers and to make money. The result was high prices, which restricted the sugar market to the upper classes, retarded the growth of the industry, and deprived the state of maximum revenues. In addition, the use of servile labor, which by 1858-1859 still constituted over 50 percent of the working force of 77,000 males and females, impeded the efficiency and productivity of the industry.[50]

Another industry of importance on the estates of European Russia and the Ukraine was liquor distilling. Older than the beet sugar industry, liquor distilling, as has been indicated earlier,[51] provided many landlords with a source of income and capital during most of the eighteenth century. The industry experienced a significant growth during the first half of the next century. By 1850, similar to the beet sugar industry, large-scale commercial distilleries were replacing the traditional, primitive, and petty local stills. The state in its quest for revenue controlled the liquor market even more tightly than sugar prices, and with similar bad effects for both the industry and the treasury.

During the late eighteenth century, liquor production in Russia more than tripled: in 1801, 42,019,432 gallons were distilled. By 1860, production had gone up approximately another 900 percent to 385,063,268.5 gallons. Russia manufactured by far a greater amount of liquor than any country in Europe.[52] Despite this significant increase in the amount of liquor produced, from 1801 to 1860 the number of distilleries in European Russia decreased from 2,489 to 723. The large-scale commercial enterprise obviously had superseded the small estate distillery. In the Ukraine, however, the local still, intended primarily to supplement the estate income rather than sustain and enrich a landlord-entrepreneur, remained the rule. Some large distilleries developed in the Ukraine; however, by 1860, 4,437 plants remained in operation out of 19,067 in 1801.[53]

Thus, by the middle of the nineteenth century, distilling brought in considerable revenue for some landlords. More capital, however, could be accumulated in the distribution than in the production of liquor. The market for liquor in Russia and the Ukraine was controlled by the state; the sale of vodka was not in the hands of the pro-

---

[50] Tikhonov, "Razvitie sveklosakharnoi promyshlennosti," pp. 152, 154; Tengoborskii, *Commentaries*, vol. I, pp. 466-67. Voblyi gives the most detailed account of state policy, see pp. 337-74. K. Kononenko, *Ukraine and Russia* (Marquette, 1958), pp. 128-30, sees the sugar excise as evidence of tsarist colonialism vis-à-vis the Ukraine. Walter Pintner blames Kankrin, *Russian Economic Policy Under Nicholas I* (Cornell, 1967), pp. 222-26.

[51] See my Chapter 1.

[52] A. Korsak, "O vinokurenii," *Obzor razlichnykh otraslei manufakturnoi promyshlennosti Rossii* (St. Petersburg, 1865), vol. III, pp. 222, 288-90, 292, 298.

[53] Korsak, "O vinokurenii," pp. 290, 296.

ducers or of government officials but, from 1795 to 1863, with a lapse of only a few years, in the profitable domain of middlemen known as "farmers" (*otkupshchiki*). Like the tax farmers of old regime France, those who came into control of liquor leases in tsarist Russia—monopolies which sometimes extended over several provinces—had the opportunity to build up enormous profits. This capital could be diverted into other business enterprises. The Gunzburg banking fortune, for example, was built initially on large liquor "farming" contracts in the south of Russia.[54] The price of liquor was very high under such a system, jumping in some cases to 600 percent of production costs. Despite such prices, the government failed to derive its maximum revenue after everyone else, including corrupt officials, had taken a cut. Production of liquor in Russia, of course, was well below plant capacity during the regime of the *otkupshchiki*.[55]

Metallurgy

At the end of the eighteenth century, Russia produced a third of the world's iron and exported more of this product than any other country. Soon after, the Russian iron industry fell into a slump from which it did not begin to emerge until the 1840's. Although there was growth that might by comparison with preceding rates be termed rapid by the 1850's (57 percent), the iron industry lagged behind other Russian manufacturing industries. Compared to the English iron industry, which was growing twelve times as fast at the same time, the Russian iron industry could only be considered stagnant. By the middle of the nineteenth century, Russia had dropped to eighth place among the major iron producing countries of the world.[56] The reasons for this relative and absolute decline have been understood by economists and historians for over a century, although the weight accorded to certain specific factors has been shifted by contemporary scholars. Many of the causes for the decay of the iron industry during the early nineteenth century apply not only to Russian metallurgy in general, but also explain why the overall process of industrialization did not accelerate during this period.

After the beginning of the nineteenth century, Russian iron began to lose its foreign market. It took over three decades for the domestic market to make up for the losses. The bottom fell out of the Russian iron market because the costs of Russian iron were too high. The basic, but not the only reason for the high cost of Russian iron, most

[54] See my Chapter 9.
[55] Korsak, "O vinokurenii," pp. 316-17, 340, 399.
[56] Figures in S. G. Strumilin, *Istoriia chernoi metallurgii v SSSR* (Moscow, 1954), vol. I, p. 420; see also Iatsunskii, in Rozhkova, ed., *Ocherki ekonomicheskoi istorii Rossii*, pp. 121-22, 166-67; Peter I. Liashchenko, *History of the National Economy of Russia to the 1917 Revolution*, translated by L. M. Herman (New York, 1949), p. 330.

historians have agreed, was the expense involved in transporting it from the Urals (where almost all iron was produced) to the ports, cities, and factories of European Russia. In addition to the problem of transport, which could not be solved until the building of railroads, the method of marketing Russian iron added needlessly to its price. As Tengoborskii indicated in the mid-nineteenth century, so long as Russian iron was marketed within the limited framework of the fair system, a few merchants at places like the national fair of Nizhnii-Novgorod, where much Urals iron was sold initially, could bolster the prices.[57]

Russian iron, however, which was sold close to the Urals or which happened to involve cheaper transport costs, was still a third higher in price than English or Belgian iron.[58] To compete with European producers, the Russian iron moguls would have to produce in larger quantities and at a lower price at point of origin. Three related factors prevented increased production and decreased costs in the iron mills of Russia. The same evils prevailed, as we have seen, in the Russian woolens industry: the use of predominantly servile labor, the failure to modernize technically, and most important of all, state policies which retarded rather than stimulated the industry. State policy was decisive because it could largely determine the organization of the labor force and the level of modernization in Russia's iron factories through its failure to institute positive measures and to abolish regressive laws. It is not easy to determine the part played by private interests, the state establishment, tradition, and bureaucratic inertia in determining government policy.[59] By keeping prices and tariffs high, the government surely was adhering to the wishes of the Urals iron manufacturers. Such favoritism eliminated competition, forestalled failure, and assured profits, but it also removed the pressures for plant modernization. A few of the very largest of the Urals industrialists had sufficient capital to introduce new technology, and did so. Many were heavily in debt to the State Loan Bank, and it is questionable whether they had the requisite funds for improvements.[60] The predominant use of servile labor of various types in both state and private iron factories was antithetical to the introduction of modern technology, machines, and the efficient organization of production. The idea of a seasonal regimentation of large masses of unskilled peasant labor (under strict military discipline and geared to the forceful extraction of mutually guaranteed work quotas) was simply incompatible with the modern factory. If the state, for conservative reasons, was reluctant to dislodge this tradition from the iron fac-

---

[57] Tengoborskii, *Commentaries*, vol. II, p. 121.
[58] Iatsunskii, in *Genezis kapitalizma v promyshlennosti*, p. 143.
[59] For a discussion of state policy in this industry, see my Chapter 6.
[60] See the data in supplement 2, Iatsunskii, in *Genezis kapitalizma v promyshlennosti*.

tories, as seems evident from its failure to effect a general serf emancipation during this period, not all of the Urals iron magnates may have been anxious to perpetuate the system, certainly not its costs. By the 1850's, some of the owners of the larger factories were pointing out that, in contrast to European capitalists, they were maintaining churches, hospitals, pharmacies, children's schools, orphanages, pensions, and other services, in some cases amounting to 30 percent of the total overhead expenses for an enterprise.[61]

Russia continued to export iron during the early nineteenth century, particularly higher grades which could not be obtained elsewhere. By the 1830's, the growth of population, cities, and military needs in Russia replaced the lost English market and the Russian iron industry slowly began to grow.[62] For 1860, Strumilin counts 179 iron factories in the Russian empire (exclusive of the Kingdom of Poland and Finland), supplied by 1,180 mines, with 152 blast furnaces and 415 puddling furnaces. Water wheels were the primary source of power in these factories, exceeding the 5,122.5 horsepower of all the steam and water turbines by almost 800 percent. These factories produced over one-half million tons of iron in 1860, about 60 percent cast iron, and most of the remainder wrought iron.[63] The Russian iron industry utilized primarily forced labor, about 65 percent of the working force at the beginning of the nineteenth century, a percentage which increased slightly by 1860. In that year, there were 136,333 workers in Russian metallurgy.[64]

Three-fourths of Russia's iron factories, and almost all of the larger ones in 1860, were located in the provinces of Perm and Orenburg in the Urals. Iatsunskii estimates the total capital of this industrial region in the 1850's at between 20 and 30 million rubles.[65] There were 110 private iron factories in the Urals. Some were worth less than 100,000 rubles; others, far more than a million. The Demidovs remained the greatest iron moguls of Russia and controlled the biggest factories in the Urals, as they had for over a century. By the middle of the nineteenth century, the total annual income of the Demidovs from their Urals factories and mines continued to be maintained at over one-half million rubles.[66] During the first third of the nine-

---

[61] Iatsunskii, in *Genezis kapitalizma v promyshlennosti*, tables, on pp. 135-37; see also A. Loransky, *Aperçu sur les institutions subsidiaires pour les ouvriers attachés aux établissements métallurgiques en Russie* (St. Petersburg, 1876), pp. 14-19.

[62] Strumilin, *Istoriia chernoi metallurgii*, vol. I, p. 420; Iatsunskii, in Rozhkova, ed., *Ocherki ekonomicheskoi istorii Rossii*, pp. 168-69. See my Appendix 2, Part 2, Table C.

[63] Strumilin, *Istoriia chernoi metallurgii*, vol. I, table 98, p. 432.

[64] Strumilin, *Istoriia chernoi metallurgii*, vol. I, p. 432; Iatsunskii, in Rozhkova, ed., *Ocherki ekonomicheskoi istorii Rossii*, table, p. 121.

[65] Iatsunskii, in *Genezis kapitalizma v promyshlennosti*, p. 133.

[66] Iatsunskii, in *Genezis kapitalizma v promyshlennosti*, p. 145. Compare

teenth century, the average annual production of the Demidov iron mills ranged from 9,000 to 13,500 tons. The Demidovs sold some of their products in stores located in all the important commercial cities and ports of the Russian empire. They continued to sell abroad. In Odessa, for the purpose of shipping their goods in the Mediterranean, they maintained a fleet of five ships, and another Demidov vessel, the "Nicholas I," was registered in an Italian port.[67]

Although Demidov iron production did not drop from eighteenth century levels, it did not grow during the first quarter of the nineteenth century. During the reign of Nicholas I, the Demidovs were among the first of the Russian iron industrialists to introduce mechanical improvements in their larger mills. Nevertheless, they sought to increase their wealth more through diversification than through intensified and modernized iron production. They not only bought estates, as they had in the eighteenth century, but copper mines and gold fields. In the 1820's, when platinum was discovered in the Urals, the Demidovs plunged into this new industry and soon controlled over 80 percent of it. By the early 1840's they were producing over 3½ tons of "white gold" a year.[68]

The Nizhne-Tagil complex in Perm province was the largest and most modern of the Demidov enterprises. Iatsunskii has provided considerable detail, taken from official surveys, on the extent of Nizhne-Tagil in the middle of the nineteenth century.[69] Although by no means typical of the Urals iron enterprises, the Nizhne-Tagil works show us the sophistication and magnitude of the larger private factory complexes in an industry just beginning to emerge from stagnation. Nizhne-Tagil was capitalized (in what very probably was an exaggerated estimate sent to the government in the early 1850's) at 3,153,000 silver rubles. This figure was based on an assessment of the estimated cost of construction of buildings and basic equipment as well as estimated annual overhead expenses. At Nizhne-Tagil, 22,000 workers were employed at 4 blast furnaces, 143 ovens of different types, 120 forges, 149 hammers, 16 blowing machines, and 25

---

with the position of the Demidovs as described in my Chapter 1. In 1812 the N. N. Demidov enterprises sold almost 2 million rubles' worth of iron, but this income was in highly inflated paper money. See B. B. Kafengauz, "Voina 1812 goda i eie vliianie na sotsial'no-ekonomicheskuiu zhizn Rossii (po materialam predpriiatii N. Demidova)," *Voprosy istorii* (1962), no. 7, p. 70.

[67] B. B. Kafengauz, "Khoziaistvo Demidovykh k kontsu pervoi treti XIX v.," *Genezis kapitalizma v promyshlennosti*, pp. 225, 229-31.

[68] Kafengauz, in *Genezis kapitalizma v promyshlennosti*, pp. 227-28; V. V. Danilevskii, *Russkoe zoloto* (Moscow, 1959), p. 278.

[69] Tables, Iatsunskii, in *Genezis kapitalizma v promyshlennosti*, pp. 123-26, 135-36; see also the article by the same author, "Materialy pravitel'stvennogo obsledovaniia zavodov chernoi metallurgii Rossii v pervoi polovine 50-kh godov XIX v. kak istoricheskii istochnik," *Voprosy sotsial'no-ekonomicheskoi istorii i istochnikovedeniia period feodalizma v Rossii* (Moscow, 1961), pp. 357-62.

rolling machines. Among other machinery used were a railroad, 7 steam engines with a total of 335 horsepower, and 3 turbines, building 68 horsepower.[70] Three steam shovels worked at Nizhne-Tagil, very probably the same American machines that had been imported and used unsuccessfully only a few years before in the construction of the St. Petersburg-Moscow railroad.[71] Thirteen dams serviced the factories, as well as 14 conduits, 6 canals, an embankment, and a dock. The number of factory buildings housing these operations, in addition to brick-making, spinning and weaving plants, bridges, storehouses, machine shops and other operational structures was not listed, but their total value was placed at 554,000 rubles. For administrative purposes, there were 2 headquarters buildings, 9 plant offices, 30 houses for guests, staff, and clergy, 8 hospitals, a secondary school, an orphanage, 5 shelters, 8 warehouses for food, 7 stables, a hothouse, 6 fire towers, 2 shops selling metal products, and a church. The annual overhead expenses at Nizhne-Tagil in the 1850's came to 433,000 rubles, and included expenses for maintaining the schools, church, hospitals, and charitable institutions; for payment of the workers' head and recruitment taxes; for pensions and awards; for the maintenance of roads, bridges, and dams; and for fire prevention and postal services.[72]

Steel during the early nineteenth century was produced only experimentally in some of the big Russian iron enterprises. The growth and scope of most of the nonferrous metallurgical industries—copper, zinc, lead, and silver—similarly was insignificant. Developments in the gold and platinum industries, however, are worthy of note. Like most other aspects of modern Russia, the gold industry dates back to Peter the Great. The mining and processing of gold, however, was a state activity of no importance until the 1820's. Beginning at this time, a large-scale, modernized gold industry was developed by private Russian capital, first in the Urals and soon after, in eastern Siberia. In 1800, Russia produced .027 percent of the world's gold; by the mid-1840's, Russia was providing 45 percent. The nearest competitor was a group of several Latin American countries, which produced 26.6 percent.[73] It was a short-lived triumph.

The rapid growth of Russian gold production in the Urals began in the 1820's, when a Russian expert, L. I. Brunitsyn, developed an

---

[70] Strumilin, *Istoriia chernoi metallurgii*, vol. I, p. 430.

[71] See my Chapter 12.

[72] More information on Nizhne-Tagil can be found in G. Ehrenberg and G. Rose, *Reise nach dem Ural, dem Altai und dem Kaspischen Meere von A. von Humboldt* (Berlin, 1837), p. 306 *et seq.*; and R. Murchison, "A Few Observations on the Ural Mountains to Accompany a New Map of a Southern Portion of that Chain," Royal Geographical Society, *Journal*, vol. 13 (1843), 269-324.

[73] Danilevskii, *Russkoe zoloto*, table 37, p. 257.

improved process for extracting gold from auriferous sand.[74] The development and character of the Russian gold industry during the reign of Nicholas I can be seen in the production statistics for state and private factories in the Urals and Siberia from 1814 to 1854. Total production in 1814 was 576 pounds (avoirdupois); by 1824, it had jumped to 7,380 pounds; by 1834, to 46,044 pounds; and by 1854, to 57,456 pounds. From 1813 to 1823, gold was produced only in the Urals, almost 85 percent by state enterprises. From 1833 to 1843, a vastly increased gold output was roughly equal in the Urals and Siberia, but private production was well over double that of the state.[75]

It was eastern Siberia where the big Russian gold boom occurred in the late 1830's and continued through the 1840's and '50's, although Urals gold production continued to rise during this same period. Not only individual private entrepreneurs, but stock companies, after the first imperial confirmation in 1842, worked to develop the Siberian fields, as well as to put up capital for prospectors. Russia's position as the leading producer of the world's gold, maintained for only a few years, was shattered by the discovery of rich gold fields in California and Australia at mid-century. The Russian industry continued to expand in the 1850's, although not at a rate comparable to the United States. Big stock companies were formed in the Urals, such as the Ekaterinburg Company, which thirteen of the biggest gold miners of Russia controlled. The Ekaterinburg Company owned thirty-six gold fields in Perm and Orenburg. Big Siberian gold companies also were formed during the 1850's.[76]

The Russian gold industry by 1860 was modernized technically in only a fragmentary way. It employed just over 58,000 laborers on a seasonal basis.[77] Far less significant, but interesting to note as a casualty of erratic state policy was the platinum industry. In the 1820's, the richest platinum fields in the world were discovered in the Urals. The Demidovs moved in to practically monopolize the industry, which was a profitable one, so long as the Russian government minted platinum money. In twenty years, Russia produced about thirty-six tons of platinum. Suddenly, in 1846, the government decided to discontinue using platinum currency. No other utility could be found for the metal at that time. The market had vanished. Production went down to almost nothing. In the late nineteenth century, European entrepreneurs moved into the field that the Russian state and Rus-

---

[74] Danilevskii, *Russkoe zoloto*, pp. 120-21.

[75] Danilevskii, *Russkoe zoloto*, tables 35 and 39, pp. 254, 259.

[76] V. Ia. Krivonogov, "Zarozhdenie i razvitie chasto-kapitalisticheskoi zoloto-promyshlennosti na Urale k seredine XIX v.," *Genezis kapitalizma v promyshlennosti*, table 2, pp. 246-48; 250.

[77] Danilevskii, *Russkoe zoloto*, p. 260; Krivonogov, in *Genezis kapitalizma v promyshlennosti*, p. 269.

sian private business had abandoned. By the eve of the Revolution, the industry was controlled almost entirely by foreigners.[78]

Fuel, Machine, and Chemical Industries

Both the coal and oil industries languished in Russia during the early nineteenth century. Although it was known that Russia had vast deposits of bituminous and anthracite coal at the time, and the value of coal for industrial and transport purposes was understood in high circles, little was done to develop the industry. The few experiments with coal for iron making came to nothing, although by 1848, Russia's beet sugar factories were using 2,160 tons of the fuel.[79] Similarly, the Russian oil industry presents a picture of neglected resources and opportunities during the early nineteenth century. With the acquisition of Baku at the end of the Napoleonic period, the Russian government found itself in possession, not only of the "eternal fires," worshipped for centuries by Zoroastrians, but also unignited surface oil pools, which could be leased for 130,000 rubles a year. Merchants traditionally had leased these pools from the khans of the area, selling most of the oil to Persia for use in lamps. During all of the prereform era, the Russian government did nothing to develop this resource, except to take over the pools for a while in order to sell the oil directly. It was hoped that this would bring in more money. The experiment did not work and was abandoned for the leasing system. Although some Russian peasants had developed a workable process for making kerosene in the 1820's, this was ignored. It was not until 1859 that the first factory for manufacturing illuminating oil from the natural substance was established near Baku. However, the Russian oil boom had to await the coming of foreign entrepreneurs in the late nineteenth century.[80]

In 1792, a foreign machinist, Charles Baird, established at St. Petersburg the first private mechanical factory to manufacture steam engines in Russia. From Baird's plant came a series of heavy mechanical monsters, the most famous of which were distinguished by dangerous vibrations and frequent breakdowns. By 1825, however, he had produced 141 industrial and other types of steam engines.[81]

---

[78] See the chapter on the Russian platinum industry in Danilevskii, *Russkoe zoloto.*

[79] Iatsunskii, in Rozhkova, ed., *Ocherki ekonomicheskoi istorii Rossii,* pp. 204-05; Tengoborskii, *Commentaries,* vol. I, p. 212; and Tikhonov, "Razvitie sveklo-sakharnoi promyshlennosti," p. 145.

[80] *Tridtsat let deiatel'nosti tovarishchestva neftianogo proizvodstva brat'ev Nobel 1879-1909* (no date or place of publication), pp. 8-10. There is another account in English, based largely on the Nobel official history, J. D. Henry, *Baku, An Eventful History* (London, no date), pp. 17-33.

[81] S. G. Strumilin, "Pervye shagi mashinogo proizvodstva v Rossii (do 30-kh godov xix v.)," *Ocherki ekonomicheskoi istorii Rossii* (Moscow, 1960), pp. 430, 435. On Baird's career see my Chapter 10.

A third of a century later, the Baird machine factory remained one of the largest in Russia, employing 1,200 workers, although by that time, it was no longer alone in this category. Of factories producing primarily steam engines which employed over 250 workers by 1860, there were at least five private establishments in St. Petersburg in addition to the Baird factory. In the same city, perhaps the largest machine producing center in Russia was the state complex at the river front suburb of Aleksandrovsk. Large private and state mechanical plants also functioned by mid-century in Moscow, Kostroma, Kiev, and Ekaterinburg, as well as a steamboat factory established by Muravev-Amurskii at Nikolaevsk in eastern Siberia.[82]

Most of these factories produced steam machinery to provide power for factories or for river transport. The more specialized needs of agriculture, industry, and rail transport found a much more tardy and feebler response in early nineteenth-century Russia. The first shop to produce agricultural machinery was set up by an Englishman in 1802. However, in the 1830's, in the Butenop enterprise in Moscow, which in the latter part of this decade employed about 200 workers, we do find an example of the relatively extensive manufacture of agricultural equipment. The Butenop plant was unique for the magnitude of its production in this field, although a few dozen much smaller shops manufacturing agricultural machinery had been set up in Moscow by 1860.[83] Industrial machinery was manufactured in Russia almost entirely for the textile factories, particularly those engaged in cotton spinning in the decades before the Great Reforms. Some of these machines were made at private establishments, but many came from the work shops of large state factories, such as the Aleksandrovsk Manufactory near St. Petersburg. Its peak production came in 1838, when it was able to sell 500,000 rubles worth of machines, most of them destined, as we have seen, for the newly founded cotton spinning concerns along the Neva River, on the outskirts of the Russian capital.[84] Although Russian machinists, the Cherepanovs, had built and operated railroad locomotives in the Urals several years before, their work, like Polzunov's steam engine of the eighteenth century, was bypassed and forgotten. The real production of steam machinery for Russian railroads did not begin until the 1840's in Aleksandrovsk, near the state cotton spinning and machine plant of the same name. The output of this mechanical and locomotive works was soon very significant, but most of the

[82] A. Ershov, "Obzor mashinostroitel'nykh zavedenii v Rossii," *Obzor razlichnykh otraslei manufakturnoi promyshlennosti Rossii* (St. Petersburg, 1862-1863), vol. II, pp. 12-76, passim.

[83] Ershov, "Obzor mashinostroitel'nykh zavedenii," pp. 53-62, 67-69; E. I. Izmailovskaia, *Russkoe sel'skokhoziaistvennoe mashinostroenie* (Moscow, 1920), pp. 3-4; Iatsunskii, in Rozhkova, ed., *Ocherki ekonomicheskoi istorii Rossii*, p. 209.

[84] Zlotnikov, "Ot manufaktury k fabrike," p. 44.

credit for the organization of production and the quality of equipment must go to foreign engineers.[85]

The Russian machine industry as a whole did not begin to grow significantly until the 1850's. In 1823, there were four machine plants in all of Russia; in 1830, there were seven; in 1845, there were fourteen; in 1851, there were nineteen; and in 1860, there were ninety-nine. These figures must be adjusted for iron foundries, some of which produced machinery, of which there were 130 in 1860. Thus, the figures for the labor force and yearly total production of the Russian machine industry on the eve of the Great Reforms—11,600 workers and 7,954,000 rubles—would have to be increased somewhat.[86] Much of this production was concentrated in St. Petersburg, and it was clear that by the mid-nineteenth century, the administrative capital of the Russian empire was defining itself as its machine producing center. Russia's main industrial center at that time, Moscow, ranked second, with at least thirty plants producing machinery. Most of the plants in either city, however, were little more than shops. The really big machine factories in Russia usually bore foreign nameplates, the imperial crest, or both. Carr and MacPherson, Harrison and Winans, Wilkins, Berman, Ellis and Butts, and Tate were some of the giants, although large-scale machine manufacturers of Russian birth, such as Ogarev, Maltsev, Shipov, and Viatkin should not be forgotten.

By the 1850's, not only did foreign engineers and businessmen play an important role in the Russian machine industry, but, more important, Russia was still buying most of her machinery from abroad, where technically superior machines could be purchased at a cheaper price. The scales were just beginning to tip in the opposite direction by that time. In the decade from 1851 until 1860, Russia imported 48,080,000 silver rubles worth of machinery and produced in her own factories and shops machines valued at 36,433,000 silver rubles. Because of wartime import restrictions, domestic production of machinery vastly exceeded the purchase of foreign products in the mid-1850's, but by 1860, without the aid of these circumstances, the value of Russian yearly output of machinery exceeded that of importation —7,954,000 to 6,716,610 silver rubles. In the 1860's, the ratio of Russian machine production to foreign purchases was approximately fourteen to thirteen for a much greater total volume of over 270,000,000 silver rubles.[87]

---

[85] See my Chapter 12 for a more extensive discussion of Aleksandrovsk.

[86] Zlotnikov, "Ot manufaktury k fabrike," pp. 44-45; Strumilin, *Ocherki ekonomicheskoi istorii Rossii*, pp. 437-39. See Appendix 2, Part 2, Table C.

[87] Strumilin, *Ocherki ekonomicheskoi istorii Rossii*, pp. 439-42; Iatsunskii, in Rozhkova, ed., *Ocherki ekonomicheskoi istorii Rossii*, p. 211; Ershov, "Obzor mashinostroitel'nykh zavedenii," pp. 10-11.

Similarly, the import of foreign chemicals began to fall after the 1830's, although Russian factories by no means ceased to depend on them. Russia produced significant amounts of potash, dyes, saltpeter, nitric and sulphuric acid, pharmaceutical chemicals, and alum by the middle of the nineteenth century. The headquarters of the Russian chemical industry was Moscow, where by 1852, thirty-five of a total of ninety plants (excluding those producing potash) were located. There were 2,413 workers in an industry which produced almost 3 million rubles worth of chemicals annually. This meant that most of Russia's chemical plants were small, the largest one in Moscow employing only sixty-six workers.[88] This was an infant industry on the eve of the Great Reforms. So it would remain when Mendeleev deplored its deficiencies at the end of the nineteenth century, a backwardness that endured in some respects long after that.

This is the essential statistical background to the development of the most important Russian industries during the early nineteenth century. Like Western countries in the early phases of their industrial growth, Russia experienced primarily a textiles industrialization, but on a much smaller scale and with much less prevalence of capitalistic forms of organization. Similarly, by 1860, there were only beginnings of a machine industry in Russia. Heavy industries, such as iron, steel, and chemicals, languished. On the other hand, with such a vast agricultural area to exploit, the development on a large scale of estate industries, such as liquor distilling and beet sugar manufacture, was natural.

Regional Distribution of Industry in the Russian Empire

From the geographical point of view, it may be argued that the industrialization of Russia was a process involving not only one but several regions or nations. It may also be stated with equal conviction that most of these regions were so closely linked by natural, commercial, cultural, and political ties that their industrial development must be viewed as the transformation of one economic unit. Facts also can be marshaled to support the thesis that the relationship of Great Russia to most of the non-Russian nationalities— reaching back even to the early period of tsarist industrialization—has been one of the exploitation of colonies by an imperialist metropolis. The problem of the nature of Russian imperialism, of course, is a complex one that has been debated at great length for many years both within and outside of the Soviet Union. No one would deny that the tsarist regime frequently exploited the non-Russian nationalities economically at the same time that they were being oppressed politically

[88] P. M. Lukianov, *Istoriia khimicheskikh promyslov i khimicheskikh promyshlennosti Rossii do kontsa XIX veka* (Moscow-Leningrad, 1948), vol. I, pp. 123, 139-42.

and Russified culturally. On the other hand, it would be difficult to conceive of the economic development of these areas in tsarist times independent of Russia, her ports, markets, and industries. It might be interesting to speculate on the development of the subject nations comprising the western borderland of the Russian empire under European influence. However the autonomous industrialization of these countries, although ideal from a nationalist point of view, was highly improbable, given the realities of power politics in the nineteenth century. The degree of economic dependence of these areas on Russia, of course varied, as did the extent of Russian exploitation and control. Finland very largely would have to be considered an exception on both counts. Quite a different interpretation, on the other hand, could be given to the economic position of the Ukraine in the tsarist empire.

Liashchenko identified what he termed eight industrial "regions" in the Russian empire by the end of the nineteenth century: the Moscow, St. Petersburg, Polish, and Uralian industrial regions; the eastern and western Ukraine; and the Baku and Transcaucasian oil and coal regions.[89] The industrial destiny of the most important of these regions was already marked out by 1860. This was not true of Baku and the Transcaucasus, an area in political turmoil during the early nineteenth century, where oil was little more than a religious curiosity. It would be several decades before the coal and iron resources of the eastern Ukraine would be united to create the steel mills of Kharkov and Iuzhovka. The vast resources of Siberia remained unexploited, except for gold; and the limited role of Central Asia as a colonial market and supplier of raw materials for Russian industry did not become clear until the 1860's.

The Polish industrial region embraced primarily the central part of old Poland (identified politically as the Congress Kingdom), which included the economic centers of Warsaw and Lodz. A detailed analysis of Polish industrialization, transportation growth, private and state enterprise is beyond the scope of this study.[90] It will suffice to emphasize that Poland was undergoing a much more rapid industrial growth than Russia and many eastern European countries during the early nineteenth century. Large quantities, particularly of textiles, were imported and exported by Polish mills to and from Russia. The industrialization of one definitely affected that of the other, although the economies of the Polish kingdom and Russia were not

[89] Liashchenko, *National Economy of Russia*, pp. 538-39. For figures on the regional distribution of Russian industry in the mid-nineteenth century, see Appendix 2, Part 2, Table H.

[90] See the bibliography of recent works in Polish and Russian cited in E. Edlitskii, "Gosudarstvennaia promyshlennost v tsarstve pol'skom v XIX v.," *Genezis kapitalizma v promyshlennosti, sbornik statei* (Moscow, 1963), pp. 278-79.

as closely linked as were those of most other non-Russian nations ruled by the tsars. The Kingdom of Poland was given a substantial degree of economic freedom and self-sufficiency when created in 1815 by the Congress of Vienna. Tariff walls were reduced—if only for a few years—in all the areas of prepartition Poland, creating a much more viable commercial unit, and facilitating trade with Russia. Economic matters within the Congress Kingdom were left pretty much in the hands of Poles. Under Nicholas I, particularly after the Polish rebellion of 1830, there was increasing restriction of Polish economic life, although the Polish government was active in the 1830's in financing industry. After 1840, these efforts were thwarted, in what was not so much a case of imperialist stunting of the economic growth of a colony for commercial reasons as of political fear that an industrialized Poland would pose a more formidable revolutionary threat to Russia. Thus, jurisdiction over the Polish iron industry was taken away from the Poles and given over to the Russian Ministry of Finances in 1866. Consequently, the state-nurtured Polish metallurgical industry was depressed for some decades.[91]

There were three industrial regions—comprehending several non-Russian peoples—which were much more closely bound with the economy of Russia and which developed rapidly during the early nineteenth century. These might best be termed the Moscow-Vladimir, St. Petersburg-Baltic, and Ukrainian industrial areas. Russia's primary center of heavy industry remained the Urals. The decline of the Urals from its eighteenth-century position as a major world center of the iron industry, and the reasons for this stagnation, have been discussed at length elsewhere.[92] It should be remembered, however, that the Urals remained one of the five major industrial areas of the Russian empire in 1860, where 85 percent of Russia's iron was produced by a fifth of the total factory labor force.[93]

The area including primarily the provinces of Moscow and Vladimir, and to a lesser degree the several provinces which surrounded them (frequently termed the central industrial region), was the birthplace of Russia's modern textile industry. The main industrial cities were Moscow and Ivanovo, in Vladimir province. Moscow was a center for the spinning and weaving of cotton, for the Russian woolens industry, particularly worsteds, and almost all of the much smaller silk industry. Much of the cotton printing industry of Russia was concentrated in Ivanovo. By 1854, over half of the factory workers in the Russian empire (excluding Poland and Finland) were located in the central industrial region; 174,599 of these workers, or well

[91] Edlitskii, "Gosudarstvennaia promyshlennost v tsarstve pol'skom," pp. 292, 298-301.

[92] See this Chapter and Chapter 6.

[93] R. S. Livshits, *Razmeshchenie promyshlennosti v dorevoliutsionnoi Rossii* (Moscow, 1955), p. 128.

over 25 percent, were concentrated in Moscow and Vladimir provinces. In 1854, the estimated total value of production of the manufacturing industries of the central industrial region was 89,059,000 rubles.[94]

The St. Petersburg-Baltic industrial area could be considered one economic unit for a number of reasons. Much smaller than the central industrial area, its industry was concentrated before 1860 in a few cities situated on the coast of the Baltic Sea and the Gulf of Finland: St. Petersburg, Riga, and Narva.[95] St. Petersburg and Riga, until Odessa caught up with the latter, were Russia's major ports: they had numerous commercial contacts with England, the United States, and other Western countries. The industries in the Baltic area were similar, although St. Petersburg was far more industrialized than any of the other cities. On the other hand, the German element in private industrial and commercial enterprise was present in St. Petersburg as well as in the Baltic states. However it was far more pronounced in the latter.

By 1860, it was clear that St. Petersburg was to be the center of the machine and railroad construction industries of Russia. There were fifteen machine plants in the city and its suburbs including several large locomotive works. Over 5,000 workers were employed in this local industry. In the Baltic states by the same year, there were nine machine plants, employing between 637 and 717 workers. Almost all were located in Riga.[96] St. Petersburg was also a center for the Russian textile industry, although taking a second place to Moscow. Cotton spinning, as we have seen, was more important in the imperial capital, with its fifteen large, for the most part mechanized mills, in which 600,000 spindles were concentrated, 50,000 more than the total number of spindles in Moscow and Vladimir provinces combined. However, the cotton weaving, printing, woolens and silk industries were far less significant in St. Petersburg than in Moscow.[97]

The textile industry had also developed a small base by the middle of the nineteenth century in the area of present-day Latvia and Estonia. By 1854, almost 40 percent of all the workers in Riga, 1,997 in number, were employed in textile enterprises.[98] Estonia was poorly developed industrially before the coming of railroads. In 1822, there were less than 900 workers and only eleven enterprises

[94] Livshits, *Razmeshchenie promyshlennosti v Rossii*, table 24, p. 131.

[95] Finland should not be included in this complex for several reasons. It was much less tightly bound to the Russian economy; Russian control, generally speaking, was very limited; and before the late nineteenth century, the Grand Duchy of Finland was insignificant industrially.

[96] Figures in Livshits, *Razmeshchenie promyshlennosti v Rossii*, pp. 106-07.

[97] Livshits, *Razmeshchenie promyshlennosti v Rossii*, pp. 95, 101-03.

[98] V. K. Iatsunskii, "Znachenie ekonomicheskikh sviazei c Rossei dlia khoziaistvennogo razvitiia gorodov Pribaltiki v epokhu kapitalizma," *Istoricheskie zapiski*, vol. 45 (1954), p. 113.

in all of Estonia. Baltic Germans practically controlled this industry, and utilized machinery and craftsmen from Germany, as well as local serfs.[99] Soon after this, a large industrial complex developed at the town of Narva. By 1867, there were 4,792 workers employed in Narva in very large woolens, linen, and cotton factories. Narva, however, was primarily an outpost of Russian capital, or rather, in large part, the capital of German entrepreneurs in Russia. It was developed by bankers, officials, industrialists, and merchants of St. Petersburg and Moscow, many of whom were of German origin. By the 1850's, Baron Stieglitz, the wealthiest banker in Russia,[100] owned a linen and a woolens factory in Narva, which combined employed over 1,000 workers. In the late 1850's, a group of Muscovite investors—merchants and industrialists, collaborating with the German promoter, Ludwig Knoop—founded the very large and modern Krenholm factory at Narva.[101]

Narva was tied very closely to the Russian market. This was less true of the other towns and factories of the Baltic provinces, until extensive construction of railroads to this area in the 1860's and 1870's linked them with distant parts of the Russian empire. Prior to this, Riga was at least partially dependent on the northwestern Russian and Belorussian provinces for raw materials and markets. At the same time, this major northern port was just as strongly linked with Europe and America, from whence its factories purchased raw and manufactured materials. Riga's factories utilized and exported Russian linen, wool, and leather, among other goods; worsted yarn was imported from Europe, woven in the Baltic region, and the cloth was sold in Russia. Like Russia's cotton factories until the middle of the nineteenth century, those of Riga wove and printed English thread and cloth.[102] Raw cane sugar and tobacco were imported from the new world. As in St. Petersburg, although on a much smaller scale, Cuban sugar was refined in Riga in several factories. In 1813-1814, over 3,000 tons of sugar were refined in the Baltic provinces, or about a third of St. Petersburg's sugar production during the same period, and about a fifth of all the sugar manufactured in the Russian empire. The sugar refining industry of the Baltic area was artificially created and sustained for almost half a century. The initial demand was stimulated by Napoleon's continental blockade, which deprived Russia of her sugar for several years. After this, the government protected the industry against the competition of both foreign cane sugar and Ukrainian beet sugar. This was done by a prohibitive tariff which ex-

[99] O. O. Karma, "Ocherk razvitiia manufakturnoi stadii promyshlennosti v Estonii," *Genezis kapitalizma v promyshlennosti*, pp. 165-86 passim.
[100] See my Chapter 10 for a general sketch of Stieglitz's career.
[101] Iatsunskii, "Znachenie sviazei c Rossei," pp. 132-34.
[102] Iatsunskii, "Znachenie sviazei c Rossei," pp. 111-12, 133.

cluded refined sugar from Russia and a domestic excise which enabled the expensive northern product to compete with the more efficiently and cheaply produced southern beet sugar. The vast superiority of the latter industry eventually proved itself, and the Baltic refineries declined as their southern rivals grew.[103]

Almost equal to the tobacco industry of St. Petersburg was that of Riga. In St. Petersburg in 1862, there were thirty-nine tobacco processing plants employing 1,795 workers; in Riga in 1854, there were fifteen plants employing 1,030 workers. The growth of this industry in Riga was probably less due to the inclination of Baltic Germans for smoking than to lower duties applied to American tobacco in preference to Havana cigars. This made it profitable to manufacture cigars in the major ports of entry for goods coming from the western hemisphere.[104]

By the end of the nineteenth century, the Ukraine had developed into a major industrial area; in the 1850's, it already constituted an important and distinct region of industry in the Russian empire, though of a different character and on a much smaller scale than what was to come. In 1860, only 11.6 percent of the total industrial production of the Russian empire issued from the Ukraine.[105] Very little of this, however, consisted of the coal and steel that were to become so important to Ukrainian industrialization several decades later. In 1860, only 96,000 tons of Ukrainian coal were produced, as compared to 24,700,800 tons in 1913. There was only one important metallurgical plant in the Ukraine prior to the Great Reforms, and this used primarily Uralian iron.[106] Ukrainian cities were feebly developed compared to Russian ones in the early nineteenth century: Kiev and Kharkov had less than 50,000 inhabitants each, and neither possessed any significant degree of industry. The industry of the Ukraine prior to the influx of foreign capital at the end of the century was situated on its agricultural estates: a woolens industry, liquor distilling, and beet sugar manufacture. In 1860, the Ukraine produced over a third of the total quantity of liquor distilled in the Russian empire, or 139,278,268.5 gallons.[107] Most of this was produced by small estate stills, for the Ukraine had not developed a large-scale commercial liquor industry to the extent that

---

[103] Figures on the growth and decline of the St. Petersburg-Baltic sugar refining industry in Livshits, *Razmeshchenie promyshlennosti v Rossii*, table 17, p. 114; and G. A. Esh, "Razvitie promyshlennosti v Latvii v pervoi polovine XIX v.," *Genezis kapitalizma v promyshlennosti*, table 12, p. 219.

[104] Iatsunskii, "Znachenie sviazei c Rossei," p. 112; Livshits, *Razmeshchenie promyshlennosti v Rossii*, table 16, p. 108. On the early industrial development of Riga, see also *Beiträge zur Geschichte der Industrie Rigas* (Riga, 1910-11), 3 volumes, published by the Riga Technical Society.

[105] Livshits, *Razmeshchenie promyshlennosti v Rossii*, p. 122.

[106] Konstantyn Kononenko, *Ukraine and Russia*, table LIV, pp. 132-33; 141.

[107] Korsak, "O vinokurenii," p. 298.

this had been done in Russia. Similarly, the woolens industry which had been developed on Ukrainian estates remained backward during the early nineteenth century, while sheep herding declined. However, the Ukrainian beet sugar industry expanded significantly during the same period, so that by 1857, 79.9 percent of all the beet sugar of the Russian empire, or over 30,000 tons, was produced in the Ukraine.[108] This is a remarkable achievement, in view of the heavy excises which the tsarist government imposed on the industry.

The first chapter of the industrialization of the Ukraine, even more sharply than that of Great Russia, reveals a picture of contrasting backwardness and growth, prosperity and stagnation. Although more richly endowed in natural resources and climate than Russia, and more favorably located for trade with Europe, the Ukraine remained poorer. While the Ukraine became a major market for Russian textile factories even before 1860, its industries were impeded by discriminatory tariffs of the imperial government. Even more vigorously than with Central Asia later on, tsarist Russia was reducing the Ukraine to a position of colonial dependency.[109]

[108] Livshits, *Razmeshchenie promyshlennosti v Rossii*, p. 118. Another good, short summary of Ukrainian industries in the early nineteenth century can be found in the first chapter of Voblyi, *Istorii sveklo-sukharnoi promyshlennosti SSSR.*

[109] Kononenko, *Ukraine and Russia*, following early Soviet and pre-Soviet Ukrainian scholars, somewhat overstates this case.

Chapter 3

Toward a Business Economy

At the beginning of the nineteenth century, there was little evidence in Russia of the commercial and financial activities which are associated with a modern business economy and the growth of industry. Commercial conditions were primitive and stagnant. Domestic trade was conducted largely through an antiquated system of transient, seasonal fairs. No more than a handful of urban markets functioned the year around, and only St. Petersburg could boast of a commercial exchange. Land and water transportation facilities were backward and slow, raising the prices of many goods prohibitively. In the realm of foreign trade, Russia followed the pattern of the European colonies, exporting raw materials to the factories of England and the continental countries, while importing finished or semifinished manufactured goods from the same sources. Wealth was siphoned off to pay for foreign luxuries or machinery. The shipping industry was virtually controlled by foreigners, as was most of the export and import trade. The little insurance which was sold came from abroad. Currency was unstable and scarce, particularly outside the main cities. Only a handful of small state banks and one stock company were in existence to facilitate borrowing and investment.

The commercial and financial revolution which would hasten the transformation of this backward system into a more mature business economy had to await the emancipation of the serfs and the growth of banking and railroads which was to come in the late nineteenth century. However, in the sixty years prior to the Great Reforms, there were important modifications in the traditional pattern. These changes paved some of the way for the emergence of capitalism in Russia. Most notably, the fair system began both to be replaced by permanent urban markets and increasingly to service Russian industry, as the domestic trade in Russian manufactured goods grew. The St. Petersburg exchange expanded and modernized, and it was clear by 1860 that the administrative center of the Russian empire was also to become its financial capital. Merchant exchanges began to appear in other Russian cities during the second quarter of the nineteenth century. During the same period, there was a significant first growth of Russian private insurance companies. Foreign trade began to expand, with Europe as well as Asia and America, and the export of wheat became significant. New ports were established and the modernization of Russian transport was initiated.[1]

[1] The subject of transport modernization will be considered in detail in Part IV of this book.

Iarmarka, Gostinnyi Dvor, and Birzha

The decline of the Russian fair (*iarmarka*) began in the early nine-teenth century. The fairs remained the most important group of markets in Russia in 1860, but in many areas, they had been replaced by nonseasonal urban markets. Moscow was the prime example of such a change. The fairs that remained by the mid-nineteenth century had themselves changed in character. By 1860, they dealt primarily with manufactured rather than agricultural goods. Factories sold their products directly at many fairs; and the old itinerant merchant was dying out.

By 1820, there were over 4,000 fairs in Russia, of which sixty-four could be considered large-scale regional or national operations, each with an annual turnover of one million rubles or more. In 1831, ten of the sixty-four large fairs exchanged goods valued at from 10 to 140 million rubles. Many of the fairs, large and small, were located in the Ukraine and the Black Earth region, although there were some important fairs in the eastern regions of European Russia, in the Caucasus, and in Siberia. In the first third of the nineteenth century, agricultural goods primarily were exchanged at these fairs. The turnover in 1831 at 1,705 Russian fairs was 563,000,000 rubles.[2]

The largest commercial fair of the nineteenth century in Russia and Europe, if not the entire world, was the Nizhnii-Novgorod fair. Originally, this fair had been established in 1624, some miles from Nizhnii-Novgorod near the Makarev monastery. Its location was such as to give it access to the great river trading routes leading to the Urals and Siberia, Central Asia, and the Baltic area. It was located "almost on the border of Europe and Asia."[3] Industrial and agricultural products from all over the world were sold at the Nizhnii-Novgorod fair, amounting to an annual turnover in the first decades of the nineteenth century of as high as 140 million rubles. By the 1850's, over three-fourths of the merchandise was Russian, largely textiles and iron. However, over 15 million rubles' worth of goods were brought in from China, Europe, the European colonies and America, Persia and the Khanates of Central Asia.[4] An American visitor in the 1840's, Charles Todd, claimed to have heard twenty different languages spoken at the Nizhnii-Novgorod fair and estimated that 200,000 merchants had come to sell and buy:

It was here that I found the cotton of Mississippi and the rice of

[2] M. K. Rozhkova, "K voprosu znachenii iarmarok vo vnutrennei torgovle doreformennoi Rossii (pervaia polovina xix v.)," *Istoricheskie zapiski*, vol. 54 (1955), pp. 299-306; P. A. Khromov, *Ekonomicheskoe razvitie Rossii v XIX-XX vekakh* (GIPL, 1950), pp. 89-90.

[3] Khromov, *Ekonomicheskoe razvitie Rossii*, p. 90.

[4] L. Tengoborskii, *Commentaries on the Productive Forces of Russia* (English edn., London, 1855-1856), vol. II, pp. 156-57.

South Carolina by the side of the cotton and rice of Bokhara . . . each brought 6,000 miles to be exchanged in the center of Russia.[5]

Despite the large amount of European and American goods sold in its stalls, the Russian and Asian flavor was predominant at the Nizhnii-Novgorod fair. Most of the merchants as late as the 1830's still wore the traditional long robes of Russia and the Orient. At one end of the main concourse of the fair stood a mosque; at the other, an orthodox church.

Although it met only in July and August, the Nizhnii-Novgorod fair was a serious commercial event of major importance to Russian merchants. The fair itself consisted of a large temporary city built on the outskirts of the small town of Nizhnii-Novgorod. Over 3,000 shops of wood and stone, restaurants, theaters, barracks, and hospitals were situated in regular blocks where over 100,000 people would be accommodated annually. At the center of these structures stood a palace for the provincial governor, who resided there every year during the fair. At the nearby river, a huge fleet of barges and river craft was moored. By land, the traffic, particularly with Asia, was spectacular. Caravans employing as many as 30,000 men would leave Orenburg.[6]

By the middle of the nineteenth century, the statistics of the Nizhnii-Novgorod *iarmarka* bear witness to two fundamental changes in the domestic commercial history of Russia. On the one hand, the official figures for 1852 show a turnover of 57 million rubles. The annual value of goods exchanged at the markets of the city of Moscow at about the same period was 60 million rubles. However, although Nizhnii-Novgorod and the other big fairs of the central industrial region of Russia were losing business to the cities, their own turnover included more industrial than agricultural goods in the middle years of the nineteenth century.[7]

The same period witnessed a growth of Ukrainian fairs. This was not, however, evidence of a more primitive or regressive commercial situation in the Ukraine, but rather an indication of the economic growth of that area and of the Russian empire in general. Like Nizhnii-Novgorod, the big Ukrainian fairs were becoming repositories of Russian industrial goods. However, in contrast to what was happening in the central Russian provinces, some of the big Ukrain-

---

[5] Charles Todd, Address on the Russian Empire, G. W. Griffin, *Memoir of Colonel Charles S. Todd* (Philadelphia, 1873) pp. 98-99.

[6] Details on the fair in the 1830's, 1850's, and early 1860's in Robert Bremner, *Excursions in the Interior of Russia* (London, 1839), vol. II, pp. 226-31, 237-54; Henry Moor, *A Visit to Russia in the Autumn of 1862* (London, 1863), pp. 157-58; and J. S. Maxwell, *The Czar, His Court and People* (3rd edn., New York, 1850), pp. 276-79.

[7] Rozhkova, "Znachenie iarmarok," pp. 307-11.

ian fairs were not so much declining as changing their nature. Rather than losing business to continuously functioning urban markets, these fairs were in the process of becoming permanent markets.[8]

The fairs of the northern Ukraine provided one of the largest markets in the Russian empire for manufactured goods from Moscow, Vladimir, and other provinces comprising the central industrial region. A fourth of Russia's cotton and woolens products were sold in the Ukraine. Its fairs also constituted an important outlet for goods from Belorussia, the Kingdom of Poland, and Riga.[9] The largest of the Ukrainian fairs were located in the north, notably the Kharkov and Romny fairs. Kharkov was ideally situated as a key Ukrainian market. It was an administrative and cultural center for the area, and was more convenient than any other Ukrainian town to both the factories of Moscow and the port of Odessa.[10] Actually, four fairs functioned in Kharkov, one for each season, lasting for from two to three weeks. The Kreshchensk fair, held in January, was the largest of these, with a turnover of 9,790,563 rubles in 1854. The largest part of this sale consisted of a wide variety of cotton and woolen goods manufactured in Russia proper. There was also a brisk trade in leather, iron, and tobacco.[11] Russian textiles also dominated the market in the next largest, although much less significant, Ukrainian group of fairs, held at various times of the year in the district of Romen or Romny in Poltava province.[12] The fairs to the south were even less important and provided a market for Ukrainian rather than Russian manufactured goods: wool and beet sugar. They were also markets for the foodstuffs and agricultural products of Bessarabia, the Crimea, Voronezh, and points east. Although fish, caviar, wax, and furs were in abundance at these fairs, European wines, imported through Odessa, could also be obtained.[13]

Traditionally, Ukrainian fairs were motley congregations of itinerant merchants from many parts of Russia and Europe who belonged to several nationalities. Russian merchants belonging to the urban guilds still dominated the scene at the Kharkov fairs in the middle of the nineteenth century. Of 5,535 merchants arriving at the Kharkov fairs in 1854, the police registered about 60 percent as Russians from the Moscow-Vladimir area, and less than a third from the southern

[8] A significant accumulation of knowledge about this process was preserved at the time by the famous Slavophile, Ivan Aksakov, who wrote a perceptive and detailed monograph on the Ukrainian fairs for the Imperial Geographical Society. The book, *Izsledovanie o torgovle na ukrainskikh iarmarkakh* was published in St. Petersburg in 1858, although Aksakov's observations and statistics pertain to the early 1850's.

[9] Aksakov, *Izsledovanie*, pp. 25, 165, 172.

[10] Aksakov, *Izsledovanie*, p. 56.

[11] Aksakov, *Izsledovanie*, pp. 61-65.

[12] Aksakov, *Izsledovanie*, pp. 97-99, 103-12.

[13] Aksakov, *Izsledovanie*, pp. 26-27.

parts of the empire. There were eight from Austria and Prussia and fourteen from the Kingdom of Poland.[14] A group of Russian peasants with goods to sell made an annual trip of several hundred miles from Vladimir province to various Ukrainian fairs. These were called *ofeni* (peddlers). Ukrainian Old Believers also circulated at the fairs as did a few Armenians. More prominent everywhere were Jews, both wealthy merchants importing goods from Europe and street hawkers.[15]

By the middle of the nineteenth century, the traditional itinerant wholesale merchant who had dominated transactions at the Ukrainian fairs was disappearing. Russian factory owners were crowding him out, by establishing shops of their own at the fairs. These shops provided not only a direct outlet for goods produced in their factories, but also for other goods which they might wish to buy and sell at the fairs. Thus, at the same time that merchants in Moscow were finding it profitable and necessary to divert their capital into industrial enterprise, industrialists were assuming the function of merchants at the Ukrainian fairs as well as in the towns. At the Kreshchensk fair of Kharkov in 1854, there were fewer Moscow merchants selling goods than agents of Moscow factories. Some of the bigger Moscow industrialists, such as the Prokhorovs, were very active at Kreshchensk; but most of these "factory outlets" were merely stands where Muscovite peasant craftsmen tried to sell goods which in all probability had been made with their own hands.[16]

Towns, such as Kharkov, which were the site of several fairs each year, were tending to become permanent urban markets. Warehouses were constructed to store goods for sale at forthcoming fairs. Merchants found it more convenient to settle in Kharkov and register in the Kharkov guilds than to travel to the city four or more times a year. Some shops preferred not to close down at all between fairs.[17]

A similar pattern had existed in Moscow for some time. The city of Moscow in the early nineteenth century had not one, but a collection of markets which operated the year around. Food was sold at numerous open-air markets, the largest being the so-named *Okhotnyi Riad*, where numerous shops and stalls provided groceries, flour, poultry, and other foodstuffs, as well as pets and household implements for Muscovites. The city's largest meat market consisted of a street about a mile in length. In the wintertime, frozen carcasses,

14 Aksakov, *Izsledovanie*, p. 57.

15 Aksakov, *Izsledovanie*, pp. 35-39. Among the Jewish merchants at the Ukrainian fairs, were numerous members of the Karaites sect, from the Crimea. According to Aksakov, since they claimed to have migrated to Russia during the Babylonian captivity, hence prior to the crucifixion of Christ, the tsarist government granted them certain commercial privileges beyond those accorded to Talmudic Jews, in view of their freedom from the guilt of Calvary.

16 Aksakov, *Izsledovanie*, pp. 20-22, 162-63, 167.

17 Aksakov, *Izsledovanie*, pp. 19-20.

sufficient to feed the entire population of Moscow for three months, were piled in circles, feet upward, in this market. The city of Moscow also had its large fish and grain markets, and, like many European cities, a "flea" market, known to the Muscovites of the early nineteenth century as the "rag" market. This exchange for junk and used articles of all types consisted of 300 small shops and stands along the old wall of the *Kitai Gorod*.

By far the most important market in Moscow was the *gostinnyi dvor* (merchant's courtyard) located in a group of buildings on the east side of Red Square, a huge oriental bazaar in place of the modern GUM. Under long and pillared, glass-roofed arcades were perhaps 6,000 shops and booths, each with its merchants, the eternal abacus, and a huckster. The shops were arranged in *riady*, or rows, according to the type of product being offered—shoes and leatherware, sweets, various types of cloth and clothing, glass, metal products, tobacco and herbs, candles, ikons, and toys, to name a few. There were well over 50 sections, with manufactured goods predominating—the products of peasant handicraft, of thousands of small urban workshops, as well as of the larger factories of the city. By the middle of the nineteenth century, some industrial concerns had established their own outlets in the *gostinnye dvory* of larger cities, similar to what they were doing at the major fairs. The Demidovs, for example, had stores in eleven cities by that time.[18]

Other Russian cities also had their fairs, stores, and merchants' courts, but a more significant market from the point of view of Russia's economic modernization was not where agricultural and industrial products were sold but the merchants' exchange (*birzha*). By the middle of the nineteenth century, there were merchants' exchanges in several Russian cities, including Moscow (1839), Odessa (1796), and Rybinsk (1811). The latter was a large Volga port, through which most of the grain and iron traffic of the major Russian canal systems passed. The Moscow and Rybinsk exchanges were late in starting and were something of a novelty in 1850. The merchants of the interior parts of the empire, far less Europeanized or emancipated from the traditions and habits of the Russian commercial class than their more cosmopolitan counterparts in St. Petersburg or Odessa, ignored the exchanges as foreign intrusions. In Moscow, from time immemorial, prior to the completion of the exchange building in 1839, merchants had gathered to do business in the *gostinnyi dvor* or in teahouses before 1812, and after the Moscow fire, in the open air of Ilinka Street. Some of the more influential leaders of the Mos-

[18] Robert Lyall, *The Character of the Russians* (London, 1823), pp. 282-83, 307, 340-41; V. K. Iatsunskii, "Geografiia rynka zheleza v doreformennoi Rossii," *Voprosy geografii*, vol. 50 (1960), p. 116.

cow business community deplored this crude and chaotic situation. After several petitions to the government, they obtained permission in 1837 to organize an Exchange Committee, and to build a hall large enough to accommodate the trading operations of the entire Moscow merchant community. The building was completed two years later, but to the dismay of the Exchange Committee, the Moscow merchants refused to use it, and continued to conduct their business out in front of its doors on Ilinka Street, even in the deep snows of winter. Attempts initiated by the Exchange Committee for the police to clear the street were unsuccessful: the merchants moved up to the sidewalk and open porch of the exchange, but would not enter its doors. It was only in the 1860's that a new generation of merchants, sophisticated by railroads, banks, and Western educations, made the Moscow exchange a major commercial center. A similar situation had prevailed for many decades in Rybinsk.[19]

The St. Petersburg stock exchange was a far more mature institution. It already had a long tradition when Alexander I came to the throne. An innovation of Peter the Great, it was founded in 1703 and was intended as a place where merchants could gather, obtain information, and make deals. The *birzha* (from the German *börse*) was naturally very much concerned with foreign trade at the beginning. Its functions did not extend beyond the commercial realm during the eighteenth century, and it remained a small, informal body, composed very largely of foreign merchants.[20]

Beginning in the early nineteenth century, the St. Petersburg *birzha* was transformed from a simple commodities exchange into a modern stock market, dealing in securities of the government and private stock corporations, and speculating with hundreds of millions of rubles. The primary reasons for its expansion can be found in the growth of the port of St. Petersburg, in government domestic borrowing, in railroad construction, and in the emergence of private stock companies in Russia during the early years of the reign of Nicholas I. A series of government decrees from 1816 to 1832 defined the organization of the *birzha*, which was regulated by the Ministry of Finances. An executive committee was set up, the qualifications and powers of the brokers were delineated, a commercial newspaper was established to facilitate the diffusion of business information, and finally, the growing stock market organization was relocated in a handsome, three-story building on Vasilevskii Island.[21]

---

[19] G. Nemirov, *Moskovskaia birzha 1838-1889* (Moscow, 1889), pp. 12-14; A. Nevzorov, "Russkie birzhi," *Uchenye zapiski Imperatorskago Iurevskago Universiteta* (1897), nos. 3, 4.

[20] A. G. Timofeev, *Istoriia S-Peterburgskoi birzhi 1703-1903* (St. Petersburg, 1903), pp. 4-8, 31, 43.

[21] Timofeev, *Istoriia S-Peterburgskoi birzhi*, pp. 69, 75, 94, 101.

The first securities to be offered on the St. Petersburg *birzha* were state bonds in 1809. Private stock was first issued for sale in the early 1830's. The exchange hall was open to all of the categories of people permitted to engage in industry or commerce in the Russian empire: guild merchants, factory owners, foreigners, and even "commercial" peasants. The first president of the stock exchange was Jacob Mollwo, a German, and his compatriots continued for many years to play an important role in its leadership and in brokerage operations. German was the language that predominated on the floor of the St. Petersburg exchange during most of the nineteenth century.[22]

Domestic and Foreign Trade

A vast domestic trade was conducted in the Russian empire during the early nineteenth century, amounting to about 900,000,000 rubles annually during most of this period.[23] Russian expansion and conquests in the seventeenth and eighteenth centuries had created a very large and variegated market. Its total volume far exceeded foreign exports, but it was a poor and primarily agricultural market. Grain, foodstuffs, lumber, and cattle were the most important objects of trade, with the highly priced manufactured goods occupying only about 10 percent of the turnover by the middle of the nineteenth century.[24] The most important commercial regions within the Russian empire were the traditional Moscow-Vladimir area and the Ukraine. The former, traversed by the Volga and other great river arteries, contained not only the largest commercial cities and fairs of Russia, such as Moscow and Nizhnii-Novgorod, but also towns that constituted centers for the grain and iron trade of the central agricultural and Uralian provinces. Ostashkov, Morshansk, and Rybinsk were the wealthiest of these. The Ukraine, in medieval times one of the important commercial areas of the world, assumed new significance for the internal trade of the Russian empire in the late eighteenth century, when the conquests of the fertile region to the north of the Black Sea and the partitions of Poland brought important new markets to Russia.[25] The tariff of 1822 closed the doors of the Ukrainian market to foreign competition for many decades, and provided a lucrative outlet for Muscovite textile manufacturers.[26] During the early

[22] Nevzorov, "Russkie birzhi," p. 12; Timofeev, *Istoriia S-Peterburgskoi birzhi*, pp. 140, 154-56. Membership lists and portraits, facing pp. 96, 189, 220.

[23] Khromov, *Ekonomicheskoe razvitie Rossii*, p. 86 for 1819, and L. Tengoborskii, *Commentaries*, vol. II, p. 153 for the early 1850's give almost the same figures. The inflation of the ruble would be about the same.

[24] Tengoborskii, *Commentaries*, vol. II, pp. 152-53.

[25] I. G. Shulga, "Razvitie torgovli na levoberezhnoi Ukraine na vtoroi polovine xviii v.," *Voprosy genezisa kapitalizma v Rossii* (Leningrad, 1963), pp. 168-69.

[26] Aksakov, *Izsledovanie*, p. 52.

nineteenth century, the Ukraine exported to other parts of the empire not only increasing quantities of its beet sugar, but also cheap grades of Ukrainian tobacco, such as *makhorka*, for the Russian lower classes to smoke and sniff. By the 1850's, between 15,000 and 18,000 tons of *makhorka* were sent from the province of Chernigov alone.[27]

The domestic market in the Russian empire, although shielded from foreign competition by prohibitive or high protective tariffs during most of the early nineteenth century was nevertheless stunted by the extremely high costs of almost all goods. These costs were occasioned not only by operating expenses at the fairs (the rental for an ideally located shop at a Ukrainian fair could run as high as 1,000 silver rubles), but primarily by expenses involved in transport. Even in the Ukraine this was a problem for Russian merchants. The trip from Moscow to the big fairs at Kharkov involved five long roads of varying quality. Only from Moscow to Tula did the merchant enjoy a macadamized highway about 112 miles long. He then entered 87 miles of less highly improved postal road. From the towns of Efreimov to Belgorod his wagons traversed what was termed a "transport" or "nonpostal" road (*nepochtovyi trakt*) for some 241 miles. A postal road 50 miles in length completed the journey to Kharkov. We have no estimate of the time consumed in this trip of almost 500 miles, half of which was very probably on dirt road, nor do we know the extent to which costs were heightened because of seasonal impediments of rain and mud.[28] Tengoborskii estimated in the 1850's that the cost of transport, capital and time investment, raised the price of agricultural goods sold in Russia by 60 percent, and of industrial goods, by 25 percent.[29]

The prohibitive costs involved in hauling heavy masses of iron, in some cases thousands of miles, from the Urals to the Western provinces of the Russian empire, were one of the major factors in the decline of Uralian industries in the early nineteenth century.[30] Not only the prolonged amount of time consumed in transport (land and water), but even more costly, the passing of goods through the hands of two or three middlemen before the time of the final sale, doubled the price of Uralian iron by the time it reached the Ukraine, Belorussia, Bessarabia, or the Caucasus.[31] The Soviet historian, V. K. Iat-

[27] G. P. Nebolsin, *Statisticheskoe obrozrenie vneshnie torgovli Rossii* (St. Petersburg, 1850), vol. I, pp. 395-96.

[28] Aksakov, *Izsledovanie*, pp. 45-46.

[29] Tengoborskii, *Commentaries*, vol. II, pp. 153-54.

[30] For a discussion of some of the other factors involved in the industrial decline of the Urals in the early nineteenth century, see my Chapters 2 and 6. On Russian exports during the early nineteenth century, see Appendix 2, Part 4, Table A.

[31] *Iatsunskii*, "Geografiia rynka v Rossii," p. 143.

sunskii, has analyzed in meticulous detail the various patterns and costs of the domestic iron trade during the early nineteenth century.[32] Most of the iron product of the Urals factories went to the Nizhnii-Novgorod fair for distribution to other parts of the Russian empire. In the late 1840's, about 92 percent of Russia's iron was purchased domestically. Most of the remaining 8 percent went to St. Petersburg and hence to the United States. The trip to Nizhnii-Novgorod took two and one-half months and cost over 11 rubles a ton. Merchant wholesalers controlled the iron trade and prices at the fair. Some of them operated on a grand scale, dealing in thousands of tons of iron and operating their own mills. From Nizhnii-Novgorod, iron was sent to many Russian provinces. Much of it was floated up the Volga to the port of Rybinsk, and from here to Ostashkov and through the newly constructed Volga-Baltic canal systems to St. Petersburg. The entire trip from factory to port took from four to six months, during which the iron might be bought and sold four times. Such conditions, Iatsunskii concludes, "graphically shows the role of transport in the economic backwardness of prereform Russia." There were two ways out of this stagnant situation: improved means of transport, and a more favorable, westerly location of iron mills. Both of these solutions were reached in the late nineteenth century, with the building of a Russian railroad network and the establishment of the Ukrainian heavy industrial complex.[33]

Russia's foreign trade during the first half of the nineteenth century was less important than domestic commerce, and was of limited significance in the international market. Toward the end of the reign of Alexander I, it amounted to about a fourth of the value of the domestic turnover, or approximately 235,000,000 rubles. During all of the nineteenth century, Russia's foreign trade accounted for 4 to 5 percent of the world total, which in the mid-1840's put Russia in sixth place among the trading nations of the world (England was first, with 22 percent).[34] The reasons for this relative commercial backwardness were for the most part geographical, continuing physical impediments to a major Russian role in world trade, which are still to some extent operative. Seaports were icebound much of the year or isolated from the main European markets. Rivers flowed into desolate areas, remote from the trade arteries of the world. In addition, Russian exports, pri-

---

[32] Iatsunskii, "Geografiia rynka v Rossii," pp. 110-45, upon which the figures in the following paragraph are based.

[33] Iatsunskii, "Geografiia rynka v Rossii," pp. 145-46; see also Alexander Baykov, "The Economic Development of Russia," B. E. Supple, ed., *The Experience of Economic Growth* (New York, 1963), pp. 413-25; and my Chapters 11 to 13.

[34] Khromov, *Ekonomicheskoe razvitie Rossii*, pp. 86-87, 98; Nebolsin, *Vneshnaia torgovlia Rossii*, vol. II, pp. 474-75; Kulisher, p. 267 gives the figure of 3.7 percent for the beginning of the nineteenth century.

marily raw materials like iron and grain, were heavy and bulky. Manufactured imported goods, on the other hand, were light and required much less space for transport. This meant that ships came to Russia with partially empty holds, greatly pushing up the cost of freight.[35]

Another characteristic weakness of Russian foreign trading operations during the early nineteenth century was the existence side by side with legitimate commerce of a vast smuggling traffic. Although the balance of trade was favorable for almost all of this period, with exports exceeding imports by a nice margin, the value of exported goods exceeded that of imported precious metals by a huge figure almost every year. The difference was accounted for by goods smuggled into the Russian empire, particularly along the western border, with vast amounts of gold and silver flowing out through the clandestine fissures. It was impossible in those days to seal off over 2,000 miles of frontier rivers and land. Even Cantonese tea, which was fantastically cheaper in Western Europe than in Russia because of the higher costs of transporting it by land rather than by sea, was smuggled in great quantities across the western border of the empire.[36] Government attempts to deal with smuggling by the use of armed force were unsuccessful. Large bands of smugglers roamed openly along the Prussian border and were not afraid to fight pitched battles with regular units of the Russian army. As the casualty lists grew, Nicholas I decided to sacrifice tariffs rather than soldiers. In the late 1830's and early 1840's, many prohibited items were removed from the tariff lists, in an attempt to eliminate the scarcities which had provided the basis for smuggling.[37]

The advantages of Russia's growing foreign trade for Russia herself were further limited by the fact that almost all of this trade was in the hands of foreigners. In the middle of the nineteenth century, a Russian merchant marine was practically nonexistent. In 1847, of 14,031 ships in Russian ports, only 12 percent flew the Russian flag, and most of these were owned by Greeks or Finns. English and German merchants controlled the ships and the trade passing through the ports of St. Petersburg and Riga; Greeks and Italians played a similar role in Odessa. Armenians, Tatars, and Persians dominated the trade between Russia and the Middle East, while Jews carried many of the goods from Eastern and Central Europe to Belorussia and the Ukraine.[38]

Thus, the general pattern of Russian foreign trade at any given time during the early nineteenth century, although showing a favorable balance, must be adjusted for the outflow of funds absorbed by the

[35] Tengoborskii, *Commentaries*, vol. II, p. 178.
[36] Tengoborskii, *Commentaries*, vol. II, pp. 182, 197, 479.
[37] Kulisher, *Ocherk istorii russkoi torgovli*, pp. 308-10.
[38] Nebolsin, *Vneshnaia torgovlia Rossii*, vol. II, pp. 462-64.

freight charges of foreign carriers and smuggling costs, a figure which, however, can only be guessed. The average total Russian export for the years 1842-1846 was 87,680,823 rubles, with imports of 79,853,979 rubles, a favorable balance when unmodified by consideration of transport costs.[39]

By far the biggest item of Russia's exports during the early nineteenth century was grain (wheat, rye, barley, and oats). At the beginning of the century (the average for 1802-1806), 10,087,000 silver rubles worth of grain was exported—1,348,000 rubles more than the next most valuable export, hemp, and almost four times as much in value as the iron export. The grain trade quadrupled during the reigns of Alexander I and Nicholas I to the level of almost a million and a quarter tons exported from 1856 until 1860: "Russia in the first half of the nineteenth century was the supplier of grain for the world market."[40] Hemp was still an important Russian export in the middle of the nineteenth century, as were flax and linen products, leather, lumber, wool, and caviar. Of industrial products, cotton goods were the most important, with an average annual export value of over 3,600,000 silver rubles during the years 1844-1846. Woolen cloth was more significant in Russia's domestic trade than her exports.[41]

The biggest part of Russia's industrial imports in the 1840's consisted of cotton thread and dyes for her factories (8,390,791 and 5,053,038 silver rubles). Significantly, Russian industrialists were importing 3,137,940 rubles worth of raw cotton by that time. The import of woolen manufactures almost equaled the export (2,990,813 to 2,848,156). Foodstuffs and luxury items were important on the Russian list of imports in the period 1842-1846, the total annual average for unrefined cane sugar, tea, coffee, fruits, tobacco, salt, and wine being 27,254,643 silver rubles. Sugar and tea were the most important of these. The value of tea imports exceeded that of machinery on a yearly average from 1842 to 1846 by 700 percent.[42]

At the beginning of the nineteenth century, Russia's foreign trade grew rapidly, imports increasing by 26 percent during the first six years of the century, exports, by 18 percent. Russia traded mainly with Europe, and most of this trade was with England. The largest part was conducted through Baltic ports—St. Petersburg and Riga. Russia exported primarily grain, linen, hemp, and iron to England,

[39] Nebolsin, *Vneshnaia torgovlia Rossii*, vol. II, p. 451.

[40] Khromov, *Ekonomicheskoe razvitie Rossii*, pp. 94-95; M. F. Zlotnikov, *Kontinental'naia blokada i Rossiia* (Moscow-Leningrad, 1966), tables 23 and 24, pp. 30-31, for figures on exports at the beginning of the nineteenth century.

[41] Figures in Nebolsin, *Vneshnaia torgovlia Rossii*, vol. II, pp. 261, 634, 642-44.

[42] Nebolsin, *Vneshnaia torgovlia Rossii*, vol. I, pp. 323-31. On the sugar trade, pp. 336-39; on the tea import, pp. 442-44. On Russian imports during the early nineteenth century, see my Appendix 2, Part 4, Table B.

and imported cotton thread and other manufactured goods from that country. English ships carried most of these goods. There was a well developed overland trade with the German states, and much smaller commercial ties with Scandinavia and the Balkans.[43]

Russia's adherence to the continental blockade of Napoleon brought both growth and disaster to her foreign trade, particularly with Europe. The average yearly total of Russian exports and imports from 1802 to 1806 was 94,900,000 silver rubles, of which 81,900,000 comprised the European trade. In 1808, the worst year of Russian foreign trade during the period of the Tilsit alliance, the trade turnover dropped to less than half of what it had been, 44,500,000 rubles. The European trade turnover fell to 36,300,000 rubles. Russia's Baltic trade was in effect destroyed by 1808, having been reduced to about one-sixth of its dimensions in the period 1802-1806.[44] The ports of St. Petersburg and Riga languished. Overland trade from Germany and the Danubian principalities also was sharply curtailed. Russia's major market, England, vanished, although a clandestine trade with England developed almost immediately. Increased commercial relations with France were no substitute for the English trade, nor did peace with Sweden in 1809 change the picture in any significant way. The Russian tariff of 1811 cut sharply into trade with France.

This commercial catastrophe was accompanied by two significant and positive developments in Russian foreign trade: the emergence of the port of Odessa, and the growth of trade with the United States. The English blockade of Europe left Odessa one of few inlets for vital goods that now could be obtained only from Asia. Cotton was the most important of these, but foodstuffs and tea were also important. Odessa also served as a port of exit for European products. Goods arriving by land from the Orient were shipped from Turkey to Odessa, and from there by river and road to the western Ukraine, eastern Europe and points west.[45]

Another factor in the early commercial growth of Odessa was the excellent administration of the Duc de Richelieu, a French émigré who served as the governor of New Russia during the Napoleonic period.[46] Richelieu's policy was to build Russia's southern trade, with

[43] Detailed figures on Russia's European trade from 1801 to 1806, from which the above have been extracted, can be found in the tables in Zlotnikov, *Kontinental'naia blokada i Rossiia*, chapter I, pp. 9-48. See also my Appendix 2, Part 4, Table E.

[44] Figures in Zlotnikov, *Kontinental'naia blokada i Rossiia*, tables 57, 59, 61, 64, and 65, pp. 290-95; in chapter 8 of his book, pp. 290-334, Zlotnikov gives a full discussion of the Russian trade picture during the period of the Tilsit alliance.

[45] Zlotnikov, *Kontinental'naia blokada i Rossiia*, p. 321.

[46] The only extensive discussion of Richelieu's commercial policies as governor of Odessa is to be found in the unpublished master's thesis by my student,

the port of Odessa as its focus. Odessa, he was convinced, was ideally located to serve as a major port, with its proximity to three major river arteries. There were few disadvantages of climate or accessibility, as in the case of the older Black Sea ports, like Taganrog and Theodosia. Detection of smugglers or pestilence was easier. To facilitate the growth of Odessa, Richelieu worked to maintain trade relations with Turkey, even in time of war with that country, and to keep the Turkish straits open to Russian commercial vessels. He was successful in this policy: while Russian and Turkish troops fought in the Balkans at the end of the first decade of the nineteenth century, Russia and Turkey traded on the Black Sea. Richelieu pleaded with Alexander I to make Odessa a free port in order to insure its preeminence among the Black Sea ports and improve its general competitive position. Although Richelieu was unsuccessful in this quest during the time of his governorship, Odessa was made a free port in 1819, and enjoyed the profits of freedom from duties for over three decades.[47] Richelieu devoted much of his energy to building Odessa into a modern city: the port facilities were improved, an efficient quarantine system was established, thousands of houses and public buildings were built, and courts and theaters were set up. By 1813, Richelieu could boast that Odessa had grown from a town of seven or eight thousand people and 400 houses to a city of 35,000, with 2,600 dwellings. While the entire turnover, of all the Russian ports of the Black and Azov seas did not exceed 1½ million rubles in 1796, according to Richelieu's report, seventeen years later the imports and exports of Odessa alone exceeded 25 million.[48] Odessa continued to grow at this rapid rate during the post-Napoleonic period. By 1838, the population had increased to 75,000. Odessa became the exporter of most of Russia's wheat, well over 90 percent of it by the middle of the nineteenth century. Two-thirds of Russia's grain, or 56,315,036 *chetverts* (337,890,216 bushels) passed through Odessa at that time. By 1850, the Black Sea trade equaled that of the Baltic. Although St. Petersburg retained its place as Russia's first port, Odessa had become the second.[49]

Another result of Russia's commercial disruptions during the Na-

---

Stanley Reifer, "The Duc de Richelieu and the Growth of Odessa 1803-1814" (New York University, 1964). Reifer's primary source is volume 54 of the *Sbornik Imperatorskago Russkago Istoricheskago Obshchestva* (St. Petersburg, 1886), which contains Richelieu's correspondence. See particularly his reports on Odessa and its trade, nos. 82, 98, and 118.

[47] Richelieu, *Correspondance et documents*, no. 118; Vernon J. Puryear, "Odessa: Its Rise and International Importance, 1815-1850," *Pacific Historical Review*, vol. III (1934), 196-97.

[48] Richelieu, *Correspondance et documents*, no. 98.

[49] Puryear, "Odessa," pp. 199, 202; Tengoborskii, *Commentaries*, vol. II, pp. 307, 416, 448. See Appendix 2, Part 4, Table G.

poleonic period was an invigorated American trade. Russia had been trading with the American colonies since the time of Peter the Great, tobacco being the main item that Americans had exchanged for Russian iron, linen, and hemp.[50] It was not until the 1780's, however, that the first American ships voyaged to Russia. The blockades of the Napoleonic period opened a wide commercial door for Americans wishing to trade with Russia. Prior to the repeal of the United States embargo in 1809, this was primarily a matter of English goods being smuggled by renegade American captains. After 1810, Russian-American trade flourished.[51] The United States needed the superior grade of hemp grown and processed in Russia for her ships.[52] High quality Russian iron was also in great demand. The coarse, tough variety of linen cloth known as raven's-duck was used in the American South to clothe slaves. The United States was Russia's biggest market for raven's duck.[53] Russia's biggest imports from the new world were Cuban sugar and cotton from the United States. By the 1840's, 98 percent of all of the raw cane sugar imported by Russia came from Cuba, to be refined in Riga and St. Petersburg. From 1842 to 1846, this amounted to over 33,000 tons.[54] Most of this was carried by American ships. By the 1850's, practically all of Russia's raw cotton came from the United States. In 1853, of a total of 34,884 tons of raw cotton imported by Russia, 32,607 tons was of American origin. Only about a fourth of this was shipped directly from the United States; the rest came through England.[55] By the 1850's, Russia's trade with the United States was significant. Although it amounted to only a fourth of her trade with England, it was surpassed only by that country, France and the German ports, and the total Asian trade. Imports far exceeded exports during most of the early nineteenth century.[56]

The Asian trade became increasingly important in the overall picture of Russian commerce during the early nineteenth century. The Asian trade comprehended Turkey and Persia, Kazakhstan, the Central Asian Khanates, and finally, China. The military victories of the

[50] Alfred W. Crosby, Jr., *America, Russia, Hemp and Napoleon, American Trade with Russia and the Baltic 1783-1812* (Ohio State University Press, Columbus, 1965), p. 5.

[51] This is the main subject of Crosby's book, see chapters 6 to 14.

[52] American-grown hemp, used mainly for baling cotton, was less durable than the Russian product because of inferior processing. It was cheaper to import the Russian product. Manila hemp had not yet come into its own. See the discussion in Crosby, *America, Russia, Hemp and Napoleon*, pp. 18-24.

[53] M. K. Rozhkova, ed., *Ocherki ekonomicheskoi istorii Rossii pervoi poloviny xix veka* (Moscow, 1959), p. 137; Nebolsin, *Vneshnaia torgovlia Rossii*, vol. II, p. 377.

[54] Nebolsin, *Vneshnaia torgovlia Rossii*, vol. I, p. 324.

[55] United States Congress, House of Representatives, 35th Congress, 1st session, document no. 85, "Consumption of Cotton in Europe," p. 62.

[56] See the table in M. K. Kuzmin, "K istorii Russko-Amerikanskoi torgovli," *Istoricheskii arkhiv* (1956), no. 6, pp. 87-90; and Nebolsin, *Vneshnaia torgovlia Rossii*, vol. II, p. 459.

1820's against the Turks and Persians opened the door of the Middle East to Russian trade. Here were new buyers for Russian cotton cloth, for which the Russian domestic market was not yet sufficiently developed. Russian industrialists sought the aid of the government in developing particularly the Transcaucasian and Iranian markets. It is debatable that tsarist policy in this area was motivated primarily by the interests of these textile manufacturers, although their influence was in evidence.[57]

The Russians had hardly begun to penetrate Persia commercially, when the market was seized by the British. As a result there was a transfer of Russian industrial exports eastward.[58] By the middle of the nineteenth century, 40 percent of Russian exports to Bokhara and Tashkent consisted of cotton goods, although the Russian-Central Asian trade did not become significant until the 1860's when the American civil war obliged Muscovite cotton manufacturers to seek raw materials as well as markets in the Khanates.[59]

Most of the Asian trade was assumed by China for a while in the middle of the nineteenth century. From 1829 to 1850, exports to China jumped from 28.9 percent of the Asian trade to 67.4 percent, or a value of 4,391,000 silver rubles. During the same period, the export to China of cotton manufactures went from 2 percent to 51.5 percent, amounting to 2,840,000 rubles.[60] In the early 1840's 70 percent of the Russian goods passing through Kiakhta, which was the focal point of the Chinese overland trade, were manufactured products, primarily textiles. The next major item, comprising 21 percent, was furs. In exchange, the Chinese sold primarily tea to Russia, over 6,000 tons in 1846.[61]

Two consequences of Russia's growing commercial bonds with the world and particularly with Europe during the early nineteenth century are worth noting. First, Russia signed a number of trade agreements with many European countries and the United States. The

[57] Tengoborskii, *Commentaries*, vol. II, pp. 439, 466. On government policy and the private cotton interests in the Middle East see M. K. Rozhkova's conclusions in *Ekonomicheskaia politika tsarskogo pravitel'stva na srednem vostoke vo vtoroi chetverti xix veka i russkaia burzhuaziia* (Academy of Sciences, U.S.S.R., 1949), pp. 382-90.

[58] Rozhkova, *Ekonomicheskaia politika tsarskogo pravitel'stva*, chapters V and VI, pp. 152-89. On the quick rise and fall of the Russo-Persian trade in the 1830's, see Marvin L. Entner, *Russo-Persian Commercial Relations 1828-1914*, University of Florida Monographs, Social Sciences, no. 28, Fall 1965, pp. 6-11.

[59] Tengoborskii, *Commentaries*, vol. II, pp. 439, 466; Rozhkova, *Ekonomicheskie sviazi Rossii so Srednei Aziei 40-60-e gody xix veka* (Moscow, 1963), table 16, pp. 60-62.

[60] Rozhkova, *Ekonomicheskaia politika tsarskogo pravitel'stva*, tables 34, 39, 55, and 58, pp. 180, 185, 301-03.

[61] Nebolsin, *Vneshnaia torgovlia Rossii*, vol. I, pp. 338-39. See Appendix 2, Part 4, Tables C, D, and F.

main purpose of these treaties was to obtain more or equal rights for Russian merchants and shippers dealing with the signatory powers.[62] As Russia's trade with more industrially advanced countries expanded, her commerce and industries were drawn into the business cycles of those countries. Economic crises that swept through Western countries began to have repercussions in Russia. This happened in 1839, in 1847-1848, and again in 1857. This was mainly a matter of foreign trade: the foreign market shriveled, and prices of certain Russian goods would fall. In all of the three European-American crises mentioned above, trading activity at the big Russian fairs significantly diminished, production in some major industries was curtailed by millions of rubles, and business activity was slower. Many factors were at work other than the ripples spreading out from depressions in Europe and the United States. Crop failures, epidemics, and wars also helped to disrupt the infant Russian industrial economy. Some Russian industries overproduced, with depressing effects on the Russian market that were apparent even before it was affected by the slackening of economic life in the West. It would, however, require another quarter century for the Russian business economy to mature to the point of crippling susceptibility to a full-fledged world crisis.[63]

Banks, Money, Stock Companies, and Insurance

The growth of capitalism and industry in Western Europe during early modern times was accompanied and stimulated by the development of numerous credit and investment institutions. Most important among these were banks, stock companies, and various types of insurance organizations. The efforts of private enterprise were prominent in creating these institutions, although state funds and monopolies frequently played a significant role. State borrowing and monetary policies also stimulated the development of banking institutions and helped to create the climate and opportunities for investment. In Russia, this financial evolution was markedly weak and uneven during the early nineteenth century. State and private banking was feeble and retarded at both the central and local levels. Money was scarce, unstable, and inflated. The state reserved most of its credit for landlords, and the largest part of the interest on state debts flowed out of the country. The channels for investment were narrow, hazardous, and neglected. Stock companies beyond isolated prototypes like the Russian-American company, made their appearance only in the 1830's, and their development before 1860 was fragmentary. The insurance business, on the other hand, witnessed a relatively rapid growth during the reign of Nicholas I.

---

[62] Kulisher, *Ocherk istorii Russkoi torgovli*, pp. 312-16.

[63] On the early crises in Russia, see A. F. Iakovlev, *Ekonomicheskie krizisy v Rossii* (Moscow, 1955), chapters 1 and 2, pp. 3-81.

The most notable of the government-sponsored banking experiments aimed at more productive ends than supporting the nobility was the State Commercial Bank, established in 1817. For twenty years prior to this, "Discount Offices" (*uchetnie kontory*) of the State Assignat (paper ruble) Bank had functioned in several Russian cities, mostly ports, to extend short-term credit to wealthy merchants. Their circle of operations was extremely limited, as were those of several private and public city banks that were established in the course of the early nineteenth century. The main business of the public city banks was mortgages, and the total initial capital of the nineteen institutions that had been chartered by 1849 did not exceed 400,000 rubles.

The system of savings and loan banks which grew out of the Kiselev reforms similarly failed to accumulate a significant amount of capital among the urban and rural lower classes. Thus, although there were 1,342 of these institutions in 1847, the capital of many was less than 1,000 rubles. In large parts of Belorussia and the Ukraine, total deposits averaged less than 100 rubles. The bulk of the depositors in provincial banks were civil servants and clergy; in some St. Petersburg banks, however, workmen and peasants made the most deposits.[64]

The Discount Offices were incorporated in 1817 into the State Commercial Bank, and new branches were opened in Riga, Ekaterinburg, and at the Nizhnii-Novgorod and Poltava fairs. The branches were allotted substantial portions of the initial 30 million ruble capital of the bank. The State Commercial Bank took interest-paying deposits, but its primary function was intended as a lending agency for commercial enterprise. It was not concerned with helping industry, although after 1824, it was permitted to do so. One Minister of Finances, Gurev, attempted unsuccessfully in 1821 to redefine the Commercial Bank as a lending agency for industry as well as commerce. Some aid, however, was being extended by the Bank in the 1840's to industries of the Urals and of the city of Kharkov. Most of the resources of the Commercial Bank, however, remained idle when they were not being siphoned off through loans to the nobility. In some years, almost all of its deposits went into the pockets of landlords.[65]

A network of public local and city banks would have stimulated industrial development in Moscow and St. Petersburg and would have facilitated the movement of capital outside of these centers to the Urals, the Baltic states, the Ukraine, New Russia, and other potential

[64] S. Ia. Borovoi, *Kredit i banki Rossii, seredina xvii v.-1861 g.* (Moscow, 1958), pp. 126-27, 242-49, 253-54.

[65] Borovoi, *Kredit i banki Rossii*, pp. 215-18, 226-27 for the history of the Commercial Bank; see also *Ministerstvo finansov 1802-1902* (St. Petersburg, 1902), vol. I, p. 45.

industrial areas, cities, and ports. Such a network was not established, nor did the government make any real attempt to encourage the development of private banks to service industry in Russia's cities and provinces. The few private banks which developed in Russia during the early nineteenth century acted as either the agents of foreign banks or merchants, or, in St. Petersburg, Moscow, and Odessa when institutions emerged which were backed primarily by Russian capital, they functioned at best as precursors of modern commercial banks. The House of Stieglitz was Russia's first great private bank. Although Baron Stieglitz invested his personal fortune in a wide range of industrial enterprises and stock corporations, the primary function of his bank was to lend money to the government or to facilitate state loans. He was the last of the great court bankers in the tradition of Jacques Coeur, the Fuggers, or more recently, the early Rothschilds.[66] Stieglitz was a German; and many German names appear in the short list of private banks operating in St. Petersburg and Moscow before 1860 —Iunker, Stern, Schultz, Pierling, and Marx among others. The extent of the operations of these "banks" can be gauged by the I. V. Iunker firm, founded in 1818, which began as part of a retail store, although by the 1860's, it had a branch in Warsaw. Greek and Italian merchants ran Odessa's early banks.[67]

More primitive banking operations were performed by the Moscow Old Believer communities, the Skoptsy of St. Petersburg, and the Jewish moneylenders of Berdichev. The Old Believers and Skoptsy handled very large sums of money, which, however, was used primarily to finance industrial and commercial undertakings of members of the sects. By the middle of the nineteenth century, there were several Jewish banks based in Berdichev, which had dealings, not only with the Ukrainian fairs, but also with banks in Polish, Baltic, and Russian cities. Most of this money was used to finance commercial undertakings, although some of the Berdichev bankers invested in the sugar industry.[68]

To meet the needs of an expanding commerce and industry, and of war, the tsarist government attempted during the early nineteenth century to increase the amount of money in circulation and to stabilize the various forms of Russian currency. The amount of silver rubles in circulation was vastly increased under Alexander I, and their weight and proportions were fixed by law. With the discovery of rich new gold fields in the Urals, Nicholas I vastly increased the amount of gold in circulation. Gold coinage during his reign amounted to

[66] For a detailed analysis of Stieglitz's industrial enterprises, see my Chapter 10.

[67] Borovoi, *Kredit i banki Rossii*, pp. 235-39.

[68] Borovoi, *Kredit i banki Rossii*, p. 237. On Old Believer, Skoptsy, and Jewish enterprise, see my Chapter 9.

327,440,382 rubles, 51 kopecks, almost eight times the sum issued under Alexander I. About 25 percent less silver was minted. Silver, along with copper, had been the mainstay of Russian hard currency. Even platinum was minted in the effort to expand money circulation and utilize Russia's newly found wealth of this precious metal; 4,251,843 rubles were issued from 1828 until 1843, when the experiment was abandoned.[69]

All of this was inadequate, and the true beginnings of a modern Russian currency must be traced to 1768, when paper money was first issued in Russia, in the form of a million *assignats*, as paper rubles were first called. A detailed exposition of the complex manipulations and fluctuations of Russian paper money that occupied the ensuing century can be found elsewhere.[70] It will suffice here to outline this history with a view to its implications for stable investment conditions in Russia. In 1777, the *assignat* was declared unconvertible, and so Russian currency remained, with a few brief and unsuccessful experiments with convertibility, for 120 years. The baleful effects of non-convertibility for economic growth, particularly foreign borrowing and investment, were to haunt all of the finance ministers of nineteenth-century Russia. By 1786, 100 million *assignat* rubles were in circulation; by 1800, 212,689,355; by 1810, 577 million; and by 1817, a peak of 836 million. From 1800 until 1817, the worth of the paper ruble in silver dropped from 66 1/4 kopecks to 25 1/6. By that time, the amount of paper money in circulation exceeded hard currency. Numerous attempts were made, beginning with the financial reform of Speranskii in 1810, to stabilize and deflate the paper ruble. Foreign loans and sales of state property were used to buy up hundreds of thousands of *assignats*, a wasteful and costly diversion of capital. The use of paper money for the payment of taxes was made obligatory. Further issuance of *assignats* was stopped, and the number in circulation was fixed several times. However, these restrictions were soon violated; the Napoleonic emergency of 1812 called for violation almost immediately after enactment. So precarious was Russian currency by the end of the reign of Alexander I, that a massive retirement of *assignats* had almost no effect on the appreciation of the ruble. At the same time, retirement orgies would cause shortages of currency, forcing the government to issue more hard money. In the early part of the reign of Nicholas I, gold and silver were made legal

[69] M. Kashkarov, *Denezhnoe obrashchenie v Rossii* (St. Petersburg, 1898), vol. I, pp. 122, 137. On the rise and fall of the Russian platinum industry, see my Chapter 2.

[70] The most exhaustive analysis, with extensive tabular material upon which this sketch is primarily based, is Kashkarov, *Denezhnoe obrashchenie v Rossii*, vols. I and II. A recent and detailed analysis of the Nicholean monetary reforms is in Walter Pintner, *Russian Economic Policy Under Nicholas I* (Cornell, 1967), pp. 184-220.

tender for taxes once again, which meant, of course, depreciation of paper money. By 1839, the *assignat* was worth only 27 1/4 silver kopecks, or just over 2 kopecks what it had been worth twenty-two years before. In that year, a program was instituted to return the ruble to convertibility, so essential to state borrowing and private investment. Russia went on a silver standard. The *assignat* was retained, but the descent of the paper ruble was halted by fixing the ratio with the silver ruble at just over 28½ kopecks. In 1843, the 595,776,310 *assignat* rubles in circulation were recalled in exchange for 171,221,802 newly designated Notes of Credit (*Kreditnye bileti*), which were convertible into silver at the same ratio. Although the inflation-tainted *assignat* soon disappeared from the scene, the Bills of Credit, issued extravagantly during the military operations and wars of the 1840's and 1850's, soon became equally precarious. By 1858, there were 735,297,006 of the new paper rubles, as opposed to 141,460,772 rubles in hard money, or less than a 20 percent ratio of silver and gold to paper. Reserves of precious metal in the state treasury were vanishing, and convertibility was once again ended. On the eve of the Great Reforms, Russian currency remained as dubious and risky a vehicle for lending, investment, and enterprise as it had during the fiscal chaos of the Napoleonic period.

Lacking banks and a stable currency to facilitate investment, little capital was attracted to industrial enterprise either from within or outside of Russia until the government began to liberalize its restrictions on corporations and to guarantee profits for concessions in the late 1850's and 1860's. Rather sizeable amounts of capital were invested in government bonds or placed in state banks during the early nineteenth century, for the government was always scrupulous and generous in paying off the state debt. Interest was high, ranging from 4 to 5 percent. The first domestic loan was floated in 1809, an insignificant sum compared to foreign borrowing,[71] but by the middle of the nineteenth century, particularly during the Crimean War, the government was selling well over 100 million rubles' worth of bonds annually to Russians. At the same time, deposits in state banks approached a billion rubles. The government used most of the money it borrowed unproductively, as will be seen in a later chapter, supporting bankrupt landlords, fighting wars, and paying interest to foreign creditors.[72] Upon occasion, it borrowed large sums from deposits in state banks, thus involving itself in a double payment of high interest for capital which was squandered. However, most of this capital sat idle in the state bank vaults awaiting enterprising borrowers who never called. The largest part of the rather substantial interest on the state debt went to foreigners. It is difficult to determine how much of the several

---

[71] On foreign loans, see my Chapter 10.
[72] See my Chapter 7.

millions of rubles representing annual interest on the domestic loans in the 1850's were used for business investment by bondholders, and how much was less productively consumed.[73]

The stunted growth of financial institutions and the absence of legal and monetary security characteristic of early nineteenth-century Russia was accompanied by a lethargic development of stock corporations. Russia's first functioning stock corporation, the "Russian Commercial Company Trading in Constantinople" was chartered in 1756, although Russian officials had been aware of this form of business organization as early as the reign of Ivan the Terrible, and had experimented with the idea in the Petrine period. However, it was the Russian-American company, founded in 1799, that popularized the idea in Russia, through the scope of its operations and their success.[74]

The early nineteenth century witnessed the first general legislation for stock companies to be developed in Russia. A *ukaz* of 1805 first clearly enunciated the limited liability of stockholders. In 1807, an imperial manifesto permitted people from all classes to form stock companies, and not just merchants. The first detailed law for Russian stock corporations was issued in 1836. This law defined the organization, rights, and responsibilities of stock companies operating in Russia. However, it was not a very liberal piece of legislation, very severely limiting the purposes and ownership of the firms that would receive charters. Its rigidity led to its desuetude: most of the charters issued for individual companies during the 1830's, 1840's, and 1850's either ignored or violated it.[75]

The easy conditions of these charters led to an initial growth of stock companies in Russia after 1836, which became even more pronounced with the impetus provided by the ending of the Crimean War and of the reign of Nicholas I. However, their development before 1870 was hardly more than experimental. From 1799 until 1836, only ten companies were established. The fact of a law, however restrictive, apparently permitted some growth of Russian stock companies after 1836. From 1836 to 1839, thirty were founded. In 1839, however, only one was established, with a capital of 300,000 rubles. The 1840's were lean years for Russian stock corporations, but there was a new spurt of development in the years of the Crimean War and im-

---

[73] See S. Ia. Borovoi's discussion of interest on the state debt, "Gosudarstvennyi dolg kak istochnik pervonachal'nago nakopleniia v Rossii," *Voprosy genezisa kapitalizma v Rossii* (Leningrad, 1960), pp. 217-28. Borovoi suggests without substantiation that the largest number of depositors and bondholders on the domestic debt by 1850 were Russian bourgeois, rather than foreign bankers or Russian nobles, and that the former would tend to invest the income more productively.

[74] This view is developed in A. I. Kaminka, *Aktsionerniia kompanii* (St. Petersburg, 1902), pp. 340-41, 352, 361.

[75] Kaminka, *Aktsionerniia kompanii*, traces the legislation in detail, pp. 378-83.

mediately following it: from 1853 to 1859, 106 companies were founded.

This involved a not insignificant investment of capital for the time, but a drop in the bucket compared to the last third of the century. During all of the early nineteenth century, a total of only 27,174,000 rubles were invested in stock, about 4 million rubles more than the same investment for the year 1870 alone. From 1855 to 1859, however, more than 300 million rubles were invested. There was another lapse in the 1860's. The peak investment for the decade was 10,545,000 rubles in 1868, the ebb, 850,000 in 1863.[76]

The history of private insurance in Russia, particularly during the reign of Nicholas I, presents an interesting contrast to the feeble developments in finance and investment. Modern insurance may be said to both reflect and affect the development of capitalism. Not only is it a form of private enterprise which generates capital for investment and provides security for entrepreneurial risks, but is an economic phenomenon which cannot appear without available fluid capital as well as some development of statistics.[77] By 1850, there were several large private insurance companies. These firms offered coverage wide enough to embrace not only marine insurance, but life, fire, and pension protection as well, to the amount of over 3 billion rubles for the period from 1827 to 1851. The private insurance companies, all of them stock companies, were backed primarily by investors from business circles in St. Petersburg, and by high-ranking government officials. They were encouraged by the government with monopolies and relief from heavy taxation and regulation. Profits were substantial.[78]

The first Russian private insurance company was established in 1827, after many unsuccessful attempts at state-sponsored insurance dating back to 1786. Influential in bringing about this early leader-

---

[76] 1858 was the exception, with 28,760,000 rubles invested. See Khromov, *Ekonomicheskoe razvitie Rossii*, appendix, table 11, p. 463; the table in Iakovlev, *Ekonomicheskie krizisy v Rossii*, p. 34; and the figures in the article on stock companies in the Brockhaus *Entsiklopedicheskii slovar.*

[77] For a discussion on the relationship of insurance to early capitalism in Europe, see J. Halperin, *Le rôle des assurances dans les débuts du capitalisme moderne* (University of Zurich, 1945). These elements were in sufficient evidence in Russia by 1850 to permit the emergence of several large insurance companies.

[78] See Paul Best, "The Origins and Development of Insurance in Imperial and Soviet Russia" (unpublished doctoral thesis, New York University, 1965), chapters I and II, which carry the story up to the end of the reign of Nicholas I. Best's dissertation is the only recent work on the subject. The older official company histories should also be consulted: *Moskovskoe strakhovanie ot Ognia Obshchestvo za 50 let sushchestvovaniia 1858-1908; V pamiat 75-ti letnago iubeleia Pervago Rossiiskago Strakhovago Obshchestva Uchrezhdennago v 1827 Godu* (St. Petersburg, 1903); and *Piatidesiatiletie Vysochaishe Utverzhdennago Rossiiskago Zastrakhovanie Kapitalov i Dokhodov* (St. Petersburg, 1885).

ship in private insurance, which was to dominate the field for the next century, was Admiral N. S. Mordvinov. Mordvinov was a vigorous proponent of domestic private insurance companies, which he hoped would stop the outflow of 100 million rubles annually to the foreign insurers of Russian property.[79] Along with Baron Stieglitz and a number of influential Russian dignitaries and businessmen, he helped gain official sanction for the "First Russian Insurance Company, Established in 1827."

This stock company, capitalized at 10 million paper rubles and engaged in fire insurance, was followed by: the "Second Russian Insurance Company, Established in 1835" (fire insurance); the "Russian Company for the Insurance of Life Pensions and Other Important Incomes" (1836); the "Salamander Insurance Association," founded in 1846 (fire insurance); in 1847, the "St. Petersburg Company for Ocean, River and Land Insurance under the Sign *Nadezhda*" (Reliance), and the "Russian Company of Ocean, River and Land Insurance and Transportation of Goods"; and in 1858, the "Moscow Fire Insurance Company." *Nadezhda* was an organization of international scope from the very beginning, having offices in the main northern and Atlantic European ports, as well as St. Petersburg, Odessa, Helsingfors, and Riga in the Russian empire. All of these firms were organized along the lines of European stock companies. By 1860, they provided the foundations for what became one of the major business operations, worldwide in scope, of Imperial Russia.[80]

[79] V. Bilbasov, ed., *Arkhiv Grafov Mordvinovykh* (St. Petersburg, 1901-1903), vol. VIII, pp. 60-62, 145-49.

[80] The American branch of one of the most important of the old tsarist companies, the *Rossiia*, still functions in Des Moines, Iowa, as the Northeastern Insurance Company.

Chapter 4

Cities and Urban Society

Growth of Population and Cities

During the early nineteenth century, continuing and accelerating the trend of the previous hundred years, the population of the Russian empire grew at a very rapid rate. This was not accompanied by extensive urbanization. Russians who lived in cities during this period continued to comprise only a small segment of the total population. Nevertheless, a few small cities of a new and purely industrial type began to appear in some areas. The two capital cities, St. Petersburg and Moscow, expanded somewhat more rapidly than others, and their social composition began to reflect a metamorphosis from primarily religious, administrative centers to industrial-commercial ones. In these larger cities, an industrial working group began to form, although it was small and still bound by strong ties to the villages of rural Russia.

From 1811 to 1863, the total population of Russia grew from approximately 41,010,400 to 74,262,750. This represents an increase of over 80 percent during the entire period. The Soviet historian, Rashin, estimates the average yearly growth during the same period at .73 percent, although great fluctuation for certain decades is evident. In the 1850's, when the Russian birthrate was the highest in Europe, the yearly rate of growth rose to 1.22 percent.[1]

The causes for these population fluctuations were both peculiar to Russia and common to many countries. Several wars and one invasion, numerous local and general famines, and a few serious cholera epidemics had great effect on the birth and death rates. Entire peoples were absorbed into the empire through conquest and diplomacy. Immigration and emigration were of little significance, but internal migration of peasants changed the statistical picture. Despite natural catastrophes and impediments of human contrivance, Russia's population, with a generally high birth and death rate, grew more rapidly than that of any European country except England, but less quickly than it would grow in the late nineteenth century.[2]

The urban proportion of this population remained small during the early nineteenth century, but the population of cities and towns did grow. From 1812 until 1857, the urban proportion of Russia's popu-

[1] A. G. Rashin, *Naselenie Rossii za 100 let 1811-1913* (Moscow, 1956), pp. 25, 41. See Appendix 2, Part 3, Table A.

[2] Rashin, *Naselenie Rossii*, pp. 136-37; P. A. Khromov, *Ekonomicheskoe razvitie Rossii v XIX-XX vekakh 1800-1917* (Academy of Sciences, U.S.S.R., 1950), pp. 80-81; L. Tengoborskii, *Commentaries on the Productive Forces of Russia* (English edn., London, 1855-56), vol. I, p. 72.

lation rose from 4.4 percent to 7.8 percent. This involved an increase of approximately 3 million people. In 1856, the urban population of Russia, according to Rashin's estimate, totaled 5,684,000; and in 1863, 6,105,000, revealing a growth rate of 120.8 percent since 1811.[3]

By 1861, the urban population of Russia was contained in 678 towns and cities (*goroda*). This estimate, made by the Soviet historian, Khromov, includes 129 towns with a population of less than 1,000. The nineteenth-century Russian economist, Tengoborskii, listed, for 1840, 733 towns within the Russian empire, including the Grand Duchy of Finland and the Kingdom of Poland, plus 1,252 villages (*miestechka* or *possady*). Of this number, there were very few purely Russian cities that could qualify as large. Seventy-two (including Archangel, Taganrog, Simbirsk, Tver, Novgorod, Tambov, Perm, and Simferopol) had a population of from 10,000 to 25,000; seventeen numbered from 25,000 to 50,000 (including Kiev, Kazan, Nizhnii-Novgorod, and Kharkov); four cities had more than 50,000 inhabitants (Tula, Odessa, Riga, and Kronstadt); and two surpassed 100,000 in 1840 (St. Petersburg and Moscow).[4]

Three major Russian cities grew very rapidly during the early nineteenth century, and came to rank among the big urban centers of the world—St. Petersburg, Moscow, and Odessa. The population of St. Petersburg more than doubled from 1800 until 1850, rising from 220,000 to 487,000. Moscow's growth was less spectacular: from 1811 until 1858, the population grew from 270,200 to 377,800. The proportion of urban to total population in 1832 in the St. Petersburg province was 74.8 percent; in Moscow, much less: 26.1 percent.[5] Odessa was hardly as populous as either of the Russian capitals. In 1863, it included 119,000 people. Its growth, however, was spectacular. In 1797, about 5,000 people of both sexes lived in Odessa, and in 1840, about 60,000—a growth rate of 1,200 percent for the entire period.[6]

The reason for rapid urban growth in certain areas of Russia during the early nineteenth century was that new cities of a commercial or industrial type were forming; and older cities were changing their character from religious and administrative centers to industrial metropolises. Large factories and working class districts were springing

[3] Rashin, *Naselenie Rossii*, p. 86; Khromov, *Ekonomicheskoe razvitie Rossii*, pp. 79-80. For European Russia, see Appendix 2, Part 3, Table B.

[4] Tengoborskii, *Commentaries*, vol. I, pp. 89-90, 112-14. For population changes in Russian cities, see Appendix 2, Part 3, Tables D and E.

[5] Rashin, *Naselenie Rossii*, pp. 11-12, 114-15. P. G. Ryndziunskii, "Gorodskoe naselenie," in Rozhkova, ed., *Ocherki ekonomicheskoi istorii Rossii pervoi poloviny XIX veka* (Moscow, 1959), p. 324.

[6] Ryndziunskii, in Rozhkova, ed., *Ocherki ekonomicheskoi istorii Rossii*, p. 324; *Odessa 1794-1894* (Odessa, 1895), p. 165.

up in their suburbs. In his study of the city, Max Weber likened Moscow in the early nineteenth century to a "large oriental city of the time of Diocletian."[7] This gross and imaginative oversimplification was based primarily on the fact of the formal existence of the institution of serfdom; Weber ignored the important socioeconomic, urban changes that were taking place within the institution and helping to bring about its dissolution. In Moscow—and even in St. Petersburg, with the official capital's sizeable administrative apparatus and bloated bureaucracy—a factory working class was forming out of furloughed and redeemed serfs. An industrial entrepreneurial class was emerging from the same social soil, and out of the old merchant class as well as foreign businessmen in Russia. Large industrial sections were forming on the outskirts of both cities by the mid-nineteenth century. Both cities also functioned as major trading centers, with large, permanent markets, stock exchanges, and a substantial concentration of commercial and industrial capital as compared to land rent.

Outside of the two capital cities of Russia, new industrial towns were forming. Perhaps the most spectacular example of this new type of Russian city was the "Manchester of Russia," Ivanovo, a center of the Russian cotton-printing industry, some 150 miles northeast of Moscow. The Russian cotton industry was also building industrial towns out of villages in Serpukhov and Egorevska in the central industrial region. Older commercial and craft towns, such as Kazan, Riga, Tula, and Narva, were assuming new industrial functions.[8]

After St. Petersburg, Riga and Odessa were the greatest ports of Russia. It was through these ports, as we have seen, that the agricultural products of the fertile western provinces of the empire flowed to Europe. The burgeoning grain trade of the early nineteenth century that made great commercial cities of Odessa and Riga created or revived many other trading cities in the Baltic states, the Ukraine, Belorussia, and the Black Sea region. Revel, Mogilev, Kiev, Berdichev, Zhitomir, Kharkov, and Taganrog were the most prominent of these. In most, however, industry remained poorly developed, and in appearance, they were scarcely distinguishable from villages.[9]

Most of the new commercial and industrial cities were concentrated in the western part of the Russian empire, although farther east and south the population of commercial centers such as Nizhnii-Novgo-

---

[7] Max Weber, *The City* (Free Press: Glencoe, Illinois, 1958), p. 200. For a critique of Weber's views of Russian cities, see P. G. Ryndziunskii, *Gorodskoe grazhdanstvo doreformennoi Rossii* (Moscow, 1958), pp. 11-13.

[8] Ryndziunskii, in Rozhkova, ed., *Ocherki ekonomicheskoi istorii Rossii*, p. 329. On Ivanovo, see the end of this Chapter and Chapter 9.

[9] A detailed account of the development of these cities can be found in Ryndziunskii, *Gorodskoe grazhdanstvo*; see also I. F. Rybakov, "Nekotorye voprosy genezisa kapitalisticheskogo goroda v Rossii," in V. V. Marvodin, ed., *Voprosy genezisa kapitalizma v Rossii* (Leningrad, 1960), pp. 232-33, 237.

rod, Samara, and Orenburg began to grow.[10] Administrative centers in this region, like Tiflis and Ekaterinburg, also showed some signs of business life. Beyond these, the majority of towns in Russia remained largely untouched by modern economic forces: administrative centers created by government order, agrarian villages, local craft and bartering centers, and sometimes a combination of all of these elements. Baron Haxthausen, writing in the late 1840's, has given perhaps the best description of the traditional Russian town as it existed everywhere in provincial Russia during that period.

> When, travelling in the interior of the empire, we approach a Russian town, we . . . enter, first, a Russian village, being the remains of the old village which was destined to be converted into a town: here still dwell the old peasants, and employ themselves principally in gardening, to supply the town with vegetables, carrying on their culture, not in enclosed grounds, but in the open fields. Passing through the village, we enter the town of Catherine II, built like one of the outer quarters of Moscow: it is composed of long, broad, unpaved streets, running between two rows of log houses one story high, with their gable ends turned to the street: here is concentrated the industrial life of the Russian population: here dwell the carters, the cartwrights, the corn-dealers: here are the inns, the alehouses, the shops, etc. Issuing from this second *quartier*, we enter the modern European town, with its straight and sometimes paved streets, and its spacious squares: we see on all hands buildings like palaces; but this part of the town has generally a deserted appearance: the streets present little bustle or animation, with the exception of the droschkies stationed in the squares and at the corners of the streets, with which no provincial capital, or even large district village, is ever unprovided. The most ancient edifices of this quarter are the public buildings: the greater number of the private houses date subsequently to 1815.[11]

Haxthausen's description also vividly portrays the divergence between city planning, which the tsarist government undertook on a comprehensive scale in the eighteenth century, and the changing economic and social realities of many Russian towns and cities by 1850. Catherine the Great was Russia's first great city planner. Her program reflected both European architectural influence and the Russian autocratic tradition. According to the Urban Statute of 1785, all Russian towns were to be planned, and each plan had to be approved personally "by the hand of the imperial majesty."[12] The style followed European planning patterns of early modern times: the medieval

[10] Rybakov, "Goroda v Rossii," pp. 232, 234.
[11] Cited in Tengoborskii, *Commentaries*, vol. I, p. 100.
[12] V. A. Shkvarikov, *Ocherki istorii planirovki i zastroiki russkikh gorodov* (Moscow, 1954), p. 84.

Russian towns with their tight and disordered clusters of Oriental kremlins and bazaars, towers, walls, moats, and churches were to be replaced by modern cities with straight, wide avenues conforming in most cases to radial or rectangular patterns, zoning for commercial, industrial, and administrative activities and for the various classes of society, and a unified architecture. Government buildings and the residences of the classes of society most closely associated with the government were to form the hub of each town or city, although the central market, or *gostinnyi dvor*, would be located in the same area. Here, the homes, offices, courts, and warehouses of the nobility, the military, and the civil service would be built in stone and on a larger scale than the rest of the city. The spacious central square would open onto a long, broad avenue traversing the center. Both would be suitable for parades.[13]

Hundreds of such plans were approved during the reign of Catherine the Great, but much of the construction of them came in the early nineteenth century. The nationalist and imperialist atmosphere, particularly of the era of Nicholas I, produced a great deal of grandiose construction elaborating on the original plans. Nowhere was this more prominent than in the central part of St. Petersburg. However, the economic changes of the period were reflected in much additional construction largely ignored by the larger city plans. Hundreds of factory and shop structures were built on the outskirts and in suburbs, by rivers or amid cemeteries and hospitals. All except the largest of these were made of wood, as were the numerous dwellings of the factory workers.

Thus, the larger Russian cities began to develop along two lines: the spacious and graceful, stone carved inner city of the state and the wealthy, and beyond its walls and plans, the ramshackle and haphazard wooden city of the factories and the poor.[14] The meticulously developed inner city gave birth to a beautiful and grim autocratic style of urban architecture and planning that awed foreign visitors, most notably the Marquis de Custine. Outside of it, another modern but planless city grew as if in isolation, bound only to the ruling city by factory pollution carried into the center by the rivers, or police spies sent out by the government into the industrial suburbs.[15]

Changes in Urban Social Structure

There were at least a dozen classes or professions (*soslovie*) in

[13] Details on Russian city planning of the early imperial period can be found in the article by Hans Blumenfeld, "Russian City Planning of the Eighteenth and Early Nineteenth Centuries," *Journal of the American Society of Architectural Historians*, vol. 4, no. 1 (January 1944), 24-33.

[14] Shkvarikov, *Ocherki istorii planirovki russkikh gorodov*, pp. 117-18.

[15] Shkvarikov, *Ocherki istorii planirovki russkikh gorodov*, p. 118. On police reports on the Moscow Old Believer suburbs, see my Chapter 9.

Russian urban society during the early nineteenth century. It is useful, without oversimplifying, to consider these classes within three general categories: the traditional and upper classes; the commercial and industrial middle classes; and the urban masses. It must be kept in mind that certain individuals and groups of people crossed lines, particularly as society in the main Russian cities began to change more rapidly. A serf might be a millionaire industrialist; a peasant servant attached to a noble's household might be working in a factory; a noble might own an industrial enterprise; and clergy as well as sectarians frequently crossed class lines.

The traditional and upper classes of a large Russian city in 1850 would consist of nobility, clergy, the military, and civil servants. In 1811, the total number of the nobility (*dvorianstvo*) in the cities of the Russian empire, according to a contemporary statistician, was 112,200. Of civil servants (*sluzhashchie, chinovniki*), there were 195,300; of the military (*voennie*), 176,300; and of the clergy, (*dukhovenstvo*), 53,200. Many nobles of course, were civil servants, and in official figures for 1858, the two categories were combined to number 281,700 in that year. The number of the military in Russian cities in 1858 was 786,000; while the clergy increased to 81,700.[16] The traditional classes of nobility, clergy, and bureaucracy thus remained a rather fixed element in the picture of Russian urban growth during the early nineteenth century, increasing in proportion to the general increase in urban population, and in some cases (the nobility and bureaucracy), declining slightly. The term "military" in the statistics of the early nineteenth century meant soldiers on garrison and police duty and retired enlisted men.[17] Some of the latter were employed in state factories. The large increase in military personnel in Russia's cities in 1858 probably indicated an increase in police and garrison forces under Nicholas I, rather than an increase in officers from the nobility residing in urban locations, since there was no corresponding rise in the figure for nobility. All in all, the traditional classes comprised a more or less steady 20 percent of the urban population of Russia during the first half of the nineteenth century. There was, of course, a much higher proportion of nobles, civil servants, and military officers and men in St. Petersburg than in Moscow; while in the old Russian capital, secular and monastic clergy, as well as religious schismatics, were in far greater abundance.[18]

The composition and numbers of the new commercial and industrial middle classes changed far more radically than the traditional

[16] Cited in Rashin, *Naselenie Rossii*, pp. 119-20.
[17] Ryndziunskii, in Rozhkova, ed., *Ocherki ekonomicheskoi istorii Rossii*, p. 283.
[18] A. I. Kopanev, *Naselenie Peterburga v pervoi polovine XIX veka* (Moscow-Leningrad, 1957), p. 25; P. V. Sytin, *Istoriia planirovki i zastroiki Moskvy* (Moscow, 1954), vol. II (1762-1812), appendix, pp. 562-63.

elements in Russian cities during the early 1800's. The classes which must be included in this general category are: the merchants (*kuptsy*), the townsmen (*meshchanstvo*), and foreigners. Russian merchants, since the eighteenth century, had been divided for tax purposes into three "guilds" (*gil'diia*). The first guild was the most privileged and expensive of the three. It was not, however, the highest legal position a wealthy merchant or industrialist could attain in nineteenth-century Russia. This was the rank of Hereditary Honorable Citizen (*potoms-tvennyi pochtennyi grazhdanin*), usually awarded to very wealthy or influential merchants and industrialists, sometimes as a special mark of recognition. Gabriel Jacob Gunzberg, a Vilna moneylender and father of the founder of the great banking house of the same name, was awarded this rank during the reign of Nicholas I on the initiative of the Minister of Finances.[19] To qualify as a first guild merchant by the 1850's, a businessman had to declare a capital of at least 15,000 rubles, and to pay a tax of several hundred rubles for his certification, in addition to other assessments. This entitled the first guild merchant to engage in foreign and domestic wholesale trade anywhere in Russia, to engage in the retail trade in the town of his residence, and to own merchant ships, banks, insurance companies, and large industrial enterprises. No less important was the second guild merchant who dominated the domestic trade of Russia. His declared capital was far less than that of the merchant of the first guild, and his industrial and commercial activities were restricted. He could engage in foreign trade only in a limited way, and could not become involved in insurance and banking. Nevertheless, the scope of business activity permitted him was great and not a few very wealthy Russian merchants were content to remain in the second guild. Those registered in the third guild were retail merchants, restricted to small-scale commerce and industry in Russia. In 1851, there were 46,279 merchants of the three guilds and Hereditary Honorable Citizens in the Russian empire, exclusive of the Grand Duchy of Finland and the Kingdom of Poland. Over 90 percent of these were merchants of the third guild. About a fourth of all three guilds were registered in Moscow and St. Petersburg, where a third of the merchants of the first two guilds were concentrated.[20]

These figures somewhat distort the picture of commercial and industrial activity in the Russian cities. The wealth of merchants of various guilds, of course, vastly exceeded what was declared for registration purposes: Tengoborskii estimates the real wealth of many Russian businessmen at ten to twenty times their declared holdings.

[19] G. B. Sliozberg, *Baron G. O. Gintsburg, ego zhizn i deiatel'nost* (Paris, 1933), p. 16. See also my Chapter 9.

[20] Kopanev, *Naselenie Peterburga*, p. 101; Tengoborskii, *Commentaries*, vol. II, pp. 166-68.

Another false image in the statistics arises from the practices of noble-men, who were given the right to register in the three guilds by a law of 1807, and who preferred to enter only the third guild. The rela-tively inexpensive fee for registration in the third guild gave most nobles the right to operate their estate and other small factories, and few of them were interested in foreign trade. Their nobiliary privi-leges remained untouched.[21]

The biggest disparity between the figures for the business of the Russian merchant and the actual volume of commercial activity in the Russian cities during the second quarter of the nineteenth century is revealed in the existence and increasing tax burden of a separate category of "commercial" (*torguiushchii*) peasants. This was the re-sult of a conservative guild reform of 1824, sponsored by the Min-ister of Finances, Count E. F. Kankrin. Kankrin's regulations aimed to shore up the position of the big merchants of the first and second guilds by increasing their commercial rights while restricting the entry of peasants into the system of merchant guilds. A separate hierarchy of commercial peasants corresponding to the rungs of the merchant guild ladder and extending below them (created in 1812) was en-larged, and a higher tax rate was imposed up and down the new scale. The peasants, of course, were obliged to obtain their masters' consents for registration. Such regulations effectively kept many peasants out of large-scale commercial and industrial activity in the Russian cities, as witnessed by the fact that there were only 4 registered in the first order of commercial peasants from 1850 to 1852. In the same year, there were 25 in the second, 2,891 in the third, and 4,395 in the fourth, totaling 7,215, as compared to seven times that number of guild merchants at about the same time. Nevertheless, the floating capital of these peasant businessmen in 1851, according to Tengobor-skii's estimate, was about 25 million rubles.[22]

Foreigners, also, were significant in the commercial and industrial activity of the big Russian cities, particularly the great ports. Even in Moscow in 1811, there were 3,285 foreign merchants as against 15,839 Russians trading in the city. According to reports for 1813, of one grouping consisting of sixty-six manufacturing enterprises in Moscow, forty-nine were owned by Russian merchants, three by no-blemen, eight by peasants, and six by foreigners.[23]

[21] A. Romanovich-Slavatinskii, *Dvorianstvo v Rossii* (St. Petersburg, 1870), pp. 263-64; Tengoborskii, *Commentaries*, vol. II, pp. 164-65, p. 167 note.

[22] Tengoborskii, *Commentaries*, vol. II, pp. 176-77; Kopanev, *Naselenie Peterburga*, pp. 93-94. For the Kankrin Guild reform, see P. G. Ryndziunskii, "Gildeiskaia reforma Kankrina 1824 goda," *Istoricheskie zapiski*, vol. 40 (1952), pp. 110-39.

[23] *Istoriia Moskvy* (Moscow, 1954), vol. III, facing p. 169; M. I. Rozhkova, "Promyshlennost Moskvy v pervoi chetverti xix veka," *Voprosy istorii* (1946), nos. 11-12, p. 90. On foreign entrepreneurs, see my Chapter 10.

Another important element of the commercial and industrial life of Russian cities during the first half of the nineteenth century was the class known as the *meshchanstvo*. The term is somewhat ambiguous, and has been translated variously as *petty bourgeois, lower middle class, burger* or *burgess*, and *townsman*. All of these European terms are imprecise and misleading when applied to Russian society. The Urban Regulation of 1785 defined the *meshchanstvo* as all representatives of the "middling sort of people" (*srednii roda liudei*).[24] The *meshchanin* has sometimes been described as an urban equivalent of the peasant in nineteenth-century Russia. His status was hereditary. He was subject to the recruit obligation and he paid the head tax, just like any peasant (although he was freed from the latter obligation in 1866, many years before the peasant's tax burden was so lightened). Actually, the *meshchanin* had a distinct position in the Russian city of tsarist times, with defined privileges and taxes, which placed him below the merchantry and above the peasants residing in the city, as well as above the *lumpenproletariat* and religious outcast population. The economic position of different members of the *meshchanstvo*, of course, did not always correspond to their legal status, ranging from moderate wealth to dire poverty, bourgeois to underworld.

The Kankrin reform of 1824, in an obvious effort to restrict and price out commercial activity for the masses, divided the *meshchanstvo* into two groups. The upper group was classified as "commercial" (*torguiushchii*). A "commercial" *meshchanin* could maintain a shop, in his home or at the local *gostinnyi dvor*, and could own inns and other small commercial and industrial establishments upon payment of a fee of 120 rubles. He could run a shop or manufacturing plant if it employed no more than eight workers. Those in the lower category of the urban *meshchanstvo* created by the Regulation of 1824 were known as "suburban" (*posadskie*) *meshchan*. The commercial and industrial activity of this group was severely limited to open-air peddling and the employment of no more than three workers.[25]

The *meshchanstvo* formed a large element of the urban population of early nineteenth-century Russia. In the city of Moscow in 1835, there were 40,354 of the local *meshchanstvo* and 6,806 registered in other cities. This far exceeded the numbers of merchants, nobles, civil and military personnel, clergy or *raznochintsy* for that year, and represented over a fourth of the number of the various kinds of peasants residing in the city.[26] Most of the *meshchanstvo* of the pre-1860 Rus-

[24] Article on "meshchanstvo," in *Entsiklopedicheskii slovar* (Brockhaus; St. Petersburg, 1892).

[25] *Istoriia Moskvy*, vol. III, p. 299.

[26] *Istoriia Moskvy*, vol. III, facing p. 169.

sian cities were engaged in small-scale manufacturing or in the petty retail trade. They peddled in the streets; they owned many of the shops. Others were craftsmen or moneylenders. The *meshchanstvo* formed a bridge between wealth and the poverty of the urban masses. For as many who were affluent shopkeepers, there were others who were wage-earning factory workers, unemployed craftsmen living in deprivation, and indigents impressed into labor for the municipality to pay delinquent taxes. From here, as previously suggested, the *meshchanstvo* faded off into the *lumpenproletariat* and the underworld of the Russian cities. The prostitute tried for murder in Tolstoi's *Resurrection* was a *meshchanka*; Admiral N. S. Mordvinov observed, of early nineteenth-century Moscow, that of some 25,000 *meshchan*, only two or three thousand were properly employed. The rest, in his view, were engaged in petty crime.[27]

The *raznochintsy* of Russian urban society of the same period were a more elusive social class and legal grouping than the *meshchanstvo*. Prior to the 1860's, there was no connotation of the déclassé intellectual in the designation. It definitely referred to the lower classes in the cities, those below the merchants and nobility and separate from craftsmen and professional people. It was sometimes identified with petty bureaucrats—clerks or servants in government offices and their children.[28] Officially, the *raznochintsy* in 1811 counted for 10,771 of the population of the city of Moscow. In St. Petersburg in the same year, they numbered significantly more: 67,000, or about a fifth of the total number of inhabitants.[29]

Many modernizing cities, with large numbers of peasants migrating from the countryside into an economy lacking sufficient industrial or commercial enterprise to absorb them, may tend to develop a bloated *lumpenproletariat*. In St. Petersburg and Moscow during the early nineteenth century, such a process was beginning. Baron Haxthausen observed this and made comparisons with the German cities in the hard years of the 1840's:

> There is no lower class in Moscow such as is found in German towns, for instance in Berlin, living in garrets and cellars. . . . Formerly there was no rabble in Moscow, and even now, this forms but a very small proportion of the population.[30]

[27] *Istoriia Moskvy*, vol. III, pp. 232-33, 261, 267; Ryndziunskii, *Gorodskoe grazhdanstvo*, pp. 24-28; and *Arkhiv Grafov Mordvinovykh* (St. Petersburg, 1901-1903), vol. VI, p. 385.

[28] See the examination of the term in Christopher Becker, "*Raznochintsy*: the Development of the Word and the Concept," *Slavic Review*, vol. XVIII (1959), 65-70.

[29] *Istoriia Moskvy*, vol. III, facing p. 169; Becker, "*Raznochintsy*," p. 66.

[30] A. von Haxthausen, *The Russian Empire, Its People, Institutions and Resources* (London, 1856), vol. I, pp. 56-57.

In St. Petersburg during the same years a much larger *lumpenproletariat* could be found living in several sections of the city. Admiral Mordvinov observed such a group on the main streets, and identified them with the *meshchanstvo*, house servants and peasants who had drifted into the city for the winter, as symptoms of a social disease which would be cured by industrial employment:

> [that there are] many growing and vigorous young people from this class sponging in the numerous Moscow lodging houses, the so-called restaurants, taverns and wine shops, or sitting in kvass shops, or staggering along the streets with hawker's trays, witnesses the fact that we have many idle unoccupied peasant hands. . . . Generally speaking, this is a sign of a disease of government which demands a cure, and the cure must be sought in the provision of a useful occupation.[31]

With the *lumpenproletariat* came slums. On one end of Vasilevsky Island, peasants, doing heavy work as porters during all of the daylight hours, slept in shacks. The first and second Admiralty sections, as they were called, presented the contrast of homes of the titled aristocracy and wealthiest merchants near the wooden huts of thousands of paupers, many of them servants.[32]

The craftsmen in most of the Russian cities of the early nineteenth century had their own form of organization, the *tsekh*. The *tsekh*, an artisan's corporation, comprehended a distinct category of Russian urban citizenship, quite apart from the merchant guilds, the *meshchanstvo* and the *raznochintsy*. It can be compared to the trade guilds of Europe in its organization and functions. The first *tsekhi,* created by Peter the Great, were based on Western models.[33] The name was derived from a German designation for the same institution—*zeche*. Peter the Great created the *tsekhi* as part of his effort to mobilize the urban population of Russia for productivity and revenue. These organizations soon became monopolies controlling the handicraft industries of the Russian cities, and fought to preserve their domains against competition from rival organizations, foreigners, and peasants.[34]

A series of laws (1721, 1785, and 1799) secured the position of the *tsekhi*, and by the early nineteenth century, they were firmly rooted as an important part of Russian urban life. Official statistics for 1858, which are incomplete, list 331,555 craftsmen belonging to *tsekhi* in the European provinces of the Russian empire; 83,006 of

---

[31] *Arkhiv Grafov Mordvinovykh*, vol. VI, pp. 384-85.

[32] Kopanev, *Naselenie Peterburga*, pp. 11-14.

[33] K. A. Pazhitnov, *Problema remeslennykh tsekhov v zakonodatel'stve russkogo absolutizma* (Moscow, 1952), p. 45.

[34] Pazhitnov, *Problema tsekhov*, p. 67; and Ryndziunskii, in Rozhkova, ed., *Ocherki ekonomicheskoi istorii Rossii*, pp. 64-65.

these were concentrated in St. Petersburg and Moscow provinces. In these cities could be found dozens of craft organizations—for butchers, bakers, and candlestick makers, as well as for iconographers, sculptors, engravers, and cigarette rollers. The *tsekh* system was divided into foreign and Russian associations. After 1818, foreigners were not permitted in the Russian *tsekhi*. Like most Western craft organizations, the *tsekhi* had a hierarchy of apprentice (*uchenik*), journeyman or foreman (*podmaster*), and master (*master*). The necessary condition of admission to a Russian *tsekh* prior to 1860 was the status of freeman.[35]

There were many serfs living during part or all of the year in Russian cities in the early nineteenth century. They formed the majority of the population. In Moscow in 1811 for example, of a total population of approximately 258,000, almost two-thirds were serfs. Of these, many belonged to various categories of the state peasantry (37,523), but by far the largest number were seigneurial serfs, numbering over 100,000. The largest category of the seigneurial serfs were listed separately in official figures as "household" (*dvorovye*) serfs. These were serfs attached to the town houses of the Moscow nobility. Of 89,540 household serfs in Moscow in 1811, 76,866 were not registered in homes. According to Soviet historians, this indicated that such serfs were not working for their masters as domestic servants, but were employed elsewhere in the city, presumably in the streets, in shops, ateliers, or factories.[36]

The large number of men in Russian cities (Moscow numbered almost twice as many men as women) would indicate furloughed *obrok* peasants employed in urban enterprises. Women, to be sure, were also involved in seasonal factory work, but whole families did not usually migrate to the city. In St. Petersburg, there were numerous seasonal construction workers as well as factory hands, coachmen, and thousands of barge haulers. In 1831, the St. Petersburg police stamped the passports of over 50,000 peasants departing from the city.[37]

During the early nineteenth century, the number of factory workers in Russia quadrupled. In 1804, Russia's factory force totaled 224,882; in 1860, 859,950. Regionally, these workers were concentrated in the Urals and in the provinces of Moscow and Vladimir. Of the 107,300 workers in Moscow province in 1860, most lived in the city of Moscow. St. Petersburg also was witness to the growth of a small factory labor force: during the early nineteenth century, the

[35] Pazhitnov, *Problema tsekhov*, pp. 99, 103, 110-12.

[36] For statistics, see *Istoriia Moskvy*, vol. III, pp. 163-64, facing p. 169; also Sytin, *Istoriia planirovki i zastroiki Moskvy*, vol. II, appendix, pp. 562-63.

[37] Kopanev, *Naselenie Peterburga*, pp. 49, 54; *Istoriia Moskvy*, vol. III, p. 165.

number of factory workers in the Russian capital expanded from 5,300 to 33,100.[38]

Of the manufacturing industries, textiles claimed the largest number of workers in the half century before the Great Reforms, particularly woolens and cotton. In 1860, according to Rashin, 120,025 workers were at work in Russian woolens factories, and 152,236 in those engaged in the manufacture of cotton cloth. The Russian beet sugar industry was built up from nothing during this period, from 108 workers in 1804 to 64,763 in 1860. Linen factory workers declined from 23,711 to 17,284 during the same years. In the mining and metallurgical industry in the Urals and elsewhere, and in both private and state factories, there were 184,900 workers. By 1860, the average number of workers in the cotton cloth factories was 127; in the sugar factories, 139; and in the woolens factories, 170. Almost a tenth of the woolens factories employed more than 500 workers; and about one-twentieth of the cotton factories were of such dimensions. In most other industries, manufacturing was done in small shops. The average number of workers in a leather goods factory in 1860, for example, was six. Contrasted to this, we have the figures for some of the largest Urals, Moscow, and St. Petersburg factories for the first third of the nineteenth century: Nizhne-Tagil, 1,605; the Chorokov factory in Moscow, 5,966; and the State Cotton factory at Aleksandrovsk, near St. Petersburg, 4,000 workers.[39]

It would be difficult to consider this rather substantial number of people working in Russian factories as a permanent, fully formed, urban working class. It might be better to define them as a transitional mass of semi-industrialized peasants. In some industries, serf labor still was dominant, or serfs represented a substantial minority of the working force. This was particularly true of the Urals metallurgical enterprises, woolen cloth manufacture, and the beet sugar industry. Large numbers of serfs were leased out by their masters for excavation work on the St. Petersburg-Moscow Railroad.[40] In other industries, however, cotton manufacturing foremost among them, forced labor had almost completely disappeared as early as the reign of Alexander I. Many factory wage earners, however, were seasonal workers, serfs migrating from their villages for the winter months.

What conditions permitted Russia's prereform labor force to develop? Forced labor in its various forms had proved inadequate as a

[38] F. Ia. Polianskii, *Pervonachal'noe nakoplenie kapitala v Rossii* (Moscow, 1958), pp. 40-41.

[39] A. G. Rashin, *Formirovanie promyshlennogo proletariata v Rossii* (Moscow, 1940), tables on pp. 26-27, 30-31, 35, 37-38, 46, and 48; M. K. Rozhkova, "Promyshlennost Moskvy v pervoi chetverti XIX veka," *Voprosy istorii* (1946), nos. 11-12, pp. 90-91. Von Humboldt gives the figure for Nizhne-Tagil as 22,000. He obviously is considering the entire complex; the figure here probably represents the largest single plant. On Humboldt, see my Chapters 2 and 6.

[40] See my Chapter 12.

source for factory workers, although not necessarily or always less productive than voluntary wage labor. In the eighteenth century, the state had reached everywhere in its attempt to meet through impressment the chronic shortage of labor—convicts, exiles, prisoners of war, tax delinquents, unfrocked monks, paupers, soldiers, children and wives of soldiers, and, of course, the state peasantry, drafted into factories in various categories.[41] These sources were rapidly drying up by the end of the eighteenth century, and the use of forced labor was declining rapidly. The system of possessional serfs was on its way out, although landlords were increasingly diverting serfs to their estate factories in the early nineteenth century, and convicts and orphans were still used in some state enterprises.

Freer forms of factory labor were becoming available by the early nineteenth century, as witnessed by the predominance of such workers in the cotton, silk, linen, and other industries. The biggest source for wage labor during this period were state and seigneurial serfs under the *obrok* obligation. As a money economy expanded in certain regions of late eighteenth-century Russia, combined with an increasing land shortage, the migration of serfs to the cities and factories for wage labor was found profitable by both the master and the servant. This was reflected in the growth of *obrok* in the central provinces and an increase in the migration of peasants in the same areas. In Iaroslav province, for example, during the early nineteenth century, 79 percent of the serfs worked under *obrok*; in the same province in 1798, 73,663 passports for peasant migration were issued. Just one village in Iaroslav dispatched 500 peasants to work in most of the important imperial cities, as far as Helsingfors.[42]

The state and crown (*udel'nyi*) serfs were in a somewhat more flexible position than privately owned peasants. The over 850,000 crown serfs, for example, were all under *obrok* by the eve of the Great Reforms; and over a quarter of the state peasants in Moscow province at about the same time were engaged in industrial work.[43] Religious dissenters were in an even freer position. For many serfs, conversion to Old Belief and employment in factories controlled by schismatic communities was the road to freedom from bondage obligations. Refugees from villages, the army, or the law could be hidden in the Old Believer factories and shops; or could be redeemed from serfdom by the Old Believers in return for an agreement to work off the redemption price in the factories. Thousands of serfs, particularly in the emerging factory suburbs of Moscow, were transformed into an industrial proletariat in this fashion.[44]

[41] Polianskii, *Pervonachal'noe nakoplenie kapitala v Rossii*, pp. 285-86, 304-05, 319.

[42] Polianskii, *Pervonachal'noe nakoplenie kapitala v Rossii*, pp. 181-84.

[43] Polianskii, *Pervonachal'noe nakoplenie kapitala v Rossii*, pp. 180-81.

[44] For a detailed account of this process, see my Chapter 9.

Conditions were bad for industrial workers in early nineteenth-century Russia, although perhaps not as deplorable as the treatment of the European factory worker of the time, according to some contemporary foreign observers.[45] Forced laborers, whether possessional serfs in Urals factories, serfs working in estate factories, or those contracted out for the railroads or other state projects suffered particularly in Russia. The working day many times exceeded twelve hours, physical punishment was common, and women and children as young as seven years of age were employed for long hours and at night work. Wage earners fared little better. The workers' responses to these conditions were frequent uprisings and violence.[46]

Three Industrializing Cities: Moscow, St. Petersburg, and Ivanovo

The beginnings of urbanization and proletarianization in Russia in the prereform era might usefully be summarized by a closer examination of three changing Russian cities: Moscow, St. Petersburg, and Ivanovo. Moscow began its metamorphosis from a religious and nobiliary center to a major industrial city of Russia in the period from 1812 to 1860. St. Petersburg during the same period was also changing character—from a purely administrative hub, a bureaucratic city, to a major port and point of concentration for the machine and cotton spinning industries of Russia. Ivanovo was transformed during the early nineteenth century from a peasant crafts village to the first new and purely industrial city of the Russian empire.

Preindustrial Moscow was a fortress and seat of government, a center for the church, and a commercial crossroads. It retained much of this character as late as the eighteenth century. Moscow was first the city of the Kremlin, of the palaces of the tsar. It was a holy city, a national shrine, a place of monks, priests, churches, and monasteries. Even in 1819, it possessed 6 cathedrals, 21 monasteries, and 274 churches, according to one contemporary count.[47] It was

---

[45] For one comment, we have Thomas Raikes, *A Visit to St. Petersburg in the Winter of 1829-30* (London, 1838), pp. 116-18: "The few English papers which the censor here permits us to receive teem with accounts of the increasing privation and distress among the lower orders with you. If a comparison were drawn between the respective situation of these classes in the two countries, I mean as to physical wants and gratifications, how much would the scale lean towards this population of illiterate slaves! The Englishman may boast of his liberty, but will it procure him a dinner? . . . The Russian hugs his slavery; he rejects any boon of liberty and clings to more substantial blessings." For other observations on the condition of Russian factory workers in St. Petersburg and Moscow (the Stieglitz and Guchkov enterprises), see my Chapters 2 and 10.

[46] For details, see the Iatsunskii-Rozhkova article in Rozhkova, ed., *Ocherki ekonomicheskoi istorii Rossii*, pp. 227-45; also *Rabochee dvizhenie v Rossii v xix veke* (Moscow, 1955), vol. I, parts I and II.

[47] Robert Lyall, *The Character of the Russians and a Detailed History of Moscow* (London, 1823), p. 80.

the home of the boyars, their retainers and servants and great palaces. Moscow, almost since its establishment in the fourteenth century, had also been a trading center. Merchants had already established themselves in the so-called Kitai Gorod next to the Kremlin, although by the eighteenth century, clergy and nobility had very largely occupied this section, and only a small minority of its residents were commercial people.[48]

During the early nineteenth century, factories began to appear, not in the central or western parts of the city, which remained official and residential, but in its eastern suburbs. By 1850, industrial districts with numerous large factories and a heavy concentration of population had developed just beyond the old gates of the city, along small rivers in what had formerly been villages, military settlements, and cemeteries (Preobrazhensk, Semenovsk, Lefort, Pokrovsk, Rogozhsk). As early as 1814, there were 253 industrial enterprises concentrated mainly in these areas, employing 27,314 workers.

This was the first great center of the Russian textile industry, with over 90 percent of its production devoted to woolens, cotton, and silk. Although most of the Moscow undertakings were hardly more than shops, there were forty-nine that employed over twenty workers and twenty-three with a working force of over one hundred.[49] Among the largest factories was the cotton manufacturing establishment of the Chorokov brothers, which in 1814 employed 5,966 workers. The largest woolens factory in Moscow and perhaps all of Russia was controlled by the Guchkov brothers. By the middle of the nineteenth century, they employed between 1,600 and 2,000 workers in several plants.[50]

The commercial life of Moscow, as has been described earlier, was concentrated in the *gostinnyi dvor*, in several other permanent markets, and along several streets and bridges. This too was departing from its traditional ways during the early nineteenth century, as can be seen from the history of Ilinka (now Kuibyshev) Street. At the beginning of the century, Ilinka Street, originally named after a monastery, was a crowded thoroughfare where one could always find large numbers of Russian merchants gathered in inns, making deals amidst a cloud of tea vapor, or bargaining out in the street itself. The Moscow *Birzha* was opened on Ilinka Street in 1839. This set the stage for the late nineteenth century, when the big private banks of Moscow

[48] P. Sytin, *Iz istorii moskovskikh ulitz* (3rd edn., Moscow, 1958), pp. 68-69. Sytin explains the name *Kitai Gorod* as a derivation from the Mongol word for "central" (*kitai*) and the old Russian word for fortress (*gorod*).

[49] *Istoriia Moskvy*, vol. III, map facing p. 148; also pp. 173-74, 178-79; and Rozhkova, "Promyshlennost Moskvy," pp. 89-90.

[50] On the Chorokovs, see Rozhkova, "Promyshlennost Moskvy," pp. 90-91; on the Guchkovs, see my Chapters 1 and 9.

were built there, and it became the financial center of the city.[51]

By the last years of the reign of Alexander I, the population of the city of Moscow exceeded 300,000 people, who occupied an area of over 31 square miles. This was divided by 1817 into 164 main and 539 side streets and 25 squares.[52] Both the population and the buildings suffered greatly from two events of the early nineteenth century —the fire of 1812 and the cholera epidemic of 1830. Three-fourths of the city was destroyed in the Napoleonic conflagration, which meant that hundreds of industrial enterprises, large and small, were obliterated. The recovery was quick. By 1817, over two-thirds of Moscow had been rebuilt, and by 1830, the number of houses exceeded the 1812 or preinvasion total of 9,158. Only sixty-two houses remained unreconstructed from the fire. During the reign of Nicholas I, the estimates for the proportion of stone houses in Moscow range from less than one-quarter to 30 percent. The city grew tremendously during the reign of Nicholas I. In 1842, there were over 12,000 houses in addition to 7,421 dwellings not classified as houses.[53]

More than most large cities of the time, Moscow was dimly lit, poorly policed, and chronically short of water. In 1817, Moscow had 4,341 street lamps as compared to 50,000 in London at that time. This left much of the city in darkness, the shadows guarded by little more than 1,000 watchmen and a handful of constables and inspectors, serving under the Head Police Master and Military Governor of the city. Moscow had few stone bridges and no metal bridge until 1859. Water came from the Moskva and Iauza rivers and was impure. Only the wealthy could afford their own wells. A few conduits with steam pumps were built, but the city remained short of water long after the early nineteenth century.[54]

Traditional Moscow society was changing by the reign of Nicholas I. The old order was decaying, as Russian and foreign observers were quick to note. Pushkin was the first to lament in romantic fashion the passing of aristocratic Moscow, writing in 1834:

And what has become of this noisy, idle, carefree life? What has become of the balls, the banquets, the buffoons and pranksters— all have vanished. . . . Now, in a silenced Moscow, huge boyars' houses stand sadly amidst vast courtyards, overgrown with weeds, and wild, neglected gardens. Under a gilded crest protrudes the signboard of a tailor, who pays the landlord thirty rubles a month

---

[51] Sytin, *Iz istorii moskovskikh ulitz*, p. 101; *Istoriia Moskvy*, vol. III, pp. 261-62, 290-91.

[52] Sytin, *Iz istorii moskovskikh ulitz*, pp. 16-17; Lyall, *Moscow*, p. 50.

[53] *Istoriia Moskvy*, vol. III, pp. 142, 151-56, 161-62, 177; Lyall, *Moscow*, pp. 65-66; Tengoborskii, *Commentaries*, vol. I, p. 106.

[54] Lyall, *Moscow*, pp. 52, 106; N. I. Falkovskii, *Moskva v istorii tekhniki* (Moscow, 1956), pp. 95-96, 125-26.

for an apartment; the magnificent ground floor has been rented by *madame* for a boarding school—it's better than nothing! Fastened to all the gates are advertisements for sale or rental, but no one buys or rents. The streets are deathlike; rarely does the tap of a carriage sound on the pavement. Young girls run to the window when one of the police chiefs with his cossacks rides by. . . .

But the Moscow which has lost its aristocratic glitter flourishes in other ways: industry, highly protected, has come to life and has developed there with unusual strength. The merchants have become rich and are beginning to live in the palaces forsaken by the nobility.[55]

According to Baron Haxthausen a decade later, the nobles had been burned out in 1812 and could not afford to restore their palaces and town houses to their former splendor:

> The palaces of the nobility, with their innumerable and lazy domestics are now occupied by the manufacturers with their equally numerous workmen. . . . If you ask, "To whom does this palace belong?" the answer is "to the manufacturer M———, the merchant C———, etc., formerly to Prince A——— or G———."[56]

If the old palaces were becoming schools, apartment houses, factories, or shops, some of their owners were themselves becoming manufacturers; and the former house servants were gone, having been sent off to earn wages in the Moscow factories.[57]

Like Moscow, St. Petersburg was a city in transition during the second quarter of the nineteenth century. The Soviet historian of the imperial capital, Kopanev, has vividly described the merging of bureaucratic with industrial St. Petersburg during this period:

> . . . the parasitical nobility and oppressed peasantry, a burgeoning bourgeoisie and newly born working class, rich merchants and insignificant traders, owners of workshops and poor handicraftsmen, the upper bureaucracy and petty chancellery clerks—all live here side by side in the same apartments and houses, not leading completely separate lives, speaking various languages . . . wearing different dress. . . . Wealth and poverty, power and deprivation of rights, idleness and exhausting labor succeeded each other here.[58]

---

[55] A. S. Pushkin, "Puteshestvie iz Moskvy v Peterburg," (1834) *Polnoe sobranie sochinenii* (Academy of Sciences, U.S.S.R., 1949), vol. II, p. 246. On the social composition of the Russian cities, see Appendix 2, Part 3, Tables C, F, G, and H.

[56] A. von Haxthausen, *The Russian Empire, Its People, Institutions and Resources* (London, 1856), vol. I, pp. 48-49.

[57] Haxthausen, *Russian Empire*, vol. I, pp. 49-50; *Istoriia Moskvy*, vol. III, pp. 158-60.

[58] Kopanev, *Naselenie Peterburga*, p. 21.

Kopanev perhaps overestimates the proximity of the various classes of St. Petersburg society. The upper classes in their town houses and palaces at the center of the city were isolated to a large degree from the factory workers in the suburbs.

The structure of St. Petersburg society in the early nineteenth century reflected economic and political differences from Moscow. Two and one-half times as many nobles and *raznochintsy* lived in St. Petersburg to serve in exalted and petty positions in the central bureaucratic apparatus of the empire. Moscow had many more merchants, but merchants of the first and second guilds were more numerous in St. Petersburg, and a far greater number of foreign businessmen were in evidence to service the world trade of the first port of Russia. There were many more craftsmen in St. Petersburg to cater to the imperial court and the tastes of a more cosmopolitan society.[59]

A new industrial St. Petersburg was emerging in the suburbs of the capital city by the 1830's. The eighteenth-century industries of the city had catered to the traditional society: shipyards for the navy, arsenals for the army, a world famous imperial porcelain factory for the tsar's court, and playing card, wallpaper, and macaroni factories for the nobility.[60]

The state and foreign entrepreneurs, beginning in the 1790's, took the initiative in building large factories engaged in more modern forms of heavy and light industrial production. Many of these factories were set up in what were then stretches of countryside just outside the gates of the city, such as the Schlüsselburg tract along the Neva where as early as 1797, the Lehman cotton printing factory employed several hundred workers.[61] Here the large state cotton spinning factory of Aleksandrovsk was established at the end of the eighteenth century. A few years earlier, Russia's first factory to produce steam machines was established in St. Petersburg by the Scottish mechanic, Charles Baird.[62] Thus, the nuclei of the two most important industries of the Russian capital—cotton and machinery—were in evidence by the beginning of the nineteenth century. By the 1840's, the Aleksandrovsk spinning factory and the Baird enterprises had been joined by the Russian Cotton Spinning Company, the Stieglitz cotton factory, the

[59] *Istoriia Moskvy*, vol. III, pp. 172-73; Kopanev, *Naselenie Peterburga*, p. 20.

[60] V. V. Pokshishevskii, "Territorial'noe formirovanie promyshlennogo kompleksa Peterburga v XVIII-XIX vekakh," *Voprosy geografii*, vol. 20 (1950), pp. 123, 126: "Vedomost sostoiashchem v St. Peterburg fabrikam, manufakturam i zavodam 1794 goda," *Sbornik Imperatorskago Russkago Istoricheskago Obshchestva*, vol. I (1867), pp. 352-61; P. N. Stolpianskii, *Zhizn i byt Peterburgskoi fabriki 1704-1914* (Leningrad, 1925), pp. 8-11.

[61] For a detailed analysis of Schlüsselburg, see N. N. Dmitriev, *Pervye russkie sitsenabivnye manufaktury XVIII veka* (Moscow-Leningrad, 1935), pp. 272-310.

[62] On Baird, see my Chapter 10.

State Aleksandrovsk Locomotive Plant, the Nobel machine works, and the several mechanical, cotton and woolen enterprises of Wilkins, Ellis and Butts, Carr and McPherson, the Duke of Lichtenberg, Thornton, Hubbard, Maltsev, and Ogarev. Most of these factories were large and highly mechanized. By 1854, 75 percent of Russia's yearly machine production issued from St. Petersburg.[63]

St. Petersburg's position as Russia's greatest port as well as the capital of the imperial government made it the natural center for financial dealings in the empire. Here, state fiscal policy was directed by the Minister of Finances. Here, the few state banks that had been established since the time of Catherine the Great functioned. It was in the Russian capital that the first central state bank would be set up in 1861. Private banks were almost nonexistent in prereform St. Petersburg, but its dominant role in Russian finance in the late nineteenth century was foreshadowed by the rapid growth of the stock exchange during the reigns of Alexander I and Nicholas I.[64]

The recorded history of Ivanovo begins in 1561, when the village bearing this royal name was given to the princely Cherkasskii family by Ivan the Terrible. The village had been settled during the turbulent sixteenth century, in part by refugees from Novgorod. In the seventeenth century, the schism left a deep and permanent mark on Ivanovo. It became, for two centuries, primarily a settlement for Old Believers. In the early eighteenth century, the village passed by marriage into the hands of the greatest of the serf-holding families in Old Russia, the Sheremetevs. By this time, Ivanovo had become a trading town, and a weaving industry had developed in most of its cottages. The reasons for these economic changes were simple. Ivanovo was favorably located with respect to the Volga trade, and the land was poor, necessitating supplementary sources of income for industrious ex-Novgorodian and *raskol'nik* peasants during the long winters. Ivanovo's first industrial entrepreneur was I. I. Grachev, a serf who established a linen plant in 1748. He was followed in this endeavor by other enterprising serfs, so that by the 1770's, the two other future big industrial families of the town, the Garelins and Iamanovskiis, were well established in business.[65]

By 1775, Ivanovo was a small manufacturing center, with a population of just over 3,200, most of it engaged in the domestic weaving industry. For some years, small groups of Ivanovo craftsmen had

[63] *Ocherki istorii Leningrada* (Moscow-Leningrad, 1955), p. 456; see also my Chapters 2 and 10.

[64] On the exchange, see my Chapter 3.

[65] For more information on the Ivanovo industrialists, see my Chapter 8. The most authoritative data on the early history of Ivanovo, upon which this account is primarily based, can be found in P. M. Ekzempliarskii, *Istoriia goroda Ivanova* (Ivanovo, 1958), vol. I, pp. 19-61, and Ia. P. Garelin, *Gorod Ivanovo-Voznesensk* (Shuia, 1884), part 1, pp. 25-42.

journeyed to Petersburg to work in the foreign-owned cotton factories of the Russian capital. The turning point for the industrial history of the town came in the late 1780's, when an Ivanovo craftsman, Osip Sokov, journeyed to the St. Petersburg suburb of Schlüsselburg to work in the cotton printing factory of the foreign firm of Lehman. Lehman had developed a secret process for the dyeing of cotton cloth with colors which would not fade. Sokov carried these secrets back to Ivanovo, they were widely adopted, and a new industry was born.[66] The continental blockade of the Napoleonic period, the burning of Moscow, and the high protective tariff of the second quarter of the nineteenth century all helped to eliminate domestic and foreign competition for the cotton finishing industry of Ivanovo. Such favorable conditions, combined with a receptivity to technological change on the part of the Ivanovo industrialists, the availability of superior grades of English thread, a benevolent policy on the part of the Sheremetev patrons toward their wealth-producing serfs, and a ready mass market for the cheaper grades of cloth produced in Ivanovo resulted in quick prosperity for the "Russian Manchester." By the mid-nineteenth century, a center for textile manufacturing was forming, the peer only of Moscow in the finishing of cotton cloth, while Vladimir province by 1858 was second only to that of Moscow in the cotton weaving industry.[67]

Ivanovo by the 1850's had become a pure industrial town, and, as such, something new for Russia; but by no means was it at that time anything more than a small city or overgrown town. The cotton printing industry, the major one in Ivanovo at mid-century, employed 5,355 workers in 105 factories, many of them small. However, a few were very large, were fully mechanized, and were utilizing steam power. The craft of hand printing cotton cloth was dying out rapidly. However, Ivanovo's six cotton weaving enterprises in 1850 employed 996 workers in factories, and 9,244 outside of these factories, presumably domestic weavers. There were 71,824 weavers in the district of Ivanovo in 1849, 8 percent of them worked in their cottages at hand looms. Ivanovo's one chemical factory employed eighty-four workers. The total production of the town's various industries—cotton spinning, weaving, printing, and chemical—came to a value of 4,957,130 rubles in 1850. By the early 1860's, according to official figures, the number of cotton printing plants had decreased radically, by two-thirds. However, according to the same statistics, total production was up by just over 20 percent, and there were six chemical

[66] Ekzempliarskii, *Istoriia goroda Ivanova*, p. 51; Garelin, *Gorod Ivanovo*, pp. 140-48.

[67] K. A. Pazhitnov, *Ocherki istorii tekstil'noi promyshlennosti dorevoliutsionnoi Rossii, khlopchatobumazhnaia, l'nopenkovaia i shelkovaia promyshlennost* (Moscow, 1958), pp. 38-39, 55-56.

plants, as well as dyeing and bleaching establishments and an iron foundry.[68]

Ivanovo by the beginning of the reign of Nicholas I traded with Russia and the world. About 1,800 tons or several million rubles worth of Manchester thread were imported from England each year. A much smaller amount of Russian thread, manufactured at the State Aleksandrovsk Cotton Spinning Factory, also was purchased by the Ivanovo weavers. Goods from the wharves and factories of St. Petersburg reached Ivanovo via the European Russian canal systems and the Volga River. They were carted in overland from the river for the last 30 miles of the journey. A much needed railroad for this final and costly link with Ivanovo was not built until the late nineteenth century. From Ivanovo's factories, printed cotton cloth was sent, in large part to Moscow, but also to the Nizhnii-Novgorod fair and the major fairs of the Ukraine.[69]

In the 1830's, Ivanovo was still a small town by modern standards, with only a few stone dwellings, surrounded by forests. Bears and wolves could be found not too far from the few dozens of streets. All of this changed rapidly in the 1840's and '50's. The trees were cut down, and the wild animals disappeared. Within Ivanovo society itself, the Schism began to decline. The younger generation became indifferent to its teachings, or departed for Moscow. Three new suburbs grew around the original village, in which both private homes and factories were built.[70] Ivanovo and these surrounding settlements were reformed by a government decree of 1853 into the township unit (*posad*) of Voznesensk. Its official population at that time was less than 3,600, although the number drawn into the industrial complex from the neighboring area probably approached 12,500. That the bulk of the workers did not live in the township itself is evidenced by the fact that it contained only 235 houses as against 402 factories, shops, and other types of buildings.[71]

Before 1861, Ivanovo was in terms of its legal and social position a village of serfs belonging to Count Sheremetev. Almost a century before this, as we have seen elsewhere, a middle class of craftsmen and industrialists had begun to form, and by the beginning of the reign of Nicholas I, the most affluent had purchased their freedom. By 1833,

---

[68] Figures for the 1840's and 1850's in Ekzempliarskii, *Istoriia goroda Ivanova*, vol. I, table, pp. 98-99, and p. 105; and B. N. Vasilev, "Formirovanie promyshlennogo proletariata Ivanovskoi oblasti," *Voprosy istorii* (1952), no. 6, table, p. 104. For the early 1860's, see *Ekonomicheskoe sostoianie gorodskikh poselenii evropeiskoi Rossii v 1861-62 g.* (St. Petersburg, 1863), section on Vladimir province, p. 65.

[69] N. Boiarkin, "Vzgliad na selo Ivanovo," *Moskovskii telegraf* (1826), part 11, pp. 111-14.

[70] Garelin, *Gorod Ivanovo-Voznesensk*, pp. 11-12, 190, 207-08, 211-12.

[71] Ekzempliarskii, *Istoriia goroda Ivanova*, vol. I, table, pp. 98-99; 103, 105.

there were 167 residents of Ivanovo who were registered in the merchant guilds, and 138 enrolled in the *meshchanstvo*. By 1855, the number of merchants had jumped to 197, while the *meshchanstvo* had diminished in number by 19. In the same year, the bulk of Ivanovo's population—4,956 peasants—remained serfs, the property of Count Sheremetev. Ivanovo's servile population, however, had declined by just over 10 percent since 1833. The few hundred people who lived in the suburbs which had formed during that period were free. Foreign craftsmen, the number of whom had doubled during the reign of Nicholas I, were still a small minority of Ivanovo's industrial class. There were 62 in 1855.[72]

After 1825, Ivanovo was governed almost exclusively by its industrial magnates. Traditionally, the Sheremetevs ruled the village through an appointed steward. Over the years, other local administrative offices developed: village delegates and overseers, a treasurer and a constable. All of these offices by the end of the reign of Alexander I were in the hands of the big factory owners, with M. I. Garelin at their head for many years. In 1854, a town council was established, which was also controlled by the Ivanovo industrialists.[73]

During most of the early nineteenth century, Ivanovo was essentially a frontier boom town, with most of the problems characteristic of rapid industrial growth in an essentially primitive rural environment. Thieves and murderers flourished almost unchecked by police, and apparently uninhibited by the moral strictures of the Old Believers. Highway robbery was common and even a local church was robbed. A small police force was established in 1817, but proved ineffective, and was abolished after one of its members was killed. Ivanovo until the late nineteenth century, like many Russian towns, was built essentially of wood and was plagued by terrible fires. In 1775, in 1793, and again in 1839, it was almost obliterated by conflagrations that consumed hundreds of structures. In 1839, 416 houses and 61 factories burned down, at a cost of over a million rubles. The Russian peasant's capacity for arson was amply displayed in the history of Ivanovo, and was met with the most severe punishments, including heavy knoutings and exile to Siberia. By the middle of the nineteenth century, many stone houses and factories were put up by the wealthier inhabitants in an effort to modify fire risks and losses.[74]

A primary school was established in Ivanovo in 1791, by Count Sheremetev. Soon after, this first school was absorbed by the Ministry of Public Instruction. By the mid-nineteenth century, it had almost 100 pupils. There were two other schools by that time, one of them established by and serving the Baburin factory. A library of 400 vol-

[72] Garelin, *Gorod Ivanovo-Voznesensk*, vol. I, pp. 213, 224-25.
[73] Garelin, *Gorod Ivanovo-Voznesensk*, vol. I, p. 190.
[74] On crime and fire, see Garelin, *Gorod Ivanovo-Voznesensk*, vol. I, pp. 154-58, 189.

umes was functioning by 1850, although an attempt to establish a vaudeville theater soon after failed. A decade later, over 100 shops were operating in a large, stone *gostinnyi dvor*. The main streets were paved with stone.[75] By a statute of 1871, Ivanovo became a city proper, and its name was changed to Ivanovo-Voznesensk. By the eve of the First World War, Ivanovo-Voznesensk had become a major industrial city of Russia, as it remains today, with a population by 1913 of 147,380, a factory working force of 33,215, and a total annual production from fifty-nine factories of 6,788,000 rubles.[76]

[75] Garelin, *Gorod Ivanovo Voznesensk*, vol. I, pp. 159, 213-15; *Goroda evropeiskoi Rossii*, pp. 63, 66-67; Ekzempliarskii, *Istoriia goroda Ivanova*, vol. I, pp. 112, 114.

[76] Ekzempliarskii, *Istoriia goroda Ivanova*, vol. I, pp. 125, 274, 281.

Part II

The State and Industrial Development

No sooner had the tsarist regime disposed of the more immediate and tangible threats posed by the French Revolution than it was faced with the novel and ambiguous challenge of the English industrial revolution. By 1815, Russia's deep involvement in European power politics, the social and economic backwardness of the country, and its political traditions all demanded a decisive initiative on the part of the state in the matter of industrial development. With the relative insignificance of indigenous private enterprise, the state was the only agent within Russia possessing the potential for undertaking the burden of industrialization. Beyond Russia's borders, foreign industrialists and financiers would soon be able and willing to play a major role in Russian development, but this would involve economic and ultimately political influences to which the tsarist government, as a great power, was loath to submit. The huge military machine which was maintained to police Europe could also act to prevent a repetition of the penetration and dismemberment of the Ottoman and Chinese empires in which Russia herself by 1860 was participating.

It was thus clear to some Russians, even as early as the Napoleonic period, that there was an urgent necessity for the Russian state to close the industrial gap with the West if it was to maintain its leadership at home and abroad. Little in the Russian political tradition stood in the way of such a major governmental intrusion into the economic life of the country. Under Nicholas I the traditional bureaucratic police despotism had matured. The regime possessed most of the instruments of coercion and faced no substantial organized societal opposition to the implementation of a major reorganization of the economy. Although heavy inertias and vested interests blocked the path, Peter the Great had shown that decisive and ruthless leadership could remove them. Mercantilism was nothing new to Russia, and the marshalling and regimentation of the labor and managerial force by the state had formed the fabric of tsarist social and economic history for over two centuries.

Despite these pressures of state interest and tradition, the tsarist regime failed to engineer or stimulate a major industrial effort in the early nineteenth century. Imperial Russia was revealed to the world in the Crimean War as a "backward" country; and it was not until at least the end of the nineteenth century that industrialization became a major aim of the rulers of Russia. The explanation for this failure of the Russian state to decisively activate and accelerate industrialization when many of the Western countries were modernizing their economies must be sought in the complex process of how economic growth begins as applied to Russia. The answer so often given to explain the inertia of Russia's government in the first half of the nineteenth century (and of many "underdeveloped" countries today) emphasizes the indolence and ignorance of the leadership, the rigidity of the society, the decrepitude of the instruments of government, and the lack of resources. All of these conditions existed in prereform Russia, but not, of course, exclusively, and it is not sufficient to explain the backwardness of the regime by collating the more blatant examples of obscurantism. Evidence can be offered that the tsarist leadership at that time was not unaware of the need for industrial progress and was willing to take steps to bring about such progress; that the society was not inflexible and was in fact changing in important ways; that the imperial bureaucracy was viable as an instrument of government; and that resources could be mobilized. The record thus merits reexamination with a view to determining precisely what the regime wanted and did not want, and what it could do and could not do.

Part II will explore three aspects of the failure of the tsarist regime to begin substantially the industrialization of Russia during the early nineteenth century. First, economic thought with specific reference to conflicting views of industrialization will be considered. How aware was the leadership of Russia—the tsars, the bureaucracy, and the ruling and educated classes—of the problem of industrialization? How willing were the rulers of Russia to implement a program of industrialization, and what specific policies were formulated? What alternative views were forwarded and how influential were they?

A second problem to be taken up in Chapter 6 focuses on the administration of industrial development in early nineteenth-century Russia. How was the tsarist administration organized on the central and local levels to deal with the novel problems of industrialization? How well equipped was the imperial Russian bureaucracy to implement industrial policy? To what extent did bureaucratic habits and patterns impede state industrial programs? What specific policies to stimulate, develop and regulate industry were put into effect and how successfully were they carried through?

Part II also discusses in Chapter 7 a third problem fundamentally connected with the failure of the tsarist government to comprehensively foster industrialization in the decades before 1860—the resources at its disposal and the priority accorded industrial policy in their allocation. To what extent was the tsarist government capable of effecting at least a beginning push toward industrialization? How adequate were its revenues? How stabile were its finances? To what extent did other policies, particularly in the realm of foreign affairs, conflict with industrialization or assume priority over it? More specifically, how did the cost of war and of the maintenance of the military machine impede a state industrialization program during the reigns of Alexander I and Nicholas I?

Chapter 5

The Industrialization Debate

The Struggle of the Freetraders and the Protectionists

The interests, motives, and issues involved in the question of the industrial destiny of Russia came to focus immediately after the Congress of Vienna in the debate, conducted largely within bureaucratic circles, between the "Freetraders" and the "Protectionists."[1] The immediate issue in this dispute revolved around the modification in the direction of free trade of the highly protective and prohibitive tariff of 1811. This tariff had aimed to stimulate infant Russian industry. The underlying issue which was debated with even greater vigor by the "Freetraders" and "Protectionists" was whether Russia should industrialize on a large scale or remain an agricultural nation. It was the first enunciation of a familiar topic of debate in the subsequent century.

On the theoretical level, the freetraders were inspired by the teachings of Adam Smith, which enjoyed wide currency among upper-ranking Russian officials during the reign of Alexander I. Russia, they argued, on the basis of Smith's theory of the international balance of trade, could not at that time develop the necessary capital for industry. She was best suited to remain primarily an agricultural supplier of raw materials to the industrialized nations of western Europe and an importer of their manufactured goods. In addition to the influence of Smith and the Physiocrats, much of the polemic of the freetraders bore the imprint of conservative nationalism, not uncolored by romantic pre-Slavophile idealizations of the Russian rural utopia. Industrialization and factory organization, it was asserted, corrupted the physical, moral, and spiritual health of the workers and led to uprisings. Economically and morally, the Russian peasant was better off under serfdom than the dehumanized English factory worker enslaved by a machine. As for the factory owners, the freetraders charged that a protective tariff favored monopolists, stimulated corruption and smuggling, and discouraged competition. It should be observed that there was no unanimity of opinion among the freetraders. Two of the most influential—Turgenev, the future Decembrist, and Heinrich Storch, the noted professor and tutor to the imperial family —were liberals who urged the abolition of serfdom.[2]

---

[1] A version of the section dealing with this debate was presented in a paper, "The Administration of Industrial Development Under Alexander I," for the first conference of the Southern Section, American Association for the Advancement of Slavic Studies, held at Duke University, October 1962.

[2] The most complete discussions of the views of the freetraders and protectionists can be found in M. Tugan-Baranovskii, *Russkaia fabrika v proshlom i nastoiashchem* (3rd edn., St. Petersburg, 1907), vol. I, pp. 267-70; and V. I. Picheta, "Fritredery i protektsionisty v Rossii v pervoi chetverti xix veka,"

The protectionists were critics of Adam Smith and his Russian apostle Storch. They argued that Russia could develop sufficient capital to industrialize, and that all the great industrial nations of Europe had at one time followed protective tariff policies. They predicted that if Russia did not industrialize, she would become an economic and even a political dependent of Europe, while with the outflow of precious metal to pay for foreign manufactures, she would follow the path of Spain into inflation, stagnation, and poverty.[3]

The struggle of the freetraders and the protectionists divided the imperial bureaucracy into factions. The very top echelons, who exercised an immediate control over tariff policy, were, with a few important exceptions, protectionists. The freetraders came predominantly from the lower ranks, and put pressure to bear on the government primarily through propaganda, both by means of the magazine which they controlled, *Dukh Zhurnalov*, and through spokesmen in academic circles. Behind the official alignment, social interests were at work. The freetraders spoke for the bulk of the nobility, within and outside of the state service, whose main interests were the preservation of serfdom and the profitable village handicraft industry, the export of Russian raw materials abroad, and the purchase of foreign-made luxuries for the affluent classes. The protectionists drew their strength from two groups: the growing Russian industrialist class, whose clamor for a high tariff to protect their enterprises did not go unheard in government circles, and great aristocrats, some of whom occupied the highest positions of state. Many of these magnate-industrialist officials and their families had since the time of Catherine the Great established factories on their estates, where they employed serf labor. Others permitted their serfs to work as hired laborers in factories which they did not personally own, while continuing to collect the *obrok* in cash from the wages of these peasants. The nobles so involved in industry were by no means numerous, but they were rich and were influential in society and at the imperial court. Typical of such magnate-industrialist officials was Count N. P. Rumiantsev, Minister of Commerce for most of the first decade of the century, who had a direct voice in the determination of trade policy and industrial development. The high tariff policy which these people endorsed permitted the industries of those who directly controlled them to survive and even flourish; while more factories under a high tariff meant more

---

Kniga dlia chteniia po istorii novago vremeni (St. Petersburg, 1912), vol. III, pp. 620-51.

[3] N. S. Mordvinov, "Nekotorye soobrazheniia po predmetu manufaktur v Rossii i o tarif," and its supplement in *Arkhiv Grafov Mordvinovykh* (St. Petersburg, 1901-03), vol. V, pp. 67-120. This was first published in 1816 and presents the most complete exposition of the protectionist position.

wages and greater income in *obrok* from those serfs who trod the roads to distant factories.

The tariff and the industrial policy of the tsarist government during the reign of Alexander I thus immediately reflected not only foreign competition, the demands of war, and the influence of European economic theory, but directly expressed the conflict of interests of social groups. Although many of the nobility and most, if not all of the merchants and industrialists could exert pressure only indirectly through petitions and propaganda, many others, including particularly representatives of the upper nobility were serving the government while at the same time being engaged in industrial enterprise. This interplay of interests has fascinated Russian historians since Tugan-Baranovskii, who first pointed out the underlying forces. Soviet historians would go beyond Tugan-Baranovskii in emphasizing the importance of the middle class in their "struggle" with the nobility.[4] In such a view, state policy was determined by social pressure. This may not have been the only factor operative, particularly with regard to the limited influence of the Russian merchants and industrialists during the reign of Alexander I. Be that as it may, the protectionists ultimately won out. The reign of free trade was a brief and transient interlude which endured for only a few years following the Congress of Vienna. A protective tariff became the rule thereafter for almost forty years. The reason that protectionism triumphed was because all of the merchant factory owners, an increasing number of landlords, and a hard core of the most influential magnates supported it, as well as leading officials who had been entrusted with major decisions about economic policy.

The struggle of the freetraders and the protectionists was the first expression of a cleavage which developed in official as well as academic and intellectual circles in Russia during most of the early nineteenth century. The two conflicting views on the industrialization question usually have been identified as those of the liberals in the one camp, opposed to the conservatives (and reactionaries). So they are presented in the recent and authoritative Soviet *History of Russian Economic Thought* in the several chapters dealing with this period by F. M. Morozov.[5] The reason for such a classification is that most of the proponents of industrialization have been seen by historians as political liberals. They advocated reform, constitutionalism, and other changes usually identified with liberalism at that time. The terms are somewhat inaccurate, not only because of the difficulty of fitting designations of Western origin, which are vague today and

---

[4] See A. V. Predtechenskii, "Bor'ba protektsionistov c fritrederami v nachale xix veka," Leningrad State University, *Uchenye zapiski*, No. 48 (1939), pp. 143-56.

[5] A. Pashkov, ed., *Istoriia russkoi ekonomicheskoi mysli* (Moscow, 1958), vol. I, part 2, pp. 5-202.

which change with the times, into an early nineteenth-century Russian context, but also because some Russians of the time, who have been considered "liberal," were not overly enthusiastic about a rapid industrialization of their country along Western lines. Few were opposed to industrialization per se; the dispute was over the method and the pace.

It would be more accurate to refer to the divergent points of view on industrialization in prereform Russia both as the struggle of Westernizers against nationalists and as industrializers versus traditionalists. The Westernizers and industrializers wished to transform Russia from an agrarian to an industrial society, modeled along Western lines, as rapidly and comprehensively as possible, but for most, within the context of the existing social order. The nationalists and traditionalists tended to envisage a unique Russian development, characterized by a slower, natural pace of industrialization, attendant to the needs of the agrarian sector of the economy and geared to the traditions of Russia. Of course, neither point of view was identified by these names at the time, there was no organized program for either side, nor had cliques formed in the bureaucracy to forward one idea or the other. Rather, the designations represent ranges of opinion in a spectrum running from moderate to extreme. Most accepted the existing political and social order; some did not.

The industrializing position was prominent where the status quo was accepted, in the upper bureaucracy, or, more specifically, at the ministerial level. This was truer of the reign of Alexander I than of his successor. These high officials never organized into a faction or "party." Rather, individuals succeeded each other in important posts for long periods of time. However, they shared a point of view, which was influential to the extent that they participated in the formulation of the main lines of government economic policy or were respected as economists. One of the earliest proponents of Russian industrialization, Count N. P. Rumiantsev, was Minister of Commerce during most of the first decade of the nineteenth century. O. P. Kozodavlev, one of the staunchest of the protectionists, was Minister of Internal Affairs during the next decade. M. M. Speranskii favored industrialization while he dominated the bureaucratic scene from 1808 until 1812. Of less influence than these officials of ministerial rank, although widely heard as the most articulate official spokesman for the comprehensive industrialization of Russia during the reigns of Alexander I and Nicholas I was Admiral, Count, and State Councillor N. S. Mordvinov. This does not exhaust the list of influential officials not directly concerned with economic policy who favored the industrialization of Russia during this period. The reformer, friend of Alexander I, member of the Secret Committee, and later, virtual dictator of Poland, Novosiltsev, was of this view. Count N. S. Vorontsov, military proconsul of the Caucasus and energetic governor of new Russia under Nicholas I, initiated a wide-ranging program for the industrial development of the latter area. Some of Nicholas I's closest and most pliant advisers, Counts Nesselrode and Benckendorf, were at least actively interested in industrial speculations, for their own gain, if not for the good of Russia.[6]

Equally influential officials of ministerial rank, considered experts in economic matters and entrusted with major responsibility for economic policy, were essentially opposed to a major industrial effort on the part of the Russian state during the early nineteenth century. The Minister of Internal Affairs upon two occasions during the reign of Alexander I, V. P. Kochubei, and the Ministers of Finances for most of the reigns of Alexander I and Nicholas I, Gurev and Kankrin, were of this view, although not without qualifications which are important to note. The Minister of State Properties and agrarian reformer of the 1830's and 1840's, General P. D. Kiselev, although not opposed to industrial development, demanded that its nature and pace be determined by the needs of Russian agriculture.

Such a diversity of views among officials who formulated and implemented policy was also characteristic of other less influential circles of the ruling elite. To this must be added the fact that the tsars were neither consistent in their views of industrialization nor in their perseverance in following through those industrial policies which had been initiated.[7] The result was that no clear-cut and comprehensive

---

[6] On Vorontsov's efforts to develop New Russia, see V. A. Iakovlev, *Biografii De Ribasa, Richilieuie i Vorontsova* (Odessa, 1894) pp. 27-29; on Benckendorf's investments, see S. Monas, *The Third Section* (Harvard, 1961), pp. 98-99; and on Nesselrode, M. K. Rozhkova, ed., *Ocherki ekonomicheskoi istorii Rossii pervoi poloviny xix veka* (Moscow, 1959), p. 176.

[7] There is little evidence that Alexander I had any significant interest in scientific or economic problems. His education under the tutelage of F. C. LaHarpe certainly was not developed along those lines. Although concerned about the improvement of Russian transport, Alexander was admittedly indifferent to technology. Machines and factories were little more than a curiosity to him, although he was concerned with conditions of his Urals metallurgical workers. Alexander was often naive in matters concerning economics: he took a fashionable interest in the teachings of Adam Smith, and embraced the "progressive" idea of free trade, apparently without understanding the harm such a policy could inflict on Russian industry. More than once, Alexander made important decisions when unaware of or indifferent to their economic consequences, as in the periods of the Tilsit alliance and the Congress of Vienna. The education of Nicholas I was much more practical. Although Storch's lectures on "Political Economy" bored him, he developed an interest in industry, and was devoted throughout his life to technical and engineering subjects. He appreciated fully the latest inventions, such as railroads. His primary commitment, however, was to war; and the development of transport and technology that took place in his reign was largely a result of that commitment. When the interests of war and industrialization clashed, it was the latter that was sacrificed. This conflict occurred most frequently and significantly in the budget. There are no studies of the economic views of the autocrats of Russia during the early nineteenth century. For fragmentary comments and

program for industrialization was formulated or implemented during the early nineteenth century, nor, for that matter was an all-embracing conservative and anti-industrial policy conceived or put into effect. Numerous individual projects, which outlined in great detail what should and should not have been done, were drawn up and submitted. Many specific policies to stimulate, develop, and regulate industry were instituted. Some were carried through effectively; others were abandoned at various points along the way. Many projects which would have helped to develop Russia industrially were turned down flatly; others moved down the tedious path of committees and reports to oblivion. Policies clearly detrimental to industrial growth were instituted. The reasons which the ministers, economists, and other administrators and writers of the time forwarded for what was desirable or undesirable, possible or impossible, provides part of the explanation for these inconsistencies of policy.

Proponents of Industrialization

Chancellor Count Nikolai Petrovich Rumiantsev is remembered in most histories as Russia's Minister of Foreign Affairs during the period of the Tilsit agreement and the last Napoleonic wars (1807-1814). The same Rumiantsev during the early years of the nineteenth century was more effective as Superintendent of Waterways (1801-1809) and Minister of Commerce (1804-1810). He left no systematic treatment of his economic ideas behind him, but his views of Russian industrialization are clear from the policies which he attempted to implement, particularly as Minister of Commerce.[8] Rumiantsev saw the key to Russian progress in the improvement of her commercial position. This in turn would stimulate domestic industry to the point where it could stand up effectively to foreign competition. Commercial improvement meant, first and foremost, the ex-

---

anecdotes, see N. Shilder, *Imperator Aleksandr Pervyi* (St. Petersburg, 1904-05), vol. I, pp. 46-47, IV, p. 614; M. Bogdanovich, *Istoriia tsarstvovaniia Imperatora Aleksandra I* (St. Petersburg, 1869-71), vol. V, p. 314, VI, p. 374; N. Riasanovsky, *Nicholas I and Official Nationality in Russia 1825-1855* (Berkeley-Los Angeles, 1959), pp. 25-27; Constantin de Grunwald, *La vie de Nicholas Ier* (Paris, 1946), pp. 26-28; B. Velikin, *Peterburg-Moskva, iz istorii Oktiabr'skoi Zheleznoi Dorogi* (Leningrad, 1934), p. 17; M. F. Zlotnikov, *Kontinental'naia blokada i Rossiia* (Moscow-Leningrad, 1966), p. 73; and A. M. Loranskii, ed., *Kratkii istoricheskii ocherk administrativnykh uchrezhdenii gornago vedomstva v Rossii 1700-1900 g.g.* (St. Petersburg, 1900), p. 56.

[8] The only studies of Rumiantsev are the short treatments in Zlotnikov, *Kontinental'naia blokada i Rossiia*, pp. 76-81; *Russkii biograficheskii slovar*, vol. XVII, pp. 504-17; *Ministerstvo finansov 1802-1902* (St. Petersburg, 1902), pp. 126-35; the collection of sketches in *Russkie liudi* (author not listed), (St. Petersburg-Moscow, 1866), pp. 297-318. On Rumiantsev's interest in the Far East and the Japanese expedition, see G. A. Lensen, *The Russian Push Toward Japan* (Princeton, 1959), pp. 130-33. On his role in Russian canal development, see my Chapter 11.

pansion of Russian foreign trade, particularly trade with Asia. Rumiantsev wished to augment not only the traditional commerce with the Middle East and Central Asia, but also to improve the Black Sea trade, develop the port of Odessa, and seek new markets in India, China, and Japan. He sponsored the Rezanov expedition to Japan, established a "White Sea Company" to expand the fishing and fur trade in the northern regions of Russia, and set up a customs house in Baku. Russia, in Rumiantsev's view, could become a first-rank commercial power and the intermediary between Europe and Asia.

When it came to the European trade, Rumiantsev was a protectionist. Like Admiral Mordvinov, he argued that Adam Smith's ideas were not applicable to Russia, that the purpose of a tariff was to encourage Russian industry, but that it should be low enough to make inroads on the smuggling traffic.

The growth of domestic trade in the Russian empire demanded first and foremost an improvement of transport facilities, in Rumiantsev's view. As Superintendent of Waterways for several years, he worked energetically to improve Russia's canal and river system. It was during Rumiantsev's stewardship during the first decade of the nineteenth century that the work of Sievers was extended to complete the most significant canal systems of the eighteenth and nineteenth centuries.

Rumiantsev hoped to strengthen the Russian middle class by extending the right to engage in commercial and industrial activity to the nobility and some of the lower classes, and by improving the social position of the Russian merchant. To stimulate business, he permitted the establishment of one of the earliest private banks in Russia. He worked to create new industries in the empire, such as the manufacture of beet sugar; and set an example on his own vast estates by establishing paper and cloth factories, as well as a steamship line.

Rumiantsev's fundamental views on industrialization may be summarized as a belief in the economic development of Russia through vigorous state action to improve conditions for industry and commerce and to facilitate the growth of a middle class engaged in private enterprise. Such an approach was elaborated with greater force and coherence by Speranskii. Speranskii emphasized domestic reform, the sphere of his greatest competence as an administrator, although he was not unconcerned with trade problems, and, like Rumiantsev, was a staunch advocate of the protective tariff. Speranskii was acquainted with contemporary economic theory, particularly Adam Smith and Sismondi, and had connections with some of the biggest Russian merchants and industrialists of the time, as well as English businessmen operating in Russia.[9]

---

[9] Pashkov, ed., *Istoriia Russkoi ekonomicheskoi mysli*, vol. I, part 2, pp. 57-58. The two most substantial recent accounts of Speranskii's views of Russian economic development, which have been utilized here, are the chapter by

Like Rumiantsev, Speranskii believed that it was important to stimulate private enterprise in Russia, and that this could be done through positive state action. First, the government had to make order out of the chaos of its finances. Otherwise industry and commerce would inevitably suffer. Inflated paper money had to be retired, and a strong currency backed by silver established. The budget had to be pruned of unproductive expenditures, and more state money devoted to industrial purposes. A central state bank as well as private banks had to be established to help finance business enterprise. Antiquated and unproductive taxes were to be eliminated. Beyond these purely fiscal measures, Speranskii thought it would be helpful for the state to liquidate its own commercial and industrial enterprises, if these proved unprofitable or were stifling private initiative. A firm foundation of legal stability with the guarantee of personal property rights were essential for the development of commerce and industry in Russia, in his view. This could be provided by and within the framework of a reformed autocratic state.

Osip Petrovich Kozodavlev was Minister of Internal Affairs from 1811 until 1819. This was a period of peacetime industrial development following the dislocations of the Napoleonic wars and invasion. Industrial problems until 1819 were largely the responsibility not, as later, of the Ministry of Finances, but of the Department of Manufactures and Trade of the Ministry of Internal Affairs. Kozodavlev was the first minister in Imperial Russia prior to Reutern for whom industrialization was a primary concern. An educational reformer under Catherine the Great, he was influenced by Speranskii, and many of his proposals in the realm of economic policy echo the ideas of the master reformer who was his contemporary. Of the two, Kozodavlev was far more vigorous a protectionist; and, unlike Speranskii, he attempted to come to grips with the problem of how the state could take an active hand in Russian industrial development without stifling private enterprise.[10]

The industrialization of Russia was the keystone of Kozodavlev's policy as Minister of Internal Affairs and the focal point of his economic ideas. In his view, it was not only desirable and possible, but

---

Morozov in the above cited volume of the Pashkov edition, particularly pp. 51-60; and Marc Raeff, *Michael Speransky* (The Hague, 1957), particularly pp. 93-105. Both of these accounts utilize primarily Speranskii's "Plan finansov," *Sbornik Imperatorskago Russkago Istoricheskago Obshchestva*, vol. 45, pp. 1-73, and both accounts are in essential agreement.

[10] The three most substantial sources for Kozodavlev's industrialization views and policies are: A. V. Predtechenskii, *Ocherki obshchestvenno-politicheskoi istorii Rossii v pervoi chetverti XIX veka* (Moscow-Leningrad, 1957), pp. 295-322; M. I. Sukhomlinov, *Istoriia Rossiiskoi Akademii* (St. Petersburg, 1882), vol. 6, pp. 191-204; *Istoricheskii ocherk ministerstvo vnutrennykh del* (St. Petersburg, 1901), vol. I, pp. 33-38.

necessary that Russia industrialize: industrialization was not a matter of prestige or domestic prosperity, but a question of state interest. Only by becoming strong industrially could Russia eliminate economic dependence on the more advanced industrial powers, and, ultimately, preserve her independence as a great power. Only the state in Russia could initiate and support an industrialization program. This did not, however, mean an over-bureaucratization of economic functions or a stifling of the businessman's initiative through burdensome regulation. The aim of the state was not to increase obstacles to business, but to remove them.[11] Free enterprise and an enlightened state industrial policy were not incompatible.

In Kozodavlev's view, the most important way by which Russian private industry could be stimulated and not thwarted by government intervention was through state tariff policy. Kozodavlev thought not in terms of a high protective tariff, but of the more extreme measure of a prohibitive tariff. Only with the absolute assurance that there could be no foreign competition would Russians establish and expand needed home industries. Free trade would ruin those Russian industries which were just getting started. On the other hand, if foreign goods were not to be permitted to compete with Russian products, foreign entrepreneurs were to be encouraged to build and operate factories in Russia. The end result would be the same for such a nationalistically oriented policy: to strengthen the domestic industrial plant and thereby achieve the economic independence of the country.

There were other means proposed by Kozodavlev by which Russian industry could be developed without rigid official regulation. The state could make substantial loans to help industries already operating or those it wished to see established in Russia. Not only foreigners, but the Russian lower classes, including all categories of serfs, could be permitted to set up industrial enterprises. Russian and foreign inventions could be publicized and rewarded with patent privileges, money and, of course, medals. Russian agricultural and industrial products could be advertised and marketed through special stores. Kozodavlev himself became the butt of jokes because of his promotion of Russian sesame seed oil. Some of this promotion was done through official publications, which he used to spread information and statistics about Russian industry and new inventions.

The similarities of the economic ideas of Rumiantsev, Speranskii, and Kozodavlev can readily be seen. All envisaged a comprehensive industrial development of Russia. All were in favor of the growth of private enterprise, but all saw the necessity for positive state action in the encouragement of industry. A strong protectionist tariff position was adopted by all three officials as one of the most important means

---

[11] Kozodavlev's project of 1810, discussed by Sukhomlinov, *Istoriia Rossiiskoi Akademii*, vol. VI, p. 195.

by which the state could stimulate home industry. All favored extension of the right to engage in business activity to classes other than the traditional Russian merchantry. All urged the government to undertake fiscal and particularly monetary reforms. Technical and agricultural improvements were unanimously viewed as necessary. Some of these ideas may have originated with Speranskii, although who influenced whom is of less importance than the similarity of ideas among the three officials whose decisions counted for most in matters of industrial policy during the reign of Alexander I.

Admiral Count N. S. Mordvinov was less influential in state circles than Rumiantsev, Speranskii, or Kozodavlev during the same period, and was outspoken and even suspect during the reign of Nicholas I. He never occupied the key ministerial posts of Finances or Internal Affairs, although he was for a while President of the Department of State Economy of the State Council. Mordvinov was respected, however, as one of the foremost economic writers of early nineteenth-century Russia. His views on the industrialization of his country were influential for a generation and form the most articulate and comprehensive body of writings on the subject that we have. Mordvinov was definitely of the pro-industrializing school of Rumiantsev, Speranskii, and Kozodavlev; but more than any other official or writer of the time, he saw the industrialization of Russia as a total social and economic process, and outlined in detail a comprehensive administrative implementation of this task. His hundreds of memoranda, letters, and several published treatises represent over a half-century of state service directed primarily to this problem and provide a guide to the industrial problems of the time, and a spelling out of the position of the industrializers in the upper bureaucracy. It will be useful to outline these ideas in some detail.[12]

As an official, Mordvinov was faced with the chronic problem of revenue deficit, the growing discrepancy between the vast political and military obligations of a major power and the inability of its im-

[12] A preliminary version of the section on Mordvinov was presented in December 1963, at the American Historical Association Meetings in Philadelphia, Pennsylvania. The session was entitled, "Two Views of Russian Economic Development, 1800-1860." The primary source for Mordvinov's economic ideas is the *Arkhiv Grafov Mordvinovykh*, hereafter cited as such. His writings have been discussed in the following works: V. S. Ikonnikov, *Graf N. S. Mordvinov* (St. Petersburg, 1873); A. Gnevushev, *Politicheskie i ekonomicheskie vzgliady Gr. N. S. Mordvinova* (Kiev, 1904); N. N. Zakolpskii, *Gr. N. S. Mordvinov, ego vzgliady na sovremennye emu ekonomicheskie zadachi russkoi zhizni* (Viazinki, 1910); I. G. Bliumin, *Ocherki ekonomicheskoi mysli v Rossii v pervoi polovine xix veka* (Moscow-Leningrad, 1940); F. Morozov, "N. S. Mordvinov kak ekonomist," in N. S. Mordvinov, *Izbrannye proizvedeniia* (O.G.I.Z.: GIPL, 1945), pp. 7-44; Pashkov, ed., *Istoriia russkoi ekonomicheskoi mysli*, vol. I, part 2, pp. 61-80; and H. Repczuk, "Nicholas Mordvinov (1754-1845): Russia's Would-Be Reformer" (unpublished dissertation, Columbia University, 1963).

poverished economy to satisfy them, resulting in debt and fiscal instability. The administrative problem of how to increase revenue was a primary source for Mordvinov's economic views. In attempting to solve it, he was led to a general theory of Russian development. Along the way, he appropriated a scientific underpinning for this theory in the teachings of Adam Smith. Mordvinov became both a follower and a critic of Smith. On the one hand, he attempted to adapt Smith's theory of wealth to Russian conditions; on the other, he became a vigorous opponent of Smith's theory of the international balance of trade and of its Russian spokesman, Heinrich Storch. This theory classified Russia among the agricultural nations destined to provide raw materials for the factories of England and other industrialized countries.

Mordvinov also studied the history of several countries for a comparative foundation upon which to place his theory of Russian economic development. Remaining an agricultural nation dependent on Europe for its manufactured goods, obstructing the productive capacities of the people by limiting education to the privileged few, Russia, he argued, could easily follow the bitter downward path of industrial stagnation and the lethargy of ignorance that had reduced Spain and Portugal from great powers to backwaters. England, on the other hand, was both the model for Russia's future and her exploiter in the present. English tariff and tax policy, protective of private capital; English science and technology; English canals and modern roads; English colonialism; and, finally, the English banking system could all be emulated by Russia. Such a modernizing effort would enable the Russians to recapture their own domestic market from English competitors and eliminate the harmful outflow of Russian silver to London. If England was the competitor of the present, America was the rival of the future, in Mordvinov's view. He had visited America at about the beginning of the Revolutionary War as a young naval student and throughout his life kept himself informed of developments in the United States. As early as 1825, he was alerting Kankrin to the threatening potential of American industrial and commercial competition.

Mordvinov's view of Russian economic modernization was based neither on the fear of revolution nor its necessity. His interest in the Decembrists, for example, focused not on the threat which they presented to the Russian state, but on how their talents in exile could be used to develop Siberia. A champion of individual and property rights and of free enterprise, Mordvinov was also a solid adherent of autocracy, orthodoxy, and nationality. He was firmly convinced that the tsarist system could modernize itself through the existing bureaucratic institutions without revolutionary changes in the political structure and without the expropriation of the existing classes and privileges.

Mordvinov based the industrialization of Russia upon a theory of her wealth. Translating the categories of the classical economists— land, labor, and capital—into a Russian idiom, he defined the wealth of his homeland in its vast but poorly exploited natural and agricultural resources, in the growth of population and educational reform to utilize fully these resources, and in the development of industrial capital and commerce to extract the maximum benefit from both. The dynamic agents in this transformation were to be the state and a vitalized capitalist class. The role of the state was to be neither too great to impede private enterprise nor too passive to permit it to languish or fail. The Russian middle class was to be expanded from above by recruiting the nobility, from below, the peasantry and *meshchanstvo*; and it was also to draw recruits from outside of Russia by hiring foreign businessmen and technicians.

What did this general program mean in terms of specific policies and their implementation? Russia's shortage of capital, Mordvinov believed, was an immediate and crucial problem, but not the result of innate political, social, and cultural deficiencies. He quite readily recognized the need for long-range social and economic reform, but he also argued that the state could create and stimulate the growth of capital by specific fiscal and commercial measures. Capital growth had been retarded as much in Russia by the ravages of the French invasion and the cost of reconstruction, by paper money inflation, by the outflow of silver for foreign luxuries, by high taxes on business, and by bureaucratic restrictions on commercial and industrial enterprise, Mordvinov argued, as by some mysterious and permanent incapacity of Russia to industrialize. A thorough reform of the tax and currency system, a protective tariff policy, as well as budgetary and fiscal housecleaning, were far more useful and patriotic measures for raising money, he argued to Heinrich Storch, than abstractions about Russia's agrarian destiny. In numerous detailed memoranda, he proposed plans for the reduction of taxes on private capital, inheritances, commercial paper, and the merchant guilds. He especially emphasized lightening the burden of the productive classes of the nation by modification of the peasant poll tax and passport obligation, particularly for peasants engaged in trade. He proposed a general progressive income tax and a defense tax. The revenue thus gained was to form a capital which Mordvinov believed would provide after a generation an interest high enough to replace all the former impositions. He fought for many years for the retirement of the paper ruble to meet inflation and foreign indebtedness through redemption on the proceeds of the sale of state land. A protective tariff, he believed, would stimulate private domestic capital and dike the outflow of precious metal for European luxuries. An austerity program among Russian consumers and at the imperial court would provide more money for Russian capital, as would a lowering of the military budget through an army reorganization which Mordvinov believed could save 60 million rubles a year. Prospecting for more gold could be done not only in the unexplored regions of Siberia but also in numerous government agencies, such as the various state banks, where large sums, he claimed, were reposing needlessly idle in bureaucratic pigeon holes.[13]

What the Russian state could not do, private domestic and foreign capital could accomplish. There was much private capital in Russia, Mordvinov believed, that remained inert "under lock and key," as he said, because of lack of credit facilities and channels of investment. The circulation of money was sluggish. One remedy was his plan for a network of private banks on the English model, particularly in the provincial cities, institutions which he believed could be activated by government subsidies and deposits, but supported in the main by local merchants and landowners. Much capital could be attracted from abroad, if the government would ease its numerous and discouraging naturalization, tax, and customs restrictions. Mordvinov listed for the tsar many profitable areas for foreign investment in Russia: canal and steamboat construction, dredging of rivers and ports, cargo insurance, irrigation of the steppe, coal and gold mining, and textile enterprise.[14]

The growth and the modernization of such a vast and isolated land mass as the Russian empire demanded an expansion of trade and this in turn depended heavily on the improvement of transport. Mordvinov saw a Russian destiny in Asia, not only with the colonization of Siberia, but a "golden path" of commerce to Central Asia and the Far East, which would vitalize and provide a market for Russian industry and at the same time strengthen her competitive position with regard to Europe. Beyond Asia were the Pacific, Alaska, California, and Hawaii, and beyond these were the Caribbean and South America. In the Russian-American Company, Mordvinov worked for the establishment of Russian supply depots and trading posts in Haiti: he saw the natives wearing Russian *rubashki* and foresaw a Panama canal. Domestic commerce required not just the improvements of Russia's traditional waterways with the building of canals and the dredging of rivers, but modern roads linking the Volga and the Don and stretching into Central Asia, steamships and, for the northern

[13] *Arkhiv Grafov Mordvinovykh*, vol. IV, pp. 171-74, 195-202, 211-16, 221-25; vol. V, pp. 11-12, 254-64. Mordvinov's plan for cutting the military budget is also analyzed in I. S. Bliokh, *Finansy Rossii XIX stoletiia* (St. Petersburg, 1882), vol. I, p. 148. See also my Chapter 7.

[14] *Arkhiv Grafov Mordvinovykh*, vol. IV, pp. 221, 225-26; vol. V, pp. 246-54, 277-78; vol. VIII, pp. 260-70.

snows, steam-heated roads (then in use in Sweden), and finally railroads connecting St. Petersburg and Moscow and traversing the Transcaucasus.[15]

The state was to be active in all this; and for the general improvement of agricultural and industrial productivity, Mordvinov envisioned a kind of central coordinating and planning agency, which he called the "Bank to Stimulate Industriousness." A staff of experts would prepare economic surveys, disseminate technical knowledge, and establish technical and agricultural schools and model farms, where such backward practices as the divided strip system could be eliminated. The directorate of the Bank would supervise long-term public works projects, state enterprises, and the development of factories and mines.[16]

The productivity of the people Mordvinov recognized as the greatest single component of the economic wealth and modernization of the Russian empire, and a significant segment of his memoranda are devoted to four major aspects of this problem: the transformation of Russian society from an agrarian to an industrial way of life, population growth, public education, and the absorption of the non-Russian nationalities.

To modernize the Russian social structure, Mordvinov wanted state legislation to increase both the productivity and the mobility of the existing classes. He envisaged not the diminution of the existing privileges of the nobility, a group which he rationalized as the guardians of the throne and of the stability and security of the empire, but the expansion of their rights to engage in business, and the lessening of their civil, military, tax, and debt obligations for this purpose. These measures, he hoped, would help to develop from the ranks of the nobility a scientifically trained agrarian managerial group and a cadre of capitalists. Russia's merchants could similarly be helped by the abolition of the cramping restrictions of the guild system, which Mordvinov believed an anachronism. Some nobiliary privileges could be extended to the merchant class, such as hereditary exemption from recruitment obligations and corporal punishment, in the effort to make their legal and social status more attractive.[17]

Mordvinov realized that the lower classes provided the source for an urban working force, and that serfdom impeded their proletarianization and prolonged Russia's agrarian poverty. Nevertheless like Speranskii, Rumiantsev, and Kozodavlev he formulated no comprehensive program for the abolition of this system. He offered only piecemeal measures for an extremely gradual and highly priced serf

[15] *Arkhiv Grafov Mordvinovykh*, vol. V, pp. 149, 173-97; vol. VI, pp. 597-690; vol. VIII, pp. 83-94, 110-13, 263-64, 375-78.

[16] *Arkhiv Grafov Mordvinovykh*, vol. III, pp. 147-78.

[17] *Arkhiv Grafov Mordvinovykh*, vol. V, p. 269; vol. VIII, pp. 39-40, 46-54.

liberation. He also urged facilitation of the urban immigration and commercial activity of *obrok* serfs, industrial training for state serfs, and the recruitment into factories of the urban *lumpenproletariat,* household servants, and other lower class city dwellers.[18]

More people would be attracted to the cities of Russia through the elimination of the urban obligation for the quartering of troops in private homes. By these measures and through state aid to several cities, Mordvinov hoped to begin to urbanize Russia, a process which he considered essential to modernization. Cities would encourage the communication of ideas, competition, the desire for a higher standard of living, and would nourish the surrounding countryside.

Underpopulation and not just serfdom hindered urbanization and the development of industry in Mordvinov's view. Part of the solution to this problem he saw in the legal encouragement of early marriage and an attack on the death rate. According to Mordvinov's statistics 50 percent of the population under thirty during the Napoleonic period were wiped out. He hoped to destroy what he considered the major peasant blights of syphilis and smallpox through the activity of the state and the Free Economic Society. Hospitals and mass vaccination programs would be established. In the absence of doctors for 92 percent of the population—the entire countryside—a large-scale program in homeopathic medicine might help. Another evil which consumed the energies and health of the Russian people was alcoholism. Mordvinov argued that it was both morally and economically desirable for the state to get out of the liquor business, while at the same time rigidly limiting and supervising the sale of vodka, in an effort to diminish drunkenness.[19]

Public education was essential to Mordvinov's program for the modernization of Russia and his approach was pragmatic and nationalistic. The "intellectual luxury" of German metaphysics and the frivolities of French culture were to be replaced by a curriculum emphasizing not only science and agricultural management, which he saw as essential to Russia's national well-being and defense, but also intensive training in Russian history, literature, religion, and language. This practical and patriotic knowledge was to be extended to the masses, through schools, public libraries, the press, the theater, and public spectacles.[20]

The peaceful assimilation of the non-Russian nationalities were part of the overall development of the empire. Mordvinov believed that the hostile peoples of the Caucasus mountains and Central Asia

---

[18] *Arkhiv Grafov Mordvinovykh*, vol. IV, pp. 203-06; vol. V, pp. 78-79, 141-45; vol. VIII, p. 257.

[19] *Arkhiv Grafov Mordvinovykh*, vol. IV, pp. 159-60, 206-09, 227-28; vol. V, pp. 205-07; vol. VIII, pp. 285-94, 651-53; vol. X, pp. 459-61.

[20] *Arkhiv Grafov Mordvinovykh*, vol. IV, pp. 405-19.

could best be assimilated by a commercial penetration which would gradually habituate these people to Russian products and tastes. Administrative policy adapted to their customs was to replace the bloodbaths of the Russian military proconsuls. Here, Mordvinov reflected the moderate nationalities approach of Alexander I and his own thirty years of experience in the Black Sea region. In the Crimea, on the other hand, where he was a powerful landlord, he argued for the dispossession of the Tatars and their dispersion to the interior steppe.[21]

Mordvinov's hundreds of memoranda and pamphlets, in which a definite pattern can be perceived, add up to a comprehensive program for the industrialization of Russia, one of the earliest to be formulated. This program agreed in its essentials with the views of Russian industrialization expressed by Rumiantsev, Speranskii, and Kozodavlev, and no doubt spelled out many reforms which these less prolific officials left unsaid. It is questionable, however, that these and many other more practical-minded administrators would have followed Mordvinov all the way in his sweeping optimism. There was little chance that such an ambitious and unrealistic plan would be even partially implemented, but it could stimulate ideas. However, the views which did receive some hearing and sympathy during the reign of Alexander I became unfashionable during the rule of his successor. Those who opposed Mordvinov's concept of the industrialization of Russia were always strong in official circles during the early nineteenth century.

Opponents of Industrialization

In the reign of Nicholas I, a conservative, traditionalist, and nationalist approach was the dominant one in economic thinking. Such an anti-industrial stand was not, however, consistent or systematic. Rather, as suggested previously, a range of opinions can be discerned in examining the views of leading officials. No one opposed the ultimate industrialization of Russia, although there were those on the one extreme who believed it would be a long time in coming and for whom the thought was unattractive and even frightening. At the other extreme, some officials supported a gradual development of Russian industry, but only as a military necessity, or if such development harmonized with the agrarian traditions of the nation.

The moderate opposition to a comprehensive and rapid industrialization of Russia during the early nineteenth century can be seen in the thinking of the two very influential officials—Alexander I's Minister of Finances from 1810 until 1823, Count Dmitrii Aleksandrovich Gurev, and Nicholas I's chief agrarian reformer and Minister of State Properties, General Count Paul Dmitrievich Kiselev. Gurev has been

---

[21] *Arkhiv Grafov Mordvinovykh*, vol. IV, pp. 162-65; vol. V, pp. 148-55, 173-97.

noted in Russian history primarily as a conservative bureaucrat who opposed Speranskii's financial reform and who was one of the leaders of the struggle against a protective tariff in the years immediately following the Congress of Vienna. Gurev supported the trade ideas of Adam Smith and his Russian followers, Turgenev and Storch. He believed that a free trade policy was sounder economically than a high tariff. It accorded with Russia's essential agrarian nature and needs, while protection might deprive Russian industrialists of incentive and lead to speculation. Gurev, as he stated in a reply to Mordvinov's *Considerations on the Subject of Manufactures in Russia and on Tariffs*, was not opposed to the industrialization of Russia but to the means which Mordvinov proposed for achieving this goal.[22] As Minister of Finances, Gurev was quite willing to advance loans to industrialists out of the state treasury or through the state commercial bank, which he founded in 1817. Like Mordvinov and Speranskii, he wished to fight inflation through the retirement of the *assignat* ruble. He was one of the earliest officials to attempt to balance the budget and increase the store of capital in Russia by heavy borrowing abroad—the *mal de siècle* of tsarist finances. In 1824, he proposed the creation, from among the state peasantry, of hereditary holders of homes and plots of land, who could freely transfer into commercial and industrial occupations —a rural social transformation of revolutionary dimensions for its own time or even two generations later.[23]

General Kiselev was formerly in the ranks of the protectionists in the question of tariff policy. Protection was a means of developing native Russian industry. He considered railroads an urgent necessity for the modernization of Russian agriculture, the improvement of domestic commerce, and the raising of the "material prosperity of the state." He saw the need for the bettering of Russian technology, for the development of technical skills, industrial occupations, and basic literacy among the masses, as witnessed by the various programs which he implemented as Minister of State Properties. More fundamentally than most officials, with the possible exception of Mordvinov, he realized that modernization required basic social reforms and a "change in the habits and customs" of the people. Nevertheless, Kiselev saw Russia's industrialization as a natural process rather than a forced one, and subordinated the development of industry to that of agriculture:

I always have and continue to insist that for Russia the truest fac-

---

[22] *Arkhiv Grafov Mordvinovykh*, vol. IV, pp. 303-07.

[23] Little has been written on Gurev's administration. There is a chapter in K. Skalkovsky, *Les Ministres des finances de la Russie 1802-90*, and discussions of some of Gurev's projects in S. Ia. Borovoi, *Kredit i banki Rossii* (Moscow, 1958), pp. 159-60; see also Predtechenskii, *Ocherki obshchestvenno-politicheskii istorii Rossii*, pp. 356-57; and *Ministerstvo finansov 1802-1902* (St. Petersburg, 1902), vol. I, pp. 30-34.

tory industry is that which is based on the products of our native soil, flourishing from the land and at the same time stimulating domestic agriculture.[24]

A much stronger opposition to Russian industrialization than what we have seen in the moderate positions of Gurev and Kiselev was offered by the former member of Alexander I's "Secret Committee" and Minister of Internal Affairs from 1802 until 1807 and again from 1819 until 1823, Count Viktor Pavlovich Kochubei. Earlier in his career, Kochubei took an interest in the development of industry in Russia. He saw Russia during the Napoleonic period as an underdeveloped country in conflict with more industrialized states in Europe. Such a weak position called for special state initiative in the form of capital aid to industry, the development of ports, and the attraction of foreign settlers to Russia.[25] As time went on, Kochubei became more pessimistic about Russia's ability to industrialize as rapidly as European countries. He sided with the freetraders in government committees, and argued that Russia had her own road of economic development and should remain an agricultural country. Russia's role, he asserted, was to serve as the "grainery of Europe." Hence, industrial goals had to be subordinate to the needs of agriculture. Kochubei urged the state to sell its factories and was opposed generally to large-scale industry. On the other hand, he viewed factories established on estates as a futile endeavor and saw no need for a domestic luxuries industry. The only industries which he wished encouraged by the government were peasant handicrafts producing basic consumer goods for the people. Otherwise, the state was to keep its hands off industry.

By far the most significant opposition in high official circles to any kind of comprehensive industrialization of Russia during the early nineteenth century came from the Minister of Finances for most of the reign of Nicholas I, Count E. F. Kankrin. In Kankrin's profoundly negative view of industrialization, and more than this, his deep-reaching conservative mood can we see, perhaps more clearly than anywhere else, the background of inconsistency, paralysis of will, and lack of motivation in the industrial policy of the Russian state during this period. Kankrin was an extremely influential figure,

[24] A. P. Zablotskii-Desiatovskii, *Graf P. D. Kiselev i ego vremia* (St. Petersburg, 1882), vol. II, pp. 199-200. More details on Kiselev's economic views in N. Druzhinin, *Gosudarstvennye krest'ian i reforma P. D. Kiseleva* (Moscow, 1946-58), vols. I and II, and "Sotsial'no-politicheskie vzgliady P. D. Kiseleva," *Voprosy istorii* (1946), nos. 2-3, pp. 33-55. See also my Chapter 16.

[25] The best summaries of Kochubei's economic views are to be found in Zlotnikov, *Kontinental'naia blokada i Rossiia*, pp. 73-76, and in the article in *Russkii biograficheskii slovar*. There are brief references in the Morozov articles in I. V. Maevskii and F. Ia. Polianskii, eds., *Voprosy istorii narodnogo khoziaistva SSSR* (Moscow, 1957), p. 221; and Pashkov, *Istoriia russkoi ekonomicheskoi mysli*, p. 39.

a close adviser to the tsar. Rarely, although the few exceptions were important, did Nicholas I refuse Kankrin's recommendations. Such recommendations were well argued, for they came from the pen not of an obscurantist, courtier, or bureaucratic nonentity, but were the words of an experienced administrator and a cultivated European. Kankrin was the son of a German bureaucrat enrolled in the Russian service, and was educated in the best German universities. He was acquainted with the latest theories of political economy, including those of Adam Smith, which he opposed, and Friedrich List's nationalist economics, which he applauded. Kankrin wrote his own treatises on economic theory, as well as books on warfare and a youthful novel.[26]

The older traditions in tsarist and Soviet historiography viewed Kankrin as a proponent of Russian industrial development. This interpretation was based largely on Kankrin's consistent support of a protective tariff, and on a memorandum which he submitted to the tsar at the end of his official career, in which he listed thirty specific policies which he had implemented to develop industry in Russia. Recent scholarship, both in the Soviet union and the United States, has revised the view of Kankrin as an industrializing minister. Most of his thirty projects to foster Russian industry have been seen as insignificant in their effect, the conservative motives of his tariff policy have been emphasized, and the anti-industrial nature of most of the major policies which he instituted as Minister of Finances as well as his consistent refusal to divert any significant funds to industrial development have been revealed.[27]

If there is such a thing as a conservative mood, then Count Egor Frantsevich Kankrin is one of history's more impressive manifestations of it. Kankrin was emotionally averse to change, and gloomily pessimistic about the consequences of tampering with the world as it is. The three mottoes to which he subscribed might be phrased: don't rock the boat; progress is questionable; poverty will always be with

---

[26] I. G. Bliumin, *Ocherki ekonomicheskoi mysli v Rossii v pervoi polovine XIX veka* (Moscow-Leningrad, 1940), pp. 138, 140.

[27] The tsarist view can be seen in Skalkovsky, *Finances russes*, pp. 67-68, and in the article on Kankrin in the *Russkii biograficheskii slovar*. Both recapitulate Kankrin's memorandum on the measures he took to develop Russian industry, as does the Soviet historian, Bliumin, *Ocherki ekonomicheskoi mysli v Rossii*, p. 141. The recent revision of this view can be seen in the contributions of F. Morozov to Maevskii and Polianskii, eds., *Voprosy istorii narodnogo khoziaistva SSSR*, pp. 216-17, and Pashkov, ed., *Istoriia russkoi ekonomicheskoi mysli*, vol. 1, part 2, pp. 36-38; see also Walter Pintner, "Government and Industry During the Ministry of Count Kankrin, 1823-1844," *Slavic Review*, vol. XXIII (1964), 45-62; *Russian Economic Policy Under Nicholas I* (Cornell, 1967), pp. 10-26, passim; and S. Ia. Borovoi, "K istorii promyshlennoi politiki Rossii v 20-50kh godakh XIX v.," *Istoricheskie zapiski*, vol. 69 (1961), pp. 280-81.

us.[28] Perhaps the best characterization of Kankrin's attitude was given by his conservative tsar. Nicholas I has left a description of a typical conference between the emperor of Russia and his Minister of Finances: Kankrin would come into his sovereign's office in slippers and stand at the fireplace, warming himself, his back to the tsar. He would almost always give one answer to the tsar's queries: "Nothing can be done, your majesty."[29]

Kankrin did not wish Russia to industrialize, nor did he believe that this would happen, at least for a very long time. He shared a view that was rather commonly held in the early nineteenth century, that some countries were destined not to industrialize; however, remaining agrarian would not adversely affect the material prosperity of the nation, provided a proper utilization of the national resources could be effected. Industrialization, Kankrin thought, was a bad thing, particularly the English example. It made a country dependent on raw materials from abroad. It created the miseries of proletarianization. Revolutionary discontent was fanned among the factory masses. In any event, Russia was not immediately threatened by such disasters, in Kankrin's view. During his time, Russia was incapable of large-scale industrialization. The domestic market was insufficient; overproduction was inevitable. Moreover, the middle class in Russia did not possess the requisite skills to assume the burden of industrialization. Without such skills, state aid to private industry would be money poured down the drain. For Kankrin, the Russian merchant class was suspect. He viewed them as ignorant people and irresponsible "speculators." He hovered over state funds protectingly when questions of business investments or loans arose. Significantly Kankrin never invested his own funds in business ventures or in stocks and bonds; they were put in the bank or used to buy real estate.[30]

Kankrin did not wish to abolish the state and private industrial enterprises that had been developed in Russia since the time of Peter

[28] See Pintner, "Kankrin," p. 60. Pintner's account and interpretation, and those of Morozov and Borovoi, all of which are in essential agreement, will be followed here. Professor Pintner's is the first full-scale published study of Kankrin and his administration. Kankrin's successors as Ministers of Finances, F. P. Vronchenko (1844-1852) and P. F. Brock (1852-1858), were bureaucratic time servers who continued the Kankrin tradition without innovation or vigor, although Brock, in the brief period of his ministry not disrupted by the fiscal chaos of the Crimean War, was of necessity more accommodating than Kankrin to Russia's growing private industrial enterprise. They will not be considered here. For brief sketches of their careers, see Skalkovsky, *Finances russes*, pp. 85-110; the article on Vronchenko by V. Sudeikin in *Entsiklopedicheskii slovar* (Brockhaus: St. Petersburg, 1892); and the article on Brock in *Russkii biograficheskii slovar*.

[29] Cited in Bliumin, *Ocherki ekonomicheskoi mysli Rossii*, p. 142. Borovoi cites another characteristic remark: Kankrin's claim that his achievement consisted "not in what he did but what he did not permit." See Borovoi, "K istorii promyshlennoi politiki Rossii," p. 281.

[30] See the biographical note on Kankrin, *Russkii arkhiv* (1866), vol. 4, p. 121.

the Great any more than he wished to expand them. He did not wish to change anything. The factories which were in existence served their purpose. Even more important was the cottage industry among the peasants, which Kankrin, like Kochubei, considered suitable for Russia, and which he wished to foster. Russia, in his view, was essentially an agrarian country. Therefore, the state should not concern itself with the questionable ventures of industrialists, but should make every effort to prop up the existing agrarian order.

Kankrin was careful to demonstrate that he was not disinterested in industry, particularly to his sovereign. Nicholas I trusted Kankrin, but felt that he was dragging his feet in the matter of industrial development, such as when the tsar overruled his Minister's opposition on the question of Russian railroads. Probably in response to this, Kankrin undertook a number of showy but inexpensive projects. The emperor was permitted to enjoy himself at industrial exhibits which Kankrin set up periodically in St. Petersburg and Moscow. Russian industrialists were made to feel important as members of the state "Manufacturing Council," established by the Minister of Finances (Kankrin was careful to see to it that the powers of the Manufacturing Council were rigorously limited). Several technical and commercial periodicals were issued, as well as a few dozen books and translations on the same subjects. All of this publicity accomplished as little as it cost, but many of Kankrin's other projects reveal a sincere interest on his part in the education of the middle and lower classes in Russia for industrial pursuits. Factory schools for children in the big private industrial concerns were encouraged. Commercial high schools for children of the middle class were established, as was Russia's first Technological Institute, set up in St. Petersburg in 1828, and personally shepherded by Kankrin through its early years.

Although Kankrin may have believed that industrialization had to begin with the education of a managerial and working class, his efforts in this direction were hardly more than gestures. The technical educational program of the Ministries of War and of Public Instruction were vastly more significant than those of the Ministry of Finances during Kankrin's term. The fact remains that most of the major policies that he instituted or opposed reveal a strong anti-industrial stand, or at best, an indifference to such matters. He opposed railroads because he believed that they were costly and impractical, and not simply because they were innovations which might upset the public morals.[31] Kankrin made it a policy, which he rarely contradicted, not to lend money for industrial enterprises, although state funds were dispersed liberally, and secretly, to estate owners. The military budget, which began to soar during the reign of Nicholas I, was ques-

[31] See my Chapters 11 and 12 for Kankrin's stand on railroads.

tioned, but never attacked. One can assume that the position of the Minister of Finances was not weakened by the gratitude of those generals, landlords, and courtiers who could open the coffers of the state treasury with relative ease.

Kankrin was a protectionist in tariff matters, as Professor Pintner has explained, because he was a conservative in temperament and outlook. Protection had been a tradition in Russia; there had been a departure from this tradition briefly in the last years of the reign of Alexander I, with dislocating effects on Russian industry. A protective tariff brought in revenue, and, if properly adjusted, prevented loss of revenue through smuggling. Kankrin did not view a protective tariff as a means for stimulating the growth of infant Russian industries, but as a means of preserving what already existed, which he believed could not compete with foreign enterprise.[32]

The Intelligentsia and the Industrialization Question

Kankrin easily stands at one end of a span of official thinking about the problem of industrialization in early nineteenth-century Russia. At the other extreme, we find Admiral Mordvinov, and between these two officials a rather rich diversity of ideas on Russia's industrial destiny. A similar diversity can be seen when we move to the economic views of other, more numerous elements from among the literate Russian public and ruling classes during the prereform era. Without attempting to survey the considerable body of Russian economic thought that developed during this period, we can for the purposes of the present study conclude by noting certain interesting contrasts and similarities between official and unofficial views of industrialization.[33] Neither the professional economists, the emerging nobiliary intelligentsia, nor the revolutionaries of the time had any more fundamental agreement about this problem than tsarist officialdom. Nevertheless, similar positions can be seen all the way down the line.

The beginnings of economics (or "Political Economy," as it was known everywhere at the time) as a serious scholarly endeavor and academic subject in the curricula of Russia's universities may be traced to the beginning of the nineteenth century. This development coincides with the publication of Adam Smith's *Wealth of Nations* in Russia (1802-1806).[34] Most of the early Russian academic economists were Smithians; their own works were commentaries on Smith,

---

[32] Pintner, "Kankrin," pp. 58-60.

[33] See the detailed analysis of early nineteenth-century Russian economic thought, based on archival materials, in Pashkov, ed., *Istoriia russkoi ekonomicheskoi mysli*, vol. I, part 2.

[34] Pashkov, ed., *Istoriia russkoi ekonomicheskoi mysli*, vol. I, part 2, p. 96. On the influence of Adam Smith in Russia, see Zlotnikov, *Kontinental'naia blokada i Rossiia*, pp. 72-73, 82-83; and Bliumin, *Ocherki ekonomicheskoi mysli Rossii*, pp. 50-58.

as well as attempts to adapt his teachings to the Russian scene. Indeed, Smith's theories became a kind of fad; and they were both misunderstood and misused. Most of the early Russian university economists and statisticians (Hermann, Kunitsyn, Arsenev, and Balugiansky, all at St. Petersburg), radical for their time in terms of political ideas, used Western economic teachings to support the thesis that Russia should remain an agrarian nation. The foremost exponent of this idea, the most significant professional economist in Russia prior to Tengoborskii, was Heinrich Storch. Storch's magnum opus, *Cours d'économie politique*, was published in St. Petersburg in 1815. In this work, although he did not exclude the possibility of an eventual and very gradual industrialization of Russia, Storch argued that it was better for Russia to invest her limited capital in agriculture. Russian raw materials could be exchanged, he believed, at increasingly higher prices for the manufactured goods of industrializing countries, such as England. Viewing state economic policy, Storch, of course, took the position of the classical economists in England, advocating free trade and laissez-faire.[35]

There was little opposition to Storch's view during the reign of Alexander I, either from academic or official sources. Outside of the universities only the telling critique of Mordvinov was heard. By the middle of the nineteenth century, the professional economists were divided on the issue of industrialization. L. V. Tengoborskii, author of the first really important full-scale study of the Russian economy, continued and refined the tradition of Storch and spelled out the position of such influential officials as Kiselev. Tengoborskii believed that there were peculiarities of Russia's economic position and development which made her industrialization a hazardous and problematical affair. It was better for Russia, in his view, to emphasize agriculture and gear her industries to the soil.[36] Tengoborskii was rebutted by the economist and later director of the State Bank in Kharkov, Professor I. V. Vernadskii, who took the position that the immediate impediments to Russia's industrialization were transitory, and that a state policy restricted to fostering agricultural industries was economically unsound. Vernadskii was not alone among Russian economists in the late 1850's in advocating more rapid industrialization, as Mordvinov had been a generation before. The Moscow University economist, E. K. Babst, was urging state policies in 1857

[35] For analyses of Storch, see Pashkov, ed., *Istoriia russkoi ekonomicheskoi mysli*, vol. I, part 2, pp. 11-16; and Bliumin, *Ocherki ekonomicheskoi mysli Rossii*, pp. 173 et seq.; Henri Storch, *Cours d'économie politique ou exposition des principes qui déterminent la prospérité des nations* (St. Petersburg, 1815). Russian problems are analyzed in volumes II and VI.

[36] L. Tengoborskii, *Commentaries on the Productive Forces of Russia* (London, 1855), vol. I, especially pp. 442-54.

which would open the doors to a full-scale development of private capitalism, banks, and railroads in Russia.[37]

The same divergence and evolution of perspectives on Russian industrialization which characterized official and academic circles during the course of the early nineteenth century can be seen among the ranks of the radical and conservative intelligentsia. The Decembrists were only casually interested in the question of industrialization. Many of them demonstrated a rather poor grasp of economics, although at least one, Nikolai Turgenev, was recognized as an economist. Some of the Decembrist leaders of greater stature, such as Pestel, expressed an interest in the development of industry in Russia; others, like Nikolai Bestuzhev, believed that his country's destiny was agrarian. All this was prior to the industrial quickening of the 1830's and 1840's; a generation later, we find the most prominent members of the radical intelligentsia—Petrashevskii, Belinskii, and Chernyshevskii—enthusiastic proponents of the development of Russian industry, banks, and railroads.[38]

The Slavophiles were neither uniformly disinterested in, nor were they rigidly opposed to industrialization. Their opponents, the Westernizers, on the other hand, were reluctant to accept an industrialization that would violate the Russian pattern of life they considered worth preserving. The problem of industrialization was central to the debate of these two groups, although not always apparent on its theological surfaces. Was Russia to modernize following the pattern of the West? Was Russia to appropriate Western capitalism, science, materialism, and all that this implied? Or was Russia to follow her own unique path to modernity? Among those Russian intellectuals of the mid-nineteenth century usually identified with Slavophilism or Westernism there were several who anticipated and endorsed the industrialization of their country, in one form or another. Prince V. F. Odoevskii, in his fictional portrayal of the fifth millennium imagined Russia and China as the industrial and scientific giants of the world. V. P. Botkin, a wealthy Moscow tea merchant and correspondent of Belinskii, immortalized himself with the proclamation, "God give us a bourgeoisie!" and dreamed that this divine gift would first become manifest in the Russian nobility, who would transform themselves into capitalists after the emancipation of the serfs. Fedor Chizhov, professor of mathematics, expert on steam engines, publisher, and capitalist, built a railroad to prove that Russian entrepreneurs could

---

[37] On Babst and the Vernadskii-Tengoborskii controversy, see Pashkov, ed., *Istoriia russkoi ekonomicheskoi mysli*, vol. I, part 2, pp. 448-49, 457-58.

[38] On the economic views of the Decembrists, see Bliumin, *Ocherki ekonomicheskoi mysli Rossii; Izbrannye sotsial'no-politicheskie i filosofskie proizvedeniia dekabristov* (Moscow, 1951), 3 vols.; and Pashkov, ed., *Istoriia russkoi ekonomicheskoi mysli*, vol. I, part 2, chapters 7 to 10.

do as good a job as foreigners. An interesting Slavophile touch involved in the mapping of the rail line was the fact that it terminated at the famous Trinity monastery in the village of Sergiev. Ivan Aksakov, of the famous Slavophile family, worked in a bank, was interested enough in economic problems to write a very thorough study of Ukrainian fairs and commerce, and urged the development of Russian industry and the Russian merchant class. A. S. Khomiakov, the Slavophile leader, who could be a mystic and the inventor of a rotary steam engine at the same time, was a proponent of the industrialization of Russia. He entertained the comforting if perhaps naive idea that Russia could appropriate and be strengthened and enriched with the products of Western science and technology, such as railroads, without being corrupted by the alien moral and philosophical principles which produced this science. Both the landlord class and the communal tradition could be adapted to conditions of industrialization, in Khomiakov's view. Herzen, of course, rejected not industrialization, but the capitalist way of doing it. In as utopian a vein as Khomiakov, he saw an alternative socialist way to modernity which could be based upon the Russian agricultural commune.[39]

The officials who advised the tsars on industrial policy during the early nineteenth century and the economists and intellectuals whose views influenced or were rejected by these officials display a divergence and hesitance not unusual for people groping with a novel and complex problem. As suggested earlier in this Chapter, two approaches to Russian economic development can be discerned from the numerous prescriptions which were offered. The Mordvinovs, Kozodavlevs, Vernadskiis, and Babsts envisaged a rapid industrial-

[39] Since this Chapter is concerned primarily with the official viewpoint, the attitudes of the Slavophiles and Westernizers toward industrialization necessarily have been touched upon in the briefest fashion. Unfortunately, most of the studies of intellectual developments in Russia during the middle decades of the nineteenth century have given only passing reference to what the intelligentsia thought about this subject. However, the Slavophiles, particularly, had much to say about the momentous economic changes that were taking place around them. See Khomiakov's letter on railroads in *Moskvitianin*, vol. 1 (1845), pp. 71-86. The pamphlet and diagram (in English) of the rotary steam engine that Khomiakov attempted to market in England can be found in the appendix to vol. III of his *Polnoe sobranie sochinenii* (Moscow, 1900): "Description of the 'Moskovka,' a new rotary steam engine invented and patented by Alexis Khomiakoff." See also V. F. Odoevskii, *4338-i god, fantasticheskii roman* (Moscow, 1926); and I. Aksakov, *Issledovanie o torgovle na ukrainskikh yarmarkakh* (St. Petersburg, 1858). In the late 1850's, Chizhov put out a journal to forward his views, *The Industrial Herald*. There are two brief, recent treatments of the economic views of some of the Slavophiles and Westernizers. On Herzen, Belinskii, Botkin, and Samarin, see Pashkov, ed., *Istoriia russkoi ekonomicheskoi mysli*, vol. I, part 2, pp. 259-60, 270-85, 384-96, 462-542. On Khomiakov, see Peter Christoff, "A. S. Khomyakov on the Agricultural and Industrial Problem in Russia," A. D. Ferguson and A. Levin, eds., *Essays in Russian History* (Archon Books: Hamden, Conn., 1964), especially pp. 141-49.

ization along Western lines. The Kiselevs, Tengoborskiis, and Slavophiles thought in terms of a more gradual, organic economic development, which would not involve a major readjustment of Russian traditions and institutions, particularly the agrarian ones. A few, like Kankrin, did not want to change at all. Another minority, like Herzen and Chernyshevskii, although eager to see the tsarist system dismantled, maintained a respect for other Russian traditions which were threatened by the massive social and economic changes that industrialization would necessitate.

Chapter 6

The Administration of Industrial Development

Reform of the Central Administration

The inability of the Russian leadership to make up its mind about industrialization and the general reluctance to change were reflected in the industrial policies that were formulated and implemented during the early nineteenth century. Despite the awareness on the part of some highly placed officials of the need for Russia to industrialize and their efforts to promote large-scale state sponsored industrialization, no comprehensive programs were carried through or even attempted. What actually came to be were numerous specific policies designed to stimulate Russian industry. Such policies emanated from various administrative establishments at different times. These efforts lacked any kind of overall plan or coordinating impulse, although the administrative machinery existed for such coordination, at least at the center of government. Some of these policies were trivial or short lived; others were of some consequence, were sustained for long periods of time, or became permanent features of state policy. In still other areas of Russian industry, nothing was done, backward conditions and ingrained evils were permitted to continue, and decay set in. The success of state industrial policies, of course, depended not only on the perception and forcefulness of the Russian leadership, but on the administrative machinery which existed or could be created to implement new programs, and on the quality of the personnel and of the training of new officials to administer these programs. The Russian military-bureaucratic tradition—its virtues and its vices—became involved in the process of industrialization.

Alexander I inherited from his eighteenth-century predecessors a number of agencies which had been established at various times to deal with problems relating to the development of Russian industry. This apparatus was not adequate to the task, nor had any attempt been made to coordinate its activities. Most of it had been created by Peter the Great, and had lapsed under his successors, particularly after the local government reforms of Catherine the Great. Many such agencies were closed at that time, only to be revived by Paul I. Most important were the Manufacturing, Mining (*Berg*), and Commerce Colleges, all originally established by Peter the Great in 1719. The first two, after shutting their doors for about ten years, were reestablished in 1796. Their main function was the administration of state owned industries or industries supplying goods for the army. The prime concern of the Manufacturing College at the beginning of the nineteenth century was the supply of cloth for army uniforms. The

Mining College supervised metallurgical factories and mines in the Urals and Moscow regions. The Commerce College concerned itself with matters of domestic and foreign trade, although for a while in the eighteenth century, it had taken over the duties of the Mining and Manufacturing Colleges as well.[1]

During the reign of Alexander I, when the problems of industrial development were increasing and becoming more urgent, the state administration was passing through a period of extensive reform and experimentation under the guidance of Speranskii, Kochubei, and others. An overhaul of the central structure was undertaken in the Ministerial reform of 1802 and 1803, in 1810 and 1811, and again in the early 1820's. In this reorganization, the various agencies for industrial development which had been inherited from the previous century or newly created in the 1800's were expanded, transposed, and consolidated to a considerable degree. There can also be discerned in the process a tendency to broaden this area of administration and give it a unity of purpose.

This can be seen in the creation of the Department of State Economy of the State Council, established in 1810 and first headed by Admiral Mordvinov, whose hand, along with that of Speranskii, we may detect in the organization and character of the agency. As part of the State Council, the main function of the Department of State Economy was to deliberate and advise upon legislative proposals. Its recommendations were then forwarded to the Emperor, who alone could promulgate law, whether he chose to follow or ignore the opinions of his State Councillors. The Department of State Economy, thus, had no executive power, but rather, served as a coordinating body for economic matters coming to it in the form of projects, complaints, reports, and memoranda. In the process of being developed into public law, they had to pass through the Department of State Economy from the Ministries, from any other official agencies, and ultimately from petitioners of the population at large. It thus came at least to deliberate upon the entire process of industrial development, so broadly was its competence defined: all factories, including mining enterprises and liquor distilleries; foreign and domestic trade; transportation; postal communication; state and private credit, involving both domestic and foreign loans; commercial and industrial privileges for the various classes of society; urban affairs; and finally, education, inventions, patents, and the general stimulation of industry. A

---

[1] On the history of the Manufacturing College in the eighteenth century, see D. S. Baburin, *Ocherki po istorii manufaktur-kollegii* (Moscow, 1939). The history of the founding of the *berg kollegia*, and its predecessors and successors during the first half of the eighteenth century is detailed in N. I. Pavlenko, *Razvitie metallurgicheskoi promyshlennosti Rossii v pervoi polovine XVIII veka* (Moscow, 1953), pp. 88-133.

sampling of some of the specific problems which the Department of State Economy discussed during the reign of Alexander I will give a better idea of the breadth and complexity of its function: a project for state insurance offices; construction of a church for one of the state factories; purchase by the government of an iron works belonging to the Demidov family; pay and feeding of workers in the Siberian salt factories; the renting of state liquor distilleries to private entrepreneurs; lapse of the patent held by the heirs of Robert Fulton to operate steamboats in Russia; permission for an Englishman to build a factory in Russia for the manufacture of a substance to prevent friction in machines; construction of a bridge across the Dnieper River; and the establishment of a "Russian Southwestern Company" with rights to the exclusive use of steam machines for the improvement of transport on certain rivers and canals linking the Black and Baltic seas.[2]

The Department of State Economy was primarily an information gathering and advisory body and had no executive power. Where some of this power had been delegated to the Ministries, there was also a tendency during the first decades of the nineteenth century to concentrate the responsibility for industrial development, although no minister ever received administrative control over the vast area which the Department of State Economy was permitted at least to survey. At the beginning of the reign of Alexander I, domestic and foreign trade, as well as water transport, were the responsibility of the same individual, Count N. P. Rumiantsev, although power was divided between the two posts which he held simultaneously, Minister of Commerce and Superintendent of Waterways. The chief responsibility for industrial development, apart from problems of trade and transport, was divided between two of the ministries established by the reforms of 1802-1803—Internal Affairs and Finances. For almost two decades following the ministerial reform, there was a reluctance to concentrate the administration of industrial development in one government agency. This was caused in part by a failure to appreciate the importance of the problem. There was also confusion as to the respective powers and purposes of the Ministries of Finances and Internal Affairs. Should the former be concerned with purely fiscal matters, or should its responsibility be broadened to include the stimulation and regulation of trade and industry? The result of this indecision was that for most of the reign of Alexander I, the Ministry of Finances shared fiscal power with an independent body, the State Treasury, while it retained control of state banks and lending agencies, the budget, revenue services, and the mint. In addition, it included in its domain the administration and regulation of state and

---

[2] *Arkhiv gosudarstvennago soveta* (St. Petersburg, 1881), vol. IV, parts 1 and 2, passim.

private heavy industry (mining and metallurgical enterprises). After 1810, it assumed charge of foreign trade and the tariff administration from the short lived Ministry of Commerce. The Ministry of Finances also picked up during the early years of the nineteenth century such seemingly incongruous duties as the administration of state lands and serfs, the salt monopoly, supervision of state forests, and control of the liquor trade.

It was not clear for many years whether the powers of the Ministry of Internal Affairs was to be limited to domestic agriculture, commerce and industry, or whether its prime functions were provincial and local government, public order, and social welfare. For about a decade, many of these latter functions were divided between the Ministry of Internal Affairs and a Ministry of Police. The latter operated from 1810 until 1819, and ran the medical administration and medical schools, the passport service, and the public charity agencies, as well as the police.

Some clarification of these conflicts and ambiguities came by 1821. The Ministry of Police had been abolished in 1819 and the Ministry of Internal Affairs had absorbed most of its powers. In 1821, the Department of Manufactures and Domestic Trade was transferred from the Ministry of Internal Affairs to that of Finances. In the same year, the State Treasury was absorbed by the Ministry of Finances. Thus, by the end of the reign of Alexander I, the Minister of Finances had become the overlord of Russian industrial development, a power maintained until the end of the tsarist regime. Under his authority came the Department of Mining and Salt, which meant the monopoly, management, or regulation, as the case might be, of most of the state and private heavy and extractive industry in the Russian empire. A similar control was exercised over Russia's manufacturing industries and domestic commerce through the Department of Manufactures and Domestic Trade. Under Nicholas I, this department was expanded and began to involve itself in the administration of river transport, excise taxes, viniculture, and trading rights. The Minister of Finances by 1825 supervised all forms of direct and indirect taxation, regulated foreign trade and the liquor business, set the tariff, and drew up the yearly budget. He controlled the state treasury, and the several state banks. One of these, the Commercial Bank,[3] was involved in the lending of money to private industry, which the Finances Minister supervised, as he did the minting of the coin of the realm and currency policy in general. He did not direct the auditing of accounts, which remained in the hands of an independent agency, the State Controller. Some powers were lost during the early nineteenth century: the administration of state lands and serfs, the most active area of government agricultural policy, passed in the 1830's into the hands

[3] See my Chapter 3.

of the newly created Ministry of State Properties, the ancestor of the Ministry of Agriculture of Stolypin's time.

To coordinate the work of this vast administrative domain and to bring it into line with the activities of other government agencies, it was seen fit early in the reign of Alexander I to make the Minister of Finances accountable in a limited way to higher state agencies representative of the government as a whole. The Department of State Economy of the State Council, as we have seen, was one such body. Earlier than its creation, the Minister of Finances was required to obtain the approval of the Committee of Ministers for major projects. This conference of the chiefs of the tsarist administration was from its beginning concerned with the yearly budget. By 1806, discussion of important financial questions was vested in a Committee of Finances. Several similar agencies functioned fairly regularly and sometimes secretly during most of the early nineteenth century. They were usually composed of several leading officials whose training and responsibilities focused on problems of the economy. The budget remained foremost in their deliberations, but other important economic legislation was discussed, such as foreign loans and basic administrative reform.[4]

The need was seen, as early as 1811, for a government agency which could gather and disseminate primarily technical information to Russian factories. In that year, the Minister of Internal Affairs, Kozodavlev, ordered a survey of Russia's industries. His observer, Senator Arshenevskii, noting the extreme technical backwardness of many Russian factories, urged the establishment of a private society or state agency for industrial information. In 1816, Arshenevskii crystallized his ideas into a project for such an agency, but it was not until 1828 that the first Russian "Manufacturing Council" was established. A law of July 11 of that year provided for the setting up of a Manufacturing Council in St. Petersburg, with a branch in Moscow, and committees and correspondents in the main industrial towns and centers of the empire. The primary purpose of the Manufacturing Council was to gather statistics on factory and peasant industry, to suggest technical improvements, to supply machinery to industrialists, and to consider patents. The Manufacturing Council had a second and important function of bringing industrialists and scientists into the government, not only for consultation, but also for actual decision making. The law of 1828 stipulated that the Council, which, as a government agency, was presided over by the Director of the Department of Manufactures and Domestic Trade of the Ministry of Fi-

---

[4] This account is based primarily upon the chapters in *Ministerstvo finansov 1802-1902* (St. Petersburg, 1902), which present a detailed exposition of the institutional growth and consolidation of the Ministry of Finances during the early nineteenth century. See particularly, pp. 38-39, 46, 218.

nances, was to be composed not only of officials but of representatives of the nobility, the merchants (six of each), and members taken from the ranks of Russia's industrialists. Professors of chemistry, technology, and mechanics were also to sit and make decisions in the Manufacturing Council. Kankrin had done his best to make it a purely consultative body, but his opposition was overridden by other officials involved in the making of the law.[5] In practice, however, Kankrin saw to it that the Manufacturing Council remained primarily an information agency. During the 1830's and 1840's, its committees and *manufaktur korrespondenty* in the provinces provided the Department of Manufactures and Domestic Trade with detailed information on the growth and decline of various industries in Russia. Beginning in 1825, in the Department's organ, the *Journal of Manufactures and Trade,* this information was published in a series of statistical articles. Detailed statistics on specific industries also were obtained by the circulation of questionnaires to factory owners. In 1852, for example, the State Council authorized the Ministry of Finances to set up a special commission for the study of the metallurgical industry. Through its various investigations, this commission accumulated a massive amount of material pertaining to the condition of Russia's iron industry in the middle of the nineteenth century.[6]

Real efforts, thus, were made to concentrate and coordinate state industrial policy during the early nineteenth century. Most of these reforms had at best a limited success. The Department of State Economy of the State Council lost its vitality with the passing of such able presidents as Admiral Mordvinov and the general atrophy of the State Council in the reign of Nicholas I. The Manufacturing Council had no power. If Nicholas I liked to wine and dine his businessmen, there was no serious thought of giving them a voice in government. Most successful were the various consolidations which by the early 1820's made the Ministry of Finances in effect the agency responsible for Russian industrial development. Such power did not prevent the appearance of paralyzing rivalries and conflicts with other big state agencies, particularly the Ministry of Internal Affairs. But the viability of this administrative reorganization is attested at least in part by the fact of its existence for almost a century. It provided

[5] For details on the history of the founding of the Manufacturing Council, see the article by A. V. Predtechenskii, "Istoriia osnovaniia manufakturnogo soveta," *Izvestiia Akademii Nauk SSSR, Otdelenie Obshchestvennykh Nauk* (1932), particularly, pp. 375-76, 382-83, 391-92.

[6] B. V. Tikhonov, "Ofitsial'nye zhurnaly vtoroi poloviny 20-kh i 50-kh godov XIX v.," *Problemy istochnikovedeniia,* vol. VII (1959), p. 156. On the 1852 investigation of the iron industry, see V. K. Iatsunskii, "Materialy pravitel'stvennogo obsledovaniia zavodov chernoi metallurgii Rossii v pervoi polovine 50-kh godov XIX v. kak istoricheskii istochnik," *Voprosy sotsial'no-ekonomicheskoi istorii i istochnikovedeniia perioda feodalizma v Rossii, Sbornik statei k 70-letiiu A. A. Novosel'skoga* (Moscow, 1961), pp. 357-62.

an effective instrument of government when a capable administrator could be found to use it. During the late nineteenth century, under Reutern, Bunge, Vyshnegradskii, and Witte, the Ministry of Finances became a dynamic instrument of industrialization. With Kankrin's deadening conservatism as the prevailing official philosophy for twenty years, Russia's industrialization was impeded rather than fostered by this agency much of the time.

The Urals Mining and Metallurgical Administration

Beyond the various general policies which it implemented to stimulate industrial growth, the Russian state concerned itself more directly with industry in two ways during the early nineteenth century. It regulated private industry and it managed its own industrial enterprises. The latter were substantial, particularly among the heavy industries of the Urals region. These various and extensive administrative functions, which were concerned for the most part with mobilizing and controlling a servile labor force, involved a large bureaucracy at the local level. Thus, the forwarding of Russian industrial development depended not only on policies conceived to nourish and not to strangle private and state enterprise, but on the caliber of the officials, particularly on the local levels, whose job it was to implement such policies. The available published sources for this kind of grass roots, petty bureaucratic history are fragmentary and contradictory, and conclusions must be based more upon specific cases for which ample documentation exists than on comprehensive statistical materials. The general picture of state administration of industrial development on the local level in Russia during the first half of the nineteenth century, as it emerges from the numerous reports of officials, legislation, eye witness accounts, and monographic studies of the subject, is one of failure. Waste, corruption, cruelty, and excessive regulation were in ample evidence. Industrial production fell, particularly in the Urals. Reforms foundered and uprisings were frequent. Soviet scholars have published extensive extracts from local reports sent to St. Petersburg of disturbances among Russia's factory workers.[7] This represents the most extensive published primary source material we have for the labor relations aspect of the administration of industrial development in early nineteenth-century Russia. What are represented in the Soviet source collections, by their very nature, are not typical conditions, but the worst situations which provoked resistance on the part of the workers. Other sources, such as the account by the distinguished German naturalist, Alexander von Humboldt, of his trip to the Urals in 1829, present a different and more positive view of the administration and working conditions of the big indus-

---

[7] *Rabochee dvizhenie v Rossii v XIX veke* (Moscow, 1955), vols. I and II for the period from 1800 to 1860.

trial enterprises in that area.[8] The weight of evidence, however, would seem to be against Humboldt.

The general dimensions of state-owned industry in the Urals during the early nineteenth century are clear. Adhering to the Petrine tradition, the government continued to operate itself a substantial number of industrial enterprises, for the most part factories producing weapons of war, military supplies, or products used by war plants. The government was strongest in the metallurgical industry, where in 1808, according to the contemporary statistician, Ziablovskii, over a third of the labor force engaged in the manufacture of Russian iron were concentrated in twenty large state factories; while over a fourth of the empire's copper enterprises, employing about three-fifths of the total number of workers in that much smaller industry, were owned by the state.[9] The Goroblagodatskii complex of state iron factories in the province of Perm was one of the more impressive state operations. Consisting of six large plants, its yearly iron production amounted to over 16,000 tons. The total labor force of these plants numbered 18,000 or about half of the population of the region.[10] The state also owned several large woolens factories in various parts of the empire, which supplied the army with its uniform cloth. A number of other military cloth enterprises, many of them owned by aristocratic families, influential officials, or wealthy merchants, used assigned state peasants and received subsidies, privileges, and protection from domestic and foreign competition. In return for this, they were obliged to supply quotas of cloth at fixed prices to the government. The most important of these "obligated" factories during the reign of Alexander I belonged to the Countess Potemkin. It employed 9,000 workers at its peak in plants located in the village of Glushkov in Kursk province.[11] Several families were similarly favored in the Urals industrial region, with grants of land and forest amounting to about 10 million acres, an assigned labor force and other privileges. The Demidovs and Iakovlevs continued to be the greatest of these state sponsored industrialist families.[12] Most of Russia's industrial

---

[8] G. Ehrenberg and G. Rose, *Reise nach dem Ural, dem Altai und dem Kaspischen Meere von A. Humboldt* (Berlin, 1837), pp. 306 et seq. on the Nizhne-Tagil establishment of the Demidovs; see also my Chapter 2, and Roderick Murchison, "A Few Observations on the Urals Mountains to Accompany a New Map of a Southern Portion of that Chain," Royal Geographic Society, *Journal*, vol. 13 (1843), 269-324.

[9] E. Ziablovskii, *Statisticheskoe opisanie Rossiiskoi imperii v nyneshnem eia sostoianii* (1808), vol. 2, p. 161.

[10] *Rabochee dvizhenie v Rossii*, vol. I, appendix, p. 822.

[11] V. Androssov, *Khoziaistvennaia statistika Rossii* (Moscow, 1827), pp. 168-69; see also K. I. Arseney, *Nachertanie statistiki Rossiiskogo gosudarstva* (St. Petersburg, 1818-1819), p. 140.

[12] M. A. Gorlovskii and A. N. Piatnitskii, *Iz istorii rabochego dvizhenia na Urale* (Sverdlovsk, 1954), p. 12. On the earlier careers of these families, see my Chapters 1 and 2.

wealth was in private hands by 1800. The revenue gained from the state metallurgical and cloth enterprises, together with the sums derived from a handful of state plants in smaller industries, was only a drop in the bucket of the total state revenue, if we exclude the money that came from state controlled salt mines and liquor distilleries. From 1800 to 1853, thirty-five privately owned iron mills were established in the provinces of Perm and Orenburg—a clear sign of economic decay. However, during the same half century, only three state plants were founded. Nevertheless, state iron production constituted about 15 percent of the total for the Russian empire (excluding Finland and the Kingdom of Poland) by the middle of the nineteenth century.[13]

The decline of the Urals during this period from one of the world's earliest and most significant centers of heavy industry into a backwater which would remain stagnant for a century was largely the result of regressive state policies and inept administration. The basic problems which confronted the Urals industrial region were the high costs of Russian iron, which precluded competition with the products of modernized European mills, and a rate of production which was insufficient to supply even the domestic market. Fundamental in creating these problems were, first, the costs of transporting Russian iron great distances by primitive, slow methods from the Urals frontier to ports and consumers in the western parts of the empire.[14] Together with this, high tariffs and other aids and privileges shielded the Urals factories from competition and discouraged inventions or improvements in production techniques. Ultimately, the state would have to take the initiative in changing both of these situations. This was not possible in the early nineteenth century, with the railroad age hardly out of its infancy, and given the protective tariff tradition that had dominated Russian trade policy since the time of Peter the Great. Lowering of the tariff would have ruined many Urals factory owners. What was possible within the limits of existing conditions was a state initiated modernization of technology and of the administration of factories. The state during the reigns of Alexander I and Nicholas I failed both to improve conditions in the factories which it owned and operated directly or to stimulate private industrialists in the Urals to do the same. A policy bound by tradition and reflecting the conservatism of tsarist despotism was followed. Reforms were directed toward the mobilization of a serf labor force along rigid military lines to provide a sufficient and disciplined supply of unskilled hands for new

---

[13] L. Tengoborskii, *Commentaries on the Productive Forces of Russia* (London, 1856), vol. II, p. 132; "Vedomost o kazennykh i chastnykh zavodakh, otkrytykh podvergshikhsia rasstroistvu i zakrytakh" (1853), *Istoricheskii arkhiv*, vol. 9 (1953), pp. 230-327.

[14] On the domestic iron market, see my Chapter 3.

mines and factories, rather than the modernization of existing organization and techniques.

The overwhelming majority of the Urals metallurgical workers at the beginning of the nineteenth century were serfs recruited for factory labor. Most of these "assigned" (*pripisnii*) serfs were owned by the state and were taken from their villages for a few months of winter work, usually, but not always, in nearby factories. A smaller number, however, were more permanently fixed at their benches. These constituted the groups known as artisans and workmen (*masterovie, rabotnie liudi*). The artisans were distinguished from the workmen by functions and skills, although both groups were recruited essentially from the same sources—orphans, children of soldiers and of factory workers, and convicts. The artisans lived under strict military discipline in barracks. The work day in the early 1800's was twelve hours, although leaves were granted during the summer, when factory production was curtailed.[15] Convicts composed the entire laboring force of some state enterprises, where they were kept under the most rigorous surveillance. They were housed in special compounds at night, and went into the mines during the daytime in chains. Their work earned them a daily allowance for food.[16]

There were only a few salaried workers in the Urals factories—about 3 percent—who were not in a status of perpetual servitude.[17] The labor force was thus essentially a seasonal corvée. Most peasants worked for only a few months and then returned to their homes. The time consumed in transit by foot to villages hundreds of miles distant might shorten even more the work years of some men. Artisans and workmen put in more time, but they never labored more than two-thirds of the year.

Curtailment of production with such a short working period was aggravated by lack of incentive under conditions of slave compulsion, and further impeded by the wasteful use of peasants during the brief time of their assignment. Most were employed in unskilled physical labor: chopping wood, digging coal, stoking furnaces, and breaking rocks, among other menial tasks.[18] Little encouragement was given to local inventors and mechanics to find ways to utilize this human labor more efficiently and to increase production with machinery. One anguished Urals machinist was forced by the persecutions of his plant manager to flee with his invention to St. Petersburg. Attempting

[15] M. Confino, "Grèves dans L'Oural au XIXᵉ siècle," *Cahiers du monde russe et soviétique*, vol. I (1960), pp. 332-33, notes. Confino provides a detailed explanation of the different categories of Urals workers in the extensive notes to his translation of documents on strikes in the factories.

[16] A. T. Kupffer, *Voyage dans l'Oural entrepris en 1828* (Paris, 1833), pp. 214, 220-21, 224.

[17] Gorlovskii and Piatnitskii, *Rabochee dvizhenie na Urale*, pp. 39, 55.

[18] Gorlovskii and Piatnitskii, *Rabochee dvizhenie na Urale*, p. 19.

to make known his plight to the Tsar, who ignored his pleas, he found himself under arrest.[19]

Although workers were treated better in state owned than in private enterprises, the administration of the former was costly and inept and many of them operated at a loss. In 1803, the Minister of Internal Affairs reported on these deficiencies. The main evils in his view were overbureaucratization and the lack of trained personnel. Profits were absorbed by a top heavy administrative staff. The lack of experience of these officials further increased costs. Operations were bogging down in paper work. Regulations hindered flexible pricing.[20] The private factories of the Urals witnessed in their management all the evils of the early industrial revolution in Europe, conditions made more onerous by a few more purely Russian methods of exploitation and punishment. Restrictive regulation, low and delayed pay, long working hours, deprivation of holidays, insufficient provisioning, infringement of contracts, poor conditions of work, and the exploitation of female and child labor were common causes of discontent and rebellion among the working force. Insubordination was met with harsh punishments, including exile to Siberia, as well as whippings with the cudgel, the lash, and the knout, and running the gauntlet of hundreds of men.[21]

The most significant attempt to reform the central and local administration of the Urals industrial region came with legislation in 1806 and 1807. The two most important laws of these years were the so-called Mining Statute and the Statute for Permanent Workers. In theory, the Mining Statute of 1806, which had been several years in preparation, was designed to remedy abuses in the administration of mines and metallurgical factories, to eliminate conflicts of government agencies, to centralize control, and to reorganize the entire administrative establishment on the local level along the lines of recently reformed Austrian and Saxon mining operations.[22] The Mining Statute was also intended to increase production and improve working conditions. The 1807 Statute for Permanent Workers was envisaged as an effort to create from among the "assigned" factory serfs a cadre of more purely industrial workers living close to factories on a permanent basis. In the actual construction and implementation of their provisions, the statutes of 1806 and 1807 were

[19] Cited from the Sverdlovsk archives by Gorlovskii and Piatnitskii, *Rabochee dvizhenie na Urale*, pp. 16-17.

[20] Cited in L. N. Nisselovich, *Istoriia zavodsko-fabrichnago zakonodatel'stva Rossiiskoi imperii* (St. Petersburg, 1884), part 2, p. 5, note 1.

[21] A. M. Pankratova, introductory essay to *Rabochee dvizhenie*, vol. I, part 1, p. 106.

[22] On the preparation for the statute, see A. M. Loranskii, ed., *Kratkii istoricheskii ocherk administrativnykh uchrezhdenii gornago vedomstva v Rossii 1700-1900 gg.* (St. Petersburg, 1900), pp. 51-53.

clearly a traditional rather than a modernizing reform. They were an effort to intensify the bondage of a large segment of the assigned factory serfs and to facilitate the mobilization of an unskilled labor force for new factories by reorganizing these workers into semi-military camps so as to maintain production levels and assure discipline. Many of the features of the so-called Mining circuits and towns established by the 1806 law may be considered industrial forerunners of the agricultural-military colonies later made infamous by Count Arakcheev.[23]

The Mining Statute of 1806, a massive piece of legislation of almost a thousand articles filling 147 pages of text, provided the basic organization and system of regulation for state and private mining and metallurgical enterprise during the remaining years of the tsarist regime.[24] It aimed to create a special administration for mines and metallurgical enterprises, separate from the ordinary civil bureaucracy. This administration was to be directed from St. Petersburg by a newly created Mining Department of the Ministry of Finances, and in the industrial regions by the provincial governors, mining inspectors (*berg inspektory*), and mining commanders (*gornyi nachal'niki*), who were to exercise a direct control over the local agencies and factories. The Mining Department was organized into a board (*gornyi soviet*), which discussed general legislative and technical problems, and an executive agency, the Mining "Expedition" (*ekspeditsiia*), which implemented primarily economic policy according to bureaucratic procedures. The state controlled iron prices. Iron manufacturers were subsidized when prices were lowered, more heavily taxed when they were raised.[25] Under the Mining Expedition were five regional administrations for the entire empire, the most important being that of Perm, the seat of Russian heavy industry. The regional administration collected taxes from private enterprises, prospected and excavated mines, registered claims, managed state forests, and provided financial aid for mine and factory owners.

Under regional inspectors and the provincial governors were the basic local units created by the Mining Statute of 1806, the Mining "circuits" and "towns." The latter designation applied to more important industrial centers of the Urals, specifically Ekaterinburg. At

[23] Gorlovskii and Piatnitskii, *Rabochee dvizhenie na Urale*, p. 65.

[24] *Polnoe sobranie zakonov Rossiiskoi Imperii* (St. Petersburg, 1825-1916), first series, no. 22208 (1806). The statute itself is preceded by a lengthy report from the Minister of Finances, outlining the defects of the existing mining administration. For discussions of the statute, see the works cited by Nisselovich and Loranskii. Loranskii provides a detailed history of changes in the Mining administration in the eighteenth century; Confino, in the notes to the article cited, a briefer summary. In 1811, the Mining Department was enlarged to include the government mint and the administration of the state salt mines. It was renamed the Department of Mining and Salt. Later in the nineteenth century, this agency was shifted back and forth among various Ministries.

[25] *Gornyi zhurnal* (1829), no. 2, p. 212.

each mining circuit (*okrug*), which usually corresponded to smaller complexes of factories, a "Mining Commander" (*gornyi nachal'nik*) was appointed. The Mining Commander had jurisdiction over all state and private factories in his circuit. He was directly involved in production matters in the state enterprises, a combination of manager and official. In other matters, his power was very nearly absolute, both for government and privately owned factories. The *politsmeistery* and *ispravniki*, who performed police and judicial functions within factories, were accountable to him. All military personnel were under his command. According to the 1806 Statute, each circuit maintained its own separate police units, military forces, and courts. The larger Mining Towns—Ekaterinburg being the first of these to be established—were run along strict military lines, becoming in effect industrial "fortresses."[26]

Although the 1806 reform had little to say about wages and hours, leaving these to the discretion of the Commanders, there was much legislation concerned with the welfare of the Urals industrial worker. Every factory was to have a school and an orphanage. Boys from the latter were to be employed in the factories after the age of seven. Hospitals were to be established for every plant employing more than 200 men. No doctors were provided for these hospitals, since few, if any, were available. Each installation received instead a *lekar* (a doctor, frequently without formal university medical training) together with medical assistants, drugs, and equipment.

The Mining Statute of 1806 provided for militarized, industrial labor camps with the appropriate discipline and means of coercion. The Statute for Permanent Workers of 1807 created an industrial forced labor cadre out of the mass of state serfs which had been assigned to the Urals factories during the eighteenth century. It had long been realized that the "assigned" peasants of the Urals factories were carrying a double burden which they could not bear. On the one hand, they had their work to perform, and quotas to meet in the factories. On the other, they continued to pay the usual serf taxes and *obrok*, as well as to serve on labor corvées for roadbuilding and other public projects. Most important to the "assigned" peasant, he had to find time to attend to his fields. This was difficult enough if his land allotment was in the immediate vicinity of the factory. Sometimes, however, he had to travel over 300 miles to get to it.[27] The 1807 Regulation was intended as a means by which the transformation of a segment of these essentially agrarian serfs into more permanent factory workers could be completed. All "assigned" peasants were relieved of factory service. However, part of this group, at the ratio of 58 to

[26] Gorlovskii and Piatnitskii, *Rabochee dvizhenie na Urale*, p. 67.

[27] Reports of mining officials, cited by Nisselovich, *Istoriia zavodsko-fabrichnago zakonodatel'stva*, part 2, p. 63.

100, were to be freed from other serf obligations and were to become a permanent working force in the Mining Towns. These "Permanent Workers," as they were called, were divided into two categories—"Foot" and "Mounted." Mounted Workers supplied horses for labor and received more provisions than those who had only themselves and their families to feed. The salary for a Permanent Worker was 20 rubles a year; his work year was fixed at from 180 to 250 days; and his total term of labor was from thirty to forty years, after which he received a pension.[28]

The Statute of 1807 was not designed to emancipate or even relax some of the obligations of this one group of Russia's servile millions, in the spirit of the Free Cultivators Statute of 1803 or the 1804 liberation of the serfs of Livonia and Estonia. The new class of workers remained in "perpetual" bondage, as the statute phrased it, with no new rights or legal status.

Actually, the old duties and state taxes of the Assigned Peasants were replaced with new bonds for the Permanent Workers which were even more burdensome than the yoke of serfdom. Although many of the former Assigned Peasants were "freed" from factory work, presumably to return to work on state lands, those unskilled serfs who were kept or brought into the factories faced more dismal prospects. As Permanent Workers, they were confronted with a new set of industrial obligations. Factory managers were given almost complete discretion in the matter of wages, hours, and jobs to which the Permanent Workers could be assigned. The 1807 Statute provided a detailed explanation of the organization of these workers. Work communities were divided into gangs of 10 and 100. The leaders of the gangs were answerable to their bosses and the latter in turn to other superiors for quotas of work met within the traditional system of "mutual responsibility" (krugovaia poruka).[29] Although provisions were made for the Permanent Workers to own cottages, vegetable garden plots, and pastures—property which most of the peasants in the state owned factories of the Urals actually came to enjoy, according to later observations—their income remained low. According to Tengoborskii's estimate at mid-century, the real net wages of the Urals worker was less than half of what workers at French or German mining installations received.[30]

---

[28] *Polnoe sobranie zakonov*, first series, no. 22498 (1807), pp. 1071-85. See also Confino, "Grèves dans l'Oural," pp. 335-36, notes, and Nisselovich, *Istoriia zavodsko-fabrichnago zakonodatel'stva*, pp. 64-72. Peasants from the immediate vicinity of a factory were classified as eligible for the new category. See Pankratova, introductory essay, *Rabochee dvizhenie*, vol. I, part 1, p. 50. According to Strumilin, the new work term was ten months. S. G. Strumilin, *Istoriia chernoi metallurgii v SSSR* (Moscow, 1954), vol. I, p. 366.

[29] *Polnoe sobranie zakonov*, first series, no. 22498 (1807), pp. 1073-74.

[30] See A. Loranskii, *Aperçu sur les institutions subsidiaires pour les ouvriers*

With the legislation of 1806 and 1807, it may be said that the regimentation of the Urals factory worker, similar to the fate of his agrarian counterpart a century before, was complete and total. On the one hand, his obligations were increased, together with the means of enforcing discipline; on the other, the relationship between lord and servant, supervisor and worker were left undefined. Such a system led to increased pressures everywhere and inevitably to abuses. The Urals factory worker offered resistance, which often took the forms of refusals to work, flight, or violence. To select one example, the workers at the industrial complex belonging to Prince Beloselskii-Belozerskii in Orenburg province (several iron factories, employing over 3,000 workers) began their resistance in July 1828, by attempting to send a petition to the Perm mining administration. In this petition, they complained of abuses by the factory superintendents: physical overwork, work on holidays and holy days, the high price of grain sold from the plant warehouse, severe punishments, and other grievances. Their emissary, a factory clerk, Tarakanov, was barbarously beaten and held incommunicado by one of the factory officials. This same official, one Hoferland, sent numerous other clerks and workers to the hospital with beatings, and even ripped off the beards of two men. About four hundred workers mobbed the administration at Hoferland's plant and forcibly freed Tarakanov. The rebellion spread to nearby establishments, and finally had to be put down with a large contingent of government troops. By 1829, the investigation of the incident had reached the desks of the vice governor of Orenburg, the Chief of the Third Section, and the Minister of Finances. The case was considered by the Committee of Ministers, which determined the guilt and punishment of the several leaders of the uprising. The ringleaders were sentenced variously to running the gauntlet of a thousand men, whippings, and life sentences to convict detachments (*arestantskie roty*). When the Tsar finally came to review the case, no clemency was given: his only revision of the sentence was to order that some of the offenders be sent to a prison regiment in Siberia, instead of one in Finland.[31]

The Department of Manufactures and Domestic Trade

Next to the mining administration, the government agency most concerned with the management, regulation, and stimulation of industry in early nineteenth-century Russia was the Department of Manufactures and Domestic Trade, as it came to be known in 1811, and for most of the subsequent century. The administrative ancestor of this

---

attachés aux établissements métallurgiques en Russie (St. Petersburg, 1876), pp. 14-19; and Tengoborskii, *Productive Forces of Russia*, vol. II, p. 128.

[31] *Rabochee dvizhenie*, vol. I, part 2, documents 6 to 13, pp. 29-61.

agency was the Manufacturing College, established by Peter the Great and active through most of the eighteenth century.[32] During the reign of Alexander I, its name was changed more than once, and its powers curtailed and then expanded. In 1819, this agency was transferred from the Ministry of Internal Affairs to the Ministry of Finances, where it remained until the closing years of the tsarist regime, when an independent Ministry of Trade and Industry was created.

The main responsibility of the Department of Manufactures and Domestic Trade during the reign of Alexander I was the development and control of all industries in Russia not under the supervision of other state agencies. This excluded from its domain primarily the mining and metallurgical enterprises of the Ministry of Finances. The Department of Manufacturing and Domestic Trade was concerned for the most part with the manufacturing and light industries of Russia, the most important of which were the expanding textile factories in several provinces. During the Napoleonic wars, the main problem to which the Department directed its attention was the shortage of woolens cloth for army and navy uniforms. There were three sources of this type of cloth within Russia: the few woolens factories operated directly by the government; numerous private factories from which the government could purchase cloth; and a few dozen so-called "obligated" (*obiazannyi*) factories. The latter were private factories supported and regulated by the government, which were required to produce fixed quotas of military broadcloth exclusively for the army and the navy. During the period of extensive military operations against the French, the Turks, and the Swedes from 1805 until 1809, shortages of this material developed. The woolens industry failed to expand during the same period: the number of new factories barely exceeded the number which closed down each year. In 1808, the government created the Central Administration of Manufactures, providing it with extensive powers and funds for the purpose of stimulating new industry and increasing cloth production. Loans and subsidies went to Russian industrialists; allotments of land, machinery and workmen were made available; legal doors were opened to encourage peasants, nobles, and religious minorities, such as the Jews, to open woolens factories; exemptions from the irksome and expensive obligation of quartering troops were extended to state woolens cloth contractors; publicity for Russian industry was provided by a publication of the Ministry of Internal Affairs, the *Northern Post*; stores were opened in St. Petersburg and Moscow to advertise and sell Russian manufactured goods; surveys of Russian industry were made, beginning in 1811; and finally, rewards, honorary civil service ranks, and numerous medals were distributed widely to enter-

[32] On the history of the Manufacturing College in the eighteenth century, see D. M. Baburin, *Ocherki po istorii manufaktur-kollegii* (Moscow, 1939).

prising souls. The results of these policies, many of them advanced and implemented by the new Minister of Internal Affairs, O. P. Kozodavlev—combined with the stimulative effects of the protective tariff of 1811—were generally favorable. By 1812, the Department of Manufactures and Domestic Trade could boast in its official organ that some Russian manufactured goods were being exported and that Russian factories could meet the domestic demand of at least the capital cities. Napoleon's invasion and the burning of Moscow was a heavy blow from which the industries in the path of French destruction took several years to recover. The situation of the "obligated" factories was improved in 1816, when the government relaxed its stifling prohibitions on the sale of surplus woolens cloth to the public.[33] After it became part of the Finances Ministry in 1819, the Department of Manufactures and Domestic Trade began to concern itself with more general problems of the stimulation of Russian industry. To facilitate the dissemination of technical and industrial information, the Manufacturing Council, as we have seen, was created in 1828, bringing private businessmen and officials from the Department together for the first time. A year later, a new official publication, the *Journal of Manufactures and Trade*, first appeared.[34]

The varied successes of the Department of Manufactures and Domestic Trade in the stimulation of private industry through loans, awards, publicity, and other encouragements were matched by its failures to properly supervise those factories which it more directly controlled. Similar to the mining administration, it adhered to traditional procedures in coping with new problems of industrial production and labor. These methods often did not work and resulted in inefficiency, waste, high costs, low production, and harsh working conditions. The Department of Manufactures and Domestic Trade assumed the main burden of administration for two types of factories: several enterprises owned outright by the state and usually engaged in the production of cloth for the armed forces, and a much larger number of "obligated" factories. The activities of the latter, as we have seen, were closely regulated by the government. Scrutiny of an example of each of these types of enterprise reveals some of the problems of factory administration with which the Ministry of Internal Affairs attempted unsuccessfully to cope.

In 1808, the Minister of Internal Affairs ordered the establishment of military woolens factories under the supervision, not of the Department of Manufactures and Domestic Trade (although this agency

---

[33] On the activities of the Department of Manufactures and Domestic Trade, see N. Varadinov, *Istoriia ministerstva vnutrennikh del* (St. Petersburg, 1858-62), especially part 1, pp. 76-79, 110-11, 222, 241; part 2, pp. 90-91, 418.

[34] B. V. Tikhonov, "Offitsial'nye zhurnaly vtoroi poloviny 20-kh i 50-kh godov xix v.," *Problemy istochnikovedeniia*, vol. VII, p. 153.

did operate a number of large woolens establishments), but of another agency within his Ministry, the Office of Public Charity (*Prikaz obshchestvennago prizreniia*). This agency, created in the eighteenth century, had charge of most of the imperial prisons, public hospitals, and workhouses for the poor. The idea presented in 1808 was to use convicts, orphans, and paupers as a labor force for a series of small state woolens factories. The use of these sources of labor was not a new concept or practice in Russia.[35] In the regulations for one of the plants, in Irkutsk, a complete plan of operations was detailed. Capital was to be supplied by funds in the Office of Public Charity, and raw materials from the nearest state factories. The latter would also dispatch a few of their craftsmen as instructors for the new plants. The finished products of the Irkutsk factory were to be supplied to provincial military units in the area, according to quota, with provision for sale on the open market of any goods in excess of the state requisitions. A small factory shop was to be set up on the premises for this purpose, and the prices of its goods were to be fixed by the government. Workers in the plant were to be clothed in special robes, housed, hospitalized, punished, and married according to detailed regulations. Although essentially slaves, they were to receive wages and the number of hours of the working day was limited. The regulation for the Irkutsk woolens factory never went into effect, although the factory itself was established, presumably under similar rules.[36] The actual factory, however, used more hired laborers than convicts, perhaps Siberian exiles. In general, the experiment in Irkutsk, as elsewhere in a few dozen tiny plants, languished.

The "obligated" Kazan woolens factory was founded by the government in the time of Peter the Great, but in the late eighteenth century came into the hands of an ex-serf of the Sheremetev family by the name of Osokin, who had made his fortune in the gold mines. The Kazan factory, however, little resembled a private enterprise: although Osokin and his heirs reaped profits, the government kept a tight grip on operations. The labor force belonged to the state, consisting largely of state serfs who had been assigned to the plant's looms. A government loan of 200,000 rubles in 1810 pulled a languishing and backward operation off the shoals of bankruptcy. Fixed quotas of cloth had to be delivered to the Kazan military district, for

[35] Orphans and old soldiers were already being used at the state Aleksandrovskii cotton spinning factory in St. Petersburg. See E. A. Tseitlein, "Iz istorii mashinogo proizvodstva v Rossii; pervonachal'noe tekhnicheskoe oborudovanie Aleksandrovskoi manufaktury," Academy of Sciences, U.S.S.R., *Trudy Instituta Istorii, Nauki i Tekhniki,* first series, issue 3 (1934), pp. 263-72.

[36] So concludes A. V. Predtechenskii, in his detailed analysis of the Irkutsk regulation, upon which this summary is based: "Sukonnye fabriki pod vedomstvom prikazov obshchestvennogo prizrenniia," *Istoricheskii sbornik* (1936), vol. 5, pp. 275-92.

which the Osokin factory was the chief source of supply, although the owners were permitted after 1816 to sell surpluses on the open market. Production was deluged with state regulations down to the last dotted "i's" and crossed "t's": how to spin, to weave, to dip, and to dye. By the beginning of the nineteenth century, the Osokins, like absentee landlords, spent most of their time in St. Petersburg, while management of the factory was left to local retainers. A three-way tug-of-war over the governing and disciplining of the workers developed among the Senate and the Department of Manufactures and Domestic Trade in St. Petersburg, the local police at Kazan, and the Osokins and their factory foremen. While the Kazan factories became notorious for their brutality and labor trouble, the Osokins sought to squelch complaints to the central government and to avoid unpopularity by shifting the burden of punishment to the shoulders of the local police and courts. The local police, as in the Urals, had one standard and traditional answer to labor commotions: severe floggings and banishment, including use of the knout and slitting of nostrils for agitators. The Ministry of Internal Affairs and the Senate, too far away in St. Petersburg to have any real control over administration in such outlying areas, usually took a liberal position which urged higher pay and shorter hours. This was ignored: it was the Osokins and the local police who usually won out and apparently cooperated. As a result of these conditions, according to the estimates of two Soviet scholars, about 70 percent of the labor force in 1801 (of which a fourth were children under the age of fourteen) were too physically debilitated to work. The work day averaged thirteen to sixteen hours and the pay 5 rubles a year presumably accompanied by a food allotment. Punishment was used as a way of maintaining production as well as discipline. The sum total of all this tyranny, brutality, interference, and mismanagement was a primitive industrial enterprise which showed almost no growth during a century of operation and served little purpose other than to supply the army poorly and devour state funds.[37]

It may be suggested by way of conclusion that the fundamental evil which vitiated the administration of industrial development in Russia during the early nineteenth century was one which affected the entire bureaucratic machine which Peter the Great had only imperfectly rebuilt and half-Westernized. However enlightened and well-organized the statesmen in St. Petersburg (and this was not always the case), officials on the local level attempted to cope with novel problems of

[37] On the Kazan factory, A. Maksimov and E. Medvedev, "Iz istorii kazan'skoi sukonnoi manufaktury," *Istoriia proletariata SSSR*, vol. 4 (16), (1933), pp. 171-206; *Arkhiv Gosudarstvennago Soveta* (St. Petersburg, 1881), vol. 4, part 2, 1395-1412; *Rabochee dvizhenie*, vol. I, part 1, documents 1-10, pp. 112-42.

industrial production and management with traditional bureaucratic methods that had been developed in earlier centuries to mobilize an agrarian economy for war by the discipline and exploitation of an enslaved peasant labor force. The state-controlled industrial enterprise of the early nineteenth century became a combination of the barracks and the estate. Soldiers, policemen, and bureaucrats performed the function of the capitalist plant owner and foremen. Military discipline and brute force more often than wage incentives were applied as a stimulant and guarantee of higher production levels. This was accompanied by the setting of quotas, the enforcement of group responsibility for these quotas, and the indiscriminate corvée of peasant and convict labor, or the use of other working groups subject for one reason or another to rigorous state discipline. Minute regulation overshadowed competitive incentives, subsidies took the place of investments, quantities of human hands were considered more important than the ingenuity of machines. State management of industry was, of course, only one aspect of state industrial policy during the early nineteenth century. It does not explain so much why Russia failed to industrialize in this period as why the state failed to modernize existing industries. To properly understand the achievements and failures of the state industrial effort as a whole, we must turn to other areas of policy.

Chapter 7

State Industrial Policy and War

A number of policies were implemented by the Russian government during the early nineteenth century, not only to improve existing industries, but also to encourage industrial growth. These policies followed mercantilist traditions long established by European countries. Most of them had been instituted in Russia during the eighteenth century, although not developed to any significance at that time. Foremost among such measures was regulation of the tariff. State aid to industry was another of far less significance. The government during the reigns of Alexander I and Nicholas I also engaged in numerous experiments aimed at the general stimulation of industrial enterprise. These ranged from the bestowing of titles and awards on businessmen to regulations which made mandatory the use of domestically manufactured paper in government offices. A listing of all of these policies would at first glance suggest an official concern with industrialization. Such was not the case during most of the early nineteenth century. The state impulse and interest wavered. Some fundamental policies were implemented consistently and vigorously and produced real results. Many others were superficial, short lived, and inexpensive, since they were intended as propaganda more than anything else. There was at no time an overall commitment to industrialization as a primary state policy. The government was never primarily concerned with industrialization. Its primary concern was war. Sometimes these concerns coincided and sometimes they conflicted. However, the capability of the tsarist government to foster a major industrial program, whatever its interests, was dictated largely by its resources. The resources of the Russian state during the early nineteenth century were determined by Russia's position as a great power, her economic backwardness, and her dependence as a primarily agrarian nation on the cycle of nature. No policies of the government, no matter how progressive, could evade the triple toll of war, poverty, and famine.

Tariff Policy

Of all state policies which affected industrial development in Russia from 1800 until 1860, the most important as well as the most vigorously and consistently pursued was that of the tariff. During almost all of this period, a high tariff was maintained, resulting in the growth of certain Russian industries. The one brief lapse from a high tariff during the last years of the reign of Alexander I proved to be crippling for Russian industry and resulted in a restoration of the tariff wall.

There are many reasons why the Russian government maintained high tariff barriers for almost all of the early nineteenth century. Patriotic or progressive motives to promote Russian industrialization were not primary, nor were officials buckling to the demands and pressures of Russian private industry. Such influences were present, and were reflected in the projects and activities of such leading officials as Mordvinov and Speranskii. The former, as we have seen, was concerned not only with the development of Russian industry, but with the inflationary effect of an unfavorable trade balance. The Russian business community often made itself heard on the matter of tariff protection during the reign of Alexander I.[1] Just as frequently, however, the government maintained or raised tariffs for conservative reasons or revised them because of diplomatic or political considerations. The tariff policy of the Napoleonic period can be seen as an instrument for fighting for or against France, as the political situation dictated. The tariff of 1811 also was designed to pull Russia out of the economic slump created largely by the political decision to adhere to the continental system. Kankrin's tariffs were aimed as much at preserving existing industrial interests as at expanding Russian industry. In some cases, this favoritism encouraged the backwardness, rather than the modernization and growth of industries. Other tariffs, which were either prohibitive or were unrealistically high, invited smuggling, with consequent adverse effects on Russian industry and loss of state revenue.

The history of Russian tariffs has been detailed in a number of works,[2] and it will suffice here to sketch the general contours of tariff policy during the early nineteenth century with a view to its impact on Russian industrial growth. The general effect of the tariffs of the first decade of the reign of Alexander I was to prevent the decay if not facilitate the growth of Russian industry under conditions of war and economic adversity, although this was not their sole and primary intent. During the last years of the reign of Catherine the Great, Russia returned to protectionism after a quarter of a century of liberal tariffs. Under Paul I, this new policy was vigorously stated in the high tariff of 1797. This tariff had three main purposes: to increase state revenue, to restore a favorable balance of trade, and to protect Russian industry.[3] The initial tendency under Alexander I was to relax

---

[1] M. K. Rozhkova, in *Ekonomicheskaia politika tsarskogo pravitel'stva na srednem vostoke vo vtoroi chetverti XIX veka i russkaia burzhuaziia* (Moscow-Leningrad, 1949), pp. 32-36, has summarized the numerous petitions in support of higher tariffs which were forwarded by Russian industrialists to the government.

[2] See K. Lodyzhenskii, *Istoriia Russkago tamozhennogo tarifa* (St. Petersburg, 1886); V. I. Pokrovskii, ed., *Sbornik svedenii po istorii i statistike vneshnei torgovli Rossii* (St. Petersburg, 1902), introductory essay; I. M. Kulisher, *Ocherk istorii russkoi torgovli* (Peterburg, 1923), chapter 16; M. F. Zlotnikov, *Kontinental'naia blokada i Rossiia* (Moscow-Leningrad, 1966), chapters 2, 4, and 6 for the tariffs of the Napoleonic period.

[3] Zlotnikov, *Kontinental'naia blokada*, pp. 56, 58-59. Kulisher, *Ocherk istorii*

some of the more rigorous articles of the 1797 tariff, which deprived the Russian nobility of foreign luxuries while encouraging smuggling. However, before a more liberal system could be developed, the 1807 alliance with Napoleon radically changed Russia's economic and commercial position, necessitating quite a different revision of tariff and industrial policy.[4]

The Tilsit treaty forced Russia to sever relations with England, traditionally Russia's main customer and supplier. The economic isolation of the continental blockade forced Russia to foster her own war industries. In some instances, however, this development was impeded by the scarcity of crucial raw materials caused by the same commercial strangulation. In general, adherence to Napoleon's system was detrimental to the Russian economy as a whole, which in turn had a depressing effect on industry. Russia's trade was disrupted, creating a passive balance of exports and imports, and a fall in the exchange value of the ruble.

This was ended by a new tariff of 1811, authored by Speranskii, who was in touch with the St. Petersburg commercial and industrial community. The aims of the 1811 tariff were similar to its predecessor of 1797: to stabilize the ruble, to make money, and to foster Russian industry. However, its extremely high duties and a vastly increased number of prohibited articles made the 1811 tariff the most vigorous one to be enacted in the eighteenth and nineteenth centuries. Almost all foreign textiles, wines, and liquors were prohibited entry into Russia, and heavy duties, ranging up to 50 percent, were imposed on those manufactured goods and luxury items which could be imported. Essential raw materials, on the other hand, were freed from all impositions.[5] The beneficial effects of this tariff were offset by the strains and ravages of the Napoleonic invasion. The growth of Russian industry from 1812 until 1814, however, was significant, and continued until 1817. Measured in terms of the number of workers and factories in the Russian manufacturing industry from 1804 until 1814, the rate of increase for the former from 1812 until 1814 was almost equal to the same rate for the entire period extending from 1804 until 1811 (from 95,200 in 1804 to 137,800 in 1811, dropping to 119,100 in 1812, and rising to 170,600 in 1814). The number of factories and plants in the same industries went from 2,399 in 1804, to 2,332 in 1812, and to 3,731 in 1814.[6]

---

russkoi torgovli, p. 303, sees the first appearance of a protectionist tendency in the tariff of 1788.

[4] On the tariff project of 1805, see Zlotnikov, *Kontinental'naia blokada*, pp. 117-28.

[5] Zlotnikov, *Kontinental'naia blokada*, discusses the 1811 tariff, see especially pp. 227, 236, 241.

[6] Figures in P. A. Khromov, *Ekonomicheskoe razvitie Rossii v XIX-XX vekakh* (Academy of Sciences, U.S.S.R., 1950), table, p. 27.

The tariff of 1811 was eulogized by Admiral Mordvinov as "a new era in the development of Russian industry," and "the true beginning of our manufactures and factories."[7] What Mordvinov actually was describing in exaggerated protectionist colors was a particular kind of tariff operating in exceptional circumstances: during a period of war preparation and reconstruction, state subsidized industries with a government market were given the chance to take root behind a wall, not only of tariff protection, but of prohibition. Under such a system, there was no chance that the prices or quality of Russian manufactured goods could be challenged, except by smuggling.

Under pressure from the European powers at the Congress of Vienna, Alexander I introduced a new tariff in 1816 which threatened the tranquility of this privileged domain. This was another case of an economic policy based on political considerations, of the subordination of domestic concerns to foreign policy interests, so characteristic of Alexander I. The Tsar could seek refuge in the liberal cliché of "free trade" and the teachings of Adam Smith, which prevailed in the Congress period. The tariff of 1816 was not so much a move in the direction of free trade as a partial substitution of the protective principle for that of prohibition. Some products were removed from the prohibition list and were permitted entry to Russia with duties ranging from 15 to 35 percent.[8] An even more moderate tariff was introduced in 1817 for the Asian trade.[9] Russia, as we have seen, had no industrial competition from Asia, and hoped to develop markets for Russian goods in China and Persia, as well as to stimulate trade generally with the far and middle eastern countries.

The European tariff of 1816 stimulated the prolonged debate in official and academic circles over free trade and Russian industrialization, which has been described elsewhere.[10] This debate had no immediate effect on government policy, because this policy to some extent had been determined by international agreements adopted at the Congress of Vienna. By the Vienna treaty, Russia was already bound to establish free trade for all parts of former Poland. There was no question that this meant the Polish provinces of the Russian empire as well as the Kingdom of Poland, Austrian Galicia, and Prussian Poland. Prussia pushed for the freer entry of her products into Russia proper. Russia, thus, was already committed in a large part of her western domains to free trade with Austria and Prussia, and the Vienna commitments were shored up with additional agreements in 1818 and 1819.[11] This paved the way for a general lowering of most

[7] Cited in I. S. Bliokh, *Finansy Rossii XIX stoletiia* (St. Petersburg, 1882), vol. I, p. 115.
[8] Pokrovskii, *Vneshnaia torgovlia Rossii*, introduction, p. xxix.
[9] *Ministerstvo finansov 1802-1902*, vol. I, pp. 148-49.
[10] See my Chapter 5.
[11] Pokrovskii, *Vneshnaia torgovlia Rossii*, introduction, p. xxx, and Kulisher,

Russian tariffs in 1819. European imports shot up as soon as the new tariff went into effect in 1820, from a value of 155,454,992 rubles in 1819 to 227,349,564 in the following year.[12] The effects were disastrous for many Russian factories, which were forced to close down. The St. Petersburg sugar-refining industry was particularly hard hit.

A new tariff of 1822 reversed this trend. This was reinforced by an 1826 tariff, which increased many import duties by 12½ percent. Tariff walls between the Russian empire, the Kingdom of Poland, and the various partition territories were raised again. This tradition continued during most of the reign of Nicholas I. In the 1830's and 1840's the Russian tariff was revised several times. Although some duties were lowered and items were struck from the prohibited list, the purpose was not to introduce freer trade but to perfect the existing protective system. Lower duties on certain goods worked to cut down on smuggling and reduced prices for essential raw materials, while goods of secondary importance which did not compete with Russian industry could safely be struck from the prohibited list.[13]

The tariffs of 1850 and 1857 mark the beginning of a new era of free trade in Russian commercial policy. The tariff of 1850 was a timid step in this direction; its successor, a definitive break with the Nicholean system. Most of the important prohibitions were eliminated in 1857, and duties were lowered considerably. This dismantling of a protective system which had endured for a quarter of a century was not anti-industrial in its intent. If such motives had been involved in the tariff of 1819, and if some Russian industrialists of the 1850's pretended to see ruin for themselves and starvation for their workers in the new policy, its basic economic purpose must be seen as the stimulation of Russian industry and commerce. Stagnant industries, it was argued, which had been carried rather than stimulated by the old tariffs would suffer; but progressive industries would gain from competition. The lowering of duties curtailed smuggling; while the shrinkage of the prohibition list lowered freight charges on Russian exports, since foreign ships no longer had to come to Russia with empty holds. Finally, with most European countries adopting free trade, Russia inevitably would have to adjust her commercial policies.[14]

Although the economic reasons for turning away from the protective system were clear, the tariffs of the 1850's, like their predecessors, were not simply a matter of revenue, or of encouraging or dis-

---

Ocherk istorii russkoi torgovli, pp. 304-05; for the Vienna provision, K. Lutostanski, *Recueil des actes diplomatiques*, vol. I, *Traités et documents concernant la Pologne* (Paris, 1918), p. 388.

[12] I. S. Bliokh, *Finansy Rossii XIX stoletiia* (St. Petersburg, 1882), vol. I, p. 146.

[13] Bliokh, *Finansy Rossii*, vol. I, p. 291; Kulisher, *Ocherk istorii russkoi torgovli*, p. 308.

[14] Kulisher, *Ocherk istorii russkoi torgovli*, p. 311.

couraging industry, or harking to landlords, but involved a complex of political, diplomatic, and even moral considerations. Lowering the tariff in 1850 was seen as a move which would improve relations with England. It was a way of forwarding Russian influence in the Middle East. It meant the end of any economic autonomy of the Kingdom of Poland. Finally, some officials urged an end to the protective system as a way of curtailing the growth of factories and an urban proletariat, a process which they observed as disruptive of the family life and morality of the peasantry.[15]

There is no doubt that the protective tariff policy which Russia followed during most of the reign of Nicholas I was beneficial to the growth of some Russian industries, particularly in the 1820's and 1830's. It helped the cotton industry to get on its feet and even to flourish in a minor way during this period. Infant Russian industries, with their crude and costly products, had no chance of successfully competing with their European rivals, as was proved by the universally depressing effect of the liberal 1819 tariff. The Russian cotton printing factories, representative of a progressive domestic industry, were stimulated by a tariff policy which kept away competition of finished English goods, but permitted English yarn and cloth to enter Russia at a price cheap enough to make it worth while to finish and sell in Russian shops. Other industries, such as Urals metallurgy, as we have seen elsewhere, were nourished in backwardness by prohibitive or high protective tariffs. Similarly, the St. Petersburg sugar refining industry was artificially maintained at the expense of Russian and Ukrainian beet sugar manufacturers.

Government Stimulation of Industry

The Russian government developed no substantial policy to finance industrial undertakings during the early nineteenth century. Under Nicholas I, or more specifically, Kankrin and his immediate successors, it was opposed to the extension of credit to businessmen. In any case, the funds available for more than token stimulation of private enterprise were extremely limited, and no significant attempt was made to divert capital from unproductive uses to industry. There were three ways that the state could help to finance private industry: through the granting of direct loans or subsidies from the treasury and other state agencies; through the intermediary of the state banking system; and through government encouragement of the development

---

[15] The various motivations of the tariff of 1850 have been examined in detail by S. B. Okun, "K istorii tamozhennogo tarifa 1850 g.," *Voprosy genezisa kapitalizma v Rossii* (Leningrad, 1960), pp. 170-81; see also Walter Pintner, *Russian Economic Policy Under Nicholas I* (Cornell, 1967), pp. 237-49, for an extensive discussion of the background of the tariff of 1850.

of private banks, particularly on the local level.[16] None of these methods were used to any significant extent during the early nineteenth century.

Direct financing of industry was practiced during the war emergency of the Napoleonic period, but was discarded as a policy under Kankrin. Funds at first were scraped together from whatever government coffers could be found, in one case, 50,000 rubles from the postal administration.[17] This kind of makeshift direct aid rarely exceeded a million rubles a year, and loans were not always repaid. In 1808 and 1809, the treasury set aside 3 million rubles for industrial credit, and such help remained substantial until Napoleon's invasion, with some positive effect on domestic factories, particularly those producing woolen goods essential for the armed forces. In 1814, funds were made available for loans up to 25,000 rubles for private metal lurgical plants. Small loans with attractive terms also were granted during the Napoleonic period to landlords and officials willing to develop new industries in Russia. Specific attempts to encourage sugar and silk factories bore little fruit.[18]

Under Count Kankrin and his successor, Vronchenko, few loans were granted to Russian industry. Kankrin, to be sure, was neither stingy nor overly cautious as a lender of state funds. Huge sums were turned over to influential grandees, who provided inadequate security.[19] It was of little consequence to him that a landlord dissipated a state loan on frivolous and unproductive expenditures; but he viewed the use of state money by a business entrepreneur for speculative purposes as harmful, if not immoral. As a result, while the gentry were given substantial aid, the several industrial loans granted during Kankrin's ministry went either to established families, victims of fires and floods, or foreigners, in whom he seemed to have more confidence than Russians, despite the fact that they too lost large sums of state money. Many industrial loan applications were refused, unless such security as stone buildings and serfs were put up. This capital Kankrin recognized as tangible; banks and stock companies were something alien and irresponsible to him, and were discouraged. Similarly, railroads were opposed as a costly and needless risk.[20]

[16] On the growth and organization of private and state banks, and other credit agencies, see my Chapter 3.

[17] S. Ia. Borovoi, *Kredit i banki Rossii seredina XVII v. 1861 g.* (Moscow, 1958), p. 135.

[18] Nisselovich, *Istoriia zavodsko-fabrichnago zakonodatel'stva*, pp. 119, 123; B. B. Kafengauz, "Voina 1812 goda i eie vliianie na sotsial'no-ekonomicheskuiu zhizn Rossii," *Voprosy istorii* (1962), no. 7, p. 77.

[19] Walter Pintner, "Government and Industry During the Ministry of Count Kankrin," *Slavic Review*, vol. XXIII (1964), 52.

[20] S. Ia. Borovoi, "K istorii promyshlennoi politiki Rossii v 20-50-kh godakh XIX v.," *Istoricheskie zapiski*, vol. 69 (1961), pp. 283-87. On financing of the early Russian railroads, see my Chapters 11 and 12.

While Minister of Internal Affairs from 1811 until 1819, O. P. Kozodavlev introduced a wide variety of measures designed to stimulate an interest in industrial enterprise among Russians, and to facilitate business activity. This was essentially a form of publicity, intended as much to advertise the government's concern with industrial development as to promote private industrial undertakings. Under Kankrin, who continued this tradition, one may suspect that many of these propaganda measures were aimed at impressing the tsar and high-ranking officials more than at reaching potential businessmen. Such policies did not involve fundamental social reform or the outlay of large sums of money: they were cheap and they were dramatic. To whatever degree they motivated individuals to embark on business ventures, which would be difficult to measure, such policies were counteracted, as has been discussed in an earlier chapter,[21] by extremely conservative social legislation. The legal walls which kept the lower classes out of business were little more than cracked by the more liberal Kozodavlev; and Kankrin promptly sealed the fissures.

Publicity meant first of all publications, and in 1811, the Ministry of Internal Affairs issued the *Northern Post* (*Severnaia Pochta*), which was designed to disseminate manufacturing news and to extol the achievements of Russian industry. Its subscription list remained small, and when the Department of Manufactures and Domestic Trade was transferred to the Ministry of Finances in 1819, it was abolished. Kankrin, however, favored government publications of this kind. In 1825, in addition to expenses for the newly founded *Mining Journal*, he began to lavish over 15,000 rubles annually on a *Journal of Manufactures and Trade*. This publication was not only to print government regulations relating to commerce and industry, but also to spread technical and managerial information. Reports about Russian factories and industrial exhibits insured publicity for government achievements in the stimulation of home industry.[22]

Industrial exhibitions were an innovation made by Kankrin. In 1829, the first pan-Russian industrial exhibition was set up in St. Petersburg, near the Exchange. Most of the items displayed were textiles: cotton, woolen, and silk yarn and finished cloth of various types. Some iron tools were included, among expensive luxury items, such as a brass inlaid grand piano, priced at 4,000 rubles, and cast iron statues, costing 1,600 rubles each. Some machinery was exhibited, such as a printing press, listed at 1,800 rubles. Consumer items were not cheap: a pair of woolen socks cost 3 rubles; an axe, 4 rubles; a scythe, 1 ruble, 20 kopecks.[23]

[21] See my Chapter 4.

[22] Nisselovich, *Istoriia zavodsko-fabrichnago zakonodatel'stva*, pp. 31-32, 37-38; B. V. Tikhonov, "Offitsial'nye zhurnaly vtoroi poloviny 20-kh i 50-kh godov XIX v.," *Problemy istochnikovedeniia*, vol. VII (1959), pp. 175-79.

[23] J. E. Alexander, *Travels to the Seat of War in the East Through Russia*

The exhibit of 1829 pleased the Tsar, who apparently delighted in exhibitions, and a second "Moscow Exhibit of pan-Russian Manufactured Products" was held in 1831. During the next thirty years, ten such exhibitions were held alternately at St. Petersburg, Moscow, and Warsaw. In 1851, a Russian display was sent to the Crystal Palace international exposition in London. This exhibit included 376 items from all parts of the Russian empire. Most of the big textile and iron manufacturers, such as the Guchkovs and the Demidovs, were represented, as were the big state iron and woolens works. However, most of the items exhibited were agricultural products or the work of craftsmen—wheat from peasants of Kostroma, spun goats' hair from the Cossack women of Orenburg, saddles from the Caucasus. Exhibit number eighty was entitled "portable soup," and featured a peasant by the name of Ezhov serving heated refreshment from a small cauldron. Machinery was rare, although there were many examples of iron and steel.[24]

Kankrin's interest in business education was reflected in the encouragement of a commercial high school in St. Petersburg and a number of other projects designed to improve the technical and organizational proficiencies of the Russian middle class.[25] Kozodavlev used a number of promotional devices to advertise Russian industry: the mandatory use of Russian paper in state offices, and the establishment of stores in St. Petersburg and Moscow which featured Russian manufactured goods. Cash prizes were given to people who opened new types of industry, but more often such awards consisted of medals or titles. The title, "Manufacturing Councillor," was created in 1811.[26]

State Finances and Industrial Development

When we turn from such peripheral programs to the crucial area of fiscal policy, we uncover the dilemma of state poverty which the rulers of Russia during the early nineteenth century were unable to resolve. The tsarist government was too poor to maintain a major

---

and the Crimea in 1829 (London, 1830), vol. I, pp. 55-56; vol. II, appendix, p. 289. Cotton and woolen cloth were plentiful and cheap at the 1835 Moscow exhibition. See Leitch Ritchie, *Russia and the Russians* (Philadelphia, 1836), p. 183.

[24] "Russia," in *Official Catalogue of the Great Exhibition of Works of All Nations* (London, 1851), pp. 295-300. On other exhibits, see Iu. Mezhenko, *Russkaia tekhnicheskaia periodika 1800-1916* (Moscow-Leningrad, 1955), p. 293; A. I. Khodnev, *Istoriia Imperatorskago Volnago Ekonomicheskago Obshchestva* (St. Petersburg, 1865), p. 295; and P. M. Lukianov, *Istoriia khimicheskikh promyslov i khimicheskoi promyshlennosti Rossii* (Moscow-Leningrad, 1948), vol. I, p. 495.

[25] Pintner, "Kankrin," p. 56.

[26] Nisselovich, *Istoriia zavodsko-fabrichnago zakonodatel'stva*, pp. 118, 121, 123; M. I. Sukhomlinov, *Istoriia Rossiiskoi Akademii* (St. Petersburg, 1882), vol. 6, pp. 199-204.

industrial effort. Such state supported industrialization, by no means unacceptable in principle to most of the leadership in Russia during that time, as we have seen, would have involved a major diversion of funds from the budget. Since the bulk of the state revenue was derived from the agrarian masses, and no other major sources of income were open to the government, this would inevitably have involved further exactions on the peasants in the form of direct and indirect taxes. The system of borrowing abroad for industrial purposes, of attracting foreign investment by creating an image of fiscal stability and maintaining a favorable balance of trade with large grain exports, was not possible in the servile Russia of the prereform period, even though it worked well later in the time of Vyshnegradskii and Witte. Foreign investment in Russia was insignificant before the late 1850's, although foreign entrepreneurs had already appeared on the Russian industrial scene.[27] A tradition of state borrowing abroad had been maintained since the late eighteenth century, but Russia's foreign debt had not yet assumed the massive proportions of the last decades of the tsarist regime, nor was such a scale of borrowing yet possible. Although Russian grain export quadrupled during the early nineteenth century, it amounted to only a third of the grain available for sale abroad and less than 2 percent of total grain production by the early 1850's. The railroads had not yet been built to move this grain from the agricultural regions to the ports, nor was there a Russian or foreign merchant marine available or willing to carry it out of the few seaports of the tsarist empire.

Nevertheless, it is not inconceivable that the tsarist government during the early nineteenth century could have so increased and diverted its existing and potential revenues as to have provided a capital surplus sufficient at least to begin the acceleration of industrial growth. Peter the Great had done this a century before. However, even had officials who, like Mordvinov, were desirous of undertaking such a policy been in the ascendency, both nature and man worked to upset budgets and plans and hold the Russian state in poverty. Russia's agrarian economy remained at the mercy of nature, of crop failures, or famines. There were severe dearths, as in 1833, one of the worst of the century. Other times, less devastating failures would last for two or even three years. The results were sharp rises in the price of grain, drastic curtailment of grain export, substantial arrears in taxes, and large state expenditures for relief of peasants and loans to landlords. In the wake of the 1833 failure, for example, not only was the average export value of grain (1833-1835) down to less than 20 percent of the amount sold in the last year before the crisis, or a loss of about 13 million rubles, but resultant tax arrears for 1834 came to nearly 15¾ millions of rubles. In the same year the government spent

[27] See my Chapter 10.

18,392,118 rubles in the purchase of grain for needy peasants and in loans to hard-strapped landlords. The total loss was about 47,000,000 rubles, or just below one-tenth of the total state revenue for that year.[28]

The ravages of nature, as serious as they were, hardly began to equal the demands of power politics or the toll of war. As a great power during the early nineteenth century, as the liberator and then the gendarme of Europe for half a hundred years, Russia was obliged to maintain a huge war machine that consumed most of the state revenue. When war came, state finances were thrown into chaos; and Russia was at war or engaged in costly and extensive military operations for about a third of the time from 1800 to 1860. She was invaded twice with tremendous devastation. She sent large armies into Europe three times, where they were engaged in major military operations. Her armies were employed in the suppression of two major and several minor insurrections within the bounds of the Russian empire. Military subsidies to foreign powers were doled out generously from the Russian treasury. The climax of this spectacular military burden and adventure was, of course, the Crimean War. The Crimean War brought the ramshackle fiscal structure of Imperial Russia to the point of collapse. At the same time, it revealed to the leadership the industrial backwardness of Imperial Russia and the need for modernization more than all of the urgings of a generation of economists and officials of the school of Admiral Mordvinov. It will be of use to trace in more detail this military-fiscal history of Russia from the Napoleonic wars to the Crimean debacle and its relationship to the failure to industrialize.

The poverty of the Russian state during the reigns of Alexander I and Nicholas I can be seen at close focus by an examination of some of the yearly budgets. In the budget for 1825, the total revenue of the Russian state was listed as 392,997,617 rubles and 59 kopecks.[29] Although not indicated, this meant inflated paper rubles, which were in wide and increasing circulation at the time, and which served as a way of concealing deficits. The total revenue was broken down into

---

[28] I. S. Bliokh, *Finansy Rossii,* vol. I, pp. 195-98. For grain exports of the middle 1830's, see L. Tengoborskii, *Commentaries on the Productive Forces of Russia* (London, 1855), vol. I, p. 245; and on state revenue, P. A. Khromov, *Ekonomicheskoe razvitie Rossii v XIX-XX vekakh* (GIPL, 1950) appendix, table 2, p. 443.

[29] Figures from A. N. Kulomzin, ed., "Finansovye dokumenty tsarstvovaniia Imperatora Aleksandra I," *Sbornik Imperatorskago Russkago Istoricheskago Obshchestva,* vol. 45 (1885), pp. 340-44. See also Ia. I. Pecherin, *Istoricheskii obzor rospisei gosudarstvennykh dokhodov i raskhodov s 1803 do 1843 vkliuchitel'no* (St. Petersburg, 1896); and Iu. A. Hagemeister, "O finansakh Rossii," document probably written early in 1856, edited by A. P. Pogrebinskii, "Gosudarstvennye finansy Rossii nakanune reformy 1861 goda," *Istoricheskii arkhiv* (1956), pp. 100-125. On the budget of 1825, see Appendix 1.

five categories: taxes (*podaty*); income (*dokhod*); duties (*poshliny*); debt payments; and extraordinary sums. Of these, the *podaty* and *poshliny*, or the direct and indirect taxes, accounted for over 90 percent of the total revenue. The *podaty* consisted almost completely of head taxes levied on the various groups of serfs, and brought in about 130 million rubles in 1825. The *poshliny* brought in over 240 million rubles, of which 126 million came from the sale of liquor throughout the Russian empire. The state salt monopoly brought in just about another 25 million. The remainder was divided among various duties on passports, guild registration fees, official stamps, and customs revenue. The remaining three categories of the state revenue—debt payments, extraordinary sums, and property income—accounted for less than 7 percent of the total, or about 25 million rubles. Thus, the two largest single sources of revenue upon which the tsarist government had to rely in 1825 were the head tax on the peasants and the liquor duty. These brought in about 60 percent of state funds in that year.

The bulk of the state income came from the peasants. The nobles paid no direct taxes, and the income derived from them through indirect taxation (mainly from import duties) could not have exceeded 10 percent of the total in 1825. The total revenue derived from import and export duties in that year was 48 million rubles, and not all of this was a tax on European luxuries purchased by the nobility. The regulation and control of business activity brought in some money for the government: the tax on commercial rights for peasants, townsmen, and merchants came to 7,405,937 rubles, 80¼ kopecks. State factories and mines (iron, copper, gold, and silver) brought in 9,047,282 rubles, 33 kopecks; and state distilleries, 2,585,000 rubles. The income from payments of debts (which would include landlord and some industrialist debtors) came to 3,339,861 rubles. Surpluses in the state banks accounted for some of the 4,095,243 rubles, 70¼ kopecks the government derived from "extraordinary sums." If we total these figures, it would appear that about 70 million rubles or only 18 percent of the total state revenue in 1825 was derived from industrial and commercial sources and from the landlord class. Foreign borrowing was insignificant in 1825. Although the tsarist government established a pattern for borrowing abroad during the early nineteenth century, the largest loan before the Crimean War, negotiated in 1820, was for 40 million rubles. The yearly average for European borrowing during the 1820's, however, came to about 1 percent of the annual revenue, although service on the total debt in 1825 was approximately 14 percent.[30]

Budgets of similar proportions to that of 1825 prevailed through

---

[30] On foreign loans, see my Chapter 10. The sale of state forests and excises levied on beet sugar and tobacco provided insignificant revenues at other times. See Hagemeister, "O finansakh Rossii," pp. 107, 111.

most of the reigns of Alexander I and Nicholas I. This was the income of a poverty-stricken, agricultural country, with few sources for state industrial capital other than what could be extracted from the peasant masses. Yet the budget of expenditures for the same years reflects the responsibilities and the ambitions of a major modern power. Expenses for 1825, which was a peacetime year, balanced out in the budget at 392,997,617 rubles and 59 kopecks, the figure for the total revenue.[31] If we consider that funds for the ordinary expenses of government, apart from military and industrial needs, were allotted to the imperial court, the church, the Ministries of Foreign and Internal Affairs, the justice and postal administrations, and servicing of the foreign and domestic state debt, we arrive at a figure of about 125 million rubles or about 30 percent of the total budget. Extravagance for nonproductive ends in this area was blatant but constant. For example, in 1825 the bill for the imperial court (which, however, supported a number of charitable institutions) was 17,665,980 rubles, 97¼ kopecks, or about five times the amount that was being expended for public schools; 54,000,514 rubles, 60 kopecks were used to service debts. The Finances Ministry was allotted 88,369,503 rubles, 88¾ kopecks in 1825. We cannot assume that all of these funds were used to aid industrial development, particularly with Kankrin at the helm by the end of the reign of Alexander I. In 1825, for example, 13,100,000 rubles were lent by the State Loan Bank of the Ministry of Finances to landlords.[32] Even if we allow for the balance being put to some productive use relative to industry, and add to this figure the bills for public instruction, war industry, and transport, we arrive at a figure of no more than 100 million rubles which might have been available in 1825 for Russian economic development, or about 25 percent of the total budget. This was a substantial figure. However the remainder, subtracting for ordinary and industrial expenditures, or 45 percent of the 1825 budget, was devoted to war. The War Ministry in that year received 145,185,669 rubles, 92¼ kopecks; the naval ministry, 20,687,144 rubles, 54¾ kopecks. If we deduct about 5 million rubles from this total for the maintenance and development of the rather extensive system of military-technical schools,[33] we have a figure of about 160 million rubles used to maintain the war machine in a peacetime year.

With such an allocation of severely limited resources, there was little chance for a state initiated acceleration of industrial development of any significance. The idea of diverting funds from the War Ministry for more productive uses was entertained several times during the early nineteenth century. In 1810, a proposal by Count

---

[31] Bliokh, *Finansy Rossii*, vol. I, table facing p. 153, estimates actual expenditures at 413,459,842 rubles.

[32] Pintner, "Kankrin," p. 51.   [33] See my Chapter 16.

Kochubei to cut down the size of the Baltic fleet was indignantly rejected as an insult to the honor of the Navy. However, in the last decade of the reign of Alexander I—peacetime years in which the military budget nevertheless was assuming immense proportions—reductions were seriously considered by special committees. In 1818, Admiral Mordvinov proposed the abolition of conscription and the substitution of a 3-ruble tax (which he believed people would willingly pay), together with an alternating year's furlough for half the army. Mordvinov estimated that these measures would save 123 million rubles a year. His interesting proposals came to nothing, as did other attempts during the reigns of Alexander I and Nicholas I to shave the budgets of the war and naval ministries. During the Crimean War, Iu. Hagemeister, a fiscal expert and high-ranking official in the Ministry of Finances, argued that the construction of a Russian railroad network would drastically curtail the size of the army and cut the military budget by a third. Full implementation of his proposals did not come, however, until the 1860's.[34]

The house of cards of Russian state finances was several times toppled by war during the early nineteenth century. During the Napoleonic period, Russia was engaged in simultaneous or successive wars with France, Turkey, England, and Sweden.[35] From 1801 until 1809, the military budget remained just under half of the total yearly expenditures. By 1813 and 1814, it was nearing the two-thirds mark. For most of this time, there was a huge deficit. Attempts were made to bridge the gap with domestic and foreign loans, capital diverted from peacetime uses, state funds originally earmarked for other purposes, inflated paper currency, foreign subsidies and reparations, and gifts from Russian subjects. Two loans were negotiated with Dutch bankers (one before the rise of the Napoleonic empire and one just after its fall). During the emergency of the 1812 invasion, the state stopped all lending and ended construction of roads and canals. The coffers of the municipalities, state banks, and even of the poor houses and seminaries were drained. Capital, as Bloch puts it, dried up. During the same emergency, the Russian merchants coughed up gifts to the government amounting to 100 million rubles. England came through (as did France later with reparations) with huge subsidies, amounting to over 132 million rubles.[36] However, the printing presses

---

[34] Projects summarized in Bliokh, *Finansy Rossii*, vol. I, pp. 148-49, 207-11. See also Hagemeister, "O finansakh Rossii," p. 123.

[35] The fiscal aspects of wars during this period are detailed and tabulated in Bliokh, *Finansy Rossii*, vol. I, passim, upon which the following summary of Russian military involvements prior to the Crimean War is primarily based. See also A. P. Pogrebinskii, *Ocherki istorii finansov dorevoliutsionnoi Rossii* (Moscow, 1954), pp. 19-21.

[36] See V. H. Storozhev, *Voina i Moskovskoe kupechestvo* (Moscow, 1914); and Zlotnikov, *Kontinental'naia blokada*, p. 338.

at the Russian mint were active enough between 1802 and 1812 to inflate the *assignat* ruble by 400 percent. On top of this came the ravages of Napoleon's invasion, the burning of Moscow, and prohibitive reconstruction costs. Although some war industries were developed in this period—a necessity arising out of the blockade of English manufactured goods—about half of the vast sums expended for the wars went into the army payroll.

During the reign of Nicholas I prior to the Crimean War, Russia did not have to bear the strain of war with the modernized great powers of Europe. However, the cost of empire building in the Middle East and police actions in eastern Europe was enough to dislocate state finances several times. On top of the bill for the wars with Turkey and Persia in the late 1820's and early 1830's, occupation expenses, and huge subsidies paid to the Sultan, came the cost of equipping the military expedition which never went to crush the Belgian revolt, and another army which put down the Polish insurrection. While this was being done, Russia was hit with a cholera epidemic. No sooner had the treaty of Unkiar-Iskellessi been signed than the Russian government was obliged to expend vast sums to meet one of the most severe crop failures of the century. During all of this period, the suppression of the Shamil revolt was draining more and more men, supplies, and money. By 1846, the Caucasus campaign had become a major military operation. In the same year, Russian troops had to be mobilized for an insurrection in the tiny republic of Cracow. Two years later, the war preparations for the 1848 revolutions in Europe, together with the costs of the subjugation and occupation of Hungary, came to over 83 million rubles. The extraordinary costs of these military adventures far exceeded existing revenue and they had to be financed by domestic bond issues and several huge foreign loans.

The Economic Impact of the Crimean War

The Crimean War was a turning point in the history of the industrialization of Russia, comparable in some ways to the Petrine reforms and the 1917 revolution. Like 1917, it marked the end of an era and a system, although not a regime. War stimulated modernization as it had in the time of Peter the Great. The key to understanding this profound change is the domestic history of Russia during the Crimean War. Such a history, as two of the foremost authorities on the war— E. Tarle in 1950, and I. V. Bestuzhev, thirteen years later—have admitted, does not exist. Fragmentary materials have been gathered by both American and Soviet historians on the Russian economy and state finances during the war, and on the views of the tsarist leadership about ending the war and about domestic reform. Nothing approaches the monograph that Tarle rightfully felt should be written on the subject.[37]

The Crimean War revealed to the world and to the leadership of tsarist Russia that the government was incapable of successfully conducting a modern war with industrialized powers, to say nothing of winning such a war. All of the wars of the early nineteenth century had exhausted the treasury and had often thrown state finances into disorder, but the government did not go bankrupt and the wars were won. Napoleon was vanquished; the Turks, Swedes, and Persians lost vast and valuable territories; the Poles and Hungarians were crushed; and Shamil was at last hunted down. The Russians (and many Europeans) had come to believe that their huge war machine was invincible; and that the state behind it, if not rich, was strong. Suddenly it became clear late in 1855, that if Russia continued in the Crimean War the state finances would collapse, the army would no longer be able to replenish its supplies and manpower, the economy itself was in danger, and that serious domestic political and social consequences would inevitably ensue from such a debacle. From this grim realization came the impulse to comprehensive reform and modernization. However mixed the success of these reforms, no one doubted that Russia's position as a great power had radically changed in the Crimean War, and that domestic policy had to be adjusted to this.

The Crimean War by no means wrecked the Russian economy: it bled the state. Two scholars who have devoted some attention to this problem have both concluded that many important areas of the Russian economy were not adversely affected by the Crimean War. According to the noted Soviet economist and historian S. G. Strumilin, the Crimean War initially was a "heavy blow" to the Russian economy, particularly to Russian industry. However, the war in his view, was not the only cause for the economic setbacks of 1854, which was the most depressed year of the Crimean War period. The 16.4 percent fall in cotton production in that year (50,000,000 to 41,800,000 rubles) he attributes to an international cotton crisis, which affected the United States as well as the Western European countries. By 1855, there was an economic upswing in the northern industrial areas, which continued on into 1856. This was caused in part, according to Strumilin, by military requisitions.[38] Professor Walter Pintner of the United States also minimizes the economic damage of the war. In this view, industry was to some extent stimulated, and commerce recovered. The greatest evil was inflation, but he sees its effects on

[37] Tarle, *Krimskaia voina* (2nd edn., Moscow, 1950), vol. I, p. 13; I. V. Bestuzhev, "Krimskaia voina i revoliutsionnaia situatsiia," M. K. Nechkina, ed., *Revoliutsionnaia situatsiia v Rossii v 1859-1861 gg.* (Moscow, 1963), vol. III, pp. 189-213.

[38] S. G. Strumilin, *Ocherki ekonomicheskoi istorii Rossii* (Moscow, 1960), pp. 478-81.

the peasantry as localized, while it benefited some landlords. The lower classes in the cities suffered somewhat more, although no class was really hard hit.[39]

The Russian state was the greatest sufferer in the Crimean War. It was unprepared to fight such a war. The leadership had failed first to understand that a modern army could not be sustained without a modern industrial plant. They had even failed to ready the army and fleet for war with major European powers. The military unpreparedness of Imperial Russia in 1853 reflects the backwardness of tsarist technology.[40] The Russian army of perhaps 800,000, according to the highest sound estimate, was outnumbered by the combined forces of England, France, and Turkey by about 200,000 men, not to mention an Austrian army of 350,000. Artillery strength was insufficient and backward, despite some reforms, such as those in the area of military-technical education under Nicholas I. Small arms were antiquated. Some Russian soldiers, as late as 1855, carried the obsolete flintlocks of an earlier age.[41] There was a shortage of ammunition, and Russia's handful of munitions plants were unequipped to meet a war time demand. There were insufficient supplies of food, uniforms, and medicine. The Russian navy was no match for English sea power. Although Russia had more ships of the line and frigates than France, the French had over five times as many steam-powered war vessels as the Russians, while the British had 150 steamers to Russia's 24 (another estimate is 52, which probably includes very small craft). Moreover, the Western powers had large fleets of modernized merchant steamers to draw upon for supplies. The Russians had almost none, although they were able to mobilize labor and skill sufficiently during the war to turn out 100 steam-driven gunboats in less than a year. Russia had no chance of competing with the British and French in other aspects of mechanized war. In 1851, there were only 19 machine factories in the Russian empire, most of them in St. Petersburg. A railroad had been planned to the Crimea before the war, but no building was done until many years later. Russia's largest railroad, the St. Petersburg-Moscow line, was used for the transport of troops and supplies between the Russian capitals during the war, but with little significant effect on the theater of operations. Railroad construction was halted completely during the war.[42] Russians walked to the front on bad roads. There was even a shortage of horses.

As the war moved into its second year—"rock bottom" for the

[39] Walter Pintner, "Inflation in Russia during the Crimean War Period," *American Slavic and East European Review*, vol. 18 (1959), 85-86.

[40] For details, see Tarle, *Vostochnaia voina*, vol. I, pp. 40-49.

[41] Bliokh, *Finansy Rossii*, vol. II, pp. 2-3; John S. Curtiss, *The Russian Army Under Nicholas I* (Duke, 1965), pp. 123-30, on the shortcomings of Russian rifles in the Crimean War.

[42] See my Chapter 13 for Russian railroads during the war.

Russian economy during the period of hostilities—industrial and agricultural production, inadequate to begin with, fell to new depths. Industrial production was stimulated to some extent by war orders in 1855; agriculture, however, suffered increasingly as thousands of horses and hundreds of thousands of men were taken from the land, and vast food supplies in the vicinity of military operations were carted off to the front lines.[43] Agricultural and industrial prices inevitably rose. Because of the insufficiency of Russian industry, the government had to buy armaments abroad. This entailed increased expenditures added to the tremendous burden of keeping the army in the field at a time when revenues were decreasing. Budgetary deficits rose by the end of 1855 to over 500,000,000 rubles. The war itself in the end cost Russia well over a billion rubles.[44] Deficiencies were met by loans and printing-press currency, with the resultant evils of inflation.

The bulk of the Russian population, except a small minority dependent on fixed wages and incomes, did not suffer from these conditions. Private industry was expanding by the final year of hostilities. Foreign trade was frustrated but not wrecked. It was the state which suffered most. It paid for more with less. By late 1855, the Russian government had been brought to its knees and the time had long since come to admit Russia's failure, explore the causes for defeat, and seriously consider getting out of the war.

To discuss these fundamental problems, a secret committee was formed several months after the death of Nicholas I, consisting of leading generals and officials, and including Nesselrode, Kiselev, and the rising and talented general staff officer and future reformer, Dmitry Miliutin. Three meetings were held in January and February of 1856.

For the second of these meetings, Miliutin prepared a memorandum, entitled, "The Danger of Continuing Military Activities in 1856."[45] This memorandum concerned itself primarily with the immediate logistical and manpower problems facing the Russian armed forces should the war be prolonged. But it also revealed in clear terms the underlying issue of the inability of a poorly industrialized country to wage modern war.

After considering the possibility that Austria, Prussia, and even Sweden might join the Western allies against Russia should the war be prolonged, Miliutin focused his discussion on the ability of Russia to meet existing or future military challenges. The first three sections of his eight-point analysis were devoted to the question of manpower.

---

[43] I. Bestuzhev, *Krimskaia voina 1853-1856 gg.* (Moscow, 1956), pp. 160-61.
[44] Bliokh, *Finansy Rossii*, vol. I, pp. 19-20.
[45] I. V. Bestuzhev, ed., D. Miliutin, "Ob opasnosti prodolzheniia v 1856 g. voennykh deistvii," *Istoricheskii arkhiv* (1959), pp. 206-08; see also Bestuzhev's analysis in M. V. Nechkina, ed., *Revoliutsionnaia situatsiia*, vol. III, pp. 194-99.

If Russia were to continue in the war during 1856, he concluded, her army could only deteriorate, because she no longer had trained reserves, the number of officers was insufficient, and the existing legal sources for conscription had been exhausted. Add to this the problem of supply, Miliutin noted later in his memorandum. There was no food left in the theater of operations. There was not enough ammunition for another Sevastopol. The stocks of weapons were almost exhausted. Even had supplies been available, Miliutin argued, the Russian transport system was inadequate to move troops, materials, or food. The Russian fleets were either trapped or destroyed, and no means of land transport connecting the center of Russia with the Crimea and rapid enough to be of help to the army existed.

In the fourth section of his memorandum, Miliutin dealt with the crucial question of war and industrialization. Russia, he argued, simply could not compete with the "inexhaustible abundance of industrialized Western Europe." Ordering weapons from America was a precarious and inadequate substitute for a modern domestic war industry. Reserves of weapons were rapidly dwindling. In the last analysis, Miliutin concluded his memorandum, Russia's finances had been brought into disorder by the war: the government simply could not pay the 300,000,000 rubles that another year of military operations would cost.

Miliutin did not go on to spell out his recommendations. The implications were clear: Russia would have to withdraw from a war which she could not sustain. Russia would have to industrialize if she were to maintain her position vis-à-vis the modern powers of the West.[46] The issue, which Mordvinov had first clearly formulated during the reign of Alexander I and which had been evaded for several decades, now had to be faced by the ruling elite of Russia. What had been considered an alternative for debate and a subject for state experimentation was now revealed as a matter of survival. State industrial policy would now have to become a major concern of the rulers of Russia. A new program and an accelerated pace of industrialization was required as an economic corollary of the Great Reforms. Agrarian poverty and war were by no means eliminated as obstacles to the modernization of Russia, but new means would be found to forestall them.

[46] A. M. Gorchakov, P. A. Valuev, as well as Alexander II were in essential agreement with these views. See A. Skerpan, "The Russian National Economy and Emancipation," in A. Ferguson and A. Levin, eds., *Essays in Russian History* (Archon: Hamden, Conn., 1964), pp. 166-67. Hagemeister, in his memorandum on Russian finances written at about the same time, particularly emphasized large-scale railroad construction as a way both of liberating the productive forces of the country and cutting the military budget. In addition, he outlined a comprehensive fiscal reform which included elimination of the head tax, transfer of state industries into private hands, and a drastic streamlining of the bureaucracy. See Hagemeister, "O finansakh Rossii," pp. 105-06, 116, 118-24.

Part III

Private Industrial Enterprise

For Baron Haxthausen, writing in the late 1840's, the Russian businessman[1] remained the traditional merchant and no less an object of romantic idealization for the famous German Slavophile than the peasant in his Commune. Haxthausen has left us a memorable image of an encounter with representatives of this class in the provincial city of Rybinsk. His host, a millionaire, was a "genuine Russian, with a beard and parted hair, and a long blue kaftan." The merchant's son, however, was clean shaven and dressed in a European suit, just as the father's house was filled with European furniture. The newly built Rybinsk exchange stood deserted, for all the local merchants preferred to transact their business, as they traditionally had done, in the local tavern, while consuming enormous quantities of tea. Here Haxthausen found his Russian middle class, "seated on benches ranged along the walls of the room, stiff and motionless, grave, silent —sipping their tea, perspiring and now and then whispering a word to each other." Although over a hundred people were crowded into the room, it was quiet, except for a European musical clock on the wall playing "di tanti palpiti."[2]

The traditional middle class in Russia, which Haxthausen encountered in the provinces where it was only beginning to change by the 1840's, had far from disappeared in the big cities. There too, the bearded merchants with their long peasant overcoats were in plentiful evidence, together with the abaci, the drunken dinners and groaning tables, and the plump wives with "round, bluish faces, fat hands, big knees, puffed lips and black teeth."[3] By the reign of Nicholas I, however, a new, Westernized industrial middle class was making its appearance in Moscow and St. Petersburg and in emerging factory towns such as Ivanovo in Vladimir province. Most of the signs of a

---

[1] The terms "businessman," "bourgeois," "capitalist," "entrepreneur," and "middle class," at the risk of imprecision, will be used interchangeably here to denote the Russian social group whose origins and specific characteristics will be delineated in the Chapters in Part III. None is fully comprehensive or applicable to Russia. "Bourgeoisie," as understood variously by a Soviet Marxist historian or a French scholar, may have a precision which the word does not carry for a non-Marxist, or outside of French culture. On the other hand, the older Russian designations, *kupets* or *promyshlennik*, are inadequate to describe the modern type of entrepreneur who emerged in the early nineteenth century.

[2] A. von Haxthausen, *The Russian Empire, Its People, Institutions and Resources* (London, 1856), vol. I, pp. 143-44.

[3] P. Vistengof, *Ocherki Moskovskoi zhizni* (Moscow, 1842), pp. 38-39; James E. Alexander, *Travels to the Seat of War in the East Through Russia and the Crimea in 1829* (London, 1830), vol. I, pp. 121-22, 177.

new social class made rich and powerful by modern industry and commerce could be seen in Russian cities as early as the 1830's. There were first of all the men of big capital. If New York had twenty millionaires by 1855,[4] Moscow at the same time had at least a dozen, St. Petersburg an equal number (although many of these were of foreign birth), and Ivanovo, three. Some of these millionaires lived in opulence, rivaling the upper nobility in the magnificence of their townhouses, and indeed in some cases buying up the costly and forsaken palaces of the titled great. In the early 1840's, according to Kopanev's estimate, one-fourth of all the large private dwellings in St. Petersburg belonged to people registered in the merchant guilds, to the city's upper middle class.[5] The new bourgeois in most cases had long since discarded his peasant robe and in fewer instances had cut off his beard. He now spoke a foreign language. His daughters, like Lipochka in Ostrovskii's dramatic portrait of a Westernizing, social climbing, Moscow merchant family,[6] were sent to dancing school and his sons to the university or on a trip to Europe. Occasionally, some young spendthrift in a guards regiment would turn out to be a wealthy industrialist's son. For business purposes, the Moscow entrepreneur of the early nineteenth century might be a member of the Merchants' Society (founded in 1813) or the Exchange Society (founded in 1831); for social purposes, if from St. Petersburg, he belonged to the Schuster Club (a German founder's name), where military men and officials mingled with wealthy merchants in a large building with billiard rooms and banquet halls.[7] The big industrialist in Moscow or St. Petersburg in 1850 went to his office in a two or three-story heated and gas-illuminated stone factory as frequently as he consigned work to men and women in their cottages in the older tradition. He maintained warehouses and shops in other cities. If he still used the abacus, by 1855 he had available in Moscow a *Handbook for Merchants, Salesmen, Clerks, and Jobbers* to guide him in the writing of business letters and the preparation of legal papers and accounts.[8]

By the late 1850's, the Moscow businessman was willing and could afford to participate in the culture that formerly had been reserved for the landed gentry. He might be a connoisseur of French wine and

[4] George R. Taylor, *The Transportation Revolution 1815-1860, Social and Economic History of the United States* (New York, 1951), vol. IV, pp. 394-95.

[5] A. I. Kopanev, *Naselenie Peterburga v pervoi polovine XIX veka* (Moscow-Leningrad, 1957), p. 103. On the changing social character of Moscow and St. Petersburg, see my Chapter 4.

[6] Alexander Ostrovskii, "It's a Family Affair—We'll Settle It Ourselves," *Plays*, translated and edited by George Rapall Noyes (New York, 1917), pp. 225-26, 258 (first published, 1850).

[7] An excellent description of these changes can be found in Edward Jerrmann, *Pictures from St. Petersburg* (New York, 1852), pp. 161-67.

[8] *Kniga dlia kuptsov, kupicheskikh prikashchikov, kontorshchikov i kommissionerov* (Moscow, 1855). The editor is identified as the "Director of the Commercial House of Vasilev."

a lover of opera, like Ivan Vasilevich Shchukin, a Moscow merchant who maintained his own room (for naps) at the newly constructed Bolshoi theater. P. M. Tretiakov, owner of a Moscow linen factory, had already begun his world famous art collection before 1860, as had several Moscow art fanciers of the middle class. Kozma Solda-tenkov, an Old Believer with a French mistress, as well as a big man-ufacturer, merchant, and investor, was one of the first great Moscow art collectors, whose cultural activities date back to the 1840's. He also financed the publication of many important foreign books in Rus-sia, including Gibbon's *Decline and Fall of the Roman Empire* and Mommsen's *History of Rome*. In this, he emulated the earlier career of Alexander Filipovich Smirdin, the St. Petersburg bookseller, pa-tron, and publisher of Pushkin, Krylov, Zhukovskii, and other famous writers of the 1830's. The Botkin tea magnates were the progenitors of the famous Slavophile, V. P. Botkin, who divided his time between literary pursuits and his warehouse. Reversing the process, the Slavo-phile intellectual, Fedor Chizhov, became a businessman at the end of the 1850's, and worked to form a private Russian railroad corporation.[9]

By the reign of Nicholas I, the new Russian middle class had ac-cumulated sufficient wealth to divert some of it to charitable causes, had the leisure to devote some time to public service, and had de-veloped an urge to do some social climbing. The Prokhorovs, perhaps the biggest industrialists of Moscow during the same period, had es-tablished schools for their workers, as had the millionaire Old Believ-er Guchkovs. Joseph Gunzburg, who founded the most important Russian Jewish banking dynasty in the 1840's and 1850's, as well as the Society for the Propagation of Culture Among the Jews, be-queathed 125,000 acres of Crimean land to charity. From 1839 to 1848, the prominent Moscow industrialist, M. I. Krasheninnikov, gave away almost one and one-half million rubles, almost all of it to the poor.[10] Urban government was largely in the hands of the Russian middle class during the early nineteenth century. The mayor's job for the city of Moscow frequently went to members of the great mer-cantile families. One such family, the Kumanins, provided three mayors during the reigns of Alexander I and Nicholas I.[11] The Rus-

---

[9] A valuable history of the cultural activities of the Moscow middle class written by a survivor is P. A. Buryshkin, *Moskva kupicheskaia* (New York, 1954), see especially, pp. 134-53; on the founding of the merchant art col-lections in mid-nineteenth-century Moscow see V. Stasov, "Pavel Mikhailovich Tretiakov i ego kartinnaia gallereia," *Russkaia starina*, vol. 80 (1893), 569-608. The *Russkii biograficheskii slovar* has excellent articles on Soldatenkov, Smir-din, Chizhov, and the Botkin family.

[10] "Mikhail Ivanovich Krasheninnikov," in M. O. Volf, publisher, *Russkie liudi* (St. Petersburg-Moscow, 1866), vol. 1, pp. 49-50. On the Prokhorov schools, see my Chapter 16.

[11] Buryshkin, *Moskva kupicheskaia*, p. 149.

sian middle class first made itself felt politically in the higher spheres of government in 1812. In that year, the merchants of Moscow put up over 1,700,000 rubles for the war chest. Nicholas I wined and dined his merchants and industrialists and invited deputations of them to his office, a gesture which until that time, as Baron Korf remarked in his memoirs, was "a rare event in our administrative history."[12] Also in 1812, a number of Russian industrialists—sugar, cotton, and linen manufacturers—petitioned the government to preserve the high tariff of 1810. Similar petitions urging the government to persevere in its protective tariff policy were issued by Russian merchants and industrialists in 1814, 1823, 1827, 1831, and 1850. The Russian middle class played a definite role in eliminating the free trade tendency that developed briefly in the last decade of the reign of Alexander I. The old line merchants also worked to eliminate competition within Russia from noble and peasant entrepreneurs. Frequently, industrialists would submit lengthy memoranda to the government which dealt not only with the tariff question, but also with more general problems of Russian industrialization. The sixth volume of the Mordvinov archives contains some of these rather well-informed discourses, written in the 1820's.[13]

If the government recognized the existence of an industrial middle class and listened to the voicing of its interests in the early nineteenth century, its political power was negligible in this period, as it would remain until the last few decades of the tsarist regime. Russian businessmen were consulted and even given minor posts and ranks in the administration, but their best route to power in prereform Russia was to climb the social ladder into the nobility. Occasionally a big industrialist or banker would have nobility bestowed upon him or even be given a title. The iron moguls of the Urals, the Demidovs, acquired nobility in the eighteenth century. The banker Stieglitz was made a baron in 1828. The baronial title of the Jewish Gunzburgs had to follow upon their wealth by a quarter of a century—nobility came to the family in 1872, but from Germany rather than Russia, although recognized in the latter country. It was easier for a rich industrialist to

---

[12] "Iz zapisok Barona (vposledstvii Grafa) M. A. Korfa," *Russkaia starina*, vol. 99 (1899), 503-04. On the tsar's banquets for the merchants, see I. N. Rybnikov, "Rossiiskoe kupechestvo na obede u Imperatora Nikolaia Pavlovich (1833)," *Russkii arkhiv* (1891), vol. 3, no. 12, pp. 563-69. On the role of the merchants in the 1812 war, see the list in V. H. Storozhev, *Voina i Moskovskoe kupechestvo* (Moscow, 1914), pp. 83-98 and P. A. Berlin, "Russkoe kupechestvo i Voina 1812 goda," A. K. Dzhiveligov, S. P. Melgunov, and V. I. Picheta, eds., *Otechestvennaia voina i Russkoe obshchestvo 1812-1912*, vol. V (Moscow, 1912), pp. 114-20.

[13] V. A. Bilbasov, ed., *Arkhiv Grafov Mordvinovykh*, vol. VI (St. Petersburg, 1902), pp. 393-441, 550-62; *Istoriia Moskvy*, vol. III (Moscow, 1954), pp. 297-301, 307-11. For a discussion of the tariff and the forces involved in the debate over free trade and protectionism, see my Chapter 5.

marry into the nobility and even into the old aristocracy than to wait for the government to award these privileges. Peter the Great's industrial middle class dissolved into the nobility during the course of the eighteenth century, and some of the great early nineteenth-century industrialist families, most prominent among them the Prokhorovs, had cast their lot with the nobility by the time of the Russian Revolution.[14]

The origins of the most important Russian industrial dynasties and of the most prominent enterprises and fortunes to be found on the eve of the First World War can be traced to the early nineteenth century, and in many cases can be pinpointed to the 1820's and 1830's. The Konovalovs, the Guchkovs, the Morozovs, the Prokhorovs, the Stieglitzes, the Gunzburgs, the Soldatenkovs, to name some of the most prominent leaders in the cultural, economic, and political life of Russia in the early twentieth century—all built their fortunes in this period. It is a period, not only of the origins of private industrial capital and an entrepreneurial class, but also the beginnings of a consumer's market for the new textile industries, together with a hired factory labor force. The scale was small: this was not the transformation that some Western European societies were experiencing at the time so much as an exotic growth in an agrarian country. As such, Russian industrial capitalism had its peculiarities, unique features which may be contrasted to the European pattern. Similar to Europe, the traditional Russian merchant class remained a source for the industrial bourgeoisie during the early nineteenth century, although on a much more limited scale than in the West. The Russian nobility continued to become involved in industry after 1800, although in different ways than in the previous century. More unique to the Russian experience, it was the lower classes—the peasants and the urban masses—which provided a major supply of industrial entrepreneurs in the early nineteenth century. Also similar to Europe, religion played a role in the rise of Russian capitalism. Many of Europe's early capitalists were of dissenting religious faiths, such as the Calvinists. Although Russian orthodoxy did not necessarily inhibit the growth of business among its adherents, we know that the dissident sects and minority religions of the Russian empire, most prominently the Old Believers, Skoptsy, and Jews, provided many of Russia's big industrial, commercial, and financial capitalists. Moreover, unlike Europe and similar to colonial areas, foreigners with business and technical skills, played an important role in the development of private industry in Russia. Thus, in contrast to the European pattern, the Russian capitalist class was recruited as much from outcasts, out-

---

[14] On the ennoblement of Moscow merchants and their marriages into the nobility, see N. P. Chulkov, "Moskovskoe kupechestvo xviii i xix vv," *Russkii arkhiv* (1907), vol. 3, no. 12. pp. 489-502.

siders, and disadvantaged elements of society—serfs, religious minorities, and foreigners—as from the indigenous commercial classes. As such, the Russian private industrial entrepreneur was par excellence a "self-made man," although perhaps not so much the "rugged individualist," seen in his Western counterpart. In Russia, the communal tradition played a not insignificant role in the growth of a factory industry and of private capital.

Chapter 8

Social Origins of the Industrial Entrepreneur

All of the classes that formed the traditional society in Russia, and all of the strata of wealth and position within these classes, contributed to the new industrial capitalist class that emerged during the early nineteenth century. Some of the wealthiest of the landed magnates and influential courtiers invested heavily in industrial enterprise on their extensive domains. Many lower ranking gentry tried to stave off bankruptcy by setting up small factories on their estates. There was a significant diversion of capital from commerce into industry on the part of the most affluent members of the Russian merchant guilds. Many craftsmen, shopkeepers, and peddlers in the towns opened small manufacturing plants, some of which were the nucleus for large industrial enterprises of the next generation. Russia had her rags to riches stories during the early nineteenth century, for it was not impossible for a few millionaire industrialists of the time to trace their origins to the *lumpenproletariat* of St. Petersburg or Moscow. There were more millionaires among the peasants, however, by the end of the reign of Alexander I. Here again, as with the middle class, a prior accumulation of capital in trade might be diverted by a wealthy serf into industrial enterprise. In many cases, however, the serf millionaires of the prereform era, began their career pounding the road, with no other assets than a knapsack filled with their wares, a few kopecks, and a furlough from their master granting them permission to leave the village to trade.

Entrepreneurial Activities of the Merchants
and Urban Lower Middle Class

Russian merchants turned to industrial enterprise or invested in industry in increasing numbers during the early nineteenth century. Not all merchants sought advancement and profits in this way by any means. Some Moscow merchants climbed by marriage into the nobility and adopted its way of life, divorcing themselves from business enterprise. Dobrynin and Bakrushin are two of the more prominent family names associated with this social and economic change.[1] Most merchants of the lowest guild,[2] preferred to engage only in trade. Of 2,789 members of the third guild registered in Moscow in 1850, just under 10 percent owned industrial plants.[3] By law, these were very

---

[1] N. P. Chulkov, "Moskovskoe kupechestvo xviii i xix v.," *Russkii arkhiv* (1907), vol. 3, no. 12, pp. 490-91.

[2] On the guild system see my Chapter 4.

[3] V. N. Iakovtsevskii, *Kupicheskii kapital v feodal'no-krepostnicheskoi Rossii* (Moscow, 1953), table 38, p. 172.

restricted in size. Those belonging to the first and second guilds, however, apparently invested very heavily in industry by the middle of the nineteenth century. In 1765, only about 2 percent of Moscow's merchants owned factories or plants. By 1849-50, 90 percent of the merchants of the first guild and 59 percent of those of the second guild controlled such property.[4]

We have no way of knowing from these figures how many of the guild members involved in industry were originally merchants who had diverted capital into factory production. Nor do we know the extent to which they involved themselves in industrial enterprise relative to commercial activity, or the way in which they diverted their capital and energies. Did they invest in stock companies? Did they become real or silent partners? Did they actively engage in management? Did they lend money to industrialists? Further difficulty in determining the commercial sources of industrial enterprise in early nineteenth-century Russia is encountered in the vagueness of the term "merchant" (*kupets*) as used at that time. A *kupets* was anyone engaged in business activity—banker, factory owner, importer, shopkeeper—and not just a commercial person. Nevertheless, it is reasonable to assume that there was a substantial change of function and investment between the overwhelmingly merchants' Moscow of 1765 and the overwhelmingly industrialists' city of 1850. According to the Soviet scholar, Iakovtsevskii, the Russian merchant class was declining as well as changing.[5] The traditional commercial monopolies and privileges were being curtailed. Peasants and nobles were granted limited rights to engage in trade, which stiffened competition. In 1842, the government further dismantled the centuries-old wall of protection that had been built around the Russian merchant class by permitting factory owners to retail their products directly in the cities and at the fairs. In little more than a decade, a marked decline in the numbers and activities of merchant middlemen was observed at many of the fairs.[6] All of this meant lower prices for the merchant, and the lure of more profits in the new industries.

The cities became magnets for Russian merchants during the early nineteenth century.[7] Such commercial migrations could become occasions for embarking on industrial ventures. The Tretiakovs were

---

[4] Iakovtsevskii, *Kupicheskii kapital*, table 38, p. 172. A. Kopanev, *Naselenie Peterburga v pervoi polovine XIX veka* (Moscow-Leningrad, 1957), pp. 102-03, lists half of St. Petersburg's 144 factories and plants as belonging to merchants in 1821.

[5] Iakovtsevskii, *Kupicheskii kapital*, pp. 177-79.

[6] See Ivan Aksakov's observations of the Ukrainian fairs during the early 1850's in my Chapter 3.

[7] M. K. Rozhkova, *Istoriia Moskvy*, vol. III, pp. 292-93, counts half of 252 Moscow merchants of all guilds as out-of-towners, half of these from out of the province. Kopanev, *Naselenie Peterburga*, lists 23 of a group of 46 St. Petersburg merchants in 1812 coming from other cities.

originally merchants of Maloiaroslavets who migrated to Moscow in 1774 and founded their fortune in the linen cloth industry. The Bakrushins were cattle drovers in the seventeenth century. One hundred years later, they moved to Moscow and in the 1830's founded a prosperous tannery and brick factory.[8]

Below the commercial families on the social ladder was a growing and variegated urban mass of menials, craftsmen, laborers, and peddlers which began to fill the Russian capitals during the first half of the nineteenth century. Many were furloughed serfs. Others were freemen of various origins, such as those classified as *raznochintsi* and *meshchanstvo*.[9] It was from this base that enterprising ex-serfs, craftsmen, construction bosses, and others were able to establish various manufacturing concerns and work their way up the ladder of urban privilege to the higher ranks of the three merchant guilds, where they had legal elbow room for expansion into large-scale industrial enterprise. According to Kopanev, the leading Soviet student of the history of the Leningrad masses, over half of the third guild merchants registered for the year 1843 came from the *meshchanstvo*.[10] Such was the case of the Naidenovs, a wealthy and influential nineteenth-century industrial family, whose most famous scion became a chairman of the Moscow stock exchange as well as a historian of the Moscow middle class. The Naidenovs derived their fortune in the manufacture of silk cloth from a dyer who came to Moscow in the late eighteenth century having quit a craftsman's job in the provinces.[11]

Heinrich Storch, Russia's most prominent economist during the reign of Alexander I, has given us a clear description of the rise of a native businessman from the urban social depths at the beginning of the nineteenth century:

This career he usually begins as a *rasnoschtsik*, a seller of things in the streets; the profits arising from this ambulatory trade and his parsimony soon enable him to hire a *lavka* or shop: where, by lending of small sums at large interest, by taking advantage of the course of exchange, and by employing little artifices of trade, he in a short time becomes a pretty substantial man. He now buys and builds houses and shops, which he either lets to others, or furnishes with goods himself, putting in persons to manage them for small wages; begins to launch out into extensive trade, undertakes contracts with the crown for deliveries of merchandise, etc. The numerous instances of the rapid success of such people almost exceed description. By these methods, a Russian merchant named Iakov-

[8] Buryshkin, *Moskva kupicheskaia*, pp. 125, 134-35.
[9] For a description of these classifications, see my Chapter 4.
[10] Kopanev, *Naselenie Peterburga*, pp. 100-02.
[11] Buryshkin, *Moskva kupicheskaia*, pp. 129-34.

lev, who died not many years ago, from a hawker of fish in the streets became a capitalist of several millions. Many of these favorites of fortune are at first vassals, who obtain passes from their landlords and with these stroll about the towns in order to seek a, better condition in life as laborers, bricklayers, and carpenters than they could hope to find at the ploughtail in the country.[12]

The Noble as Entrepreneur and Investor

During the early nineteenth century, some Russians believed that the new capitalist class should be drawn from the top as well as the bottom of Russian society. Admiral Mordvinov argued that nobles as well as peasants should be attracted to business pursuits. One enthusiast appealed in 1812 to the nobility to shed their military functions and enter commercial and industrial enterprise as a service to the fatherland.[13] Reflecting these sentiments, legislation during the Napoleonic period relaxed prohibitions on noble entry to the higher merchant guilds.[14] Recently, some Soviet scholars have suggested that the Russian noble during the prereform period was becoming more "bourgeois" than had previously been thought.[15] To what degree was the Russian landlord becoming a businessman? The question is an important one. Much of the wealth of Russia was concentrated in the hands of this class. The industrialization of Russia would depend to a large degree on how much of this wealth was expended (to use Rostow's phrase) on "roads and railroads, schools and factories rather than on country houses and servants, personal ornaments and temples."[16] Several questions must be answered to determine the nature and significance of nobiliary enterprise in Russia during the early nineteenth century. First, a phenomenon which goes back to the eighteenth century:[17] were nobles continuing to set up factories on their estates with the aim of producing for a market? What caused them to engage in industrial enterprise? Did they have the necessary capital? Did they have the requisite skills? To what extent were landlords investing their wealth in business ventures? Were they able and willing to do this? Did their estate finances and way of life provide surpluses which could be diverted into productive invest-

[12] Heinrich Storch, *Picture of St. Petersburg* (London, 1801), pp. 271-72.

[13] P. A. Berlin, *Russkaia burzhuaziia v staroe i novoe vremia* (Moscow, 1922), pp. 74-76, cites the book by Levshin, *Russkii Polnii fabrikant i manufakturist* (Moscow, 1812).

[14] A. Romanovich-Slavatinskii, *Dvorianstvo v Rossii* (St. Petersburg, 1870), p. 263.

[15] Kopanev, *Naselenie Peterburga*, p. 111. From 1833 to 1838, the number of nobles registered as merchants in St. Petersburg increased only by 6, from 35 to 41.

[16] W. W. Rostow, *The Stages of Economic Growth* (Cambridge, 1960), p. 19.

[17] See my Chapter 1.

ment? Were there signs during the early nineteenth century that the pattern and mentality of extravagant consumption which prevailed among the upper nobility were giving way to attitudes more favorable to saving, profit making, and organization of resources?

Some of the answers to these questions can be found in the last chapter of the history of the estate (*votchinal*) factories which came in the period 1820-1870. The fall in grain prices in the last years of the reign of Alexander I caused an expansion of the number of *votchinal* factories in the attempt of landlords to more profitably utilize their peasant labor in industrial pursuits.[18] Only the wealthier strata of the nobility had sufficient working capital to build factories large enough to elicit the cooperation of the government, which in most cases was necessary to the survival of the enterprise. Most of the estate factories founded during the early nineteenth century manufactured coarse woolen cloth which was sold to the army for uniforms at high prices. Sugar refineries also were established on estates during the reign of Nicholas I. The larger ones received state subsidies; the small ones were primitive operations with a very low productivity.[19] Even these were beyond the means of most landlords, whose industrial activities were limited to small stills and tanneries for purely home consumption. A family as relatively wealthy as the Lunins, owners of almost a thousand serfs, were able to build a small plant employing only forty-two of their peasants, and could afford to maintain this for only a few years.[20]

The names of owners of some of the estate factories developed during the early nineteenth century and the size of the operations give some idea of the status of the nobility engaged in industrial enterprise—Khovanskii, Gagarin, Uvarov, Trubetskoi, Iusupov, Kurakin, Shcherbatov, Bariatinskii, Saltykov, and Potemkin, among others. Both the Gagarin and Uvarov factories employed 1,000 workers by the 1850's. More modest and typical was the linen factory of Prince Shcherbatov in Iaroslavl, which employed eighty serfs. These magnates were able to exert their influence to procure a lion's share of lucrative, protected, state-subsidized industries. Tugan-Baranovskii gives the figure of seventy-four of ninety-eight woolens factories in 1809 in the hands of the nobility, of which nineteen were owned by titled grandees.[21]

Votchinal factories employed primarily serfs, including many

[18] M. Tugan-Baranovskii, *Russkaia fabrika v proshlom i nastoiashchem* (St. Petersburg, 1898), vol. I, pp. 107-09, 116-17.

[19] See my Chapters 2 and 16.

[20] B. D. Grekov, "Tambovskaia imenie M. S. Lunina v pervoi chetverti xix v.," *Izvestiia Akademii Nauk SSSR, Otdelenie Obshchestvennykh Nauk* (1932), pp. 623-34.

[21] Tugan-Baranovskii, *Russkaia fabrika,* vol. I, pp. 28, 108-09; A. Pogozhev, "Votchinnye fabriki i ikh fabrichnye," *Vestnik Evropy,* vol. 138 (1889), pp. 13, 18-20.

women and children. On some estates, serfs worked off their *barshchina* obligation in the factory instead of in the fields. This usually amounted to three days a week. On other estates, they might work the entire week, being paid in cash, produce, or even in the use of land. The work day was twelve to fourteen hours; the work year, eight to nine months. Some estate factories employed two shifts.[22]

B. D. Grekov's researches into the estate finances of the Decembrist Lunin during the last years of the reign of Alexander I have provided us with a wealth of detail and insight into the functioning of a small *votchinal* factory. A small woolens "factory" (as it was called) was established on Lunin's Tambov estate in 1817. The factory employed eight men, sixteen women, and eighteen children. What the children did beyond accompanying their parents to the factory, it is difficult to say. Some helped the women to spin. The plant engaged in all the main aspects of wool production: spinning, weaving, and dyeing. There were a few looms, a press, and a dyeing machine. Beyond these simple implements, the numerous processes involved particularly in the spinning of wool were done by hand. The finishing of the cloth was sometimes turned over to another factory.

The Lunin factory was not a self-sufficient estate operation by any means. Almost all of the wool had to be purchased, which accounted, together with other raw materials, for over half of the cost of operation. The woolen cloth was sold at local fairs, which involved additional costs of transport and rental of stalls. Finally, the wages of the serfs consumed 46.1 percent of costs. This left a profit of 2,001 rubles, 47½ kopecks in 1820, which represented, however, about 30 percent of the gross for that year. The gross amounted to only 4 to 5 percent of the total income of the Lunin estate. However, maintenance costs, which were not calculated with the operating expenses, must have cut deeply into the profits, because a price fall in the early 1820's occasioned the closing of the factory in 1825.[23]

Whether most of the small estate factories were as short-lived as Lunin's we do not know. The larger ones were more durable. Some *votchinal* factories founded in the late eighteenth century were still functioning a century later. But the lord was gone. In many cases, the noble sold out after the emancipation of the serfs to industrialists of the newer breed. By 1889, of 204 factories functioning on estates in the Moscow district, only 6 percent were still owned by nobles.[24]

Such an attrition is testimony to the fact that the *votchinal* enterprises were far more a part of the old Russian bureaucratic serf order than a beginning of industrial capitalism. The noble factory owner of the early nineteenth century remained essentially a variant within the

---

[22] Pogozhev, "Votchinnye fabriki," pp. 11-13.
[23] Grekov, "Tambovskaia imenie M. S. Lunina," pp. 623-36.
[24] Pogozhev, "Votchinnye fabriki," pp. 20-21.

pre-industrial society. Rarely did he participate in the running of his factories or acquire managerial skills. Nor did he make any serious attempt to invest in private enterprise. Projects for stock companies were drawn up and discussed by landlords concerned with the improvement of the rural economy and the industrial growth of the country; but nothing ever came of these projects.[25] When the actual opportunity to buy stock was presented to Russian nobles, it was passed up. We have no general statistics on business investment in early nineteenth-century Russia to fully substantiate such a conclusion. However, if the lists of investors available for certain of the early Russian stock companies are examined, it can be seen that, although token purchases by titled aristocrats and government dignitaries were made, the bulk of the investors in these commercial and industrial ventures were from the Russian middle class or the foreign colony.[26]

If we examine the budgets of the wealthiest Russian landlords during the last years of serfdom we find that productive investments were subordinate to the main aim of paying for an extravagant and cumulative consumption, and the debts that these consumptive excesses had accumulated over decades and generations. Indeed, consumption and borrowing had become so ingrained and institutionalized, that any significant removal of funds from customary expenditures became highly improbable. Some landlords might have been more businesslike and experimental in the marshaling of funds; a few would qualify as aggressive profit seekers. Nevertheless, all was turned over to the maintenance of the traditional establishment. Here again, no general statistics exist to support conclusions. We do, however, have detailed studies and figures on the finances of certain landlords, some of moderate wealth, some of the richest in Russia. The Russian Revolution opened numerous family archives, and since then, analyses have been made of the Sheremetev, Kurakin, and Lunin budgets during the early nineteenth century, as well as several descriptions of the economy of the Iusupov estates and factories at that time. There is no evidence that these budgets are either typical or exceptional, although their remarkable similarity in many important ways indicates a pattern.

Any study of the budgets of the wealthy titled aristocracy must be prefaced by the observation that most of Russia's landlords were poor, many of them desperately so. A substantial number even in

---

[25] See E. H. Kusheva, "Proekt uchrezhdeniia aktsionernogo 'Obshchestva Ulucheniia Chastnogo Sel'skogo Khoziaistva' 30-kh godov XIX v.," *Istoricheskii arkhiv* (Moscow, 1951), vol. VII, pp. 46-95.

[26] See A. A. Preobrazhenskii, "O sostave aktsioncrov Rossiisko-Amerikanskoi Kompanii v nachale XIX v.," *Istoricheskie zapiski*, vol. 67 (1960), pp. 286-98. There is a list of stockholders on pp. 295-98; also, *Piatidesiatiletie Vysochaishe Utverzhdennago Rossiiskago Zastrakhovaniia Kapitalov i Dokhodov* (St. Petersburg, 1885), pp. 90-92.

the middle of the nineteenth century lived like and indeed *with* their serfs, at a bare subsistence level that precluded any kind of enterprise or investment. This majority of landlord paupers, however, controlled only a tiny fraction of Russia's agricultural wealth. Most of the remainder of the nobility—below the 3 percent who owned almost half of the seigneurial serfs—could never make ends meet. Always hard pressed for cash, they had no capital reserves to sustain investments and enterprises. They languished in a pattern of chronic borrowing, pinching of their peasants, and the most backward and uneconomical methods of producing and selling—all in a desperate effort to get hold of sufficient funds to maintain their estates. To the high costs of inefficient management and transportation were added those of a Western way of life, the amenities of which they had come to desire and demand. Many of these middling landlords thus were brought to the brink of ruin, not because of the proverbial Russian profligacy, but because of the inability if not the impossibility of adjusting their primitive estate economies to the money demands of Westernization. However, those who controlled the largest part of Russia's wealth in land and souls—the small minority of great magnates—had immense surpluses, almost all of which were squandered from the point of view of business investment.[27]

The Sheremetevs, with over 200,000 serfs, were the greatest landlords of old Russia. Nikolai Petrovich Sheremetev, who died in 1809, and his son, Dmitri Nikolaevich Sheremetev, who administered the family domains for the rest of the prereform period, had no interest either in state or military service, or in expanding their wealth. They were *grands seigneurs* of the old school whose primary occupation, economically speaking, was to spend the family fortune. The father concentrated on building palaces; the son found religious solace in extravagant philanthropy. Apart from their eccentricities and obsessions, both spent the largest amount of their annual income on payment of debts and on maintenance of the household. These were constant and increasing costs, which absorbed most of the Sheremetev money unproductively, since little attempt was made to amortize the debts or to cut back on the numerous foreign teachers, entertainers, and professionals, or their expensive salaries. The bulk of the Sheremetev income came from the *obrok* of their empire of peasants. In 1859, this amounted to 589,000 rubles, out of a total annual income of 702,800 rubles. The pittance gained from sale of produce testifies to the lack of commercialization of Sheremetev agriculture in

[27] See M. Confino, *Domaines et seigneurs en Russie vers la fin du XVIII*ᵉ *siècle* (Paris, 1963) for an analysis of the economic plight of the poorer Russian landlords at the end of the eighteenth century. A more comprehensive discussion of the seigneurial economy of the time and of the distribution of nobiliary wealth can be found in Jerome Blum, *Lord and Peasant in Russia from the Ninth to the Nineteenth Century* (Princeton, 1961), pp. 367-85.

the prereform period—18,400 rubles. Another drop in the bucket of 14,800 rubles is designated in the 1859 budget analysis as income on "capital," presumably some kind of investment, whether in real property, loans, or industry, it cannot be determined. However, in 1838, this income was much higher, 143,300 rubles. In 1859, nothing was invested in this way; 736,700 rubles were required for debt payments, which thus exceeded the income for that year by 33,900, a discrepancy which had to be met by still more borrowing. In fact, 338,200 rubles were consumed in personal, household, and estate expenses, exclusive of charity and administrative costs, which totaled 266,800 rubles.[28]

Prince Kurakin was a noted diplomat of the Alexandrine period, a dignitary of the highest rank for whom the cost of living and entertaining was high. He accumulated a debt of 7 million rubles. Like the Sheremetevs, he was a builder of palaces and gardens. He maintained a huge staff: administrators, bookkeepers, clerks, doctors, medical assistants, German gardeners, French secretaries, English riding masters, craftsmen, musicians, and architects, in addition to hundreds of serfs and hired help used for menial work and in factories. This amounted to 800 people, and cost the Prince, together with his regular household expenses, 191,900 rubles a year in the 1820's, out of a total income of 541,000. Most of the remainder was absorbed, as with the Sheremetevs, in interest, amortization, doweries, gifts, charity, gambling losses, and construction. In the end, Kurakin was obliged to mortgage his entire estate to a government bank for thirty-seven years. Prior to this, he made numerous attempts to expand the income of his properties. Possessing far fewer serfs than the Sheremetevs (about 5,000), he had no opportunity to live off the *obrok*. Like many other Russian landlords of the early nineteenth century, Kurakin went into the business of selling wheat, hemp, fruits, and other produce. This was accompanied by attempts to improve agricultural methods. To further increase his revenue, Kurakin built a woolens factory, which, however, proved to be unprofitable and was closed. Plans for a station house and inn on Kurakin property located on the Kiev highway came to nothing.[29]

The Iusupov budgets during the early nineteenth century present interesting contrasts and resemblances to those of Prince Kurakin and Count Sheremetev. Unlike his contemporaries, Boris Nikolaevich Iusupov, who ruled the family domains during the reign of Nicholas I, was the most entrepreneurial of the great Russian magnates. More than any other wealthy Russian landlord, the Iusupovs attempted to

[28] V. Staniukevich, *Biudzhet Sheremetevykh, 1798-1910* (Moscow, 1927), pp. 9 17, and table, pp 22-24.
[29] "Usad'ba nachala XIX v., iz zapisok arkhitektora V. A. Bakareva," *Krasnyi Arkhiv*, vol. 78, pp. 254-62.

industrialize their estates, and derived a major part of their income from their factories. On the other hand, the Iusupovs consumed with an extravagance that can only be called magnificent. They borrowed with equal flourish.

By the beginning of the nineteenth century, the Iusupov holdings constituted a kind of agrarian empire: in 1806, 198 villages, in 9,039 square miles of property (222,143 *desiatinas*), where 17,239 serfs served the family interest.[30] A central and local administration was created to rule this empire. At the hub were the Moscow and St. Petersburg chancelleries, which sent out inspectors to regional administrations. The center for the Iusupov administration in the Ukraine was a major economic center in itself: a town of 2,320 inhabitants with shops, warehouses, factories, mills, barracks, administrative buildings, a tavern, and a hospital.[31]

The cost of maintaining this administration was great, but did not even begin to match the personal expenses of Nikolai Borisovich Iusupov, a retired dignitary of the Catherinean era. In 1820, in addition to the usual staff of foreign professionals, he hired an entire Italian opera company, which by 1824, was costing him 24,000 rubles a year.[32] To finance this kingly scale of living, Iusupov bought estates, borrowed money, mortgaged serfs, but above all he built factories. By his death in 1831, he had mortgaged over half of his serfs and owed 2,542,042 rubles. However during the first third of the nineteenth century, from 25 to 50 percent of the Iusupov income came from several estate factories. These factories produced primarily wool for the government, but also silk for the consumer market. Attempts were made to increase production by the introduction of machinery, but the Iusupov profits depended basically on state orders.[33] Boris Nikolaevich Iusupov succeeded to the family estates in the 1830's. His Soviet historian has classified him as "landlord entrepreneur" who quit the state service in 1837 to devote himself entirely to his properties, who was interested in making money, and who introduced many reforms in the Iusupov administration.[34]

Mikhail Lunin, the Decembrist, was far less affluent than the Iusupovs, Kurakins, and Sheremetevs. Nevertheless, his finances follow a similar pattern. Of an income of 37,593 rubles from the summer

[30] K. V. Sivkov, "Biudzhet krupnogo sobstvennika-krepostnika pervoi treti xix v.," *Istoricheskie zapiski*, vol. 9 (1940), appendix, p. 152.

[31] A. N. Nasonov, "Iz istorii krepostnoi votchiny xix veka v Rossii," *Izvestiia Akademii Nauk SSSR*, VI series (1926), p. 504.

[32] Nasonov, "Krepostnaia votchina xix veka," p. 501.

[33] Sivkov, "Biudzhet krupnogo krepostnika," pp. 147-48; A. N. Nasonov, "Khoziaistvo krupnoi votchiny nakanune osvobozhdeniia krest'ian v Rossii," *Izvestiia Akademii Nauk SSSR, Otdelenie Gumanitarnykh Nauk*, VII series (1928), pp. 367-70.

[34] Nasonov, "Krepostnaia votchina xix veka," pp. 511-12.

of 1823 to that of 1824, 83.6 percent was consumed for personal expenses and debts. The tiny factory that was set up to increase income, as we have seen, was of little help. The mainstay of the estate in Tambov was its grain crop, although some *obrok* was obtained from a smaller estate in Saratov. In the years of bad harvests and falling prices of the mid-1820's, the Lunin estate was desperately short of cash, and the feeble industrial ventures had to be abandoned.[35]

The Serf Entrepreneur

During the early nineteenth century, a new type of industrialist emerged from the social group in Russia presumably least expected to produce him. Where the landlord entrepreneur to a large degree failed to modernize, the serf industrialist established himself as a fixed and prominent part of the Russian social scenery, as a modern type of capitalist, and as an important factor in the emerging textile industry. The paradox of a slave millionaire—of the lord who owns not the capital but the capitalist, and of the serf who is the master of hundreds of hired laborers—has easily attracted the interest of historians in both Russia and the West since Tugan-Baranovskii.[36] There is near unanimous concurrence as to the significance of this phenomenon and no lack of convincing reasons for its appearance have been provided.

Several historians would agree that the combination by the late eighteenth century, particularly in the north of Russia, of increased circulation of money, population rise, decreased productivity of land, and the growing appetite of a Westernizing nobility for the cash necessary to buy European and other manufactured products, led to an increase in the transmission of peasant obligations into a money *obrok*. These sums could be obtained more readily by those lords who permitted their serfs to work for wages in factories or at handicrafts within the peasant hut.[37] Not only was an industrial labor force in the making but also a group of peasant craftsmen and busi-

---

[35] Grekov, "Tambovskaia imenie M. S. Lunina," pp. 483-84, 493, 640.

[36] Tugan-Baranovskii, *Russkaia fabrika*, 102-03; Joseph Kulischer, "Die kapitalistischen Unternehmer in Russland (insbesondere die Bauern als Unternehmer) in den Anfangsstadien des Kapitalismus," *Archiv für Sozialwissenschaft und Sozialpolitik*, vol. 65 (1931), pp. 309-55; more recently, F. Ia. Polianskii, *Pervonachal'noe nakoplenie kapitala v Rossii* (Moscow, 1958); Roger Portal, "Du servage à la bourgeoisie: la famille Konovalov," *Revue des études slaves*, vol. 38 (1961), 143-50, and "Origines d'une bourgeoisie industrielle en Russie," *Revue d'histoire moderne et contemporaine*, vol. VIII (1961), 35-60; Henry Rosovsky, "The Serf Entrepreneur in Russia," *Explorations in Entrepreneurial History*, vol. VI (1953-1954), pp. 207-29, and Dmitri Shimkin, "The Entrepreneur in Tsarist and Soviet Russia," *Explorations in Entrepreneurial History*, vol. II (1949-1950), pp. 24-34.

[37] See Rosovsky, "The Serf Entrepreneur," pp. 209-11; Polianskii, *Pervonachal'noe nakoplenie kapitala*, pp. 77-78; and Portal, "Origines d'une bourgeoisie industrielle," pp. 42-43.

ness entrepreneurs. It has been suggested that the eighteenth-century peasant was far from being devoid of property consciousness or inept commercially, although peasant entrepreneurship may have been stifled by a state policy which aimed to hold the peasant within a burden-bearing group such as the commune.[38] The huts of the energetic and the shrewd did expand into shops and hence into factories. Ambitious Russian craftsmen, such as the founder of the Garelin fortune at Ivanovo could send peasants to smuggle out, after employment at foreign cotton mills in Russia, the secrets and skills of new processes of cloth printing. This knowledge enabled them to modernize and expand their enterprises. The fire of 1812, which destroyed the textile industry of Moscow, was a boon to the serf craftsmen of the famous Sheremetev village of Ivanovo to the northeast, many of whom were able to begin their entrepreneurial careers with capital gleaned from highly accelerated earnings prompted by this catastrophe.[39]

For the noble who owned such an enterprising soul, as D. S. Mirsky has most felicitously described it, this was the "goose who laid the golden egg." The price of such a productive slave came high, and the redemption sum of a few serf millionaire-industrialists and their families sometimes grew to immense fortunes—of such proportions that the lord, pressed for cash, finally could not resist.[40] For the serf, the protection of a great name fortified by privileges of nobility provided a shield from competitors and from the state that made it worthwhile and tempting up to a certain point to remain in bondage. But with expanding mechanized industry, the fish grew too big for the pond: in the decade after 1825, for example, fifteen Ivanovo industrialists bought themselves out of bondage. The last and only previous redemption had been in 1795.[41]

The nobility, particularly those influential grandees such as the Sheremetevs whose villages were being transformed into prosperous factory towns and whose pockets were being lined with peasant gold, as well as modernizing bureaucrats, such as Mordvinov and Rumiantsev, were reluctant to see the new industry impeded. This had its effect on state policy. The efforts of merchants in the eighteenth and early nineteenth centuries to forestall through state restriction the invasion by peasant entrepreneurs of their privileged precincts in the guild system and to bar peasants from industrial

---

[38] Shimkin, "The Entrepreneur," p. 27.

[39] Tugan-Baranovskii, *Russkaia fabrika*, pp. 97-98. On Garelin, see the sketch in Ch. Iuksimovich, *Manufakturnaia promyshlennost v proshlom i nastoiashchem* (Moscow, 1915), vol. I, pp. 215-16.

[40] Kopanev, *Naselenie Peterburga*, p. 94, gives a range of from 400,000 to 1,000,000 rubles.

[41] P. M. Ekzempliarskii, *Istoriia goroda Ivanova* (Ivanovo, 1958), vol. I, p. 97.

pursuits were never fully successful, any more than were the attempts to keep the nobility out of industry.

The classic example of the success story of peasant captains of industry can be seen in the history of Ivanovo, which during the early nineteenth century was transformed by serf industrialists from a small village belonging to Count Sheremetev to the textile city which came to be known as the "Russian Manchester."[42] Of the half-hundred Ivanovo serf entrepreneurs who attained the affluence sufficient to match the high price for their freedom, three families overshadow all others as the undisputed leaders of the new business community—the Grachevs, the Garelins, and the Iamanovskiis.[43]

The Grachevs, along with the Garelins, were the first of Count Sheremetev's serfs to move from the hut to the factory—as early as 1751, when they set up the first small plants in Ivanovo for the printing of cotton cloth. Garelin was one of the first to send local peasants to work in the Schlüsselburg factory of the English manufacturers Chamberlain and Cuzzins in order to learn and appropriate secret new techniques for cotton printing. It was Grachev, however, who first reached the "big time," having attained by 1795 the wealth that bought his freedom (for 130,000 rubles) as well as his registration in the first merchant's guild. By 1798, his factory housed 121 workers. An expanded plant with machinery employed, in 1807, 722 wage-earning serfs. The Garelins, also profiting from their own active quest for new techniques and machinery as well as from the Moscow fire in 1812, were operating the third largest factory in Ivanovo by 1817, which numbered 1,407 workers. In addition, Garelin came to own an entire peasant village and all its inhabitants—that of Spaskoe, although he did not buy himself out of bondage until 1828.[44]

The Iamanovskiis were the first family of the Ivanovo bourgeoisie, having a declared capital of 300,000 rubles and owning large tracts of land as well as the largest factory complex in the area. This consisted of twenty-four stone and wooden buildings, including three three-story stone structures, which housed the special cloth printing operations and the machinery. In addition to these plants and several warehouses, ten buildings were reserved for housing the workers, who numbered 1,402 men and 85 women (wives of the male workers). Iamanovskii lived in the finest private residence in Ivanovo, drove

---

[42] On the town itself, see my Chapter 4.

[43] The industrial history of Ivanovo has been detailed briefly and most recently by Roger Portal, "Origines d'une bourgeoisie industrielle." Portal consulted the Sheremetev archives. In addition to the recent Soviet history by Ekzempliarskii, there is also a collection by Iu. F. Glebov and V. M. Sokolev, *Istoriia fabriki bol'shoi ivanovskoi manufaktury* (Ivanovo, 1952). The older history, by one of the big Ivanovo industrialists, is Ia. Garelin, *Gorod Ivanovo-Voznesensk* (Ivanovo, 1885), 2 vols.

[44] Rosovsky, "The Serf Entrepreneur," pp. 217-19.

around in carriages, was attended by Kirghiz houseboys and, if Turgenev's description of Ivanovo hospitality applies to his household, entertained his guests in a parlor furnished with mahogany pieces while gracing his meals with champagne.[45] Ivanovo's Soviet historian, Ekzempliarskii, quotes an even more enthusiastic report in 1827 by the magazine *Moscow Telegraph*, which very probably resulted from a visit to either the Iamanovskii or Grachev abode;

> You are visiting a banquet of an Ivanovo resident . . . a vast hall, adorned by furniture of fine wood, upholstered with silk material and gilded in the latest style, filled with inhabitants of Ivanovo village of both sexes. Everywhere you see glitter, lamps, the richest of carpets, stands holding silver plates, silken drapes with gold painting and fringes, expensive crystal; everywhere lacquer, silver and bronze, all in wonderful purity. Not only floors, windows and doors, but as well stairways and several houses varnished. . . .[46]

As Tugan-Baranovskii expressed it, the serf millionaires were "juridically as much without rights as the lowest beggar from among their workers," although in practice their powers were far more extensive.[47] However, the lord could both give and take away, and might take away at any time that which he had given. In practice, the lords did all of this. One serf of Count Sheremetev, who had become a multimillionaire hat manufacturer in Moscow, in a splendid act of conspicuous consumption, priced his own freedom at 800,000 rubles.[48] Most of the others, however, did not find justice or reprieve in such prohibitive redemption prices, and like the Morozovs, scrimped for years to raise the necessary sums. Most of the serf industrialist magnates, whose possession of extensive real and personal property including peasants might never be disputed while they remained in bondage, found upon the purchase of their personal freedom that they no longer owned the land, machinery, or factory buildings that they had so painfully developed. Like their less enterprising brother serfs later in 1861, they had to buy their own property and it did not come cheap. The lord was, thus, doubly enriched at the time that he decided to let go of his Midas-slave: in addition to the fortune that he harvested from personal redemption came a lucrative income in rents and sales of property. The redeemed serf, of course, kept his private fortune and his profits.[49] In the end in many cases, he regained his properties, rebuilt his fortune, expanded his enterprise, and aspired to

---

[45] Ekzempliarskii, *Istoriia goroda Ivanova*, pp. 71, 77, 80; N. Turgenev, *La Russie et les Russes* (Brussels, 1847), vol. II, pp. 127-28.

[46] Ekzempliarskii, *Istoriia goroda Ivanova*, p. 81.

[47] Tugan-Baranovskii, *Russkaia fabrika*, p. 99.

[48] Polianskii, *Pervonachal'noe nakoplenie kapitala v Rossii*, p. 87.

[49] As in the case of the Konovalovs. See Portal, "La famille Konovalov," p. 150.

new empires. It would be tempting to inject romantic irony into the history of Russian industrialization by concluding that the lord quickly ran through his windfall and slid into poverty and bankruptcy, while his ex-serf accumulated new wealth and power. The new class replaces the old. Such was not the case with the Sheremetevs, although we do have the instance of the Kondratevs, industrialists belonging to the ancient titled house of Bibikov, many of whom remained in bondage right up to the emancipation, but who in the 1880's bought the Bibikov palace and moved into it.[50]

If the price for absolute personal and economic freedom came high, the lord was careful not to restrict his industrialist slave to the degree that the latter's enterprise and incentive might be seriously impeded. Protection and power were in fact bestowed liberally. A great noble name was a legal shield, a kind of extended freedom in itself, which the emancipated serf no longer possessed in the more cramped legal categories of the merchantry. Entire streets in the prereform merchant sections of Moscow and St. Petersburg were observed by Nikolai Turgenev to have "Sheremetev" and "Orlov" inscribed on the name plates of the houses.[51] Nor did Count Sheremetev, apparently, always closely restrict or scrutinize the business deals of his serf industrialists. Grachev, for example, was able to acquire properties through merchant associates and so build up a private domain beyond the control or even the knowledge of his master.[52] The Sheremetevs also, in effect, handed over to their major industrial magnates the local government of the factory villages. In Ivanovo, this meant necessary police power —the power of the Grachevs, Iamanovskiis, Garelins, and others to impose discipline on their factories.[53]

Ivanovo was not the only new serf industrial complex in Russia during the early nineteenth century, nor were the Sheremetevs the only noble family who benefited from the new phenomenon. Factories were rising in numerous other villages in Vladimir, Kostroma, and Moscow provinces. The Sheremetev industrial empire itself extended beyond the village of Ivanovo. There were the villages of Pavlovo and Vorsma near Nizhnii-Novgorod with hardware factories, and numerous enterprises of Sheremetev serfs in the capital cities. In St. Petersburg, a Sheremetev serf operated a fruit market on the Nevskii Prospect with a capital of 3 million rubles.[54] The Saltykovs, Riumins, Kurakins, Bibikovs, Orlovs, and Khrushchevs were other great noble families who profited from the emergence of the new entrepreneurial class.

In St. Petersburg, the peasant entrepreneur found opportunity in

[50] Rosovsky, "The Serf Entrepreneur," pp. 221-22.
[51] Turgenev, *La Russie et les Russes*, vol. II, p. 125.
[52] Rosovsky, "The Serf Entrepreneur," p. 219.
[53] Ekzempliarskii, *Istoriia goroda Ivanova*, pp. 78-79. See also my Chapter 4.
[54] Kopanev, *Naselenie Peterburga*, p. 94.

catering to the complex needs of the administrative hub of the empire and the craving of the nobility for European style luxuries, rather than in supplying the mass market for cheap cloth. An official report for 1794 lists eighty-three factories and plants in St. Petersburg, almost all engaged in the production of luxuries (gold work, silks, tobacco, hats, brewing, etc.). Included in this list were Vasily Samoilov, a serf of Count V. G. Orlov, who operated a candle-making shop, and Semen Borin, belonging to Count N. P. Sheremetev, who was engaged in the manufacture of corkscrews.[55] Kopanev calls the peasant building contractor a "characteristic figure" of early nineteenth-century St. Petersburg, resulting from the extensive construction in that period of monumental state and private edifices. For example, such a contractor, Gregory Kesarin, expanded his carpentry service for St. Isaac's cathedral from three partners in 1818 to 400 employees in 1834, during the same period advancing himself up the social ladder of the merchant guilds. Elsewhere in the same city there was the famous Savva Iakovlev, an ex-fish huckster and probably ultimately an ex-*obrok* serf, whose factory by 1801 employed almost 3,000 workers. Iakovlev's linen product was good enough to become famous in Europe, and his fortune in the hands of his son had grown by the mid-nineteenth century to over 60 million rubles.[56]

It was in Moscow province, however, that the new textile factories and their owners multiplied most rapidly. By 1861, within a 250 mile radius of Moscow there were dozens of villages repeating on a smaller or sometimes very nearly an equal scale the history of Ivanovo. In at least three vicinities, over 4,000 workers were employed, over a dozen utilized 500 to 2,000, and another dozen factory centers were peopled by from 300 to 500 workers.[57]

It was in these villages as in the cities of Ivanovo and Moscow that some of the wealthiest and most famous industrialist families of tsarist Russia founded their enterprises in the early nineteenth century. Such is the story of the Morozovs, Alekseevs, Naidenovs, the Konovalovs and the Prokhorovs, all of which follow a similar pattern. Serf craftsmen (in the case of the Prokhorovs, a liberated ecclesiastical serf who was able to climb into the petty bourgeoisie of Moscow in the late eighteenth century and become a big industrialist by the 1830's) establish shops in villages near or on the outskirts of Moscow, expand their enterprises during the period following the Moscow fire and the

---

[55] "Vedomost sostoiashchem v St. Peterburg fabrikam, manufakturam, i zavodam 1794 goda," *Sbornik Imperatorskago Russkago Istoricheskago Obshchestva*, vol. I (1867), pp. 352-61.

[56] Kopanev, *Naselenie Peterburga*, pp. 95-96, on Kesarin. On Savva Iakovlev, see Iuksimovich, *Manufakturnaia promyshlennost*, pp. 141-42; and Jerrman, *St. Petersburg*, pp. 160-63.

[57] See "Ekonomicheskaia karta evropeiskoi chasti Rossiiskoi Imperii nakanune reforma 1861 g.," *Istoriia SSSR* (Moscow, 1956), vol. I, appendix.

protective tariff of the 1820's, buy their freedom soon after, train their sons in the business, set up branches and commercial operations in other parts of the empire, and install machinery. By 1861, they have entered the ranks of the leading textile manufacturers in Russia, usually with a headquarters at Moscow.[58]

[58] Iuksimovich, *Manufakturnaia promyshlennost*, gives useful summaries of the founding of the Moscow textile dynasties. On the early history of the Prokhorov factory in Moscow, see N. A. Rozhkov, "Prokhorovskaia manufaktura za pervye 40 let ego sushchestvovaniia," *Istorik marksist*, vol. 6 (1927), pp. 79-110.

Chapter 9

Religious Origins of the Industrial Entrepreneur

The Moscow Old Believers[1]

As Moscow began to industrialize during the early nineteenth century, the old Orthodox and national shrine of Russia experienced a finale of Russian religious history. Moscow during this same period became a center of the Old Believers; *raskol'niki*, scattered for over a century on the frontiers of Russia, began to flock back to the ancient capital. The two events are linked. Many of the private industrial entrepreneurs in Moscow were Old Believers. The focus of their business activities was the textile industry. Here, the peculiar beliefs, way of life and organization of the larger communities of the schismatics seemed admirably suited to the accumulation of industrial capital, the provision of incentive for master and worker alike, and the mobilization of the lower strata of Moscow and the surrounding countryside into a factory labor force.

During the early nineteenth century, the Old Believer movement continued and even expanded as a major force in the life of the people of Russia. Perhaps as high as a third and no less than a fifth of the peasants had embraced it. It was a power which the state feared and fought and which even the revolutionary leaders acknowledged to be a vital element of peasant and urban life and a vehicle for the destruction of the old order in Russia.[2] The Old Believer entrepreneurs emerged in Moscow during the reigns of Alexander I and Nicholas I from the two main factional streams which flowed from the schism of the seventeenth century—the Priestists (*Popovtsy*) and the Priestless (*Bezpopovtsy*), or, more specifically, the great communities which became the national centers in Moscow of these two factions, the Rogozhsk and Preobrazhensk communities of "cemeteries" (*kladbishcha*; so called because the communities were built around the sites of Old Believer burial places). These communities were established in the late eighteenth century in what at that time were outskirts and vil-

---

[1] A version of the section dealing with the Moscow Old Believers appeared in the *Slavic Review*, vol. XXIV (1965), 407-24.

[2] See Anatole Leroy-Beaulieu, *The Empire of the Tsars and the Russians* (New York, 1896), vol. III, pp. 358-59. Leroy-Beaulieu's perceptive study of the Russian schismatics is still very usable. On the numbers of Old Believers in the nineteenth century, see Serge Zenkovsky, "The Ideological World of the Denisov Brothers," *Harvard Slavic Studies*, vol. III (1957), p. 64; and John Curtiss, *Church and State in Russia 1900-1917* (New York, 1940), p. 138. A conservative estimate of the dissenting population of Russia about 1850 would be nine million. The official figure was less than a million, a bureaucratic attempt to hide the fact of major religious disunity.

lage suburbs of Moscow but in the nineteenth century became the city's main industrial districts. According to one of the best known students of Old Belief of the last century, P. I. Mel'nikov, the *raskol'-nik* segment of the population of Moscow and its suburbs jumped from about 20,000 in 1800 to 186,000 by 1848, about half of the total number of inhabitants. Most of these people worked in factories controlled by Old Believers or at home work farmed out by the same industrialists. The elders of the communities controlled the factories; for 1838, 138 families of the Rogozhsk Cemetery were registered in the first and second merchant guilds, and many were Hereditary Honorable Citizens as well as Commercial and Manufacturing Councillors,[3] dignities which designated only the most important and wealthiest mercantile and industrial entrepreneurs at that time in Russia.

It took a century of religious dissent to give birth to these industrialists. The religious history of the first period of the Russian Schism—from the Nikonian revolution to the reign of Catherine the Great—is one of persecution, flight, dispersal, and factionalism. There is also an economic history of Old Belief during this same time. The Priestists, the moderate wing of the original schismatics, who continued to accept the notion of a priesthood and of a true church and who were unwilling to go to the extremes of torture, incarceration, or self-inflicted death in the face of government persecution, fanned out to the forests of the west, south, and east, to the Ukraine and Poland, to the lower Volga, the Don, the Urals and western Siberia, and even a few to China.[4] By the end of the eighteenth century, hundreds of thousands of Priestists had set up communities in these desolate areas, groups which, although largely self-sufficient, maintained contact with each other and with religious centers that had developed, such as the monastery at Kerzhenets (near Nizhnii-Novgorod). In return the religious centers received financial support from such wealthy communities as Ekaterinburg, where Old Believers owned most of the private metallurgical industry and numbered, according to most estimates, some 150,000, or the lower Volga area, where they came to control the east-west trade, the fairs, and the shipbuilding industry.

Labor, money, and commercial information apparently circulated along with religious teachings in this frontier world of the Old Believers. Not only spiritual but economic cooperation was necessary to sur-

---

[3] P. I. Mel'nikov, *Polnoe sobranie sochinenii* (2nd edn., St. Petersburg, 1909), vol. III, 204-06. Mel'nikov was better known under the pen name of Andrei Pecherskii. In addition to his numerous studies of the Old Believers, he wrote a fictional trilogy about them.

[4] F. C. Coneybeare, *Russian Dissenters* (Cambridge, Mass., 1921), pp. 101-05; P. Miliukov, *Outlines of Russian Culture* (Philadelphia, 1942), vol. I, p. 61; V. V. Andreev, *Raskol i ego znachenie v russkoi narodnoi istorii* (St. Petersburg, 1870), p. 149.

vive in the face of a hostile government and a wild frontier environment.[5] It was a recapitulation of the commercial history of many of the world's harried, migrant, and sometimes pioneer religious sects. Yet the tsarist government, rigorous in matters of political submission and ideological conformity, was indulgent with the Old Believers when it came to taxes and other pecuniary obligations. This policy was no doubt influenced by the problems of assessment and collection in the hinterland of Russia, where even the military arms of the tsar could not always stretch. The Old Believers paid only the "double" head tax and were exempt from many of the commercial, military, and labor obligations that burdened the Orthodox peasants and merchants. Catherine the Great expanded these exemptions to a general policy of toleration. Under her "enlightened despotism," they were invited to return from frontier banishment, and measures were taken toward further legalization of their position.[6] With such concessions, the Old Believer communities grew and prospered. But the state could always reverse itself and launch out on new persecutions. The period of toleration inaugurated by Catherine the Great and continued by Alexander I was ended by Nicholas I. Persecution intensified during the last years of his reign, when a police terror was imposed on the *raskol'niki*. The commercial and industrial fruits of the earlier period, however, endured.

The history of the Priestless faction of the schism during the eighteenth century carries us deeper into the ideological and organizational background of the entrepreneurial activities of the Old Believers. The economic prosperity of the Priestless was encouraged by the same external factors of frontier cooperation and eventual state tolerance that we have seen in the case of the Priestists. The peculiar doctrines and way of life of the Priestless sects were equally decisive in determining their business future. The Priestless fled to the north rather than to the south to escape the troops of the tsar. As Miliukov and Nikol'skii point out, their isolated communities in the wilderness, the lack of government control, the weak influence of Orthodoxy, and the scarcity of priests were conducive to a nonhierarchical type of religion, to simple, puritanical religious services, and to self-sufficient, hard-working, and austere religious communities.[7] One of the most important of these early communities of the north, was the Vyg Commune, the birthplace of the "Shore Dweller" (*Pomortsy*) faction. Vyg established the organizational pattern that would be followed by many of the later Priestless communities. The community was headed by an elected council of elders, who controlled its religious and economic life. As time went

[5] N. M. Nikol'skii, *Istoriia russkoi tserkvi* (Moscow-Leningrad, 1931), pp. 218-21, 275.

[6] Nikol'skii, *Istoriia russkoi tserkvi*, p. 275; Andreev, *Raskol*, p. 155.

[7] Miliukov, *Outlines of Russian Culture*, pp. 61-63; Nikol'skii, *Istoriia russkoi tserkvi*, p. 234.

on, the elders became businessmen and businessmen became elders. Vyg became a federation consisting of a large number of industrial and agricultural communities and subsequently expanded from agriculture and ironmaking until it handled much of the fishing, whaling, and commercial activity of the north. Wherever they traded, the Shore Dwellers set up communities.[8]

Developing at about the same time as the Shore Dwellers, closely akin to them, but irreconcilable on certain issues, was the Theodosian faction of the Priestless schismatics, named after its founder, the Novgorod clerk Theodosii Vasil'ev, who died in prison in 1711. The Theodosians during the eighteenth century were the most puritanical of the main branches of Old Belief. In varying degrees at different times they remained hostile to the state, to private property, to sex and marriage, to rituals, to dealings with people of other beliefs, to priests and church hierarchy, and to tobacco, alcohol, coffee, tea, potatoes, Western dress, and the shaving of beards.[9] In the course of a century and a half of secularization most of these attitudes were modified or obliterated. The austere, puritanical outlook, however, endured long enough to help in the creation of sober, diligent communities throughout the north of Russia, where hard work and asceticism soon produced large reserves of capital. The prohibitions on sex, marriage, and family life were soon, of necessity, revised or evaded, but the concept of communal property and the prohibition of familial inheritance were not eliminated in practice, as we shall see, until the mid-1800's, allowing for almost a century of accumulation of vast capital in the treasuries of the communities, a fund which usually fell into the hands of the merchant elders of the groups.

Such was the case when the Theodosians founded their wealthiest and most important community, the Preobrazhensk Cemetery, in a suburb of Moscow in 1771. The story is a dramatic one. Moscow was

[8] On the Vyg Commune, see Zenkovsky, "Denisov Brothers," pp. 52-64; and P. G. Liubomirov, *Vygovskoe obshchezhitel'stvo* (Moscow-Saratov, 1924).

[9] Nikol'skii, *Istoriia russkoi tserkvi*, pp. 236-37; Andreev, *Raskol*, p. 157; Ryndziunskii, "Staroobriadcheskaia organizatsiia v usloviiakh razvitiia promyshlennogo kapitalizma," *Voprosy istorii religii i ateizma*, vol. I (1950), pp. 189-90. Although I cannot agree with some of his interpretations, Ryndziunskii has had access to the archives and has provided many new facts on the economic activity and the ideology of the Moscow Theodosian community; his article ranks with the more general work by Nikol'skii. An earlier study of the Theodosian community by O. Rustik, "Staroobriadcheskoe Preobrazhenskoe kladbishche (kak nakoplialis kapitaly v Moskve)" *Bor'ba klassov*, nos. 7-8 (1934), pp. 70-79, is of less value. Pierre Kovalevsky, in "Le Raskol et son rôle dans le développement industriel de la Russie," *Archives de sociologie des religions*, vol. III (1957), pp. 37-56, and Valentine Bill, in *The Forgotten Class: The Russian Bourgeoisie from the Earliest Beginnings to 1900* (New York, 1959) are the first scholars in the West to have raised the question of the business significance of the Old Believers, but in their general surveys, neither has explored the Moscow communities in any depth or detail.

being ravaged at the time by a cholera epidemic. Il'ia Kovylin, a brick merchant and Theodosian, seeing the plague as a visitation of God for man's sinful departure from the true religion, set up a pesthouse, cemetery, and place of refuge and prayer for his co-believers in Moscow. Catherine the Great, following her policy toward Old Ritualists and seeing the settlement as a useful and enlightened social service, legalized the Preobrazhensk community. This was the signal for the return of schismatics to the holy capital of pre-Nikonian days. At almost the same time the Priestists established their own community at the Old Ritualist Cemetery of the suburban village of Rogozhsk. As Old Believers flocked to Moscow and the fame of the communities spread, they expanded their operations. To the refuges for the old and sick were added numerous chapels, shops, and homes. The Moscow organizations were soon recognized as supreme by the other schismatic communities of the empire. Further legal guarantees and privileges were obtained, as in 1808, when Alexander I permitted the expansion of commercial activities by the Preobrazhensk community. By this time the growing wealth of the two schismatic centers was finding new outlets in the textile and other industries. Many of the Moscow cloth manufacturing enterprises of the early nineteenth century were founded by the Old Believers, or, rather, by the industrial entrepreneurs who emerged at this time from among the elders of the local communities or who joined the sect to get hold of capital. Utilizing the unique system of capital and labor which the ideals and organization of the Moscow schismatic groups made possible, a new class of textile industrialists appeared in the city. In the end, the second generation deserted the Old Believer communities which had provided their capital but which often prohibited them from investing profits for personal gain, while the schism itself, under the double shock of this secularization and of renewed state oppression in the last years of the reign of Nicholas I, fell into decline.

Several unique methods were employed by the Theodosian community in Moscow to build up its capital, gather its labor force, and manage its industries. They are a commentary both on the growth of private enterprise and the decay of a religious utopia, as well as an example of the disintegration of the communal principle before the force of materialistic individualism. At the beginning of the nineteenth century the Preobrazhensk community was still largely the embodiment of a social and religious ideal—the national center of a religious cult, a democratic society (which was later to be compared by some to institutions in the United States), and a refuge for the needy and the elderly supported by contributions of the faithful and the wealthy, given to enable the community to continue its charitable works and to spread the Theodosian teachings.

As a national religious center it had obtained by the turn of the century one vast source of income in the monopoly on the manufacture and distribution of sacred art and religious articles—icons, crosses, incense, holy oil, rare manuscripts, sacred books, candles, and the like. A profitable business developed from the shrewd buying and selling of religious antiques and from the manufacture and sale of imitations, copied in the ateliers of the community and sold in shops at Moscow and at the great fairs. Candles proved an important source of revenue, as they did for the Orthodox Church at that time. Members of the sect were required to use only candles manufactured at Preobrazhensk. Another source of income for the Moscow Theodosian community was the public baths built by the industrialist Grachev and used by the workers of the Old Believer factories and shelters for an admission price of 4 to 5 kopeks.[10]

In addition to this income, money poured into the Preobrazhensk treasury from schismatics in all corners of Russia in the form of gifts and bequests. The Malyshevs, for example, a wealthy merchant family, made an annual donation of 50,000 rubles and added to this a gift of 300 poods of sturgeon.[11] Legacies, however, provided the major funds for an initial capital expansion sufficient to serve as a foundation for industrial ventures. To join the commune and to enjoy the use of its shelter entailed the signing over of one's entire estate. A small amount of the total might be withheld for the personal needs of a member, but on his death even this reverted to the common fund. The Moscow police reports on the schismatic communities for 1845 provide the example of one elderly man, Semen Fomin, who bequeathed 35,000 rubles to the Theodosians upon entering their home for the aged, reserving the sum of 4,000 for himself. Upon his death, his relatives attempted in vain to secure the balance of this sum.[12] In other instances we see that

---

[10] A. A. Titov, ed., "Dnevnye dozornye zapisi o Moskovskikh raskol'nikakh," June 10, Oct. 7, Dec. 16, 27, 1845; March 8, 9, May 9, July 6, 1846; Jan. 28, Feb. 3, March 25, 1848, in *Chteniia v obshchestve istorii i drevnostei Rossiiskikh* (1885-86, 1892), section entitled "Smies," hereafter cited as "Patrol Reports," referring in all cases to the section, "Smies" of this source. These police reports are the most valuable primary source available for the economic activities of the Moscow Old Believers during the reign of Nicholas I. The published collection consists of more than four hundred printed pages of almost daily official observation, primarily of the Priestless communities from 1845 to 1848. Needless to say, the police were hostile to people they considered fanatics, and did not always distinguish between fact and rumor. The Soviet scholar, Ryndziunskii, who has had access to the original manuscripts, finds omission and distortion in the Titov edition. The economic history contained in the published documents remains reliable, I have concluded, on the basis of comparison with Ryndziunskii's own facts, quotes, and interpretation, and with the other accounts and sources, as well as on the basis of strong internal evidence. For comparison, see notes 15 and 28 below.

[11] V. Kelsiev, *Sbornik pravitel'stvennykh svedenii o raskol'nikakh* (London, 1860), vol. I, p. 55; Patrol Reports, Aug. 5, 1847.

[12] Patrol Reports, May 12, 1845.

the commune understood these legacies to be total, to include every kopek, every stick and stitch of the member's property: icons, clothing, cash, and particularly precious metals and stones. The gold and silver objects were melted down into ingots and added to the community's treasury. The commune did not hesitate to assert its claims aggressively. In one case, in the middle of the night immediately upon the death of a merchant obligated to the group, and in an effort to foil his relatives, the Preobrazhensk Cemetery dispatched its own horses and carts to haul away the deceased's property. A coachman was regularly maintained for this purpose.[13]

As the monetary capital of the commune accumulated, it was found expedient to lend to both the rich and the poor, the enterprising and the desperate. Such loans were attractive to borrowers, since they involved little or in many cases no interest. The condition of the loan was conversion to the Theodosian creed and discipline. Larger business loans usually meant the reversion of the borrower's entire estate to the commune upon his death. For serfs the loan of a sum to cover their redemption and recruitment obligation meant employment in a Preobrazhensk factory to pay off their debt. The size of some of these loans indicates the wealth of the Preobrazhensk community by the mid-nineteenth century. In 1847 the Nosov brothers, already owners of a woolen factory, were lent 500,000 rubles by the Moscow Theodosians, with no interest to pay for the first three years and a 4 percent rate thereafter. They received the sum upon their conversion to the sect.[14]

The disposal of the capital of the Preobrazhensk community—estimated to be as much as 12 million rubles at one point—was given to caretakers selected from among its wealthiest supporters. Since the organization was not permitted legal ownership of real and movable property, these men in fact came to use most of the vast capital of the commune as they saw fit, and it was used to expand their own enterprises and holdings. In the case of two of the most prominent leaders, Grigor'ev and Guchkov, this meant the creation of millionaires. Most of the first generation of Old Believer capitalists remained within the discipline and habits of their religion—they observed its rites and planned to turn over their vast fortunes to the commune. However, power over the large amounts of capital they had established could be used in quite a different way by their more materialistic sons and prospective heirs.

The treasure chest which acted as a magnet for businessmen even more powerfully attracted workers to the industries allied to the Preobrazhensk community. In 1846 the police reported the following kind of talk in villages several miles outside of Moscow: "Formerly our vil-

[13] Patrol Reports, May 2, 12, Dec. 7, 29, 1845; Kelsiev, *Sbornik o raskol'nikakh*, vol. I, p. 9.

[14] Rustik, "Staroobriadcheskoe Preobrazhenskoe kladbishche," pp. 75-76.

lage was all Orthodox, but preachers from the Preobrazhensk Cemetery began to visit us and to corrupt the women and children. The men, working in the factories, returned converted to Old Belief. These and others forsook the Church. Our priests hold their tongues about the fact that the conversions were well paid for."[15]

As perhaps a more compelling lure, conversion to Old Belief was a road to freedom for some peasants. It was also, according to the police reports, a release from land hunger and its resultant poverty and want in both private and state villages. Word that someone might readily provide a loan of money which could buy both liberty and security and might also be used to liquidate debts or pay one's way out of military obligations could not long remain hidden. Lists of rich Theodosian industrialists willing to put up a peasant's redemption were posted or circulated in Moscow.[16] The price of these loans was again conversion to Old Belief and employment in the creditor's establishment to work off the debt. This might take a lifetime of low wages. Apparently the workers as well as the industrialists preferred this form of free labor over factory employment as *obrok* serfs. One master was a lesser evil than two for all concerned—or three, since the industrialist in some cases was purchasing not only a redemption from the lord but freedom from the tsar's army.

Other segments of the labor force did not always come knocking willingly at the doors of future employers. Some had to be enticed, and many were pushed by hard necessity. Many girls and children, who made good candidates for the textile industry, were actively recruited in the villages. A number of women left the countryside for summer employment in the Theodosian industries, and some would remain hidden in workshops in Moscow or were smuggled to other cities until they could obtain urban passports. Orphans and impoverished women from the Moscow *lumpenproletariat* were brought into the community in large numbers. Pregnant girls were taken in, their children to be cared for and educated in the teachings of the sect. Free apartments were provided for many of these people, who would work at home or in the factories of the Preobrazhensk industrialists. In one section of the Lefort suburb, the industrial magnate and leader of the Moscow Theodosians, Guchkov, owned a block of thirty such houses. Elsewhere, in the area surrounding the city, the Old Believers went so far as to squat on state land, where they built factories and houses.[17] Furthermore, a schismatic community could become a hideout for lawbreakers. In Leroy-Beaulieu's words, it "offered a safe refuge to sectarians under pursuit, to deserting soldiers, to vagabonds sporting forged papers. In

---

[15] Patrol Reports, Aug. 1, 1846; also quoted in Ryndziunskii, "Staroobriadcheskaia organizatsiia," p. 209.
[16] Patrol Reports, Jan. 3, 1846.
[17] Patrol Reports, July 10, 11, Nov. 27, Dec. 24, 1845; Jan. 16, March 7, 1846.

this crowd of outlaws, the wealthy leaders always found workers at half price and blind tools."[18]

The fugitive could be hidden among the ranks of the Theodosian factory proletariat. A new urban identity could be provided in the passport of a deceased *meshchanin*, or officials could be bribed to turn over the papers of dead soldiers. A few Theodosian craftsmen became expert passport forgers. If the police were hot on someone's trail, he could be smuggled to some distant Theodosian community or refuge, as far away as Poland if necessary.[19] A kind of "underground railroad" operated in the cities of the Russian empire, most of which contained Theodosian communities in close contact with Moscow centers. The predominance of Old Believers in the coach transport business on Russian roads and highways facilitated communication in this fugitive network. The laborers in the factory of an Old Believer were also placed in a special tax category which released them from certain bothersome municipal obligations levied on ordinary workers (contributions to sickhouses, for example).[20]

If all of this made the factories of Preobrazhensk attractive, one should not describe the proletarianization of schismatic Moscow as a process whereby the leaders of the Theodosian community cynically squeezed greedy peasants, starving children, and criminals. The religious element was not absent from the motivations of employer or worker, any more than in the case of many of the businessmen who gave and borrowed from the capital of the community. Master and servant were bound not only through promissory notes but also by ties of belief and bonds forged by the state persecution they shared. They protected each other. The richer industrialists set up schools and chapels where the teachings of Old Belief could be instilled and perpetuated. For example, preachers were sent into the Guchkov factory after mealtime to spread the true religion to the workers. The habit of reading holy scripture in the mornings and evenings before and after work, or at spare moments in the shops, was cultivated by all age groups. A woman received a special salary from Guchkov to convert his factory girls to Old Belief.[21] The result was a religious training the keenness of which was noticeable to Russians and foreigners alike. Eventually, secularization would dissipate this bond of faith between workers and employers, just as it would erode the religious ethic of the businessman.

Near to the Theodosians, the equally significant Rogozhsk Priestist community, located in an eastern Moscow suburb a few miles away, followed a similar socioeconomic pattern in the building of capital and

---

[18] Leroy-Beaulieu, *Empire of the Tsars*, vol. III, p. 354.
[19] Patrol Reports, Jan. 21, Feb. 5, 10, July 5, Nov. 29, Dec. 8-10, 20, 1845; March 15, 1847.
[20] Ryndziunskii, "Staroobriadcheskaia organizatsiia," p. 205.
[21] Patrol Reports, March 15, 1845; March 7, July 15, 1846.

a labor force through conversions, legacies, concealment, forged passports, and interest-free loans.[22] The Rogozhsk community, even as Mel'nikov described it in decline in the late nineteenth century, remained an impressive example of a highly organized business and charitable organization. In addition to the cemetery and several churches and chapels, the walled compound contained many poorhouses and homes for the aged of both sexes, convents, an orphanage, a school, an insane asylum, and a reception center, many of these equipped with central kitchens and dining halls. These establishments were supported by the community treasury, although some received money from wealthy merchants and industrialists, who also endowed several dozens of families living in small private homes erected in the same area. At the center of the enclosure was a larger two-story structure which served as the administrative center of the Rogozhsk community. This building contained a large meeting room for the forty-odd elders and caretakers of the organization, business offices, a kitchen and dining room, archives, a crypt, and a rich library of rare books and manuscripts.[23] In the 1830's over one thousand people were estimated to have been living within the Rogozhsk enclosure proper. The number that passed through its shelters and settled into a new urban way of life in the factories, shops, homes, and apartments of the surrounding area was much greater; in 1825, the larger congregation numbered perhaps 68,000. In this larger area were located the establishments of at least seventy-four industrialists who during the same period were connected with the community.[24]

The Theodosian community at nearby Preobrazhensk was even larger and more impressive than the Rogozhsk enclosure. As Baron Haxthausen saw it in the late 1840's, there were "two enormous fortress-like quadrangles: high walls and towers, large arched gateways, above which rose the numerous cupolas of several churches." Behind the massive gates, taken from an abandoned palace of Peter the Great, were shelters for the poor and aged, hospitals, madhouses, stores, kitchens, and stables, as at Rogozhsk. Unlike the family arrangements of the Priestist community, the Theodosian community segregated the sexes, with one quadrangle reserved for the women. Each quadrangle housed at least a thousand inmates. Fifty to sixty persons occupied each dormitory, which was connected to a chapel. No children were to be seen.

The Preobrazhensk community had more than one hundred officers, ranging from the Prior, Treasurer, and Curators at the top to numerous

22 Patrol Reports, Dec. 19, 1844; Mel'nikov, *Sochinenie*, vol. III, pp. 237-38.
23 Mel'nikov, *Sochinenie*, vol. III, pp. 225-36.
24 "Rogozhskoe kladbishche," in *Entsiklopedicheskii slovar*, vol. XXVI (Brockhaus-Efron; St. Petersburg, 1899), pp. 892-93; S. V. Bakhrushin, in *Istoriia Moskvy* (Moscow, 1954), vol. III, p. 295.

clerks and servants for the various shelters and chapels. An iconographer was retained. The Prior (*nastoiatel'*) was the formal head of the community, but the police reports refer to the richest industrialist of the Moscow Theodosians as his "co-ruler." The actual title of the several wealthy businessmen who ruled Preobrazhensk along with the Prior was "Curator" (*popuchitel'*). The leading businessman controlled the economic life of the community and owned many houses and tracts of land. He ran its industries. The big merchants and industrialists, together with other leaders of the community, formed a council of twenty-six in the 1840's, which met every Friday morning to discuss and conduct the business and government of Preobrazhensk. It should be noted that this organizational pattern with its merchant control was repeated in the communities of other sects of Old Believers in the Moscow suburbs, even the very small ones. A nearby splinter community of only thirty-five "marrying" Shore Dwellers had the merchant Morozov as its chief Curator and custodian of a capital of over 80,000 rubles.[25]

By the mid-nineteenth century, the area around the Preobrazhensk community became the most heavily industrialized part of Moscow. Most of the enterprises were small in scale, not much larger than shops. The recent Soviet student of the Moscow Theodosians, Ryndziunskii, considers only thirty-two of more than two hundred establishments located in the bordering Lefort suburb to have been true factories, that is, by his definition, employing more than twenty-five workers. Among these, of course, were included some very large operations for their times, such as the main Guchkov factory, with a force in the 1840's of nearly one thousand, a number which doubled by the end of the reign of Nicholas I. The Alekseev factory, also located in the Lefort district, employed 645, and there were several others which counted a staff of over one hundred.[26]

The walled compounds which housed the chapels and shelter houses of the Preobrazhensk and Rogozhsk communities thus became large-scale operations which served both as the headquarters of nationwide cults and the nerve centers of local industrial complexes. "They became a combination of convent, seminary, and chamber of commerce, a consistory and an exchange.[27] Not just shrines for pilgrims from distant parts of the empire, the Moscow communities were convenient as well to Old Believer merchants from provincial Russia as financial

---

[25] A. von Haxthausen, *The Russian Empire, Its People, Institutions and Resources* (London, 1856), vol. I, pp. 275-76; Patrol Reports, Dec. 11, 1846; Jan. 20, Feb. 10, June 11, 1847.

[26] Ryndziunskii, "Staroobriadcheskaia organizatsiia," pp. 205-06, 209; Rustik, "Staroobriadcheskaia Preobrazhenskoe kladbishche," p. 72.

[27] Leroy-Beaulieu, *Empire of the Tsars*, vol. III, p. 354. The heavy industrialization of the Preobrazhensk area can be seen in *Istoriia Moskvy*, vol. III, map facing p. 320.

centers where business could be transacted and deals made, new ventures launched. From the Moscow suburbs, Theodosian influence spread to an estimated thirty-eight villages or hamlets in the area of the capital, while the Priestists of Rogozhsk fanned out to dominate the important Russian fairs as far as Siberia and Central Asia.[28]

"The firm and stable organization of these rude masses," commented Baron von Haxthausen on his visit to the Preobrazhensk Cemetery at mid-century, "which has already lasted so long, without any definite system, theology, nobles, or priesthood, is something marvellous. The remarkably powerful spirit of association and the unparalleled communal institutions which have sprung from it, alone explain the phenomenon.[29]

This romanticization, with its Slavophile overtones, was written at a time when the Old Believer communities of Moscow actually were undergoing a rapid disintegration, a process which had been in evidence for at least two decades and one which Haxthausen himself elsewhere recognized.[30] The communal solidarity of Preobrazhensk and Rogozhsk was giving way to a spirit of capitalist individualism and private-property consciousness, while the puritanism, piety, and nationalism of the first century of the Schism were losing the battle with Westernism, secularism, and materialism.

The general causes and obvious symptoms of this disintegration were in evidence by the 1830's. The growth of large personal fortunes and involved business holdings, as well as simply a general rise in the material situation of many members, particularly of the Theodosian community, caused frustration within the cramping restraints of the old puritanism. A few members still held to the injunction of celibacy, but many wished to have conjugal unions and families dignified by formal community recognition. There was a growing reluctance to obliterate private estates that had been built up painfully over the years or to surrender fortunes the fruits of which people had been accustomed to enjoy and which they had jealously come to consider rightful and exclusive inheritances. The result of these growing tensions was the withdrawal of members of the Theodosian creed to join other sects, such as the Shore Dwellers, who recognized marriage. Some withdrew to form new, small splinter groups like the Moninists, whose allowance of marriage invited the secession of a number of wealthy merchants from the Preobrazhensk Cemetery as early as 1812. Some of the Theo-

[28] Patrol Reports, Aug. 1, 1846; see also Ryndziunskii, "Staroobriadcheskaia organizatsiia," p. 209.

[29] Haxthausen, *Russian Empire*, vol. I, p. 277.

[30] Haxthausen, *Russian Empire*, vol. I, p. 272: "The Starovertsi in the large cities—Moscow, St. Petersburg, and Riga—merchants and manufacturers who have grown rich, only remain true to their sect for the first generation; the next cut off their beards, throw off the kaftan, and put on coats; and with the old customs and dress, their religious notions also disappear."

dosians of St. Petersburg made an even earlier and far more radical break; they joined the Westernized society of the capital, adopting its fashions in European clothing, abandoning the old prohibitions, and even marrying outside the sect.[31]

This foreshadowed a general tendency among all of the Old Believer industrial communities by the 1830's and 1840's. Like the "fathers" and "sons" Turgenev described among the nobility and intelligentsia during the same period, a new materialistic and Westernizing second generation emerged from amidst the Old Believers. Businessmen rather than religious leaders, they found Westernization far more conducive to their profit-making and their pastimes than the old Russian austerities. Like the Nihilists, they repudiated their heritage. As Leroy-Beaulieu later reflected on a process that continued for some decades:

> To the great scandal of good provincial souls, young Old Believers are already seen in Moscow smoking, shaving, dancing, frequenting the theaters. Wealth, which has begun the Raskol's social emancipation, will end by accomplishing its intellectual emancipation also, so that, after having been temporarily a source of strength, money and the conditions it creates will become a cause of weakness and undermine the Raskol's doctrines and principles.[32]

In vain the "fathers" of the schismatic suburbs of the old capital, like their Slavophile contemporaries in the salons of the Moscow aristocracy, attempted to preserve the past. In 1846 we see Semen Kozmin, one of the Theodosian leaders of the old generation, banishing from the chapels and from among the new arrivals to the community all who were wearing European clothing or who sported Western fashions.[33]

The tsarist government unwittingly accelerated the secularization of the schismatic middle class of Moscow through persecution. The Old Believer communities came under increasing police surveillance in the 1840's in the fear that they were hotbeds of heresy, subversion, and corruption. The fact of cloistered communal living and the existence of conjugal bonds unsanctified by the marriage sacrament were compounded by rumors and lurid reports of sexual immorality and concubinage concealed behind the walls of Preobrazhensk and Rogozhsk. Politically the Theodosians had long before compromised themselves in the eyes of the state by the suspicious dealings of certain of the Moscow community with Napoleon in 1812.[34] It was also believed by many that the Old Believers were engaged in counterfeiting, profiteering, and other criminal activities.

[31] Patrol Reports, Dec. 1844; Nikol'skii, *Istoriia russkoi tserkvi*, pp. 237-38.
[32] Leroy-Beaulieu, *Empire of the Tsars*, vol. III, p. 343.
[33] Patrol Reports, Jan. 15, 1846.
[34] Kelsiev, *Sbornik o raskol'nikakh*, vol. I, pp. 36-38; Patrol Reports, March 7, 1846.

In 1847, after two decades of harassment, the government struck with full vigor. The asylums and homes of Preobrazhensk and Rogozhsk were seized and put under direct state administration. The altars of the church were padlocked. Some leaders were arrested and banished. Finally, the Theodosians were forced to marry officially, an obligation which many no doubt welcomed.

The reaction to this persecution was no longer resistance, suicide, and flight, as had been the case a century earlier, but rather compromise, disavowal, and indifference. In the 1850's, many leaders of the Theodosian community rejoined the Orthodox Church in the *Edinoverie* movement, a kind of halfway house for the Old Believers sponsored by the government to recapture dissenters for the official faith.[35] Others had become secularized and Westernized businessmen for whom religious duties were of little concern and who abandoned the precarious status of Old Believer with ease. A half century of heavy tsarist oppression descended on the Moscow *Raskol'nik* communities, but they managed to survive it, as well as to endure the 1917 revolution and the atheist regime which followed. Over 100,000 Old Believers of the two main sects still inhabit Moscow,[36] and Rogozhsk, with its impressive Pokrovskii cathedral and numerous icons, still stands. The state superintendent of the Old Believers is the descendant of a wealthy Moscow manufacturing family.

The story of another such family—the Guchkovs—during the last century of tsarism epitomizes this entire area of Russian social and economic history. Four generations of Guchkovs illustrate three stages of social evolution: the original accumulation of capital by the religious leader of a dissenting group; the building of an industrial empire by his secularized, capitalist sons and grandsons; and, finally, a fourth generation making a decisive move from business to politics. It is a story that is not unique to Russia, but the Russian overtones are unmistakable.

The founder of what became one of the great industrial fortunes in Moscow was Fedor Alekseevich Guchkov, an *obrok*-paying serf who was permitted by his master to migrate to the city at the end of the eighteenth century to set up a weaving shop. In less than three decades he had developed one of the largest woolen factories in Russia and had put up the small fortune necessary to buy himself and his family out of serfdom. Fedor Guchkov's devotion to business was surpassed by his loyalty to the Preobrazhensk community, which he had joined and of which he remained one of the leaders until his political exile in the repressions of the last years of the reign of Nicholas I. Devout in his belief, he was content to retain his beard and peasant-overcoat and an essentially old-Russian religious and personal life. His factories he

[35] Nikol'skii, *Istoriia russkoi tserkvi*, p. 296.
[36] W. Kolarz, *Religion in the Soviet Union* (London, 1961), pp. 140-41.

viewed as congregations of the faithful and as schools as much as business enterprises. In 1825 he transferred to his sons, who had been trained in the business, the control of his factories. The elder Guchkov continued to assume a major responsibility for the business affairs and the exchequer of the Theodosian community. Since his own property and enterprises were bound intimately with the financial affairs of the group, as a way of both conforming with government property restrictions and deceiving the state as to the holdings of the community, Guchkov's sons soon came to assume a major voice in the disposal of the Preobrazhensk purse, although they stood outside the formal religious leadership of the group. Even after 1847, when they became converted to the less restricting Shore Dweller sect to further consolidate the family fortune, they retained this control. By 1853, the main plants of the Guchkovs employed 1,850 workers and were mechanized, producing goods to the value of 700,000 rubles yearly. In addition, they were founding new factories and farming out work to hundreds of homes and shops in the Preobrazhensk area.[37]

Ivan and Efim Guchkov were modern businessmen who dressed in Western clothing, received Western educations, and traveled to Europe. They devoted themselves fully to the expansion of their enterprises and fortunes, and when their religious background became an obstacle or a disadvantage, it was sacrificed to the interests of the business. Their conversion to the Shore Dweller sect was followed in 1853 by their rejoining the Orthodox Church in the *Edinoverie* movement. Efim's son, Ivan, remained in the business but also served in urban government posts and in the imperial administration. The fourth generation was essentially *rentier*—they closed down the family business, invested their money in stocks and bonds, and turned their energy and enthusiasm almost wholly to politics. Nikolai Guchkov was the mayor of Moscow for several years. Aleksander Guchkov—adventurer, public servant, liberal politician of the last years of the tsarist regime, Octobrist leader in the Duma, and Minister of War for the Provisional Government—best represents the final variant of the several generations of the Russian schism and of the nineteenth-century Russian middle class. It is interesting to note that one of Guchkov's colleagues in the early leadership of the government of 1917 was the liberal Minister of Trade and Industry, A. S. Konovalov, heir to another famous textile enterprise, which also had been founded by a serf and Old Believer in the early nineteenth century.[38] The small Russian in-

[37] Patrol Reports, 1845-46, passim; Ryndziunskii, "Staroobriadcheskaia organizatsiia," pp. 204, 208, 214, 218-19.

[38] For details on the early Guchkov family history, I am indebted to Mr. Louis Menashe, who has examined a family chronicle, formerly owned and probably written by the late Aleksander Guchkov and now in the possession of Madame L. Csaszar of Paris. See also Patrol Reports, July 15, 17, Aug. 21, and Nov. 5, 23, 1847, for some interesting data on Fedor Guchkov's property and

dustrialist bourgeoisie had attained partial political power, if only briefly.

The business activities of the Old Believers provoked both hostility and sympathy on the part of their contemporary Russians and in the subsequent century produced a variety of interpretations as to the motivations and significance of the *raskol'nik* entrepreneur. Policemen saw crime at the source of the Old Believer's wealth—counterfeiting, smuggling, profiteering in scarce goods, and the raiding of legacies; "the milch-cow of rascally millionaires," said one.[39] For some observers, the appeal of Old Belief for factory workers and entrepreneurs alike was purely a materialistic one, a new way of getting money and labor rather than a better road to salvation. P. I. Mel'nikov, a lifetime student of the movement, concluded:

> Its propagandizing was done not in the chapels and retreats of the Rogozhsk and Preobrazhensk cemeteries, but in factories, plants, in shops and stores. Sermons were given not from the pulpits of Rogozhsk priests or Preobrazhensk preceptors, but from spindles and machines. The preaching of the schism acted not on the heart, not on the mind of the adepts, but on their pocketbooks. Not hopes of felicity beyond the grave, but a true accounting of the good things of this world brought new converts to the Rogozhsk cemetery. In these forceful sermons, not a single word was uttered on religious subjects; the discourse turned rather on rewards, salaries, loans, the paying of debts, redemption from serfdom, and the buying off of military service obligations. Such sermons were irresistible.[40]

Other writers, during the Populist period, viewed the business activities of the *raskol'niki* sympathetically as a democratic expression of the Russian people against the state, a kind of economic struggle following upon the earlier religious and political resistance of the schismatics. The revolutionary intelligentsia of the same era saw potential allies in the Old Believers. In our own century Soviet historians have alternated between praising the Old Believers as a progressive democratic movement in conflict with tsarism and condemning them as capitalistic exploiters operating behind a screen of religion.[41] In the West such distinguished scholars as Leroy-Beaulieu and Max Weber both

industrial holdings, his factory school, mortgage buying, and serf redeeming. On the Konovalov's, see Roger Portal, "Du servage à la bourgeoisie: la famille Konovalov," *Revue des études slaves*, vol. XXXVIII (1961), 143-50; and Ch. Iuksimovich, *Manufakturnaia promyshlennost v proshlom i nastoiashchem* (Moscow, 1915).

[39] Quoted in Leroy-Beaulieu, *Empire of the Tsars*, vol. III, p. 340.

[40] Mel'nikov, *Sochinenie*, vol. III, p. 206. Brief statements of the main interpretations of tsarist times can be found in Mel'nikov, *Sochinenie*, vol. III, pp. 209-11; and Andreev, *Raskol*, pp. 160-61.

[41] For the Soviet views, see note 9 above and a discussion in Kolarz, *Religion in the Soviet Union*, pp. 129-31.

suggested comparisons of the social status, ethos, and prosperity of the Russian Old Believers and sectarians with European Calvinists, Quakers, and Methodists and such groups as the Copts, Parsees, and Armenians of the Orient.[42] It should be noted, however, that none of the authors in the West devoted any comprehensive or systematic study to the problems and relationships of Russian business and religious history; they have given us only passing references. What might appear to be a tempting model in the Weberian analysis of the Protestant ethic and the rise of capitalism in Western Europe could easily be misleading when set in the Russian context. At any rate, if his few observations of the Old Believers and sectarians provide food for thought, Weber never attempted an application to Russia of his more general theories of entrepreneurship.

The history of the Moscow Old Believers suggests the following conclusions. Making themselves felt in their surroundings like outcast religious and national minorities in many parts of the world, they played a limited but not insignificant role in initiating the commercial and industrial modernization of the hitherto traditional agrarian society of the Moscow region. Persecuted, relegated to a position of social inferiority, cut off from the normal channels of political, bureaucratic, and agrarian power and privilege, yet consigned to an outcast legal status which opened to them a commercial freedom not permitted the traditional, recognized classes of society, the Moscow Old Believers, as a matter of belief and survival, closed ranks in austere, disci-

---

[42] Leroy-Beaulieu, *Empire of the Tsars*, vol. III, pp. 338-39: "The *Starovier*, who does not smoke and drinks little, finds in temperance and economy a short cut to competence. Yet this is only a partial explanation. There is a reason of a higher order, one which we encounter in most religions, in almost all races which have long been downtrodden. Persecution and disqualifying laws, by debarring oppressed sects from taking any interest in public affairs, turn them perforce into the channel of private enterprise—into commerce. Their financial capabilities, strengthened by practice and accumulated by heredity, and by becoming a sort of natural gift or inborn faculty. The Jews all over the world, the Armenians in the East, the Parsees in India, the Copts in Egypt, are, in their different ways, living illustrations of this one law.

"The mercantile prosperity of the Old Believers compares favorably with that of sundry Protestant sects in England and the United States. There are certain religious forms laid out on simple lines, inculcating severe, even morose, moral principles, which are suited to certain social classes and to a certain mediocre average of culture, doctrines of what might be called a bourgeois—some would say a 'philistine'—stand and which easily fit the mind of the merchant or businessman and lead to fortune by a surer and more regular road. In the *Raskol'nik* as in the Puritan, the Quaker, or the Methodist—in the Great Russian as in the Anglo-Saxon—practical sense goes very well with the theological mind, and a turn for business is not incompatible with religious delusions."

See also, Max Weber, *Wirtschaft und Gesellschaft* (4th edn., Tübingen, 1956), vol. I, p. 292; and *The Protestant Ethic and the Spirit of Capitalism* (New York, 1958), pp. 39, 189-90, 197. Weber also had pertinent observations in his studies of Oriental society and of the city, although no other direct comments on the Russian religious dissenters.

plined, self-sufficient religious communities. These communities came to assume many of the commercial and, at the beginning of the factory age in parts of Russia, industrial functions of the society. Money, as Leroy-Beaulieu observed, became "its *nervus rerum*, the ruble has all along been its great weapon, for self-defense and conversion."[43]

The significance of the Old Believers for the formation of a Muscovite industrial working force in the early nineteenth century is comparable to the role attributed to the enclosure movement in England or to the Irish migration to the United States. For all the differences in tradition and geography, each was an important part of the process of getting peasants off the land and into cities, shops, and factories. To be sure, the extent to which the Theodosian community facilitated this modernizing function is by no means equal to that of the transatlantic Celtic migration or the English enclosures and poor laws, even if we add to the Theodosian community the several tens of thousands of workers in the equally significant Rogozhsk community, as well as the Shore Dweller and other smaller schismatic and sectarian factions in Moscow. Nevertheless, through this process, a substantial segment of the textile enterprises of the city and the surrounding towns could undergo a first stage of industrialization and the formation of a factory working class.

In the case of the Moscow schismatic enterprises, the institutional aspect was more important than the ideological in the accumulation of capital and the organization of production. Not individual capitalists moved by a worldly ascetic "calling" in the accumulation of wealth in business affairs so much as a group capital through legacies, contributions, and a communal way of life and enterprise determined the economic expansion of the Moscow Old Believers. The Russian communal tradition, glorified by the Slavophiles and the *narodniki*, asserted itself, although not for long. Money and commerce brought with it materialistic individualism, property consciousness, and the appearance of a class of secularized, private entrepreneurs.

Jewish Enterprise and Banking

The Old Believers were persecuted religious sects, outcast minorities lacking full protection of the law, who withdrew for survival into self-sufficient cooperative communities and began to accumulate the money which provided their only protection and power. The result was the creation of an industrial bourgeoisie and the growth of a modern textile industry and a working class in the Moscow suburbs. To what extent was this process repeated by other outcast religious minorities and sects in the Russian empire? Little is known of the economic activities of the Georgian and Armenian minorities of the Caucasus

[43] Leroy-Beaulieu, *Empire of the Tsars*, vol. III, p. 339.

or the Moslems of Central Asia. However significant the commercial traditions of these peoples, their function in the industrial development of the Russian middle east would have to await the quickening of the economic growth of this area in the last decades of the nineteenth century. Little has been written about the history of capitalism among the Protestant Germans of the Baltic provinces. Soviet scholars recently have provided brief studies of the industrial development of Estonia in the late eighteenth and early nineteenth centuries. Concerning the Baltic German merchants, L. A. Loone concluded that their enterprises "were smaller and usually short lived." The largest factories were established by Russians, and in even larger number by European Germans, Germans from St. Petersburg who had been naturalized as Russians, and Baltic barons, such as the Ungern-Sternbergs. O. O. Karma, however, found German entrepreneurs and craftsmen running the largest Estonian factories during the first quarter of the nineteenth century. In Riga, which was the major industrial and commercial center of the Russian Baltic by 1850, Germans controlled the business life and the local government. They owned many of the sugar refineries, cigar and candle factories, breweries, and other industries important to the city, which were founded in the 1830's, '40's, and '50's.[44]

More information is available on the business activities of the Russian Jews during the first half of the nineteenth century. Similar to the official and unofficial slander of the Old Believers, antisemitic bias has distorted some of this material. By the reign of Nicholas I, the Jews were far from being wealthy exploiters of the Christian masses of Russia's western borderlands, a sin of which they were later accused. A large minority of the 1,041,301 Russian Jews in 1847 had come to constitute a *lumpenproletariat*—unskilled, unemployed, and stuffed into ghettos. Another substantial group roamed the countryside as peddlers or smuggled goods across the European frontier. Thousands worked as tailors. A smaller number ran saloons.[45] A small group became wealthy through the export trade. Here, the statistics are flagrantly contradictory. A frequently cited figure from the mid-nineteenth-century tsarist statistician, Koeppen, indicates that in 1851, 467 Jews were first guild merchants. This would amount to about one-fourth of the total number of the wealthiest merchants in Russia at

[44] See L. A. Loone, "Iz istorii promyshlennogo perevorota v Estonii," *Voprosy istorii* (1952), no. 5, pp. 94-95; O. O. Karma, "Ocherk razvitiia manufakturnoi stadii promyshlennosti v Estonii," *Genezis kapitalizma v promyshlennosti* (Moscow, 1963), pp. 166-68, 171-72, 185. On Riga, see Alfred Bilmanis, *A History of Latvia* (Princeton, 1951), pp. 240-41; Technischer Verein zu Riga, *Beiträge zur Geschichte der Industrie Rigas* (Riga, 1910-11), vols. I-III; G. A. Esh, "Razvitie promyshlennosti v Latvii v pervoi polovine XIX v.," *Genezis kapitalizma v promyshlennosti*, especially pp. 214, 219.

[45] See the figures in Salo Baron, *The Russian Jew Under Tsars and Soviets* (New York, 1964), pp. 98, 102-03, 114.

that time. The Soviet scholar, Iuditskii, however, found an 1852 Kiev manuscript which listed only sixty-eight Jewish first guild merchants.[46] Iuditskii's statistics pertained to the eleven western provinces of the Russian empire, where the Jewish population was concentrated. Since first guild Jewish merchants were not permitted business dealings outside of the pale until 1859, this figure could be taken as representative of all Jewish merchants of the highest guild in Russia. Iuditskii's figures are borne out by another official report of 1849-1850. The author[47] of this report, which dealt specifically with Jewish society in Russia, believed that the "chief and most cherished activity of the Jews is commerce." However, he had to admit that only 3.47 percent of the Russian Jewish population (excluding those in Volhynia) were engaged in such pursuits. The remainder, according to the same report, were involved in agriculture or belonged to the urban masses. Although the tsarist regime encouraged Jewish agricultural colonization, over 90 percent of Russia's Jews remained in towns or cities during the early nineteenth century.[48] It can be concluded that most of these were either paupers or petty shopkeepers and craftsmen.

Out of this impoverished mass, a small group of wealthy entrepreneurs and financiers emerged during the nineteenth century. This Jewish bourgeoisie was to play a not insignificant role in the industrialization of the Western provinces of the Russian empire. Similar to the serf industrialists of Moscow and Ivanovo, they emerged in the 1820's and 1830's as an economic force, particularly in the Ukraine and Belorussia.

Two scholars, one in the Soviet Union and one in the United States, have revised the traditional view held by Dubnow and others of the insignificant role of Jewish industry in Russian economic development during the nineteenth century. The Soviet historian Iuditskii, utilizing archives in Kiev and of the tsarist Department of Manufactures and Domestic Trade, accorded the Ukrainian Jewish industrialists of the early nineteenth century an "important place in the subsequent development of the textile industry in that area." Professor Salo Baron, surveying the entire century, sees a "major participation of Jewish entrepreneurs in Russian industrial development."[49]

The origins of this industrial bourgeoisie, as Iuditskii points out,

[46] Baron, *The Russian Jew*, table, p. 104; on Koeppen, see P. A. Berlin, *Russkaia Burzhuaziia v staroe i novoe vremia* (Moscow, 1922), pp. 70-71.

[47] Identified by G. B. Sliozberg as B. Miliutin. See G. B. Sliozberg, *Pravovye i ekonomicheskie sostoianie evreev v Rossii* (St. Petersburg, 1907), p. 113. The report is entitled: *Ustroistvo i sostoianie evreiskikh obshchestv v Rossii* (St. Petersburg, 1849-1850).

[48] Baron, *The Russian Jew*, pp. 96-97, estimates only 100,000 by 1900.

[49] A. D. Iuditskii, "Evreiskaia burzhuaziia i evreiskii proletariat v tekstil'noi promyshlennosti pervoi poloviny xix v.," *Istoricheskii sbornik* (1935), p. 117; Baron, *The Russian Jew*, p. 106. On Dubnow's view, see S. Dubnow, *History of the Jews in Russia and Poland* (Philadelphia, 1916), vol. I, p. 363.

can be traced to the reign of Alexander I in time, and in place to the great estates of Russian Poland as well as the ghettos of such cities as Vilna, Berdichev, and Brody. The Jews of this area had traditionally maintained business contact with the local landlords, serving as stewards, cashiers, commercial agents, and rent collectors. By the early nineteenth century, some of the great Polish magnates of the area, following the pattern of the Russian nobility, established factories on their estates to process various products of the land. Some also built woolens factories. During the Napoleonic war years and the decade following, Jewish entrepreneurs leased some of these estate factories, or built new ones on rented land. In Kiev province, for example, a Berdichev Jew, Lisanskii, leased in the late 1820's a woolens factory owned by Count Potocki-Kalinowski. The plant consisted of four buildings and employed 276 men.[50]

These emerging Jewish entrepreneurs obtained their capital from at least three sources other than what they were able to accumulate as local dealers—general store, inn or saloon keepers. Many Jews were active traders at the Ukrainian fairs. At some, they dominated the commercial life. Most, however, were impoverished peddlers who crowded the streets. The Slavophile, Ivan Aksakov, has left us a vivid picture of this commercial *lumpenproletariat* of Russian Poland in the 1850's:

> Jews are especially numerous at the Ilinsk fair: like locusts, they descend on the city, selling goods in stores and in shops, in huts, under sheds and from tents, wholesale and retail, behind counters, peddling, and in private homes. Then the Sabbath comes: the Jews disappear, and in the city is a deathly silence . . . around each Jewish wholesale merchant a hundred petty, poor Jews crowd, who secure goods from the wholesale store to sell . . . they lend to commerce a certain feverish vitality, running, bustling, making deals, accompanying each word with rapid gestures; everywhere, their quick, guttural speech; everywhere, with each step, they stop visitors with offers of goods.[51]

From this struggle for survival wholesale merchants had already emerged by Aksakov's time, as well as Jewish bankers, contractors, and teamsters who worked with them. The biggest of these merchants were wealthy entrepreneurs who belonged to the Russian guilds and conducted trade not only at the major Ukrainian fairs, but in Belorussia, and beyond, at the Leipzig fair and in Austria.[52]

A second source for Jewish industrial capital in the Ukraine during the early nineteenth century were the funds accumulated by money-

---

[50] Iuditskii, "Evreiskaia burzhuaziia," pp. 116, 123-24.

[51] Ivan Aksakov, *Izsledovanie o torgovle na ukrainskikh iarmarkakh* (St. Petersburg, 1858), p. 36.

[52] Aksakov, *Izsledovanie o ukrainskikh iarmarkakh*, p. 36.

lenders. Berdichev, a Jewish center in the Ukraine, had over eight banks by 1849, with business running into hundreds of thousands of rubles yearly, and financial ties throughout the Russian empire. Some of the bigger Berdichev moneylenders were in fact private bankers by the mid-nineteenth century and were branching out into industrial ventures. The Halperins are a case in point.[53]

A most important source of support and money was the Russian government. The tsar's armies during the Napoleonic period were desperately short of cloth. The government was willing to pay well for army woolen cloth and to lend money to those willing to produce it. Moreover the government during the reign of Alexander I began to evince an interest in teaching useful occupations to the Jewish paupers of the western borderlands. This could be done in factories. Jewish entrepreneurs were encouraged to petition for loans and contracts, which they did.

With the state smiling upon it, the Jewish woolens industry of Russian Poland grew rapidly. By 1828, there were seventy-five woolens factories owned by Jews in this area, producing almost 320,000 yards of cloth. This put Jewish entrepreneurs in the forefront of the most important industry at that time in the Ukraine. Volhynia was the center. Perhaps the biggest Jewish woolens industrialist of Volhynia in the late 1820's was Joseph Bernstein, who owned twelve factories employing 740 men.[54]

The Jewish woolens factories of the Ukraine did not develop within the walls of tight-knit religious communities similar to the Old Believer textile enterprises of Moscow. Nevertheless, their labor force, numbering 2,185 by the late 1820's, consisted almost entirely of coreligionists in many factories. Some factories were intended to provide jobs and teach crafts to the paupers of the ghetto as well as to make money. The wealthiest Jews assumed the role of protectors of their less fortunate brethren.[55]

Another estate industry from which Jewish entrepreneurs could build large-scale enterprises was beet sugar refining. Several great sugar fortunes were founded in the mid-nineteenth century by Jews. Railroads also offered an opportunity. The first of the several Jewish railroad kings of the Russian empire—the Warsaw banker, Herman Epstein—was active in the financing of railway construction in the 1840's. The next decade witnessed the rise of the powerful Jewish banking house of Gunzburg in St. Petersburg. These were the foundations for the major role that the Russian Jewish businessman came to

[53] Iuditskii, "Evreiskaia burzhuaziia," pp. 108-12, 116-17; on Berdichev banking, see also S. Ia. Borovoi, *Kredit i banki seredina xvii v. – 1861 g.* (Moscow, 1958), p. 237.
[54] Iuditskii, "Evreiskaia burzhuaziia," pp. 119-20, 125.
[55] Iuditskii, "Evreiskaia burzhuaziia," pp. 113, 129, 133.

play in tsarist capitalism and the industrialization of the western part of the Russian empire by 1900. By the end of the century, he had a dominant position in railroads in that area, as well as steam transportation on the rivers. He controlled substantial sectors of the petroleum, sugar, and textile industries. His banking activities were of international significance.[56]

The making of a Russian capitalist and the founding of one of the great Jewish fortunes in the early nineteenth century is typified by the career of Baron Joseph Gunzburg. Like the Russian Guchkovs, Morozovs, Konovalovs, or Ryabushinskiis, the Gunzburgs during the course of a century moved from obscurity, poverty, and a life framed by religious traditions and concerns, to business wealth, political involvement, humanitarian activities, and the patronage of art and scholarship.

The Gunzburgs,[57] in the course of the fifteenth to eighteenth centuries, moved from Portugal to Bavaria to Poland, picking up their name along the way from the Bavarian town of Gunzburg, near Ulm. The family was a rabbinical one of great repute, with notable scholarly representatives. In the late eighteenth century, Naphtal Herz Gunzburg broke with this tradition to enter business life, the first in his family to do so. Why he did this and what his new activities were we do not know. We can surmise that the economies of Russia and Poland were changing rapidly at the end of the eighteenth century, and that new commercial opportunities presented themselves for the enterprising member of an outcast minority.[58] The last years of the Napoleonic wars found Naphtal Herz's son, Gabriel Jacob, in Vitebsk, where Joseph (Evzel) Gunzburg, the founder of the Gunzburg banking fortune, was born in 1813. Joseph Gunzburg learned business as the cashier for a big landlord. Through the influence of this magnate and the esteem with which the Gunzburg family was held in the Jewish communities of western Russia, Joseph was able to obtain highly lucrative government liquor concessions. By the late 1840's, he controlled the liquor trade for the Ukraine and the Crimea, a vast and wealthy sinecure. His friendships extended up to the Minister of Finances,

[56] Detailed in Baron, *The Russian Jew*, pp. 106-13.

[57] The best accounts of the early history of the Gunzburgs, upon which I base this analysis are: G. B. Sliozberg, *Baron G. O. Gintsburg, ego zhizn i deiatel'nost* (Paris, 1933) and the articles on the family in *Evreiskaia entsiklopediia*, vol. VI (St. Petersburg, no date). There is a French edition of the biography, *Baron H. O. de Gunzbourg, sa vie et son oeuvre* (Paris, 1933). There are many spellings of the name.

[58] Professor Bert Hozelitz summarizes the general process in his critique of Sombart's *The Jews and Modern Capitalism* (Glencoe, Illinois, 1951), introduction to the American edition p. xxiv: "Not the legal philosophy or the religious rationalism of Judaism were responsible factors for the development of capitalism, but the growth of opportunities for gain from commercial and financial transactions, the need to adapt to a foreign, hostile world. . . . Not the Jews as they were made capitalism, but capitalism made the Jews what they are."

Vronchenko, and it was seen to it by the latter that the Emperor awarded Gabriel Jacob Gunzburg the prestigious title of Hereditary Honorable Citizen.

In 1859, not without Gunzburg's influence, the tsarist government lifted partially the Pale restrictions of the Russian Jews. First, guild merchants and holders of university degrees were permitted residence and business privileges in other cities of the empire. By this time, Joseph Gunzburg had become a spokesman and protector of the Jewish community in Russia as well as of his own vast commercial interests. The 1859 edict was the beginning of a series of laws during the reign of Alexander II which opened the Pale barriers for the Russian Jews. In the same year, the banking house of Joseph Gunzburg was established in St. Petersburg. Soon after, the greatest bank until that time in Russia, Stieglitz and Company, was liquidated, when its owner, Baron Alexander Stieglitz, became president of the newly created Russian State Bank.[59] The Gunzburg bank inherited much of the Stieglitz business and soon became one of the major banks of St. Petersburg and of Europe. The House of Gunzburg maintained connections with the great Jewish bankers of Hamburg, Berlin, Frankfurt, and Paris. It set up its own branch in Paris, as well as the first commercial banks of Kiev and Odessa. It was destined to take an important hand in the financing of Russian railroads.

By the 1850's, Joseph Gunzburg's son and successor, Horace Gunzburg, was taking over the direction of the family enterprises. The father retired to Paris in 1857, building a home on the Rue Tilsit. He became increasingly involved in philanthropic activities. He also continued to act as a spokesman and leader of the Russian Jewish community. In 1863, he founded the Society for the Propagation of Culture Among the Jews in Russia, for which he acquired about 125,000 acres of Crimean land for agricultural colonization. In 1872, along with his son, he was made a Baron by the Duke of Hesse-Darmstadt, a hereditary title, which was recognized by the Duke's brother-in-law, Tsar Alexander II. Russia had her first and only titled nobleman of the Jewish faith. When Joseph Gunzburg died in 1878, his will had two appropriate stipulations: his sons, to inherit his legacy, had to retain both their Jewish religion and their Russian citizenship. Although the next generation of Gunzburgs resided in Paris and married into the high society of the Second French Empire and the Jewish banking aristocracy of Europe, they followed their father's intention of remaining the protectors and patrons of the Russian Jewish community.

The role of the Jewish businessman in the creation and development of industrial capitalism in Russia may be compared and contrasted with that of the Old Believer. It also may be likened to the evo-

---

[59] See my Chapter 10 for a history of the House of Stieglitz.

lution of the Jewish entrepreneur in Europe, although there are important differences. The Old Believer and the Jewish entrepreneur in Russia share a common historiographical fate: both were neglected by the twentieth-century German sociologists of religion and capitalism. Like Weber's exclusion of the Russian schismatics from his investigations, Werner Sombart, in his classic study, *The Jews and Modern Capitalism*, did not include Russian Jewry. However, many of the reasons he gives for the involvement of the European Jews in modern business life (if other of his explanations are questionable)[60] would apply to the Russian case. The Russian Jews were strangers in the land, a foreign element injected into a traditional, agrarian society—isolated, hated, persecuted, and unsure of protection from the authorities. The sword was always over the Russian Jew's head, even if the blade did not fall until the pogroms of the late nineteenth century. In such a position of intrusion, insecurity, and poverty, he had to work harder than the others to establish himself and his people:

> While the natives are still in their warm beds, the newcomers stand without in the sharp morning air of dawn, and their energy is all the keener in consequence. They must concentrate their thoughts to obtain a foothold, and all their economic activities will be dictated by this desire.[61]

The Russian Jew had to be ready to pull up stakes at any time. Indeed many of the Jewish masses in the Russian empire were itinerant—peddlers, or the most unfortunate, drifters, "luftmenschen," as they were called.[62] For the more ambitious and affluent, this meant, as Sombart has suggested, a store of fluid capital—gold and precious metals, but better than this, money and negotiable instruments. And so Sombart would trace the evolution of moneylending to banking to finance capitalism. Indeed, this is the road that several of the big Russian Jewish entrepreneurs took during the nineteenth century. Few were machine technicians like many of the English and Scottish industrialists in Russia, or managerial wizards, like the German, Knoop.[63]

The Russian Jew, even more than the Old Believer, was excluded from the normal avenues of advancement, power, and privilege in early nineteenth-century Russia. The professions were for the most part closed to him, as were the military and civil services. And so his energies were turned into the economic and particularly commercial sphere in an agrarian society. Within the Pale, the doors to wealth were open to him—doors which the nobility scorned in terms of any direct involvement, and which the lower agricultural classes were too pre-

---

[60] See the introductory discussion by Hozelitz in Sombart, *The Jews and Modern Capitalism*.

[61] Sombart, *The Jews and Modern Capitalism*, p. 176.

[62] Baron, *The Russian Jew*, p. 114.

[63] See my Chapter 10.

occupied, too poor, or were in various ways unsuited to traverse. Thus, the Jew assumed the economic functions of the community in the western part of the Russian empire: he became the peddler on the road and at the fair, the proprietor in the general store and the inn, the cashier on the estate.[64] With few exceptions, he refused to become a farmer, despite encouragement from his own leaders as well as repeated official exhortation.

Unlike the Old Believer, the Russian Jew had to fight to gain the right to participate in commerce and industry on a national or international scale. This right was not won until the 1860's. Unlike the Jews of Germany, Holland, or England, the Russian Jews were largely a poverty stricken mass jammed into squalid cities in Russian Poland. In Germany by the end of the nineteenth century, a fourth of the boards of directors of electrical, mining, and brewing firms with a capital of 3 million marks or more were Jews; in England at the same time, half of the big bankers were Jewish.[65] In Russia, only a very few were able to battle their way to the top. These men were individualists, leaders, self-made men of importance.

Unlike the Old Believers, the Jews had no communal form of life or group capital to provide a base for industry. The Russian Jews had the ghetto and the Pale, which, if nothing else, provided a common way of life, an identity, a sense of kinship, and a mutual dependence. This was a factor in the employment of Jews in Jewish factories, in the cooperation of Jewish businessmen, and in the securing of economic privileges for their people by the businessmen-leaders of the Russian Jewish community.

Skoptsy Capital

Of the Russian sectarians, the most persecuted, despised, and perverse were also the best organized and perhaps the wealthiest, numbering among them several millionaire industrialists and financiers, and constituting a fabulously rich underground kingdom which extended from Siberia to Rumania. These were the infamous Skoptsy, the fanatical mystics whose practices of castration and female mutilation brought down upon their heads the severest of government retaliations. Outlaws and outcasts of two regimes until they were stamped out by the Soviet government after a Leningrad trial in 1930, the Skoptsy developed not only a hardy will to survive, but as well an organizational vigor and entrepreneurial initiative that enabled them to accumulate capital perhaps more rapidly than any of the other

---

[64] Similar to Poland, Hungary, and other parts of eastern Europe. On Transylvania at the end of the nineteenth century, see Raymond Recouly, *Le pays magyar* (Paris, 1908), cited in D. Warriner, ed., *Contrasts in Emerging Societies* (Bloomington, Indiana, 1965), p. 91.

[65] Figures in Sombart, *The Jew and Modern Capitalism*, pp. 105, 113-14.

sectarians or the schismatics. The historian of Russian religion, Nikol'-skii, has given the fullest explanation for the rise of the Skopets capitalist:

> . . . entering into the sect and undergoing castration, [the Skopets] at the same time cut himself off completely from the entire world. . . . He broke with a family or with the possibility of family life, had to refrain from heavy agricultural work, for which he had become incapable. He was cut off from the peasant milieu and was obliged to forsake it. He had to go to the city, where he found outcasts from the normal world like himself. In this peculiar milieu, he revised to the point of unrecognizability all his former ideals, changed his attitudes and aspirations, created for himself a new form of social life with a new ideology. . . . There appeared merchants' and industrialists' ships in Kostroma, Saratov, Samara, Tomsk, Tula, and other cities. Peasants who had been castrated in the countryside drifted to all these cities: here was a ready-made working mass for the Skoptsy-capitalists, to whom it remained only to exploit their obedient flock. The bonds of abnormality were quickly transformed into an unbreakable economic dependence, propped up by the religious halo which surrounded the boss-prophet.[66]

Leroy-Beaulieu offers the less likely explanation, which apparently he derived from the Skoptsy themselves, that the elimination of sexual passion and the diminution of the expenditures, efforts, and time demanded by family life enabled the Skopets to devote all his energies to the accumulation of money, fast growing sums which were fed back to other members of the sect equally eager to add to this capital. "This preeminently mystical sect, these illuminates ahungering for prophecy, have not proved wanting in the positivism, in the mercantile spirit characteristic of the great Russian and the Raskolnik."[67]

Skopism originated in the eighteenth century, an extreme version of the Khlysty sect. Its prophet was Kondraty Selivanov, who managed to mutilate hundreds of peasants before being arrested, flogged, and banished. One of his disciples, Luginin, set up the first Skoptsy "ship" in Moscow, and at the same time established a factory. Soon after, Skoptsy ships, factories, and commercial and financial houses were springing up in all the main cities of Russia, particularly in St. Petersburg, which became a kind of center for the new sect, as did Moscow for the schismatics. One reason for this Skoptsy concentration in the capital was the particular favor which the aged and repatriated leader Selivanov enjoyed from Alexander I, who had personally interviewed and taken a liking to this strange mystic.[68]

---

[66] Nikol'skii, *Istoriia russkoi tserkvi*, pp. 298-99.
[67] Leroy-Beaulieu, *Empire of the Tsars*, vol. III, pp. 433-34.
[68] Nikol'skii, *Istoriia russkoi tserkvi*, pp. 299-301.

During the ascendency of Selivanov, members of the Skoptsy entered the crafts as jewellers and goldsmiths. They also plunged into commerce and industry, and soon numbered several powerful merchants in the sect. More important, they expanded into the budding financial world of Russia. They became noted, not only as moneylenders, but as bankers and investors as well. At one end of the range of their financial activities, money was lent to small merchants, for whom default, it was alleged, could open to them the choice of joining the sect in lieu of payment. Other large sums might be used to buy candidates for Skopism from among the poor and bankrupt. One nineteenth-century author reports that in 1825, the Russian police cracked down on a large gang of prominent Skoptsy who were engaged in counterfeiting and smuggling gold specie.[69] At their height of power before a state persecution was inaugurated in the 1840's, the Skoptsy were estimated to have numbered over two thousand adherents. They owned banks and conducted various other financial operations in the main cities and fairs of the empire. There was even for a while in St. Petersburg an institution called the Bank of the Skoptsy. Their financial world stretched to Bucharest, where many of them settled after the Russian Revolution. The Skoptsy were active in the St. Petersburg exchange in the early nineteenth century and numbered several millionaires. There was a famous case in 1868, when the police discovered a treasure of 30 million rubles in the house of a deceased Morshansk Skopets, Plotitsyn.[70]

Arrests, confiscations, and a series of group trials and banishments broke the back of the Skoptsy in European Russia during the late nineteenth century. Despite this, they continued to flourish in Siberian communities, establishing factories and prospering commercially. Among the defendants in the Soviet Skoptsy trial of 1930, which marked the end of their history in Russia, were three ex-millionaires.[71]

Like the Old Believers, the Skoptsy lived as a religious community, in which all individual wealth was bequeathed to the group. A large capital quickly grew, which could be used for loans to merchants, for other investments, or for helping members of the sect. Far more subject to persecution than the Jews, the Skoptsy preferred the more fluid forms of capital and tended toward moneylending and banking. Here the similarities end. The Old Believers and Jews were outcast minorities in an agrarian society who turned their energies as individuals and groups into the channels of commerce and industry which remained open to them. They made a lasting impression on Russian economic

---

[69] Kelsiev, *Sbornik o raskol'nikakh*, vol. III, p. 226, note.

[70] I. Rapoport, *Les faits de castration rituelle. Essai sur les formes pathologiques de la conscience collective* (published doctoral thesis, University of Paris, 1945), pp. 55-60, 70-72.

[71] Rapoport, *Faits de castration rituelle*, p. 72.

life. The Skoptsy were as much outlaws engaged in fund raising for an underground society as they were business entrepreneurs. In this, they resemble the later Russian revolutionary organizations, who usually were adept in getting hold of substantial sums of money. The Skoptsy, necessarily few in number and transient in their way of life, were a fleeting, if interesting, epiphenomenon of Russian industrial history.

Chapter 10

The Foreign Entrepreneur

No church without a priest
No barracks without a bug
No factory without a Knoop[1]

So went one version of the popular and caustic nineteenth-century comment on the industrial empire which had been created in Russia by the German, Ludwig Knoop. Knoop symbolized the foreign intrusion into Russian industry. A European born and trained business wizard, his achievements—dating back to the early 1840's—in the creation of new industrial enterprises and the mechanization of old ones made him a millionaire and a baron. His talent for procuring much of the capital necessary for the modernization of cotton manufacture in Russia and for doing things in a big way generally is and has been of interest to several of the historians of Russian industry.[2] What Knoop built, as significant and instructive as it is, should not however be taken as a real measure of the role of the foreign entrepreneur in the development of private and state industrial enterprise in early nineteenth-century Russia, which was much less spectacular. Foreign control of Russian industry during the reigns of Alexander I and Nicholas I was only a fraction of what it would be in the heyday of imperialism at the end of the century. Foreigners very nearly controlled Russia's external trade before 1860, but not her industry, where Russian private and state capital were of greater significance. Nevertheless, many of the patterns of foreign entrepreneurial activity in Russia were established early in the nineteenth century, and not a few of the great foreign industrial fortunes were founded at this time.

Statistics on the role of foreigners in the overall industrial growth of Russia during the early 1800's are almost nonexistent—Russian statisticians and officials did not think in such terms until much later in the century. Beyond a few figures which census takers in the ports and capital found it useful to gather, the picture of foreign industrial enterprise in Russia at this time has to be reconstructed from facts that can be gleaned about individual concerns. However, before these facts can be evaluated, the elusive term "foreign enterprise" has to be pinned down. Taking into account the vagaries of imperial Russian law in this mat-

[1] Cited in K. A. Pazhitnov, *Ocherki istorii tekstil'noi promyshlennosti dorevoliutsionnoi Rossii, sherstiannaia promyshlennost* (Moscow, 1955), p. 103.

[2] Schulze-Gävernitz sees in Knoop a combination of John D. Rockefeller and Richard Awkwright. For details on Knoop's career, see Gerhardt von Schulze-Gävernitz, *Volkswirtschaftliche Studien aus Russland* (Leipzig, 1899), pp. 90-97; and Ch. Iuksimovich, *Manufakturnaia promyshlennost v proshlom i nastoiashchem* (Moscow, 1915), vol. I, pp. 204-08.

ter, the line between a foreign businessman operating in a country of which he is not a subject, and a permanent immigrant ought to be made, but this has not always been done. Andrew Carnegie, born and raised in Scotland, is not considered a foreign entrepreneur by historians of the United States. Ludwig Knoop, on the other hand, who came to Russia before he was twenty, who became a Russian subject and a baron, and who remained in the adopted land that had enriched him for over half a century until his death, is considered a foreigner by most historians of Russian industry. Other factors complicate the definition of the entrepreneur in Russia. Would membership in a religious or national minority of the Russian empire, for example, define a businessman operating within its borders as a foreign or a Russian entrepreneur? How does one classify the foreign entrepreneur with a base in Russia, but with extensive industrial, commercial, and financial interests abroad? Although there are numerous clear-cut instances of foreign entrepreneurs, who—like the American railroadmen, Joseph Harrison and the Winans brothers—come to Russia, pile up a fortune, and just as quickly, gather up their treasure and leave,[3] it is clear that many of the non-Russian enterprises in Russia during the early nineteenth century could not properly be called foreign, or could only partially be considered as such. In the broadest sense, as will be used here, the foreign entrepreneur in Russia can be defined as the subject, originally of another nation, who brought capital, as well as managerial and technical skills acquired elsewhere, to the Russian industrial scene. In the narrowest sense, which will *not* be used here— since such types were almost nonexistent in the early nineteenth century—the foreign enterprise in Russia can be defined as those concerns which were controlled from abroad, the bulk of the product of which accrued to foreign subjects or people outside the Russian empire.

The Foreign Role in Commerce, State Loans, and Private Enterprise

Another obvious distinction which must be made in the definition of foreign industrial enterprise in tsarist Russia is the difference between investment in trade and in factories. The large-scale European import and export trade of Russia during the early nineteenth century was almost entirely in the hands of English and German concerns based in St. Petersburg. In the same port in 1838, of the twenty-nine largest commercial houses whose yearly import volume alone exceeded a value of 2 million paper rubles (nine exceeding 5 million), thirteen concerns are classified by Amburger as German, eight as English, three as Swiss, one as English-German, and four as Russian. Most of this number, of course, had become or were in the process of becoming Russian subjects.[4] Some of the same merchants began to build factories

---

[3] See my Chapter 12 for details on the Harrison-Winans activities.
[4] Eric Amburger, "Der fremde Unternehmer in Russland bis zur Oktoberrevolution im Jahre 1917," *Tradition*, 2nd year (1957) no. 4, table III, p. 353.

or to invest in Russian industry; many others did not. The bulk of foreign enterprise in Russia before 1860 was commercial.

A distinction must also be made between foreign enterprise based in Russia and the migration of foreign capital to Russia. Huge sums of money began to flow into the tsarist empire during the late eighteenth and early nineteenth centuries in the form of subsidies and loans to the Russian government. Most of this money was used for war, to put armies in the field, but by the 1840's, large proportions of borrowings at home and abroad were being channeled into peacetime, state-sponsored industrial development. This investment did not, however, exclude military objectives, since most of it went into Russian railroads. Between 1769 and 1862, forty-five loans were obtained by the tsarist government, involving hundreds of millions of rubles. The money was supplied by wealthy banking houses, primarily in Amsterdam and London. In the late eighteenth century, almost all the loans were secured in Holland, although some money was obtained from Italian bankers. During the Napoleonic period, the Russian government was directly subsidized by England; most of several million pounds was used to equip and pay Russian troops. After 1815, most of the money obtained abroad by the Russian government came from the coffers of the houses of Baring and Rothschild in England.[5]

The Barings were marketing Russian bond issues in England as early as 1818. English investors bought half of the Russian bonds issued in that year, amounting to 2 million pounds. In 1820, joined by the Hope banking house of Amsterdam, the Barings took a much larger Russian loan of 40 million rubles. Again in 1832 and 1833, the English bankers, whose profit motives apparently were not greatly inhibited by adverse public opinion or political considerations, took a hand in advancing to the Russian government 3 million pounds. This sum helped to pay the bill for the repression of the Polish uprising. By this time, the Barings were cooperating with the premier Russian banking firm of Stieglitz and Company in the sale of Russian iron to the United States. In the late 1840's, the Barings, together with the Amsterdam banking house of Hope, came to the aid of the St. Petersburg-Moscow railroad with a loan of 5½ million pounds.

For the next decade, Baring and Company maintained its Russian contacts, even during the Crimean War. The English bankers were, thus, in an excellent position, almost immediately following the Peace of Paris, to join in a financial operation almost unprecedented in its scope in Russian or in European banking history. Together with bankers in St. Petersburg, Amsterdam, Warsaw, Berlin, and Paris, including the powerful Péreires and a contingent of French bankers, all connected with the Crédit Mobilier, the Barings undertook to finance the most ambitious single railroad undertaking hitherto seen in Europe—

[5] B. Ischchanian, *Die ausländischen Elemente in der Russischen Volkswirtschaft* (Berlin, 1913), table, pp. 196-97.

a network of almost 1,500 miles of railroads for the European part of the Russian empire. This project was estimated to cost a billion francs. One of the earliest of the larger foreign stock companies to operate in Russia, the Grande Société des Chemins de fer Russes was formed to meet these costs, with shares to be marketed by the participating bankers in Europe and Russia. The backing of the Russian government soon after was assured. British firms were to supply some of the rails, and two representatives of the house of Baring were appointed to the board of directors. In 1859, Thomas Baring became a vice president of the company.[6]

The Rothschilds became interested in Russia as early as the period of the Congress of Vienna, at which international council Solomon Rothschild began negotiations for a loan to the Russian government. In 1822, the Russians received 6 million pounds, or 43 million rubles worth of Rothschild gold from the family banks in London and Paris. In addition to interest payments, Solomon and James Rothschild were awarded the distinction, coveted by them, of the Russian order of St. Vladimir.[7]

The passing of only a few years found the Rothschilds much more deeply involved in the financing of European governments, while at the same time, Russia and the European powers had begun to drift away from the harmonies of the Congress period. When the tsarist government in 1828 sought a loan from the Rothschilds to finance war against the Turks, the request was promptly turned over to Metternich. His suggestion that Russia be refused was heeded. A second issue, which was to cloud the relationship of the house of Rothschild with the Russian government for the remainder of the tsarist period, appeared in these loan negotiations of the first years of the reign of Nicholas I—the mistreatment of the Jews in Russia.[8]

Soon after the passing of Nicholas, we see James Rothschild paying a visit to Russia for the specific purpose of investigating prospects for railroad investment. Before the passage of many months, however, in September 1856, the rival French house of Péreire brothers seized the opportunity from the Rothschilds with the creation of the Grande Société des Chemins de fer Russes. The latter had to content themselves with a Russian loan of 15 million pounds in 1862.[9]

It is obvious that the major source of capital for the early Russian railroads came from abroad, primarily through borrowing by the Rus-

---

[6] On the Barings and Russia, see Ralph Hidy, *The House of Baring in American Trade and Finance, 1763-1861, Harvard Studies in Business History* (Harvard, 1949), vol. xiv, pp. 64, 108, 139, 407, 435, 499, 517.

[7] E. Corti, *The Rise of the House of Rothschild* (New York, 1928), pp. 279-80.

[8] Corti, *Rise of the Rothschilds*, pp. 371-72.

[9] Ischchanian, *Ausländischen Elemente*, p. 197; Rondo Cameron, *France and the Economic Development of Europe* (Princeton, 1961), p. 276.

sian state and European investment in stock companies. The Russian railroads before 1861 were also heavily dependent on foreign industrial entrepreneurs operating in Russia, both in terms of track construction and the manufacture of locomotives and rolling stock. The role of the foreign entrepreneur in many other industries in early nineteenth-century Russia was much less significant. There are few general statistics on the foreign involvement in Russian industry from 1790 to 1860, but local statistics, together with data on foreign enterprises in specific industries and the industrial activities of particular national groups in Russia give some indication of its importance in the Russian economy of the period.

The first volume of the *Collection of the Imperial Russian Historical Society* includes a list of the factories and plants in the city of St. Petersburg in 1794. This tabulation indicates the nationality of the entrepreneurs as well as the type of manufacture in which they engaged. Of 162 "factories" and "plants," 31, or just about 20 percent were owned by people who are indicated as being of non-Russian nationalities—almost all of them French, German, or English. We may conclude that most of the "plants" were little more than shops, and that many of the "factories" were not much larger. This is borne out by the type of manufacture of the various factories: potato (8), macaroni (2), silk (7), lace (14), hats (12), and so on, down a list primarily, but not exclusively, consisting of luxury items.[10] St. Petersburg industry of the 1790's was for the most part concerned with supplying the nobility and the imperial court with the utensils and frills sought by an upper-class urban society. It is natural that a substantial number of European craftsmen would be imported to make such objects, but it is interesting that in Russia's most western city at the end of the eighteenth century, the foreigners formed only a small minority of the total number of factory and shop owners. This is not to deny that there were large and important foreign industrial enterprises in St. Petersburg at the end of the eighteenth century. Chamberlain and Cuzzins, Englishmen who founded one of Russia's earliest cotton weaving and printing factories in 1753, under the most privileged conditions, were still operating at the end of the century a large enterprise near St. Petersburg, which was providing a school for Russian craftsmen and furnishing several future factory owners with production secrets. A number of other foreigners—Englishmen and Germans—followed the lead of Chamberlain and Cuzzins during the last decade of the eighteenth century by setting themselves up in the Russian cotton industry.[11] This

[10] "Vedomost sostoiashchem v St. Peterburg fabrikam, manufakturam i zavodam 1794 goda," *Sbornik Imperatorskago Russkago Istoricheskago Obshchestva*, vol. I (1867), pp. 352-61.

[11] Anton Crihan, *Le capital étranger en Russie* (Paris, 1934), pp. 77-79; Tugan-Baranovskii, *Russkaia fabrika v proshlom i nastoiashchem* (St. Petersburg, 1898), vol. I, p. 61.

did not, however, prefigure a foreign control of this industry during the reigns of Alexander I and Nicholas I, although foreigners—men like Knoop, Wilson, and Stieglitz—played a most significant role in the development of various of its branches. By 1863, the spinning of cotton in Russia in the fifty-five largest factories with over one and one-half million spindles was very largely controlled by Russians.[12] Foreign entrepreneurs, on the other hand, pioneered and dominated in the Russian machine industry until mid-century. Nevertheless, in the total scheme of industrial enterprise and investment on the eve of the Great Reforms, if the few general figures we have can be considered a reliable guide, the foreign involvement would appear to be relatively minor. At that time, there were seventy-eight stock companies in Russia, with a total capital of 72 million rubles. Foreign capital amounted to 9,700,000 rubles, or not more than 15 percent. By 1889, this had climbed to less than a quarter, and by 1914, to about a third of the total industrial investment.[13]

The Legal Position of the Foreign Entrepreneur

There are no precise figures on the foreign element of Russia's population in the early nineteenth century. However, available local statistics and estimates provide some guide as to the occupation and national distribution of foreigners residing in Russia as this relates to industrial enterprise. By mid-century, for example, there were at least sixty thousand foreigners in St. Petersburg out of a total population of almost half a million. The largest proportion of these foreigners had become Russian subjects. Well over half were of German origin. Poles, English, and French constituted the most important other foreign colonies, but were much smaller in number. The police reports on foreigners in St. Petersburg in 1843, which counted only non-Russian subjects, numbered them at 14,006. About half of these arrivals, according to the Soviet authority on the subject, Kopanev, were professional people and household servants—doctors, druggists, and tutors, but also craftsmen and supervisory personnel for factories.[14] A partial record of the passport registration of Frenchmen who journeyed to Russia in the 1840's shows similar occupational distributions of newly arrived foreigners. For the last half of 1846, excluding August, and all of 1847, there were just over two hundred French visitors to Russia. The number of machinists, industrial workers, and businessmen—almost all of the latter engaged in commerce—was easily matched by the number of household workers or the number of tourists. Four

---

[12] A. Sherer, "Khlopchatobumazhnaia promyshlennost," *Obzor razlichnykh otraslei manufakturnoi promyshlennosti Rossii* (St. Petersburg, 1863), vol. II, pp. 462-68.
[13] Crihan, *Le capital étranger*, pp. 239-40; citing N. V. Ol, *Inostrannye kapitaly v Rossii* (Petrograd, 1922), pp. 12-13.
[14] Kopanev, *Naselenie Peterburga*, pp. 20-21.

chemists, three engineers, three machinists, one agronomist, and one bank official arrived in Russia from France in late 1847, but with them came twenty-two *artistes*.[15]

By the 1840's, it is probable that most of the foreign industrial entrepreneurs who had been established for several years in Russia had become Russian subjects. Imperial edicts of the early nineteenth century, particularly those issued under Nicholas I, made it increasingly difficult for foreign businessmen to operate factories in Russia without relinquishing their foreign citizenship. This had been possible under Catherine the Great, when the first legislation on foreign industrial enterprise in Russia appeared. The urban statute of 1785 permitted foreigners to establish and operate "factories" and "plants" in Russia on the same basis as Russian subjects. Restriction of foreign businessmen began with Paul I, who limited their commercial activities to the cities of Moscow and St. Petersburg. A major revision of the legal status of the foreign entrepreneur in Russia and a further restriction of his sphere of business activities came with the manifesto of 1807. According to this law, a foreigner who wished to do business in Russia had to register as a "resident merchant" (*zaiezhii kupets*) or as a "foreign merchant" (*inostrannii gost*). The former was a temporary wholesale trading privilege, which permitted import and export merchants to operate under the jurisdiction of the customs house and in the merchants' exchange, but nowhere else, and only for a period of one year. The "resident merchant" then had to become a "foreign merchant," or terminate his commercial activity, or leave Russia. The "foreign merchant" was defined as a non-Russian of "incomplete citizenship" (*nepolnoe grazhdanstvo*). He was registered in coastal or border cities, could own a residence in such a city, and was obliged to pay a tax on declared capital which exceeded 50 thousand rubles. He could acquire and operate factories, was permitted the use of free and hired labor in such establishments, could buy from Russians (except peasants), and could sell the products of his factory both within Russia and abroad. In 1824, the scope of industrial activities of the foreign entrepreneur in Russia was further limited. According to a regulation of that year, his trading was curtailed not only with the peasantry, but also with all levels of the urban population below the second guild of merchants— the *meshchanstvo*, commercial peasants, and others. He could not buy and sell in other towns in Russia. Finally, he could not buy or rent any kind of factory without special permission from the Tsar himself.

The Regulation of 1824 was directed primarily at foreign merchants and aimed to restrict the activity of those who had become industrialists. By 1826, however, it was apparent that some foreigners who were not registered merchants engaged in commerce had set up factories on

---

[15] M. Cadot, "Les débuts de la navigation à vapeur et l'émigration française en Russie," *Cahiers du monde russe et soviétique*, vol. IV (1963), pp. 388-89.

a smaller scale, since a *ukaz* of this same year permitted a foreign *fabrikant* to register in the second or third Russian merchant guild for a period of ten years, without having to become a Russian subject. At the end of this period, he was obliged to do so or to sell his enterprise.

It is clear that such a restrictive system, combined with the police surveillance and bureaucratic harassment for which Nicholean Russia was notorious among foreign visitors, did not make the country an inviting home for the European capitalist. His taxes were high, and he had little or no protection, either from Russian competitors or from arbitrary actions of the state. The best he could hope for was something less than the cramped situation of the native Russian merchant or industrialist. This was far, to say the least, from the capitulations in Turkey, extraterritoriality in China, or the Mixed Courts of Egypt. Nor did it approximate the Russian *ukaz* of June 1860, which swept away this system and in effect opened the doors of Russia to the foreign entrepreneur. The foreigner, by the new legislation, was permitted entrance to all the Russian merchant guilds on terms of equality with Russian businessmen, and could own and bequeath real and personal property.[16]

As unattractive as the earlier system might have been to many foreign entrepreneurs, it was not always rigidly or consistently enforced, nor did it eliminate the possibility for some individuals of making large profits in Russia. Other forces, including specific government policies, worked to attract foreign entrepreneurs to the Russian empire during the early nineteenth century. And where necessity dictated, or court influence paved the way, exceptions could be made and special privileges bestowed. The high tariff maintained for over a quarter of a century after 1822, although designed to protect Russian industry from the competition of cheap foreign goods, also attracted foreign entrepreneurs to establish themselves in Russia. There was profit to be had in avoiding the high Russian tariff and in underselling highly priced and inferior goods manufactured by Russians. About the time of the lifting of the British government's ban on the exportation of machinery (1842), a number of businessmen from the "workshop of the world" saw in Russian cotton mills a fertile field for the profitable application of English mechanical skills and the newest English spinning machinery. Several large firms were established, including a few corporations. With efficient, imported managerial staffs and superior machinery, the English concerns were able to expand rapidly and make money.[17]

When the Russian government so desired, it could not only except a foreign enterprise from burdensome restrictions, but could secure it

---

[16] The legislation is summarized in "Ministerstvo finansov, departament torgovli i manufaktur," *Istoricheskii ocherk oblozheniia torgovli i promyslov v Rossii* (St. Petersburg, 1893), pp. 104-05, 107-08, 130, 134, 142-43.

[17] Leland Jenks, *The Migration of British Capital to 1875* (New York, 1938), p. 183.

from all threatening competition and provide for generous, if not extravagant, profits. Some foreign enterprises became heavily subsidized charges of the government. A classic example of this favoritism was the British cotton printing concern of Chamberlain and Cuzzins, which flourished for a century. Established in 1753, the English firm was given a monopoly on the production of calico in Russia, a state loan of 30 thousand rubles, and tariff protection against English cloth. Chamberlain and Cuzzins could import materials and equipment without paying duty, and were assigned 300 state serfs to labor in their factory.[18] Sometimes the government would encourage the foreign entrepreneur by indicating in various ways that he would have no difficulties in Russia. The English merchants, Crown and Danielson, for example, who had established a brewery in St. Petersburg in 1795, were commended by the state and awarded a gold medal in 1818, in view of the interest of the Minister of Internal Affairs in the manufacture of English porter in Russia.[19]

French, English, and German Entrepreneurs

It is possible and instructive, from the limited figures we have, to study and compare the foreign entrepreneurs operating in Russia during the early nineteenth century in terms of nationalities. French, English, and German businessmen dominated the scene. Although there were American and Swedish names of great significance in Russian industry before 1860—Winans and Nobel[20]—they were almost alone among the capitalists of their respective countries in making the trip to Russia to set up factories. In general, as indicated by the enterprises for which we have data, the French entrepreneur in Russia tended to engage in the production of consumer goods—the luxuries of France, which the upper classes of Russia were accustomed to demand. The Englishman's way to the ownership of industrial enterprises in Russia was usually through his technical proficiency, his mastery of the secrets of industrial machinery. The German industrialist in Russia was more often than not a merchant by origin: he brought capital and the techniques of banking and finance to Russian industry.

At mid-century, a French visitor to Russia, Xavier Marmier, re-

[18] Peter Liashchenko, *A History of the National Economy of Russia to the 1917 Revolution* (New York, 1949), p. 334.

[19] P. N. Stolpianskii, *Zhizn i byt Peterburgskoi fabriki 1704-1914* (Leningrad, 1925), p. 32.

[20] On the Winans enterprises in Russia, see my Chapters 12 and 13. The foundation for the Nobel oil empire in the Caucasus during the late nineteenth century was laid before 1860 in St. Petersburg. Immanuel Nobel (father of the inventor of dynamite) accumulated and lost a fortune manufacturing machinery and armaments. See Eric Berengren, *Alfred Nobel, the Man and his Work* (London, 1962), pp. 4-18, and *Mekhanicheskii zavod Liudvig Nobel 1862-1912* (no author, date, or publisher), pp. 1-4.

marked that, although the biggest bankers in Russia were Germans or Englishmen, the finest stores for luxury items and costume jewelry were owned by French or English merchants. There was, he observed, a large French colony of tailors, hairdressers, and milliners. The existence at that time of a Committee for Charity for the French of St. Petersburg would indicate a significant number of French immigrants of limited means and skills who were finding it difficult to make their way in the Russian capital, rather than a colony of affluent factory owners.[21]

There were some exceptions to this general picture in Moscow. An Alsatian, Steinbach, established a mechanized cotton printing plant in that city in 1825, which by the eve of the Great Reforms employed 650 workers with an annual production valued at 9 million rubles. In 1846, another French citizen (also very probably an Alsatian) Hubner, established a cotton printing plant in Moscow, which he soon mechanized and expanded. However, French industrial entrepreneurs seemed to be more attracted to Poland and the Ukraine than to Russia proper. In 1833, a Frenchman named Girard founded a linen manufactory near Warsaw. Two years later, one of his compatriots, Louis Gaver, set up a cotton-spinning mill with steam machinery near Lodz. A Belgian, Charles Cheibler, also established himself industrially at Lodz.[22]

Far more important than the French to the early development of Russian industry, although less numerous, were technicians and capitalists from England and Scotland. These men played an important role in the mechanization of the cotton industry in Russia and dominated her infant machine industry during the early nineteenth century. The Englishman's initial capital was his knowledge of machines. When, in the early 1840's, the English government lifted its prohibition on the export of machinery, a golden opportunity was presented to enterprising British businessmen familiar with the latest techniques in the manufacture of textiles. Bringing the most advanced business techniques and the most highly skilled machinists of the age to Russia, it was possible for them to outstrip most of the local competition and to accumulate substantial profits. Thus, we see several large textile concerns being founded in St. Petersburg in the 1840's, owned and managed by English entrepreneurs and their staffs. Typical was the Hubbard cotton-spinning factory, founded in the Russian capital in 1844. In 1852, Hubbard, together with another Englishman, Egerton, incorporated the Petrovskii Mills with a capital of 1,200,000 rubles. Other large English concerns stimulated by the Russian technological lag of the 1840's were the firms of John and

---

[21] Cadot, "Les débuts de la navigation à vapeur," pp. 395-96, 398.

[22] Crihan, *Le capital étranger*, pp. 80-81, 83-85; Iuksimovich, *Manufakturnaia promyshlennost v proshlom i nastoiashchem*, vol. I, p. 293.

Joseph Shaw (spinning and weaving factories in St. Petersburg) and of James Thornton, whose woolen-cloth establishment, founded in 1841 and incorporated in 1866, became one of the great industrial enterprises in the Russian capital in the late nineteenth century.[23]

It was almost inevitable that the English would come to play a dominant role in the development of the Russian machine industry, either as managers of state enterprises, or as entrepreneurs in their own right. Not forgetting the important mechanical establishments of the Swede, Immanuel Nobel, the Duke of Liechtenberg's locomotive plant (both in St. Petersburg), the state locomotive and railroad car plant at Aleksandrovsk, near St. Petersburg, managed by the American contractors, Harrison and Winans, and the large, Russian-owned Shipov plant in Kostroma, most of the important machine factories in Russia before 1860 were in the hands of Englishmen. In St. Petersburg, with the exceptions noted above, all of the big machine producing concerns or iron foundries had English or Scottish names on the doorplates— Carr and McPherson, Baird, Wilkins, Ellis and Butts, and Isherwood. In Moscow, the mechanical plants of Smith, Bromley and of Bukteev and Williams numbered among the largest.[24]

One of the wealthiest and most important of the English-speaking machinists of early nineteenth-century St. Petersburg was Charles Baird. A product of the industrial and technological revolution in England and Scotland, Baird applied his skills in Russia for over half a century, from 1786 until his death in 1843. A keen business sense accompanied the finest mechanical training available at the time; and the several industries which Baird left behind him under the direction of his son, Francis, remained among the largest in St. Petersburg for many years. His career in many ways typifies that of the English industrial entrepreneur in prereform Russia and provides a striking example of the technician's way to industrial prominence in the empire of the tsars.[25]

---

[23] Crihan, *Le capital étranger*, pp. 81-82; Jenks, *The Migration of British Capital*, p. 183.

[24] R. S. Livshitz, *Razmeshchenie promyshlennosti v dorevoliutsionnoi Rossii* (Moscow, 1956), pp. 104-07.

[25] Baird's contemporary and compatriot, General Wilson, was an important figure in the expansion and mechanization of the Russian textile industry in the early nineteenth century. However, Wilson preferred to restrict his talents and ambition to state service, rather than embark on private ventures. Son of an Edinburgh blacksmith, he went to Russia with his parents during the reign of Catherine the Great, where he was trained by Gascoigne, director of the Imperial Armaments Plant at Kolpino, who also trained Baird. In the early nineteenth century, Wilson superintended the Aleksandrovsk plant, the largest state cotton-spinning enterprise in Russia. Aleksandrovsk also served as a training establishment for machinists from various parts of the Russian empire. Wilson also had a hand in managing private textile enterprises in the St. Petersburg area. However, he remained in the Russian state service for almost three-quarters of a century, achieving the rank of General and a pension when he retired at the age of ninety.

Part III: Private Industrial Enterprise

Baird's career began in one of the northern ramparts of the English industrial revolution. In Scotland, at Carron, near Falkirk, one of the world's first iron works to smelt with coal was founded in 1760. By the end of the eighteenth century, the Carron works was a gigantic operation for its time, employing over two thousand workers. It became famous throughout Europe and developed into a training ground for machinists.[26] It was here that Charles Baird received his technical and business education. In 1786, he accompanied a director of the Carron works, Gascoigne, to Russia, where the latter was invited to modernize Russian iron and cannon foundries.

In less than a decade, Baird turned to his own private ventures. In 1792, in partnership with an Englishman, Morgan, he developed Russia's first steam machine factory, which became as well one of the largest iron foundries in the Russian capital. It was here that Russia's first steam engines and steam-propelled industrial machines were produced, numbering 141 by 1825. In addition Baird was available and competent to undertake special jobs for the government: gun carriages, the iron roof of St. Isaac's cathedral, machinery for the St. Petersburg mint, a huge angel for the top of the Alexander I monument, and several suspension bridges for the city.

For these special assignments, Baird received his share of Vladimir and Anna crosses of the lesser degrees, and in 1811, the rank of Chief Foundry Manager (*oberhüttenverwalter*), eighth class. His millions were obtained elsewhere. The first step on this road was taken in 1815, when Baird's factory produced Russia's first steamship, the *Elizaveta*, operating from Kronstadt to St. Petersburg. He received a ten-year monopoly for this line, which applied to passengers and freight. It was from the latter that he accumulated his fortune. Sailing vessels could not compete with the steam transport monopolized by Baird, so that almost the entire local transfer of goods entering and leaving the port of St. Petersburg fell into his hands. For many years, his vessels dominated the waters around St. Petersburg. By 1842, ten steamers were operating on the Kronstadt-St. Petersburg passenger line alone.

Aided in the beginning by a government monopoly, Baird took the precaution to expand in various directions on his own. He purchased land near the waterfront behind the Admiralty building, where he set up an industrial complex, including an iron foundry, a saw mill with steam machinery, a porcelain works, a wharf, and a sugar manufactory. For the latter enterprise, Baird hit upon the ingenious idea of finding a nonanimal substitute for bullock's blood, a substance hitherto essential to the process of purifying sugar. It was thus possible for the Scotsman to sell his product very profitably during Lent and fast days, when it was in great demand, without fear of competition from the sugars refined with forbidden animal substances.

[26] A. M. MacKenzie, *Scotland in Modern Times* (London, 1941), pp. 22-23, 102.

Baird employed a large number of English technicians and workmen in his factory, probably numbering in the hundreds by the middle of the nineteenth century. He also used Russian serf labor, by agreement with landlords residing in St. Petersburg. According to one contemporary observer, Baird's factory became a workhouse for troublesome household serfs. At least one hundred of these unfortunate ex-domestic servants were working at the Scot's establishment at any one time, without pay: he obliged himself only to feed them and to turn over a small fee to their masters.[27]

By 1860, the Baird machine works, then owned by the founder's son, Francis (1802-1864) was one of the largest in Russia, if not the world. The plant employed twelve to fifteen hundred workers and used eight steam-propelled machines, in addition to dozens of cranes, punches, and other types of apparatus. The yearly value of the mechanical products of the plant, in fulfillment of both private and state orders, was estimated at 500,000 rubles.[28]

The Englishmen who dominated the machine construction industry of St. Petersburg in the early nineteenth century, who owned many of the great textile factories along the banks of the Neva, and whose great commercial houses controlled much of the import-export trade of the port built magnificent houses near a quay along the river which became known as the "English quay." An English colony of wealth and influence isolated itself in the surrounding area. Not far across the waters, on the Vasily Ostrov, a German colony, comparable in opulence, had developed. Here one could find German shops and taverns, the mansions of German merchants and industrialists, or the residences of German academicians and professors. Most of the Germans in the Vasily Ostrov were merchants or manufacturers, the majority from the eastern German states or the Baltic coast, although the big German ports and commercial cities also had their representatives in the St. Petersburg suburb.[29]

The German's path to industrial enterprise in early nineteenth-century Russia ran through the merchant's office rather than the machine shop. Russia had gathered her share of German scientists since the early eighteenth century, but when it came to industry, it was capi-

---

[27] On Baird, the main sources, in addition to the article in the *Russkii biograficheskii slovar*, are Robert Bremner, *Excursions in the Interior of Russia* (London, 1839), vol. I, p. 261; "Vospominanie Przhetslavskago" *Russkaia starina*, vol. II (1874), p. 471; James E. Alexander, *Travels to the Seat of the War in the East Through Russia and the Crimea in 1829* (London, 1830), vol. I, p. 33; J. G. Kohl, *Russia and the Russians in 1842* (London, 1843), vol. II, pp. 18-20.

[28] A. Ershov, "Obzor mashinostroitel'nykh zavedenii v. Rossii," *Obzor razlichnykh otraslei manufakturnoi promyshlennosti Rossii* (St. Petersburg, 1863), vol. II, pp. 42-43.

[29] On the English and German suburbs of St. Petersburg during the early nineteenth century, see Kohl, *Russia in 1842*, vol. II, pp. 218-19, and Bremner, *Excursions in Russia*, vol. I, pp. 256-57.

tal that the Germans knew how to provide rather than technical skills and knowledge. Over many years, the Germans had mastered the techniques for accumulating capital as merchants trading out of northern Russian and Baltic ports. By the early nineteenth century, a few of them were becoming bankers as well. Many diverted their capital into Russian industrial enterprise.

Not all the Germans in prereform Russia who demonstrated an interest in industrial investment were "bourgeois." Some German aristocrats, particularly during the reign of Nicholas I—Baltic barons or influential courtiers and state servants—saw industry as a profitable channel for the investment of their wealth. Count Nesselrode bought 36,000 rubles worth of stock in the Russian Cotton Spinning Company in the 1830's. Count Benckendorff became involved in several enterprises in Russia and the Baltic area, including steamships and insurance. One contemporary estimated that this earned him half a million rubles a year.[30] The Duke of Liechtenberg, son of a Bavarian princess and Eugène de Beauharnais and married to the daughter of Nicholas I, was an influential and wealthy courtier who took an enlightened interest in Russian industrial development. Liechtenberg was more a scientist than a businessman, who conducted experiments in electricity, wrote papers for the Academy of Sciences, and served as Director of the Imperial Mining Institute. In the early 1850's, he financed a locomotive plant in St. Petersburg which undertook to supply 100 locomotives for the St. Petersburg-Warsaw Railroad, then in construction. The Liechtenberg plant also supplied the Tsarskoe Selo Railroad at the time.[31]

Nesselrode was Russian Foreign Minister; Benckendorff was Chief of Gendarmes; and Liechtenberg a son-in-law of the Tsar. It was from these positions of court influence and bureaucratic power that their fortunes were derived and their industrial investments protected. More typical of the German industrial entrepreneur in Russia during the early nineteenth century was the merchant from Lübeck, Kiel, or Hamburg who moved to St. Petersburg or Archangel as a commercial agent. The profits gained from this activity might be invested in ships, or he might buy into Russian industry. In the very early 1800's, sawmills, rope factories, iron foundries, and particularly sugar refineries were seen as profitable ventures by the Germans. After 1830, as with the English, cotton cloth was the industrial lure. This is the commercial-industrial pattern which can be seen in the history

---

[30] Cited in S. Monas, *The Third Section* (Harvard, 1961), pp. 98-99; on Nesselrode's investments, see M. K. Rozhkova, ed., *Ocherki ekonomicheskoi istorii Rossii* (Moscow, 1959), p. 176.

[31] B. F. Brandt, *Inostrannye kapitaly ikh vliianie na ekonomicheskoe razvitie strany*, part 2: *Inostrannye kapitaly v Rossii* (St. Petersburg, 1899), p. 18; on Liechtenberg's scientific and business activities, see the article in *Russkii biograficheskii slovar.*

of such prominent German firms in early nineteenth-century Russia as Brandt, Knauff, Knoop, and Stieglitz.[32]

By far the most significant German entrepreneurs in Russia from the beginning of the reign of Alexander I until 1860 were the Barons Ludwig and Alexander Stieglitz. The story of this father and son is one of commercial agents of German background who go on to build a Russian fortune in industry and finance (and pick up Russian ranks and titles along the way). It follows the general pattern of the German businessman in the tsarist empire during this period.

Ludwig Stieglitz was born in western Germany in the town of Arolsen where his father, Bernard Stieglitz, was a merchant. The father's commercial operations were widespread enough to require his enrollment in the merchantry of Hamburg. Bernard Stieglitz also acted as court agent for the princes of Waldeck. The Stieglitzes were originally a Jewish family who had traded in Germany for generations. The elder Stieglitz had become sufficiently Germanized, however, to convert to Lutheranism, and his son's Jewish heritage was little emphasized in his upbringing.[33] It was a German-trained businessman who left the West in his early twenties to make his fortune in Russia.

He began as a stockbroker in St. Petersburg, initiating a lifelong attachment to the exchange (*birzha*) in the Russian capital. In 1803, Stieglitz was able to borrow the equivalent of 100,000 rubles from one of his German banker uncles. With this, the commercial house of Stieglitz and Company was born.[34]

By the end of the Napoleonic period, Ludwig Stieglitz was easily the biggest importer and exporter in St. Petersburg, a position which the firm maintained throughout the reign of Nicholas I. In the ten years from 1824 to 1833 inclusive, the total value of goods imported and exported by the house of Stieglitz amounted to 226,088,617 rubles. The yearly total climbed as high as 30,294,932 rubles during this period (1831), and by 1838 had reached 54,720,973 rubles. The Stieglitz commercial operation was based in St. Petersburg, but in the 1830's and 1840's, the firm was also officially listed for Odessa, Kherson, Taganrog, Radziwillow, Narva, and Moscow.[35] By this time, Stieglitz was making deals with English and American bankers and merchants. During the early 1830's, the house of Stieglitz joined the Barings of England in the trading of large cargoes of iron, wool, hemp,

[32] Amburger, "Der fremde Unternehmer in Russland," p. 344. See also his article on the Brandts in *Neue Deutsche Biografie*, vol. II, pp. 593-94.

[33] B. von Maydell, "Die Stieglitz aus Arolsen," *Deutsches Familienarchiv*, vol. V (1956), pp. 62-63.

[34] For details on Stieglitz's early career, see the article in *Russkii biograficheskii slovar*.

[35] *Gosudarstvennaia vneshnaia torgovlia*: see the annual reports 1824-60, passim. Each contains the names of import-export houses, the amounts of their yearly trade, and the cities in which they trade.

and tallow. In a 1831 arrangement, they joined forces to buy 12,000 tons of Russian iron, which Stieglitz consigned to American commission merchants. In other cases, the Barings might do the consigning.[36]

The house of Stieglitz was Russia's first great private bank.[37] However, it did not act formally as a banker for the St. Petersburg business community in the manner of a modern commercial or industrial credit institution. Ludwig Stieglitz limited his lending activities almost exclusively to the tsarist government, while spreading his personal investments through a wide range of Russian industries. He became the Russian court banker of the reigns of Alexander I and Nicholas I, or, in the words of Lamanski, Alexander Stieglitz's collaborator and successor as president of the Russian State Bank, the "sole and exclusive banker of the Russian government."[38] It was through Stieglitz that the Tsar obtained his money from the great banking houses of Europe; and foreign bankers attempting to move into the Russian field had first to deal with the house of Stieglitz. Even the Rothschilds had to come to terms with so influential a bank, and by the 1840's had developed a social as well as a financial relationship with the Stieglitzes. In 1846, a German consular official in Paris could report that Alexander Stieglitz was a guest at the Rothschild palace, in the company of such exotic international luminaries and potential borrowers as Ibrahim Pasha. For his own part, the younger Stieglitz was coming to be called the "Rothschild of the East," and the "Rothschild of Russia."[39]

The first big state loan which Stieglitz and Company placed with London and Amsterdam bankers was the 40 million ruble pledge of 1820. Twenty years later, the house of Stieglitz, after 1843 in the hands of Alexander Stieglitz, contracted with the same European firms, Baring and Hope, to provide sums for the initial construction of the St. Petersburg-Moscow Railroad, three loans, amounting to 42 million silver rubles. During the Crimean War, the Berlin and Amsterdam bankers, Mendelsohn and Hope, cooperated with Stieglitz to provide 100,000,000 silver rubles to supply the Russian war machine. After the war, the house of Stieglitz was involved in the billion-franc financing of the Grande Société des Chemins de fer Russes.[40]

While functioning primarily as a court banker, along the lines of the Fuggers or the early Rothschilds rather than those of a modern commercial banker, Ludwig Stieglitz did not hesitate to distribute his capi-

[36] Hidy, *House of Baring*, pp. 138-39.
[37] For a general discussion of banking in early nineteenth-century Russia, see my Chapter 3.
[38] "Iz vospominanii E. F. Lamanskago," *Russkaia starina*, vol. 162 (1915), p. 338.
[39] P. Emden, *The Money Powers of Europe in the 19th and 20th Centuries* (New York, 1938), p. 170; von Maydell, "Die Stieglitz aus Arolsen," pp. 78-79; Kohl, *Russia in 1842*, vol. I, p. 363.
[40] Ischchanian, *Ausländischen Elemente*, pp. 196-97; Cameron, *France and the Economic Development of Europe*, p. 276.

tal liberally to a number of industrial and agricultural undertakings. By the 1820's, he had acquired several factories, which were producing such items as stearine candles, sugar, linen, and mineral water. He invested in a steamship line operating between St. Petersburg and Lübeck. He purchased estates in several parts of the empire, particularly the Black Sea area, where he embarked on the raising of Merino sheep. In the 1830's, Ludwig Stieglitz founded one of the largest cotton-spinning factories in St. Petersburg, a five-story stone affair, with heating, and gas illumination. He imported the largest machinery yet to be used in eastern Europe, entrusting it to an English plant manager. By mid-century, he was also the owner of linen and woolens plants in Narva which employed over a thousand workers. Stieglitz appeared to some to be a benevolent "capitalist" for his time. A foreign visitor was astounded by workers singing on the job and by the "healthy look of these people, as compared with the wretched, sickly, demoralized factory laborers that are to be found in the manufacturing districts of Belgium, France and Germany." The well-being of Stieglitz's workers was also observed and commended by Nicholas I, who made official note of it.[41]

The elder Stieglitz was a pioneer of private insurance in Russia. As early as 1822, he joined several St. Petersburg businessmen in submitting to the government a project for a stock insurance company to be called the "Phoenix." However this plan came to nothing. In 1827, along with Admiral Mordvinov and a number of dignitaries and merchants, he participated in the founding of the "First Russian Insurance Company," as it was called. This was a fire insurance company, with a capital of 10 million paper rubles for which 10,000 shares of stock were issued. Its success was assured by a government-bestowed twenty-year monopoly in the cities of St. Petersburg, Moscow, and Odessa. Stieglitz was a director of this company from its founding until his death in 1843. He was also associated with the Russian Company for the Insurance of Life Pensions and Other Important Incomes and Monetary Capital. This company, founded in 1835, was concerned mainly with the insurance of pensions for beneficiaries, children, and army recruits. It was capitalized at 4 million paper rubles. Stieglitz was the biggest single investor in this firm, having purchased 1,500 shares, which brought him control of 7½ percent of the stock and cost him 300,000 paper rubles.[42]

Ludwig Stieglitz was a life-long member of the St. Petersburg Stock

---

[41] Kohl, *Russia in 1842*, vol. II, pp. 20-21.

[42] Paul J. Best, "The Origins and Development of Insurance in Imperial and Soviet Russia" (unpublished doctoral thesis, New York University, 1965), chapters I and II, which carry the story up to the end of the reign of Nicholas I. See also *Piatidesiatiletie Vysochaishe Utverzhdennago Rossiiskago Zastrakhovanie Kapitalov i Dokhodov* (St. Petersburg, 1885). See my Chapter 3 for the general background on private insurance in Russia during the early nineteenth century.

Exchange, where his Russian career had begun as a broker. He remained active in its trading and its charitable activities until his death. A foreign observer has provided us with a portrait of the elderly Russian banker at work in the *birzha* in his last years: "His shrewd, sparkling eyes, his short, stout, Napoleon figure, and his old, simple green surtout are to be seen daily in the middle of the exchange."[43]

In 1834, Stieglitz contributed 10,000 rubles to a capital formed by members of the stock exchange, the income of which went to pay the tuition for six students of the St. Petersburg Commercial School, the Technological Institute, and the School of Commercial Navigation. Stieglitz's contribution was exceeded only by that of the Demidovs and one or two other very wealthy St. Petersburgers. Previously, in 1827, he had demonstrated his interest in the St. Petersburg Commercial School, of which he was a trustee, by a donation of 10,000 rubles for its library. In 1840, Stieglitz money paid for a new three-story stone building for this same school. His other charities included a children's hospital and an orphanage. For his contributions to the Russian war chest in 1812, Stieglitz received a bronze medal.[44]

By the end of the reign of Alexander I, the German merchant who had prospered in the empire of the tsars was becoming increasingly Russianized. In 1826, Stieglitz was made a hereditary Baron of the Russian Empire, and thereafter assumed a number of posts in the Ministry of Finances. In 1828, he became a member of Kankrin's newly created Manufacturing Council and during the final fifteen years of his life, he sat on three government committees dealing with commercial and banking matters.[45]

When he died in 1843, Baron Ludwig Stieglitz left a fortune of 30 million rubles, which was far exceeded by his holdings in land, ships, warehouses, factories, and other properties. One contemporary estimate of his wealth placed it at approximately seventy-five million rubles.[46] This immense estate did not make Baron Stieglitz the richest man in mid-nineteenth century Russia, nor was he the only millionaire of that time. There were industrialists who were richer, but the greatest wealth was still in land holdings. Stieglitz did, however, create Russia's first great banking fortune.

All of the wealth and position of the father passed to the son in 1843. Alexander Stieglitz had been raised as an upper-class Russian of German background. He had been privately tutored in classics in St. Petersburg and had graduated from Dorpat University, rounding out his education with travel in Europe.[47]

[43] Kohl, *Russia in 1842*, vol. II, p. 363.
[44] A. G. Timofeev, *Istoriia S-Peterburgskoi Birzhi* (St. Petersburg, 1903), pp. 134, 218; facing p. 220.
[45] *Russkii biograficheskii slovar*, article on Ludwig Stieglitz.
[46] Kohl, *Russia in 1842*, vol. I, p. 363.
[47] *Russkii biograficheskii slovar*, article on Alexander Stieglitz.

Following in his father's footsteps, Alexander Stieglitz continued in the role of industrialist, philanthropist, imperial court banker, and leader of the St. Petersburg Exchange. He served as president of the latter for over a decade. Railway financing was a continuing concern of his in the 1840's and 1850's. Massive new loans for the construction of the St. Petersburg-Moscow railway were provided by the house of Stieglitz. Other large sums were secured for the Russian military effort in the Crimean War. With the restoration of peace in 1856, Stieglitz again became active in Russian railroads and European high finance. France was in her first fever of industrial capitalism and Russia was ready for her first railroad boom. It was to involve large-scale, privately financed construction. The Stieglitzes joined with the great banking houses of France and Germany to form the billion-franc Grande Société des Chemins de fer Russes. In the same year, Baron Stieglitz put 2 million rubles into a Russian stock company for a suburban rail line running from St. Petersburg to Peterhof. That this Russian businessman, baron and state councillor had not forgotten his father's German background was evidenced by the waiting room for the St. Petersburg terminal of the railroad—a version of the refectory of a German castle, complete with vaults and buttresses. The new railroad earned 20,000 rubles in its first month of operation, which brought a substantial profit and a St. Stanislaus Order of the first class to Stieglitz. The line was soon after extended to port facilities at Oranienbaum, and a spur was built to Krasnoe Selo and hence to Gatchina and Warsaw.[48]

Alexander Stieglitz continued and extended the educational and charitable activities begun by his father. He carried on support of the St. Petersburg Commercial School and established a technical drawing and craft school bearing his own name. As a result of banking services performed for the government during the Crimean War, Stieglitz was promoted to the high civil service rank of Actual State Councillor. Although this title was largely honorary, his ties with the Ministry of Finances were long-standing and intimate. He hobnobbed with the most important dignitaries in the Russian capital, particularly Ministers who also happened to be of German backgrounds—Reutern and Nesselrode. The Stieglitz palace on the English quay became in the 1850's the frequent scene of society balls and musical soirées.[49]

The creation of the State Bank in 1860 presented Stieglitz with the opportunity of actually functioning in an important administrative capacity within the Ministry of Finances. The State Bank was designed as the central bank of Russia. Its main functions were to stabilize the currency and to provide capital for industrial development. It was

[48] Von Maydell, "Die Stieglitz aus Arolsen," p. 84; *Kratkii istoricheskii ocherk nachala i rasprostraneniia zheleznykh dorog v Rossii po 1897 vkliu chitel'no* (St. Petersburg, 1898), vol. I, pp. 72-73.

[49] Von Maydell, p. 83.

thus a modern institution and it was deemed fitting to put a business-man rather than a bureaucrat at its head. At a dinner given by Count Nesselrode, Reutern offered the job to Stieglitz. The latter, as the wealthiest private banker in Russia, was the ideal figure for such a post.[50] By education and experience, however, although an adept businessman, he was not qualified as an economist and fiscal expert who could probe the complexities of Russian state finances. Baron Stieglitz was well aware of his shortcomings, and accepted the post of Director of the Russian State Bank only after being assured that the real work of administration would be in the hands of an assistant, Lamanski. Lamanski, an able administrator, succeeded Stieglitz in 1866 to become the leading state banker in Russia for many years, at least until the appearance of Bunge on the bureaucratic scene.

Stieglitz's resignation in 1866 did not signal his return to private banking. When appointed head of the State Bank, he had liquidated his financial empire. He now retired to a rentier's life in his St. Petersburg palace, with the comforts of an income estimated at three million rubles a year. His total fortune, apart from real property, upon his death in 1884, exceeded one hundred million rubles.[51] Ludwig Stieglitz's original capital in 1803 had been increased a thousandfold.

The Stieglitzes did not continue in the shipping, banking, manufacturing, railroad, and insurance businesses of Russia which they had helped to found and develop. Philanthropists and rentiers, some married into the aristocracy, while others wrote books on Slavophilism. The family name died out before the Revolution. The reign of the House of Stieglitz was of short duration, little more than two generations—half a century. This pattern was characteristic of Russian capitalism rather than unique, and was to be repeated many times in the late nineteenth and early twentieth centuries. The Guchkovs by the fourth generation dissolved their enterprises and plunged into politics. The Konovalovs and Riabushinskiis combined big business and political activity. The younger Riabushinskiis, like the Botkins, found new sources of dedication in science. Savva Morozov befriended the Marxists and was cast out of his family concern when he attempted to turn it into a profit-sharing organization. The Prokhorovs entered the nobility just before World War I. The railroad king, Von Derviz, retired to ostentatious idleness on the Riviera. Another great Russian railroad magnate, Bloch, abandoned business life and became a scholar and pacifist writer. Some of the Tretiakovs and Gunzburgs turned to the arts and philanthropy, as did one of the famous Russian capitalist patrons at the turn of the twentieth century, Savva Mamontov.[52] One

[50] "Iz Vospominanii E. F. Lamanskago," p. 339.

[51] *Russkii biograficheskii slovar*, article on Alexander Stieglitz.

[52] On the railroad magnates of the late nineteenth century, see Valentine Bill, *The Forgotten Class* (New York, 1959). On Russian capitalism in the last

can argue that the later generations of the great industrialist families of Europe and America have done all of these same things. However, it may be suggested that the Western capitalists had a greater staying power than their counterparts in Russia, excluding the final blow of revolutionary expropriation. Some Rockefellers have gone into politics; others have remained in business. The Fords, Du Ponts, and Krupps have rarely wandered from the office. Russian capitalism did not seem to "stick." This could already be seen—as in the case of the Stieglitz family—at its very beginning.

---

decades of tsarism: Roger Portal, "Industriels Moscovites, la section cotonnière (1861-1914)," *Cahiers du monde russe et soviétique* (1963), vol. IV, pp. 5-46 and I. F. Gindin, "Russkaia burzhuaziia v period kapitalizma, eie razvitie i osobennosti," *Istoriia SSSR*, vol. 7 (1963) no. 2, pp. 57-80; (1963) no. 3, pp. 37-60.

Part IV

Transportation

"With a railroad, St. Petersburg will be in Moscow, and Moscow will be in Kronstadt!" So proclaimed Nicholas I on January 25, 1842, to a delegation of seventeen awe-stricken Russian merchants, tears running down some of their faces. The St. Petersburg businessmen had been given an unprecedented invitation to come to the tsar's office and express their gratitude for his recent decision to build a railroad between the two Russian capitals.[1] By the expression, "St. Petersburg will be in Moscow," the Gendarme of Europe meant that in the event of an insurrection, a fully equipped regiment could be moved by railway in less than a day from cheaper Moscow garrisons to St. Petersburg. When he said, "Moscow will be in Kronstadt," however, the Tsar was expressing his awareness of the tremendous commercial advantages of rapid transport between the interior of Russia and its ports. A clearer appreciation of Russia's transport needs was voiced at about the same time by the tsar's leading railroad engineer, Paul Mel'nikov. In an article in the official *Journal of Ways of Communication*, Mel'nikov argued that a railroad network would shrink Russia sixteen times.[2] Industrializing Russia shared with the United States the problem of bigness. The world's largest empire could never industrialize without effective rapid transportation. Industrialization demanded the binding of Russia's grain, ore, coal, and wood, its cities, markets, and ports, and the moving of manufactured goods and raw materials, imports and exports, by new and efficient means of transport. Modern war required a quickened pace for the marshaling and movement of armies; and after December 1825, it was reassuring to know that rebellions could be stifled more easily by the electricity of the telegraph and the steam of locomotives than by nocturnal maneuvers in the streets of the capital and barracks exhortations.

The modernization of Russian transportation, however, began not with railroads in the 1830's but with canals in the reign of Paul I. The early nineteenth century may be considered the golden age of canal construction in Russia. Most of the important canal systems of European Russia were completed in the reigns of Alexander I and Nicholas I. Roads were not developed as extensively during the same period. Only a few important highways had been built when the railroads came to Russia to overshadow them. The early Russian railroads had

---

[1] "Iz zapisok Barona (vposledstvii Grafa) M. A. Korfa," *Russkaia starina*, vol. 99 (1899), pp. 503-04.

[2] Cited in S. A. Urodkov, *Peterburgo-Moskovskaia Zheleznaia Doroga, istoriia stroitelstvo 1842-1851* (Leningrad, 1951), pp. 34-35.

commercial and military value; their construction and operation also form important first chapters in the history of Russian industry and technology. A generation of Russian railroad engineers were trained by the building of the St. Petersburg-Moscow railroad. These engineers went on to build much of the Russian rail network of the late nineteenth century. Railways require machinery: the history of the first Russian railroads is also the story of the birth of steam technology and a machine industry in Russia.

In at least two important ways the first Russian railroads set the pattern for the transportation history of Russia during the remainder of the tsarist period as well as the early years of the Soviet regime. Russia remained dependent on foreign technicians, both by importing machinery which Russians could not operate and by bringing in the makers of the machines themselves. The locomotives, rolling stock, track, and embankment of the St. Petersburg-Moscow railroad could not have been built without the help of American engineers. Later, for the building of large parts of the railway network of European Russia, French and German engineers were used. The first major Russian railways were state controlled. The state put up most of the money. Army engineers were used to do the building, together with foreigners retained by the government. The lines were operated by the Department of Railroads of the state transport administration. Although Russia was to have its share of privately owned railroad lines in the late nineteenth century, financed and managed by Russians and foreigners, by the end of the tsarist period state control was reasserted. The military motive in such circumstances remained a prominent one in the building of Russian railroads.

Chapter 11

From Rivers to Rails

Canals and Highways

The traditional highways of Russia since before the coming of the Varangians had been her vast network of rivers. As commercial pressures for improved transportation intensified in the early nineteenth century, it was natural that an initial reliance would be placed on the ancient water links of the northern and southern seas and of Europe and Asia. Canals, as Peter the Great had first pointed out, would bring a new life and capacity to the river system with which to meet the demands of a growing industry and trade. Modern roads connecting the main cities of Russia would hasten communications, if they could not substantially augment the volume of goods which inched their way across the empire on animal and man-drawn river barges.

Russia in the early nineteenth century, very much like the United States during the same period, witnessed an era of transport experimentation which manifested itself primarily in the construction of canals and to a lesser degree improved roads. The causes, problems, and magnitude of this prelude to rail transport in both countries were roughly approximate, but there were differences worthy of note. In the United States, the "turnpikes" preceded the canals, were short-lived, unprofitable, and never of great significance, until the coming of the automobile a century later ushered in a new era in road building. American canals, a mixed product of state and private enterprise, were a going concern for several decades following the opening of the Erie Canal in 1825. In the end, they lost out to the cheapness and speed of the railroad freight carriers. In Russia in the early nineteenth century, the first flurry of canal building preceded the building of highways. Unlike those of the United States, the Russian highways remained insignificant. Even today, they are only beginning to rival the railroads. Canals in Russia, a large-scale state enterprise since the beginning, continue in Soviet times to be major transport arteries for cargo and passengers, although they offer little competition for the Russian railroads. Physical geography partially explains the differences: Russia has the most extensive and navigable river system in the world. The ten largest of thousands of navigable rivers extend for a distance of over 20,000 miles. The beginning of the history of modern transport in Russia must, then, be traced back to waterways.[1]

By a *ukaz* of February 27, 1797, Paul I created the post of Super-

---

[1] A. Lebed and B. Iakovlev, "Transportnoe znachenie gidrotekhnicheskikh sooruzhenii SSSR," Institute for the Study of History and Culture of the U.S.-S.R.," Munich, *Issledovanie i materialy*, series 1, vol. 14 (1954), p. 9.

intendent of Waterways. The Superintendent of Waterways was put in charge of a Department of Waterways, which was opened in March 1798. This was an independent transport agency, which was organized along bureaucratic lines of procedure, following the shift away from the collegial principle under Paul I. The Superintendent was in full command of his agency, responsible not to the President of one of the Colleges, but to the Senate. He was assisted by a board, consisting of four civil and military officials. Under them worked a staff of engineers, mostly military men. On the local level, the Department of Waterways established offices wherever needed. Inspectors were sent out to supervise the canal systems. The Speranskii reforms of 1809-1810 embraced the transportation establishment, which was enlarged and consolidated. The Superintendent was made responsible for roads and ports as well as waterways. The Russian empire was divided into ten districts for the purpose of supervising canals, roads, bridges, dams, and other elements of the transport system. An engineering school was established.[2] During the last decade of the reign of Alexander I, the educational and research activities of the transport administration were enlarged. By the time of the creation of a Department of Railroads under Nicholas I, the Main Administration of Ways of Communication, as it had come to be called, was equivalent to a ministry in all but name. This designation came in 1865.[3]

The transport administration, like the Ministry of Finances, was fortunate enough to attract during the nineteenth century some of the best administrative talent both within and outside of Russia. Its superintendents during the early years, from 1797 to 1833, would appear at first glance to have been products of the traditional court-bureaucratic favoritism and nepotism. At the helm in this period were three counts, a prince, and a duke (one a brother-in-law and one an uncle to the tsar). Actually, the first three Superintendents of Waterways were able administrators, all vigorous proponents of canal construction. Count Jacob Johann Sievers organized and ran the transport establishment from 1797 until 1800. Although this Livonian German was practically a septuagenarian, he remained one of the most experienced and vigorous of Catherine the Great's administrators. A provincial reformer, he had pioneered in canal construction in the 1760's while serving as the Governor of Novgorod. Sievers was charged with the building of a major canal system under Paul I. The infirmities of old age did not restrain him from a personal inspection of the proposed route, and he was carried by stretcher when and where he could no

---

[2] On the early history of the Institute for Engineers of Ways of Communication, see my Chapter 16.

[3] The early administrative history of the transport establishment is summarized in *Kratkii istoricheskii ocherk razvitiia i deiatel'nosti vedomstva putei soobshcheniia za sto let ego sushchestvovaniia 1798-1898* (St. Petersburg, 1898), pp. 13, 17-18, 29-32.

longer walk. Sievers was almost immediately followed as Superintendent from 1801 until 1809 by Count Nikolai Petrovich Rumiantsev,
whose advocacy of Russian industrialization and transport modernization has been discussed elsewhere.[4] Under Rumiantsev's tutelage, the
most extensive canal construction in Russia during the entire nineteenth century took place. Rumiantsev was succeeded by a young
cousin and brother-in-law of Alexander I, Prince George Paul Oldenburg. Although Oldenburg, like Rumiantsev, had no technical training
or experience in the field of transport engineering, he was an active
reformer, humanitarian, provincial governor, and wartime leader. His
three years as Superintendent of Ways of Communication witnessed
the opening of the two most important canal systems of European
Russia and the reforms which provided the foundation for the transport administration during the remainder of the tsarist period.

Oldenburg was followed upon his death by two transport experts,
both of them foreign engineers. The first was François Devolant, a
Belgian trained as a military engineer in the Dutch colonies of the new
world. Devolant entered the Russian scene in 1787 as a military engineer, soon rising to the rank of general. During the early years of the
reign of Alexander I, he gained fame as the builder of the Mariinskii
canal system. As Superintendent of Ways of Communication from
1812 until his death in 1818, he worked with Arakcheev to improve
Russian highways. Devolant was succeeded by a distinguished Spanish
engineer, Augustine de Bethancourt. Bethancourt became known as
an expert on canals and steam engines in Spain and France before he
entered the Russian service in 1808. As Superintendent of Ways of
Communication from 1819 to 1823, Bethancourt worked to introduce
steam transportation to Russian rivers and to improve the transport
educational system.

Bethancourt was succeeded by Alexander Frederick, Duke of
Württemberg, whose nephew was the Emperor of Russia. Württemberg had held several posts in the Russian civil administration, but
had no engineering experience. Although it has been claimed that the
only words of Russian which he knew and used were *"sto palok"*
("100 lashes"),[5] much in the way of heavy transport construction
(perhaps because of this) was achieved during his ten-year administration. A huge canal system was cut, which linked the Volga
River and the White Sea as well as the commercial center of Rybinsk

[4] On Rumiantsev's views, see my Chapter 5. Glimpses of Sievers' work as a
transport administrator are recorded in a compilation of his diary by K. L.
Blum, *Eines Russischen Staatsmanns, des Grafen Jakob Johann Sievers Denk-
würdigkeiten zur Geschichte Russlands* (Leipzig, 1858); and P. L'vov, "Prichina
naimenovaniia Mariinskago kanala," *Otechestvennye zapiski* (1820), part 4,
pp. 108-24. Sievers was succeeded briefly by a temporary replacement, Count
G. G. Kushelev.

[5] V. Virginskii, *Tvortsy novoi tekhniki v krepostnoi Rossii* (Moscow, 1957),
p. 321.

with the port of Archangel. Russia's first major highway, connecting St. Petersburg and Moscow, was completed by Württemberg.[6]

The foreigners, Devolant, Bethancourt, and Württemberg were followed at the helm of the Russian transport administration by war heroes and tough soldiers rather than technicians. It was not until after the death of Nicholas I that Russian engineers were appointed to head this agency. Much had been accomplished during the first three decades of the century, particularly in the modernization of internal waterways. Seven water transport systems, or twenty-nine canals of varying lengths amounting to about 500 miles, had been added to the Vyshnevolotsk system started by Peter the Great. This sole survivor of the eighteenth-century system was itself improved and enlarged. Most of the new canals were located in the western part of the Russian empire. The building of a Siberian canal system, as well as the construction of massive, sea-going canals and hydroelectric complexes had to await the Soviet period. However, the European Russian system was created essentially under the tsars in the early nineteenth century.[7]

Peter the Great's Vyshnevolotsk canal system united the Volga and the Baltic. This series of canals, lakes, and rivers extended for about 865 miles and was narrow, shallow, dangerous to navigate, unusable part of the year, and was constantly falling into disrepair. A much needed alternative system to connect the Volga and the Baltic was started in 1799. A major combination of canals, lakes, rivers, conduits, reservoirs, locks, dams, and bridges, including a hospital and a school, was planned to permit a safer two-way traffic of larger vessels. Construction took nine years and cost 450,000 rubles. The cost was sustained by the dowager empress, and the system named "Mariinskii" after her. Improved during the nineteenth century, it came to consist of twenty-seven locks and was just over 700 miles long.[8] A third Volga-Baltic system, called the "Tikhvinskii," after its main canal, was completed in 1811. The Baltic and the Dnieper had already been connected in 1804 by the Berezina system of eighteen rivers, lakes, and canals. In the same year, the Oginski system was completed to connect the Dnieper and the Niemen. In 1830, the Augustus system connected the Niemen with the Vistula in the Kingdom of Poland, and in 1841, the Vistula was connected with the Dnieper and Bug to

---

[6] On Devolant, see L'vov, "Prichina naimenovaniia Mariinskago Kanala," and on Bethancourt, Oldenburg, and Württemberg, the articles in *Russkii biograficheskii slovar*.

[7] Lebed and Iakovlev, "Znachenie gidrotekhnicheskikh sooruzhenii SSSR," pp. 12, 41-42.

[8] On the Mariinskii canal, see two other articles by the contemporary, Pavel L'vov, "Vzgliad na Mariinskii kanal," and "O sisteme plavaniia po Mariinskomu kanalu," *Otechestvennye zapiski* (1820), part 2, pp. 163-88, and (1821), part 5, pp. 278-79; also Lebed and Iakovlev, "Znachenie gidrotekhnicheskikh sooruzhenii SSSR," pp. 20-23; and *Kratkii istoricheskii ocherk razvitiia vodianykh i sukhoputnikh soobshchenii i torgovykh portov v Rossii* (St. Petersburg, 1900), pp. 156-58.

link the Black Sea with Danzig and Königsberg. The Volga and the White Sea, as mentioned, were linked in the rapid time of three years (1825 to 1828) by the Duke Alexander of Württemberg system, consisting of five canals, six lakes, and seven rivers.[9]

Russia's rivers required maintenance and improvement like any man-made road or canal. The Dnieper rapids were an ancient problem, which was largely solved by 1850 through the circumvention of treacherous areas with canals. The northern Volga presented more difficult problems of meandering and shallows, so that much in the way of dredging and dams remained to be accomplished by the end of the reign of Nicholas I. The lower Volga had human obstacles: the millennial plague of pirates. These brigands were cleared by Alexander I's gunboats.[10]

River and canal roads were wide ones upon which bulk cargo could be carried: this was their great virtue. From 1825 until 1850, according to the official reports, the value of cargo on all interior waterways multiplied by about 250 percent, from 55,445,000 to 138,000,000 rubles.[11] The greatest shortcoming of water transport in the vastness of Russia as in the United States was slowness of movement. Heavy cargoes were hauled in barges by animals—and in Russia by humans—although small sailcraft were found useful on the rivers. The trip from north to south and east to west, as has been detailed in an earlier chapter, took months and sometimes years.[12]

Steam motive power was one answer to this problem which was seized upon by both Russians and Americans, although somewhat less enthusiastically by the former. Nevertheless, some government engineers, forward-looking landlords, and enterprising merchants actively encouraged river steamship experimentation. Nicholas I permitted the forming of private river steamship companies. After the fruitless venture of Robert Fulton in Russia, a landlord named Evreinov in 1823 built the 84 foot, 60 horsepower *Volga*, which could handle a cargo of up to 900 tons. Prior to this, Evreinov had experimented with small, steam-propelled vessels capable of making the trip from Astrakhan to Astrabad in twelve days. After the government granted permission for private river steamboating enterprises in 1843, at least one Russian company, the "Mercury" was formed to navigate the Volga. In the same year, the first steamboat service on Lake Ladoga was instituted.

---

[9] Details and maps in Lebed and Iakovlev, "Znachenie gidrotekhnicheskikh sooruzhenii SSSR," pp. 19, 24-27; see also the official report, "Istoricheskoe obozrenie putei soobshcheniia i publichnikh zdanii s 1825 po 1850 god," *Sbornik Imperatorskago Russkago Istoricheskago Obshchestva*, vol. 98, pp. 532-41. See map in my Chapter 2.

[10] *Sbornik Imperatorskago Russkago Istoricheskago Obshchestva*, vol. 98, p. 541; *Istoricheskii ocherk vedomstva putei soobshcheniia*, p. 55.

[11] *Sbornik Imperatorskago Russkago Istoricheskago Obshchestva*, vol. 98, p. 552.

[12] See Chapter 3.

These were only token gestures. No real capital was advanced for steam navigation of the Russian rivers during the early nineteenth century, and in the latter half of the century, railroads assumed the job. By 1850, there were only ninety-nine steamboats on the principal Russian rivers, lakes, and inland seas out of a total of 57,000 vessels.[13]

The quest for more rapid transport—if not for cargo, at least for passengers and troops—led to experimentation with improved roads which could withstand those pressures of nature and human traffic that quickly reduced dirt paths to impassable bogs of mud and dust. In both the United States and Russia, wooden plank roads and the far more durable stone macadam highways were constructed during the prerailroad years of the early nineteenth century. This was done on a fairly extensive scale (for the time) of several thousand miles. The wooden plank road was itself a Russian innovation which came to the United States through Canada in the 1830's. The Russian government took its first real interest in macadamized highways in 1816, when the tough Count Arakcheev was appointed to head a new committee for the planning and supervision of highway construction. In the same year, the building of the first Moscow-St. Petersburg highway was initiated, but with a termination date which was stretched out over two decades. Nicholas I hastened somewhat the completion of this important link—to 1833. A labor force for the construction of the road was provided by a corvée of soldiers and military colonists, rather than contracted *obrok* serf wage laborers. This was a precedent that was partially followed in the building of the early Russian railroads. Soon, a daily stagecoach operated in both directions between Moscow and St. Petersburg. By 1850, Moscow had been connected by similar modern highways with Iaroslav, Nizhnii-Novgorod, Riazan, and Brest-Litovsk. According to the official report of that year, 100 cities had been united by 4,841 and 3/4 *versts* (about 3,228 miles) of highways, with another 1,518 *versts* in construction.[14]

As with the United States during the same period, such roads, although providing a more rapid means of transport than canals during part of the year, were by no means a satisfactory answer to Russia's transport and commercial problems in terms of either speed or capacity. It took almost three and one-half days for a coach and horses to gallop over the new highway from St. Petersburg to Moscow. The fare was 70 rubles. Exorbitant freight charges, as we have seen, pushed sky

[13] "Iz zapisok Barona Korfa," *Russkaia starina*, vol. 100 (1899), p. 274; Virginskii, *Tvortsy novoi tekhniki*, pp. 331-32; and *Istoricheskii ocherk vedomstva putei soobshcheniia*, pp. 54-56 on river steamboats. See also M. K. Rozhkova, ed., *Ocherki ekonomicheskoi istorii Rossii pervoi poloviny xix veka* (Moscow, 1959), p. 271.

[14] "Istoricheskie obozreniia putei soobshcheniia," *Sbornik Imperatorskago Russkago Istoricheskago Obshchestva*, vol. 98, pp. 554-58; *Kratkii istoricheskii ocherk deiatel'nosti vedomstva putei soobshcheniia za sto let ego sushchestvovaniia 1798-1898 gg*, pp. 44-47.

high the prices of Russian goods by the time they had completed the long trek from the interior parts of the empire to the westerly markets, where they had to compete (not very successfully) with cheaper foreign products. By the 1830's, however, railroads using steam locomotives were operating in England, and a growing number of experiments with this new mode of transport were taking place in Europe, in the United States, and even in Russia.

The Railroad Debate of the 1830's

During the same period a debate over the usefulness and desirability of railroads in Russia spilled over from official chancelleries to the press and the general educated public. High ranking representatives of the bureaucracy, such as Mordvinov, Kankrin, and Benckendorff, became involved. Influential Russian merchants and industrialists pressed for railway links, not only between the two capitals, but also from Russia's interior to the Black Sea. Academicians and scientists published articles and books in which the economic and technical advantages of railroads were systematically presented to the public; while Russian engineers began to explain the new invention in the classrooms of the Institute of Engineers of Ways of Communication. In 1835, Paul Mel'nikov, a young officer and lecturer in this school, who was to become a builder of the St. Petersburg-Moscow railroad and later Minister of Ways of Communication, published the first technical treatise on railroads to appear in Russia.[15] Outside of official, business, and academic circles, intellectuals in the Moscow salons, like the Slavophils Tiutchev and Odoevskii and the poet Pushkin, looked upon the new devices with alternating romantic hopes and practical misgivings. Prince Odoevskii, in his fictional Russia of the fifth millennium, saw electric subways under the Caspian Sea and the Himalayan mountains.[16] To these voices were joined those of a numerous contingent of Russian journalists and foreign promoters. The railroad debate of the 1830's is significant and revealing for several reasons. Most of the technical and economic problems which would beset the construction of Russia's first railroads were aired. Similar to the struggle of the freetraders and the protectionists over tariff questions twenty years before, the disputants ultimately had recourse to arguments involving fundamental questions of Russia's industrial destiny.[17] The urgency of Russia's modernization was once more heralded to official circles with new and more compelling facts and conclusions. Many of these ideas reflected general standpoints in the debate then forming between the Slavophiles and the Westernizers. The

[15] P. P. Mel'nikov, "Svedeniia o russkikh zheleznykh dorogakh," *Krasnyi arkhiv*, vol. 99, p. 135.

[16] V. F. Odoevskii, *4338-i god, fantasticheskii roman* (Moscow, 1926), p. 16.

[17] On the debate of the freetraders and the protectionists, see my Chapter 5.

railroad debate of the 1830's in some respects might be called a reflection in the area of technology of this larger dispute.

Many of the proponents of railroads presented not only general technical and economic arguments supporting their feasibility and necessity, but formulated specific projects as well. One of the earliest and most extravagant of these came from a young officer, Golievskii, who in 1837 proposed to the Emperor a scheme for two large, transecting rail lines, which with their spurs would connect St. Petersburg, Moscow, Kiev, Odessa, Warsaw, and the Austrian border with some 3,600 *versts* of track. This network, which, if realized, would constitute by far the largest in the world, was to cost the state very little, according to the visionary Golievskii, since it could be financed by a special head tax and built by serf corvées provisioned from local estates.[18] A year later, a similar project was offered by N. N. Muraviev. Muraviev was far more accurate in his predictions than he was practical in his proposals. For the future, he rightly foresaw that in forty years Russia would have a system of railroads, not only in the western provinces, but extending into Siberia as well. However, he unrealistically proposed in 1838 that the state, which had only just permitted the completion of a sixteen-mile experimental line from St. Petersburg to the suburban summer palaces of the tsars—a railway financed by private investors—should undertake itself the entire burden of a vast network, which would connect St. Petersburg, Moscow, Kazan, Warsaw, and Odessa.[19] Such a project would cost hundreds of millions of rubles and was well beyond the tsarist government's fiscal capacity. The most radical railroad thinking of the 1830's from the technical point of view was that of the academician B. S. Jacobi. Jacobi was experimenting in St. Petersburg with electric engines in the 1830's, and envisaged their application to rail transport. Seemingly, the most bizarre plan was contained in the proposals of a Russian official, Frederick Fick, who suggested a rail line with passenger cars drawn by teams of humans, presumably serfs. Since human motive power was still used extensively in Russia in the hauling of barges along the rivers and canals, there was nothing unusual about Fick's proposals. Like many of his contemporaries, he was apprehensive about the high speeds attained by steam locomotives and saw human propulsion as a kind of safety factor for passenger transport.[20]

N. S. Mordvinov's views of rail transport were far more practical from the economic point of view. Although he went so far in the

[18] Urodkov, *Peterburgo-Moskovskaia zheleznaia doroga*, pp. 55-56.

[19] Mel'nikov, "Svedeniia o russkikh zheleznykh dorogakh," *Krasnyi arkhiv*, vol. 99, p. 161; M. Krutikov, ed., "Pervye zheleznye dorogi v Rossii" (official documents), *Krasnyi arkhiv*, vol. 76, pp. 122-26.

[20] On Fick, see B. Velikin, *Peterburg-Moskva, iz istorii Oktiabr'skoi zheleznoi dorogi* (Leningrad, 1934), p. 44; on Jacobi, my Chapter 16 and N. A. Figurovskii, *Istoriia estestvoznaniia v Rossii* (Moscow, 1957), vol. I, part 2, pp. 142-44.

1830's as to envision a Transcaucasus railroad, most of the time he argued that the building of a Russian rail system was possible only through foreign investment in private stock companies.[21] By far the most coherent economic arguments advanced in support of Russian railroads in this first debate came in 1839 in an article by one Safonov, printed in the influential *Syn Otechestva.* Safonov believed that the primary utility of railroads in Russia was the fact that they provided a bond of rapid freight transport between her ports and her industrial and agricultural centers. Furthermore, the construction of railroads helped to develop technology in Russia. On the basis of these considerations, he proposed a rail line which would run from St. Petersburg to Moscow and thence to the provinces of Tambov and Saratov, thus making possible connections with the commercial routes and agricultural areas of central Russia and the lower Volga as well as the Urals industrial complex.[22]

All of these proposals were turned down flatly by the Russian government. Opposition to Russian railroads in the 1830's was widespread, not only among journalists and engineers, but in the upper echelons of the bureaucracy. Ranged against the aging and outspoken economist Mordvinov, the agrarian reformer Kiselev and the policeman Benckendorff (who, however, had certain reservations about railroads as a gendarme, if not as an investor) were almost the entire Committee of Ministers.[23] Kankrin remained a staunch enemy of railroads, and was seconded not only by succeeding Ministers of Internal Affairs, Perovskii and Stroganov, but even by the Superintendent of Ways of Communication, Baron Toll. The tsar, however, wanted a railroad, at least between St. Petersburg and Moscow. Beyond this he would not go, nor was he fully convinced of the usefulness—particularly military—of railroads, or of their technical feasibility. Apparently he was willing to experiment and to listen for quite some time to the debate among his officials and engineers before coming to that resolution of the "supreme will" which would decide the issue once and for all.

Some of the opinions of the opposition were concerned with planning, financing, and administrative implementation. The validity of railroads per se was not questioned. Others, voicing a kind of technological Slavophilism, attacked railroads as a moral and political evil which threatened the security of Russia. The general tone of all the

[21] V. Virginskii, "Bor'ba vokrug podgotovki k stroitel'stvu pervoi bol'shoi russkoi zh-d. magistrali Peterburg-Moskva," *Istoricheskie zapiski*, vol. 32 (1950), pp. 74, 77-78; V. A. Bilbasov, ed., *Arkhiv Grafov Mordvinovykh* (St. Petersburg, 1901-03), vol. IX, pp. 43, 86, 145, 169-70 for the Mordvinov proposals.
[22] Virginskii, "Bor'ba vokrug podgotovki russkoi zh-d. magistrali," *Istoricheskie zapiski,* vol. 32, pp. 74-76.
[23] Mel'nikov, "Svedeniia o russkikh zheleznykh dorogakh," *Krasnyi arkhiv,* vol. 99, pp. 162-63.

voices of dissent reflected the conservatism of intellectual and official circles of the Nicholean period: resistance to change, to innovation, to departure from past procedures, to threats to economic or bureaucratic vested interests, to experimentation or needless risks, and to extravagance in ideas or money matters. The poet Pushkin, along with Mordvinov, Speranskii, the engineer Mel'nikov and other partisans of railroads, mainly raised questions as to whether the state or private corporations, Russians or foreigners, should assume the burden.[24] Other critics looked to their pocketbooks: what would be the effect of railroads, asked one group of sceptics—including for obvious reasons investors in the St. Petersburg-Moscow stagecoach lines, which brought in millions of rubles each year—on the highway transport business and on the numerous peasant coachmen therein engaged? Count Kiselev raised questions on this point; and an article appearing in 1835 in the journal, *Publicly Useful Information*, claimed to report the apprehensions of peasant coachmen about railroads and steam engines.[25]

A general distrust of machines was reflected in the widespread view that railroads could never conquer the snows and freezing temperatures of Russia and that a speed of forty *versts* (about twenty-seven miles) per hour was dangerous. Although ready to admit the usefulness of railroads in Europe and the United States, many felt that Russia was not ready for them. A book on railroads published in 1838 argued that Russia possessed neither the density of population, the industry, nor the educational level demanded for freight and passenger railroads. Sharing this belief was the Superintendent of Ways of Communication, Baron Toll, who argued that Russia was basically an agricultural country which did its shipping once a year after harvest, and with such a schedule, railroads would be impractical. He further argued, as did many engineers, such as General Destrem, a leading transport official, that canals were Russia's mainstay of transportation.[26] Underlying these arguments was the belief that Russia's economic destiny was fundamentally agricultural, not industrial.

Kankrin is reputed to have argued against railroads on the ethical and political grounds that frequent rapid transport would increase "the restless spirit of our age." More often, however, we see him attacking from his customary and stronger position of cost. Why empty the state treasury to build a railroad to Odessa when the winds of the

[24] Velikin, *Peterburg-Moskva*, pp. 25, 33-34.
[25] Urodkov, *Peterburgo-Moskovskaia zheleznaia doroga*, p. 38.
[26] A. Pravdin, "On Iron and Paved Roads" (1838), cited in Urodkov, *Peterburgo-Moskovskaia zheleznaia doroga*, p. 40. On the official views, see M. Krutikov, ed., "Pervye zheleznye dorogi v Rossii," *Krasnyi arkhiv*, vol. 76, pp. 125-26; and Mel'nikov, "Svedeniia o russkikh zheleznykh dorogakh," *Krasnyi arkhiv*, vol. 99, pp. 161-63.

Russian rivers and the Black Sea are free?[27] Baron Toll expressed the most reactionary fears of Western political ideas when he opposed Muraviev's project on the grounds that railroads were democratic and would help to spread the subversive tendency of egalitarianism in Russia. Other officials similarly pondered the disasters which would follow from having serfs and nobles sitting next to each other on the same bench of a crowded passenger car. Inevitably, there appeared the perennial Russian argument that railroads would increase the number of foreign tourists, including revolutionaries, and thus cause an influx of dangerous Western ideas. This fear was voiced by the Minister of Internal Affairs, Perovskii, who concluded that the cost of policing the Russian railroads would be exorbitant. For his part, the Chief of Gendarmes, Benckendorff, was not apprehensive about railroads from a police perspective. In fact, a St. Petersburg-Moscow railway would tend to reduce the potentially dangerous overcrowding of factory workers in these cities as industrialists began to build plants in the countryside near the rail lines.[28]

The Tsarskoe Selo Railroad

Many of the technical objections to Russian railroads were refuted by the success of the first Russian railroad, completed in 1837. This was the famous Tsarskoe Selo line, which connected St. Petersburg and the summer resorts of the tsars and St. Petersburg society at suburban Tsarskoe Selo and Pavlovsk. Count Kankrin sarcastically dismissed this experiment as an expensive toy which served little function except to connect "the capital with the cabaret." The parsimonious Minister of Finances was no doubt stung by the bill for almost a million rubles, or about one-fifth of the total cost of the railroad, which had been allotted for the construction of restaurants and dance halls in Tsarskoe Selo and Pavlovsk.[29] The first Russian railroad cannot be considered to have been much more than an excursion line. Nevertheless, it was a significant beginning step. It demonstrated beyond all reasonable doubt that a railroad could function in the rigors of the Russian climate. More important, it was built with the intention of providing the preparation as well as the first segment of a trunk line between St. Petersburg and Moscow.[30]

[27] Velikin, *Peterburg-Moskva*, p. 45.
[28] On the views of Toll, Benckendorff, and Perovskii, see Virginskii, "Bor'ba vokrug podgotovki russkoi zh-d. magistrali," *Istoricheskie zapiski*, vol. 32, pp. 74, 84; Mel'nikov, "Svedeniia o russkikh zheleznykh dorogakh," *Krasnyi arkhiv*, vol. 99, p. 174; and A. I. Shtukenberg, "Iz istorii zhelezno-dorozhnago del v Rossii, Nikolaievskaia doroga mezhdu Peterburgom i Moskvoiu 1842-1852," *Russkaia starina*, vol. 46 (1885), p. 315.
[29] Franz Anton von Gerstner, *Berichte aus den Vereinigten Staaten von Nordamerika* (Leipzig, 1839), pp. 61-62.
[30] Virginskii, "Bor'ba vokrug podgotovki russkoi zh-d. magistrali," *Istori-*

Technically speaking, the Tsarskoe Selo line was not the first road of iron rails to be placed on Russian soil, nor were its foreign-built engines the first steam locomotives to belch smoke into the Russian air. From 1806 until 1810, a Russian mechanic by the name of Peter Frolov built and operated a cast iron railway for horse-drawn wagons. This line was several miles long, and was intended to service an iron factory in the Urals. In 1833, in another Urals plant, two other Russian-trained inventors, a father-and-son team, the Cherepanovs, built steam engines capable of moving at the rate of eight to ten miles per hour and of carrying forty passengers as well as cargos of eighteen tons. The achievements of Frolov and the Cherepanovs were not miracles performed by untutored serfs, building complex machines with their bare hands in a gloom of illiteracy and backwardness. The Russian inventors were as educated, traveled, and as conversant in the latest technical advances as most of their contemporaries in the West. Frolov attended the Mining Institute in St. Petersburg. M. Ye. Cherepanov was in England at the time that George Stephenson was making locomotives and may well have examined the Englishman's work. The Cherepanov experiments remained isolated, however, and had little effect on the mainstream development of Russian transport. Although some officials were acquainted with them, they did not influence the state's decision to utilize foreign personnel, machinery, and techniques in the building of both the Tsarskoe Selo railroad and the St. Petersburg-Moscow line. The government so opted less because of the blindness and "cosmopolitanism" of the unpatriotic ruling circles of Russia than because Russian inventions did not provide an effective substitute for foreign technology and organization of production.[31]

The original scheme presented to the Russian government in 1835 by Gerstner, the builder of the Tsarskoe Selo railroad, had been far more ambitious than the sixteen miles of track, three stations, twelve locomotives, forty-four passenger and nineteen freight cars that constituted the completed operation. He had proposed a network that would connect St. Petersburg with Moscow, Nizhnii-Novgorod, Kazan, and possibly Odessa, and which would then be linked to steamship lines on the Volga River and Caspian Sea. Cargo, he argued, could be moved rapidly from Central Asia to the Baltic in ten to fifteen days, and—a prospect more appealing to Nicholas I—a large contingent of troops, horses, and equipment could be shuttled from Moscow garrisons to St. Petersburg in about twenty-four hours. Russia's agriculture and industry would be stimulated, commerce with Asia would

---

cheskie zapiski, vol. 32, p. 75; C. Kreeft, *First Russian Railroad* (London, 1837). The latter was an advertisement for the company.

[31] On the Cherepanovs and Frolov, see the chapters in Virginskii, *Tvortsy novoi tekhniki.*

grow, a favorable balance of trade with Europe could be achieved, and European and American railroad progress would be overtaken.[32] This was a revolutionary engineering concept for its time. Only in the United States had it been imagined that such distances could be spanned by rails and locomotives. The plan was rejected by the government committees formed to consider it in 1835. However it was not so much the technical audacity of Gerstner's proposals that repelled the Russian officials as the toughness of his bargain.

Franz Anton Ritter von Gerstner was a typical prodigy of the early days of industrial capitalism and the infancy of the world's railroads, half genius and half scoundrel. His plans, energies, and unscrupulousness were set to a larger scale from the beginning, when he abandoned a Viennese academic career to build the first continental European railroad. This was an eighty-mile line completed in 1832, which connected Linz in upper Austria to Budweis (Budejovice) in the southwest part of today's Czechoslovakia. Dismissed before the completion of this line over money matters, Gerstner soon turned his eyes toward the expanses and rubles of Russia, where he was invited in 1834 by the Chief of the tsar's Corps of Engineers, General Chevkin. After completing a survey of the Russian terrain, he presented his offer to the government. It was at best an arrogant bargain: a railway network, beginning with a St. Petersburg-Moscow line, which itself was to cost 75 million rubles. Gerstner was to have an exclusive twenty-year monopoly on the construction of all railroads in Russia, and was to own in perpetuity for himself and his heirs the St. Petersburg-Moscow line. In order to retain these vast advantages, he was to be held accountable only for the construction of one hundred *versts* (about sixty-seven miles) of track during the first four years of his contract.[33]

An offer of such outrageous disproportions of profits and responsibilities could hardly meet favor in the Russian committees to which it was submitted, consisting as they did of officials already prejudiced against railroads on technical and political as well as budgetary grounds. The proposal passed from a larger council of ministers and elder statesmen to a smaller one, set up to consider it in greater detail. This committee consisted of Speranskii, Kankrin, and Toll. In the process, the idea of a Russian railway network was whittled down to a modest plan for an experimental railroad from St. Petersburg to Tsarskoe Selo, to be financed by Gerstner privately. Gerstner's own

[32] Report of Baron Toll, *Krasnyi arkhiv*, vol. 76, pp. 90-98; Velikin, *Peterburg-Moskva*, p. 31.

[33] On Gerstner and his proposals see Mel'nikov, "Svedeniia o Russkikh zheleznykh dorogakh," *Krasnyi arkhiv*, vol. 99, pp. 142-44; Gerstner's own *Berichte aus den Vereinigten Staaten*; Krutikov, ed., "Pervye zheleznye dorogi v Rossii," *Krasnyi arkhiv*, vol. 76, pp. 86-87; and Shtukenberg, "Nikolaievskaia doroga," *Russkaia starina*, vol. 46 (1885), p. 310.

share of the profits was brought down to similar proportions. That even this fragment of the original proposal was saved can be attributed to at least three people. According to the engineer Mel'nikov, who was close to the events of 1835, Nicholas I and Speranskii remained railroad partisans, and apparently did not wish to sacrifice the fundamentally sound idea of a St. Petersburg-Moscow railroad because of the inacceptability of Gerstner's particular offer. How pleasant it would be, the tsar remarked to the committee, to dine with the governor of Moscow and return to St. Petersburg the same night.[34] The Tsarskoe Selo railroad at least was a first step in this direction, both technically and geographically: it was an affirmation and a beginning. Count Bobrinskii, an influential aristocrat, wealthy manufacturer of beet-sugar, and a champion of Russian railroads, secured most of the necessary financial backing for Gerstner, who by himself would have found it difficult to inspire confidence and raise the necessary funds. A stock company, consisting at the beginning in 1836 of Gerstner, Bobrinskii, and two prominent merchants, was formed. Significantly, Count Benckendorff soon after became the company's president and the Third Section thereafter took an interest in its affairs.

Construction of the Tsarskoe Selo railroad was begun in the spring of 1836 and completed in the fall of 1837, exceeding Gerstner's original estimates by nearly a year in time and hundreds of thousands of rubles in expenses, despite favorable conditions. According to Mel'nikov, it was an easy construction task.[35] There were no problems of gradings, inclines, or bridges of any major proportions. The rails were imported from England, as were the locomotives, although a few came from Belgium. The construction engineers were mostly colleagues of Gerstner from the Austrian empire, while the operating engineers came with their equipment from the British Isles. These human and mechanical imports, together with the elaborate resorts of foreign design built at the Tsarskoe Selo and Pavlovsk stations, explain the higher cost of the railroad, but not the delay in building it. The first Russian railroad was built by the hands of a corvée of unskilled Russian labor, consisting of 2,500 serfs and 1,400 soldiers.[36]

The line was officially opened on October 30, 1837, when Gerstner, at the throttle of a locomotive pulling an eight-car train, carried the tsar and an entourage of Russian and foreign dignitaries on the thirty-five minute trip to Tsarskoe Selo.[37] This gala maiden voyage was

[34] Korf documents in Krutikov, ed., "Pervye zheleznye dorogi v Rossii," *Krasnyi arkhiv*, vol. 76 (1936), pp. 98-101; Mel'nikov, "Svedeniia o russkikh zheleznykh dorogakh," *Krasnyi arkhiv*, vol. 99, pp. 150, 154-55.

[35] Mel'nikov, "Svedeniia o Russkikh zheleznykh dorogakh," *Krasnyi arkhiv*, vol. 99, pp. 155-60.

[36] Velikin, *Peterburg-Moskva*, p. 37; Virginskii, *Tvortsy novoi tekhniki*, p. 326.

[37] Velikin, *Peterburg-Moskva*, p. 39.

without mishap, although such good fortune and high mechanical performance apparently did not long persist. According to Joseph Harrison, the American who a decade later was building the engines and cars for the St. Petersburg-Moscow railway, ". . . they could not make things go even with English enginemen. They ran off the track, had collisions, broke axles and [had] all kinds of trouble, even to killing people and having some of the enginemen arrested."[38]

The passenger who safely reached the end of the line at Pavlovsk Park just beyond Tsarskoe Selo was greeted by a large, circular station, designed by an English architect, a tower, the clock of which remained illuminated at night, a hotel, a restaurant, game rooms, parks, and dance bands playing fashionable waltzes from Germany.[39] The Tsarskoe Selo railroad was more, however, than a dangerous way to get to a pleasant Sunday afternoon outing. With the initial kinks ironed out, it proved that railroads could both be built and operated successfully in Russia. Debate over Russian railroads now had to exclude the "why?" and was limited to the more productive questions of "where?" and "how?" The "where" that Gerstner and others never had far removed from mind when building the Tsarskoe Selo railroad was a St. Petersburg-Moscow line. A pamphlet issued in 1838 to publicize his company in Europe states this as a fact,[40] although the railroad which a decade and a half later did connect St. Petersburg and Moscow did not utilize the line connecting "the capital and the cabaret." Nor was Ritter von Gerstner on hand. Frustrated in Russia, he turned to the United States for a new world to conquer; and he died in Philadelphia a few years later, full of schemes for American railroads.

---

[38] Joseph Harrison to William Winans, Jan. 28, 1852, Joseph Harrison Letter Books in the possession of the Historical Society of Pennsylvania, Philadelphia, Pennsylvania, hereafter cited as Harrison, *Letter Books.*
[39] Velikin, *Peterburg-Moskva,* pp. 37, 42.
[40] Kreeft, *First Russian Railroad* (London, 1837).

Chapter 12

The Building of the St. Petersburg-Moscow Railroad

Planning, Organization, and Financing

After the completion of the Tsarskoe Selo experiment in 1837, the next step in Russia's railroad evolution was generally conceded to be a line which would connect the two capitals. The task was viewed as a formidable one. The immensity of such a project in the 1840's is dwarfed by the image of the gigantic transcontinental systems of the United States, Europe, the Middle East, and of Russia herself in the late nineteenth century. When completed in 1852, however, the St. Petersburg-Moscow railroad was in fact a notable technological achievement. The state locomotive plant at Aleksandrovsk near St. Petersburg equaled any in Europe and America. At that time, American railroads had not yet reached Chicago; and the short lines then operating in Europe could not hope to match a double track railway 400 miles long.

As the idea of such a line began to take root, at least among engineers and businessmen, the flow of projects and plans into the offices of the Main Administration of Ways of Communication increased. The new proposals were more practical than the earlier dreams of Gerstner and others for covering Russia with vast webs of rail. They focused on the concrete problems and specific benefits to be derived from a railroad which would connect the two capitals. The most important of these came from a Moscow landlord and promoter, A. A. Abaza, who in 1838 published a thirty-six page brochure entitled, "Thoughts of an Inhabitant of Moscow on the Possibility of Establishing a Stock Company for Building a Railroad from St. Petersburg to Moscow." At about the same time, Abaza submitted a project to the government. In the spring of the same year, a committee, consisting of the Ministers of Internal Affairs, Finances, the Superintendent of Ways of Communications, and the Chef de Gendarmes, was formed to consider it.

In addition to the general arguments, which, as we have seen, a number of other writers advanced in favor of railroads—improvement of communications, trade, agriculture and industry, military and administrative efficiency—Abaza asserted that the combined population of Russia's two capitals, which by 1838 had reached 850,000, not only demanded but made profitable the building of a passenger and a freight railroad connecting them. Specifically, he proposed a double track line with animals hauling freight on one of the tracks, while on the other, steam locomotives were to be used for a combined passenger and postal line. Freight loading stations would be situated at approximately fifteen-mile intervals on the one line; while the passenger railway would have several stations with hotels, as well as facilities for changing locomotives. Foreseeing the actual future with near accuracy, Abaza claimed that such a line could be built in six years (the actual construction took eight). He argued for inviting capable foreign engineers to build the rails, engines, and rolling stock in Russia, where the plant they established could become a center for an indigenous machine industry. This in fact happened. He believed that a private Russian stock company could finance what he saw to be a 120,000,000 ruble undertaking (a little less than the actual cost). Although Russian private capital had played a dominant role in the Tsarskoe Selo line, the state, through the floating of loans with foreign bankers, contrary to Abaza's plan, would finance the actual St. Petersburg-Moscow railway. Foreign capital, in turn, would back the big railroads of the 1850's and 1860's.[1]

In a committee dominated by Kankrin and Toll, Abaza's project got a cool reception and soon was rejected. However, by this time, Russian officialdom could no longer follow a passive course in the railroad issue for its own part, even if it could continue for a while to rebuff private promoters. A first positive act, in 1839, was to send two promising young Russian railroad engineers, Mel'nikov and Kraft, to the United States for a year's study of American techniques and achievements in the new transport technology.

At the time of his American assignment, Paul Mel'nikov had already built a foundation for his future role as the leading Russian engineer involved in the construction of the St. Petersburg-Moscow railway line, and later in 1865, the first Minister of Ways of Communication. By 1839, he had seventeen years of service in the Corps of Engineers behind him. For several of these years, he had been a professor in the state academy for transport engineers, a specialist in railroads. Four years before, he had written the first technical treatise on railroads of Russian authorship. From 1837 until his American trip, he had spent fifteen months in Europe, engaged in the study of rail technology there. He had talked to George Stephenson and other leading continental engineers.

The United States offered much greater possibilities for a Russian railroad engineer. As Mel'nikov himself recognized, its vastness, its many river arteries, its climate, and its underpopulation all more closely approximated Russian conditions than what he had found in

---

[1] Abaza's memorandum in M. Krutikov, ed., "Pervye zheleznye dorogi v Rossii," *Krasnyi arkhiv*, vol. 76 (1936), pp. 108-17; see also the publication, *Mysli moskovskago zhitelia o vozmozhnosti uchredit obshchestvo na aktsiiakh dlia sooruzheniia zheleznoi dorogi ot S. Peterburga do Moskvy*, by A . . . ia A . . . (St. Petersburg, 1838).

Europe.[2] Moreover, the United States was leading the world in track and engine construction: as early as 1835, almost four times as much railroad line existed on this side of the North Atlantic as in Great Britain. This was a natural consequence of size and precisely the problem the Russians were seeking to solve. The Americans were also developing a railroad technology more suitable to Russian conditions: improved locomotives, capable of hauling heavy burdens of freight for long distances were being manufactured in the shops of Baltimore and Philadelphia.

Mel'nikov and Kraft traveled extensively in the United States, from Massachusetts to Ohio and the South, contacting engineers, inventors, and businessmen. It was an impressive experience, and it is difficult to square the assertion by Soviet scholars that this trip was only of secondary importance with Mel'nikov's own enthusiastic statements. Much later, he could still marvel at America's ability to build 16,000 miles of railroads in thirty years, despite a civil war.[3] He returned to Russia in 1840, convinced that railroads were a necessity of far greater urgency for both countries than for Europe, the compactness of which allowed for greater dependence on canals for the transport of freight. Although he continued to believe that canals were important to Russia's commercial transport, Mel'nikov by 1840, as we have noted, was arguing very cogently that a railroad network using steam power would shrink the Russian empire to a sixteenth of its size.[4]

Upon his return to Russia, Mel'nikov fulfilled his official duties by submitting a bulky technical report on American railroads to his superiors. By this time, however, the St. Petersburg-Moscow railroad had become a cause for him and he impatiently decided to carry the issue beyond the Corps of Engineers and even the Superintendent of Ways of Communication to the Tsar himself. To achieve this, he contacted the influential Count Bobrinskii, who had played so important a role in the Tsarskoe Selo railway and who was known as a friend and promoter of railroads.

Bobrinskii, however, was negotiating with a group of German bankers and investors who had recently gained attention for their role in the building of the Leipzig-Dresden railway. Like Gerstner's scheme before them and many such foreign proposals to follow, the German offer called for extensive privileges and returns. These demands split

[2] P. P. Mel'nikov, "Svedeniia o russkikh zheleznykh dorogakh," *Krasnyi arkhiv*, vol. 99 (1940), pp. 164-65.

[3] Mel'nikov, "Svedeniia o russkikh zheleznykh dorogakh," *Krasnyi arkhiv*, vol. 99, p. 166; V. S. Virginskii, "Bor'ba vokrug podgotovki russkoi zh-d. magistrali Peterburg-Moskva," *Istoricheskie zapiski*, vol. 32 (1950), pp. 77-78.

[4] Cited from the Journal of Ways of Communication by S. A. Urodkov, *Peterburgo-Moskovskaia zheleznaia doroga, istoriia stroitel'stva 1842-1851* (Leningrad, 1951), pp. 34-35. On Mel'nikov's view of Russian canals, see V. S. Virginskii, *Tvortsy novoi tekhniki v krepostnoi Rossii* (2nd edn., Moscow, 1962), p. 323.

the committee of March 1841, which was appointed to consider the plan. Although all members of this committee were veteran partisans of Russian railroads, Mel'nikov, Kraft, and A. A. Abaza (the author of the 1838 brochure on a railroad project) opposed private foreign control of construction and urged that the Russian government assume the burden. Count Bobrinskii and General Chevkin, a leading engineering officer, wished to create a private company similar to the one which had financed the first Russian railroad as well as the Warsaw-Vienna line, the construction of which had begun two years before. The competition was obviously uneven, very probably bitter, and may have resulted in Mel'nikov's transfer during the summer of 1841 to a job developing steam navigation on the Volga to keep him out of the way.[5] This did not, however, facilitate acceptance of the German proposal, which, after lengthy negotiations, came to nothing.

Mel'nikov, meanwhile, had time in the summer to prepare, together with Kraft, a detailed technical project for a St. Petersburg-Moscow railroad. This plan described a two-track railroad similar to the Abaza proposal of 1838 in that the freight line would use animals hauling cargoes weighing about 180 tons at a speed of ten miles per hour. A second passenger line would have steam locomotives which were capable of carrying a lighter cargo of 5,640 poods (about 203,604 pounds) at twenty-four miles per hour. Mel'nikov predicted a tremendous volume of freight and passengers for the year-round service between the capitals. According to his calculations, this was to bring in an annual income of 5,730,000 silver rubles at a cost of 3,150,000 and an initial construction capital (for the earthworks, bed, rails, locomotives, cars, bridges, and buildings) of 43,026,000 silver rubles.[6]

A second committee, consisting mainly of engineers and private businessmen, reported on Mel'nikov's project in December of 1841, with the objections that he had both underestimated the construction and operating costs and overestimated the profits by millions of rubles, although they agreed in other respects with the project.[7]

Nicholas I was now ready to have all of the arguments pro and con arrayed before him, or perhaps he had made up his mind already. Early in January of 1842, he summoned the highest-ranking transport engineers and officials as well as his ministers into final conferences on the question of a St. Petersburg-Moscow railroad. He frequently attended these sessions in person. As usual, most of the ministers ranged themselves firmly against such a project for the various financial, technical, climatic, and political reasons which have been dis-

[5] Mel'nikov, "Svedeniia o russkikh zheleznykh dorogakh," *Krasnyi arkhiv*, vol. 99, p. 171.

[6] Krutikov, ed., "Pervye zheleznye dorogi v Rossii," *Krasnyi arkhiv*, vol. 76, pp. 127-47; Urodkov, *Peterburgo-Moskovskaia zheleznaia doroga*, pp. 62-68.

[7] Krutikov, ed., "Pervye zheleznye dorogi v Rossii," *Krasnyi arkhiv*, vol. 76, pp. 127-47.

cussed elsewhere. The railroad supporters included, as on previous occasions, Bobrinskii and Chevkin. Also among their number was a new power in the Main Administration of Ways of Communication, of whom more will be said later, Count Kleinmikhel. There were heated discussions. In the final meeting, according to the memoirs of the contemporary engineer, Shtukenberg, Nicholas listened to the various arguments with a "knitted brow." At the conclusion, he abruptly declared that the "supreme will" recognized the need and feasibility of the quick construction of a St. Petersburg-Moscow railroad. Since his ministers were not in sympathy with this idea, he felt it necessary to appoint a special committee to see the job through. The issue was decided.[8]

What motivated Nicholas I to override his ministers and favor the railroad? Military considerations were uppermost, most students of the subject would agree. According to Mel'nikov, Nicholas stated that it was cheaper to garrison guards regiments in Moscow and a railroad meant that these units could safely be stationed at such a distance, because they could be brought into action in the Baltic capital with full supplies and horses in less than twenty-four hours.[9] To be sure, the Tsar was not unmindful of commercial and industrial considerations and so expressed himself to a delegation from the St. Petersburg business community.[10]

The statutes of February first, sixth, and eighth of 1842 set up the initial administrative machinery for the St. Petersburg-Moscow railroad. At the very top, a special Railroad Committee was established, under the presidency of the heir apparent, the Grand Duke Alexander, and including the Ministers of Finances, State Property and Internal Affairs, the police chiefs, the head of the corps of transport engineers, and finally Bobrinskii and Kleinmikhel. This committee was empowered to head the railroad organization and make all the final decisions; in practice, it became a nominal body that did little of the actual work. Placed directly under it was the Construction Committee, a smaller group headed by Benckendorff and including Kleinmikhel and a few private businessmen, as well as the four Russian officials most sympathetic to railroads and knowledgeable about them: Chevkin, Bobrinskii, Mel'nikov and Kraft. In August of 1842, this commission and most of its personnel were absorbed into a newly created Department of Railroads, headed by a transportation official, K. I. Fisher, who was

---

[8] A. I. Shtukenberg, "Iz istorii zhelezno-dorozhnago dela v Rossii, Nikolaevskaia doroga mezhdu Peterburgom i Moskvoiu 1842-1852," *Russkaia starina*, vol. 46 (1885), pp. 314-15.

[9] Virginskii, "Bor'ba vokrug podgotovki russkoi zh-d. magistrali," *Istoricheskie zapiski*, vol. 32, p. 89; see also Krutikov, introduction to Mel'nikov, "Svedeniia o Russkikh zheleznykh dorogakh," *Krasnyi arkhiv*, vol. 99, p. 133.

[10] Korf, "Iz zapisok Barona Korfa," *Russkaia starina*, vol. 99 (1899), pp. 503-04, cited at the beginning of my Part IV.

directly responsible to the Superintendent of Ways of Communication. Responsibility for the new railroad was thus more completely absorbed into the regular transport administrative apparatus, which in 1842 became the domain of Count P. A. Kleinmikhel. The St. Petersburg-Moscow railroad was now completely in the hands of a man who, according to one of his contemporary subordinates, had never even seen a locomotive.[11] Although Nicholas I, in a private conference with Mel'nikov and Kraft, declared that his office was always open to them, this direct communication and supervision was never in fact exercised. Occasional opinions might be solicited, usually when they coincided with those of Nicholas I, but it was his favorite Kleinmikhel upon whom he completely relied and through whom he conveyed his will.

Count P. A. Kleinmikhel can be considered a classic example of the old bureaucratic school in Russia. He was a brute who got things done by driving his laborers beyond the last ounce of their energy and by intimidating and abusing his subordinates with harsh insults and dire threats. He was poorly educated, arbitrary and a rapacious bribe taker. For all this, he was shrewd and pushing, capable of sizing up character and of getting the most (at the highest cost) out of the Russian people—of using the bureaucracy as an effective instrument, blunt and unwieldy as it might be. A protégé of the martinet Arakcheev, many of whose characteristics he shared, he came to the attention of Nicholas I as the man who could rebuild the Winter Palace in record time. This massive structure had been gutted by a fire in the 1830's, and Kleinmikhel's reconstruction made new records, not only in terms of the time saved, but also in the number of workmen's lives sacrificed to such practices as moving men out into sub-zero temperatures from rooms stiflingly overheated for winter painting and decoration. Kleinmikhel was absolutely obedient to his sovereign in the successful execution of orders and this was Nicholas I's ideal of a state servant. Such matters as graft, cruelty, and universal unpopularity were overlooked as natural side products of the system. When Kleinmikhel was dismissed by Alexander II because of his widespread unpopularity and unsuitability in the new reform atmosphere of the late 1850's, he responded with a characteristic remark: "The sovereign finds it necessary to have me removed in view of public opinion. What does this mean? Doesn't he have his own opinion?"[12]

The actual construction of the railroad was organized into two ad-

---

[11] Delvig, memoirs, cited in Virginskii, "Bor'ba vokrug podgotovki russkoi zh-d. magistrali," *Istoricheskie zapiski*, vol. 32, p. 90. For details on the general administrative organization of the railroad construction, see Shtukenberg, "Nikolaevskaia doroga," *Russkaia starina*, vol. 46 (1885), pp. 316-18.

[12] A. I. Delvig, *Polveka russkoi zhizni, vospominaniia A. I. Delviga 1820-1870* (Moscow-Leningrad, 1930), vol. II, pp. 50-51. On Kleinmikhel, see the same work and V. Panaev, "Vospominaniia Valerian Aleksandrovich Panaeva," *Russkaia starina*, vol. 107 (1901), pp. 31-66.

ministrative domains. For the putting down of the bed and track and the building of bridges and stations, the distance between St. Petersburg and Moscow was divided equally into Northern and Southern Commands (*direktsii*). Mel'nikov headed the Northern, extending from St. Petersburg to Bologoe; Kraft, the Southern, which extended from this point on to Moscow. To Mel'nikov and Kraft were assigned a group of young engineering officers, several of whom would achieve a later fame, not only as builders of the Russian rail network of the late nineteenth century, but also as literati and intellectuals. Shtukenberg, Panaev, and Delvig were the most notable of this company, who were assigned the immediate supervision of the several Subdivisions (*uchastki*) within each of the two main commands. At the recommendations of Mel'nikov, Major George Washington Whistler, an American railroad pioneer, was invited to be advisory engineer at a salary of 60,000 rubles per year (about $12,000 in the exchange value of the time).

A Russian legend which circulated around the globe in the nineteenth century told of the "straight line" railroad from St. Petersburg to Moscow. According to the story, Nicholas I decided the dispute which had arisen among his officials over the precise route the line was to take by throwing a ruler on the map. "Make the road straight," he was supposed to have commanded (allowing for curves corresponding to the bumps where his fingers extended beyond the ruler). The autocrat of Russia thereby exhibited the arbitrariness of the despot and revealed the servility of his subjects that so many foreigners took as characteristic of the tsarist autocracy and the Russian mind, solving one group of problems and raising a host of others. The truth behind the legend was known in the nineteenth century. In a country as flat as Russia, with no large bodies of water and only one range of low hills between St. Petersburg and Moscow, a nearly straight railroad is the practical one to build. Nicholas I, in the winter of 1841-1842, dispatched Mel'nikov and Kraft at the head of a group of engineers to report on the best possible route for the railroad. The final choice narrowed to two alternatives: the most direct line possible between the two capitals or a longer line which would curve to the city of Novgorod. Mel'nikov's report argued for the straight line as 50 miles shorter and 17 percent cheaper to build. This apparently was in agreement with the personal views of Nicholas I, who was more interested in the shortest and cheapest possible military link of his two principal cities than of the economic development and private interests of the province of Novgorod. According to Panaev, it was at this point and in this context that he made the famous remark that was soon after misinterpreted.[13]

---

[13] Panaev, "Vospominaniia," *Russkaia starina*, vol. 107 (1901), pp. 35-37.

Other organizational questions, such as the location of freight and passenger stations in St. Petersburg and the width of the bed were more quickly decided. There remained the difficulty of financing construction. The government that had elected to build the largest railway in the world was badly equipped to do so, not only from a technical but from a fiscal point of view. On top of the crushing burden of the military machine and the wars of Nicholas I were the obvious costs of foreign debts and the hidden ones of fiscal mismanagement and inflation. The railroad which was to cost at least eight million silver rubles a year to build had to be financed during the very period of the currency reforms of 1839, 1841, and 1843 when hard money was scarce. The only way out of this financial dilemma was additional foreign loans, supplemented by whatever other funds could be obtained from domestic sources—loans from the state banks and treasury bonds. From 1843 until the completion of construction, five massive loans were obtained from foreign bankers—for the most part Englishmen in cooperation with the Russian House of Stieglitz. Foreign borrowing totaled 76,300,000 rubles, the actual cash value of which came to 70,285,096 silver rubles. Domestic loans totaled 21,980,000 silver rubles. The interest on these sums was staggering: estimates of the actual cost of construction range from 66,849,537 to 74,540,372 silver rubles, the balance of the loans going back to the bankers, making a total cost that climbed far over one hundred million rubles by the 1850's. The highest single expenditure after interest payments was for the earthworks and track, which cost about thirty-five million silver rubles, while bridges and tunnels ran to almost nine and one-half million. Over four millions went out in the contract made with foreign locomotive engineers. The construction costs of the first major Russian railroad thus came to average out at five times as much per *verst* as the later railways built in Russia.[14] Foreign engineers were an expensive item, but the greatest costs arose from a lack of proper planning and a tendency to corruption on the part of Russian officials. The highest price was in the end the one levied on the peasants digging the earth and swamp between St. Petersburg and Moscow.

Construction of the Line

The engineering problems involved in the construction of 400 miles of track between St. Petersburg and Moscow were far more formidable than they might have appeared to the casual observer of the deceptively smooth and monotonous Russian terrain separating the two capitals, or to some technically untutored transport official perusing inaccurate maps from within a government chancellery. There were scores of streams and rivers, some with deep gorges that had to be

---

[14] For accounts of foreign investment and financing, see my Chapter 10; and Urodkov, *Peterburgo-Moskovskaia zheleznaia doroga*, pp. 92-98.

spanned with bridges as high as 130 feet. Long and deep passes—the largest a mile in length and 100 feet in depth—had to be cut through ravines made of rock-like clay. The way was blocked with several huge swamps, which had to be filled and traversed, and hundreds of lakes through which engineers had to needle the track, along narrow isthmuses. Paths had to be cut through several deep forests, teeming with eagles, bears, and wild animals that seemed not to be disturbed by the roar of a steam engine. All of these obstacles had to be surmounted during six months out of the year, for from October until May, only gunpowder blasts could break the frozen earth.[15] Beyond these natural impediments, there were the novel technical problems involving the use of new excavation equipment, the procurement and processing of materials for rails, ties, and trestles, determination of the gauge and inclination of the track, of water supply, of switches and signals, and of the disposition of repair, passenger, and freight stations. The technical situation was further complicated by problems of a bureaucratic nature: corruption, ignorance, mismanagement, the waste of money and labor, and improper planning.

The overcoming of all these problems and the carrying out of the construction of the St. Petersburg-Moscow line to a successful conclusion was largely the work of two engineers. The first of these was Mel'nikov and the second, Major George Washington Whistler, formerly of the United States Army Engineers. The role of both of these railroad pioneers was obscured in their own time and afterward. Russian historians, both before and after the Revolution, have done much to establish Mel'nikov as a highly talented engineer, teacher, and administrator, thus helping to puncture the myth of a mid-nineteenth-century Russia so technically and educationally backward as to be incapable of producing railroad engineers of any distinction. That Whistler was called in from the United States as an advisory engineer for the construction of the first major Russian railroad does not alter the picture or prove that Russia was utterly dependent on foreign skill in the development of technology and transportation, nor does it diminish the stature of Mel'nikov. Whistler was not a capitalist profiteer, upon whose talents ignorant Russians had to rely for a scandalous price. He was an experienced railroad construction engineer, whose help for a relatively modest compensation was sought by the tsarist government at the recommendation of Mel'nikov, who respected him and became his friend. The esteem of his Russian colleagues and the sacrifice of his life to cholera while still in the service of Russia in 1849 (during epidemic conditions) are further proofs of his integrity and ability. These were sentiments which were not always directed toward his American colleagues called in to establish a loco-

[15] Shtukenberg, "Nikolaevskaia doroga," *Russkaia starina*, vol. 48 (1885), pp. 311-18.

motive factory for the line. Soviet historians have practically ignored Whistler's role in the construction of the St. Petersburg-Moscow railroad. The American documents which relate to this subject clearly establish his role as a primary one. The story of the building of the first major Russian railroad thus properly begins with a reassessment of the careers and ideas of the two leading engineers.

By the time he was assigned to supervise the Northern Command of the St. Petersburg-Moscow line, Pavel Petrovich Mel'nikov was already known and respected among Russian engineers, if not in the higher spheres of the bureaucracy or by the emperor, as the most brilliant and experienced of the younger generation of Russian engineers. For several years, he had lectured and published in the fields of applied mechanics and railroad technology. Prior to exclusive preoccupation with railroads, he was known as an expert on water transport and as the designer of a new type of dome for the Troitskii Cathedral. From 1837 until 1840, as we have seen, he studied the railroad systems of Europe and the United States.

The goal of a far-flung network of railroads in Russia had become something of a mission for Mel'nikov by the time he began work on the St. Petersburg-Moscow line. This goal he retained through the construction period of the railroad and on into the lull of the 1850's, when he was inactive officially, although he took the time to organize a private company for the steam navigation of the Volga and Don rivers. In 1862, he was appointed head of the transport administration, soon after becoming Russia's first Minister of Ways of Communication, when this establishment was raised to the status of an independent ministry. Mel'nikov was the first railroad engineer who had worked up from the bottom to such an exalted post, one hitherto usually reserved for imperial favorites or bureaucrats. During his administration, the Moscow-Kursk railway was built, the first step toward the Black Sea and toward the network that Mel'nikov hoped would unite European and Asiatic Russia.[16]

His contemporary and subordinate in the Northern Command during the construction years of the 1840's, Valerian Panaev, enthusiastically described Mel'nikov's administrative capacities: "Mel'nikov's system of administration was distinguished by a complete absence of formalism, bureaucratism, and pedantry." Paper work was at a minimum: Mel'nikov supervised directly, traveling everywhere along the route of construction, sharing the rigors of the Russian climate with his engineers, while attempting to boost their morale. He attended to minute detail on the spot, whenever he could, but encouraged initia-

[16] For Mel'nikov's career and Russian evaluations see his memoirs, "Svedeniia o Russkikh zheleznykh dorogakh," *Krasnyi arkhiv*, vol. 99, pp. 127-99; the chapter in Virginskii, *Tvortsy novoi tekhniki*; and Panaev, "Vospominaniia," *Russkaia starina*, vol. 107 (1901), pp. 60-65.

tive in his subordinates, who, Panaev claims, loved, esteemed, and even "worshiped" him. He contrasts Mel'nikov's administration to the pedantic and "Germanic" bureaucratic regime of Kraft in the Southern Command.[17] Panaev's view was seconded by his contemporary engineers. Soviet historians have argued along similar lines that Mel'nikov was both a capable and popular administrator and the best engineer in Russia.

In reconstructing the achievements of Mel'nikov, recent writers have given little more than passing mention to George W. Whistler, although it was on the recommendation of Mel'nikov himself that the American engineer was called to Russia as advisor for the construction of the railroad. Whistler's Russian contemporary, the engineer Shtukenberg, was more observant. He recalled in his memoirs that Whistler had earned "general esteem" and that "his recommendations were always clear, well-defined, fully knowledgeable, and useful." He included Whistler with Mel'nikov and Kraft as a preceptor of the young Russian engineers assigned to study and work with the railroad. Nicholas I recognized the American's achievements by awarding him the Order of St. Anna.[18] Whistler's first American biographer, Vose, overestimated when he assigned Whistler the major credit for both planning and construction of the St. Petersburg-Moscow railroad and its equipment.[19] Nevertheless, the fact remains that Whistler had built railroads before he came to Russia; Mel'nikov and Kraft had no such experience.

Whistler's American career began with West Point and the U. S. Army Engineers, where, like Mel'nikov, he developed an interest in railroads. Private companies were building rail lines in the United States in the late 1820's, at a time when native engineering skills were still scarce. It was the federal government's practice to lend out experienced officers such as Whistler to private corporations. Whistler helped to build several lines in this period, the most famous being the Baltimore and Ohio. At about the time that Mel'nikov was beginning to teach and write about railroads in Russia, Whistler resigned his military commission and entered private business, concerned with both railway and locomotive construction. His most famous achievement, during the six years prior to his departure for Russia, was the Western Railroad

---

[17] Panaev, "Vospominaniia," *Russkaia starina*, vol. 107 (1901), p. 63.

[18] Shtukenberg, "Nikolaevskaia doroga," *Russkaia starina*, vol. 46 (1885), p. 319; George W. Whistler to General J. G. Swift, April 8/20, 1847, the Joseph Gardner Swift papers in the possession of the Manuscript Division, New York Public Library, hereafter cited as *Swift mss*. On Russian opinion of Whistler, see also Joseph Harrison to Mrs. Anna Whistler, April 18, 1850, Joseph Harrison, letter books in the possession of the Pennsylvania Historical Society, hereafter cited as Harrison, *Letter Books*. The most recent American biography is Albert Parry, *Whistler's Father* (New York, 1939).

[19] George L. Vose, *A Sketch of the Life and Works of George W. Whistler* (Boston, 1887), p. 35.

of Massachusetts (Worcester to Albany), where he acted as chief engineer.[20]

Word of Whistler's work first reached Mel'nikov on his trip to the United States in 1840, and it was his name that came to mind when the Russians began to seek a foreign expert as consulting engineer for the construction of the St. Petersburg-Moscow line. An officer was sent to the United States to engage Whistler, who accepted promptly, arriving in Russia in the summer of 1842. His salary came to $12,000 per year (60,000 rubles), certainly substantial for its time compared to the wages of his Russian officer colleagues, but meager, when placed against the millions that the American locomotive contractors later took out of Russia. Whistler refused a Russian military commission, believing quite correctly that his income, position, and influence would be much superior as a private citizen. An American of the age of Jackson, Whistler was embarrassed and amused by the medal he later received, and apparently was treated as a social inferior by his Russian subordinates, most of whom were nobles. According to one story, the tsar was concerned about this snobbishness, and to remedy it, on a day when Whistler and his engineers were paying a visit to an art gallery, went up to Whistler and walked arm-in-arm with the American through the gallery and in plain sight of all the officers. In an instant and thereafter, the relationship between Whistler and his Russian subordinates changed.[21]

Whistler became aware, as the job progressed, that he was by no means going to emerge from it a wealthy man, although he and his family lived well enough in Russia, renting a large villa just outside St. Petersburg on the way to Peterhof. By 1846, his hopes did not extend beyond a total savings that might earn him $1,000 a year: "My money affairs are not so prosperous as I could wish, or as many may think; notwithstanding, I do my best in the way of economy."[22] His death in Russia in 1849 left his wife and children, including the boy who was to become the famous painter, in pinched circumstances; and we hear a few years later of the unsuccessful attempts of Mel'nikov and his American friends to obtain a final additional salary settlement for his widow.[23]

Whistler divided his time in Russia between surveys of the road construction and meetings with the Construction Commission in St. Petersburg. His work, he observed in 1845, consisted for the most part of preparing plans and defending them before this state agency: the gauge of the rail line, materials for the bridges, opinions on foreign projects, and many technical aspects of the embankment and track. He

[20] Vose, *Whistler*, pp. 16-23.   [21] Vose, *Whistler*, pp. 39-40.
[22] Whistler to Swift, May 18, 1844; April 26, 1845; May (no date), 1845; May 20, 1846, *Swift mss.*
[23] Harrison to Mrs. Whistler, Oct. 3, 1850, Harrison, *Letter Books.*

also undertook outside jobs for the government, being consulted for fortifications, docks, a large iron bridge spanning the Neva, and other engineering tasks.[24] Whistler, like Mel'nikov, viewed Russia as a country urgently in need of improved transportation. He recognized that Peter the Great had made a beginning in the improvement of transport, but added: "nothing has been done since." Looking to the future, he believed that a long time would pass before railroads were extended beyond Moscow, but rightly predicted that when this came about, they would move toward the Black Sea. Steamboats on the Volga, Whistler felt, would suffice for the eastern trade from the Caspian Sea.[25]

Upon his arrival in Russia in 1842, Whistler undertook a survey of the entire route. Research by Russian engineers over the same area prior to the actual beginning of construction continued through 1843. According to Panaev, there were no decent maps of this part of Russia, large stretches of which apparently were wild and uncharted. This sometimes later resulted in costly mistakes—in one instance, the building of a very large bridge, which might have been avoided.[26] Some of the work was eliminated by a path which had been cut through a large forest area by Peter the Great in 1712, in an abandoned first effort to connect Moscow and his new capital by improved road.[27] Problems of climate, in addition to those of topography, haunted the construction, as they had the planning of the railroad. Beyond the short working year the Russian winter enforced, Whistler had to cope with dry summers, which exhausted the water supply from small streams along the way and necessitated its very costly transport over long distances. The heavy snows made imperative the construction of a higher bed— from six to ten feet in most places. To accommodate the two tracks, each consisting of a five-foot gauge with six feet between them, the bed was made thirty feet wide. Added to this were swamps and gullies which necessitated some 260 miles of banks and 116 miles of passes, not to mention hundreds of bridges and underpasses of various sizes. All of this, according to Whistler's estimate, involved the removal of about 60,000,000 cubic yards of earth.[28]

The excavation, begun in 1844 and not completed until 1849, was done for the most part in sand and clay, when the picks and shovels did not encounter a rare outcropping of flagstone or even the occasional bones of prehistoric animals. Summer rains made the digging, almost completely hand work, difficult, and the cold weather made it

24 Whistler to Swift, May 5, 1845, *Swift mss.*; Vose, *Whistler*, p. 38.
25 Whistler to Swift, Oct. 28, 1844; Jan. 18, 1847, *Swift mss.*
26 Panaev, "Vospominaniia," *Russkaia starina*, vol. 107 (1901), p. 38.
27 Velikin, *Peterburg-Moskva*, pp. 51-52.
28 Shtukenberg, "Nikolaevskaia doroga," *Russkaia starina*, vol. 48 (1885), pp. 321-22, 329; Whistler to Swift, Jan. 18, 1847, *Swift mss.*

impossible.[29] The first steam shovels to be used in Russia were imported, four in number, by Whistler. They came from the United States, the invention a few years before of the Massachusetts engineer, Otis, and were accompanied by an American operator, William Crane. Whistler probably intended these cumbersome steam machines for heavy excavation work in the deepest passes, such as the Kuznetsov cut in the Valdai Hills, over a mile long and almost 100 feet deep. They were used for about three years with a fair degree of success, according to Shtukenberg. Mechanical breakdowns, lack of repair facilities, inexperienced handling of the machinery, and the hostility of private contractors engaged for the excavation (who were obliged to maintain and repair the steam shovels which competed with their serf diggers) all worked to cause the government to abandon the new devices. "These solitary foreigners," as the Soviet scholar Krutikov expresses it, "lost in the many thousand-man army of serfs with shovels and wheelbarrows," were perhaps premature for a Russia, economically and mentally habituated to mass labor corvées. In the end, they were sold and put to work in a Urals mine.[30]

The period of construction was also dragged out by the need to construct some twenty-six miles of bridges, numbering 188, in addition to dozens of tunnels. Some of these structures were major engineering feats for their day. The Vereba River bridge, built to span a huge gorge, was unmatched for its type in Europe or America; 175 feet high and 1,925 feet long, it was the first application in Russia, in the last days before the age of iron and steel bridges, of the new American method (the Howe system) of combining stone foundations and high wooden trestles.[31] The Russians were duly proud of this achievement, and set up a special station at one side of the bridge, where train passengers could debark to a spot along the gorge which permitted a full view of the span. The engineer, Zhurovsky, received a promotion and a St. Vladimir cross, although several of his colleagues, according to Panaev, had done nearly as well on the rivers Msta, Tsna, Tvertsa, Volga, and Skhodna.[32] Apparently, there was no shortage of capable bridge specialists among the Russian corps of engineers, although Whistler had his doubts. He saw waste, corruption, and inefficiency in the Msta River bridge, 875 feet in length, which cost $360,000 and three years of work, as contrasted with the 1,260-

---

[29] Shtukenberg, "Nikolaevskaia doroga," *Russkaia starina*, vol. 48 (1885), p. 329.

[30] Note by Shtukenberg, "Nikolaevskaia doroga," *Russkaia starina*, vol. 50 (1886), pp. 443-45. See also the discussion by M. Krutikov, ed., "Polozhenie rabochikh na postroike Peterburgo-Moskovskoi zheleznoi dorogi 1843-1851 gg.," *Krasnyi arkhiv*, vol. 83 (1937), p. 46. Velikin, *Peterburg-Moskva*, p. 70, identifies the inventor by the name "Otis."

[31] Shtukenberg, "Nikolaevskaia doroga," *Russkaia starina*, vol. 50 (1885), pp. 334-36.

[32] Panaev, "Vospominaniia," *Russkaia starina*, vol. 107 (1901), pp. 58-59.

foot Connecticut River bridge in the United States, which was completed in one year and cost $120,000.[33]

The Russians were meticulous and overcautious. They paid an additional price in time and money for this. Nicholas I wanted elaborate safety precautions, no matter what the expense. He believed that Americans were careless and questioned Whistler not only on the hazards of various aspects of the railroad, but also suspiciously in 1844, about a recent explosion on the American warship, the *Princeton*, in which several high-ranking American officials were killed. Whistler reacted to all this with his own version of Russian overcautiousness.[34] Nevertheless, throughout the construction and operation of the St. Petersburg-Moscow railroad, carelessness on the part of the workers and technicians, Russian and foreign, was harshly punished. The result was greater safety, although several disasters occurred after the line was opened.

Elaborate safety precautions were expensive, as was the 400-foot right of way for the railroad, and the beautifully cultivated banks, with slopes so regular that Whistler was prompted to observe that they "look on the ground like a problem in descriptive geometry on paper."[35] Famous architects were engaged to build elaborate terminals in the two capitals, and roundhouses with repair shops and large passenger stations were set up at fifty-mile intervals. Four classes of stations, numbering thirty-seven in all, were sprinkled across the wilderness, wherever water was needed for the trains, although they were located near towns when this was possible. The larger stations and roundhouses were built on the so-called American model—a large waiting room located between an expanded interval of the two tracks and a high, circular domed roundhouse, 210 feet in diameter, with room for eighteen locomotives. The elaborate St. Petersburg passenger terminal cost a million and a half rubles. All stations, large or small, had attractive landscaping for which the bill was another half million rubles.[36]

There was much debate among officials and engineers over the more novel technical questions of rails and tracks. Wood was the cheapest and best material for ties and could easily be obtained through contractors from the surrounding forest. The most inexpensive rails of good quality were imported from England, although some officials wanted to use higher priced equipment manufactured in the Urals. One Russian factory owner tried unsuccessfully to get the contract. In the end, both English and Russian iron were used.[37]

---

[33] Cited in Albert Parry, *Whistler's Father*, p. 229.

[34] Whistler to Swift, May 4, 1844, *Swift mss.*

[35] Whistler to Swift, Oct. 28, 1844, *Swift mss.*

[36] Shtukenberg, "Nikolaevskaia doroga," *Russkaia starina*, vol. 46 (1885), p. 327, vol. 49 (1886), pp. 97-103; Vose, *Whistler*, p. 32.

[37] Urodkov, *Peterburgo-Moskovskaia zheleznaia doroga*, pp. 83-89.

Whistler argued eloquently for a five-foot rail gauge and was seconded by Mel'nikov. In a lengthy report to Kleinmikhel in 1842, he tried to prove that the narrower four-foot, eight-inch English gauge had no rationale other than the fact that it was the first to be used and had been continued for purposes of uniformity. More practical for Russia, thought Whistler, would be a gauge a few inches wider, which would be adequate for high speeds of thirty-five miles per hour, but which would cost no more. A width beyond five feet, such as the six-foot gauge of the Tsarskoe Selo railroad, would involve the greater expenses of a wider bed, heavier rails, and larger cars. He went on to suggest the American "H" rail as the simplest and best.[38] Whistler's recommendations were accepted and the five-foot gauge became standard for Russia and unique in Europe, a fact of dubious future military significance.[39] Such considerations had not, however, entered into the American engineer's conceptions in 1842.

Problems of Bureaucracy and Labor

The shadow of Russian bureaucracy fell gloomily over the construction of the St. Petersburg-Moscow railway, presenting problems as formidable as any of the geographical or technical obstacles to the progress of the line. Whistler was particularly sensitive to these problems, since in his previous experience, he had been relatively unhampered by restrictions of bureaucratic mentality and organization. His letters bear witness to this, in the frequency and vigor of his observations, particularly on the higher spheres of the Russian railroad administration, its strengths and weaknesses, abuses and virtues. The young Russian engineers subordinate to Whistler, particularly Panaev, also felt the pressure of the bureaucratic machine and its representatives at lower levels, and they have given us a sharply focused picture of its day-to-day operation. Finally, Soviet historians have abundantly reconstructed the administration of the railroad's labor force, the conditions of the workers, and their reactions to the pressures and brutality of officialdom.

At the pinnacle of the railroad administration, almost from the beginning of construction, stood Count Kleinmikhel, whose background and character have already been sketched. Kleinmikhel remained in this commanding position for over a decade. He ruled his subordinate generals, engineers, contractors, policemen, and laborers with an iron hand, which extended frequently from the top councils of the

---

[38] "Report of George W. Whistler to His Excellency, the Count Kleinmikhel on the Gauge of Russian Railways," Sept. 9, 1842, St. Petersburg, typewritten copy in the Manuscript Division of the New York Public Library, New York, N. Y. Virginskii, *Tvortsy novoi tekhniki*, p. 337, gives Mel'nikov the credit.

[39] The German Army during the Second World War had no difficulty in rapidly putting down an additional rail to accommodate the gauges of its trains.

administration to the day-to-day work in the various subdivisions concerned with the construction. Whistler respected Kleinmikhel within the context of a system which he despised:

> I am sometimes puzzled with this Count Kleinmikhel. He is certainly one of the most, if not the most unpopular of men in Russia—he possesses more of the confidence of the emperor than any other, that in some degree may account for it.—When I say confidence, I mean he is made more use of—he is more useful.
>
> . . . a man of great industry—in availing himself of the labor of others—a man of such universal usefulness that he has played a most singular . . . part. At one time chief of the College of Physicians, at another, Chief of the Academy of Arts—then Chief Architect of the Palace—not that he knows anything of physics or the fine arts, but that he has the faculty [to render] order out of disorder.[40]

Directly subordinate to Kleinmikhel was the Construction or Technical Commission of the Railroad Department of the Main Administration of Ways of Communication, an administrative agency entrusted with the major decisions on engineering and technical matters. This commission consisted of a dozen high-ranking transportation officers, headed by General Destrem. Destrem formerly had been one of Napoleon's engineers, and had come to the Russian service by way of an arrangement made at the Peace of Tilsit. In the 1830's, he had been a vigorous opponent of railroads. According to Whistler, who was also a member of the Commission, Destrem now always sided with him in the disputes that frequently arose in the conferences of this group. General Chevkin, later to become Superintendent of Ways of Communication succeeding Kleinmikhel, as part of furthering his own ambitions and maneuvering for the latter's job, opposed the recommendations of the American. This typical situation of intrigue and rivalry inevitably meant delay in construction. Since Kleinmikhel held all of the power, much time was wasted in futile obstruction and argumentation over matters that did not count. Whistler's suggestions were always approved in the end, he discovered, when it was known that he would take the responsibility for them.[41]

Away from the St. Petersburg bureaus, the actual building of the railroad, as has been mentioned, was divided into a Northern and a Southern Command under Mel'nikov and Kraft respectively. The Kolomenets River separated the two Commands and each was further divided into six Subdivisions of varying lengths, from four and one-half to sixty-eight *versts*. These in turn were cut into some thirty Dis-

---

40 Whistler to Swift, April 4, 1844, *Swift mss.*
41 Whistler to Swift, April 4, 1844, *Swift mss.*

tricts, usually of twelve to sixteen *versts* each. Junior officers were usually placed in command of these various sections. In addition, a cumbersome civil bureaucracy was attached to each Subdivision, numbering, according to the estimate of Panaev, about fifty officials and forty horses for each sixty *versts*: supervisors and their assistants, accountants, clerks, foremen, and timekeepers. The central office at the village of Chudov, claims the same engineer, whose task probably kept him out of doors much of the time, had its box of Chateau Cliquot and other champagnes and wines to ease the hardships of office life along the construction site.[42]

Whistler was unnerved by this enormous machine which he had ample opportunity to experience at all levels. In his letters to his father-in-law, General Swift, in 1844 and 1845 (reminiscent of the contemporary observer of Russian autocracy, the Marquis de Custine, whose book he had read with disapproval), he attempted to comprehend and explain it:

> In a country like this, success is almost the sole criteria of merit—much credit following success, and a single failure obliterates all merit—this intimidates the many while it inspires a sort of desperate energy in the few that makes them firm believers in the catholic principle that the end justifies the means. Not only is the will of the Emperor the law of laws, but the very whim of the Emperor is the law of these few—indeed I might say all—for it is quite apparent in the perfect submission of the many as it is in the energy of the few.[43]

The Russian bureaucracy, Whistler noted, was "the most servile of all services." No one, including generals, escaped the grossest humiliations. There was no redress of wrongs, only flattery and fawning:

> . . . 'tis worse than useless to complain—necessity put them in their places and necessity keeps them there. They must endeavor to please at all hazard, for in no other way can anything be expected. The Emperor gives to whom he pleases, and others in authority do the same—the mass is ground that the few in authority may secure their places by annual displays of munificence.

Corruption was flagrant and imbedded in a bureaucratic system which seemed to Whistler (in the vivid images of a railroad engineer) to have assumed a despotic control, momentum, and law of its own:

---

[42] Panaev, "Vospominaniia," *Russkaia starina*, vol. 107 (1901), p. 39.

[43] Whistler to Swift, April 4, 1844; April 26, 1845, *Swift mss.* On Custine, Whistler wrote (April 8/20, 1843, to Swift) that one had to allow for the exaggerations of travelers and the vanity of "a Frenchman who thinks he writes well." The book, nevertheless, in Whistler's view, gave a good picture of Russian society. He notes that it was banned in Russia.

. . . the machine is in motion—governed by certain laws—be they good or bad—and not even his majesty could with impunity interfere with it—fear keeps everybody within his orbit, but he should be crushed as his work certainly would be if he got in the way of the great car.[44]

Mismanagement, corruption, and capricious financing all contributed to prolonging the construction schedule. Whistler's letters from 1845 to 1847 are a chronicle of frustrated expectations as to the date of completion of construction, and of his possible departure from a situation that was becoming increasingly unpleasant for him. Had the railroad been completed by the original deadline, the year 1848, the American engineer might have escaped with his life. In 1845, he was still hopeful that this plan could be fulfilled, and noted in a letter to Swift that more than half of the earthworks for the entire line had been put down. By the spring of 1846, he was adding an additional year to his original estimate. That November, the first section of track, extending from St. Petersburg to Kolpino, was completed. A ball was held to celebrate the occasion.[45] A few months later, at the beginning of 1847, Whistler complained that the construction budget had been cut by a third, from 15 to 10 million silver rubles, which meant a prolongation of the work schedule by yet another year. The money, he suspected, had been diverted for the expenses of the previous year's travels of the imperial family. "So they do here," he observed, "no troublesome members of Congress to call for information."[46]

Not much more than a year later, Whistler was cut down by cholera. The Russian government negotiated in Washington for an American replacement, another army engineer, who arrived in Russia around the beginning of 1850, less than a year before actual completion of construction.[47]

One of the main tasks of the bureaucratic apparatus of the St. Petersburg-Moscow line—cooperating with a special police auxiliary—was the marshaling and disciplining of the huge labor force. The first major Russian railroad like its midget predecessor, the Tsarskoe Selo line, was built by hand. The few imported American steam shovels failed to compete, not with the efficiency of 50,000 peasant picks and shovels, but with the social and political system which made them necessary. From one perspective—that of the misery and deprivation

[44] Both passages cited from Whistler to Swift, April 26, 1845, *Swift mss.*

[45] Journal of Thomas Winans, Nov. 22, 1846, the Winans papers, now in the possession of the Maryland Historical Society, Baltimore, Maryland, hereafter cited as Winans, *Papers.* The information above was based on typed copies or abstracts found among the Winans papers, the original source of which the author has been unable to locate.

[46] Whistler to Swift, Dec. 19, 1845; May 20, 1846; Jan. 18, 1847, *Swift mss.*

[47] Harrison to Mrs. Whistler, Nov. 21, 1849, Jan. 2, 1850; Harrison to George Prince, Feb. 10, 1850, Harrison, *Letter Books.*

involved—the organization and working conditions of the laborers on the St. Petersburg-Moscow Railroad resembled those of their contemporary Irish diggers and Chinese coolies who put down the eastern and transcontinental lines of the United States. From the perspective of the state regimentation and exploitation of a massive slave force, the building of the St. Petersburg-Moscow line could also be compared to the monument building and irrigation works of the ancient oriental despotisms. What might have remained very largely a submerged social history has been revealed recently by the work of Soviet historians, whose special interest in the history of labor has resulted in the publication of a number of primary sources and studies relating to the working conditions and the responses to their plight of the laborers on the early Russian railroads.[48]

The number of workers varied from year to year: at times, the figure would climb over 60,000; at others, below 40,000. These figures are taken from the peak of the warm season: as the winter set in, the total dropped rapidly. In October 1844, only 32,000 were employed. Construction, of course, ceased almost completely in the deep winter. Most of the ordinary laborers were serfs, obtained from government domains or private estates, particularly from the areas of Vitebsk and Smolensk. Some soldiers from regular regiments were used—more extensively, as Major Whistler observed, when the parade season was over. Those formerly designated as military colonists, in the 1840's known as "cultivating soldiers," were also utilized. Hard-up peasants who had drifted to the cities were hired, and a few Polish political prisoners were put to work on the construction.[49]

The engineer-litterateur, Panaev, has described the pathetic slavishness and degradation of the Belorussian peasants who came to dig for him:

> These were the most unhappy people in all the Russian land, who less resembled people than working cattle, from whom inhuman strength was demanded in their labors, one might say, without any reward. The downtrodden aspect and so to speak idiocy of these people, difficult to describe, was aggravated by almost no knowledge of the Russian language. . . . When I saw these people for the first time at the works, I was struck by the following: Each person,

---

[48] See particularly Krutikov, ed., "Polozhenie rabochikh na postroike Peter-burgo-Moskovskoi zheleznoi dorogi 1843-1851 gg.," *Krasnyi arkhiv*, vol. 83 (1937), pp. 43-106; and the more recent Soviet collection of documents, *Rabochee dvizhenie v Rossii v xix veke*, vol. I, part 2, 1826-1860 (Moscow, 1955), pp. 398-414.

[49] Various estimates of the numbers and composition of the excavation workers in: Urodkov, *Peterburgo-Moskovskaia zheleznaia doroga*, pp. 100-01; Shtukenberg, "Nikolaevskaia doroga," *Russkaia starina*, vol. 48 (1885), pp. 324-25; Krutikov, ed., "Polozhenie rabochikh," *Krasnyi arkhiv*, vol. 83, pp. 58-61; and Whistler to Swift, July 21, 1846, *Swift mss.*

before passing me, bowed, so that his back came to a horizontal position; then, with mincing steps, he hastened up to me, seized the cloth end of my cape, kissed it with the words, "I kiss you *pan* colonel," and withdrew in the same position.[50]

Although, as mentioned, ordinary soldiers and military colonists were used on the construction, their price, in the form of special wages, was high. For the bulk of the labor force, the government resorted to a contract system for the engagement of lots of peasants. For local jobs or for much larger jobs—entire sections of the construction —merchants, landlords, and officials would compete (by bidding and by intrigue) for work contracts. In these contracts, certain quotas of work would be promised in return for fixed sums from the government. In some cases, contractors would bid to provide groups of skilled and unskilled workers at specified wages. In others, local landlords would bring their own serfs to the job and remain with them. In his memoirs, Panaev recalls two of these, Klodt and Bunicki, who brought some 270 men to work. The former was, in the Russian engineer's view, a decent man; the latter, however, ". . . was in the full sense of the word an exploiter of negroes."[51] The biggest contractors for the northern part of the line were Baron Korf, of an important official family, succeeded by an equally powerful Baltic Baron, Ungern-Sternberg. The latter provided 10,000 diggers. For the southern part of the line, the big contractors were primarily rich merchants, who would make deals with local landlords. By 1845, all contracts for the earthworks were in the hands of a few of these speculators in human misery.[52] The extent to which contractors could make up for low bids and could enrich themselves out of the pockets of their work gangs is to some extent measured by the desertions and uprisings which came to characterize the construction.

A contract drawn up in 1844 between the department of railroads and the merchant, Ivan Kuzmin, illustrates some of the conditions which contractor and worker were obliged to observe or tempted to evade. The workers had to be between the ages of twenty and forty-five and in good health. As soon as the warmer weather began, they were ordered to appear for 150 working days. After the stipulated beginning date, the contractor was obligated to supply the food. The proposed diet was porridge or gruel with smelts or beef. The workers were to have time off on Sundays and six holy days each season. Two hours each day were allotted for meals, and rest periods were designated. The workers, however, were obliged to meet fixed quotas.

[50] Panaev, "Vospominaniia," *Russkaia starina*, vol. 107 (1901), pp. 39-40.

[51] Krutikov, ed., "Polozhenie rabochikh," *Krasnyi arkhiv*, vol. 83, pp. 46-48, 51-52; Panaev, "Vospominaniia," *Russkaia starina*, vol. 107, p. 40.

[52] Urodkov, *Peterburgo-Moskovskaia zheleznaia doroga*, pp. 99-100, 105-06, 117; Shtukenberg, "Nikolaevskaia doroga," *Russkaia starina*, vol. 48 (1885), p. 320.

There were deductions in salary for failure to do so, as well as cuts for work stoppage because of rain and for idling on the job. There were additional deductions for care of the sick. The workers had to supply their own clothing for all kinds of weather, but the contractor was supposed to make provision for at least two baths a week.[53]

The fact that the workers, organized into labor groups or *artels*, were bound to meet fixed quotas by the traditional Russian system of mutual responsibility (*krugovaia poruka*) meant longer hours and harder work than the already disadvantageous terms stipulated by the contracts. During the reign of Nicholas I, this system was being extended from the peasant villages and the Urals factories to various transport enterprises. Just prior to the construction of the St. Petersburg-Moscow Railroad, it had been applied to the Volga barge-haulers.[54] What the *artels* could not enforce, the contractors could, aided by the railroad police. Docking of salaries and other more severe penalties, such as whippings, punctuated the demands for discipline.

All of this meant a dawn to dusk working day, and a salary for the least skilled majority of the laborers which averaged 12 kopecks a day.[55] Pay was given only for work performed, although payrolls were not always met on time. The basic tasks of the unskilled laborers were digging and hauling earth, rock breaking, the cutting of trees, and swamp clearance. According to Velikin, the equivalent of 100 miles of swampland were drained or dammed in the process of construction.[56] This amounted to one-fourth of the total length of the line.

In addition to their clothing, the workers had to provide their own shelter, which consisted of tents and huts. Crowded and unsanitary living conditions, bad food, and insufficient clothing, combined with the pollution of swamps, led to disease. Scurvy, dysentery, and feverous lung infections were frequent, climaxed by the outbreak of cholera. From the beginning, infirmaries were set up and a medical staff was assigned to the line. However, there were never more than a hundred medical attendants of various types on duty at any one time, many with insufficient experience. The greatest number of beds available did not exceed 1,600, and budgetary cuts at times reduced these already inadequate facilities. For example, from July to November 1844, almost five thousand men were sick. During the cholera epidemic, as many as five men a day died in one infirmary alone. The death toll for the entire construction of the railroad ran into the thousands.

If the workers had few medicines and drugs, it was seen to it that

[53] In Krutikov, ed., "Polozhenie rabochikh," *Krasnyi arkhiv*, vol. 83, pp. 52-58.
[54] Krutikov, ed., "Polozhenie rabochikh," *Krasnyi arkhiv*, vol. 83, p. 104.
[55] Wage figures in Urodkov, *Peterburgo-Moskovskaia zheleznaia doroga*, p. 108.
[56] Velikin, *Peterburg-Moskva*, p. 67.

alcohol was abundantly available to them, for a price. Leases for vodka taverns located close to the construction site, lucrative for the owner and the Russian government alike, were liberally granted by the Minister of Finances, although both the construction engineers and the railroad police, for obvious reasons and to no avail, opposed such a policy.[57]

The civil and technical administration of the railroad, the workers' *artels*, the labor contractors and serf owners, and in addition, several chaplains with portable army churches proved insufficient to control and discipline the working force, and police units were called in. The officially stated purpose of the railroad police force was surveillance of the contractors and supervision of the welfare of the workers. It was obvious from its size—seventy-two men and nineteen officers headed by a Major General, Prince Beloselskii-Belozerskii—that the gendarme command of the St. Petersburg-Moscow Railroad was intended primarily to impose discipline and quell disorders.[58]

The major cause for discontent among the workers was fraud on the part of the contractors and poor working conditions. Most frequently, their reaction to a particularly intolerable situation would be desertion of the job, sometimes a mass walk-off, either to petition higher officials in the cities, or to return to the villages. Violence could break out in the course of protestation. A police report for November 15, 1843 describes one such scene, when 1,500 peasants, who had gathered for the day's work, began to riot when it was announced that their wages would be lowered. Some officials were pommeled and one foreman was threatened with an ax while the crowd shouted "hurrah!" The police reaction to these incidents was quick and severe, and sometimes involved mass floggings.[59]

The labor conditions prevailing on the construction of the St. Petersburg-Moscow Railroad were too flagrantly abusive to escape the attention of Russian society and the emerging intelligentsia. The bitter taste persisted for many years. More than a decade after the completion of the line, Nekrasov was inspired to write his famous poem, *The Railroad*. The grim images of Nekrasov's lines, in turn, incited the younger generation of revolutionaries of the 1860's and 1870's:

> We, in the heat, in the frost strained our sinews
> Toiled with our shoulders eternally bent

[57] The medical history and the problems of epidemic and alcoholism are summarized in Urodkov, pp. 121-36; for documents on the same matter, see *Rabochee dvizhenie*, vol. I, part 2, pp. 395-96.

[58] Shtukenberg, "Nikolaevskaia doroga," *Russkaia starina*, vol. 48 (1885), p. 324; on the portable chapels, see Urodkov, *Peterburgo-Moskovskaia zheleznaia doroga*, p. 147.

[59] *Rabochee dvizhenie*, vol. I, part 2, pp. 327-28, 330-33, 335-36, 389-93 for this and other typical outbreaks and police reports of incidents.

Lived in mud-hovels, were sodden and frozen
Fought with starvation, with scurvy were spent
Cheated we were by the quick witted foreman
Flogged by the masters, and ground in the soil
All we endured and were patient, God's Legions
Peaceable children of toil.[60]

However closely Nekrasov's image approximates the truth of the worst conditions of forced labor in the construction of the St. Petersburg-Moscow Railroad, some strikingly different scenes of voluntary effort have also become known to us. Panaev described one such drama of mass enthusiasm on the part of the peasants reminiscent of Soviet propaganda films. The time was the spring of 1850, the place, a construction site somewhere near the midpoint between St. Petersburg and Moscow, with the deadline for completion of the line rapidly approaching, and much digging still to be done. Neither Kleinmikhel's dire threats, nor Mel'nikov's dynamite in an attempted mid-winter excavation had produced results. Suddenly, the peasants of the surrounding countryside came to the rescue:

> Hardly had the peasants sowed the summer fields than, as if to answer a call through the whole surrounding countryside, there appeared before us thousands of people with their womenfolk. The muzhiks dug the earth with plowshares and the women dragged it away, some in socks, some on mats, some in their skirts or even simply in the hems. In one month, the excavation was cut for one road without slopes . . . and the possibility of opening on time was insured.[61]

[60] *Poems by Nicholas Nekrassov*, translated by Juliet M. Soskice (Oxford, 1929), p. 190. On the inspiration for this poem and its influence on Plekhanov and others, see N. Nekrasov, *Polnoe sobranie sochinenii* (Moscow, 1948), vol. II, notes, pp. 680-83.

[61] Panaev, "Vospominaniia," *Russkaia starina*, vol. 107 (1901), pp. 42-43.

Chapter 13

Locomotive Development, Operational Problems, and Railroad Planning, 1840-1860

The Aleksandrovsk Locomotive Plant

By far the greatest technical problem facing the Russian government in the construction of the St. Petersburg-Moscow Railroad was that of providing the locomotives and rolling stock. There were three alternatives available: for Russians to build the machines themselves in Russia; for the government to import finished locomotives and cars from abroad; or for foreign engineers to be contracted to build the necessary equipment in Russia. The first alternative was not feasible: Russia possessed neither the locomotive engineers, nor machinists, nor skilled workmen who had sufficient training in the construction and operation of the new machines. The primitive locomotives which the Cherepanovs operated during the 1830's and 1840's as workhorses for Urals factories were hardly known and never adapted for long-range transportation purposes. Another Urals locomotive, built in 1839 by Russians under the direction of a foreign machinist, ended its career at an industrial exhibition.[1] Locomotives, together with their drivers, had been imported from England and Belgium for the Tsarskoe Selo Railroad. This was the cheapest and most reliable alternative; but in the long run, it would place Russian railway transport in a state of dependence on foreign industry and technology. The St. Petersburg-Moscow Railroad would become a foreign enterprise in a technologically stagnant Russia. The third alternative—the employment of foreign engineers to build the locomotives, cars, and the facilities for construction and repair in Russia—was far more expensive than the second. In the long run, however, it meant the birth of a Russian railway industry independent of foreign controls and prices, as well as the training of a cadre of Russian locomotive engineers, operators, and machinists. Such a plant could become a school for Russian machine technology, the influence of which might extend beyond the exclusive needs of railroads and carry the technological development of Russia a step forward. Such were the ideals of Mel'nikov, and in a private conference with Nicholas I, he was able to persuade the Tsar to take this alternative for the provision of motive power for his railroad.[2]

Another factor which favored the construction of equipment in Russia was the existence of at least the physical nucleus for a Russian

---

[1] V. S. Virginskii, *Tvortsy novoi tekhniki v krepostnoi Rossii* (2nd edn., Moscow, 1962), p. 328.

[2] Virginskii, *Tvortsy novoi tekhniki*, p. 334.

railroad machine center in the Aleksandrovsk iron foundry located at the Neva River on the outskirts of St. Petersburg. Although the existing machinery at Aleksandrovsk was antiquated and had to be replaced for the purposes of the new operation, the physical plant, less than twenty years old, was in good condition and well suited for large-scale factory production. Plans were made to utilize this plant as a locomotive construction and repair center for the St. Petersburg-Moscow railroad. In 1844, the administration of the "Aleksandrovsk Main Mechanical Works," as it was newly named, was transferred from the Ministry of Finances to the Department of Railroads in the Main Administration of Ways of Communication in preparation for the new tasks.[3]

By this time, at the suggestion of Whistler and Mel'nikov, the American locomotive firm of Harrison, Eastwick, and Winans had been invited to bid for the construction contract. Their nearest competitor was a Belgian firm, which quoted a fee almost 40 percent higher than that of the Americans and could not guarantee the construction of more than a fourth of the equipment in Russia. Harrison, Eastwick, and Winans offered to build all of the equipment, engines and rolling stock, in Russia, at a cost of 12,000 silver rubles per locomotive and 425 to 512.50 per car. This meant a contract totaling 4,400,000 silver rubles. When it was signed, the Americans obligated themselves to build 165 twenty-five ton locomotives and tenders, 2,500 box and platform cars of eight wheels, 76 eight-wheel passenger and mail cars and 1 sixteen-wheel car for the emperor's personal use.[4]

They were called upon to supply their own tools and machines, which could be imported free of duty. They were to be supplied with Russian workmen, some of whom they were expected to train as machinists, enginemen, and conductors. To facilitate construction, they were permitted for the six-year term of their contract the full use and control of all the buildings and equipment of the Aleksandrovsk works. Police supervision of the area remained the responsibility of the Russian government.[5]

The firm of Harrison, Eastwick, and Winans consisted of four part-

[3] Joseph Harrison, *The Iron Worker and King Solomon* (2nd edn., Philadelphia, 1869), appendix, pp. 53-54, hereafter cited as Harrison, *Memoirs*. The appendix to the second edition contains Harrison's memoirs of his Russian and American careers. See pp. 49-138. For the early history of the Aleksandrovsk works, see P. Bezrukikh, *Stoletnii gigant, istoricheskii ocherk proletarskogo zavoda 1826-1926* (Leningrad, 1929).

[4] Harrison, *Memoirs*, pp. 51-52; Urodkov, *Peterburgo-Moskovskaia zheleznaia doroga*, pp. 81-82. According to Harrison's figures, the silver ruble was worth about seventy-five American cents in the 1840's.

[5] Shtukenberg, "Nikolaevskaia doroga," *Russkaia starina*, vol. 46 (1885), p. 319; *Polnoe sobranie zakonov Rossiiskoi Imperii*, second series (1844), no. 17761.

ners: Joseph Harrison and Andrew Eastwick of Philadelphia, and the brothers Thomas and William Winans of Baltimore. The Winans name was the most renowned of the three in American railroad history, for the father of Thomas and William was Ross Winans, who had built the locomotives and cars for the Baltimore and Ohio line, one of the most important of the early American railroads. The elder Winans also helped to develop the modern American railway passenger coach, and the heavy duty "Camel" locomotives, which enabled the B. & O. to penetrate the West. Some of these were used in Russia in the 1850's.[6] Absorbed in his American enterprises, he elected to send his two sons to Russia, young men who by the 1840's were trained locomotive engineers beginning their careers.

When he departed for Russia, Joseph Harrison already had behind him a career in American locomotive engineering and a prominent place in the early history of American railroads. He overshadows Eastwick, a Philadelphia inventor and businessman about whom little is known, and the Winans brothers, at least for the first ten years of the history of the Aleksandrovsk *zavod*. Later the Winans would assume a primary role in the enterprise. Harrison quit the venture at mid-century. Like many mechanical engineers at the beginning of the technological revolution, Harrison was a self-made, self-educated man of humble means who trained himself in the shop. Beginning at the age of fifteen, he worked as an indentured apprentice in several machine shops over a period of ten years, rising to a foreman's position and a salary of twelve dollars a week. During this time, he mastered the principles of steam engines. In 1834, he transferred to the Long and Norris locomotive works in Philadelphia, pioneers in the construction of the new machinery in that city. Through trial and error, many mechanical failures and near fatal accidents (he barely escaped being crushed by a derailed locomotive near the Dismal Swamp in Virginia), Harrison became a master builder of railroad steam engines, and by 1837 had become a partner in the Philadelphia firm of Harrison and Eastwick, "investing my skill, the only capital I ever had."[7]

By this time, he had helped to design improved locomotives and such inventions as the equalizing beam, a very important device which adjusted the pressure of the engine's driving wheels to the unevenness of the track, thus permitting a more rapid and a safer transit.[8] Harrison's greatest achievement was his design, for the Reading Railroad, of the "Gowan and Marx," the first Mogul-type

---

[6] John Stoves, *American Railroads* (Chicago, 1962), p. 32.

[7] Biographical details from Harrison, *Memoirs*, pp. 115-28.

[8] Harrison gives original credit to Eastwick, although most histories attribute this important innovation to him. Improvements were patented by Harrison in 1838. See Angus Sinclair, *Development of the Locomotive Engine* (New York, 1907), p. 147; and J. S. Bell, *The Early Motive Power of the Baltimore and Ohio Railroad* (New York, 1912), p. 36.

locomotive and the most efficient light-weight freight engine that had yet been constructed in the world. The Gowan and Marx, weighing eleven tons, was able to haul 101 cars with a cargo of 423 tons for fifty-four and one-half miles in about five and one-half hours. This indicated an average speed of nearly ten miles per hour. The cost was forty cents per ton, an unprecedented achievement for the time. It was this performance which attracted the attention of Mel'nikov and Kraft, then visiting the United States; and it was an adaptation of the Gowan and Marx Mogul which the American later built for the St. Petersburg-Moscow railway.[9]

Harrison embarked for Russia early in 1843 to face problems of finances, bureaucracy, and labor that were almost totally new to him and unrelated to his American experience. He joined forces with the Winans brothers en route. Several months of conferences and bidding ended in December 1843 with the gaining of the contract by the Americans. They were faced almost immediately with money problems. They had no capital of their own to buy the machinery and raw material their contract required them to supply, but the Russian government would permit advances on their fee of no more than 300,000 rubles at a time, to be paid only after six months following any contracted bill. This was double the usual period of credit extended by business firms at that time. Harrison was fortunate in this predicament. The Urals iron magnates, the Demidovs, offered to supply him whatever of their products he could use on his own terms of payment, an offer which he readily accepted. For the necessary foreign machinery, Harrison made a special trip to England, where he was able to persuade the prominent Welsh iron monger, William Crawshay, to supply a substantial part of his machinery and goods on the Russian government's terms and with no security other than his contract.[10] Other English firms followed the lead of Crawshay, and later the Americans obtained additional machinery from the United States as well. By keeping his production ahead of schedule, Harrison was able to pay all of his bills before they came due. For ordinary expenses at the plant, since there were few private banks of deposit in Russia, he was obliged periodically to haul large bundles of cash from government offices in St. Petersburg. He sometimes carried as much as 130,000 rubles in one hundred-ruble notes—"a package nearly a foot square," commented Harrison, who was constantly fearful of robbery on the long and lonely open coach ride from the capital back to Aleksandrovsk.[11]

---

[9] On the Gowan and Marx, see Sinclair, *Locomotive Engine*, p. 146; and Joseph Harrison, *The Locomotive Engine and Philadelphia's Share in its Early Improvements* (rev. edn., Philadelphia, 1872), p. 52.

[10] Harrison, *Memoirs*, pp. 49-53, 79-84.

[11] Harrison, *Memoirs*, pp. 131-35.

The Aleksandrovsk plant, which the Americans were ultimately to run for eighteen years, was perhaps the least of their problems. Extending for a quarter of a mile along the Neva, close to the St. Petersburg-Moscow highway and about eight miles from the capital, it included several sturdy buildings, an iron works, a sawmill, docks, a workers' village complete with cemetery and church, and a large villa for the use of Harrison and his family. To this complex, the Americans added a car works and a spur from the nearby St. Petersburg-Moscow railway line upon which locomotives could be tested and moved.[12] According to the Statute of March 1844, the mechanical operations at the Aleksandrovsk works were under the exclusive supervision of the firm Harrison, Eastwick, and Winans, although in practice Major Whistler had a final responsibility. All other aspects of the administration of the factories were organized in a military manner. There were closed gates and a pass system, entrusted to a *politsmeister*, who was assisted by several clerks and noncommissioned officers, and forty-five military guards. These consisted for the most part of old soldiers, who were used frequently in tsarist days for this kind of duty. In times of emergency, such as during a cholera epidemic in 1848, when workers, crazed with fear, were deserting the plant in large numbers, a special guard of 200 mounted Cossacks was brought up to reinforce the regular police. The Cossacks were encamped within the walls of the works. The functions of the factory police were defined as keeping order, guarding property, seeing that the work was done, and watching the accounts, in that order. In addition to the police regulations, which comprise most of the articles of the Aleksandrovsk statute, provision was made for an infirmary with a doctor and several assistants. A school with one teacher and forty students for the children of the craftsmen was stipulated, as part of the government's obligation, while the Americans were required to maintain in repair, at their own expense, the houses of the workers.[13]

On one of his rare visits to the Aleksandrovsk plant, Nicholas I, standing in front of a crowd of a thousand peasants, commented to Harrison of his workers: "They are very good people, but they will get drunk!"[14] The Tsar was exaggerating an obvious, but not a fundamental problem: drunkenness, which was severely punished, was probably the least of the problems which Harrison and his associates faced in the supervision of several hundred Russian workers. Lack of skill, ignorance, poverty, and pilfering were greater evils, but Harrison

[12] Harrison, *Memoirs*, pp. 54-55; Anna M. Whistler Journal, Aug. 19, 1844, in the possession of the Manuscript Division, New York Public Library, hereafter referred to as *Journal of Anna Whistler*.

[13] Harrison, *Memoirs*, pp. 53-56; J. Harrison to Henry Harrison, July 4, 1848, Harrison, *Letter Books*; *Polnoe sobranie zakonov*, second series (1844), no. 17761.

[14] Harrison, *Memoirs*, p. 77.

believed that he had overcome these shortcomings by higher wages and good treatment. It is interesting to note the monthly wages at Aleksandrovsk. According to the second American contract of 1850, they were listed, according to skill, as the following:[15]

Rank	*Monthly Wage*
Master Mechanic	33 rubles, 16 3/4 kopecks, plus 3 poods of rye flour
Foreman	17 rubles, 29 kopecks, plus 3 poods of rye flour
Carpenter	8 rubles, 12 1/2 kopecks, plus 2 poods of rye flour
Workman	7 rubles, 51 1/4 kopecks, plus 2 poods of rye flour
Apprentice	2 rubles, 65 1/2 kopecks, plus 1 pood of rye flour

A master mechanic at the first Russian locomotive works in 1850 was thus earning about half of what Harrison himself earned only fifteen years before as a "highly paid" machine shop foreman in the United States (excluding the payment in food). However, he brought home little more than one-third of the salary of the skilled mechanics imported to Aleksandrovsk from England.[16] Although these were high wages for the time, considerably better than the remuneration of the laborers on the track excavation, they were not high enough to prevent labor trouble only a decade later.[17]

In addition to Englishmen, the Aleksandrovsk plant employed a number of Swedes, Germans, and several Americans. The bulk of the workers consisted of Russian men and boys, about a third of whom were state serfs, assigned to the locomotive factory with wages. The remainder of the Russian personnel were presumably *obrok*-paying seigneurial serfs who were hired as wage laborers. The work day began at six in the morning and ended at seven-thirty in the evening, including Saturdays until seven, with two hours for meals. This equalled a sixty-eight and one-half hour work week.[18] However, a large number of religious holidays, to Harrison's dismay, substantially

[15] This is "Table A" of a copy of the contract now among the Winans papers; see also Harrison, *Memoirs*, p. 56. These figures compare roughly with those extracted recently from documents in Soviet archives. See R. Zelnick, "An Early Case of Labor Protest in St. Petersburg: the Aleksandrovsk Machine Works in 1860," *Slavic Review*, vol. XXIV (1965), 513.

[16] Harrison to Alexander Sterling, June 30, 1851, Harrison, *Letter Books*.

[17] See Zelnick, "An Early Case of Labor Protest," pp. 507-20.

[18] "Table A" of the contract of 1850, Winans, *Papers*; Harrison, *Memoirs*, pp. 53-56; *Journal of Anna Whistler*, Aug. 19, 1844.

diminished the yearly total of working days. This tradition was of special benefit to the state serfs, who were paid for thirty-six such holidays, although they could elect to work on some of them. The other serf workers had only thirteen holidays, during which time the plant was closed.[19]

In 1848 and 1849, the cholera epidemic which carried off Major Whistler ravaged the Aleksandrovsk plant. At its height in 1848, Harrison estimated that several hundred people a day died of the disease in St. Petersburg, while at the Aleksandrovsk workers' village, there were five or six deaths a day among its population of 2,000. The small infirmary which the statute of 1844 had established was obviously inadequate, and two hospitals were attached to the factory. The greatest problem, as far as the progress of work was concerned, was the departure of hundreds of the workmen for their villages in the interior of Russia, a panic which the government attempted to stop by armed force. Since most of the contracted locomotive and car construction had been completed by 1848, this human tragedy did not represent a major economic crisis for the railway, and the abatement of the epidemic by the end of 1849 found the plant functioning normally.[20]

Harrison in his memoirs relates a conversation with the aristocratic railroad promoter, Count Bobrinskii, after the signing of his first contract in 1843:

"So you have signed a contract with the government."

"Yes," I replied.

"I am very happy to hear it," he said; "they will never let you complete it," meaning that red tape and even more serious troubles with the officials could wear us out before the contract term was ended.[21]

Similar to Whistler, Harrison had a long and frustrating experience with bureaucracy. He was directly approached for graft, in one instance by an inspector who wished to authorize and then share with the Americans the pilferings from a grossly padded account. Harrison asserts that he refused this proposition and reported the matter to Colonel Mel'nikov. The latter had the inspector removed. As soon as the Americans had established a reputation for incorruptibility, Harrison observed that the officials ceased to harass them with frequent inspections and in fact became lax in their duties.[22]

On top of their difficulties with the Russian government, friction developed among the Americans themselves. Harrison and the Winans brothers not only found it impossible to work with Eastwick, but

---

[19] Harrison to Charles Harrison, April 6, 1846, Harrison, *Letter Books.*

[20] Harrison to Samuel Poulterer, June 6, 1848, June 16, 1848; Harrison to William Poulterer, Nov. 20, 1849, Harrison, *Letter Books.*

[21] Harrison, *Memoirs,* pp. 57-58.   [22] Harrison, *Memoirs,* pp. 59-62.

developed a vigorous animosity toward him. "He has been our mill-stone, our incubus, my contempt and disgust," wrote Harrison. In 1850, just after the completion of the principal construction on the line and the signing of a new contract between Harrison, the Winans brothers, and the Russian government for the repair and maintenance of the rolling stock, Eastwick sold his interest to William Winans and returned to Philadelphia a wealthy man.[23]

In the day-to-day administration of the factory, Harrison had the opportunity to observe the same harsh discipline and overcautiousness on the part of the Russian officialdom that had attracted the attention and criticism of Whistler. In 1844, he observed in a letter to America:

> Many of our operations with the government are new to them and they are so fearful of going wrong that they take up a great deal of time in arranging the best way to accomplish things so as to make matters work sure and easy for them and for us.[24]

Another waste of time and money resulted from the rare but elaborate imperial inspections. In March 1847, Nicholas I, accompanied by the Grand Dukes Alexander and Constantine, the Duke of Württemberg (then Viceroy of Poland), Generals Benckendorff and Kiselev, and several other ministers, spent several hours at the Aleksandrovsk plant. It took three weeks of tidying and prettifying, including the planting of evergreens in front of the factory door—all at a cost of some two thousand rubles—to prepare for this royal outing. This was an expensive and time-consuming ceremonial gesture which was incomprehensible and irritating to the Americans.[25]

Harrison, like Whistler, considered himself a "plain republican," a term which both men used when contrasting themselves to the pomp and display of the Russian court and upper officialdom. Perhaps this was the spirit and style of the Jacksonian democracy in which the American engineers had been educated as well as a role which Europeans and Russians in the age of De Tocqueville expected them to fulfill. Whistler was awarded an Anna Cross at the 1847 inspection, which he hesitated to wear, while Harrison for his services to Russia, was given the more plebeian accolade of a diamond ring. Antimonarchist in his political philosophy, sympathetic to the revolutionaries of 1848, a solid mid-century Victorian, he turned his back on the corruption of Russian officialdom. To be sure, he had no material need to yield to it; his legitimate compensation from the Russian government

---

[23] Harrison to Samuel Poulterer, Sept. 29, 1850; Harrison to his wife, Oct. 4, 1850, Harrison, *Letter Books*; Ellis P. Oberholtzer, *Philadelphia. A History of the City and Its People* (Philadelphia, 1912), vol. II, p. 159, note 3.

[24] Harrison to G. Ralston, Aug. 19/31, 1844, Harrison, *Letter Books*.

[25] Harrison to S. Poulterer, March 7/20, 1847, Harrison, *Letter Books*; Whistler to Swift, Oct. 28, 1844, *Swift mss.*

was ample and generous, to say the least. This money moved in a fairly steady flow, during his seven years in Russia, to Philadelphia, where Harrison was amassing a substantial fortune in real estate.

Despite the various problems of financing, labor, and bureaucracy, and unlike the slow progress of track construction, production at the locomotive works remained ahead of schedule. By December 1845, or two years after signing the first contract, an expanded operation employing 1,600 skilled workmen was turning out ten cars a day and one locomotive a week. Both passenger and freight locomotives, the latter with an extra third pair of driving wheels, were built—all equipment with interchangeable parts. Also in regular production were passenger cars fifty-six feet long and capable of holding from thirty to eighty passengers; many more eight-wheeled freight cars, thirty feet long; and a large number of platform cars, designed by William Winans, which could be used for the transport of military units. An added luxury and showcase was a sixteen-wheeled private car for the use of the tsar, 84 feet long, with a sleeping compartment, a luxuriously furnished parlor, a kitchen, wine cellar and dining room, refrigeration, and a hot water boiler.[26]

By the summer of 1847, the original contract was only a few months short of completion, a year ahead of time, with two locomotives being produced every six days. Harrison could boast that ". . . this beats our old operation at home and it is about two engines a month ahead of any establishment in any country we have knowledge of." Even earlier than this, Whistler could call the Aleksandrovsk plant, ". . . the finest establishment in all Europe."[27] It was by far the best in Russia, and provided a training center for a whole generation of Russian machinists. It flourishes today, renamed the Proletarian Locomotive Repair Plant and the October Car Repair Plant.

With release from the burden of building a fleet of locomotives and cars from the ground up as well as a machine industry to maintain them, Harrison and William Winans had the time after 1849 to devote themselves to other engineering projects. Harrison assisted the Russian engineer, Kerbedz, in building across the Neva River in St. Petersburg what he described as the longest cast iron bridge in the world—1,100 feet long and 77 feet wide, with seven arches, and spans ranging from 107 to 156 feet. The construction of the bridge was begun in 1843 by English engineers who abandoned the task half finished. It was resumed and completed at the end of the decade by

[26] Figures and descriptions in: Whistler to Swift, Dec. 19, 1845, *Swift mss.*; Harrison to William Winans, April 12, 1851, Harrison, *Letter Books*; Vose, *Whistler*, pp. 34-37; and Albert Parry, *Whistler's Father* (New York, 1939), p. 322.
[27] Harrison to S. Poulterer, July 26/Aug. 7, 1847, Harrison, *Letter Books*; Whistler to Swift, May 5, 1845, *Swift mss.*

Harrison and Kerbedz. Harrison lost money on this contract, which apparently did not seriously dent the fortune he had accumulated in Russia, but was further compensated by the Order of St. Anna and a gold medal bearing the inscription: "For Zeal."[28] His Russian experience was enriched by the opportunity to observe the spectacle of the opening of the bridge. Nicholas I appeared in public on the twenty-fifth anniversary of his accession to the throne, in defiance of the popular superstition that death or assassination would prevent him from ruling more than twenty-five years. A huge crowd thronged around the bridge for the ceremony. Nicholas suddenly turned to the mass of peasants and townsmen and shouted: "Let the people come on!" In a moment, the bridge was inundated with the human flood, and Harrison feared for his life, that of the emperor, and for the stability of the bridge itself under the impact of this stampede. However, the crowd passed uneventfully over the bridge and merged with another mob coming from the other side.[29]

The mid-1850's were a time of war for Russia, and the inventive mind of William Winans was turned to the service of the Russian navy in the Crimea and Black Sea. He helped to build—perhaps in collaboration with Nobel and Putilov—seventy-five gunboats, 111 feet in length, displacing 176 tons, using steam power and screw propellers, which attained a speed of ten knots. According to Winans, these vessels performed well. However, they were only preliminary to a favorite dream of the Winans family: a "cigar" boat (a steamship with a spindle shaped hull), a concept far in advance of its time. Winans wrote a report for the **Grand Duke Constantine**, the progressive Minister of Naval Forces, on how the cigar boat could be adapted as a warship. In other plans, he envisioned a fighting vessel with disappearing guns, torpedoes, and watertight "cells like a bee hive," that would make it unsinkable.[30]

At the time of the outbreak of the Civil War in the United States, the firm of Winans, Harrison, and Winans were nearing the end of their first contract for the repair and remounting of the locomotives and rolling stock of the Nicholas railroad. This first contract had been concluded in 1850 for a term of twelve years. A second contract was made in 1865, and remained in force until 1870, when the railroad was converted from a state enterprise into a private stock company. Both contracts were extremely advantageous for the Americans, as

[28] Harrison, *Memoirs*, p. 70; J. Harrison to S. Poulterer, Oct. 24, 1850, Harrison, *Letter Books*.

[29] Harrison, *Memoirs*, pp. 72-74; Korf, "Iz zapisok Barona Korfa," *Russkaia starina*, vol. 102 (1900), p. 517.

[30] William to Thomas Winans, Nov. 26/Dec. 8, 1858; March (undated), 1859; June 2, 1861; July 25/Aug. 6, 1861; Sept. 7, 1861, Winans, *Papers*. On the gunboats, see also *Mekhanicheskii zavod Liudvig Nobel 1862-1912* (no date or place of publication), p. 3.

can be seen from the provisions of the first, a printed copy of which has been preserved among the Winans family papers. In return for the servicing, painting, and overhaul of all machinery, Harrison and the Winans brothers received a generous allowance (for example, according to the estimate of Bayard Taylor, $700 for the greasing of the wheels on an ordinary train making one trip between St. Petersburg and Moscow). The costs were guaranteed by numerous articles of a tightly written agreement of ninety-five paragraphs, and were kept at a minimum by guarantee of the free use of the Aleksandrovsk factory complex, as well as of the repair shops along the line.[31] William Winans was estimated to have netted a million rubles a year on these contracts, or a total of twenty-five million rubles by 1870, when he made a profitable settlement with the government upon the liquidation of the railroad as a state enterprise. Harrison probably made less, but certainly enough by 1859 to make it necessary for the Winans brothers to offer him 240,000 English pounds sterling to sell out his interest.[32]

It was obvious by the end of the second decade of the American venture in Russia that the initiative was passing to William Winans. Eastwick was out by 1850, and Harrison and Thomas Winans soon after returned to semiretirement in the United States. William, engrossed in his holdings, speculations, and lawsuits in Russia, never returned to his native Baltimore. He was consolidating his railroad empire with "a passion." When the Russian government began to hedge, prior to the second repair contract, on the large sums that were passing from the state treasury into his hands, he called the famous Baltimore railroad lawyer, John H. B. Latrobe, into the case. Latrobe was paid the extravagant fee of $60,000.[33]

It was apparently necessary for Winans to get Harrison out of the firm to permit full scope for his ambitions, and in 1858 the latter was offered 20,000 pounds sterling a month for all of the following year. Harrison accepted, and the Winans brothers became the sole participants in the third American contract of the 1860's.[34]

The reaction of many of the Russian engineers to the Winans

[31] Harrison, *Memoirs*, pp. 67-69, 94-99. The Winans papers (no. 51271) include a printed copy of the 1850 contract.

[32] Delvig, *Polveka russkoi zhizni*, vol. II, p. 262; William Winans to Joseph Harrison, Dec. 29, 1858, Winans, *Papers*.

[33] John Semmes, *John H. B. Latrobe and His Times* (Baltimore, 1917), pp. 471-73.

[34] William to Thomas Winans, Dec. 23/Jan. 4, 1858; Jan. 2/14, 1859; Jan. 7/19, 1959, Winans, *Papers*. In 1859, Winans wrote his brother Thomas, who was in Baltimore, that he was "particularly anxious for Harrison to accept," and, a few days later: "I am *devilish anxious* that he should accept my proposition, and I have a pretty strong hope that he will, 240,000 p.s. besides what he has already got ought to satisfy him. Were I in his place, I would *jump at such an offer*." (Underlining [italics] by Winans in a letter to his brother, Thomas, Jan. 7/19, 1859.)

arrangements were mixed. General Mel'nikov, who by this time had become Minister of Ways of Communication had been William's personal friend and colleague for over two decades and apparently felt that the Russian government was receiving full value for an admittedly highly priced service. He supported Winans as did some other engineers and directors of the private railroad corporation formed in 1870. Other officials, such as General Chevkin and the engineers, Baron Delvig and Valerian Panaev, saw Winans not only as a swindler who was bleeding the Russian government of millions, but as a criminal who was doctoring obsolete machinery to gain even more illicit income. It would be difficult to substantiate these accusations, although it is obvious that the Winans and Harrison were able to carve substantial fortunes out of their two or three decades in Russia—tens of millions of dollars, which enabled all of them to retire to a life of opulence at an early age. There is no doubt that their services came high, but at the time they were crucial and hard to find.[35]

Operation and Impact of the St. Petersburg-Moscow Railroad

On August 20, 1850, prior to the public opening, the Emperor of Russia boarded the imperial car of the St. Petersburg-Moscow line for his first railroad trip between the two Russian capitals. He was certainly not the line's first passenger. Significantly, Russian soldiers were the first to be accorded this hazardous honor. The Tsar had been preceded by a troop movement on the fifteenth of the month. The earliest completed section of the railroad, the St. Petersburg-Kolpino run, had been used for experiments in military transport for over two years. Thousands of tons of freight had also been carried over this section, and in 1848 and 1849, 80,000 pilgrims had been conveyed to the shrine of St. Nicholas at Kolpino by the new steam locomotives.[36]

The Tsar was accompanied by the entire imperial family—"three generations of the reigning Romanov house," in what was intended as a "triumphal passing," as the engineer, Shtukenberg, recalled it. The royal travelers were situated in the special, blue imperial car, eighty-four feet long, a "comfortable and luxuriously decorated rolling house." At the Vyshnii Volochok station, the Tsar disembarked. A crowd of peasants surrounded him on the platform, shouting "hurrah!"

[35] On the contemporary Russian and later Soviet views of the Americans, see: Delvig, *Polveka russkoi zhizni*, vol. II, pp. 259-62, 325-26, 355-56; Panaev, "Vospominaniia," *Russkaia starina*, vol. 108 (1902), pp. 403-05; Virginskii, *Tvortsy novoi tekhniki*, pp. 340-41. On the legal proceedings of the 1860's between the Americans and the Russian government, see *Proshenie i prilozhenie predstavlennye ego imperatorskomu velichestvu gosudariu Imperatoru Aleksandru II, amerikanskimi grazhdani Uainans, Garrison i Uainans otnositel'no ikh iska na rossiiskoe pravitel'stvo* (London, 1863).

[36] Panaev, "Vospominaniia," *Russkaia starina*, vol. 107 (1901), p. 43; Parry, *Whistler's Father*, p. 289.

Nicholas I was in high spirits. Walking up to the locomotive, he turned to the people and exclaimed: "Here is a little horse I've gotten for you!" The Tsar then held out his nephew, a small boy, to the peasants, and again a great hurrah! went up, accompanied by caps flying into the air. At another station, viewing one of the colossal, domed locomotive sheds that had been built for the line, Nicholas exclaimed in French: "C'est un panthéon! C'est un temple!"[37]

These opening festivities unfortunately were not unaccompanied by anxious moments, omens of many breakdowns and catastrophes that were soon to come. At about mid-point in the Tsar's first trip, the imperial train appeared to be stalled on the 125-foot heights of the Vereba River bridge. The American engineers at the throttle, Bartner and Winans, discovered to their horror that some workman had adorned the rails along the bridge with slippery black oil paint to make the sovereign's view more pleasing. Soon after, at the end of September, the Empress and her entourage were making the return trip to St. Petersburg and came very close to losing their lives in the darkness because of a siding switch that had been left unturned. Only the quick thinking of one of the sentinels on duty at the next switch averted a royal tragedy. The first major wreck came in the late fall of 1850, a head-on collision which killed at least one engineman.[38]

Only a few passengers were on hand to be injured in this accident, because the line had not yet been opened to the public, and was restricted to the carrying of mail, to experimental troop movements, and to the conveying of a few curious dignitaries. When passenger service was installed late in 1851, over a year after the Tsar's first trip, the railroad was still far from completion. Many passenger stations remained windowless, numerous water tanks were missing, and locomotives had to be kept in the open air in several stations. Since the telegraph line parallel to the track had not been completed, passengers, in the event of the frequent breakdowns or accidents, ran the risk of being stranded for an entire day before help, solicited by hand car or even on foot, could arrive. In the sub-zero winter wilderness between St. Petersburg and Moscow, rather grim situations could develop in unheated cars, lacking both food and water.

"So badly arranged was this road at first," complained an English visitor,

> that when we went to St. Petersburg by it, we were kept thirty-six hours in the midst of the Valdai Hills in twenty-eight degrees of cold [Réaumur] without anything to eat or drink. Some of the third class passengers were obliged to be brought into the first class

[37] Shtukenberg, "Nikolaevskaia doroga," *Russkaia starina*, vol. 49 (1886), pp. 115-17, apparently there at the time, describes the trip and its perils.
[38] Shtukenberg, "Nikolaevskaia doroga," *Russkaia starina*, vol. 49, (1886), pp. 118-20; Harrison, *Memoirs*, pp. 84-86.

wagons, lest they should be frozen to death; and a poor peasant's child died in her arms from the dreadful severity of the weather. Some of the passengers (one of them an officer in the army) fainted; and all of this through the negligence of the authorities.[39]

This anguished tourist's account was echoed by one of the Russian engineers assigned to supervise a section of the operating line: "There was such confusion that it is impossible to imagine or describe it," Valerian Panaev recalled, admitting that the local commanders, most of them Russian transportation engineers, were of little help. They had received "literally only one lecture" on steam locomotives. Panaev had to read a French text on the subject to acquaint himself on the job. He was not, however, permitted by the American engineers to tamper with the machinery.[40]

Under such conditions, trains kept poor schedules, and the duration of a trip between the Russian capitals in the early days of the line was closer to a day than the eighteen hours which had been originally planned. In 1866, the trip still consumed twenty hours. The apprehension of the passengers over the perils of their journey may have distracted them somewhat from annoyance over regulations which required attendance at the railway station a full hour before departure, passports, and special police authorizations. Slowly but appreciably, however, the St. Petersburg-Moscow Railroad began to improve. Safety measures were taken: one government regulation prohibited private wooden structures closer than 280 feet from the railroad stations because of the danger of flying sparks from the locomotives. The American engineer, Harrison, observed that the railroad came to be run on the "principle of military discipline—prompt and severe punishment and no excuses." Two drunken workmen, one of them a foreigner, who had caused a collision, were flogged publicly and sentenced to work, ball and chain, in the Kronstadt naval yard for a term of three years. The result of such severe measures, Harrison acknowledged, was a lower accident rate than in any other country.[41] By the end of the 1850's, another American, a famous journalist, lecturer, and world traveler, Bayard Taylor, who had seen his share of railroads in Europe and the United States, could describe the "Nicholas Railroad," as it had come to be known after 1855, as punctual, operated with "utmost precision and regularity," although slower than its for-

---

[39] *The Englishwoman in Russia* (author not given) (London, 1855), p. 25; on early conditions of the line, see Panaev, "Vospominaniia," *Russkaia starina*, vol. 107 (1901), pp. 43-46.

[40] Panaev, "Vospominaniia," *Russkaia starina*, vol. 107 (1901), pp. 47-48.

[41] On the running of the railroad, see Korf, "Iz zapisok Barona Korfa," *Russkaia starina*, vol. 103 (1900), p. 44; J. F. Loubat, *Narrative of the Mission to Russia in 1866 of the Honorable Gustavus Vasa Fox* (New York, 1873), pp. 208, 213; Shtukenberg, "Nikolaevskaia doroga," *Russkaia starina*, vol. 49 (1886), p. 125; and Harrison, *Memoirs*, pp. 87-88.

eign rivals, and "in its construction and accessories, the finest railway in the world."[42]

A third foreign observer, an Englishman, Lawrence Oliphant, who traveled on the St. Petersburg-Moscow line just before the Crimean War, was fully alerted at this early date to the military purposes of the railroad. He wrote in 1854:

> Russian railroads seem to be meant for Russian soldiers; and it is the facility thus afforded of moving large bodies of men that invests this mode of communication in Russia with an importance which does not attach to it in Great Britain or perhaps any other country in Europe to an equal extent.

> When St. Petersburg, Moscow, Odessa, and Warsaw become connected, Russia assumes an entirely new position with regard to the rest of Europe. A few days, instead of many months, will then suffice to concentrate the armies of the north and south upon the Austrian or Prussian frontiers. Through this same quarter of the world many hundreds of years ago, poured those barbaric hordes which overran civilized Europe—it would indeed be a singular testimony to the spirit of the age if the next invaders made their descent by means of railroads.[43]

Oliphant does not mention any of the large troop movements which took place on the St. Petersburg-Moscow line during the time of his visit, although his remarks would indicate that he had seen or heard of them. Experimental transport of military personnel was instituted as soon as the first section of the line, extending from St. Petersburg to Kolpino, was completed in 1848. In June of that year, 250 recruits were dispatched by railroad to the Russian capital. Later in the same year and in 1849 and 1850 entire regiments were being carried along completed sections of the line. In the summer of 1851, two months before the opening of the railroad to civilian passenger service, the first transfer of a large, fully complemented and equipped military unit over the entire length of the line was executed. This included the moving of infantry battalions from the Preobrazhenskii and Semenovskii regiments together with artillery units. In all, nine trains, numbering fourteen to nineteen cars each, were used. In 1852, the entire Seventeenth Infantry Division was moved between the two Russian capitals in trains dispatched at two-hour intervals.[44]

By this time, open and closed platform cars designed for the trans-

[42] Bayard Taylor, *Greece and Russia* (New York, 1859), pp. 373-74. On Taylor, see M. Herzberg, *The Reader's Encyclopedia of American Literature* (New York, 1962).

[43] L. Oliphant, *The Russian Shores of the Black Sea* (London, 1854), p. 16.

[44] G. N. Karaev, *Vozniknovenie sluzhby voennykh soobshchenii na zheleznykh dorogakh Rossii 1851-1878* (Moscow, 1949), pp. 26-27, 31, 36; Shtukenberg, "Nikolaevskaia doroga," *Russkaia starina*, vol. 49 (1886), p. 125.

port of infantry and cavalry were in regular use. The closed cars contained stalls for two horses; on the open platform cars, three rows of benches were installed, capable of holding sixty infantrymen with equipment. With such improvisations, the War Ministry, in whose hands military transport by rail had been placed, moved 836,500 troops, 58,200 horses and 11,000 wagons on the St. Petersburg-Moscow line between 1852 and 1856. Much of this activity related to the transport of reserve units, supplies, ammunition, and weapons for the Crimean War.[45]

Such figures underscore the military motives so pronounced in the early Russian railroads, and they lend strength to the claim made by Soviet historians that Russian planning and experimentation in the field of military rail transportation preceded that of the Germans.[46] Such a priority, however, is of little significance: planning, however farsighted, did not build railroads to the south of Russia and the Caucasus, where troops and supplies were so urgently needed in the Crimean War, although a railroad to Theodosia had been surveyed two years prior to the outbreak of hostilities. The Crimean War pointed up not Russia's feeble successes in the realm of military transport on its only major rail line, but rather, Russia's weaknesses and backwardness in railroad construction generally.

Although it was not the foremost consideration in the minds of the planners, the commercial potential of the St. Petersburg-Moscow Railroad was far from overlooked. The straight line of the track indicated preference for a through traffic of military personnel and freight between the two Russian capitals, but was not intended to foster the stagnation of commercial centers in north central Russia. As the engineer Shtukenberg later pointed out in defense of the straight-line concept, the cities that were bypassed—Novgorod the most important among them—were too far away from the track to really suffer competition. They continued to flourish as commercial centers. Towns located on the nearby St. Petersburg-Moscow highway, such as Valdai, did lose their trade to the railroad. To compensate for this, however, the line stimulated the growth of new industrial centers, such as Vyshnii Volochok.[47]

Almost two million pounds of freight were carried along the early experimental road to Kolpino in its first year of operation (1847-1848). The rolling stock of the completed line at the time of its opening consisted of almost three times as many freight as passenger cars, or 2,570 enclosed and platform vehicles. In the early 1850's, three freight trains a day were dispatched from St. Petersburg, carrying

[45] Karaev, *Vozniknovenie sluzhby voennykh soobshchenii*, pp. 27-29, 32, 40.
[46] Karaev, *Vozniknovenie sluzhby voennykh soobshchenii*, pp. 21-22.
[47] Shtukenberg, "Nikolaevskaia doroga," *Russkaia starina*, vol. 49 (1886), pp. 126-27.

mainly Russian raw materials and imported foreign goods—tea, tallow, fur, and cotton.[48] The volume of freight transport was increased over the years, so that by 1874, the Nicholas line carried the greatest amount of commercial cargo of any of the forty-seven railways operating by that time in Russia. This amounted to over two and one-quarter million tons.

In the same year, 1,626,000 passengers were carried between the two Russian capitals, which made the Nicholas railway second in Russia (next to the St. Petersburg-Warsaw line) in terms of numbers of passengers carried.[49] In the early years of its operation, despite growing passenger and freight revenues, the Nicholas line did not, however, realize anticipated profit expectations. One reason for this was the absence of a railway network to feed in freight from the interior of Russia. This was partially solved in the 1860's with the completion of the Moscow-Kursk and Moscow-Riazan lines, which resulted in a doubling of revenue from that of the 1850's. Another reason for the failure of the line to pay off in a big way was the persistence of low rates and fares combined with prohibitive operating expenses. The staff alone was a weighty burden, numbering about 3,000 from the very beginning. The American engineers who had built the original locomotives and rolling stock for the line, as we have seen, were able to conclude follow-up contracts for maintenance which guaranteed extravagant profits for them. It was only in the late 1860's that the Russian government was able to buy its way out of this unprofitable arrangement, but this cost 5½ million rubles. By this time, the line had been sold to the European-controlled Grande Société des Chemins de fer Russes, although it was later taken over again by the Russian government.[50]

At the time of the completion of the St. Petersburg-Moscow railway, there were about five hundred miles of track in the Russian empire. By 1870, there were over 5,000. For several years, until the completion of the midwestern and transcontinental lines in the United States and the St. Petersburg-Warsaw line in the Russian empire, the Nicholas railway remained the largest in the world and the best equipped, according to the testimony of many foreign observers. This did not mark the beginning of the modernization of Russian railway transport in any quantitative sense. Russia had decades to wait for a comprehensive rail network, even for the European part of the empire. The significance of the Nicholas railroad is that it demonstrated

[48] Urodkov, *Peterburgo-Moskovskaia zheleznaia doroga*, pp. 153, 156; Oliphant, *Russian Shores*, p. 15.

[49] Figures on freight in I. S. Bliokh, *Vlianie zheleznykh dorog na ekonomicheskoe sostoianie Rossii* (St. Petersburg, 1878), vol. I, table, pp. 66-67.

[50] Bliokh, *Vlianie zheleznykh dorog na Rossii*, vol. I, pp. 3-5; Urodkov, *Peterburgo-Moskovskaia zheleznaia doroga*, p. 168; Shtukenberg, "Nikolaevskaia doroga," *Russkaia starina*, vol. 49 (1886), p. 121.

the feasibility of a major railway for military, freight, and passenger transport in the physical conditions of Russia.

Planning for a Russian Railway Network in the 1850's

One year after the full opening of the St. Petersburg-Moscow line for commercial use, planning began in earnest for the construction of a rail network in European Russia, with the formulation of a project to connect the commercial centers of the central and western provinces of the empire. The idea of a Russian rail network was first broached in the early years of the reign of Nicholas I by such pioneer proponents of the modernization of Russian transport as Admiral Mordvinov, the Ritter von Gerstner, and others. The decision to build a major line between the Russian capitals almost immediately encouraged promoters and planners to press for other lines. For the decade beginning in 1843, plans were considered to connect the Don and Volga rivers, St. Petersburg and several Baltic ports, Kharkov and the Black Sea port of Theodosia, Odessa, and Warsaw, and most important, Moscow and Odessa. The initial project for a Russian rail network, which was forwarded in 1852, proposed several main lines radiating out from the Russian capitals so as to connect them with Odessa, Kiev, Theodosia, Kharkov, Kursk, and Rostov in the south; Brest, Warsaw, Smolensk, and Riga in the west; and Nizhnii-Novgorod and Kazan in the east. The network was to be built in three stages, which, when completed, would unite the main industrial and agricultural regions of European Russia. Siberia and Central Asia were not included in these plans, the first detailed projects for these more ambitious undertakings appearing in 1858.[51]

Not all of this planning came to nothing. In the winter of 1850, immediately upon the completion of the St. Petersburg-Moscow line, a special committee headed by the Grand Duke Alexander was set up to consider the building of a railroad from the Russian capital to Warsaw. Late in 1851, Nicholas I began to press the slow-moving committee for action. According to Baron Korf, he considered the strategic importance of the line an urgent matter.[52] The Tsar had similar feelings about a line to the Black Sea, and in the same year, ordered Mel'nikov to look into the matter. The latter project produced no immediate results, but construction was begun on the Warsaw line in 1852. By the following year, a first section of this railway had been

[51] The various projects enumerated in Karaev, *Vozniknovenie sluzhby voennykh soobshchenii*, p. 25; Shtukenberg, "Nikolaevskaya doroga," *Russkaia starina*, vol. 46 (1885), p. 313; *Vsepoddanneishii otchet po vedomstvu putei soobshcheniia za 25 let c 19 fevralia 1855 do 19 f. 1880 goda* (St. Petersburg, 1880), p. 47.

[52] "Iz zapisok Barona Korfa," *Russkaia starina*, vol. 103 (1900), p. 48.

completed, at a cost of 18 million rubles. The Crimean War brought an end to all railroad planning and construction in Russia.[53]

With the conclusion of the Crimean War, the railroad history of Russia entered a new phase beyond the scope of this account. The innovations and the continuities of the new period may be suggested by way of conclusion here. The initial method of state financing and control of railroad construction and operation was abandoned after the death of Nicholas I for experiments with private enterprise. With the imperial confirmation in 1857 of the Grande Société des Chemins de fer Russes, Russia became the happy hunting ground for foreign investors, capitalists and, engineer-entrepreneurs. The Americans who worked on the St. Petersburg-Moscow railway in the 1840's may be considered the vanguard of this economic invasion. The Winans family, as we have seen, continued to lead the attack during the first railroad boom of the 1860's.

The charter of the Grande Société also marks the beginning of the reconstruction of a unified rail network in European Russia, the realization of the plans of the early 1850's. Russian private entrepreneurs as well as foreigners caught the railroad fever after the Crimean War. In 1858, Baron Stieglitz financed the building of a St. Petersburg-Peterhof suburban line with a spur to Krasnoe Selo. This was the nucleus of the future Baltic railroad. In 1861, a Russian company undertook the construction of a railroad from Moscow to the Monastery of the Holy Trinity in Sergiev. Fedor Vasilevich Chizhov, the well-known Slavophile, was the moving force behind this attempt to pit Russian against foreign capital. Although this manifestation of "business" Slavophilism got off to a bad start, it eventually made a fortune for Chizhov and his associates.[54] Later the line was extended to Iaroslav and assumed major economic significance. In the Ukraine and New Russia, the railroad fortunes of the great German and Jewish tycoons—Von Derviz, Von Meck, Poliakov, and Bloch—were in the making on the eve of the Great Reforms.

During the same period, French railroad engineers replaced Americans, shortly in turn to be themselves replaced by Germans. The French had little to learn, in their view, from the Nicholas railroad, except from its mistakes and flaws. They saw the railroad as an expensive and dangerous operation. There were too many stops and too few trains. The waiting rooms were not designed properly: if trains from both directions happened to be in the same station, people frequently entered the wrong train. The wide American gauge neces-

---

[53] Krutikov, *Krasnyi arkhiv*, vol. 99, p. 134, introductory essay; *Otchet po vedomstvu putei soobshcheniia*, p. 72.

[54] For details on Chizhov and the Moscow-Sergiev line, see J. N. Westwood, *A History of Russian Railways* (London, 1964), pp. 45-48.

sitated expensive, slow-moving cars. Actually, Russia's gauge problem was more a question of disparity than of impractical size. By 1860, there were four gauges in use, varying from three and one-half feet to six feet. The changes corresponded to succeeding waves of foreign engineers: the Austrians built with one, the Americans another, the French a third, and the Germans a fourth.[55]

European engineers by 1860, however, were no longer dominating the railroad scene in Russia. Other areas of Russian engineering would remain heavily dependent on foreigners for almost another century; the construction of the St. Petersburg-Moscow railroad had at least provided a school for several leading engineers, whose contributions to the building of an empire-wide railway network in the late nineteenth century were notable. K. I. Shernval, who as a newly commissioned lieutenant in the transport service commanded a construction section of the St. Petersburg-Moscow line, later became famous as the builder of the Finland Railroad. Simechev, another section commander in the 1840's went on to superintend the construction of the Moscow-Kursk Railroad. Baron Delvig, whose engineering career began in the same way, became the first director of the Moscow-Sergiev line. Shtukenberg, who like Delvig and Valerian Panaev, divided his later career between literature and engineering, became a high official in the transport ministry and served on the Technical Construction Committee of the Ministry of Internal Affairs. He wrote numerous articles on railroads and other technical subjects, and was one of the early proponents of the construction of railroads in Asiatic Russia. Mel'nikov, as we have seen, after a brief involvement with the privately financed development of commercial steam transport in south Russia on the Volga, Don, and Black Sea waterways, returned to state service in the 1860's as the first Minister of Ways of Communication.[56]

The Nicholas railroad, for all its faults, proved that rail transport had come to Russia to stay. At least a decade before the Great Reforms and the railroad boom beginning in the 1860's, the state had accepted this idea. Railroad development became henceforth a major state policy, although the state would continue to give priority to the military over the industrial and commercial uses of the new means of transport. By the late 1850's, private enterprise, both foreign and domestic, saw the potential for Russian railroads and was willing to invest heavily in their financing. As with the construction of the St. Petersburg-Moscow Railroad, state guarantees and concessions cut

[55] For the criticisms of the French engineers see E. Collignon, *Les Chemins de fer Russes de 1857 à 1862* (2nd edn., Paris, 1868), pp. 60-65; on the gauges, *Vsepoddanneishii otchet po vedomstvu putei soobshcheniia*, p. 47.

[56] On the later careers of these Russian engineers, see the memoirs of Delvig, Mel'nikov, Shtukenberg, and Panaev cited in this Chapter.

the foreign entrepreneur's risks down to nothing, encouraged delay, inefficiency and corruption, and facilitated the amassing of huge profits. The foreigners were needed, not only for their capital, but, more important, for their engineering skills, and in these two costly roles Europeans and Americans were prominent in Russian railroading for many years to come. A cadre of skilled Russian engineers, however, was in evidence from the time of the completion of the Nicholas railway.

The Russian intelligentsia also had come to accept railroads by the mid-nineteenth century. The Slavophiles were among the first to recognize their value. Chizhov, as we have seen, became a railroad magnate. Earlier, the Slavophile leader, Aleksei Khomiakov, in an article written for *Moskvitianin* in 1845, endorsed railroads as inevitable and necessary for the development of the industry, public well-being, and security of his homeland. It was possible, Khomiakov argued, for Russians to appreciate and enjoy such material products of Western science as railroads without absorbing the moral evils of European culture.[57]

Important elements of the left wing intelligentsia at mid-century also came to support the modernization of land and water transport in Russia. Chernyshevskii, in the pages of *Sovremennik*, saw railroads and river steamers as important signs of the inevitable industrialization of Russia, which he believed had begun in earnest after the Crimean War. In his articles and reviews, he called for increased railroad construction to stimulate Russian industry. One of his projects was a line which would connect the Don coal basin and river. "In ten years," he predicted in 1857, "we will have at least 4,000 *versts* of railroad; and in thirty years, by the most conservative estimate, 30,000 *versts*."[58] Chernyshevskii's prophecy was correct.

[57] A. S. Khomiakov, *Moskvitianin*, vol. I (1845), pp. 71-83.
[58] N. G. Chernyshevskii, *Polnoe sobranie sochinenii* (Moscow, 1948), vol. IV, pp. 303, 744-45, 847.

Part V

Technology

It would be difficult if not impossible to understand the industrialization process without a consideration of technology. However, the relationship of technology to economic growth is a complex one. Equally difficult to grasp is the relationship of social and cultural development to the emergence of technology.[1] In the most general terms, technology can be defined as the application of scientific knowledge to practical life. At least three aspects of technological development can be distinguished in any society: the educational, the creative, and the practical. The *educational* factor involves the development and diffusion of knowledge: the establishment of schools at all levels, the advance in research and experimentation, the allocation of resources to support scientific and educational activity, and finally, the existence of a general cultural and political atmosphere in which scientific training and exploration can move forward. The *creative* aspect of the larger process is close to what historians traditionally have defined as technology: the conceiving, making, and developing of inventions and the elaboration of new techniques. The *practical* aspect of technology is concerned with the application and use of these inventions and new techniques in industry, transportation, war, and other nonabstract human activities—with industrial innovation as well as state-sponsored modernization programs.

Technology, so defined, cannot be thought of as independent of economic processes. It both reflects and affects economic growth. Technological progress, in terms of research, invention, or application, may be dependent upon subsidization, military necessities, or the incentives and pressures of a consumer's market. Without the significant play of one or more of these factors (without excluding the

[1] Most recently, these subjects have been explored by Jacob Schmookler, *Invention and Economic Growth* (Harvard, 1966); Everett E. Hagen, *On the Theory of Social Change* (Homewood, Illinois, 1962); and C. E. Black, *The Dynamics of Modernization* (New York, 1966). The definition of technology employed in this book is an adaptation and simplification of the complex and refined uses of the word employed by Professors Schmookler, Hagen, and Black. For Schmookler's several approaches to, or dimensions of "technology," see Schmookler, *Invention and Economic Growth*, pp. 1-8. For Hagen's much broader definition, in line with his concern, not solely with the relations of inventions to economic growth (as is Schmookler), but the general process of the beginning stages and preconditions of accelerated economic growth, see *Theory of Social Change*, pp. 11-12. Black's even broader definition of technology is related closely to his concept of Modernization, in his view a result of the "unprecedented increase in man's knowledge, permitting control over his environment, which accompanied the scientific revolution." See Black, *Dynamics of Modernization*, pp. 7, 11.

contribution of individual creativity), its development will be stunted. The Russian case is a clear indication of such a dissipation of knowledge and individual genius in an unreceptive environment. Technological progress, in turn, has obvious effects on economic and industrial growth. But technology cannot be seen apart from the expansion and diffusion of scientific knowledge, and both are positively and negatively effected by the cultural as well as the political milieu in which they operate.

All of these factors come into play in the history of Russian technology during the early nineteenth century. Obviously there was no comprehensive and rapid technological progress in Russia from 1800 to 1860 sufficient to warrant identification with a "technological revolution" or "drive to technological maturity."[2] The development of Russian technology in the prereform era, similar to other aspects of Russian economic progress and backwardness at that time, must be considered a preparatory stage, prior to more accelerated change. Technological growth was stunted in this period of Russia's history. As we have seen in earlier chapters, the consumer market and in turn, Russian industry, were extremely disorganized and limited, except possibly the cotton industry after 1830. In such a situation, there was only the most modest incentive for technological innovation, and a very small field for the application of new inventions and processes. The state was either unable or unwilling to divert major resources into industry or for the significant development and application of military and industrial technology. Russia, however, enjoyed the advantage of being able to use and copy the end products of European technology, so that by the middle of the nineteenth century, there was some application of industrial technology which was comparatively significant for its time.

Although the economic basis of Russian technology was extremely weak during the early nineteenth century, the intellectual foundations were more important. Russia was heavily dependent on foreign technicians—particularly English, Scottish and American machinists —as she would be for another century.[3] Although costly at the time, this imported, trained cadre was in the long run an asset for Russian industrial development. They mechanized factories, built railroads and weapons, and trained Russians. However, Russian science, both abstract and applied, developed significantly during the early nineteenth century. Most of the important Russian scientists of this period were interested in the development of technology—industrial, much less than military. All, however, maintained contact with the main-

---

[2] W. W. Rostow, author of the latter term, sees the "drive to technological maturity" in Russia from 1890 to 1950. See his *Stages of Economic Growth* (Cambridge, 1960), p. 67.

[3] See my Chapters 10 and 13.

stream of European scientific research. Although Europe remained the world's center for the advanced study of science and technology during the early nineteenth century, the Russian universities and engineering schools, with substantial state encouragement, were able to provide by 1860 comprehensive and up-to-date training in the main branches of applied science and technology. The political and cultural atmosphere in Russia during the early nineteenth century, with brief lapses into extreme reaction, did not however smother science and technology. Private societies and publications, although on a limited scale, began to disseminate scientific and technical knowledge. A small technical intelligentsia was developing in Russia by 1860. The masses, however, remained very largely illiterate and technically untutored, although a few schools had been set up to raise them to a functional level for an industrialized society. Thus, of the three aspects of technological progress defined here, the first, the educational, was the most significant in early nineteenth-century Russia, and will be considered at greatest length: state policy, the cultural and political environment, literacy, elementary technical training, the dissemination of technical knowledge, university research for industry, the contact of Russian and European scientists, the establishment of engineering and technical institutes, and the growth of military technical education. The creative phase of technology in Russia before 1860 was one of economic stagnation and the frustration of inventiveness: the achievements of Russian inventors, and the problems which they faced at that time, in the fields both of military and industrial technology will be considered in Chapter 16. The practical application of Russian technology in the prereform era, allowing for Russia's dependence on foreign technology with the latter's superior capacity for development and innovation, was at best partial. This application of technology, particularly to Russian industry, will also be evaluated in the last part of this book.

Chapter 14

The Dissemination and Advance
of Technical Knowledge

State Educational Policy

The greatest impetus and at other times the most potent threat to technical education in early nineteenth-century Russia came from the state. It was the state which initiated, during the first decade of the reign of Alexander I, the educational reforms that followed on the creation of the first Ministry of Public Instruction in 1802. While Russia struggled against Napoleon for several years following this date, the domestic scene was witness to a vigorous and creative impulse in the building of new schools, in new enthusiasm on the part of students and expanded faculties, in educational experimentation, and in scholarship. The serious shortcomings of this reform were balanced by the achievement of most of its basic aims. Most historians of Russian education would agree that the initial plan for the establishment and systematization of public education in Russia from the local elementary school to the level of the university was largely attained by 1825.

These early educational reforms of Alexander I not only provided in the new system a foundation for all levels of nonmilitary technical education[1] in Russia, but as well emphasized technical training as a fundamental concern of the program. This was manifest both within the public schools and universities and in the development of technical and engineering schools. Other tendencies, however, became prominent during the last half of the reign of Alexander I, which worked to counteract and inhibit the initial encouragement of technical education. This reaction was transmitted from within, mainly emanating from high-ranking educational officials. One reason for the sometimes contradictory tendencies or even abrupt reversals of educational policy during the early nineteenth century was that the educational reforms of 1802-1804 had created a highly centralized system which was susceptible to ministerial despotism. To the Ministers of Public Instruction and particularly to their immediate subordinates, the curators of the six vast educational districts which comprehended most of the Russian empire, were entrusted impressive administrative powers. These powers extended not only down through a chain of deans, inspectors, and principals all the way to the parish school level, but also outward from school administration to censorship controls of the press, libraries, theaters, and other centers of

---

[1] The reforms and development of military-technical education at all levels in early nineteenth-century Russia will be discussed later in this Chapter and in Chapter 15.

intellectual life. Although at the beginning, the universities had been granted limited autonomy, by the 1820's this had largely been usurped by the ministers and curators. These leading educational officials were responsive, of course, to the autocratic power of the tsar, but when the "Supreme Will," as he was termed in official documents of the time, chose to be indulgent or indifferent, the same officials could become subject to a number of other pressures and incitements. These ranged from changes in the climate of opinion, both within and outside of Russia, to personal ambitions, obsessions, and fears, or to commitments and intrigues within the bureaucratic machinery. During the early nineteenth century, with few exceptions, the Ministers of Public Instruction and the district curators—not always in agreement with each other, with the emperor, or with public opinion—did not fail to assert their administrative powers with vigor and sometimes fanatical determination. The officials involved could be extremely capable, upright, enlightened, and moderate, or they might just as easily be unscrupulous, self-seeking, or overzealously committed to religious and nationalistic enthusiasms and to various political and educational dogmas. Some combined many, if not all, of these characteristics. One need think only of such ministers or curators of the reigns of Alexander I and Nicholas I as Prince Adam Czartoryski, M. L. Magnitskii, Prince A. N. Golitsyn, Admiral A. S. Shishkov, or Count S. S. Uvarov, among a number of lesser-known figures, to see the widest range of character, talents, and ideals, but seldom the grayness of bureaucratic nonentity. Educational policy during this period tended to be modified in accord with the views and personalities of the succeeding Ministers of Public Instruction (and sometimes by especially powerful district curators) as much as by previous traditions, policies, and precedents. In certain periods, such as the reaction of the 1820's, even the tsar seemed to permit the contradiction of his own views.

The influence of educational officials was particularly strong in the area of technical education. It has been customary in recent histories of Russian education to divide the early nineteenth century into an initial era of reform followed by a long period of reaction and the decay of schools, the latter period beginning in the decade after 1815 and ending with the death of Nicholas I. His reactionary image is seen to dominate the period.[2] The history of technical training does not adhere strictly to this pattern, and tends to accord more with views and policies of the various educational officials. Thus, the initial encouragement of technical training in Russian schools (the work of

---

[2] See Nicholas Hans, *History of Russian Educational Policy* (London, 1931), p. 61; W. H. E. Johnson, *Russia's Educational Heritage* (Pittsburgh, 1950), p. 87. These scholars have entitled their chapters on the period of Nicholas I, "The Reaction," and "The Long Period of Reaction."

such members of Alexander I's Secret Committee as Count Paul Stroganov and N. N. Novosiltsov, who were very much interested in the advancement of science and inventions) ended in the early 1820's. A decade of disruption and interference ensued, expressed in the obscurantism and rash policies, notably of M. L. Magnitskii, although the highest official position held by this scourge of Russian education in the last years of the reign of Alexander I was that of Curator of the Kazan Educational District. A. S. Shishkov, Minister of Public Instruction from 1824 until 1828, continued the destructive policies of Magnitskii, leaving the mark of a reactionary septuagenarian mind, particularly in the area of censorship. However, in the 1830's and 1840's, we witness a new period of mixed tendencies, as seen in the state encouragement of both classicism and technology in the Russian public school curriculum. In this essentially moderate and reformist phase can be seen the hand of the Minister of Public Instruction from 1833 until 1849, Count S. S. Uvarov. Uvarov's policies persisted and were even to some extent reinforced in the area of technical education despite the return of reaction in other spheres, which followed the revolutions of 1848 and Uvarov's replacement by Prince P. A. Shirinskii-Shikhmatov. With the closing of the reign of Nicholas I, a new period began characterized by a more relaxed atmosphere conducive to scientific development, and with more pronounced state encouragement of technical education under a liberal Minister of Public Instruction, A. S. Norov. During most of the early nineteenth century, the two tendencies which threatened the continuance and expansion of technical education in Russia can be summarized in the two words, "Conservatism" and to a much lesser degree, "Classicism." Depending on the particular educational official implementing these tendencies, however, the definition of these terms could vary greatly. Conservatism could often mean reaction but at other times might encourage modernist tendencies in the sciences and humanities. Classicism, similarly, could be either rigid and hostile or accommodating to scientific, technical, and practical education.

Neither of these tendencies was evident to any marked degree in the initial educational statute of 1804 which set the pattern for the Russian public education system of the nineteenth century. At all levels of the system, from the university through the lyceum, the gymnasium, the district school, and the parish school, a practical education was emphasized with a particular focus on technology and related subjects. This utilitarian impulse was apparent, even before the drawing up of the statute of 1804, in the discussions of Alexander I's Secret Committee. In the statute itself, Professor Hans has demonstrated the influence of Condorcet's essays on public instruction, an influence which was transmitted probably through Count Paul Stroganov, who had received a rather unique and thorough French education, both before and during the French Revolution. Condorcet's plan, written a little more than a decade prior to the Russian one, emphasized a utilitarian and egalitarian education, in terms almost identical in some instances to provisions of the Russian statute of 1804. This was particularly true with regard to courses in statistics, technology, and commerce, which in the Russian and French schemes, were very largely to replace classical languages and studies. The latter subjects occupied a central place in the curriculum of the Polish public school system, upon which the Russian reform was in the first instance based. However, Condorcet's proposals for a practical education were actually expanded upon in the Russian statute of 1804 to include training in Agriculture and Industry, as well as in Commerce and Statistics in the lower and middle schools, with a strong emphasis on Applied Mathematics, Chemistry, Physics, Medicine, Mineralogy, Agriculture, and "Technology with Application to Trade and Industry," in the universities.[3] This was specifically implemented in the 1804 statute by the creation of a special new Faculty of Physical and Mathematical Sciences at Moscow University, which included in its teaching program the above subjects, as well as other natural sciences. This department was copied soon after in the six universities which had been created in the Russian empire by 1820. At about the same time, a program of public lectures were given for the first time at Moscow University. Beyond one European History course, the offering was practical in scope: Natural History, Experimental Physics, and "Commerce and Money."[4]

For the next major level of the public school system, the gymnasium, the statute of 1804 continued an emphasis on science and technology, again with a focus on practical, industrial application. Courses were offered in Applied Mathematics, Experimental Physics, and the "Foundations of Commercial Science and Technology." Visits to factories and workshops were recommended for gymnasium students. The district schools were also ordered to teach "Technology Relating to Local Conditions and Industry"; and the parish schools at the lowest level of the educational hierarchy were included in the general program of technical education by a recommendation for teaching "Short precepts on Agricultural Management."[5]

Some of the more general features of the reform of 1804 were of significance for the development of technical education in Russia.

[3] Hans, *Russian Educational Policy*, pp. 41-50 (with comparative charts). On Stroganov and the question of French-inspired utilitarian education, see also S. V. Rozhdestvenskii, *Istoricheskii obzor deiatel'nosti ministerstva narodnago prosveshcheniia 1802-1902* (St. Petersburg, 1902), p. 33.

[4] A. Vucinich, *Science in Russian Culture: A History to 1860* (Stanford, 1963), pp. 192-93, 196.

[5] Rozhdestvenskii, *Obzor ministerstva narodnago prosveshcheniia*, pp. 64-65; N. Hans, *The Russian Tradition in Education* (London, 1963), p. 23.

For one thing, it provided education for pupils of all social classes and both sexes who could meet the academic requirements. Placing the Russian public school system on such an egalitarian basis was meaningless, unless tuition was to be waived for many students, scholarships provided, and other exceptions made for the poor. Such measures were taken in a limited way during the early nineteenth century in the middle and higher schools, including such technical and scientific schools and institutions as the Mining Institute, the School of Shipbuilding, and several institutes of forestry and veterinary medicine.[6]

The centralization of the public school system characteristic of the statute of 1804 had constructive as well as destructive potential for the development of scientific and technological education. The law until the 1830's subordinated the gymnasiums and the district and parish schools to the universities and curators in scientific as well as administrative matters. Thus, the universities had the intellectual resources of several provinces at their disposal for cooperative ventures, particularly in the realm of the natural sciences.[7]

Despite the strong utilitarian emphasis, the early educational reforms of Alexander I were designed to provide a general education, not a specialized technical one. Hence, schools devoted exclusively to instruction in purely technical and engineering subjects of various kinds were supposed to remain independent of the Ministry of Public Instruction. The Ministry was to have only general coordinating powers over these institutions, which were to be supported and operated by other ministries. In practice, however, the education administration came to control a number of technical schools and maintained a special interest in medical and military schools.[8] Many of the latter were also schools of engineering. Significantly, the central scientific institution of the Russian empire was placed under the Ministry of Public Instruction. An 1803 reform of the Academy of Sciences called for emphasis on practical, technical, and experimental activities, as well as cooperation with industry.[9]

A few secondary schools of quality, which offered some technical training, were founded during the period of Alexander I's early educational reforms. In 1805, the government confirmed the establishment of the Iaroslav (later Demidov) School of Higher Sciences, which owed its existence to contributions from the Urals industrial magnate, P. G. Demidov. This school was defined as a "lyceum,"

---

[6] Hans, *Russian Educational Policy*, pp. 52-54.

[7] N. A. Figurovskii, ed., *Istoriia estestvoznaniia v Rossii* (Moscow, 1957), vol. I, part 2, p. 25.

[8] Rozhdestvenskii, *Obzor ministerstva narodnago prosveshcheniia*, p. 78.

[9] Rozhdestvenskii, *Obzor ministerstva narodnago prosveshcheniia*, p. 97. The technical activities of the Academy of Sciences will be discussed later in this Chapter.

which placed it above the gymnasiums and just below the main universities of the empire in rank. Although it later became an exclusive preparatory school for law and the state service, the initial offering of the Iaroslav lyceum emphasized some practical and technical training, including courses in Mathematics, Chemistry, Technology, and the "Science of Finances." The Tsarskoe Selo Lyceum, founded five years later, and intended primarily to polish aristocrats and train them for high positions in the government service, nevertheless offered Statistics, Commercial Science, and Technology in the junior half of its six-year program. In the three final years, which were equivalent to a higher education, a Physics Mathematics Faculty was established, following the pattern of the new university system.[10]

The founding of the Tsarskoe Selo Lyceum marks the end of a decade characterized by a modest expansion and improvement of technical schools and education in Russia. No new technical schools were established from 1810 until 1828. By the earlier date, it was possible for some people to obtain at least the rudiments of a technical education at any level of the public school system in the Russian empire. Within the limits of one's purse and the state scholarship system, this could apply to a noble attending the exclusive Tsarskoe Selo Lyceum, a merchant's son attending public lectures at Moscow University, or a peasant in a parish school. The foundations for technical education in Russia through a state educational system had been laid. Although in 1810, the success of the early educational reforms of Alexander was still questionable, by 1825, it was clear that the original plan had in the main been achieved, despite over a decade of war followed by a wave of obscurantism. In 1825, Russia had 6 universities, 3 lyceums, 57 gymnasiums, 370 district schools, and 600 parish schools. This was well over four times the number of schools which had existed in the empire of the tsars in 1801. Only on the district and parish level did the reform fail to meet the objectives of the original plan, although this was somewhat compensated for by the existence of 360 private schools.[11] To be sure, this 1825 total of 1,411 schools and 69,629 students was a small figure: as Professor Johnson has pointed out, "public education had hardly made a dent in the

---

[10] Rozhdestvenskii, *Obzor ministerstva narodnago prosveshcheniia*, p. 75. On the three most important of the lyceums or secondary schools, see K. Golovshchikov, *Pavel Gregorevich Demidov i istoriia osnovannago im v Iaroslave uchilishcha 1803-1886* (Iaroslav, 1887); Charles Nicolle, *Établissement du Lycée Richelieu à Odessa* (Paris, 1817); and I. Ia. Seleznev, *Istoricheskii ocherk Imperatorskago byvshago Tsarskosel'skago nyne Aleksandrovskago Litseia za pervoe ego platidesiatiletie c 1811 do 1861 god* (St. Petersburg, 1861).

[11] Hans, *Russian Educational Policy*, p. 58; on a specific district (St. Petersburg), see S. V. Rozhdestvenskii, ed., *S.-Peterburgskii Universitet v pervoe stoletie ego deiatel'nosti, 1819-1919. Materialy po istorii S.-Peterburgskogo Universiteta* (Petrograd, 1919), vol. I, no. 196, pp. 551-62; no. 201, pp. 594, 601.

orthodox hide of Russia,"—that is, in the 4,266 churches, monasteries, and seminaries functioning during the same period.[12] There was a long road to be traversed before Russia could build up an adequate complement of native engineers and technologists or educate the masses to the demands of technology in an industrialized society. Within the context of the first decade of the nineteenth century in Europe, however, the early educational reforms of Alexander I do signify a substantial initial effort on the part of the state.

The intellectual and political atmosphere in Russia during this period was favorable to the development of science and technology. Scientists occupied an honored place in society. They were encouraged to come to Russia from European universities, and did so in substantial numbers, particularly from Germany. The new Russian universities grew up in an atmosphere of relative freedom. Scientific research, technical publications, inventions, and scholarly societies were encouraged and subsidized by the state.[13]

This last expression of the Enlightenment in Russian education came to an end in 1816, when the Ministry of Public Instruction was merged with the Holy Synod and other administrative agencies which dealt with religious matters. The Russian educational system was placed on radically new foundations of religion, classicism, conservatism, and nationalism, accompanied by an administrative centralization which vastly increased the powers of the ministers and their curators. Clear signs of the change had appeared several years before 1816. Extreme conservatives and intellectuals, such as Joseph de Maistre, interested themselves in Russian education. His memoranda, eloquent indictments of the evils of modernity, captured the attention and respect of high-ranking educational officials and courtiers close to the imperial family and the Tsar. De Maistre railed against the dangers of science and, less than a decade after their inception, vigorously attacked the operation and spirit of the educational reforms of 1802-1804.[14] Elsewhere, within the higher levels of the educational administration, a new breed of officials—aggressive, articulate, and conservative—made their appearance.

The first of these to achieve prominence, Prince A. N. Golitsyn, was the most moderate. Golitsyn was a cosmopolitan aristocrat, a mystic, and a humanitarian with a sincere and abiding interest in the spread of education among the poor. His primary aim, however, was not to bring science and modern knowledge to Russia, but to recast the entire public educational system along the religious lines enunci-

[12] Johnson, *Russia's Educational Heritage*, pp. 77, 82.
[13] Vucinich, *Science in Russian Culture*, pp. 189, 193-95.
[14] Joseph de Maistre, "Quatre chapitres sur la Russie: Chapitre deuxième—de la science"; "cinq lettres sur l'éducation publique en Russie," *Oeuvres complètes de J. de Maistre* (Lyon, 1893) vol. I, particularly pp. 164-65, 168-69, 307.

ated by the Holy Alliance in the field of foreign affairs. For this purpose, he was entrusted with vast powers, as head of a newly created Ministry of Spiritual Affairs and Public Instruction. This agency incorporated all of the churches, synagogues, mosques, theaters, and libraries of Russia into the state educational system. Golitsyn, in effect, controlled the intellectual life of Russia from the university lecture hall to the village chapel. During his administration, there was no direct attack launched on science and technology in the universities. However, the program in technology and commerce which had been developed in the gymnasiums and district schools during the early educational reforms of Alexander I was permitted to lapse. Courses in Commercial Science and Technology, as well as courses in the humanities and social studies, were dropped from the curriculums of these schools. Ancient languages and Bible study, the latter of particular concern to Golitsyn (who was the moving force of the Russian Bible Society), were emphasized.[15]

In 1824, Golitsyn was succeeded, or rather, overthrown, by a clique of extreme reactionaries and careerists, whose policies dominated the Russian educational administration for four whirlwind years of purge and persecution. M. L. Magnitskii, who became the Curator of the Educational District of Kazan, and very nearly destroyed its university, believed that science was a carrier of the disease of materialistic ideas from the West. He recommended that the teaching of science be harmonized with the Holy Gospel and that the natural order be represented as a reflection of the divine. One of Magnitskii's colleagues, the Curator of the Kharkov Educational District whose obscurantism bordered on primitive superstition, interrupted a Physics lecture with the hypothesis that the triangle at the tip of a lightening belt represented the Trinity.[16] Similar repressions were being conducted at St. Petersburg University by its reactionary Curator, Dmitrii Runich.

The Minister of Public Instruction from 1824 to 1828 was Admiral A. S. Shishkov, an aged relic from the days of Catherine the Great, and an extreme nationalist reactionary. Like Magnitskii, Shishkov believed that science was a carrier of subversion and hoped that Russian educators would work to bring it in line with holy teachings. He called for control of the lecture hall by approved teaching guides,

[15] Rozhdestvenskii, *Obzor ministerstva narodnago prosveshcheniia*, pp. 133-34, 144-47; E. Karnovich, *Zamechatel'nye i zagadochnye lichnosti xviii i xix stoletii* (2nd edn., St. Petersburg, 1893), pp. 423-25. On Golitsyn, see also Alexandre Sturdza, *Oeuvres* (Paris, 1844), vol. III, pp. 146-69.

[16] Figurovskii, ed., *Istoriia estestvoznaniia v Rossii*, vol. 1, part 2, p. 26. On Magnitskii in this period, see E. Feoktistov, *Magnitskii, Materialy dlia istorii prosveshcheniia v Rossii* (St. Petersburg, 1865), especially pp. 68-69, 71. See also Karnovich, *Zamechatel'nye lichnosti*; and V. Zaleskii, "K stoletiiu Imperatorskago Kazan'skago universiteta (1804-1904), Period goneniia nauky 1819-1826," *Zhurnal ministerstva narodnago prosveshcheniia* (1903), pp. 41-130.

and of the press by the most rigid censorship Russia had ever seen. Shishkov extended this system to the masses, because he felt that knowledge was a dangerous thing for the common man. Moral precepts, he argued were all the people needed.[17] This boded ill for technical education and was reflected in the school statute of 1828, a product of the final year of Shishkov's administration. According to this new ruling, religious and nationally oriented subjects were to be emphasized in the gymnasiums, district schools, and parish classrooms, while courses in commerce, natural science, agriculture and technology were either to be eliminated or only to be offered with special permission from higher up.[18]

Technical education was not necessarily incompatible with a religious emphasis within the school system, nor did it have to be at odds with the nationalist and conservative tendencies which dominated the educational scene in Russia for almost two decades following the Napoleonic era. Hence it was not singled out for destruction by the enemies of liberalism, secularism and cosmopolitanism in the educational administration, and survived the period of extreme reaction in the 1820's. This period was nonetheless one of stagnation and reversal for technical education as it was a time of disaster for many other areas of Russian education. The blight which ravaged the sciences, humanities, and social studies when extreme obscurantists came to control the administration of Russian education inevitably extended to applied science and technology.

A new period, which extended over most of the 1830's and 1840's, was one of growth and progress in scientific and particularly technical education in Russia. It was dominated by the ideas and personality of the Minister of Public Instruction from 1833 until 1848, Count S. S. Uvarov. Uvarov's education and earlier career easily indicated the broader path that Russian education would follow under his tutelage after the obscurantism of the 1820's, a trend which would not only restore but favor technical education at all levels. Beginning his state service in the Napoleonic period as a diplomat, Uvarov soon displayed literary and scholarly interests. These were reflected in youthful essays on classical subjects, which from an early age became his major intellectual interest. They were also echoed in Uvarov's policy as the Curator of the St. Petersburg Educational District. One of his first acts upon appointment to this post in 1811 was to urge the expansion of classical education in Russia. Uvarov also developed an interest in science and technology during this earlier period of his

---

[17] Rozhdestvenskii, *Obzor ministerstva narodnago prosveshcheniia*, pp. 166, 177, 180; Karnovich, *Zamechatel'nye lichnosti*, p. 440. See also "Vospominanie ob Aleksandre Semionoviche Shishkove," A. G. Gornfeld, ed., *Sobranie sochinenii S. T. Aksakova* (St. Petersburg, 1909), vol. III, pp. 333-95.

[18] Hans, *Russian Educational Policy*, pp. 68-70.

career, which was both reflected and developed by his nomination to the presidency of the Academy of Sciences in 1818 and his appointment in 1822 as Director of the Department of Manufactures and Trade of the Ministry of Finances. It need not be reiterated that Uvarov imbibed deeply of the nationalistic, conservative, and religious tendencies of the 1820's. On the other hand, his struggle against the obscurantists did cost him the curatorship of the St. Petersburg Educational District, even though it shielded the Academy of Sciences from the same destructive forces.

The result by 1833 was a very complex and sophisticated man, whose policies as Minister of Public Instruction reflect the various influences and experiences of his career. He developed a rather remarkable and consistent system of education which might easily be described as an attempt at change while remaining the same. Uvarov's program was aimed first at inculcating the conservative, nationalist values of Nicholas I and consolidating the existing social order in Russia. At the same time it was designed to foster a liberal and humanistic education for Russian youth. Such an education would be shuttered carefully against subversive ideas from Europe, but would advance and expand scientific investigation and technical education for all levels of Russian society.

The philosophy underlying this system as well as its consequences for technical education in Russia during the second quarter of the nineteenth century can be seen clearly in the memorandum which Uvarov submitted to Emperor Nicholas I in 1843, entitled, "A Decade of the Ministry of Public Instruction 1833-1843."[19] Uvarov here reiterated the basic postulates which he had set down for the Russian educational system upon his assumption of the ministerial post ten years before, the fundamental principles of "Orthodoxy, Autocracy, and Nationality." These tenets the Russian educational system would foster and they would save Russia from the "rapid decline of religious and civil institutions in Europe." Socially, such an educational system was correct only when it was harmonized with the existing divisions of society, so as to train people for their particular station in life. Intellectually, the historical experience of most enlightened peoples indicated that classical education was the best way to improve the minds of the young and to inculcate the wisdom of the ancient world upon which Russian religion itself was based.

On the other hand, Uvarov argued, it would be one-sided and harmful to neglect the general tendency toward industrialization by failing

---

[19] *Desiatiletie ministerstva narodnago prosveshcheniia 1833-1843* ("Memorandum submitted to the Sovereign Emperor Nicholas Pavlovich by the Minister of Public Instruction Count Uvarov in 1843 and returned with His Majesty's own inscription: 'Read with Satisfaction.' "), (St. Petersburg, 1864), see particularly pp. 1-4, 20-22, 29, 86-87. On Uvarov's career, see Rozhdestvenskii, *Obzor ministerstva narodnago prosveshcheniia.*

to provide an education which could adjust the basic principles of general science to the "technical needs of handicraft, factory and agricultural industry." To these ends, Uvarov cited the achievements of a broad policy which was being implemented during his ministry in Russian universities as well as in lower schools. To improve the science of agriculture in Russia and to prepare teachers in this subject, chairs of Agronomy were being opened in the universities. In the large cities where no universities existed, public lectures in the same subjects were being offered. Lectures in Agricultural Management and Forestry were being offered at St. Petersburg University and at Moscow, while at Dorpat, in addition to such courses, a special school for agricultural management was being set up. St. Petersburg was training three students to teach agricultural management, and Dorpat was sending eight young men abroad to complete their training for the teaching of agronomy. Model farms were proposed for some universities. In the Richelieu Lyceum in Odessa, chairs in Agricultural Management and Forestry were being established, while at the gymnasium in Mitau, a course in the latter was planned.

The Russian universities, Uvarov's report continued, were offering public lectures in Technology as part of the Ministry of Public Instruction's program for the improvement of industry. St. Petersburg University, Russia's pedagogical center, undertook to prepare six students for the teaching of technology in various schools. Moscow University was establishing courses in Technical Chemistry, Machine Construction, and Practical Mechanics. Public lectures were being read at St. Vladimir and Dorpat Universities in Applied Chemistry, Mechanics, and other technical subjects. Below the university level, vocational classes and sections were being established in several gymnasiums and district schools—in Tula, Vilna, Kursk, Riga, Kerch, and Kolomensk, among other cities—to bring technical and other practical instruction to industrial workers. Recognizing Moscow as an important industrial center, the Ministry of Public Instruction introduced a similar program, not only in some of the gymnasiums, but also in Sunday classes in district and parish schools, where instruction in technical drawing was made available to industrial employees. Provision was made in several cities for business training. Also, special measures were taken to supply textbooks translated from foreign languages, as well as machines, models, and laboratory equipment.

Uvarov's successor from 1848 until 1853 was Prince P. A. Shirinskii-Shikhmatov, who two decades before had been a protégé of Admiral Shiskhov. His appointment signifies an attack on Uvarov's policies and a partial return to the anti-Western and religious emphasis of the 1820's. This was stimulated by the reactionary panic which gripped Russia following the revolutions of 1848. However, the program in technical education in the universities and lower schools which Uvarov had been developing since the mid-1830's was not disrupted by the new reaction. With the liberal arts under suspicion and with the almost complete removal in 1849 of Uvarov's classical program from the Russian educational system, practical education, including technical subjects, was given a new emphasis. Prince Shirinskii-Shikhmatov could report to the Tsar in 1851 that public lectures in Technology and related subjects continued to be read in all of the Russian universities. St. Petersburg University continued to prepare special students to teach Technology in the growing number of vocational classes in the public schools, and in the gymnasiums, the teaching of Greek was being replaced by courses in Natural Science.[20] In addition to public lectures in General Technology, which were given at almost all of the Russian universities in the early 1850's, courses in Practical Mechanics and Applied Chemistry had become universal. Moscow and Dorpat universities, the two oldest and most advanced in the empire, were able to offer more sophisticated courses, such as the Theory of Steam Machines at the former and Agronomical Chemistry at the Baltic university. The growth and popularity of the public lecture system can be seen in the registration and attendance for courses in Technology, Technical Chemistry, and Mechanics at the University of Kharkov in 1852 and 1856. In the earlier year, the Chemistry courses averaged 35 to 150 students, with 15 to 30 in Mechanics, and 40 enrolled for Technology. In 1856, 275 attended the lectures in Technical Chemistry and 139 were registered for the Technology course. The same period witnessed a continuation of the trend in vocational education, with "real" classes established in the district school at Riga and in the gymnasiums at Vilna and Bielostok in the subjects of Chemistry, Technology, and Mechanics.[21]

The emphasis on classical education was partially reinstated under Shirinskii-Shikhmatov's successor as Minister of Public Instruction, A. S. Norov, whose administration from 1854 until 1858 largely coincided with the beginning of the liberal era of Alexander II. Norov's policies reflected this new tendency, as well as his own interests as an amateur archaeologist and classicist, a scholar of sorts, who had learned Hebrew and who had visited and studied religious sites of the world of antiquity. Much more important than this, however, was the influence of N. I. Pirogov, the internationally famous surgeon and Professor at Dorpat, national hero of the Crimean War, and pioneer in Russian pedagogical theory. Norov immediately recognized Pirogov's original ideas, incorporated them into official policy and

[20] *Izvlechenie iz vsepoddaneishago otchela ministra narodnago prosveshcheniia za 1851 god* (St. Petersburg, 1852), p. 41.

[21] *Otchet ministra narodnago prosveshcheniia*, 1852, pp. 32, 41-42, 50, 61, 68, 71, 79; 1854, pp. 5, 44, 51, 62, 69; 1856, pp. 43, 48, 53.

appointed him Curator of the newly created Odessa Educational District. Pirogov was opposed to an exclusively practical and specialized education, at least on the primary and early secondary school level, and opted for classical training at this stage. A world famous scientist himself, neither he nor Norov were opposed to the training of scientists, engineers, and technologists in Russia. Nor was Pirogov, the man who had operated on Garibaldi's wounds, at all akin to the reactionary or even moderate nationalists of previous decades whose main concerns were the erection of systems of restrictions and propaganda designed to shield Russian youth from Western influences. He was of a new generation of pedagogical writers deeply interested in the future of education who were able to raise the level of the educational debates in Russia to a plane that had not existed previously in an earnest and profound attempt to evaluate the merits and relationships of humanistic and specialized, practical education.[22]

A new era was approaching for both scientific and technical as well as liberal education in Russia, which carries us into the period of the Great Reforms and beyond the scope of this study. The flowering of science and the expansion of technology and technological education at all levels in Russia which comes after 1860 can be attributed in part to the spirit of liberalization and modernization which accompanied the Great Reforms. The roots of this development, however, must be found in the policies and tendencies of the sixty years which preceded the emancipation statute. Apart from the obscurantist blight of the 1820's, the damaging effects of which on scientific and technical education in the Russian schools were not serious or prolonged, the study of technology and related subjects was encouraged and expanded by the Russian state at all levels of the public education system for over half a century. This system from its very inception was strongly oriented toward scientific and utilitarian studies, and after 1830, this emphasis was reaffirmed within the framework of the conservative, class restricted system of Nicholas I and Count Uvarov. The classical tradition which was introduced at that time presented less of a threat to scientific and technical education than the ideological interference of obscurantist bureaucrats. With the development of technical studies in the universities, the establishment of technical schools, and the setting up of a "real" or vocational program in the lower schools during the reign of Nicholas I, continued expansion and cooperation rather than the warfare of science and technology with the humanities was the trend indicated for Russian education. The trend was affirmed by the teachings of Pirogov and the Great Reforms themselves.

[22] On Pirogov and Russian educational theory of this period, see Hans, *Russian Tradition in Education*, pp. 28-85. For a sketch of Norov, see Rozhdestvenskii, *Obzor ministerstva narodnago prosveshcheniia*, pp. 339-42.

Elementary Technical Training

The industrialization of Russia was dependent on an expanding cadre of technicians, particularly at the lower levels, to provide the skills essential for the application of technology to industry and war. This elementary kind of technical education meant not just experience with new processes, or proficiency in the operation and maintenance of new machinery: underlying this was the basic problem of the literacy prerequisite for technical operations of minimal sophistication. No major solution to these problems was achieved during the early nineteenth century in Russia, although numerous attempts were made by the state, private societies, and individuals to raise the levels of literacy and technical proficiency. By the middle of the century, about 1 percent of Russia's children were in schools. This meant about five hundred thousand pupils in a few thousand schools, most of them operated by the several ministries of the government or by the church. A few were run by private families or societies. A number of elementary technical schools received both official and private support. The province of Tula, as seen in the late 1850's by the educational authority and theorist, Ushinskii, exemplifies the general situation.

The province of Tula had a population of 1,125,517 in the mid-nineteenth century, of which about 10 percent was concentrated in the towns, the most important city being Tula, the ancient and famous arms manufacturing center. The province had twenty-nine schools (one gymnasium, two district schools, twenty-one parish schools, and five private educational institutions). A total of 2,112 students attended these twenty-nine schools, corresponding to the national average of the time of 1 percent. In the city of Tula were located the Alexander Corps (a military school), a seminary and, among the elementary schools, a school for the sons of arms workers, with 485 pupils; a government supported children's shelter bearing the name of Tsar Nicholas I, with 159 pupils; another such shelter for the daughters of arms makers, named after the Tsar's brother, the Grand Duke Michael, with 53 pupils; and a privately endowed "Love of Work" Home for 20 girl boarders.[23]

One of the more notable attempts to provide elementary and basic technical education for Russia's peasant masses during the early nineteenth century came with the Kiselev agrarian reforms of the 1830's and 1840's. P. D. Kiselev was a vigorous proponent of education for the peasants. He saw that the literacy rate of the agrarian masses

[23] *Arkhiv K. D. Ushinskogo* (Moscow, 1960), vol. II, pp. 207-11; on general statistics, see N. A. Konstantinov and V. Ia. Struminskii, *Ocherki po istorii nachal'nogo obrazovaniia v Rossii* (Moscow, 1949), p. 85; and Alexandre de Krusenstern, *Précis du système, des progrès et de l'état de l'instruction publique en Russie* (Warsaw, 1837), pp. 410-13. On the development of elementary education in the early nineteenth century, see Appendix 2, Part 5, Table A.

would have to be raised if other aspects of his reform of the state peasants were to be realized. Since the basic aim of the reform was the creation of an enlightened peasantry receptive to modernization in the countryside, this presupposed not only peasants who could read and write, but also farmers trained in modern techniques of rural management, able to utilize new processes and handle agricultural machinery. Hence, two educational systems were planned by the Minister of State Properties in the late 1830's and early 1840's: a system of primary schools, and a system of educational farms.[24]

Originally, Kiselev proposed the establishment of about two thousand primary schools, one for the central village of each *volost*. The schools were free, open to any healthy young peasant eight years or older. He attended school for three years during the winter for six hours a day, and was taught the three R's combined with a strong dosage of religious teaching, since in most cases the teacher of necessity would be a local priest. Two hundred fifty rubles were to be supplied to each school yearly to maintain the premises and pay the teacher and his assistant. Each school was to construct a garden for purposes of agricultural training.

The reality did not rise to the level of such expectations, but the actual accomplishment of the Kiselev primary school reform for the state peasants was significant. In 1842, there were 11,386 pupils in 226 schools, and by 1856, 112,460 peasants were being educated in 2,536 of the "parish" schools of the Ministry of State Properties. By 1854, 19,653 of these pupils were girls. These rather impressive statistics must be modified by the fact that many of the Kiselev schools had almost no students, while others had bad teachers and no equipment. The priests who did the teaching naturally taught religion to the exclusion of more practical rudiments of a primary education. The school system itself was inhibited by bureaucratism and opposition by the church.

In 1839, the Ministry of State Properties began to plan for the practical education of the state peasantry in modern agricultural methods as well as the training of peasant boys in useful trades. A promising idea for a system of model educational farms was developed in the law of 1841. The approach was practical: 75 to 150 state and seigneurial serfs between the ages of seventeen and twenty were to be brought for a term of two years to several large model farms. Each was designed to serve about five provinces. Each farm had on its staff a clergyman, a teacher of grammar, a veterinarian, a medical assistant, a cattle expert, a horticulturist, and a shopmaster to care for tools.

---

[24] The definitive study of the Kiselev reforms, based on exhaustive archival study is N. M. Druzhinin, *Gosudarstvennaia reforma Kiseleva*. On the primary and agricultural schools of the Ministry of State Properties, see especially vol. II, pp. 52-57, 236-62; also Konstantinov and Struminskii, *Nachal'noe obrazovanie v Rossii*, pp. 83-85.

The pupils were to live simply, retaining their peasant clothing and eating peasant food, while they were instructed on the job in improved agricultural techniques and the use of new tools. In the summer, they were to apply this knowledge working in the fields; in the winter, they were to be taught to read and write while being drilled in the catechism. The most successful students were to be relieved of their recruitment obligation and were to be returned at the end of the training period to their home villages to spread agricultural knowledge.

The flaw in this seemingly practical and enlightened scheme was that the trained peasants were given no help by the Ministry of State Properties or by local officials once they left the school. Over 8,000 pupils were enrolled in the educational farms program of the 1840's and 1850's, but the 1,373 who successfully completed the course were thrown back into the rural struggle for survival, where insufficient land or income prevented meaningful application of their knowledge. Kiselev's plan for the training of peasant youth in useful trades was also deprived of sustaining government support and came to nothing. Although 50,335 state serfs were registered as apprentices to craftsmen in 1856, many peasants quit the masters or returned home insufficiently trained. The Ministry of State Properties also established a few crafts schools as well as several schools to train selected peasants in the rudiments of rural administrative law so that they could serve as village clerks. The number of trained students that issued from these schools was negligible. The same fate greeted a handful of horticultural schools set up in various provinces.

Beyond the elementary grammar and technical schools of the Ministries of State Properties and Public Instruction, most of the other Russian ministries by 1850 maintained schools which could provide literacy and primary technical training. The Ministry of War was most active in the area of primary education, in the mid-1830's training annually over twice the number of children as the Ministry of Public Instruction, and three times the number of children in religious schools, or almost 170,000.[25] Most of these schools accommodated orphans or the children of soldiers. Begun under Paul I, they were expanded during the first quarter of the nineteenth century, and just before the death of Alexander I given a military organization. In these cantonists brigades and battalions, as they were called, children from the ages of six to eighteen were taught to read and write and prepared for the various branches of the military service, where most of them went upon graduation. The Ministry of War also maintained small elementary technical schools at its various arsenals, munitions plants, and armaments works.[26]

The main Administration of Ways of Communication also de-

---

[25] Krusenstern, *Instruction publique en Russie*, pp. 285, 413.
[26] Krusenstern, *Instruction publique en Russie*, pp. 273-83.

veloped an elementary school system during the early nineteenth century, although on a much smaller scale than the program of the War Ministry. These "circuit" or "conductors" schools, as they were designated at different times, were also designed to provide elementary training in Grammar, Mathematics, and Technology for the children of soldiers and civil servants employed by the transport administration. The students were prepared for employment as technicians and officials on state canals, roads, and railroads. The schools were located in the provinces, near transport installations and canals, where the students could receive practical training. The program was never extensive, nor was it adequate to meet the growing needs of Russian transport. The first school, established in 1812, had only fifteen students. By 1856, there were only 600 students in eight schools. In addition, there was a small telegraph school, Russia's first, set up in the early 1840's. Here, some children of military colonists were taught to read Russian and then to transmit messages by a Russian code system. They trained at the telegraph line connecting Kronstadt and St. Petersburg and afterward were put to work on the Warsaw line.[27]

The Ministry of Finances maintained a somewhat larger system of elementary and middle schools in the mining and metallurgical centers of the Urals and Siberia. The Mining Statute of 1806 required that each factory employing more than 200 men establish an elementary school.[28] After a quarter of a century, there were fifty-six such schools, with 189 teachers and 4,034 pupils, a small fraction of the laboring population of the Urals. The children of workers and petty officials were eligible for these schools. They attended a five-year program, and at the age of twelve were dispatched either to the mines and factories to work, or to technical training in the field of metallurgy in several small "middle" schools (Barbaul, Nerchinsk, Ekaterinburg, Petrozavodsk, Lugansk, and St. Petersburg).[29] Kankrin also supported a commercial high school in Moscow and vocational classes for the study of technical subjects in several of the district public schools.[30]

The Ministry of Internal Affairs maintained about sixty elementary schools for orphans, the poor, and children of petty bureaucrats. Over ten thousand pupils were involved. The same ministry established several small schools for medical assistants during the early years of the reign of Nicholas I. The Empress also maintained large foundling homes in St. Petersburg, Gatchina, and Moscow, which cared for about 50,000 orphans. Many of these children were sent to state schools, were apprenticed to craftsmen, or were trained in state fac-

[27] *Kratkii istoricheskii ocherk uchebnykh zavedenii vedomstva putei so-obshcheniia* (St. Petersburg, 1900), pp. 4-22, 29-30.

[28] See my Chapter 6.

[29] Krusenstern, *Instruction publique en Russie*, pp. 310-13.

[30] Rozhdestvenskii, *Obzor ministerstva narodnago prosveshcheniia*, pp. 274-75.

tories. The most famous of the state factories which employed orphan apprentices was the Aleksandrovsk cotton spinning mill, where in 1836, 629 children worked.[31]

With the more rapid development of the Russian textile industry in the 1830's and 1840's, many Moscow industrialists established factory schools. This interesting experiment in privately sponsored elementary education in industrial technology and plant management for the children of factory workers pleased Nicholas I and was encouraged by the Minister of Finances. By 1845, according to Ushinskii's estimate, there were twenty-one such schools in Moscow with 1,420 pupils. Some of the biggest industrialists of the time—the Guchkovs and the Prokhorovs, among others—were involved in this educational venture. The impulse was short lived. Official fear of the factory proletariat in the reaction to the 1848 revolutions, and the economic blows to Moscow industry of the international cotton depression of the 1850's, the Crimean War, and finally, the American Civil War, all worked to decimate the ranks of these schools. By 1856, there were only four; by 1866, the largest and oldest of the Moscow factory schools, belonging to the Prokhorov enterprises, was reduced to half-a-hundred pupils.[32]

The history of this earliest of the private Russian trade schools is instructive. The founder, Timofei V. Prokhorov, was a kind of Russian Andrew Carnegie. He even wrote a discourse, "On Wealth," which, like the American steel magnate's *Gospel of Wealth*, forwarded the idea of plutocratic responsibility.[33] Prokhorov rebuilt his father's textile enterprise after the scourge of the Moscow fire, and this famous "Factory of the Three Mountains" soon became one of the largest in Russia. In 1816, Prokhorov set up a small trade school for the children of his workers and of the Moscow poor, which by 1830, helped by an influx of orphans of the cholera epidemic, had grown to 100 pupils. Prokhorov, according to his biographer, Terentev, was not acting solely out of humanitarian or patrimonial motives. He had visited factories in Germany and saw the need for technical training in Russia. In 1831, he drew up an elaborate proposal for a technical school for the lower-class children of Moscow It was designed to train not only 100 skilled workers a year for the city's factories, but also a number of plant managers through a longer program. Both Prokhorov's business associates and the government, who were supposed to finance the project, remained indifferent, and

[31] Krusenstern, *Instruction publique en Russie*, pp. 336, 346, 371.

[32] Ushinskii, *Arkhiv*, vol. II, pp. 192-93; *Istoriia Moskvy* (Moscow, 1954), vol. III, p. 236.

[33] P. N. Terentev, *Kratkii istoricheskii ocherk deiatel'nosti Prokhorovskoi Trekhgornoi Manufaktury po tekhnicheskomu obshchemu obrazovaniiu rabochikh 1816-1899 gody* (Moscow, 1899), p. 3.

he decided to build the second Prokhorov school out of his own pocket. A Stroganov town house was purchased and converted into classrooms, shops, and dormitories. The school provided an elementary education as well as courses in Mechanical Drawing, Machine Construction, and Industrial Chemistry. It was open to adults and children in the Prokhorov employ and to children of the poor in the area. The Tsar apparently visited the school in the 1830's, was pleased with what he saw, and thereafter it flourished, at least for two decades. Over 100 students attended annually, working with several teachers. A small women's professional school also was established by the Prokhorov family about 1840.[34]

Scientific Societies and Technological Publications

One gauge, not only of the dissemination of technical knowledge, but of the receptivity of culture to technology, is the growth of societies and learned organizations, state-sponsored and private, with an active interest in scientific and technical subjects. Another manifestation of an increasing national interest in technology comes with the appearance of publications and periodicals dealing with technical subjects. With the establishment of a national educational system during the reign of Alexander I, there was some expansion of scientific societies. Two great scientific societies, one state-sponsored and one private, had been established in the eighteenth century: the Academy of Sciences and the Free Economic Society. While these groups expanded their scientific and technical activities, a number of other organizations interested in science were established in St. Petersburg and Moscow. The year 1805 saw the birth in the latter city of the Physics-Mathematics Society and the Moscow Naturalist Society. In 1811, a Mathematics Society was founded at Moscow University; and in 1817, the Mineralogical Society began functioning in St. Petersburg. Most of these societies had technical and industrial interests: the Moscow Naturalist Society, for example, evinced an interest in Russian industrial development from its very inception.[35]

Another phenomenon of the early nineteenth century in many parts of Russia was the growth of agricultural societies. Next to the Free Economic Society, the most important of these was the Moscow Agricultural Society, founded in 1818. In the 1830's and 1840's, in addition to the Agricultural Society of South Russia (1828) and the Agricultural Society of South Eastern Russia (1848), agricultural societies were established in Kazan, Iaroslav, Lebediansk, Kaluga,

---

[34] See Terentev, *Deiatel'nosti Prokhorovskoi Manufaktury*, pp. 1-25, passim and appendix 2.

[35] Figurovskii, *Istoriia estestvoznaniia v Rossii*, vol. I, part 2, pp. 28-29. On the Moscow Naturalist Society, see V. A. Varsanofeva, *Moskovskoe obshchestvo ispytatelei prirody i ego znachenie v razvitii otechestvennoi nauki* (Moscow, 1955).

Iurevsk, and in the Caucasus. The smallest of these societies (Iaroslav) had 81 members and correspondents; the largest (Moscow) had 491. Many of these groups published reports and papers, which reveal an interest in agronomy, farm machinery, rationalization of production, estate manufacturing, and other aspects of the modernization of agriculture.

The most important scientific society in Russia at the beginning of the nineteenth century was the Imperial Academy of Sciences. The Academy received a new statute in 1803, which ended its educational functions and officially defined it as the highest scientific body in the Russian empire. The statute of 1803 also emphasized the practical role of the Academy in helping to improve Russian industry, arts, and crafts. It was ordered to publish a periodical devoted to technology, which appeared soon after, bearing the title, *Tekhnologicheskii Zhurnal*.[36]

The Academy was neglected during the period of the Napoleonic wars, but received a new life in 1818 with the appointment of S. S. Uvarov to its presidency. For the next two decades, the future Minister of Public Instruction worked to develop the Academy as the central scholarly institution of the Russian empire. In 1841, it was united with the Russian Academy. This newly amalgamated body, which endured until a decade after the Russian Revolution, pursued linguistic, philological, literary, and historical as well as scientific and mathematical studies. The Pulkovo observatory, which was to gain world prominence among astronomers by the 1840's, was set up by the Academy in 1835.[37] Uvarov, as we have seen elsewhere, was interested in the development of Russian technology. During his presidency, research in Applied Science was encouraged. With the work of academicians Ostragradsky, Schilling, Petrov, Lenz, and Jacobi, the Russian Academy of Sciences became one of the world's pioneers in the new field of Electricity. Several inventions important to the harnessing of electrical power were developed at the Academy during the 1830's.

The Free Economic Society during the early nineteenth century became increasingly interested in technology, industry, and a wide variety of subjects related to Russian economic development. Admiral Mordvinov, who was the Society's president for many years, was particularly responsible for focusing its attention on problems of technology and industry. Many of the landlord members were interested not only in agricultural machinery, but in improved techniques for profitable estate industries. The Society financed the publication

[36] *Istoriia Akademii Nauk SSSR* (Moscow-Leningrad, 1964), vol. II, pp. 14-15; G. A. Kniazev and A. V. Koltsov, *Kratkii ocherk istorii Akademii Nauk SSSR* (2nd edn., Moscow-Leningrad, 1957), pp. 28-29.

[37] *Sto let Pulkovskoi Observatorii, sbornik statei* (Moscow-Leningrad, 1945), pp. 6-11.

and translation of studies on improved methods of liquor distilling, beet-sugar production, and soap manufacture.[38] Beyond the bounds of rural estates, it offered prizes for inventions and for discoveries of coal, and sponsored public lectures on Chemistry and other technical subjects. A machine shop, which took orders from the government and private citizens, was established in 1824. In 1861, a committee of the Society discussed the question of combining several existing technical schools into a polytechnical institute.[39] However, this advanced type of school, already in existence in France since Napoleonic times, was not realized in Russia until the beginning of the twentieth century.

The Moscow Agricultural Society particularly reflected the concerns and curiosity of landlords who were turning their production toward commercial markets and who wished to develop and modernize agricultural industries. The Society received money from the Ministry of Finances for several of its projects, and cooperated with manufacturers in Moscow and professors at Moscow University. Professor P. Pavlov, the noted agronomist, was very active in propagandizing for this organization. He edited its technical journal, the *Notes for Agricultural, Plant and Factory Managers*, and in 1826, the Society published his textbook, *Agricultural Chemistry*.[40] The Moscow Agricultural Society was particularly interested in modernizing the Moscow woolens industry and concerned itself actively with the technology of sorting, dyeing and bleaching wool. Like the Free Economic Society, it was interested in the beet-sugar industry, but also in Caucasian silk worm culture. It even considered proposals for growing American tobacco in Russia. Schools and model farms were set up for agriculture and beekeeping, and along with the government, the Society provided money in the 1830's to help establish a private factory manufacturing agricultural machinery.[41]

It is difficult to gauge the impact of the Free Economic Society and the Moscow Agricultural Society, as well as the smaller provincial societies, on the development of agricultural and industrial technology in prereform Russia. Obviously, the activities of these societies were limited to an upper circle of progressive and relatively wealthy landlords, particularly in the larger cities, where such societies, with their exhibits and lectures, principally functioned. Nevertheless, a substantial amount of information was gathered and disseminated,

[38] A. I. Khodnev, *Istoriia Imperatorskago Volnago Ekonomicheskago Obshchestva* (St. Petersburg, 1865), pp. 142, 347, 352.

[39] Khodnev, *Volnoe Ekonomicheskoe Obshchestvo*, pp. 232, 244, 280, 322, 356.

[40] Stepan Maslov, *Istoricheskoe obozrenie deistvii i trudov Imperatorskago Moskovskago Obshchestva Sel'skago Khoziaistva so vremeni ego osnovaniia do 1846 goda* (Moscow, 1846), pp. 59-61.

[41] Maslov, *Moskovskoe Obshchestvo Sel'skago Khoziaistva*, pp. 55-57, 67, 85.

particularly in the 1830's, 1840's, and 1850's. This reflected growing interest and would have some cumulative effect by the end of this period.

The periodical press grew rapidly in Russia during the early nineteenth century. Along with this, the number of regularly published journals devoted exclusively or in part to technical subjects increased significantly.[42] Lisovskii tabulates a total of 567 periodicals which began publication in Russia from 1796 to 1860. According to his figures, there were 108 in 1796 and 675 in 1860. Mezhenko lists 415 technological periodicals issued in Russia between 1800 and 1916, of which 26 appeared before 1861.[43] His figure includes periodicals which were concerned primarily with technology. However, numerous journals of a more general nature, published during the early nineteenth century, contained articles or sections devoted to technical subjects. These included industrial and commercial journals, periodicals dealing with military and naval subjects, official periodicals published by various ministries, agricultural journals, magazines of general interest, and serial publications of universities and learned societies. The number of such periodicals published between 1800 and 1860 would be about double Mezhenko's figure. There is no precise way to determine the degree to which this small but not insignificant increase in periodicals devoted in whole or in part to technology indicates a growing interest in and diffusion of technical knowledge among the educated classes in Russia. What people read, as contrasted to what they bought, would be, of course, impossible to determine. Length of publication would indicate some sustained interest. Many technical journals in early nineteenth-century Russia were short lived, lasting only a few years or less; some endured for decades. Government subsidy, however, undoubtedly was a factor in the longevity of some official journals.

The first purely technical journal in Russia was of such nature.[44] This was the *Technological Journal*, which came out of the 1803 reform of the Academy of Sciences. The 1803 statute ordered funds for such a publication. The first issue of what was planned as a quarterly appeared in 1804, and publication continued until 1820. The

[42] Numerous textbooks, monographs, and translations appeared at the same time and provide another indication of the growth of interest in and diffusion of technical knowledge. Nevertheless, at the beginning of the century, the number of published books devoted to theology easily outnumbered those devoted to natural science by two to one. This type of publication is discussed in Chapter 15.

[43] N. M. Lisovskii, *Bibliografiia russkoi periodicheskoi pechati 1703-1900* (Petrograd, 1915); Iu. A. Mezhenko, *Russkaia tekhnicheskaia periodika 1800-1916* (Moscow-Leningrad), pp. 253-95.

[44] Technical material first appeared much earlier, in the *St. Petersburg Gazette*, published by the Academy of Sciences beginning in 1711. See my Chapter 1.

aim of the *Technological Journal,* as stated in the first issue, was the dissemination of scientific knowledge that could be applied practically. It was to include translations from foreign works and articles by Russian authors. Thus, in the first volume, one finds articles on chemistry, agriculture, steel processing, and meteorology, as well as descriptions of factories in Germany and in the Urals, and of a new English steam engine.[45]

Two years later, another state-sponsored technical journal appeared. This was the *Journal of Useful Inventions in Arts, Crafts and Trades and the Latest Discoveries in the Natural Sciences,* published by the Moscow provincial gymnasium and edited by P. M. Druzhinin. Druzhinin stated the purpose of his journal as follows:

> . . . to acquaint our factory managers with inventions of every type which are made in other lands for the improvement of factories and plants . . . to give knowledge to our readers of domestic industry . . . the history of inventions and a description of our most important factories and plants.[46]

The *Journal of Useful Inventions* lasted only three years. More durable was Russia's first privately published journal devoted primarily to technology, the *Journal of Generally Useful Information,* which was issued from 1833 to 1839 and again from 1847 to 1859. This periodical concerned itself, not only with general problems of industry and agriculture, but also with industrial technology, railroads, steam navigation, and such inventions as the electric telegraph.[47]

More important than the few purely technical journals as disseminators of this kind of information were the official periodicals supported by various government agencies. The Ministry of Internal Affairs was the first to publish such a periodical, the *Northern Post* (1809-1819), which included reports on new inventions. However, after 1825, several such organs appeared, with solid financial support from the government and substantial circulations. Of these, the *Mining Journal,* the *Journal of Manufactures and Trade,* the *Journal of the Ministry of State Properties,* and the *Journal of Ways of Communication* took a substantial interest in technology.

The *Mining Journal,* first issued by the Ministry of Finances in 1825, and still in publication today, served as the official reporter for new state mining regulations. Almost from the beginning, however, an elaborate system of eighty-four correspondents and their assistants was established in the various mining regions and metallurgical factory centers of the empire to service the *Journal.* For this purpose, a

---

[45] See *Tekhnologicheskii zhurnal,* vol. I (1804), parts 1-4, passim.
[46] Cited in Mezhenko, *Russkaia tekhnicheskaia periodika,* p. 94.
[47] A. G. Dementev, A. V. Zapadov, and M. S. Cherpakhov, *Russkaia periodicheskaia pechat 1702-1894 g.g., spravochnik* (Moscow, 1959), vol. I, p. 225.

central editorial board also was established. The *Mining Journal* was allotted 10,000 rubles as an initial capital with a yearly operating subsidy of 5,000. It published articles on a wide variety of subjects relating to mining and metallurgy: Mineralogy, Chemistry, Machine Technology, Coal Geology, and on several new processes.[48]

Similar to the *Mining Journal*, the *Journal of Manufactures and Trade*, also issued by the Ministry of Finances and first published in 1829, reported official regulations. Its most important function in this respect was as a patent journal. It also published reports on new inventions and technical improvements in provincial industries. These were submitted by a group of government machinists who were sent out from 1843 to 1857 by the Department of Manufactures and Domestic Trade to the factories of Russia to gather information and give advice.[49] A third important official publication, the *Journal of the Ministry of State Properties*, issued monthly from 1841 to 1864, concerned itself with agricultural technology and estate industries. The *Journal of Ways of Communication* commenced publication in 1826, and may be considered an almost exclusively technical periodical.[50]

Military and naval journals, which contained articles on the technology of land and sea warfare, first began appearing in 1800, with the publication of the *Naval Notes*, issued by the Admiralty College and edited by Admiral Shishkov. However, only one issue of the *Naval Notes* appeared, and it was not until 1828 that a new, more technical publication, the *Notes of the Scientific Committee of the Naval Staff*, was issued. This publication concerned itself with problems of shipbuilding, naval armament, and astronomy. Two years after its demise in 1845, the *Naval Collection*, a St. Petersburg monthly, began publication, which continued until the 1917 Revolution. Russia's first military-technical publication was the short lived *Artillery Journal* (1808-1811), which included material on artillery, munitions, and powder factories. Publication was resumed in 1839, and in 1858, the *Military Collection*, which included similar subject matter, was first issued. This also endured until the Revolution.[51]

Several short-lived industrial-commercial journals were published in Russia during the early nineteenth century. Some of their names reflect the middle-class audience for which they were designed: the *Moscow Telegraph* (1825-1834); the *Northern Ant* (1830-1833); the *Merchant* (1832-1835); the *Leaflet on Industry, Craft, Art and Factories* (1838-1839); the *Business Agent* (1840-1855); the

---

[48] B. V. Tikhonov, "Ofitsial'nye zhurnaly vtoroi poloviny 20-kh i 50-kh godov xix v.," *Problemy istochnikovedeniia*, vol. VII, pp. 176, 180-81, 183.

[49] Tikhonov, "Ofitsial'nye zhurnaly," pp. 153, 158-59.

[50] Tikhonov, "Ofitsial'nye zhurnaly," pp. 186, 191, 193.

[51] Mezhenko, *Russkaia tekhnicheskaia pechat*, p. 165; Dementev, et al., *Russkaia periodicheskaia pechat*, pp. 126-27, 202, 320-21, 358.

Journal for Stockholders (1857-1860); the *Industrial Herald* (1858-1861); the *Industrial Leaflet* (1858-1859); and the *Producer and Industrialist* (1859-1861). These periodicals often included articles on science, technology, transport, and mention of new inventions.[52]

Serial publications of Moscow and Kazan universities, of the Free Economic Society, the Moscow Agricultural Society, and other agricultural societies also contained information on Russian and European technology.[53] This was also true of the more general journals, devoted primarily to literary, historical, and philosophical questions. *Fatherland Notes* (1818-1820, 1839-1884) contained in its early issues the first article on the history of technology in Russia—a life of the eighteenth-century machinist and inventor, Kulibin—as well as a description of a Tula armaments plant. Later, it included sections on science, agriculture, and industry. The better-known *Reader's Library* (1834-1865) had similar sections, and included articles by von Humboldt and Pirogov. Both *Muscovite* and *Contemporary* had articles devoted to science, industry, transport, and technology.[54]

[52] Dementev, et al., *Russkaia periodicheskaia pechat*, pp. 185, 213, 222, 270, 293, 344, 357-58, 365, 386.

[53] B. V. Tikhonov, "Obzor 'zapisok' mestnykh sel'skokhoziaistvennykh obshchestv 30-50kh godov xix v.," *Problemy istochnikovedeniia*, vol. IX, pp. 93-97.

[54] Dementev, et al., *Russkaia periodicheskaia pechat*, pp. 166, 231, 242, 273, 296.

Chapter 15

Technical Education and Research

By the mid-nineteenth century, of the seven universities which were functioning in the Russian empire, the three most easterly and purely Russian institutions—Moscow, St. Petersburg, and Kazan—were the first to develop programs in science and technology. Dorpat was also an important scientific center, located in one of the several areas of the world most prolific in the production of scientists, the Baltic region.[1] However, until the late nineteenth century, Dorpat was very largely a German university. Although within the Russian empire, supported and controlled by the Russian government, taking in a substantial number of Russian students, and including some Russian scientists of distinction on its faculty even before 1860 (Pirogov most prominent among them), Dorpat nevertheless remained German in culture. Classes were conducted in German, and the staff was composed overwhelmingly of German-born and German-trained professors, teaching a student body consisting in the majority of Germans from the Baltic provinces.[2] During the same period, the universities of Kharkov and St. Vladimir in Kiev established science faculties, departments of Technology and Agriculture, scientific laboratories, and programs of public lectures on technical subjects. A broad tradition of scientific research and teaching did not, however, take root at these institutions until the late nineteenth century.[3] The Polish University of Vilna, which had begun to flourish as a scientific center very early in the same century, was closed after the revolt of 1831. The scientific tradition at the University of Helsinski reached far back into the eighteenth century. Helsinski was one of the finest universities in the Russian empire and received ample support from the Russian government. Indeed, it was rebuilt after a disastrous fire of 1827 largely by Russian private and state contributions. The Grand Duke and future Tsar Alexander II was its Rector. However, although Helsinki contributed a few great scholars to Russia, it was essentially a

[1] H. T. Pledge, *Science Since 1500* (New York, 1959), map, facing pp. 72-73.
[2] On Dorpat's role in Russian scientific and educational development, see E. V. Petukhov, *Imperatorskii Iurevskii byvshii Derptskii Universitet za sto let ego sushchestvovaniia 1802-1902* (Iurev, 1902), vol. I, appendix, pp. 1-8; and E. E. Martenson, *Istoriia osnovaniia Tartuskogo (b. Derptskogo-Iurevskogo) Universiteta* (Leningrad, 1954), pp. 104-05.
[3] *Otchet ministra narodnago prosveshcheniia*, 1851, pp. 32-35, 42, on Kharkov and Kiev Universities; on Kiev University, see also M. F. Vladimir-skii-Budanov, *Istoriia Imperatorskago Universiteta Sv. Vladimir* (Kiev, 1884), vol. I, pp. 226-27, 340, 379, 383-85, 440, 443; on Kharkov, *Kharkovskii Gosudarstvennyi Universitet im. A. M. Gorkogo za 150 let 1805-1955* (Kharkov, 1955), pp. 38-45.

Swedish University in the early nineteenth century, bound to the Scandinavian West by language, scholarship, and culture.[4]

Moscow University

By the middle of the nineteenth century, Moscow University was Russia's greatest institution of higher learning, although it ceded primacy as a center of pure and applied science to St. Petersburg University and to the several engineering, military, medical, technological and scientific schools, and research centers located in the imperial capital. The growth and quality of its faculty, library, and laboratories, the scope and variety of its curriculum, the richness of its publications in several fields, the multiplication of allied scientific and scholarly societies, and above all, the memoirs and testimonies of numerous of its students reveal Moscow University, at least as early as the 1830's, as a vigorous educational institution and for some, a focus of intellectual and political ferment.[5] If it was a seedbed for the Russian intelligentsia during this period, it was also moving into the European scientific community, developing closer ties with the educational centers of Germany, France, and England. The main flow of knowledge still moved eastward. No European student would go to Moscow University in 1850, certainly not to study the sciences, while Russian scientists and engineers before 1860 still had to make a final pilgrimage to the educational centers of Europe. It was here that the most advanced specialized knowledge necessary to crown a higher education and fully prepare a student for original research and practical work could be obtained. On the other hand, Moscow University by 1850 no longer had to import the finished academic product from the German universities, which had been the prevailing practice in the eighteenth century and at the time of the Russian educational reforms of 1802-1804. In most of the fields of pure and applied science as well as of Technology and Agronomy, Russians could be trained for the largest part of their university work—some for all of it— at Moscow. The senior professors of this Russian institution by the 1850's were making important contributions to the mainstream of science in Europe through publication and by participation in international scientific conferences.

In the sciences, Moscow University was strong in the fields of Mathematics, Physics, Chemistry, Geology, and Biology, although inferior to St. Petersburg and even to Kazan in all but the last two of these subjects. There were no Lobachevskiis, Ostrogradskiis, or

[4] See E. Berendts, *Imperatorskii Aleksandrovskii Universitet v Finliandii* (St. Petersburg, 1902), pp. 12, 18-19, 30-31.

[5] See P. A. Zaionchkovskii and A. N. Sokolov, eds., *Moskovskii Universitet v vospominaniiakh sovremennikov* (Moscow, 1956) and Alexander Herzen, *My Past and Thoughts* (London, 1924), vol. I.

Petrovs at Moscow University during the early nineteenth century. However, many of the leading scientists and educators of Russia, some having made major contributions to their respective fields and having earned international reputations, belonged to the Moscow faculty—N. D. Brashman and D. M. Perevoshchikov in Applied Mathematics; K. F. Rouillier in Zoology; R. G. Heimann and A. A. Ivovskii in Chemistry; M. F. Spasskii in Geology; P. I. Strakhov in Physics; and M. G. Pavlov in Agronomy, to name several of the most prominent. Moreover, Moscow, more than any other university in the Russian empire, was increasingly emphasizing the technical and industrial aspect of its science curriculum and the practical orientation of its scientists by the middle of the nineteenth century.

This was clear at a very early time, in the educational regulations of 1804, which provided for a special Physics-Mathematics Faculty at Moscow University. The organization of this faculty became a model for all the Russian universities, but nowhere were the technical aspects of this program implemented more fully than at Moscow. The 1804 statutes created a separate sciences faculty consisting of eight departments. In addition to Chemistry, Botany, Mineralogy, Astronomy, and Pure Mathematics, there were to be professors and courses in Experimental and Theoretical Physics, Applied Mathematics (which consisted very largely of courses in Mechanics), Agricultural Management, and an eighth department of "Technology, Relating to Commerce and Factories." Although the new faculty was made a section of the general Faculty of Philosophy in the university reform of 1835, its offerings were expanded to include courses in Physical Geography, Geology, Forestry, and Architecture. In 1850, the Physics-Mathematics Faculty was again separated from the liberal arts (History-Philology) section, while the Department of Philosophy was destroyed in the wave of reaction of the last years of the reign of Nicholas I.[6] This administrative subordination of the sciences to philosophy in part reflects another influence—of Romantic German metaphysics, notably the *Naturphilosophie* of Schelling—which was sweeping through the Russian universities in the 1830's and 1840's. Although Schellingism, which subordinated the truths of empirical science to higher speculative verities, easily tempted students and professors alike out of the laboratory and into the realm of philosophy, it did not present a significant threat to the experimental scientific tradition in the Russian universities in the long run. For some, it helped to kindle an interest in natural science. At Moscow University, some professors could ignore the new philosophical fashions and continue to keep abreast of the latest research in experimental sci-

[6] N. A. Figurovskii, ed., *Istoriia estestvoznaniia v Rossii* (Moscow, 1957) vol. 1, part 2, pp. 33-34; A. F. Kononkov, *Istoriia fiziki v Moskovskom Universitete 1755-1859* (Moscow, 1955), pp. 149-50.

ence. Others could find the truths of philosophy and the more prosaic findings of the laboratory completely compatible. Professor M. G. Pavlov, the brilliant agronomist, is a striking case in point. A disciple of Schelling, he nevertheless was a vigorous partisan and a pioneer of practical experimental work in the area of scientific agriculture.[7]

It was a policy of Moscow University as early as 1804 to offer a program of public lectures which emphasized the practical side of science for a popular audience. To Strakhov's course in Experimental Physics, first given in 1804, were added courses in Chemistry, Arithmetic, and Natural History in the following year. After 1835, public lectures in technical subjects became a feature of the entire university and school system in Russia and a major affair at Moscow University. Professor R. G. Heimann of the Chemistry Faculty, for example, gave public lectures in Technical Chemistry for eighteen years, a course which came to number hundreds of listeners each year. According to the mid-nineteenth-century historian of Moscow University, Shevyrev, Heimann's classes included nobles, factory managers, merchants, and "even peasants."[8]

From the beginning of the century, there was a continuous offering of regular courses in technology and scientific agriculture at the university, read by specialists occupying the chairs of Technology and Agricultural Management. By 1848, the Professor of Technology, Ershov, was boasting that his newly developed course in Practical Mechanics put Moscow University in the company of four European institutions—Cambridge, Paris, Munich, and the Royal College of London—as the only existing universities where such study was offered.[9]

The university reform of 1835 encouraged the development of scientific laboratories, and several Moscow University professors took advantage of this. Under Professor Dvigubskii, aided by Moscow machinists, the physics laboratory was expanded. Numerous instruments were ordered from Europe, such as apparatus for electrical experiments and a first daguerreotype. Professor Denisov developed a technological laboratory in the 1820's, which numbered over 200 pieces, including industrial equipment. Professor Linovskii founded an agricultural laboratory in 1846, which by the mid-1850's included over 1,700 instruments, models of agricultural tools, surveying implements, plants, and seeds. The chemistry laboratory, founded in the late 1830's, reflects Moscow's growing status as an industrial center,

---

[7] On the influence of Schellingism, see A. Vucinich, *Science in Russian Culture* (Stanford, 1963), pp. 280-86, 331. Pavlov will be discussed at greater length later in this section.

[8] S. Shevyrev, *Istoriia Imperatorskago Moskovskago Universiteta* (Moscow, 1855), p. 569.

[9] Figurovskii, *Istoriia estestvoznaniia v Rossii*, vol. I, part 2, p. 102.

for it became the concern, not only of the university chemists, but also of the factory owners of the city. In 1854, they arranged for the transfer to the university of chemical equipment from the laboratory of the Moscow section of the Manufacturing Council, with the proviso that the University Chemistry Department provide analyses for the Moscow factories.[10] Backing up the laboratories was the University Library, which by 1855 exceeded 100,000 volumes.

It was the Department of Applied rather than of Pure Mathematics which stood out at Moscow University by 1860. Applied mathematics for the Moscow professors in the early nineteenth century meant Mechanics with a special emphasis on Practical Mechanics. M. I. Pankevich, who was Professor of Applied Mathematics from 1791 until 1812 and who taught courses in Mechanics, wrote his Master's thesis at Moscow (in Latin) on the "Principles of Steam Machines." This was published in 1788 and was the first treatise on this subject to appear in Russia written by a Russian. In 1846, N. D. Brashman, then the leading Professor in the Faculty of Applied Mathematics, succeeded in having a chair of Practical Mechanics created.[11]

Brashman was unquestionably the most important figure in the fields of Mathematics and Mechanics at Moscow University during the early nineteenth century, a teacher and scientist with an international reputation. Born in Moravia in 1796, he was educated at Vienna University and the Vienna Polytechnical Institute before coming to Russia in 1824 to teach at St. Petersburg and then at Kazan University. In 1834, he was invited to the Applied Mathematics Faculty at Moscow University, where he remained for over thirty years. Brashman's prime interest was Mechanics, a field in which he published and taught both in Russia and Europe. He is known to have read papers before a British scientific society, which were later published. In Russia, he is credited with having brought the teaching of Mechanics at Moscow University into its own. Russian mathematicians of future distinction, such as Chebyshev and Somov, were numbered among his students. Brashman's research and publication focused on Mechanics, and his only textbook, which appeared in 1853, was his *Course in Mechanics*. He was particularly interested in Technology and worked with Ershov, the Professor of Technology at Moscow, to develop a teaching program in Practical Mechanics.[12]

[10] Shevyrev, *Istoriia Moskovskago Universiteta*, pp. 438, 515, 520, 420; I. S. Galkin, ed., *Moskovskii Universitet: kratkii istoricheskii ocherk* (Moscow, 1955), p. 42; Kononkov, *Istoriia fiziki*, pp. 110-17.

[11] *Biograficheskii slovar professorov i prepodavatelei Imperatorskago Moskovskago Universiteta za istekaiushchee stoletiia, sostavlennyi trudami professorov i prepodavatelei* (Moscow, 1855), vol. II, pp. 202-08; *Istoriia Moskovskogo Universiteta* (Moscow, 1955), vol. I, p. 141.

[12] On Brashman, *Biograficheskii slovar Moskovskago Universiteta*, vol. I, pp. 99-102; *Russkii biograficheskii slovar*; and Figurovskii, *Istoriia estestvoznaniia v Rossii*, vol. I, part 2, pp. 98-99.

A. S. Ershov, Professor of Technology at Moscow University in the 1840's and '50's, was an interesting and significant figure in the history of Russian technical education during the nineteenth century. His background and career provide an instructive contrast to the life and works of Brashman. Ershov was a Russian, born in the Russian empire in 1818 and educated in a Russian gymnasium. His higher education was received at the St. Petersburg Technological Institute and the Institute of Engineers of Ways of Communication, followed by a Master's degree at Moscow University in Pure and Applied Mathematics. He then went abroad for advanced studies in Practical Mechanics. In the early 1840's, Paris was a center for research and study in this field and Ershov attended courses in Mechanics and the Theory of Machines. His summers were spent visiting factories in France, Germany, Switzerland, and England. Upon his return to Russia, Ershov taught all aspects of the subject of Mechanics at Moscow University, but was particularly interested in Practical Mechanics. It was Ershov who taught the first course in Practical Mechanics to be offered at the university, in 1846. Ershov was also concerned with the technical problems of industry and sought to attune the university study of practical mechanics to the needs of Russian factories. His interest in the development of Russian industrial technology was expressed in 1862 in the report which he wrote for the Ministry of Finances on machine production in the Russian empire.[13] He also wrote on such diverse subjects as the electric telegraph and the factories of Ivanovo. His interest in Russian technical education was expressed not only in his researches and writings on European technical schools, but also in the 1860's, when he accepted the directorship of the newly founded Moscow Superior Technical School.[14]

Ershov's predecessors in the Moscow University Department of Technology going back to the first years of the nineteenth century were A. Chebotarev, I. A. Dvigubskii, and F. A. Denisov. All three were born in Russia and received their primary, secondary, and most of their university educations in the Russian school system. Like Ershov, Dvigubskii and Chebotarev completed their studies at European universities. Denisov was trained entirely in Russia. All three were particularly interested in the application of technology to Russian industry. Denisov, who was interested in chemical technology, served as an advisor to several factories. In 1822, he delivered an address at the university on the subject, "The Influence of Chemistry on the Success of the Manufacturing Industry." In 1807, Chebotarev lectured to Russian factory managers on aspects of bleaching, dyeing, and finishing cloth. Dvigubskii gave the first course

[13] On Ershov's report, see my Chapter 16.
[14] On Ershov, *Biograficheskii slovar Moskovskago Universiteta*, vol. I, pp. 326-28; and Figurovskii, *Istoriia estestvoznaniia v Rossii*, vol. I, part 2, p. 102.

in Chemical Technology at Moscow University. His textbook for this course stressed the importance of technology for the economic and industrial growth of Russia. Most of the second part of the same text was devoted to the technology of some of the principal Russian manufacturing industries. After 1813, Dvigubskii gave Saturday evening lectures on industrial technology, presumably designed for people engaged in Moscow manufacturing. For ten years he edited a journal, the *New Magazine for Natural History, Physics, Chemistry, and Economic Information*, which included descriptions of the latest European inventions.[15]

Professor M. G. Pavlov is often remembered as the professor of Alexander Herzen who would stand by the door of the classroom and ask the entering student: "You wish to know nature? But what is nature? What is it to know?"[16] It is clear from such statements that Herzen and his fellow students were going to receive from this convinced Schellingist professor a full dosage of the latest German philosophy which they craved. Herzen was bored by Pavlov's lectures on agriculture, although greatly impressed by his philosophical observations. However, in the 1820's and 1830's, it was scientific agriculture for which Pavlov was already famous in Russian educational and scholarly circles. It was the development of modern agricultural methods and agronomical education in Russia that became the professor's prime endeavor as a scientist, although he indulged himself freely in German metaphysics as a teacher of general science courses or the proprietor of an intellectual salon.

Pavlov was educated in Kharkov and Moscow, and then in 1818, like so many other Russian scientists of his time, was sent to Europe to complete his studies. In Pavlov's case, this meant natural history and scientific agriculture. Returning in 1821 to teach at Moscow University, he became active, not only as a fashionable and influential exponent of Schellingism, but also as a serious teacher of Agronomy who urged the closer unity of theory and practice in Russian science. As a scholar and experimental scientist in the Russian countryside, Pavlov set up the first Russian agricultural station near Moscow in 1822. In addition to publishing several textbooks and treatises on scientific and comparative agriculture, Pavlov edited the Journal, *The Russian Farmer*. He became active in the Moscow Agricultural Society and directed its agricultural schools and model farms, which were working to spread scientific agriculture throughout the Russian empire.

Pavlov's successor in the Department of Agricultural Management

---

[15] On Dvigubskii and Chebotarev, *Biograficheskii slovar Moskovskago Universiteta*, vol. I, pp. 290-94, vol. II, p. 551; Kononkov, *Istoriia fiziki*, pp. 87-92, 105-17.

[16] Cited in Martin Malia, *Alexander Herzen and the Birth of Russian Socialism* (Harvard, 1961), p. 69.

at Moscow University, Ya. A. Linovskii, was almost equally famous in Russian scientific circles, and, like Pavlov, directed himself to matters of the practical improvement of agriculture, maintaining a particular interest in soil reclamation. Linovskii was educated at Kiev and Moscow universities and then sent abroad by the government for intensive study of scientific agriculture and the techniques of model farms in Germany, Belgium, France, England, and the Italian peninsula. To help popularize scientific agriculture in Russia, Linovskii prepared a course and textbook called *Conversations on Scientific Agriculture*.[17]

The most famous popularizer of technical subjects at Moscow University was Professor R. G. Heimann, who in 1836 was asked to develop a simplified public lecture course in Technical Chemistry for Russian factory managers, one which would not presume a prior knowledge of physics. Heimann, son of a Vilna doctor, and educated in Medicine and Chemistry at Vilna and Moscow universities, apparently had the talent for making his subject understandable and palatable to large audiences of Muscovites from outside the University. His course was given almost regularly each year from 1836 until 1854, its enrollment growing from fifty to nearly five hundred. In 1851, Heimann joined Professors Solovev, Granovskii, Shevyrev, and other popular and distinguished Moscow University lecturers to offer part of a public course in Literature, History, and Science. He delivered three lectures, which attempted to attract an audience to the fundamentals of Physics and Chemistry with the bait of classical subject matter, under the title: "A Quick Look at the Four Elements of Antiquity in Their Physical, Chemical, and Physiological Relationship." The lectures were published by the University in 1852.[18] In addition to these courses, Heimann regularly taught Organic Chemistry in the University, and in 1849, he offered a course dealing with general Industrial Chemistry. This course may have prompted a textbook which Heimann published, entitled, *Course in Mechanical Chemistry for Moscow Factory Managers*. In 1835 and again in 1843, he served Moscow industrialists as the advisory expert in chemistry for the national manufacturing exhibitions of those years. He served the government in 1841 on an inspection trip of factories in the cities of Ivanovo and St. Petersburg, and in 1843, as a member of the Manufacturing Council of the Ministry of Finances. For this agency, he conducted a survey of Russian chemical plants, together with recommendations for improvements. In addition to his academic and official

---

[17] On Pavlov and Linovskii, *Biograficheskii slovar Moskovskago Universiteta*, vol. I, pp. 458-62; Galkin, *Moskovskii Universitet*, p. 41; *Istoriia Moskovskago Universiteta*, vol. I, pp. 152-53; Kononkov, *Istoriia fiziki*, pp. 156-58.

[18] "Beglii vzgliad na chetyre stikhii drevnikh v otnoshenii fizicheskom, khimicheskom i fiziologicheskom," *Publichnye lektsii professorov Geimana, Rule, Soloveva, Granovskago, Shevyreva* (Moscow, 1852).

activities, Heimann became involved in a Moscow private industrial enterprise. In 1836, he became the director and supervisor of plant production of a corporation engaged in the manufacture of stearine candles. By mid-century, this company was producing and exporting a product worth two million rubles annually.[19]

The Chemistry Department of Moscow University, during the reign of Nicholas I particularly, shared the industrial and technological interests of Professor Heimann. Givartovskii, who completed his scientific training in Germany, studied not only Medicine and Practical Chemistry, but also Technology, Metallurgy, and industrial techniques. In Moscow, he followed his colleague, Heimann, into the stearine candle business, becoming plant chemist and doctor and later technical director of the factory. Professor N. E. Lyashkovskii, a Pole educated in Europe and Russia, who taught Organic Chemistry, also read a public course in 1852 on "Organic Substances Important in Technology." Like Givartovskii, he was involved in the Russian industrial exhibition of 1853 and was also active in the Moscow Agricultural Society.[20]

A pattern of development can be seen in the careers of the leading scientists at Moscow University sketched above, one which corresponds to the educational background of many of their colleagues and to most of the Russian universities and scientific institutions during the early nineteenth century. The two notable exceptions are Dorpat University and the Academy of Sciences. This pattern would indicate a gradual, although far from complete emancipation of Russian science from a dependence on Europe, the beginning of a Russian scientific tradition in research and in education, and an emphasis on applied science, particularly industrial technology. Before 1825, Moscow University was still a kind of colony of European science. Its science departments remained heavily dependent on Europeans who had been imported at the conclusion of their training, usually from universities in France and in the German-speaking lands. After 1825, this situation began to change. It was, of course, an era of nationalism. In the rivalry between Russian and foreign professors that soon appeared, it was the Russians on the Moscow University Science Faculty, as well as those at Kazan and St. Petersburg, who began to gain an advantage over the Germans, although this was not true at the Baltic German center of Dorpat or the German-dominated Academy of Sciences. After 1825, the Minister of Public Instruction as well as Tsar Nicholas I supported a policy of training a generation of Russian scholars and scientists to fill in the gaps left by the Magnitskii

[19] *Biograficheskii slovar Moskovskago Universiteta*, vol. I, pp. 177-78; Galkin, *Moskovskii Universitet*, p. 42.
[20] *Biograficheskii slovar Moskovskago Universiteta*, vol. I, pp. 197-99, 475-79.

witch hunt. Count Uvarov a few years later encouraged the sending of Russian students abroad for the advanced training in scientific fields that could not yet be obtained in Russia. As primary, secondary, and university education improved in the Moscow Educational District and elsewhere, this became the pattern for Russian scientists during the reign of Nicholas I. Upon achievement of a Master's degree in Russia and perhaps some doctoral work, a promising student would go, at government expense, to European universities and to scientific and technical training centers, particularly those of France and Germany. The student would then, usually after two or three years, return to Moscow or some other Russian university or technical school to teach and work, continuing to maintain his contacts with the European scientific community, contributing to it, and, in some cases, achieving international recognition. A few foreigners remained at Moscow University by the mid-nineteenth century, as we have seen —Brashman, Heimann and others—although almost all had become Russianized to a considerable degree. It was possible also for a few Russian professors of distinction by 1850 to have received all of their training in Russia, and this tendency was to grow. Europe, however, for Russians, as well as for students from most other countries in both of the world's hemispheres, would remain the world's scientific and educational hub until 1914.

In his memoirs, Alexander Herzen provides an interesting and significant recollection of the teaching of science at Moscow University during the second quarter of the nineteenth century:

> German philosophy had been grafted on Moscow University by M. G. Pavlov. The Chair of Philosophy had been abolished since 1826. Pavlov gave us an introduction to Philosophy by way of Physics and Agricultural Science. It would have been hard to learn Physics at his lectures, impossible to learn Agricultural Science; but they were extremely profitable.[21]

Herzen's remarks are misleading, not only in terms of Professor Pavlov, whose interest in metaphysics, as we have seen, did not prevent him from becoming one of the leading practical agronomists in Russia, but also with regard to both the students and faculty at Moscow University. Herzen obviously was bored when Pavlov lectured on Agricultural Science and other purely technical subjects. However, his statements should not be taken to indicate that Moscow's "Science" courses were merely cloaks to disguise fashionable philosophical ideas from Europe, which German or German-educated academicians could provide for the diversion and spiritual development of disaffected young Russian nobles, such as Herzen (or A. S. Khomia-

[21] Herzen, *My Past and Thoughts*, vol. II, p. 113.

kov, who preceded him as a student at the University by several years).

The later careers and views of these two aristocratic Russian intellectuals, both of whom were enrolled at the Physics-Mathematics Faculty while at Moscow University, provide an interesting, although not typical, commentary on the effects of a scientific education of the 1820's and 1830's at this school. Neither became a professional scientist, despite the fact that both had selected this area as the major subject of their higher education. However, they retained a proficiency in scientific topics and maintained a life-long interest in science, including applied science and technology. Herzen was very much concerned with the relationship of science and philosophy—how one could vitalize the other. He was desirous of bringing science down from the clouds of metaphysics, pure theory, specialization, and professionalism. Khomiakov also nurtured throughout his life the scientific education which he had begun at Moscow University in the early 1820's. As befitted a wealthy landlord, he was very much interested in scientific agriculture, technology, and the progressive management of estates. He was active for many years in a provincial scientific agricultural society, built a sugar factory on his lands, and became something more than an amateur physician and machinist, attempting to sell in England a rotary steam engine of his own invention. As a Slavophile, Khomiakov envisaged a harmony of liberal and scientific education in Russia. He saw no contradiction to his conservative and nationalist views in the importation of Western technology, as in the matter of railroads, which he saw as inevitable and beneficial for his country.[22]

Scientific education at Moscow University during the early nineteenth century, however, was neither designed for, nor limited to, a few noble intellectuals like Herzen or Khomiakov, whose lives would be devoted largely to nonscientific activities. The statistics which are available would indicate that during the second quarter of the 1800's, the Physics-Mathematics Faculty had become a major branch of Moscow University, both in terms of its position among the other faculties and its popularity with the students. In the decade following 1825, there were 119 matriculated and nonmatriculated students in Physics-Mathematics, compared to 173 of similar standing in Literature, 510 in Law, Theology, History and Politics, and 521 graduated physicians and Doctors of Medicine. From 1836 until 1854, there were 458 students in the Physics-Mathematics Faculty, as compared to 294 in History-Philology, 802 in Law, and 958 in Medicine. Thus, by the mid-nineteenth century, Moscow University was still training a large

[22] P. Christoff, *A. S. Xomjakov* (Mouton; The Hague, 1961), pp. 23, 105, 184-86. See also my Chapters 5 and 13. On Herzen, his *My Past and Thoughts*, vol. II, pp. 128-29.

number of civil servants, as was to be expected, but it was also training a far greater number of students in the sciences than in humanistic subjects, and was serving as a major center for the preparation of physicians. Herzen's fellow students of science at Moscow University were far from being landlords and nobles like himself who would find in the science program a way of studying European philosophy and of finishing a liberal education. In a report for the academic year 1826-1827, of a total of fifty students enrolled in the Physics-Mathematics Faculty, nineteen were nobles, fifteen children of civil servants, twelve came from merchant, lower middle class or craftsmen's families, and four from clerical homes, orphanages, or undesignated backgrounds. It would be reasonable to conclude from these figures that over half of the students studying the sciences at Moscow University during this period were of a social background which would indicate that they intended to make practical use of their training in business, education, or state service.[23]

If the professors of the Physics-Mathematics Faculty at Moscow University during the early nineteenth century included philosophy in their lectures on scientific and technical subjects, this was not reflected in their publications, which tended to emphasize Applied Science and Technology. A bibliography of the publications of this faculty from 1790 to 1860 includes many monographs, theses, textbooks, articles, and addresses which deal with technical matters. At least nine members of the faculty wrote on such subjects during this period. Most prolific in this matter was Herzen's professor, M. G. Pavlov, who wrote two editions of a textbook, a book-length monograph, and four articles, all dealing with agricultural management and experimentation. Some of the technical subjects treated by other members of the Moscow Physics-Mathematics Faculty in their publications were electrodynamics, the construction of dams, steam machinery, and industrial technology. Two of these works were masters' theses, part of a total of ten prepared at the university between 1814 and 1826.[24]

St. Petersburg University

The city of St. Petersburg, the administrative heart of Imperial Russia, became its center for technological and scientific training and research during the early nineteenth century. The government preferred to establish its main engineering and technological institutes there, as well as to train its teachers, officials, and doctors and to gather the scientific minds of Russia near the center of the administrative and military apparatus. Here, Russia's first higher school of

---

[23] Figures from Shevyrev, *Istoriia Moskovskago Universiteta*, pp. 572, 574; *Istoriia Moskovskago Universiteta*, vol. I, p. 113.
[24] Kononkov, *Istoriia fiziki*, p. 41 and appendix, pp. 283-97.

technology, her two most important engineering schools, the Medical-Surgical Academy, and numerous military and naval schools were located. All offered science courses and numbered trained scientists on their faculties. Finally, there was the Academy of Sciences itself. St. Petersburg University fit into this pattern by 1850 as an important scientific center, most notably in the fields of Mathematics and Physics.

Established as a university as late as 1819, St. Petersburg was slow in developing a strong program in scientific research and the teaching of science. The last of the major Russian universities to be founded under Tsar Alexander I, its early formative years coincided not with a reformist period, as at the beginning of the reign, an atmosphere from which the other Russian universities derived strength and encouragement, but under the shadow of the reactionary Dmitrii Runich, Magnitskii's counterpart in the St. Petersburg Educational District. It was not until the late 1830's that the University emerged as a scientific center. With world recognized mathematicians like Buniakovskii, Chebyshev, and Somov, and a physicist of the stature and reputation of Heinrich Lenz as its Dean, the Physics-Mathematics Faculty of St. Petersburg far surpassed that of Moscow University in these crucial fields by the mid-nineteenth century. Like the Academy of Sciences, with which it had many close bonds, St. Petersburg University tended to emphasize theory over practice. Unlike Moscow, however, with all of the technical and engineering schools then functioning in St. Petersburg, it was not the only place in the city where the best practical training could be obtained.

It was not until the general university reform of 1835 that any significant program in technical education was developed at St. Petersburg University. A small Physics-Mathematics Faculty had been created in 1824, which offered courses in Physics, Chemistry, Mathematics, Theoretical Mechanics, and "Economic or Applied" Botany, but no lectures in Technology, Agricultural Science, Applied Mechanics, or Technical Chemistry. The two leading professors in this faculty during the 1820's, Chizhov in Mathematics and Shcheglov in Physics, were interested in technological research: the former published a book on Practical Mechanics in 1823 and the latter edited, from 1824 until 1831, a journal which reported on technological among other scientific matters. However, no impulse to provide for a program in technical and practical subjects, either from above by the university and the state educational administrations, or from below by the students, was in evidence in the first decade of St. Petersburg's existence.[25]

---

[25] V. V. Grigorev, *Imperatorskii St. Peterburgskii Universitet v techenie pervykh piatidesiati let ego sushchestvovaniia* (St. Petersburg, 1870), pp. 24-25, 50, 61, 70-71.

The reform of 1835 expanded the Physics-Mathematics Faculty to include seven chairs: Zoology, Botany, Mineralogy and Geology, Chemistry, Physics and Physical Geography, Astronomy and Geodesy, and Pure and Applied Mathematics. In addition, three chairs for more purely practical studies—Agricultural Science and Forestry, Technology and Technical Chemistry, and Civil Architecture and the Art of Construction—were joined to the Juridical Faculty. Since the Juridical Faculty in 1835 was concerned primarily with legal and administrative preparation for state service, it can be assumed that the new departments were providing technical training which would be used by future government personnel and hence were administratively subordinated to the Law Schools, rather than attached to the Sciences Division.[26]

A further impetus to technical training came in 1839 with the creation of a "Real Section" of the University. This new section, which was supported in part by funds from the Ministry of Finances, was intended to train teachers of technology for the public education system. Two modest programs, since they involved only six students each time, were set up, in the period 1841 to 1843 and again from 1849 to 1851. Professors and instructors from the regular science departments, from the newly created chairs in Technology and Agricultural Science, as well as engineers from outside the University were utilized. Thus, three officers from the Corps of Engineers of Ways of Communication lectured on Applied Mechanics, Architecture and Drawing, while two university instructors, Voskresenskii of the Chemistry and later of the Technology Faculty, and Usov of Agricultural Science, lectured respectively on Technical Chemistry and Technology. In the second "Real" program of 1849-1851, the noted mathematician, Chebyshev, lectured on Practical Mechanics.[27]

The Chair of Agricultural Science and Forestry of St. Petersburg University was occupied from its founding in 1836 until 1859 by Professor S. M. Usov. Usov's education departs from the pattern of training for most Russian scientists and technologists during the early nineteenth century. He received his entire education in Russia, obtaining his Master's degree from St. Petersburg University in 1839. Usov specialized in the study of scientific agriculture and industry, which according to one biographical note, he knew "not only from books, but as well on-the-job, having spent several years occupied with commercial matters and managing a factory." This training was reflected in his academic and scholarly activities, as well as in public service. The former included courses in Agriculture, Technology, and Commercial Accounting, textbooks and translations in the field of scientific agriculture and cattle breeding, and editorship of the

[26] Grigorev, *St. Peterburgskii Universitet*, pp. 171-213, passim.
[27] Grigorev, *St. Peterburgskii Universitet*, pp. 116, 176-77.

Agricultural Gazette and *Mediator, A Newspaper of Industry, Agricultural Management, and Real Science.* The latter involved a statistical mission for the Ministry of State Properties on industry and commerce in the Ukraine, New Russia, the lower Volga area, and Siberia.[28]

Usov's successor to the Chair of Agricultural Science and Forestry in 1859 was A. V. Sovetov, whose educational background was perhaps more typical of the times: he was a product of the Vilna Seminary, but also of the first Russian higher agricultural school, the Gorygoretskii Agricultural Institute. Sovetov went on to study beet-sugar manufacturing on one of the estates of Count Bobrinskii, and completed his education at farms and agricultural institutes in several localities in eastern and western Europe. He obtained a Master's degree at Moscow University in 1859.[29]

What happened to the graduates of the "Real" programs at St. Petersburg University? At least two of them, for whom we have some records, returned to the University to teach in its newly formed Department of Technology and Technical Chemistry. P. A. Ilenkov, a graduate of the first Real Section of 1841-1843, completed his education in Practical Chemistry in schools and factories in various German principalities and in France. Training in the laboratory method under eminent professors at Berlin, he organized in 1849, partly at his own expense, a first small chemical laboratory for student research at St. Petersburg University. Ilenkov's successor, M. V. Skobikov, a graduate of the 1849-1851 Real Section, was trained entirely in Russian schools and factories. In addition to teaching Technology at the University, he edited, for the Department of Manufactures and Domestic Trade of the Ministry of Finances the journal, *Manufacturing and Metallurgical News.* Skobikov was concerned with problems of the agrarian and industrial modernization of Russia. In addition to his work for the Free Economic Society, this can be seen in some of his publications, such as an article published in the late 1850's in the *Industrial Herald*, "The Frontiers of Technology and Their Significance for the Development of the Productive Strength of a People and Their Culture."[30]

By the mid-nineteenth century, the center of mathematical studies in Russia had moved from Kazan and Moscow to St. Petersburg. The foundations had been established in the imperial capital and its university for a Russian school of mathematicians which was to become world famous. Physics and chemistry were also greatly strengthened at St. Petersburg in the 1840's and 1850's. Although the practical, technical, and industrial orientation among the leading

[28] Grigorev, *St. Peterburgskii Universitet*, pp. 171-72.
[29] Grigorev, *St. Peterburgskii Universitet*, p. 173.
[30] Grigorev, *St. Peterburgskii Universitet*, pp. 174-76.

scientists at St. Petersburg was far less marked than at Moscow University, these men were not unconcerned with the practical application of their work, and some of their colleagues were ready to develop the military and industrial implications, particularly of mathematical research.

Pafnuty Chebyshev is a case in point. Chebyshev, educated in Russia at Moscow University, was world famous by 1850 for his work with prime numbers. During this early period of his career, Chebyshev became a part of the Western scientific community, visiting universities and academies in Europe during most of his summer vacations, establishing lifelong relationships with European scientists, and publishing extensively in French in European scientific journals. One of Chebyshev's earliest teaching assignments at St. Petersburg University was a course in Practical Mechanics in the Real Section from 1849 to 1851. After this, he maintained an interest in machinery, and particularly in the synthesis of motion in experimental and practical types of mechanisms. To this end, Chebyshev built many machines and devices for transforming motion, including sorting and paddling machines and a hand-powered wheelchair. In the early 1850's, he studied mechanics in Europe, and later added to his publications with several works on machinery and other practical subjects—on cogwheels, centrifugal regulators, and the drawing of maps, among other subjects. In one article, he articulated his view that practical science was essential to the advancement of pure science because it revealed "new subjects for research or new aspects of subjects already well known," as well as posed "questions which are really new for science, thus urging upon research completely new methods."

In his concern for the practical application of science, Chebyshev was also interested in the theory of probability and its uses for insurance rates and military recruiting. He was a member of the government Military-Scientific Committee, and in the late 1850's conducted artillery experiments. A decade later, some of Chebyshev's mathematical formulae were utilized by a Russian artillery officer, Major General N. Maevskii, in experiments conducted at the Krupp works in Essen. These experiments were concerned with the measurement of the gas pressure of gunpowder in artillery weapons.[31]

The other great mathematician at St. Petersburg University during the mid-nineteenth century (although his period of maturity and

---

[31] On Chebyshev, A. Vassilief, *P. L. Tchébychef et son oeuvre scientifique* (Turin, 1898), pp. 9-10, 48, 50; I. V. Kuznetsov, ed., *Liudi russkoi nauki* (Moscow, 1961), pp. 132-36; A. V. Predtechenskii and V. Ia. Golant, *Kolybel russkoi nauki* (Leningrad, 1959), pp. 129-34; V. V. Danilevskii, *Russkaia tekhnika* (2nd edn., Leningrad, 1948), pp. 203-04; Grigorev, *St. Peterburgskii Universitet*, pp. 184-85; and N. Maevskii, Royal Academy of Literature and Art, Belgium, *Mémoires*, vol. 21 (1870), no. 4.

fruition as a scholar extended from the 1840's to the 1880's) was V. Ya. Buniakovskii. Buniakovskii was perhaps most responsible for transforming St. Petersburg into Russia's mathematical capital by the end of the reign of Nicholas I. A brilliant lecturer, he came to the university by way of extensive study of mathematics and mechanics at the Sorbonne, where he obtained his doctor's degree in 1825. Beginning his teaching career in military, naval, and engineering schools (including the Mining Institute and the Institute of Engineers of Ways of Communication), Buniakovskii became a Professor at St. Petersburg University in 1846. His research work in the 1840's was in the theory of probability, which led to publication and government consultation on numerous practical matters of interest to him. He wrote on population questions in Russia, the death rate and longevity, and on insurance and banking statistics. Buniakovskii was also interested in computing instruments, and built accounting machines and other devices for mathematical measurement.[32]

St. Petersburg University carried on its faculty from 1838 until far into the second half of the nineteenth century the "grandfather of Russian Chemistry," A. A. Voskresenskii, so called because several famous Russian chemists of the late nineteenth and early twentieth centuries, including Mendeleev and Menshutkin, were his students. His education followed a pattern which was not infrequent for Russian scientists in the early nineteenth century, as other cases have indicated. It began in a seminary and was completed, after distinguished work at the St. Petersburg Pedagogical Institute, in the laboratories of the great German chemists—Von Liebig and others —of the period. Voskresenskii's early teaching experience was gained in gentry military schools, but also in the Institute of Engineers of Ways of Communication and the other advanced engineering schools in St. Petersburg. This preparation easily qualified him for the teaching of Technology at St. Petersburg University, and we find him teaching Technical Chemistry in the first Real Section of 1841-1843. In 1846, Voskresenskii was appointed to the newly created chair of Technology at the University.

Voskresenskii's interest in the practical application of chemistry extended to his research work, according to the testimony of Mendeleev, the greatest of his students. The "grandfather" of Russian chemistry made detailed analyses of Russian coal and proved that the Russian substance was equal in quality to imported varieties and fully practical to use. It would be reasonable to suppose that Mendeleev's interest in Russia's coal deposits and other crucial natural resources was derived from Voskresenskii. Like Mendeleev, Voskresenskii was also interested in the application of chemistry to agri-

---

[32] Kuznetsov, ed., *Liudi russkoi nauki*, pp. 116-18; Predtechenskii, *Kolybel russkoi nauki*, p. 129.

culture, and his university address of 1854 was devoted to this subject.[33]

A second founder of Russian chemistry who trained many important students at St. Petersburg University during the early nineteenth century was N. N. Zinin (1812-1880). Zinin's most famous student was A. M. Butlerov. He also instructed Mendeleev and acted as a private tutor for Alfred Nobel. Nobel had much to learn from Zinin, who was interested in explosives. During the Crimean War, Zinin performed some of the earliest known experiments with nitroglycerin for the Russian War Ministry.

Zinin came to St. Petersburg University at the height of his career. He had been trained at Kazan University and in the major chemistry laboratories of Germany. In 1847, he was appointed to the Chair of Chemistry at the St. Petersburg Medical-Surgical Academy, and it was through Zinin's efforts that this medical school was transformed into a first-class scientific center with a good laboratory. Zinin was essentially a practical chemist, and his greatest work was the production of aniline from nitrobenzine. This provided the basis for the manufacture of numerous dyes, drugs, and other valuable industrial materials.[34]

Perhaps the greatest chemist of the nineteenth century, and Russia's greatest scientist after Lomonosov and Lobachevskii, was beginning his mature career at St. Petersburg University in the years just before the Great Reforms. This was D. I. Mendeleev, who began lectures and laboratory work in chemistry at the University in 1857. His training included childhood experiences in his family's glass factory near Tobolsk, as well as soil and coal research with Voskresenskii. This background disposed Mendeleev as much to technical chemistry and the application of science to the industrialization of Russia, as it did to his later basic theoretical research on the periodic system of the elements, for which he is better known. As early as the first years of his teaching, Mendeleev was publishing articles in industrial journals on such subjects as iron metallurgy. Mendeleev continued to develop this interest, both as a state servant and a private entrepreneur, so that by 1900, he was easily the foremost expert on problems of technology and industrialization in Russia.[35]

E. C. Lenz came to St. Petersburg University in 1835 as an academician of international reputation. His major contributions were made in Russia's highest scientific institution in the field of elec-

---

[33] Kuznetsov, ed., *Liudi russkoi nauki*, pp. 434-38; Grigorev, *St. Peterburgskii Universitet*, pp. 194-95.

[34] On Zinin, see Kuznetsov, ed., *Liudi russkoi nauki*, pp. 441-46; Erik Bergengren, *Alfred Nobel, the Man and His Work* (London, 1962), p. 14.

[35] Grigorev, *St. Peterburgskii Universitet*, pp. 196-97; D. I. Mendeleev, *Problemy ekonomicheskogo razvitiia Rossii* (Moscow, 1960).

tricity. The Russian Academy of Sciences, with the work of Lenz, Schilling, and Jacobi, was one of the world's pioneering institutions in the study of electric power and its practical application to transport, communication, and industry. Lenz's major contributions will be considered elsewhere; however, his contributions to the teaching of science at St. Petersburg University will be discussed here. Lenz taught Physical Geography and Physics for thirty years at St. Petersburg, and became the most renowned member of its Faculty of Physics and Mathematics, Dean of this school, and ultimately Rector of the University. Physical Geography had been his first scientific interest, had carried him around the world on the Russian-sponsored Kotzebue expedition of 1823-1826, and had prompted studies of the water levels of the Caspian Sea. However, it was his courses and public lectures on Physics and particularly on Electricity and Magnetism that were best known at the University. These lectures were based on original research, accompanied by experiments, and were presented in a clear and forceful way in good Russian. Lenz worked to improve the University's physics laboratory, to develop scientific organizations at the school, and to encourage Russian scientists, although he was of German background and had been trained at the essentially non-Russian universities of Dorpat and Helsinki. He may be considered the founder of the School of Physics at St. Petersburg University.[36]

If the faculty at St. Petersburg University made it a center for research in Mathematics, Chemistry, and Physics by 1850, and if a program of technical studies had been developed, student interest remained weak. The famous Semenov-Tian Shanskii, a student in the Physics-Mathematics Faculty from 1845 until 1848, states that there were never more than eight students in the advanced courses in this faculty. St. Petersburg University was dominated until at least the 1860's by young men preparing for government service. Never more than seven students in any one year prior to the middle of the century attended the Science Faculty. In 1850, there were seven students in Physics-Mathematics and 119 in Law. (The Chairs of Agriculture and Technology at the time were attached to the latter, although there are no figures for the number of students then taking these subjects.) In 1860, there were forty students in Physics-Mathematics and ninety in Law.[37] Of the few graduates of the Physics-Mathematics Faculty, however, many were scientists of the first order—Ilenkov, Usov,

[36] On Lenz's work in the field of electricity, see my Chapter 16; on his academic career, memoirs of P. P. Semenov-Tian Shanskii in V. V. Mavrodin, N. G. Skladkevich, and L. A. Shilov, eds., *Leningradskii Universitet* (Leningrad, 1963), vol. I, p. 41; Vucinich, *Science in Russian Culture*, p. 303; Grigorev, *St. Peterburgskii Universitet*, pp. 191-93.

[37] Semenov-Tian Shanskii in Mavrodin, ed., *Leningradskii Universitet*, pp. 41-44; Grigorev, *St. Peterburgskii Universitet*, appendix V.

Mendeleev, and Semenov-Tian Shanskii himself. Almost all became professors at St. Petersburg University and leaders of the future generation in both science and technology.

Kazan University

If a Mendeleev might reasonably be expected to emerge from the relatively sophisticated scientific center that St. Petersburg University had become by the 1850's, the appearance of Lobachevskii at Kazan a quarter of a century before would appear to be premature and exceptional. All of the circumstances of the early decades of Kazan University seemed designed to stifle the development of science: a frontier city thousands of miles from the scientific centers of Europe and from the main Russian universities themselves; imported German professors, few of whom knew Russian, and who lectured in Latin to poorly prepared provincial Russian students who had difficulty in following their words, to say nothing of their ideas; the Magnitskii holocaust of the 1820's, a reaction which very nearly brought the university to physical destruction, followed by thirty years of militarism. Yet Kazan produced Lobachevskii, and was in part responsible for the originality of his thought; and it was largely because of Lobachevskii that Kazan survived its trials and became a scientific establishment of the first rank in Russia.

The weaknesses of Kazan University were not as damaging as they might at first appear. The German faculty, if initially isolated by language from its students, was eventually able to establish communication and to be understood. Most of this same faculty were highly trained men, products of the best scientific centers of Germany, and for a long time superior to the growing minority of their Russian colleagues. From the very beginning, they aimed to make Kazan a mathematics center, which they were able to do in two decades. Technology was stressed at an early time, a chair being created in 1808 for technological and agricultural subjects. The industrial aspect of these studies was emphasized in the new name given to the chair in 1812: "Technology and Science Relating to Commerce and Factories." The early technology professors, however, were not as successful as their German countrymen who were teaching mathematics, nor did they remain long. The first appointee, Wuttig, returned to Germany in 1812, after only four years at Kazan. His successor, Von Breitenbach, who lectured to nearly empty classrooms in German, was appointed by the Minister of Finances to the Forestry Institute, after having been purged by Magnitskii.[38]

---

[38] N. N. Bulich, *Iz pervykh let Kazan'skago Universiteta 1805-1818* (2nd edn., St. Petersburg, 1904), vol. I, pp. 4-9, vol. II, pp. 484-94; M. K. Korbut, *Kazan'skii Gosudarstvennyi Universitet imeni V. I. Ulianov-Lenina za 125 let 1804/5-1929/30* (Kazan, 1930), vol. I, pp. 15-17.

Chartered in 1804, Kazan University got off to a slow start during the Napoleonic war years. It was beginning to take hold in the postwar period. In the five years from 1814 to 1819, the enrollment jumped from 42 to 161. Then Magnitskii appeared. Although the reactionary curator persecuted some professors and left the library in a shambles, he was not out specifically to destroy science and technology at Kazan, and the damage, although severe, was not irreparable at the time of his fall from power.

Magnitskii was followed as Curator of the Kazan Educational District by a typically Nicholean appointment. This was Musin-Pushkin, an ex-cavalry colonel whose main concern was to run Kazan University as much like a military unit as possible. However, he did not understand intellectual matters, and was less of a threat to the sciences and technology in this respect than Magnitskii, who knew his philosophy and science well. Fortunately for the University, Musin-Pushkin turned such matters over to Lobachevskii, who became the administrative head, or Rector, in 1827, a post he held until 1846.[39] Lobachevskii thus had almost twenty years to rebuild Kazan University and transform it into a major scientific center of the Russian empire.

Lobachevskii was a product of Russia and indeed of Kazan itself. He began his education in that city, and completed it at Kazan University, where he remained for the rest of his life as Professor, Dean, and then Rector. The German professors at Kazan during the first years of its existence, particularly Bartels, provided Lobachevskii with a solid foundation in mathematics and natural science. They did not, apparently, inculcate along with this training the precepts of Romanticist German metaphysics. Lobachevskii was thus kept free of what might have become a philosophical encumbrance to his scientific development and remained on the more solid ground of eighteenth-century empiricism. This circumstance, in the opinion of some scholars, accounts in part for the originality of his mathematical thinking.[40]

The pioneer of non-Euclidian geometry, unrecognized outside of Russia for his scientific achievements for many years, was also a superb administrator, hailed in his own time as the savior of Kazan University. His inaugural speech as Rector in 1827 indicated the humanistic and practical direction that education at the school was to take once the damage wrought by Magnitskii was repaired.[41] The

---

[39] Korbut, *Kazan'skii Universitet,* vol. I, pp. 25-26.

[40] Vucinich, *Science in Russian Culture,* pp. 318-23; on early influences, see V. Г. Kagan, *Lobachevskii* (Moscow-Leningrad, 1944), p. 39; E. F. Litvinova, *N. I. Lobachevskii, ego zhizn i nauchnaia deiatel'nost* (St. Petersburg, 1895), pp. 24-26.

[41] N. I. Lobachevskii, Speech of July 5, 1828, "On the Most Important

library was restored, new buildings were put up, a scientific journal was founded, physics and chemistry laboratories were built, as well as an astronomical observatory, an anatomical theater, a clinic, and a botanical garden. Lobachevskii was even on hand to mobilize the students to fight fires and epidemics. For the expansion of technology, new departments of Mechanical and Chemical Technology, Agriculture, Forestry, and Architecture were created. In the early 1840's, Lobachevskii fought unsuccessfully to keep the courses in Agricultural Science and Technology in the Science Faculty, rather than transfer them, as many professors wished, following a trend in other Russian universities, to the Finances Faculty. Lobachevskii believed that students entering technical fields needed a solid foundation of basic science, but his plan of organization was not adopted until after his death.[42]

Outside of the University, Lobachevskii worked to develop a district trade school. He joined the Kazan Economic Society and read reports on scientific agriculture, cattle feeding, and mill construction. He also experimented with soil temperature and invented a special thermometer for its measurement.[43]

The Early Engineering and Technological Institutes

Professional training in engineering and technology in Russia dates back essentially to the early nineteenth century. As in other areas of Russian modernization, Peter the Great attempted to blaze the trail in these fields, but without much success. The few eighteenth-century technical schools languished, and it was not until the educational reforms at the turn of the century that the training of engineers and technicians in Russia assumed more than an experimental significance. Several of the most important research and educational institutions in basic fields were founded in the early 1800's, particularly during the reign of Alexander I. Many have survived until today as important schools. The first school of transport engineers was created in 1810, and the first technological institute in 1828. The first military engineering institute was established in the same period (1819), followed a decade later by the first schools of civil engineering and architecture. These last two were combined in 1842. In 1830, the Michael Artillery School, an important military-technological center, was founded in St. Petersburg. Russia's first medical academy and her first forestry school were created at the turn of the century (1798 and 1803). The first equivalent of an agricultural college—the Gorygoretsk Institute—was developed in the early 1840's. A surveying school, a naval mechanical

Subjects of Education," L. B. Modzalevskii, ed., *Materialy dlia biografii N. I. Lobachevskii* (Moscow-Leningrad, 1948), pp. 321-27; Kagan, *Lobachevskii*, pp. 62-63.

[42] Korbut, *Kazanskii Universitet*, vol. I, pp. 49-50, 52, 67.

[43] Kagan, *Lobachevskii*, pp. 213, 244; Litvinova, *N. I. Lobachevskii*, p. 49.

school, and a school of mining and metallurgy were inherited from the eighteenth century and expanded into professional training establishments for military and civilian engineers and technicians.

Similar to the Russian universities, the engineering and technical schools of the early nineteenth century endured evils which stemmed from conditions in the state and society of the time. Reaction and obscurantism were less of a threat to these schools than other obsessions of the age. Militarism, reflected in the reorganization of engineering establishments as officer training schools, was one of the Nicholean "reforms" which consumed in military subjects and exercises valuable class hours that might have been devoted to specialized technical study. An impediment more serious than this was the disinterest of educated Russian society in the practical education of the younger generation. This indifference was combined with a universal inadequacy of preparatory or general education. These two conditions were reflected in the technical schools in their attempt to combine professional with liberal arts training, the gymnasium with the engineering school. The result many times tended to be less a cultivated engineer than a socially adept but professionally untutored product of a finishing school.

The curricula of the main engineering schools, however, were not seriously enough perverted by these influences to prevent the training of many skilled technicians. The early nineteenth-century tradition was sufficient to provide a substantial basis for the reforms of the 1860's, which reorganized Russia's higher technical schools into university-level institutions of advanced and specialized training.

The problems, frustrations, and achievements of the formative period of Russia's technical schools can be seen in the history of the Mining Institute (or the Institute of Engineers of the Mining Cadet Corps, and the Institute of the Corps of Mining Engineers—its various names during the early nineteenth century). It is known today as the Leningrad Mining Institute. The Mining Institute was founded in St. Petersburg in 1774. It had been preceded by several schools for the training of technicians in mining and metallurgy, originally established by Peter the Great and his Urals collaborators, Hennin and Tatishchev. These schools were set up in the various factory complexes of the Urals, the most important located at the industrial and administrative center of Ekaterinburg. This institution, which never provided much more than a training in the basic fundamentals of mathematics and mechanics, survived the trials of the post-Petrine period, thanks to Tatishchev, but was inadequate for the task of advanced technical training.[44]

With the establishment of the Mining Institute in the Russian capi-

---

[44] "Gornii Institut za 150 let, kratkii istoricheskii ocherk," *Gornii zhurnal*, 99th year (1923), 668-69; Virginskii, *Tvortsy novoi tekhniki v krepostnoi Rossii* (2nd edn., Moscow, 1962), p. 88.

tal half a century later, it was hoped that specialized training of a theoretical and practical nature in mining and metallurgy could be provided for young men. Prospective students would receive their general education in the liberal arts and in science and mathematics at Moscow University, and then move on to a more specialized training at the Mining Institute in courses in Mechanics, Hydraulics, Mine Surveying, and other such technical subjects. For practical education, a model mine, which later became a popular sight for tourists, was built near the school building.

From the very beginning, a sufficient number of qualified students could not be found, and the Mining Institute was obliged to become a secondary school which could provide a general education for engineering aspirants, as well as a higher technical school.[45] This changed the character of the Mining Institute for almost a century, although it did not spell the end of its development and growth in the fields of mining and metallurgical engineering. It broadened the purposes of the school, but what was intended as a necessary, secondary and preparatory activity was to become for a number of years and for many of the students the primary function and value of the school.

The Mining Institute was not neglected in the educational reform movement of the early years of the reign of Alexander I. A statute of 1804 aimed to reorganize and expand the existing institution so as to bring it up to the level of the Russian universities, and at the same time, create a first-rate gymnasium out of its lower classes. The military element was also introduced at this time. The school was renamed the Institute of Engineers of the Mining Cadet Corps, and the students were obliged to wear uniforms and assume cadet ranks. However, the new Cadet Corps was not yet turned into a closed officer-training school for the nobility. Military subjects were not taught, and many of the students were children of officers in the mining administration who were supported by state or private scholarships. In the upper classes, the number of specialized subjects in the offering was broadened in 1804 and again in 1817 to include Mechanics, Management, and Mining Law. New courses in the sciences were added, internship in the St. Petersburg factories and provincial mines was required, and the faculty was improved with the inclusion of members of the Academy of Sciences as well as experienced mining engineers and machinists. Many of the faculty continued to be imported from abroad: the Mining Institute would find it necessary to rely heavily on foreign professors for most of the reign of Alexander I.[46]

[45] "Gornii Institut," p. 670.
[46] A. Loranskii, *Istoricheskii ocherk Gornago Instituta* (St. Petersburg, 1873), pp. 48, 65; "Gornii Institut," pp. 671-72; L. N. Nisselovich, *Istoriia zavodsko-fabrichnogo zakonodatel'stva Rossiiskoi Imperii* (St. Petersburg, 1884), vol. I, part 2, p. 40.

The first two of the four classes of the Institute were primarily a gymnasium offering a general foundation in arts and sciences, French, German, and Russian grammar, and such subjects as Music, Dancing and Fencing, which might be expected to produce a polished engineer and gentleman. By the early 1820's, the Institute of the Mining Cadet Corps, which numbered over four hundred students, had in fact become famous as a finishing school for the nobility. The best dancing and fencing masters in St. Petersburg were on its faculty, and the student theater was so accomplished that several graduates of the Mining Institute went on to become famous actors, singers, and dancers. Final examination time at the Institute was not so much a test of engineering proficiency as a display, before the social elite of St. Petersburg, of choral singing, poetry recitation, overtures and symphonies performed by the student orchestra, trick marching, fencing with rapiers and swords, the polonaise, the minuet, and the gavotte.[47]

It is clear that the Mining Cadet Corps was becoming a fashionable gymnasium, but by 1825, attempts were being made to restore its prestige as an engineering school. In 1825, under a capable director, E. V. Karneev, and with the support of the Minister of Finances (then Count Kankrin), reforms were instituted. A periodical, the *Mining Journal*, was founded, with members of the school's faculty as its editors.[48] As has been seen in the cases of other Russian schools and universities at the time, public lectures dealing with scientific and technical subjects were given in the Institute in the 1830's. New courses in Paleontology, Geology, Mineralogy, and Chemistry were added to the senior program for the school.[49]

In a new reform of 1834 the school was again renamed—this time it was called the Institute of the Corps of Mining Engineers—and transformed from a finishing school into a closed military-training institution. Preparatory training was maintained, but military subjects were added, military discipline was intensified, and the program of studies was lengthened. The military tendency was reaffirmed in a statute of 1848.

According to some contemporary testimony, the reforms of Nicholas I did not mean a decline in the technical education which the Institute provided.[50] It prolonged the course of studies and substituted the parade ground for ballroom frivolities. What was required was not a drastic reform or improvement of the existing technical program, but the elimination of educational elements nonessential to the higher

---

[47] For a brilliant description of one of these ceremonies, see Loranskii, *Ocherk Gornago Instituta*, pp. 67-70.
[48] On the founding of *Gornii zhurnal*, see my Chapter 14.
[49] Loranskii, *Ocherk Gornago Instituta*, pp. 76-79, 84, 87-88.
[50] "Gornii Institut," pp. 673-74.

training of engineers, and which could be obtained elsewhere. This surgery was performed by the statute of 1866, which in effect eliminated the general education program under which the Mining Institute had labored for almost a century, as well as the militaristic, exclusive character which it had acquired, particularly under Nicholas I. Around the nucleus of a sound engineering education which its higher faculties offered, an open, nonmilitarized, university-level engineering institute was created in 1866, with scholarships, university rights, and a minimum entering age of sixteen instead of twelve.[51]

The Institute of Engineers of Ways of Communication was founded in 1800 to meet pressing needs for the modernization of Russia's transport system. In the early years of the nineteenth century, this meant engineers who could build and maintain the canals and highways that had been developed since the late 1790's by Sievers and Rumiantsev.[52] At the time, France was the source of the most advanced knowledge of these subjects, and both the models and the recruiting ground for the faculty of the new Russian transport school were the French École des ponts et chaussées and the École polytechnique, established during the Revolution. By agreement with Napoleon during the Tilsit period, four French engineers were sent to Russia. During the next decade, several other French engineers, graduates of the École polytechnique, joined the faculty of the Russian school. More than 36,000 rubles worth of books and equipment were acquired in Paris. The Institute of Engineers of Ways of Communication thus remained basically a French school in its early years, with many of the classes conducted in the French language. This went on until 1830, when most of the French members of the faculty were obliged to leave Russia for political reasons. However, foreign influence in the school extended beyond the French professors and went right up to the top. The first superintendent was a Spanish engineer of international reputation and later Superintendent of Ways of Communication, Lieutenant General Augustine de Bethancourt. He was succeeded by a German, the Duke of Württemberg, also destined to head the transport administration.[53]

The school was generously endowed by the government, and initial help included a splendid building purchased from Prince Iusupov for 350,000 paper rubles. The building remains today, with two stories added, housing the Academician V. N. Obraztsov Institute of Engi-

---

[51] Loranskii, *Ocherk Gornago Instituta*, pp. 124-27.
[52] See my Chapter 11.
[53] S. Timoshenko, "The Development of Engineering Education in Russia," *Russian Review*, vol. 15 (1956), 173-74; S. M. Zhitkov, *Institut Inzhenerov Putei Soobshcheniia Imperatora Aleksandra I, istoricheskii ocherk* (St. Petersburg, 1899), pp. 6-8, 36-37; Vucinich, *Science in Russian Culture*, pp. 198-99.

neers of Railroad Transportation.[54] In addition to the regular lecture halls, workshops, and laboratories, a collection of model machines and a library which included maps of rivers, canals, and roads of the Russian empire were installed in the school not long after its founding.

In its development during the reigns of Alexander I and Nicholas I, the Institute of Engineers of Ways of Communication followed in many ways the pattern of the Mining Institute and other Russian technical schools of the period. As early as 1823, it became a closed military training school, with the usual courses in Military Science and the Catechism added to the curriculum, together with sessions of military drill and gymnastics and the imposition of strict military discipline, ranks, and uniforms. Supplementary regulations of 1830, 1844, and 1849 extended the militarization of the school. In 1831, as in the Russian universities and other higher technical schools, public lectures were offered. Notable among the first of such offerings was a course on the "Impossibility of Building Railroads in Russia," delivered in French by a French engineer. In 1826, following hard upon the *Mining Journal*, the first issue of the *Journal of Ways of Communication* appeared, in French and Russian.[55]

Militarization, as in the case of the Mining Institute, did not, however, seriously intrude upon technical instruction; while the transition from foreign to Russian teaching was easily accomplished. The French engineers had done their job well: a generation of competent Russian engineers had been trained by 1830. By that time, there was as well a pool of scientific talent in the Academy of Sciences to draw upon. Ostrogradskii, for example, came to teach at the Institute of Engineers of Ways of Communication, and by the beginning of the reign of Nicholas I, its mathematics instruction was considered to be at as high a level as that of St. Petersburg University.[56] The first generation of Russian transport engineers was headed by P. P. Mel'nikov,[57] who joined the Institute's faculty in the 1830's. Mel'nikov developed the earliest research and teaching in the new field of railroad transport during this decade. In the 1840's, the construction contingents of the St. Petersburg-Moscow railroad became in effect practical workshops of trainees from the Institute of Engineers of Ways of Communication. The school encountered most of its difficulty in this period from the higher transport administration, which had passed into the hands of the crude and brutal court favorite, Count Kleinmikhel, a man ignorant of engineering matters. Under Alexander II, similar to the

[54] E. Sokolovskii, *Piatidesiatiletie Instituta i Korpus Inzhenerov Putei Soobshcheniia* (St. Petersburg, 1859), vols. IX, XII; Gregory P. Tschebotarioff, *Russia, My Native Land: A U.S. Engineer Reminisces and Looks at the Present* (New York, 1964), p. 343 and pictures, nos. 58 and 59.

[55] Zhitkov, *Ocherk Gornago Instituta*, pp. 40-42, 51, 66.

[56] Zhitkov, *Ocherk Gornago Instituta*, p. 38.

[57] On Mel'nikov, see my Chapter 12.

Mining Institute, the Institute of Engineers of Ways of Communication was reformed into a university-level school for the advanced study of transport engineering.

One of the most interesting of the technical schools to be founded in Russia during the early nineteenth century was the St. Petersburg Practical Technical Institute, the first technological institute in Russia and one of the world's earliest. It was founded in 1828, has continued to educate technicians in Russia until the present day, and is now functioning under the name, the Lensoviet Technological Institute. In its conception, purpose, and development during the reign of Nicholas I, it represents a departure from the pattern to which most of the other engineering and technical schools of the time adhered. The curriculum of the St. Petersburg Practical Technical Institute was never militarized, nor did it ever attempt to train army officers of any kind. Its student body was not restricted to the children of nobility, nor was it set up to serve either as a finishing school for the sons of socially prominent families or a training place for civil servants.

The St. Petersburg Practical Technical Institute escaped these various pitfalls of the period because it had become a kind of pet project of the Minister of Finances, Count Kankrin. It was his brainchild, it was through his initiative that it was founded, and it was he who preserved its peculiar character until the institution was well enough established to sustain itself.[58] The fundamental purpose of the St. Petersburg Practical Technical Institute was to train young people who could act as supervisors and technicians in Russia's factories. The education was to be a practical one, which would utilize the factories of the Russian capital in its training program. Students were to be taken from all classes of society—excluding the peasantry—particularly the children of merchants, shopkeepers, craftsmen, and lower-rank bureaucrats. Entering the Institute at the age of fifteen, they followed a six-year program of formal training, followed by internship in Russian factories and advanced training in Europe for the most promising students. The general education in the first two years was limited (after required study of the Catechism) to those basic courses in natural science, mathematics, and modern languages considered indispensable to advanced technical training. Beginning with the third year, courses in technology with particular emphasis on processes employed in the textiles industry and on the construction of machinery were introduced. To make the training as pragmatic as possible, a chemical laboratory and various kinds of workshops were

---

[58] This sketch of the early years of the St. Petersburg Practical Technical Institute is based on its only history by A. A. Voronov, *Istoriia Tekhnologicheskogo Instituta 1828-1917* (Leningrad, 1928), pp. 12-65.

established. These shops were devoted primarily to the spinning, weaving and dyeing of cotton, wool, and linen, the processing of metals, and the building of steam engines and other types of machinery. Students were required to spend their mornings in the classroom, and their afternoons from two until eight working in the shops. Practical training included visits to local factories.

Kankrin kept a close eye on the Technological Institute and introduced a number of measures to enhance the practical nature of the training. Not only were new workshops that duplicated the processing in the main Russian industries set up at his insistence, but managers of the state-owned factories in the St. Petersburg area were drawn into the administration and curriculum planning of the school. By 1833, professors from the Mining Institute and the Michael Artillery Institute were teaching at the Technological Institute. The Minister of Finances ordered the school to construct its own steam engines and agricultural machinery in 1835, although prior to this he had been content to have the students learn from horse-drawn machines. In 1836, Sunday classes in Mechanical Drawing and other technical subjects were conducted by the faculty, as well as public lectures, designed as semester courses, in Industrial Chemistry. These lectures were poorly attended. The regular program at the school, however, grew. From 1837 until 1843, 129 graduates were sent into Russian factories as supervisors of various ranks, although complaints frequently were heard that the graduates had insufficient practical experience to function properly as industrial managers.

The Practical Technical Institute continued to grow after Kankrin's death, expanding its faculty and student body. However, similar to the other technical and engineering schools established in Russia during the first half of the nineteenth century, it did not attain university rank as a school for advanced, specialized training, until a statute of 1862, which provided for a Master's degree in Mechanical and Chemical Technology. As such, it has remained for the past century, incidentally accruing status as a center for the underground revolutionary movement in the last decades of the old regime, and as one of Lenin's earliest contact points in St. Petersburg.

Beyond the fields of metallurgical and transport engineering and industrial technology, a number of schools offering instruction in other areas of technology were established or reformed, particularly during the reign of Nicholas I. The Architecture School was established in 1830, followed two years later by the School of Civil Engineers. These schools were united in 1842 to form the Construction School. Its primary aim was to train engineers in the construction of buildings, roads, bridges, and dams. Like most of the other Russian engineering schools of the period, the Construction School served as a gymnasium for its junior classes, supported its students by state scholarships, was restricted to children of nobles or bureaucrats, and was militarized under Nicholas I.[59]

Two other schools in early nineteenth-century St. Petersburg which offered technical training were the Constantine Surveying School, founded in 1779 and reformed as a closed military school with a four-year program in 1835; and the Forestry Institute, opened in Tsarskoe Selo in 1803 and moved to St. Petersburg in 1811. Starting as a *Realschule*, the Forestry Institute developed advanced training, and by 1859, it was offering special courses to university students.

Russia's first state agricultural school was established near Pavlovsk in 1799, but lasted only four years. The Akkerman School of Horticulture was set up in Bessarabia in 1832 to train state settlers in the cultivation of grapes and the art of wine-making. In the same year, an Agricultural School to provide elementary education and training in farm management for 250 young peasants was established. In 1836, another state agricultural school was founded on the government estate of Gorygoretsk in Mogilev province. This was the basis for the first and only advanced agricultural school in Russia before the 1860's. The school was opened to students of all classes, except seigneurial peasants. It was designed to provide two types of training: instruction in the fundamentals of agricultural management and more advanced study of agronomy. The elementary students were taught to cope with a wide range of problems: irrigation, surveying, forestry, and horticulture, among several others. The advanced section studied Chemistry, Zoology, Botany, Rural Economics, Agronomy, and Veterinary Medicine.[60]

The Gorygoretsk school became increasingly concerned in the 1840's with the training of state peasants, as part of the reform instituted by the Minister of State Properties, P. D. Kiselev. In 1843, the number of pupils at Gorygoretsk was tripled, to equal 122. After 1848, when the school was reformed into an Agricultural Institute, the student body was again increased. By 1853, there were 222 students, although the number of graduates was meager: in 1848, eleven, in 1853, fifty-seven. Moved to St. Petersburg in the 1860's, Russia's first agricultural institute was later returned to its original home in Mogilev in Soviet times, and is now functioning as the Belorussian Agricultural Academy.[61]

---

[59] Zhitkov, *Ocherk Gornago Instituta*, p. 114; *Ocherki istorii Leningrada* (Moscow-Leningrad, 1955), vol. I, p. 805.

[60] Alexandre de Krusenstern, *Précis du système, des progrès et de l'état de l'instruction publique en Russie* (Warsaw, 1837), pp. 330-31, 336, 349.

[61] N. Druzhinin, *Gosudarstvennye krestiane i reforma P. D. Kiseleva* (Moscow, 1958), vol. II, p. 236; see also the article in *Bol'shaia sovetskaia entsiklopediia*.

Military Technical Education

During the early nineteenth century, the most important educational enterprise of the tsarist government in terms of state expenditure and numbers of students, particularly for the lower classes, were not the public or church schools but the military ones. In 1836, the number of students enrolled in schools under the jurisdiction of the Ministry of Public Instruction accounted for less than half of those attending the military schools or schools operated by the Ministry of War. Most of the War Ministry's pupils were recruits or children of soldiers. They received an elementary education. In addition to this, about 10,000 young men were being educated in higher level military and naval schools, for which 6,887,000 rubles were expended in 1836, a few hundred thousand less than the budget for the Ministry of Public Instruction for that year. Almost all of the students in the Russian military schools under Nicholas I were supported by the state.[62]

In 1800, Russia had only two military schools, the First and Second Cadet Corps. The latter had absorbed the Engineering and Artillery School established by Peter the Great. A naval cadet school had also functioned since Petrine times. Under Alexander I, a network of military schools for the Russian nobility was developed in the main cities and provinces of the Russian empire. Cadet and *iunker* schools were established in Tula, Tambov, Kharkov, Mogilev, Smolensk, Orenburg, Warsaw, Tulich, and Kalish. To these soon after were added the Imperial Page Corps, the Tsarskoe Selo Lyceum (originally a military school), a topographical school and a cadet corps for Finland, a quartermaster school, a school for scouts, and a school for Siberian cossacks of the line at Omsk. Several military schools supported by the local nobility were also founded during the reign of Alexander I—in Vilna, Tiflis, Kazan, and several smaller cities. Nicholas I added to this system by building ten new cadet schools in provincial locations. All of the cadet schools primarily trained line officers. More advanced military technical schools were also developed during the early nineteenth century. A Military Medical Academy was established in St. Petersburg in 1798. An advanced school for military engineers was set up in the same city in 1816. In 1830, the Michael Artillery School was founded. By 1854, there were over 16,000 students in twenty-two Russian cadet schools, not counting the doctors, artillerists, engineers, and other military specialists who had been trained by the War Ministry establishment.[63]

[62] Krusenstern, *Instruction publique en Russie*, tables, pp. 285, 413.

[63] M. Lalaev, *Istoricheskii ocherk voenno uchebnykh zavedenii* (St. Petersburg, 1880), pp. 36-47, 90; *Stoletie voennago ministerstva 1802-1902* (St. Petersburg, 1902), vol. X, part 1, *Glavnoe upravlenie voenno-uchebnykh zavedenii, istoricheskii ocherk*, pp. 82, 100-02; Krusenstern, *Instruction publique en Russie*, pp. 209-15.

Military technology was considered important and given a prominent place in the curricula of the War Ministry schools. Even in the
cadet schools, both in the capitals and in some of the provinces, several technical subjects were taught. In the First and Second Cadet
Corps, in St. Petersburg, and the Tambov Military School, for example, courses were offered in Mathematics, Physics, Mechanics, and
Hydraulics.[64] In the military and naval technical schools—the Main
Engineering School, the Naval Cadet Corps, the Military Medical
Academy and the Michael Artillery School—an advanced program in
science and technology with more than a purely military application
was offered.

The Main Engineering School, the first school to provide advanced
training for military engineers in Russia, was founded in St. Petersburg in 1816, having been preceded by an elementary military
engineer's school set up in 1804. It was favored by Nicholas I, who
was interested in engineering and who had been appointed its inspector in 1819. As with other engineering establishments in Russia, the
Main Engineering School aimed to train both technicians (or "conductors" as they were known) and engineer officers. While the first
four classes of technicians studied basic mathematics, the upper two
classes of officers applied themselves to Physics, Applied Chemistry,
Applied Mathematics (the study of machinery was the focus of this
course), and Descriptive Geometry Applied to Stone-Cutting and to
Carpentry. Student-engineers were also called upon to write on such
problems as hydrotechnology applied to canals and rivers.[65]

The Naval Cadet Corps, founded in Moscow in 1701 by Peter the
Great, had grown during 125 years not only into Russia's main academy for the training of naval officers, but also into an important
center for higher technical training. The school was reorganized in
1826 to provide a six-year program for the more than 500 students
then enrolled. The early grades followed the usual pattern of providing a gymnasium-level education in fundamentals, while the upper
classes followed courses in Navigation, Astronomy, Mechanics, Naval
Architecture, and Hydraulics. In 1827, the Emperor Nicholas I Naval
Technical School was formed as an advanced officers' program within
the Naval Cadet Corps. The purpose of this program was to train
superior students and officers in the sciences and technology. Its quality was evidenced by the appointment of such distinguished scientists
as Buniakovskii, Lenz, and Ostragradskii to the faculty. These professors offered courses in Differential and Integral Calculus, Analytic

---

[64] *Stoletie voennago ministerstva*, vol. X, part 1, pp. 68, 81.
[65] *Stoletie voennago ministerstva, Glavnoe inzhenernoe upravlenie, istoricheskii ocherk*, vol. VII, part 1, pp. 152-59, 170-71, 216; Krusenstern, *Instruction publique en Russie*, pp. 242-43.

Mechanics, Physics, and Chemistry. Courses in Naval Construction and Artillery were also part of the three-year program.[66]

The original purpose of the Military Medical Academy in St. Petersburg, which was Russia's first medical college (established in 1798), was to train doctors, veterinarians, and pharmacists for the army and navy. As such, it was formally a military school, administered by the War Ministry during much of the early nineteenth century. Actually, it served, not only as the main medical training center in the Russian empire, beyond universities such as Dorpat, but also, from the beginning, as a scientific and technical center as well. One of the great Russian physicists of the nineteenth century, V. V. Petrov, taught his specialty at the Military Medical Academy from 1802 until 1833. N. N. Zinin, one of the founders of Russian chemistry, joined the faculty in 1847.[67]

If the St. Petersburg Military Medical Academy was more than a training center for army doctors, the Michael Artillery School, established in the same city in 1820, was a technical school, rather than simply a school for line artillery officers. The history of Russian artillery schools dates back to Peter the Great, but was witness to periods of decline, one after Peter's death, and one in the early years of the nineteenth century. In 1820, the tsar's brother, the Grand Duke Michael, took the initiative in establishing a school which could provide not only the rudiments of artillery training for line officers, but also, for the senior students, the best education available in higher mathematics, science, and technology. The emphasis on advanced mathematical training at the Michael Artillery School was evidenced by the presence of Ostragradskii on the faculty in the 1840's. Technology also was emphasized by 1830: Applied Mechanics and Ballistics were taught and the students were required to intern in armaments and metallurgical factories. P. P. Mel'nikov, the pioneer of Russian railroad engineering, was brought in during the 1830's to lecture on Mechanics and Hydrotechnology, as well as his own specialty in the new transport technology.[68]

The first director of the Michael Artillery School was Major General A. D. Zasiadko, an experienced artillery officer of the Napoleonic period, and one of the first Russian scientists to experiment with military rockets. It is significant that Zasiadko was appointed head, not only of the new artillery school, but also of the St. Petersburg arsenal,

[66] *Entsiklopedicheskii slovar*, articles on the Emperor Nicholas I Naval Technical School and the Naval Cadet Corps; Krusenstern, *Instruction publique en Russie*, pp. 266-70.

[67] *Stoletie voennago ministerstva, Imperatorskaia Voenno-meditsinskaia Akademiia, istoricheskii ocherk*, vol. IX, pp. 21-32, 36, 105, 114.

[68] A. Platov and L. Kirpichev, *Istoricheskii ocherk obrazovaniia i razvitiia Artilleriiskago Uchilishcha 1820-1870* (St. Petersburg, 1870), pp. 44-46, 112, 117-19, 122, and appendices, nos. 9, 15, 32.

its laboratory, and the Oktensk munitions plant. Zasiadko not only taught and encouraged the development of ballistics at the artillery school, but also established the first rocket manufactory in Russia in 1826. His greatest pupil and later a professor at the Michael Artillery School was Major General K. I. Konstantinov. Konstantinov was appointed director of the St. Petersburg Rocket Manufactory in 1847 and was one of the world's pioneers in the development of the mechanized mass production of rockets with standardized parts. By the 1860's, he was recognized as an international authority in the field of gunpowder rocket dynamics.[69]

[69] Platov and Kirpichev, *Razvitie Artilleriiskago Uchilishcha*, pp. 35-37; A. A. Kosmodemianskii, *Konstantin Tsiolkovskii, His Life and Work* (Moscow, 1956), pp. 50-51; Virginskii, *Tvortsy novoi tekhniki*, pp. 345-72. See also, *Mikhailovskaia Artilleriiskaia Akademiia i Uchilishche* (St. Petersburg, 1889), p. 80.

Chapter 16

The Application of Technology

Industrial Technology

In an 1862 report to the Minister of Finances on the Russian machine industry, A. S. Ershov, Professor of Technology and Practical Mechanics at Moscow University, noted:

> We are beginning to outlive the age when the fate of our mechanical plants was in the hands of foreigners and we lived by the beck and call of foreign minds and worked with foreign machines.[1]

Ershov's optimism was premature; at least three-quarters of a century had yet to pass before Russia would no longer be dependent on foreign technology. His report nevertheless recognized a fact: that by the middle of the nineteenth century, domestically manufactured as well as imported machinery and machine power, though not chemical technology, were being applied in limited but increasing degrees to Russian industry.

Cotton manufacture, the most modernized of Russia's industries in the early nineteenth century in other respects, was also the most progressive in the utilization of machinery. It was St. Petersburg, Russia's machine-producing center,[2] which also became the focal point for a mechanized cotton-spinning industry during the reign of Nicholas I. In the 1830's, in addition to the state-owned Aleksandrovsk plant, the large private cotton-spinning enterprises of Stieglitz, Maltsev, and the Russian Cotton Spinning Company came into being, equipped with Belgian, Russian, and, after 1842, British machinery. The yarn manufactured in these highly concentrated factories was made almost entirely out of American cotton and was sold to weavers who congregated for the most part in the Moscow region. The hand loom continued to prevail in mid-century in this branch of the Russian cotton industry. However woven cotton cloth was printed and finished in such factory centers for the final stages of the processing as Ivanovo. Here, the larger enterprises were mechanizing during the last two decades of the reign of Nicholas I. Ivanovo also had several chemical, dye, and bleach factories by the time the Great Reforms began.[3] Looking at the total picture of the mechanization of the Rus-

---

[1] A. Ershov, "Obzor mashinostroitel'nykh zavedenii v Rossii," *Obzor razlichnykh otraslei manufakturnoi promyshlennosti Rossii* (St. Petersburg, 1862-1863), p. 90.

[2] Details on the machine industry of Russia during the early nineteenth century can be found in Chapter 2.

[3] *Ekonomicheskoe sostoianie gorodskikh poselenii evropeiskoi Rossii v 1861-62 g.* (St. Petersburg, 1863), section on Vladimir province, p. 65.

sian cotton industry by 1860, we see 1,150,000 spindles in operation in the tsarist empire (excluding Finland and the Kingdom of Poland) in that year. The same industry was served by machinery capable of 9,725 horsepower, over 3,000 horsepower higher than the next most heavily mechanized branch of Russian industry (metallurgy), and over 7,500 horsepower higher than the total application of steam machine power estimated for Russian industry and all other uses in 1831. By 1850, over 43,000,000 pounds of raw cotton were imported by Russia, about seven times the quantity of yarn imported in the same year.[4]

Partial mechanization had taken place in other Russian industries by the mid-nineteenth century. The woolens industry was beginning to introduce advanced types of machinery and steam power by the 1850's. This applied more to worsteds and to the industries of Moscow than to the coarser grades of woolen cloth manufactured in many parts of Russia. In the worsteds industry, some jacquard looms were being used; and at the beginning of the Crimean War, of just over 100 woolens factories in the district of Moscow, there were twenty steam engines operating with a combined horsepower of 513. There were fifty-eight machines powered by horses and water in the same factories, totaling 576 horsepower.[5] Outside of Moscow, water wheels and animals provided almost all of the power for the manufacture of woolen cloth. The dyeing of Russian wool remained primitive. Except in the case of a few large enterprises, dyes had to be imported. Weaving was done very largely by hand. Nevertheless, the several processes that go into the making of woolen yarn were mechanized to a significant degree by the 1840's. A government report of 1845 provides considerable detail on this subject. The report deals with mechanization in 613 factories engaged in the production of the coarser varieties of wool. Many of these factories were large for the time, the average number of workers being 143. There were 771 willowing machines in 472 of the factories; in 96, the wool was cleaned by hand, and 50 did no willowing at all; 221 factories had fulling machines; 396 had no equipment for shrinking cloth. Most of the factories (481) had carding machines (3,290); in 80, the wool was combed by hand. Machine spinning was universal, with 8,344 machines and 402,935 spindles in 548 factories. Weaving was done on hand looms in almost every factory reporting. This involved 29,397 workers at 18,337 looms. Most plants did not engage in the process of napping woolen cloth; of the 250 that did, 142 used 814 machines and 108 trimmed

[4] V. K. Iatsunskii, "Rol otechestvennogo mashinostroeniia v snabzhenii priadel'nym oborudovaniem russkikh fabrik v pervoi polovine xix v.," *Istoricheskie zapiski*, vol. 42 (1953), p. 281; A. Sherer, "Khlopchatobumazhnaia promyshlennost," *Obzor promyshlennosti Rossii*, pp. 462-63.

[5] N. I. Falkovskii, *Moskva v istorii tekhniki* (Moscow, 1950), p. 301.

by hand. Similarly, 258 factories had 1,029 shearing devices; 55 sheared by hand; and 305 did no shearing at all. There were 229 brushing machines in 154 factories; 331 plants had 721 presses. Most plants did no steaming, but 94 had 107 machines for this task.[6]

The Russian woolens industry by the middle of the nineteenth century was thus far from being modernized technologically, but it was also far from being primitive. The government report of 1845 also demonstrates that the process of mechanization in industry is a very complex one that cannot be evaluated properly by the historian if only the introduction of steam power or other more dramatic forms of modern motivation are taken into account. However, these are the things that tend to leave their imprint on the history of technology.

In industries of the Moscow area other than cotton and wool, some steam machines were in evidence, although not very many, by the middle of the nineteenth century: in the brewing and linen industries, to name the most important. What other machines these factories used, we do not know. Moscow's fifty odd candle factories by 1858 were using special machines of recent invention. Russian chemists by that time had helped to develop a few stearine candle factories.[7]

The Ukraine in the 1840's saw the introduction and rapid growth of steam-powered machinery in the beet sugar industry. In Chernigov, Kiev, Kharkov, and Podolia provinces from 1848-1849 to 1860-1861, the number of plants which converted from the use of fire to the more efficient use of steam in the refining of sugar rose from 30 to 114. This represented more than two-thirds of all the steam refineries in the Russian empire—223 (primarily small estate plants) continued to use fire. The Soviet historian, Iatsunskii, has contrasted from archival data the old and new types of beet sugar factories in the 1840's. The traditional estate operation used horses and hand power to refine beet sugar with fire. The process took place in a one-story wooden building, in which just over three and one-half tons of sugar were produced each year. The whole operation was worth about 1,600 rubles. The modern sugar factory was valued at 70,000 rubles and produced 180 tons of sugar annually. A 12-horsepower steam engine powered a grating machine and four presses, together with a steam activated water pump. A stone factory building 175 feet long and 39 feet wide housed 92 workers.[8]

The Urals metallurgical industry remained backward technically during the early nineteenth century although the very largest enter-

---

[6] V. K. Iatsunskii, ed., "Materialy o sostoianii sukonnoi promyshlennosti Rossii v 1845 g.," *Istoricheskii arkhiv* (1956), no. 4, pp. 82-126.

[7] Falkovskii, *Moskva v istorii tekhniki*, pp. 293, 312, 385. On the dyeing of wool, see my Chapter 2, and on stearine candle factories, see Chapter 15.

[8] V. K. Iatsunskii, "Pomeshchichi sakharnye zavody v Rossii v pervoi polovine xix v.," *Akademiku Borisu Dmitrievichu Grekovu ko dniu semidesiatiletiia, sbornik statei* (Moscow, 1952), p. 347.

prises were able to introduce some machinery. Steam power was conspicuously absent: only 123 machines, totaling 2,788 horsepower, were operating by 1859. This represented 4.7 percent of the total amount of power utilized. There was little significant production of steel before 1860, despite the achievements of talented individual experimenters, such as P. P. Anosov.[9]

Railroads were by nature highly modernized examples of technology in terms of steam locomotives and rolling stock, but the steam engine on rail or river was still an oddity in Russia in 1860—a few hundred steamboats and locomotives moved among tens of thousands of horses.[10] The application of machinery and chemicals to agriculture was even more retarded, a condition which persisted far beyond the early nineteenth century. The Russian peasant relied on hand tools until the twentieth century and even today lacks sufficient chemical fertilizer. The handful of farming machines that were manufactured in Russia by 1860, and the much larger quantity that were imported, were together insignificant in the total picture of the primitiveness of Russian agriculture.

Occasional technical achievements and the progress of mechanization in certain industries must be etched into the massive backdrop of primitive ways which still largely characterized the Russian industrial scene in the mid-nineteenth century. The power of water, the rays of the sun, the strength of animals, dyes and acids which nature rather than the laboratory could provide, and the labor of human hands still dominated Russian industry in 1860. Even in some of the most progressive areas of Russian manufactures by that time—the cotton industry—79 factories, employing 39,316 workers, were mechanized, while 972 establishments, employing 89,575 workers, used hand labor. The yearly output from the obviously larger mechanized factories, however, exceeded that of hand production by 14,400,000 rubles or just above twice as much. In the iron mills of the Urals in 1859, over 95 percent of the power was derived from water as opposed to the few steam engines which supplied the remainder. Even in the largest enterprises with the largest concentration of new machinery, steam power never accounted for more than 10 percent of the total. Despite government and university encouragement through public lectures for factory managers and advice from chemistry professors, the development of chemical technology in Russian industry remained backward until the late nineteenth century. Plant laboratories were rare or primitive; and soda, sulphuric acid, and oil chemical dyes were neither being produced nor utilized to any significant degree.[11]

---

[9] V. V. Virginskii, *Tvortsy novoi tekhniki krepostnoi Rossii* (2nd edn., Leningrad, 1962), p. 236.

[10] On transport technology, see Chapter 13.

[11] Figures from S. G. Strumilin, *Ocherki ekonomicheskoi istorii Rossii*

Within the context of time and place—statistics confined to the early nineteenth century and to Russia—a number of conclusions about the backwardness as well as the progressiveness of Russian technology would have to be modified by figures drawn from the later periods of Russian and Soviet history, as well as from the technological development of other countries during the same, earlier, and later periods. It is commonplace to compare machine production and utilization in Russia in 1860 with that of England in the same period. More useful perspectives might emerge from a comparison of Russian applied technology in 1860 to that of England at the beginning of the nineteenth century, a time when the latter country was in the midst of the "industrial revolution." However, a more definitive assessment of the relative position of Russian technology in the half century before the Great Reforms would have to go beyond the uniqueness of England—the first to industrialize, the "workshop of the world" by 1860, a much smaller country than Russia, with a smaller population, less resources, and radically different problems of economic development. Such was not the case with the United States, whose conditions and problems of industrialization more closely approximated those of Russia although here too there are important contrasts.

Although the first steam engines were made in England in the eighteenth century, several decades before this happened in Russia (if we exclude the claims made for Polzunov), it was not until the 1820's that the mechanical engineer and the machine factory made their appearance in industrialized areas, such as London, Manchester, and Glasgow. In such cities, we find several factories of this type appearing in the decade before 1830.[12] Thus England preceded Russia in the early development of a machine industry by no more than a quarter of a century. Her chemical industry, however, preceded that of Russia by well over fifty years: it was not until the 1890's that the Russian chemical industry experienced any significant growth.

In 1810, according to the census of that year, the total value of machinery manufactured in the United States was $6,144,466, or almost the value of Russian-made machinery in 1860. By 1860, the United States produced over two hundred million dollars worth of agricultural, industrial, transport, and household machinery in almost four thousand factories and shops. According to Bishop, in the year 1857, the Russian government granted twenty-four patents for in-

---

(Moscow, 1960), p. 452; S. G. Strumilin, *Chernaia metallurgiia v Rossii i v SSSR* (Moscow-Leningrad, 1935), pp. 221-22. On chemical technology, P. M. Lukianov, *Istoriia khimicheskikh promyslov i khimicheskoi promyshlennosti v Rossii do kontsa xix veka* (Moscow-Leningrad, 1948), vol. I, p. 477; L. F. Haber, *The Chemical Industry During the Nineteenth Century* (Oxford, 1948), pp. 137-39.

[12] J. H. Clapham, *An Economic History of Modern Britain* (Cambridge, 1950-52), vol. I, pp. 152, 154-55.

ventions, eighteen of them to Russians. In the United States for the same year, 2,900 patents were granted. American chemical production had a good beginning by 1860.[13] By 1912 in Russia, the total domestic production of machinery amounted to between 200,000,000 and 210,000,000 rubles, while 150,000,000 to 160,000,000 rubles' worth of machinery was being imported from abroad. Forty percent of all agricultural machines, amounting to a value of over 43,000,000 rubles, were imported from the United States in 1912, and in the period 1898-1918, the value of imports for agricultural machinery increased seven and one-half times. Russia thus remained heavily dependent on imported machinery, not only in the early nineteenth century, but also far into the twentieth and into the period of Communist rule.[14]

The most progressive and highly mechanized of Russia's industries during the early nineteenth century, cotton manufacture, utilized 1,150,000 spindles in 1860, 350,000 less than Austria, 550,000 less than the Zollverein states of Germany, over 5,000,000 less than the United States, and more than 26,000,000 less than England. Russia was by that year the world's sixth largest spinner of cotton. Thirty years later, by 1890, the number of spindles in Russia had more than doubled; and by 1910, 8,306,000 spindles were operating in the Russian cotton spinning industry. Hand labor, still a dominant factor in weaving in 1860, declined rapidly in the last decades of the nineteenth century, from just over 40 percent of the entire cotton industry in 1866 to about 8 percent in 1894-1895.[15] England experienced a similar decline in hand labor in her cotton industry a half-century before. One estimate for 1830 gives 240,000 hand looms to 55,000 to 60,000 power looms. By 1850-1851, this proportion had been reversed. As in Russia, the use of steam power in industry was just beginning in England and in the United States by 1800. Water power continued to dominate over steam in England until the second quarter of the nineteenth century and in the United States until mid-century.[16]

A distinctive characteristic of Russian industry which can be traced

---

[13] John L. Bishop, *A History of American Manufactures from 1608 to 1860* (Philadelphia, 1860), vol. II, pp. 162, 460-61; on American, English, and Russian chemical production, see Haber, *Chemical Industry*, pp. 54-55, 138-39.

[14] A Raffalovich, *Russia: Its Trade and Industry* (London, 1918), pp. 202-04; Harry Schwartz, *Russia's Soviet Economy* (2nd edn., New York, 1954), p. 266.

[15] Sherer, "Khlopchatobumazhnaia promyshlennost," p. 455; P. A. Khromov, *Ekonomicheskoe razvitie Rossii v xix-xx vekakh* (Academy of Sciences, U.S.S.R., 1950), appendix, table 9, pp. 460-61; P. I. Liashchenko, *History of the National Economy of Russia to the 1917 Revolution* (New York, 1949), p. 422.

[16] D. D. Cunningham, *The Industrial Revolution* (Cambridge, 1942), pp. 626-27; Clapham, *Economic History of Modern Britain*, vol. II, pp. 28-29, 143; Victor S. Clark, *History of Manufactures in the United States* (New York, 1929), vol. I, p. 403.

back to as early as the 1830's and which became a permanent feature
was the concentration of production and hence of mechanization. It
was not unusual for the larger cotton spinning plants in Russia to exceed in size not only those of the United States, but of England as
well. A mill with over 20,000 spindles was regarded as "gigantic" in
the United States in 1830. During the same decade, as we have seen,
several such large-scale factories were built in St. Petersburg, some
exceeding 40,000 spindles. In 1860, the largest cotton spinning plant
in Philadelphia, which at that time was considered the foremost textile
manufacturing city in the United States, had 27,000 spindles, while
the city and its suburbs claimed 400,000. In 1858, the four largest
factories in St. Petersburg had a quantity of spindles equal to the total
for all of the Philadelphia area and the Neva factory alone operated
160,000.[17]

The foregoing materials suggest at least two general conclusions.
First, that by the middle of the nineteenth century, the production and
use of machinery and chemicals to promote the industrial growth of
Russia was no more than beginning to develop momentum. Rapid
and massive technological development was at best only in sight on
the horizon, and in agriculture, that horizon was not even in sight and
would not be until the next century. Russia's machine industry was
in an infant stage compared to what it would become even before the
collapse of tsarism or compared to the mechanical progress of the
United States by 1860. The chemical industry was even more retarded, and remained in the backward state that was to grieve Mendeleev a generation later. Russian heavy industry and most light industry remained as if fixed in backwardness. Traditional ways dominated the scene. The horse, the sail, the hand loom, the water wheel,
and the human barge hauler were the rule, and the intrusion of the
new machines and processes were more often than not the work of
foreigners come to Russia or, even more frequently, imported products of factories and laboratories in Europe and America.

A second conclusion which may be drawn from the statistics of
early nineteenth-century technology both in Russia and in other countries is that, despite its backwardness, the empire of the tsars was far
removed from a primitive stage of the development and the application of machinery and chemistry in the world environment of the
early industrial revolution. Russia was not significantly behind England or the United States by 1860 in the application of steam power
to certain key industries and, in fact, had profited from several decades
of American and English experimentation. By the same year, Russia
was a major world producer of cotton cloth, and was not more than

[17] Clark, *Manufactures in the United States*, pp. 547, 559; Sherer, "Khlopchatobumazhnaia promyshlennost," p. 462.

twenty-five years behind England in the mechanization of this major area of early industrialization. The heavy concentration of both private and state enterprise in Russia, beginning in the second quarter of the nineteenth century, resulted in the creation of some of the world's largest, most productive, and most modernized individual factory units. By the mid-nineteenth century, Russian-born mechanics were building and producing machinery, the quantity of which at least equaled, and sometimes surpassed the volume of machines imported. The level of research and teaching of applied chemistry in the main universities was high by this time. Problems of climate, distance, and training would inhibit the Russian chemical industry for a long time, but all the essential industrial chemicals were being produced and consumed in limited quantities before 1860.

The statistical picture of Russian industrial technology in the early nineteenth century is thus one which combines many elements of backwardness with some clear signs of development. The explanation for both of these contrasting elements, of course, must be sought in a number of complex factors, some of which elude the quantitative measures of machine production and applied technology. Russian scholars of the 1860's had already found the answers to some of these larger questions: in 1862, Professor A. Ershov of Moscow University, in the report to the Minister of Finances on the progress of machine factories in Russia cited at the beginning of this chapter, gave a comprehensive and enlightening review of the strengths, weaknesses, and needs of machine construction in the Russian empire at that time. Ershov saw the basic economic problem of the Russian machine industry in foreign competition and the high cost of coal and iron. This applied whether these materials were obtained in Russia, where scattered resources made prices prohibitive, or whether they were imported, still at high prices. Such a situation, combined with the problem of the relatively low degree of specialization in Russian industry, made Russian manufactured machinery expensive. It could not compete with European machinery, but European machinery, on the other hand, was not always readily adaptable to Russian conditions. Beyond these problems of resources and trade, Ershov saw great obstacles to the development of a Russian machine technology in the realm of management and labor. There were all the damaging effects of the legacy of serfdom, the lack of technical training, insufficient cadres of craftsmen, and drunkenness. Russian plants were poorly managed and the larger factories were too few in number to provide training ground for enough skilled workers. The Russian workman had far too many holidays to permit competition with the laborers of Protestant countries in Europe.[18]

[18] Ershov, "Mashinostroitel'nye zavedeniia v Rossii," pp. 85-87.

Inventions

Russia was capable of producing notable inventors in the eighteenth century—Polzunov and Kulibin, among others.[19] However, no contribution was made to the development of Russian technology at that time, because nothing was done to exploit their inventions, either commercially or militarily. Short-lived efforts and experiments were quickly forgotten, and the records and models were buried in the archives for a century. Similarly, in the early nineteenth century, with a higher educational level, increased state support, and greater contact with world scientific community, Russian inventors made important contributions. Again, however, with rare exceptions, no significant practical application of their work followed, and although Russians profited from European and American experience, news of Russian inventions almost never reached other countries. Thus, it came to be assumed that Russia played no role in the history of inventions.

In the last years of the Stalin period, a group of books, monographs, and pamphlets was published on the history of Russian inventions in tsarist times which asserted, not only the progressiveness of Russian technology in the eighteenth and nineteenth centuries, but also sometimes made extravagant claims that the Russians were the first to build many important modern inventions.[20] These claims were not just a bizarre expression of Stalinist nationalism. Monographs revealed material long obscured in archives and voiced legitimate resentment on the part of Soviet historians of Russian science and technology over the indifference to their findings in Western histories.[21] In post-Stalin times, Soviet historians have continued to assert, although more modestly, Russia's role in the history of technology and inventions in the eighteenth and nineteenth centuries. A. A. Zvorykin, in a recent article, had this to say:

> In spite of social and economic conditions which were unfavorable for her development in the eighteenth and nineteenth centuries (serfdom and its vestiges, which retarded scientific progress), Rus-

---

[19] See Chapter 1.

[20] See V. V. Danilevskii, *Russkaia tekhnika*; A. V. Iarotskii, *Elektromagnitnii telegraf—velikoe russkoe izobretenie* (Moscow, 1953); V. S. Virginskii, *Russkie izobretateli Cherepanovy—sozdateli pervoi parovoi rel'sovoi dorogi v Rossii* (Moscow, 1953); V. P. Nikitin, *Vedushchaia rol otechestvennoi nauki i tekhniki v razvitii elektricheskoi svarki metallov* (Moscow, 1953); G. I. Bolovin, *Vklad otechestvennykh uchenykh v sozdanie provodnoi sviazi* (Moscow, 1961); N. Ia. Konfederatov, *Vydaiushchaiasia rol russkikh uchenykh v razvitii elektrotekhniki* (Moscow, 1954), and *Universal'nii parovoi dvigatel—velikoe russkoe izobretenie* (Moscow, 1951); and A. G. Arenberg, *A. S. Popov, izobretatel radio* (Moscow, 1951), among others.

[21] See Virginskii, *Tvortsy novoi tekhniki*, introduction to the first edition; C. E. Black, "Mechanical Technology in Russia Before World War I," paper delivered at the American Historical Association Meetings, December 1961 (the author has kindly given me a copy).

sia advanced and she had, similar to other countries, illustrious engineers, scientists, and inventors, whose works have contributed to the scientific and technical development of humanity.[22]

During the early nineteenth century, Russian inventions were stimulated basically in three ways. First, following the eighteenth-century tradition in connection with Russian industry, the Urals continued to provide new inventions, although the Moscow and St. Petersburg textile and machine industries also stimulated the development of new machines and processes. Military needs also provoked the development of new weapons, particularly in the periods of the Napoleonic and Crimean wars. Finally, the Academy of Sciences conducted research which resulted in more sophisticated inventions which paralleled developments in Europe and America at the same time. The Russian government supported much of this work, at least in the initial stages. The inventors were usually academicians, professors, or military and civil engineers and mechanics in the state's employ and service.

A *ukaz* of 1801 provided for medals and cash awards for new inventions. The first Russian patent law came in 1812, but was extremely limited. A patent lasted for only ten years, after which a new invention could be exploited by anyone. The fee for such a patent was high: 1,500 rubles. Partly as a result of this law, only thirty-six patents for inventions were granted during the entire reign of Alexander I. The law was revised in 1833.[23]

In a smaller way, the state fostered new inventions at the industrial complex which it directly owned and operated in Aleksandrovsk, a suburb of St. Petersburg. Here, by the 1840's, were located one of the largest cotton spinning factories in the Russian empire, an iron foundry, machine shops, and one of the most important early locomotive works in Europe.[24] Not only were textile and railroad machinery developed at the Aleksandrovsk plants, but model equipment was demonstrated, machinists from many parts of the empire were trained, and metal products, ranging in sophistication from bolts to locomotive roundtables and parts of iron bridges, were produced.[25]

The money which the Russian government invested in its Aleksandrovsk plants financed inventions designed almost exclusively for industrial and commercial uses. It was willing to spend much more money supporting the plans and projects of inventors of military weapons (submarines, balloons, explosives, etc.) although reluctant

[22] A. A. Zvorykine, "Remarques sur l'histoire des inventions et de la pensée scientifique et technique russes des xviiie et xixe siècles," *Contributions à l'histoire russe, Cahiers d'histoire mondiale*, special issue (1958).

[23] L. N. Nisselovich, *Istoriia zavodsko-fabrichnogo zakonodatel'stva Rossiiskoi Imperii* (St. Petersburg, 1884), vol. I, part 2, pp. 30, 99; N. I. Falkovskii, *Moskva v istorii tekhniki* (Moscow, 1950), p. 451.

[24] For details, see Chapter 13.

[25] B. F. Brandt, *Inostrannye kapitaly v Rossii* (St. Petersburg, 1899), p. 17.

to invest in the development of these weapons after the initial stages of research—in many cases just after the first working models had been built. The one exception was gunpowder rockets. Designed by the talented military engineer and pioneer in this field, General A. D. Zasiadko, rockets were manufactured in substantial quantities at state arsenals and used effectively as early as the Russo-Turkish War of 1828-1829.[26]

More typical is the history of projects and working models of submarines during the reign of Nicholas I. Russia's first submarine was built in 1835 by Adjutant General K. A. Shilder, a trained military engineer, who was well known in Russia and Europe for his work with explosive mines.[27] Although he started on his own, the Russian government helped Shilder to complete his submarine, with a grant of 13,448 rubles. Later, he was again aided in the building of a second undersea warship. Shilder's submarines were small craft, powered by four large wheel-operated cars. They could stay away from a pontoon base for seventy-two hours and had crews of eight men. They were armed with underwater rockets with a range of 300 feet, and a long, bowsprit harpoon cannon, to which a powder mine wired to a detonation battery inside the submarine was attached. When the harpoon mine was pushed into the hull of a ship below the water level, the Shilder submarine would withdraw to a safe distance and the mine would be detonated by an electric charge. This invention, advanced and sophisticated for its time, was deprived of funds after the second model was built in 1838, and the experiments were forgotten.[28] A third Russian submarine, built at the end of the Crimean War by a German inventor, Wilhelm Bauer, came to nothing, as did several projects for undersea craft submitted by Russians during that period.[29]

The Urals industrial complex continued to stimulate inventive efforts on the part of craftsmen and engineers employed in the metallurgical factories, as had been the case in the eighteenth century. The inventors were generally better trained after 1800, having the advantage of new and enlarged technical schools. However, the craftsman-inventor, whose training and experience was confined to the Urals, was still in evidence. Just as many of the military inventions were not developed, many of the industrial innovations in machinery and various kinds of processing were not used. Nevertheless, as private industry developed in the Moscow-St. Petersburg region as well as in parts of the Urals, the value of some inventions was im-

[26] Virginskii, *Tvortsy novoi tekhniki*, pp. 349-55.
[27] Karl Marx, for example, wrote of him. See G. M. Trusov, *Podvodnye lodki v russkom i sovetskom flote* (Leningrad, 1963), p. 39.
[28] Trusov, *Podvodnye lodki*, pp. 38-44.
[29] Trusov, *Podvodnye lodki*, pp. 48, 54-57.

mediately grasped, and they were exploited, sometimes with significant results.

The Russian steel industry remained technically in a backward and experimental stage. Although two accomplished engineers, P. O. Anosov and P. M. Obukhov, developed new processes for making high-grade steel in quantity, their experiments were very largely ignored in the 1840's and 1850's. Only in the following decade did Obukhov establish the first steel plant in St. Petersburg that bore his name.[30] A quarter of a century earlier, two Russian craftsmen, born and trained exclusively in the Urals, fathered important inventions which influenced the course of at least one major industry. In 1837, Ignatii Safonov invented one of the world's earliest water turbines. This machine, which provided double the power of the largest of the existing water wheels with the same consumption of water, was soon being used in three large plants in the Urals. As we have seen in an earlier chapter, Lev Brunitsyn's discovery of a new process for extracting gold from auriferous sand in 1814 resulted a few years later in a boom for the Russian gold industry.[31] In the Moscow industrial region, Jacquard looms and spinning jennies imported from Europe were far superior to Russian-made textile machinery operated during the early nineteenth century, although mechanics employed in several Russian factories in Moscow and St. Petersburg attempted to make improved versions of the foreign models.[32]

Some of the most important and sophisticated inventions to come out of Russia during the early nineteenth century originated in the Academy of Sciences. The Academy, by this time one of the important scientific centers of the world and attuned to the newest areas of research, developed at a very early date an interest in electricity. Experimentation in this field may be considered the Academy's most important contribution to technology during this period. As was the case in other areas of Russian technology, particularly during the reign of Nicholas I, the government's interest did not match that of the inventors. Although some research was encouraged and subsidized, no funds were made available for the practical application of new inventions on any significant scale. Little publicity leaked out to Europe and America, the models were stored away in exhibit cases, and the experiments were soon forgotten.

Research, experimentation, and invention in the field of electricity was the work of four Russian academicians during the early nineteenth century: V. V. Petrov (1761-1834), E. K. Lenz (1804-1865),

[30] Danilevskii, *Russkaia tekhnika*, pp. 95-96, 102-04; Zvorykine, "Histoire des inventions Russes," p. 196.

[31] On the gold industry, see my Chapter 2; on Safonov, Danilevskii, *Russkaia tekhnika*, pp. 300-02.

[32] Tikhonov, "Ofitsial'nye zhurnaly," p. 154.

P. L. Schilling (1786-1837), and B. S. Jacobi (1801-1874). Only one of these men, Petrov, was a native Russian. Lenz and Schilling were Baltic Germans, the sons of nobles and Russian state servants educated at German-influenced schools such as Dorpat or in universities in the Germanies proper. Jacobi was the son of a Prussian banker, who studied at Berlin and Göttingen universities. The bulk of the research and teaching of these men, of course, was done in Russia, and it was at the Academy of Sciences in St. Petersburg that their most important work was accomplished.

V. V. Petrov's experiments with electricity and illumination at the beginning of the nineteenth century would have been of the utmost significance for the history of technology had they been known outside of Russia, and had there been proper understanding of his discoveries within Russia as well as adequate financial support for their development. Petrov was unsuccessful in his attempts to gain such official support, and his published findings, as far as Europeans and Americans were concerned, remained concealed within the Russian language (he was the first academician to write exclusively in Russian).[33] Petrov himself, although born in provincial Russia, and educated in Kharkov and St. Petersburg, but not abroad, could read French, German, English, and Latin.[34] Influenced by the work of Volta, he built a large battery only a few years after the Italian's discoveries. The battery was first operated in St. Petersburg in 1802. From his experiments with this and improved batteries, Petrov produced electric arcs and studied the potential of electricity for illumination and metallurgy.[35]

The theoretical foundations for electric machinery were built by the research of E. K. Lenz in the early 1830's. Lenz was a member of the world community of scientists in the fullest sense of the word, complementing the work of Faraday in England and actually collaborating with other noted English scientists. As a physicist, his discoveries had a profound influence on later basic research in Europe. Next to Mendeleev, he is the Russian scientist of the nineteenth century best known in the West.[36]

During the 1830's, Schilling and particularly Jacobi were building electrical machinery at the Academy of Sciences. Schilling has been

[33] Vucinich, *Science in Russian Culture*, p. 206.

[34] Danilevskii, *Russkaia tekhnika*, p. 328.

[35] On Petrov, see V. P. Nikitin, *Vedushchaia rol otechestvennoi nauki i tekhniki v razvitii elektricheskoi svarki metallov*; S. I. Vavilov, *Akademik V. V. Petrov 1761-1834* (Moscow-Leningrad, 1940), especially pp. 191-201; and V. S. Virginskii, *Tvortsy novoi tekhniki*, pp. 166-81.

[36] There is a biography in English written prior to the development of Russian studies in this country: Wilbur Stine, *The Contributions of H. F. E. Lenz to Electromagnetism* (Philadelphia, 1923); for a brief Russian account of the significance of Lenz's work in technology, see I. Ia. Konfederatov, *Vydaiushchaiasia rol russkikh uchenykh v razvitii elektrotekhniki*, pp. 9-10.

recognized, at least in Russia, in both tsarist and Soviet times, as the inventor of the electric telegraph. His claim would appear to be stronger than that of Samuel Morse or of Cooke and Wheatstone. Schilling was a scientist and inventor, a Baltic Baron educated in Germany, who had been working with electromagnetism and telegraph devices in collaboration with European scientists since the Napoleonic period. His electric telegraph was first publicly demonstrated in 1833, a decade before that of Morse.[37] In contrast, Morse was an artist and a more or less amateur inventor whose telegraph was built and developed with the help of trained American scientists. Both inventors devised a code. The difference and significance of the two inventions can be seen in the respective development and practical application. Morse received relatively generous support from Congress at the start, and private business soon after fully appreciated the commercial possibilities of his invention. Schilling's telegraph was demonstrated in Germany, and almost immediately inspired and was developed by two English experimenters, William Cooke and Charles Wheatstone. Lines were soon put down in many parts of England. In Russia, government support was given to Schilling to build a line from St. Petersburg to Kronstadt, a project which ended upon his death the following year. A few experimental lines were built around the Russian capital in the 1840's, but lack of development of the invention as compared to its development in the United States ended in the irony of the Russian government's decision to use the Morse telegraph for the first big line which paralleled the St. Petersburg-Moscow railway.

Academician B. S. Jacobi carried on not only the work of Schilling on the telegraph, but also that of Lenz in the application of electric power to machinery. Jacobi's first machine, an electromagnetic engine producing continuous circular motion, was built in 1834. In 1838, with support from the Russian government, he demonstrated an electric powered boat—which he called an "elektroboat"—on the Neva River. Jacobi's engine used 320 galvanic batteries which produced three-fourths of one horsepower. He later built a model for an electric locomotive. His inventions received publicity in Russia and Europe, and the potential of the electric engine, particularly for military uses,

---

[37] Nicholas I dispatched the first message on the new Russian telegraph line, which connected the Winter Palace with a nearby government building—not the dramatic and pompous, "What hath God wrought!" of Morse, but the much more casual (perhaps presaging the lack of seriousness with which the Russian government would estimate the new invention), "Je suis charmé d'avoir fait ma visite à M. Schilling." See the article on Schilling in the *Russkii biograficheskii slovar*; other biographical information in Virginskii, *Tvortsy novoi tekhniki*, pp. 301-02; Charles Singer et al., eds., *A History of Technology* (Oxford, 1954), vol. IV, pp. 655-60; and A. V. Iarotskii, *Elektromagnitnii telegraf, velikoe russkoe izobretenie* (Moscow, 1953).

was voiced. However, soon after, the Russian government, as in other instances, balked at the expense of developing Jacobi's invention, dismissing the existing machine as impractical.[38]

In the late 1830's, at about the time of the electrical experiments of Schilling and Jacobi, the Slavophil poet and writer, Prince V. F. Odoevskii, imagined the technological future of Russia. He set down his dreams in a novel-fantasy, *The Year 4338*. Odoevskii's work belongs in part to the genre of utopias, but it can also be considered a primitive forerunner of Russian science fiction.[39] His Russia of the forty-fourth century has surpassed the entire world in the development and application of science. With the Western nations in decline in this Slavophile vision, only China approaches and at the same time emulates the Russians. Electric trains speed through huge tunnels cut under the Himalayan mountains and the Caspian Sea, and electric airships traverse the Russian atmosphere, where the Russian winter has been subdued by a system of mammoth air conditioners. The telegraph, electric light, and camera are items of everyday life. Horticulturists produce a tree bearing dates, peaches, and cherries. The populace is amused by exotic musical instruments which use water flowing softly over crystal balls. People are tranquillized by special gases. Scientists, of course, have a strong position in the government. Although Halley's comet threatens to destroy the earth in the following year, no one worries, because Russia's scientists have devised guided missiles to intercept it.

Russian technology was far removed from Odoevskii's dream at the time that he wrote. In fact, there was hardly enough technological advance to permit such a utopia even to be imagined. In technology, as in other areas of modernization in Russia in the middle of the nineteenth century, there was little more than a beginning. However, it would be difficult to understand Russia's later technological development and the way in which she developed without consideration of these foundations.

[38] On Jacobi, Virginskii, *Tvortsy novoi tekhniki*, pp. 298-317; *Istoriia Akademii Nauk S.S.S.R. 1803-1917* (Moscow-Leningrad, 1964), vol. II, pp. 68-77.
[39] V. F. Odoevskii, *4338-i god, fantasticheskii roman* (Moscow, 1926).

Conclusion

How does the prereform era fit into the history of the industrialization and economic growth of Russia? One answer comes from contemporary Russia. Many Soviet historians and economists have attempted to move the beginning of the Russian "industrial revolution" (*promyshlennii perevorot*) back to 1830, not, however, without qualifications or dissent. This group includes S. G. Strumilin, V. K. Iatsunskii, and the late M. F. Zlotnikov, who were among the more important scholars involved in a lengthy debate on this subject after World War II. The thesis, advanced by one Russian historian in 1950, that the industrial revolution in Russia began at the end of the eighteenth century, was given sober consideration.[1] Such contentions were not new or uniquely Soviet: Tarle had been able to publish essentially the same ideas in the last years of the old regime.[2] It may be asked by the uninitiated: how can scholars talk seriously about an industrial revolution beginning in Russia a century or more before the first five-year plan? The answer, of course, is to be found in the definition of terms more than in historical facts. However, it should be pointed out that Soviet historians have unearthed from their archives a valuable fund of materials to prove their point, which makes study of this development in their historiography extremely useful.

The adequacy of the term "industrial revolution"—even as it applies to economic developments in England in modern times—has been questioned by many scholars. Arnold Toynbee's classic definition of the industrial revolution in England,[3] with its neat succession of inventions, changes in population and agriculture, the growth of factories, and the landmarks in economic thought from 1760 to 1830, has inspired a generation of history textbooks, but seems dated today. Moreover, the term industrial revolution is not always clearly distinguished from the broader idea of economic modernization. By 1830, England may be said to have completed her first industrial revolution, but she was not economically modernized before at least another half century had passed. Even today, Soviet Russia has not completely modernized economically in several important respects;

---

[1] B. Iakovlev, "Vozniknovenie i etapy razvitiia kapitalisticheskogo uklada v Rossii," *Voprosy istorii* (1950), no. 9, pp. 91-104. On the industrialization debate, see K. A. Pazhitnov, "K voprosu o promyshlennom perevorote v Rossii," *Voprosy istorii* (1952), no. 5, pp. 68-76; S. G. Strumilin, "Promyshlennii perevorot v Rossii (1830-1860 gg.)," *Ocherki ekonomicheskoi istorii Rossii* (Moscow, 1960), pp. 445-57; V. K. Yatsunsky, "Promyshlenii perevorot v Rossii," *Voprosy istorii* (1952), no. 12, pp. 48-70; and M. F. Zlotnikov, "Ot manufaktury k fabrike," *Voprosy istorii* (1946), nos. 11-12, pp. 31-48.

[2] Ye. Tarle, "Byla li Ekaterinskaya Rossia ekonomichesku otstaloiu starnoiu?," *Sochineniia*, vol. IV (Moscow, 1958), pp. 441-68.

[3] Arnold Toynbee, *The Industrial Revolution* (Boston, 1956). The work was first published in 1884.

and pockets of backwardness are etched everywhere in the economic surface of the developed world. Nevertheless, one can choose to define "industrial revolution," not as a change in the society as a whole,[4] but as a change within industry alone—the appearance of machinery, factories, wage workers, etc.—in an economy which remains overwhelmingly agricultural. This is the definition that most Soviet historians tend to use. It permits them to see the threshold of an industrial revolution at the beginning of the reign of Nicholas I, a time when Russia was sunk in economic backwardness by any modern standards.

Recently, economists (particularly in the United States) have attempted to broaden the concept of an industrial revolution, rather than to narrow or reject it. Maintaining the essential idea of accelerated and comprehensive economic growth, they have used such terms as "takeoff," "spurt," "big push," or "critical minimum effort" to embrace a much broader social and economic process than that which nineteenth-century writers viewed as an industrial revolution. One need not accept the inevitability and universality of such dynamic economic happenings to posit, as most scholars in the West have done, that extensive and rapid industrialization cannot be observed in Russia prior to the 1880's, or, at the furthest limit, the last third of the nineteenth century.[5] Prior to this, Russia was essentially a backward, agricultural country.

At the same time, an accumulation of processes and pressures had brought Russia to the beginnings of her industrialization. By 1860, she was at the point at which more rapid economic growth was possible and imminent. The preparatory forces were less visible and spectacular than the changes usually associated with an industrial revolution. Some were the continuation or the culmination of related economic processes first set in motion generations or even centuries before; others were new phenomena, small in scope, but more clearly the first signs of the industrial age in Russia. Hence, it would be more appropriate to characterize the early nineteenth century in Russia as a period of foundation and preparation (as well as stagnation), than as one of overt change. Needless to say, this constitutes a most important part of Russian economic history, not only for the submerged contours of growth, but also for the more deeply hidden ones of back-

[4] R. Portal, "The Problem of an Industrial Revolution in Russia in the Nineteenth Century," translated and abridged by Sidney Harcave for his anthology, *Readings in Russian History* (New York, 1962), vol. 2, p. 28. Portal discusses the Soviet industrialization debate at some length at the beginning of his article.

[5] See Portal, "Industrial Revolution"; W. W. Rostow, *The Stages of Economic Growth* (Cambridge, 1960); and Alexander Gershenkron, "The Early Phases of Industrialization in Russia: Afterthoughts and Counterthoughts," W. W. Rostow, ed., *The Economics of Take-off into Sustained Growth* (London, 1964), pp. 151-69.

wardness. Hence, Marx's concept of the original accumulation of capital, rather than the Soviet Marxian formulations of an industrial revolution under serfdom; or W. W. Rostow's postulation of the pre-conditions for the takeoff, rather than his theory of the takeoff would be more useful tools for analyzing such a period. This is not to equate the two concepts, or to accept without serious qualification and amendment the applicability of either to Russia. It is rather to con-sider for their usefulness the two theoretical approaches to Russian economic development in the early nineteenth century most widely current today.

Marx was concerned with explaining how industrial capitalism emerged from sources prior and external to industry. In its most simplified definition, this meant for him the breakdown of an agrarian society from which emerged an industrial labor force, a group of in-dustrial entrepreneurs, and a fund of capital which could be diverted into industry. He focused his analysis on the spectacular economic changes and social dislocations that were apparent, particularly in England and Holland, in the sixteenth and seventeenth centuries: the detachment of the peasants from the land and their reduction to propertyless wage earners and consumers; the vast accumulation of capital by European nations through the acquisition of colonies; the freeing of the merchant class from medieval restrictions and its sub-sequent growth in the flourishing commercial conditions of early modern times; and the emergence of powerful nation states, whose taxing powers and borrowing proclivities created large national debts, piled up reserves of interest for investment, and facilitated the de-velopment of financial institutions.[6]

Marx's concept of the original accumulation of capital, like Toyn-bee's exposition of the industrial revolution becomes more flexible or more rigid, depending on the use to which it is put. His analysis was oriented toward the early modern history of Western Europe. It emphasized factors, which, although relevant to the early economic growth of Russia at a later time, were of lesser significance there, or played a very different role than in Europe. Soviet historians have tended to apply Marx's formulations rather dogmatically to the Rus-sian situation, without any attempt to seriously revise or elaborate upon the original ideas. The concept becomes unwieldy and stretched. In Russia, proletarianization of the peasants began even under the system of serfdom, and proceeded on a scale and at a tempo quite different from the European experience. These changes were still oc-curring in the twentieth century. Colonialism was never an important factor in the process of capital formation, although it did operate in a

---

[6] A recent edition of the essential selections from Part VIII of *Capital* ("The So-called Original Accumulation") can be found in Otto Feinstein, ed., *Two Worlds of Change* (New York, 1964), pp. 105-62.

limited way during the nineteenth century in Russia's relations with the Ukraine and Central Asia. Commercial capital was diverted into industry in the early nineteenth century, as it was previously in Europe, but hardly on the same scale. The emergence of the industrial entrepreneur during the same period was a complex social, economic, and cultural process, unique in many ways when compared to earlier developments in Europe. Interest on the state debt played a much less significant role in capital accumulation. Private and state banking and other credit institutions to facilitate investment were poorly developed in the prereform period and emerged at a later time, almost simultaneously with the industrial revolution, rather than before it. Thus, the concept of the original accumulation of capital, when applied to Russia, functions awkwardly. Moreover, it can ignore as much as it distorts, in terms of the manifold creative and negative functions of Russia's already highly developed autocratic state, the impact of war and power politics, the role of foreign capital and enterprise, the introduction and modernization of transportation facilities, and the role of technology in economic growth. To Marx must go the credit for being one of the first to develop in any comprehensive way the concept of preconditions and preparation for industrialization. He dealt with fundamental problems of capital formation, enterprise, and labor, which must be brought into any consideration of the origins of industry. However, to be usable as a tool for the analysis particularly of non-Western societies in the past century, his insights must be revised and brought up to date, something which has not been done in the field of Russian studies.[7]

Rostow's focus is more purely economic than that of Marx, who was concerned basically with the problems of social change and the exploitation of the lower classes of Europe and the colonial peoples. The concept of the preconditions for the takeoff is also more immediately concerned with the setting and causes for rapid economic growth than the Marxian explanation of the foundations of the capitalist system. Nevertheless, Rostow, like Marx, does take into account the appearance of the entrepreneur, the growth of commerce, colonialism, the development of financial institutions, and the mobilization of capital for investment. However, where Marx emphasizes the social aspects of agriculture in the proletarianization of the peasantry, Rostow focuses on the agricultural economy and the growth of food production to feed cities and to export. The most important innovation in Rostow's analysis of the preconditions for the takeoff, and his main concern, is his exploration of the role of the state. This is a nat-

---

[7] For a recent discussion of Soviet and European uses of the concept of the original accumulation of capital, see Alexander Gershenkron, "Rosario Romeo and the Original Accumulation of Capital," *Economic Backwardness in Historical Perspective* (New York, 1962), pp. 90-118.

ural result of Rostow's incorporation of non-Western societies in his study. Marx was concerned with the nations of Western Europe where capitalism emerged in early modern times; Rostow looks to Russia and Japan, where the government played an important role in economic development in the nineteenth and twentieth centuries. Thus, the period of the preconditions for the takeoff in the Rostovian analysis emphasizes the creation of a strong national state, the role of nationalism and war in the stimulation of industrialization programs, the emergence of political leadership dedicated to modernization, taxation, public education, the transfer of rent consumed unproductively by the traditional landowning class to the state for industrial investment (which implies state-sponsored agrarian reforms), and finally, the assumption by the state of the burden of building railroads, canals, and other forms of costly "social overhead capital."[8]

Rostow's concept of the preconditions for rapid and sustained economic growth has been subject to much criticism. I will not need to comment on this criticism at any length here. It will suffice to summarize in a general way some of the most significant limitations of his analysis as it applies to Russia in the nineteenth century. These limitations have been underscored by several scholars in recent years. First, it has been argued that Rostow fails to take into account the contrasts in various societies in the preindustrial period and the sometimes radically different weights of the forces of progress and backwardness (Gershenkron).[9] Along the same lines, it has been suggested that an analysis such as Rostow's tends to equate different periods of history in different areas, when and where many of the preconditions for industrialization were dissimilar (Kuznets).[10] Third, it has been asserted that the Rostovian schema is too narrowly economic, and that it fails to take into account adequately the influence of political tradition (Black).[11] Finally, Rostow has been charged with establishing as preconditions for rapid economic growth developments which in many societies take place simultaneously with this growth (Hagen).[12]

Keeping these criticisms in mind, since they are very pertinent to Russian economic development, one must nevertheless recognize Rostow's concept of the preconditions for the takeoff as fundamentally sound and useful when applied to Russia. Most of the facts which have been presented in this book would validate the Rostovian

[8] W. W. Rostow, *The Stages of Economic Growth*, pp. 6-7, 17-31, 65-66, 98.
[9] Gershenkron, "The Early Phases of Industrialization in Russia."
[10] Simon Kuznets, "Underdeveloped Countries and the Preindustrial Phase in Advanced Countries," *Two Worlds of Change*, pp. 1-21.
[11] C. E. Black, *The Dynamics of Modernization* (New York, 1966), p. 191.
[12] Everett E. Hagen, *On the Theory of Social Change* (Homewood, Illinois, 1962), pp. 517-19.

scheme. However, they can also serve to qualify and amend it, as well as to fill in a number of details.

The idea of economic progress began to emerge among the ruling elite of Russia during the early nineteenth century, particularly among high ranking officials like Admiral Mordvinov and Count N. P. Rumiantsev, administrators who were immediately concerned with economic policy. However the traditionalist view tended to prevail in state circles during the reigns of Alexander I and particularly of Nicholas I, and state policy aimed at developing industry was fragmentary and experimental. Nationalism tended to be associated as much with tradition as with progress. The Crimean War placed a tremendous burden on the Russian state, and the necessity and urgency for modernization was brought home to those who ruled Russia, as is clear from the Miliutin and Hagemeister memoranda written during the war years.

Education for a modern society, both technical and primary, saw its beginnings in the reign of Alexander I. Technical research was conducted in the universities and the Academy of Sciences, engineering schools and technological institutes were founded, and a public education system was set up. Russian scientists were part of the European scientific community. An intellectual foundation for technology was built, but no material basis for the development of this technology was provided, either by the state or through the commercial market. Russia remained dependent on foreign engineers and equipment for the limited application of technology to industry and war that occurred during the prereform era.

The industrial entrepreneur made his appearance in Russia during the early nineteenth century. Many of the biggest industrial firms which played an important role in the industrial revolution of the late tsarist period can be traced to the period from 1820 to 1860. The Russian capitalist was recruited not so much from the ranks of the commercial middle class as from the servile peasantry and outcast religious groups. This was testimony both to the persistence of the traditional agrarian society and its decay. Russia's industrial middle class was small compared to Western countries, and it did not supersede the old land-based elite in social and political authority until much later, when Russia was in the midst of her takeoff. Although the extent of private capital was small, the ability of the new Russian entrepreneurial groups to mobilize this capital through communal property and cooperation, as in the case of the Old Believers, was great. Foreign enterprise and investment appeared in Russia during the early nineteenth century, but did not assume major proportions until Russia's industrial takeoff at the end of the tsarist period.

Financial institutions to facilitate capital accumulation and investment were poorly developed in prereform Russia. There was some development of insurance, but private and state banking did not expand in any significant way until the late nineteenth century. Stock companies began to develop in the 1830's, but had to await the more favorable financial and legal climate of the emancipation era to expand in appreciable numbers and resources.

The scope of Russia's domestic and foreign trade widened during the early nineteenth century. A European market for Russian wheat began to grow, as did a limited Russian, Ukrainian, and Asian market for Russian textiles and some other industrial goods. Along with the growth of domestic markets came a change in their traditional functions. Permanent urban markets, which could better service a growing commerce and industry, began to replace the fairs. Direct retail outlets for industrial enterprises invaded the domain of the old itinerant merchants.

Modern industrial enterprises appeared in Russia during the early nineteenth century, but on a much larger scale than Rostow would attribute to them in the preconditional period. This was particularly true of Russia's cotton industry. By 1860, Russia ranked sixth in the world in the spinning of cotton, and possessed a highly concentrated, mechanized, capitalistic form of this industry. Factors that need to be taken into account in explaining this rapid growth in certain industries in a period supposedly preliminary to this kind of development are the lateness of Russia's industrialization, which permitted her to utilize the industrial technology and the cheaper semimanufactured products of the more advanced countries of the West, such as England. England's industrial revolution affected Russia's. However, the rapid growth of Russia's cotton industry during the second third of the nineteenth century, as well as some other areas of textile manufacture, was not repeated in her heavy industries, which remained either stagnant or undeveloped. Accelerated growth of some of these industries did not take place until the late nineteenth century, and some, like the chemical industry, remained backward even during Russia's industrial revolution.

A small machine industry had to be built in Russia during the early nineteenth century, not only to meet the needs of existing factories, but also to service the first railroads. The prereform era, going back to the turn of the century, witnessed the beginnings of the buildup of social overhead capital in Russia. The major canal systems of European Russia were built in the period extending from the reign of Paul I to that of Alexander II. Road and highway construction was much less important. The railroad age in Russia began in the 1840's, with the construction of the first major line, the St. Petersburg-Moscow railroad. The state assumed the major role in financing and organizing these costly projects, which were viewed as essential to the economic progress and military security of the country. Although this buildup of social overhead capital stimulated the growth of auxiliary industries and technical education in Russia, its success remained dependent on foreign engineering skills, and in the post-reform period, on foreign capital as well.

By 1860, the contours of Russia's economic backwardness as well as the main lines which her economic growth would take were apparent. Russian society remained very largely traditional, and acted as a very powerful brake on industrialization. The landed nobility retained its privileged position and its hold on the income of over half of the peasantry. Its generally conservative approach to social change and economic development pervaded official circles, and its excessively consumptive style of living prevented the diversion of any significant segment of the vast wealth it controlled into productive industrial investment. The institution of serfdom prevented a large-scale mobilization of the peasantry into an industrial labor force and retarded agricultural productivity. There was little urban growth or significant expansion of the small hereditary and seasonal industrial proletariat within the cities. The emancipation of the serfs in 1861, however, did not so much constitute a revolutionary breakdown of the old system as it symbolized fundamental changes in the traditional Russian social order that were developing during the entire nineteenth century. Mobility for millions of peasants had developed under the decaying serf system through the practice of peasant furloughs, cash *obroks*, and voluntary redemptions. After 1861, the commune continued to act as a brake on peasant mobility. The commercialization of Russian agriculture also began before 1861.

As significant as traditional Russian society was in keeping Russia a backward country during the early nineteenth century, it must be considered only one of the factors contributing to this backwardness. As has been pointed out by several scholars, Russia's natural poverty served as a major impediment to her industrialization.[13] Poor climate, a disadvantageous location for participation in world trade, a lack of ports, a dispersal of resources, and Russia's immense size all worked to limit the unification of minerals and fuels necessary for the development of heavy industry, as well as the linkage of granaries with the cities and ports prerequisite for economic growth. The construction of a railroad network in European Russia which could minimize some of these problems was begun in the 1840's but not completed until the 1880's.

The state played a major role, not only in industrializing Russia under the tsarist and Soviet regimes, but also in impeding this indus-

---

[13] Alexander Baykov, "The Economic Development of Russia," B. E. Supple, ed., *The Experience of Economic Growth* (New York, 1963), pp. 413-25; Roger Portal, "La Russie industrielle à la veille de l'emancipation des serfs," *Études d'histoire moderne et contemporaine*, vol. V (1953).

trialization. In Russia, the building of an effective, centralized national and nationalistic state, which Rostow sees as a major feature of the preconditional period and as necessary for the takeoff, was achieved centuries before this in the traditional period. National unity, a large, centralized bureaucracy and army, regimentation of the various classes of society, a strong degree of control of cultural and economic life—all of the factors deemed characteristic of a modern industrializing society—were evident in "feudal" Russia. Such a mobilization of the society, of course, was limited in comparison to the twentieth-century world by the absence of sophisticated communications technology, but a remodeling of the state apparatus and the extension of its powers more completely over the entire nation was performed by Peter the Great and several of the Westernized tsars who followed him. However, this entrenched despotic tradition acted as a detriment to Russian industrialization as well as a determinant of it. During the early nineteenth century, as in later periods, it alternately impaired and stimulated, although it did not halt the development of science and technology. The harsh, militaristic methods of labor exploitation characteristic of the traditional agrarian despotism were found deficient when applied to the running of factories. Overbureaucratization, favoritism, caprice, brutality, corruption, and all the other evils of the system were extended to the new area of economic policy. The capitalist middle class was stunted and oppressed by the bureaucratic regime and very largely excluded from participation in it. The requirements of industrialization were given second priority to the war needs whose fulfillment was demanded by the old school military elite. This tradition continued to determine the bureaucratic, exploitative character of Russia's industrialization after 1860.

The period from 1800 to 1860, thus, can be seen as one of preparation for more rapid industrial growth, with the peculiarities and exceptions to various other theories of economic growth that have been noted. The period from 1860 to 1890 is more difficult to define, since it mixes important elements of the preconditional phase with those of the industrial revolution. However, this later period is a subject for a subsequent volume.

Glossary

APTEKARSKII PRIKAZ. Bureau of Apothecaries, a state agency of Muscovite times.

ARESTANTSKAIA ROTA. A convict detachment, a form of organization for prisoners in imperial Russia.

ARSHIN. A linear measure equal to 28 inches, applied particularly to cloth production in tsarist industrial statistics.

ASSIGNAT (ASIGNATSIONNYI RUBL'). A form of unconvertible paper currency issued by the Russian government during the late eighteenth and early nineteenth centuries.

BARSHCHINA. The labor obligation of the Russian serf.

BERG INSPEKTOR. A state inspector of mines and metallurgical enterprises in tsarist times.

BEZPOPOVTSY. The Priestless faction of the Old Believers who in the early nineteenth century controlled industries, particularly in Moscow.

BIRZHA. A commercial stock exchange, a place for business transactions in tsarist Russia.

BURLAK. A human hauler of barges on Russian rivers.

CHETVERT. A dry measure equal to about six bushels.

DESIATINA. A land measure equal to 2.7 acres.

DOKHOD. A form of tsarist state revenue, largely rents and proceeds from the sale of liquor produced in government distilleries and of precious metals from government mines.

DUKHOVENSTVO. The clergy in Russian official statistics of the nineteenth century.

DVORIANSTVO. The status of nobility in tsarist Russia.

DVOROVYE LIUDI. Landless serfs who worked in the household of the lord before the 1861 emancipation. In the early nineteenth century, some serfs attached to the town houses of the nobility were furloughed for factory work.

FABRIKA. One form of designation for a factory in tsarist statistics.

GIL'DIIA. An administrative and tax classification for Russian merchants and industrialists in tsarist times. During the early nineteenth century, there were three "guilds," each of which paid different registration fees and had commensurate economic privileges.

GORNAIA EKSPEDITSIIA. The Department of Mines, a central administrative agency dating back to the eighteenth century.

GORNYI NACHAL'NIK. A Mining Commander. During the early nineteenth century, usually a military officer given extensive police, judicial, and managerial powers over a given complex of private and state factories.

GORNYI SOVIET. A central board of the tsarist mining administration.

GOROD. A city or larger town.

GOSTINNYI DVOR. A marketplace, an urban commercial center in old Russia in which shops, stalls, and arcades were more or less permanently established in a special structure or location.

IARMARKA. A fair, a large commercial center operating for a short period each year.

INOSTRANNYI GOST'. A foreign merchant. A foreigner doing business in Russia on a semi-permanent basis during the nineteenth century, to whom certain rights of commerce and of Russian citizenship were extended.

ISPRAVNIK. A judicial officer in tsarist state-owned iron mills.

KITAI GOROD. The commercial center of old Moscow, located near the Kremlin.

KREDITNYI BILET. A note of credit, a form of tsarist paper money which succeeded the *assignat* in the 1840's.

KRUGOVAIA PORUKA. Mutual responsibility. For most of the tsarist period, the joint responsibility of groups of peasants and workers for money and labor obligations.

KUPETS (KUPTSY, KUPECHESTVO). A merchant, or, more generally, a businessman belonging to one of the guilds.

LEKAR. An intern or medical assistant with some experience and training who served as a physician in tsarist hospitals.

MANUFAKTUR KORRESPONDENT. An official of the Ministry of Finances during the early nineteenth century who gathered information on Russian industries.

MASTEROVYE LIUDI. Artisans, a category of skilled factory serfs in the state enterprises of the early 1800's.

MESHCHANIN (MESHCHANSTVO). An urban inhabitant of lower class origin in the nineteenth century, not enrolled in the merchants guilds but permitted limited commercial rights and subject to the head tax and to military service. The registered urban lower class collectively, as distinguished from peasants, merchants, and nobles.

MESTECHKO. A small town, larger than a village.

NASTOIATEL'. A prior or superior, the religious head of a community of Priestless Old Believers.

NEPREMENNYI RABOTNIK. A permanent or perpetual worker, a new category of state serf created in 1807 for continuous rather than seasonal work in Uralian metallurgical factories.

OBIAZANNAIA FABRIKA. An obligated factory in the early nineteenth century, a private factory supported and regulated by the state, supplying quotas of goods to the government at fixed prices.

OBROK. The serf obligation in money or kind.

OFENIA. A peddler in nineteenth-century Russia, usually seen in rural areas.

OKHOTNYI RIAD. An open air food market in nineteenth-century Moscow.

OTKUPSHCHIK. A lessee, with particular reference to those individuals during tsarist times who were granted a monopoly for the sale of liquor in certain regions.

OKRUG. A tsarist administrative division used, among other places, in mining regions.

POCHTOVYI TRAKT. A postal road.

PODAT'. A direct tax levied by the tsarist government.

PODMASTER. A journeyman or foreman in nineteenth-century Russian craft organizations.

POLITSMEISTER. A police chief in tsarist mining and metallurgical complexes.

POOD, see PUD.

POPOVTSY. The Priestist faction of the Old Believers who in the early nineteenth century controlled industries in the city of Moscow.

POPUCHITEL'. The curator or business manager of a community of Priestless Old Believers.

POSAD. A small town, usually commercial or suburban, inhabited by members of the urban lower and middle classes as classified in tsarist times.

POSHLINA. A duty levied by the tsarist government on imported goods as well as certain domestic products.

POTOMSTVENNYI POTOCHNYI GRAZHDANIN. Hereditary Honorable Citizen. A title created in the early nineteenth century and granted to merchants for service or distinction, also to military and civil servants not promoted to hereditary or personal nobility.

PRIKAZ OBSHCHESTVENNAGO PRIZRENIIA. An Office of Public Charity, a government agency which aided the poor in various ways in imperial Russia.

PRIPISNOI. A special category of registered or assigned peasants during the eighteenth century, usually those residing in villages in the vicinity of metallurgical factories who were obliged to perform winter work in these factories.

PUD. A weight measure equal to about 36 pounds avoirdupois or 40 Russian pounds.

PROMYSHLENNIK. An entrepreneur.

RABOTNYE LIUDI. Unskilled factory serfs in Russian state enterprises of the early nineteenth century.

RAZNOCHINETS. Members of the urban lower and middle classes in the prereform period, although not registered in any of the existing administrative groups. A petty civil servant, a commoner, a person not of noble origin.

RAZNOSHCHIK. A peddler or hawker, usually in nineteenth-century Russian cities and towns, a petty retailer of goods in the streets.

RAZRIAD. A subdivision within a particular class in the tsarist administrative order, such as one of the rankings within the category of *meshchanstvo*.

REMESLENNIK. A craftsman.

RIAD. A stall or small shop where goods were sold, or a row of similar structures offering the same products within a larger marketplace.

SHOSSEINAIA DOROGA. A highway.

SLOBODA. A suburb, a village located on the outskirts of a city. In the nineteenth century, an industrial suburb.

SLUZHASHCHIE. Government employees, particularly clerks.

SOSLOVIE. People of the same occupation, rights, and status, such as members of the Russian nobility, or of craft organizations.

TORGUIUSHCHII KREST'IANIN (TORGUIUSHCHII MESHCHANIN). Members of the lower rural and urban classes permitted limited commercial rights during the prereform era.

TSEKH. An association of craftsmen or tradesmen in tsarist times.

UCHENIK. An apprentice.

UCHETNYI KONTOR. A discount office, a branch of the State Assignat Bank during the early 1800's.

UDEL'NYI. Property and peasants belonging exclusively to the imperial family in the time of serfdom. In Moscow, almost all of these serfs by the middle of the nineteenth century held furloughs which permitted them to work in factories.

VEDRO. A liquid measure equal to approximately 13 quarts.

VERST. A measure of length equal to approximately two-thirds of a mile (.662).

VOENNYE. Military personnel in official statistics of the early nineteenth century.

VOTCHINNAIA FABRIKA. A factory utilizing serf labor, established by a landlord on his estate.

ZAIEZHNII KUPETS. A foreign merchant or industrialist operating in Russia during the early nineteenth century on a more temporary basis than the *inostrannyi gost'*.

ZAVOD. One form of designation for a factory in tsarist statistics.

Appendices, Bibliography, and Index

Appendix 1

The Imperial Budget of 1825

Register of Revenue and Expenditure of the Government
in the Year 1825[1]

REVENUE

I. *Taxes*

	Rubles	Kopecks
Head taxes on townsmen and craftsmen	8,225,739	60
Head tax on people of free status inhabiting cities and seigneurial lands in the Baltic and the several western provinces	793,844	40

Head tax and *obrok* on single homesteaders and other state peasants

	Rubles	Kopecks		
	75,833,749	70½		
On those enlisted in military colonies	384,350			
Head tax on Little Russian Cossacks who have been reorganized into quartered troops	1,716,288			
			77,934,428	50½
On crown peasants and peasants assigned to places in particular agencies, a single head levy			2,435,675	86
On seigneurial peasants and household people, the same single head levy			38,749,759	45½

Taxes of a special nature and denomination:

On foreign craftsmen located in the capitals	56,600			
Prison ordinance and other income from the following provinces: Volynia, Podelia, Minsk, Kiev and Mogilev	151,127	73½		
Returns from the Commander's estates, transferred from the capital of the order of St. John of Jerusalem	6,625			
The same such taxes of special designation for Georgia and from other regions absorbed from Persia	1,221,697	36		
			1,436,050	9½
Total			129,575,497	91½
Minus arrears			3,500,000	
			126,075,497	91½

II. *Economic Income*

	Rubles	Kopecks
From estates belonging to the state, leased or awarded	2,674,656	52¼
From state forests	2,319,100	
From state lands, mills, fisheries, and other items under *obrok*, including *obrok* incomes from Georgia	2,109,411	91¾

	Rubles	Kopecks		
Gold, silver, and copper mined at state mining establishments, including income from mineralogical establishments in Georgia	4,108,187	76¾		
From melting copper money of old mintage into ingots and selling these at market prices	2,154,400			
For iron, shells, and various other objects cast at state metallurgical plants for the military and naval departments	3,211,694	56¼		
			9,474,282	33
Realization and profits for spirits produced in the state distilleries for the liquor farmers of the Siberian provinces			2,585,000	
			19,162,450	77

III. *Duties*

Liquor leases for the Siberian and the three New Russian provinces, including excises on inns and on vodka made from grapes	7,176,049	2		
On spirits sold in the towns and districts of the 29 Great Russian provinces	108,041,800			
Excise on brewing and on distillation of vodka from grapes, fruits, etc.	2,476,755			
Duties on various certificates: liquor dealers, plant owners, brewers, keepers of ale houses, grape wines, restaurants, and various other revenues of this type	1,858,535			
			112,377,090	
From liquor leases, collected by special regulations in the following provinces: the two Little Russian, seven Western and two Lithuanian provinces, together with capital and smaller cities	4,309,400			
Excises and other fees in the three Baltic and two Lithuanian provinces, in the district of Belostok and the land of the Army of the Don	1,938,520			
For the sealing of spirits made from grapes in the French manner in Kiev Province and the Army of the Don	30,000			
			6,277,920	

From the sale of state salt	24,996,599	83½
Tithe on private gold and silver mines, mills for smelting copper, iron, for extracting minerals, *obrok* on blast and copper smelting furnaces	2,605,817	29½
Customs duties on imported and exported goods	48,000,000	
Postal fees	9,181,950	
Road tolls	744,850	
For government stamps, bills of exchange, and promissory notes	7,054,950	
From seals issued for the right to trade: to merchants of the three guilds and commercial townsmen and peasants	7,405,937	80¼

	14,460,887	80¼

For passports		4,475,850	
Duties on title deeds and various chancellery fees	9,499,850		
From brokers' books	257,700	9,757,550	

	240,324,563	95¼

IV. Debt Payments

From various people, in payment of sums loaned to them	3,339,861	25

V. Extraordinary Sums

Revenues from Bessarabia	1,500,000	
Earned by the Commercial and Loan Banks	2,000,000	
Various balances and occasional incomes	595,243	70¼

	4,095,243	70¼
Grand Total	392,997,617	59

EXPENDITURES

I. Debts

For the payment of state debts	54,000,574	60

II. Expenditures of the Ministries and Administrations

The Imperial Court	17,665,980	97¼

For Clerical Affairs

The Grecorussian faith	3,821,792	92½
Foreign faiths	429,994	7¾

Appendix

For the Ministries

Public instruction	3,608,749	88¾
War	145,185,669	92¼
Supplementary premiums on silver sent for the pay of troops in the Kingdom of Poland and Georgia	2,600,000	
For the construction of military settlements	1,716,288	
For metals designated for manufacture in state metal-lurgical plants for the war department	1,947,392	58¼
Group taxes for peasants joining the military colonies	384,350	80
	151,833,701	30½
Naval	20,687,144	54¾
For metals designated for manufacture in state metal-lurgical plants for the naval department	1,264,301	98
	21,951,446	52¾
Foreign affairs	4,639,503	24½
Internal affairs	15,170,146	18½
Finances	88,369,503	88¾
Justice	5,537,974	97¼
Main administration of Ways of Communication	8,661,880	
Main administration of Post	4,821,307	
State controller	485,062	½
Total	380,997,617	59
For extraordinary expenses	12,000,000	
Grand Total	392,997,617	59

Signed in His Imperial Majesty's Own Hand:
"Alexander"

St Petersburg
11 December 1824

Minister of Finances Lieutenant General Kankrin

Source for Appendix 1

¹ A. M. Kolomzin, editor, "Finansovye dokumenty tsarstvovaniia Imperatora Aleksandra I," *Sbornik Imperatorskago Russkago Istoricheskago obshchestva*, vol. 45, pp. 340-45.

Appendix 2

Part 1: Russian Industry in the Eighteenth Century

Table A

Production of Iron and the Number of Iron Plants
in Russia in the Eighteenth Century[1]

Date	Poods of pig iron produced	Poods of cast iron produced	Number of plants (state and private)
1710	316,000	156,000	41
1720	610,000	300,000	52
1730	957,000	553,000	28
1740	1,530,000	1,020,000	35
1750	2,009,300	1,330,600	42
1760	3,663,300	2,271,200	62
1770	5,105,900	3,204,500	76
1780	6,718,000	3,761,100	93
1790	7,836,600	5,387,600	104
1800	9,787,800	6,153,500	109

Table B

Production of Woolen Cloth and the Number of Woolens
Manufacturing Plants in Russia, 1725-1815[2]

Date	Number of plants	Total production in arshins
1725	11	49,300
1741	13	600,007 (coarse varieties only)
1773	59	no figures
1815	261	4,103,408

Table C

Production of Linen Cloth and the Number of Linen
Manufacturing Plants in Russia, 1725-1812[3]

Date	Number of plants	Total production in arshins
1725	7	1,200,000
1741	35	no figures
1763	79	7,192,000 (four main types of linen 1761-63 average)
1812	214	15,362,296

Appendix

Table D

Distillation of Liquor in State and Private Plants
1754-1801[4]

Date	Total production in vedros
1754	3,792,471
1775	2,946,105
1801	9,167,173

Sources for Part 1

[1] Compiled from S. G. Strumilin, *Istoriia chernoi metallurgii v SSSR* (Moscow, 1954), vol. I, appendices 3-8, pp. 459-92; tables 34, 35, and 39, pp. 180-81, 197.

[2] Compiled from K. A. Pazhitnov, *Ocherki istorii tekstil'noi promyshlennosti dorevoliutsionnoi Rossii: sherstianaia promyshlennost'* (Moscow, 1955), tables 1, 2, 4, and 5, pp. 16, 22-26, 35-36; E. I. Zaozerskaya, *Manufaktura pri Petre I* (Moscow-Leningrad, 1947), appendix 6, pp. 171-73.

[3] Compiled from K. A. Pazhitnov, *Ocherki istorii tekstil'noi promyshlennosti dorevoliutsionnoi Rossii: khlopchatobumazhnaia, l'no-pen'kovaia i shelkovaia promyshlennost'* (Moscow, 1958), tables 43-45, pp. 167-68, 170-71, 174; Zaozerskaya, *Manufaktura pri Petre I*, appendix 4, pp. 167-68.

[4] Figures from A. Korsak, "O vinokurenii," *Obzor razlichnykh otraslei manufakturnoi promyshlennosti Rossii* (St. Petersburg, 1865), vol. III, pp. 232, 288-89.

Part 2: Russian Industry in the Early Nineteenth Century

Table A

Increase in the Number of Factories and Workers, 1804-1860[1]

Type of Industry	Number of plants			Number of workers		
	1804	1830	1860	1804	1830	1860
Textiles	1006	1351	2416	69,742	184,333	303,832
Sugar	10	57	467	108	1,607	64,763
Iron	28	198	693	4,121	19,889	54,832
All others	1646	3706	5986	20,117	46,425	81,891
Total	2680	5306	9562	90,379	252,253	505,408

Table B

Production of Sugar in Russia and the Ukraine, 1813-1857[2]

Date	Number of plants	Number of workers	Total production (in poods)
1813-14	50	962	717,046
1848-49	340	42,851	907,104
1855-57	395 (1855-56)	71,798 (1856-57)	2,105,880
1860-61*	401	—	1,322,037 (plus 7 Russian pounds)

* Beet sugar only

Table C

Production of Pig Iron in Russia, 1801-1860
(exclusive of the Kingdom of Poland
and the Grand Duchy of Finland)[3]

Date	Private plants	State plants	Total (poods)
1801	9,208,000	960,000	10,168,000
1810	7,887,000	1,074,000	8,761,000
1820	7,955,000	274,000	8,229,000
1830	9,703,000	1,738,000	11,441,000
1840	10,244,000	1,281,000	11,525,000
1850	11,792,000	2,100,000	13,892,000
1860	16,046,000	2,152,000	18,198,000

Table D

Growth of the Russian Machine Industry, 1851-1865, and the Role of St. Petersburg[4]

Year	Number of plants	Number of workers	Total production in rubles
1851	19	1,349	478,000
1852	28	3,180	2,305,000
1853	27	3,261	2,340,000
1854	29	3,813	2,065,000
1855	35	5,251	3,995,000
1856	31	6,604	3,865,000
1857	35	6,982	4,011,000
1858	46	7,602	4,199,000
1859	86	8,526	5,260,000
1860*	99 (15)	11,600 (4920-6695)	7,954,000 (6,217,000)
1865	126	17,284	11,720,000

* Figures in parentheses are for St. Petersburg in 1860. The total value of production is approximate, since no information was available for seven plants.

Table E

The Russian Cotton Industry, 1804-1860[5]

Year	Plants	Total workers	Total product in rubles	Spinning	Weaving	Finishing	Import of cotton fibre in poods
1804	199	8,181					
1814	430	40,203					
1825	484*	47,021*					32,000
1852	835**	126,500**	45,281,000	15,648,000	14,208,000	15,425,000	62,000
1860			71,117,000	28,670,000	19,343,000	23,104,000	1,835,000
							2,840,000

* Calico and chintz industries only
** Figures for 1854

Table F

The Russian Linen Industry, 1815-1860[6]

Year	Total plants	Total workers	Total production in arshins	Rubles
1815	222	33,363	15,764,651	
1825	196	26,832	16,165,000	
1835	186	26,801	18,867,000	
1852	112	12,450		
1860	117	17,284		6,103,395

Appendix

Table G

The Russian Woolens Industry, 1815-1860[7]

Year	Number of enterprises	Number of workers	Total production in rubles
1815	261	51,290	785,000*
1820	304	57,703	
1830	389	67,241	
1852	657	106,851	29,077,000**
1860	706	120,025	39,024,000***

    * assignat rubles, 1812-1815
  ** silver rubles, 1850
*** silver rubles

Table II

Geographical Distribution of the Manufacturing Industry in the
Russian Empire in 1854 (exclusive of Poland and Finland)[8]

Area	Number of enterprises	Number of workers	Total production in rubles
Central provinces	4,426	305,483	89,059,000
Northwest provinces	806	26,507	30,791,000
Northern provinces	237	4,354	804,000
Volga provinces	92	8,760	1,576,000
Southern provinces	1,863	62,063	11,490,000
Western provinces	693	14,957	6,188,000
Northern Caucasus	163	931	479,000
Transcaucasus	333	1,728	372,000
Urals	558	19,911	3,835,000
Kazakhstan and Central Asia	17	70	43,000
Western Siberia	186	930	756,000
Eastern Siberia	80	564	123,000

Sources for Part 2

[1] Compiled from P. A. Khromov, *Ekonomicheskoe razvitie Rossii v xix-xx vekakh* (1950), pp. 31-32; A. G. Rashin, *Formirovanie promyshlennogo proletariata v Rossii* (Moscow, 1940), pp. 26-27, 30-31. These figures do not include adjustments for the entire metallurgical industry.

[2] Compiled from K. G. Voblyi, *Opyt istorii sveklosakharnoi promyshlennosti SSSR* (Moscow, 1928), vol. I, tables 5, 9, and 13, pp. 84, 158-59, 160-61, 169, 179, 182; E. N. Andreev, "O sveklosakharnom proizvodstve," *Obzor razlichnykh otraslei manufakturnoi promyshlennosti Rossii* (St. Petersburg, 1862), vol. I, p. 18.

[3] Compiled from S. G. Strumilin, *Istoriia chernoi metallurgii v SSSR* (Moscow, 1954), vol. I, table 89, p. 367.

[4] M. F. Zlotnikov, "Ot manufaktury k fabrike," *Voprosy istorii* (1946), no. 12, p. 45; R. S. Livshits, *Razmeshchenie promyshlennosti v dorevoliutsionnoi Rossii* (Moscow, 1955), table 15, p. 106.

[5] Compiled from K. A. Pazhitnov, *Ocherki tekstil'noi promyshlennosti dorevoliutsionnoi Rossii: khlopchatobumazhnaia, l'no-pen'kovaia i shelkovaia promyshlennost'* (Moscow, 1958), tables 1, 5, 7, 8, and 10, pp. 17, 32-33, 38, 57; Khromov, *Ekonomicheskoe razvitie Rossii*, p. 47, and appendix, table 7, pp. 434-39; Livshits, *Razmeshchenie promyshlennosti v Rossii*, table 11, p. 92.

[6] Compiled from Pazhitnov, *Khlopchatobumazhnaia, l'no-pen'kovaia i shelkovaia promyshlennost'*, table 46, p. 176.

[7] Pazhitnov, *Ocherki istorii tekstil'noi promyshlennosti derevoliutsionnoi Rossii: sherstianaia promyshlennost'* (Moscow, 1955), tables 4, 5, 13, 24, pp. 35-36, 72, 119, 122.

[8] Compiled from Livshits, *Razmeshchenie promyshlennosti v Rossii*, table 24, pp. 131-34.

Part 3: Population and Social Structure in the Early Nineteenth Century

Table A

Total Population, 1811-1863[1]

Years	Registered male population of the Russian empire*	Total population of the Russian empire**
1811	20,863,100	41,010,400
1838	24,978,700	61,490,100
1851	28,555,400	69,033,300
1863	—	74,262,750

* taxable male population only
** males, females, and children of all classes

Table B

Urban Population, 1811-1863[2]

Years	Total urban population of European Russia	% of urban to total population in European Russia
1811	2,765,000	6.61
1825	3,329,000	
1838	4,666,000	9.27
1856	5,684,000	
1863	6,105,000	9.98

Table C

Class Distribution of Registered Population, 1816-1857[3]

Classes	1816	1835	1851	1857
Nontaxable population (*dvorianstvo,* clergy and others)	—	1,639,104	1,849,895	2,588,783
Kuptsy	84,388	119,364	175,434	178,475
Meshchanie	733,126	1,259,424	1,588,554	1,727,123
Peasants				
Free	78,885	123,146	196,629	173,195
State	6,316,136	7,724,290	9,749,408	10,964,849
Crown	915,125	1,148,395	1,257,672	846,995
Private	9,770,695	11,251,994	11,539,159	11,373,407
Temporary tax exempt population	61,309	102,864	177,101	156,338

Appendix

Table D

Population Changes in Selected Cities,
1811-1863[4]

Cities	1811	1840	1863	% growth 1811-1863
St. Petersburg	335,600	470,200	539,500	1.6
Moscow	270,200	349,100	462,200	1.7
Riga	32,000	60,000	77,500	2.4
Kiev	23,300	47,400	68,400	2.9
Odessa	11,000	60,100	119,000	10.8
Rostov-Don	4,000	12,600	29,300	7.3
Kharkov	10,400	29,400	52,000	5.0
Nikolaiev	4,200	28,700	64,600	15.4
Mogilev	5,800	17,600	48,200	8.3
Minsk	11,200	23,600	30,100	2.7
Berdichev	7,400	35,600	53,200	7.2
Astrakhan	37,800	45,900	42,800	1.1
Saratov	26,700	42,200	84,400	3.2
Vilno	56,300	64,500	69,500	1.2
Kazan	53,900	41,300	63,100	1.2
Tula	52,100	51,700	56,700	1.1
Orel	24,600	32,600	35,000	1.4
Iaroslavl'	23,800	34,900	27,700	1.2
Kursk	23,500	30,500	28,600	1.2
Kaluga	23,100	35,000	34,700	1.5
Kishinev	—	42,600	94,100	—
Tbilisi	—	29,900	60,800	—

Table E

Comparative Tabulation of Cities[5]

Ten most populated cities in 1811		Ten most populated cities in 1863	
1. St. Petersburg	335,600	St. Petersburg	539,500
2. Moscow	270,200	Moscow	462,500
3. Vilno	56,300	Odessa	119,000
4. Kazan	53,900	Kishinev	94,100
5. Tula	52,100	Saratov	84,400
6. Astrakhan	37,800	Riga	77,500
7. Riga	32,000	Kiev	68,400
8. Saratov	26,700	Nikolaiev	64,600
9. Orel	24,600	Kazan	63,100
10. Iaroslavl'	23,800	Vilno	69,500

Appendix

Table F

Class Distribution of Urban Population[6]

Classes	1811 Number	1811 % of urban population	1840 Number	1840 % of urban population	1858 Number	1858 % of urban population
Dvorianstvo	112,200	4.2	246,500	5.0	281,700	5.2
Clergy	53,200	2.0	53,200	1.1	81,700	1.9
Kuptsy	201,200	7.4	219,400	4.5		
Meshchanie	949,900	35.1	2,284,200	46.8	3,051,600	54.7
White Collar	195,300	7.2				
Military	176,300	6.5			786,000	14.1
Peasants					1,128,900	20.2
Raznochintsy	1,017,700	37.6	2,078,900	42.5	193,000	3.5
Others					40,200	0.7
Total	2,705,800		4,887,000		5,583,000	

Table G

Class Distribution of Population in St. Petersburg[7]

	1801 Number	1801 % of total city population	1831 Number	1831 % of total city population	1869 Number	1869 % of total city population
Dvorianstvo	13,200	6.5	42,900	9.6	94,600	14.2
Clergy	500	0.2	1,900	.4	6,100	0.9
Kuptsy	14,300	7.1	6,900	1.5	22,300	3.3
Meshchanie	23,400	11.6	56,200	12.5	140,900	21.2
Raznochintsy	35,000	17.3	63,100	14.1		
Peasants	50,500	25.0	117,500	26.2		
Serfs	26,100	12.9	98,100	21.9		
Military	39,100	19.4	45,800	10.2		
Foreigners	—		13,000	2.9	21,300	3.2
Others	—		2,900	.7	174,000	26.1
Total	202,100		448,200			

Table H

Class Distribution of Population in Moscow[8]

	1788-1794		1834-1840		1871	
	Number	% of total	Number	% of total	Number	% of total
Nobility	8,700	4.9	15,700	4.7	48,200	8.0
Clergy	36,600	2.0	8,200	2.5	11,200	1.9
Kuptsy	11,900	6.8	17,000	5.3	29,200	4.8
Meshchanie	9,100	5.2	75,300	22.5	153,900	25.6
Raznochintsy	17,600	10.1	27,700	8.3		
Peasants	53,700	30.7	84,500	25.2	260,400	43.2
Serfs	61,300	35.0	37,000	20.0		
Military	7,000	4.0	33,700	10.1		
Foreigners	2,200	1.3	4,800	1.4	6,900	1.1
Others					92,200	15.4

Sources for Part 3

[1] Compiled from V. M. Kabuzan, *Narodonaselenie Rossii v XVIII—pervoi polovine XIX v.* (Moscow, 1963), tables 6 and 17, pp. 136-37, 159-63; *Statisticheskii Ezhegodnik Rossii* (Petrograd, 1915), p. 151.

[2] A. G. Rashin, *Naselenie Rossii za sto let* (Moscow, 1956), tables 50 and 56, pp. 86, 98. The urban population refers only to the forty-nine provinces of European Russia.

[3] Kabuzan, *Narodonaselenie Rossii*, tables 95 and 96, pp. 134-37.

[4] Rashin, *Naselenie Rossii*, tables 53 and 54, pp. 89-93. Population given for Tbilisi is that of 1825.

[5] *Ibid.*

[6] Rashin, *Naselenie Rossii*, tables 80, 82, and 84, pp. 119-21.

[7] Rashin, *Naselenie Rossii*, tables 89 and 91, pp. 126, 129.

[8] Rashin, *Naselenie Rossii*, tables 87 and 88, pp. 124-25.

Part 4: Foreign and Domestic Trade in the Early Nineteenth Century

Table A

Exports (in silver rubles), 1802-1860[1]

Selected items	1802	1820	1840	1860
Wheat	1,158,000	7,100,000	11,074,000	37,508,000
Rye	1,600,000	1,750,000	622,000	12,117,000
Other cereals, flour, etc.	420,000	2,040,000	2,890,000	14,947,000
Total grain	3,178,000	10,890,000	14,586,000	64,572,000
Vegetable oil	446,000	1,750,000	118,000	89,000
Seeds, all sorts	718,000	3,650,000	7,820,000	15,868,000
Wood and wood products	412,000	1,128,000	2,657,000	4,975,000
Tar and resins	75,000	252,000	344,000	317,000
Potash	296,000	702,000	701,000	858,000
Horses, cattle, pigs, etc.	414,000	367,000	1,756,000	1,741,000
Fat and lard	2,752,000	13,700,000	15,620,000	18,221,000
Bristle, mane, down, and feathers	225,000	1,151,000	2,035,000	3,155,000
Leather	701,000	1,495,000	3,537,000	2,394,000
Furs	720,000	2,120,000	1,728,000	2,294,000
Wax	103,000	683,000	346,000	—
Caviar and fish	88,000	183,000	289,000	542,000
Fish glue	83,000	429,000	420,000	444,000
Metals and metal products	1,370,000	5,350,000	2,872,000	2,569,000
Platinum	—	—	—	209,000
Flax, hemp, and their products	5,590,000	16,180,000	21,427,000	28,764,000
Wool	275,000	350,000	4,386,000	19,748,000
Silk	—	134,000	296,000	1,574,000
Paper products	363,000	—	1,450,000	4,008,000
Total export	18,100,000	63,200,000	85,431,000	181,383,000

Appendix

Table B

Imports (in silver rubles), 1802-1860[2]

Selected items	1802	1820	1840	1860
Grain	16,900	22,000	1,082,000	269,000
Rice	—	49,200	229,000	901,000
Fruits, nuts, etc.	402,000	1,586,000	3,036,000	7,121,000
Spices	79,500	346,000	436,000	765,000
Tea	536,000	1,580,000	2,594,000	6,895,000
Coffee	302,000	2,440,000	1,211,000	3,768,000
Tobacco	54,300	339,000	1,357,000	3,581,000
Sugar	1,589,000	13,100,000	8,400,000	5,355,000
Alcohol	820,000	8,550,000	6,426,000	9,294,000
Olive and vegetable oils	201,000	1,165,000	1,705,000	6,193,000
Horses, cattle, poultry	203,000	870,000	994,000	4,453,000
Cheese and butter	43,700	151,000	188,000	1,518,000
Furs	128,000	565,000	1,105,000	2,997,000
Leather	5,700	126,000	257,000	1,713,000
Fish and caviar	210,000	1,420,000	1,542,000	4,076,000
Salt	478,000	950,000	2,210,000	4,516,000
China, crockery, earthenware, glass	75,000	199,000	71,000	1,787,000
Coal	14,000	64,000	611,000	2,956,000
Metal, zinc, steel, pig iron, copper, etc.	245,000	830,000	1,629,000	5,656,000
Instruments, machines, tools	168,000	1,378,000	1,978,000	12,991,000
Cotton and cotton products	2,440,000	14,780,000	15,667,000	30,583,000
Wool and wool products	2,100,000	6,480,000	4,417,000	7,565,000
Silk and silk products	1,000,000	5,060,000	7,166,000	6,599,000
Chemicals and pharmaceutical products	160,000	1,330,000	1,832,000	3,078,000
Dyes	850,000	4,040,000	6,224,000	9,230,000
Jewelry	132,000	279,000	1,562,000	421,000
Total import	13,050,000	70,080,000	78,128,000	159,303,000

Table C

Trade Across the Asian Frontier:
Exports (in rubles), 1815-1860[3]

Selected items	1815	1840	1860
Grain, flour, etc.	57,000	279,000	521,000
Leather and hide	550,000	900,000	764,000
Fur	1,110,000	1,836,000	973,000
Metals, metal products	547,000	428,000	828,000
Wool products	390,000	3,642,000	3,316,000
Silk	42,000	65,000	1,249,000
Cotton products	154,000	2,140,000	3,882,000
Total export	3,460,000	11,066,000	13,352,000

Appendix

Table D

Trade Across the Asian Frontier:
Imports (in rubles), 1815-1860[4]

Selected items	1815	1840	1860
Fruits and spices	13,000	205,000	725,000
Tea	1,160,000	2,496,000	6,895,000
Sugar	—	256,000	568,000
Horses, domestic animals, cattle	164,000	851,000	4,087,000
Furs	213,000	488,000	881,000
Cotton	2,220,000	3,421,000	3,944,000
Silk	418,000	797,000	973,000
Total import	4,530,000	9,387,000	21,122,000

Table E

Trade Distribution, 1849-1853[5]

Average yearly export		Average yearly import	
Countries	% of trade	Countries	% of trade
Great Britain	49.2	Great Britain	33.9
Low Countries	7.6	Prussia	11.2
France	7.1	France	10.8
Europe, Turkey, Greece	6.7	United States	10.1
Prussia	5.5	Hanseatic Cities	7.8
Austria	5.2	Europe, Turkey and Greece	6.3
Italy	4.5	Low Countries	5.2
United States	2.5	Spain and Portugal	4.3

Table F

Trade Distribution along the Asian Frontier,
1849-1853[6]

Average yearly export		Average yearly import	
Countries	% of trade	Countries	% of trade
China	60	China	43.8
Kirgizian steppes	16.8	Persia	23.6
Persian	8.1	Kirgizian steppes	13.0
Asiatic Turkey	7.2	Asiatic Turkey	5.2
Bukhara	3.2	Bukhara	4.3

Appendix

Table G

Distribution of Trade Among Ports[7]

Ports	Number of ships			Tonnage		
	1802	1850	1860	1802	1850	1860
Baltic ports	2,768	3,423	5,188	418,092	634,002	915,250
Black Sea ports	706	2,590	4,595	73,204	487,244	1,052,332
White Sea ports	236	547	697	59,976	112,104	108,864

Sources for Part 4

[1] Compiled from *Sbornik svedenii po istorii i statistike vneshnei torgovli Rossii* (St. Petersburg, 1902), table V a, pp. 103-17; *Gosudarstvennaia vneshnaia torgovlia* (St. Petersburg, 1860). See also G. P. Nebol'sin, *Statisticheskoe obozrenie vneshnei torgovli Rossii* (St. Petersburg, 1850). Until 1840, the value of foreign trade was given in *assignat* rubles in the sources. In the export and import tables, the value of assignat rubles has been converted into silver rubles for 1802 and 1820 on the basis of 1.00 silver ruble = 3.50 assignat rubles.

[2] Compiled from *Sbornik svedenii po istorii vneshnei torgovli Rossii*, table V b, pp. 119-41. The grain figure for 1802 includes the import of rice.

[3] Compiled from *Sbornik svedenii po istorii vneshnei torgovli Rossii*, table VIII a, pp. 169-75.

[4] Compiled from *Sbornik svedenii po istorii vneshnei torgovli Rossii*, table VIII b, pp. 177-85.

[5] *Sbornik svedenii po istorii vneshnei torgovli Rossii*, p. xxxii.

[6] *Ibid.*

[7] *Sbornik svedenii po istorii vneshnei torgovli Rossii*, p. xxxv.

Part 5: Education in the Early Nineteenth Century

Table A

Total Number of Schools and Pupils, 1804-1856
(including technical schools in 1837)[1]

Date and category	Number of schools	Pupils
1804		
Schools under the Ministry of Public Instruction	499	33,481
Military schools	15	29,000
Church schools	100	15,000
Special and technical schools	13	31,775
Total	627	109,256
1824		
Schools under the Ministry of Public Instruction	1,411	69,629
Military schools	117	102,295
Church schools	544	50,000
Special and technical schools	46	41,300
Total	2,118	263,223
1837		
Schools under the Ministry of Public Instruction	1,681	85,707
Military technical schools	2	320
Naval technical schools	5	1,924
Other military schools	145	177,737
Church schools	711	67,024
Technical schools:		
Of the Ministry of Finances	72	6,221
Of the Ministry of Internal Affairs	32	2,220
Of the Ministry of State Properties	68	1,070
Of the Ministry of Ways of Communication	3	665
Of the Ministry of Justice	1	200
Factory schools of the Empress Maria	3	670
Commercial high schools	2	325
Total	181	11,371
Other special schools	126	116,493
Total	2,851	460,576
1856		
Schools under the Ministry of Public Instruction	2,335	125,667
Military schools	—	—
Church schools	—	—
Primary schools of all types	3,225	—
Factory and railroad elementary schools	6	—

Sources for Part 5

[1] Compiled from Alexander Krusenstern, *Précis du système, des progrès et de l'état de l'instruction publique en Russie* (Warsaw, 1837), pp. 308-426; *Izvlechenie iz otcheta ministerstva narodnago prosveshcheniia za 1856 god* (St. Petersburg, 1857), table 1, 140-41; Imperatorskoe volnoe ekonomicheskoe obshchestvo, G. Fal'bork and V. Charnoluskii, editors, *Nachal'noe narodnoe obrazovanie v Rossii* (St. Petersburg, 1900), vol. III, tables 234 and 295, pp. 190, 245. Figures exclude the Kingdom of Poland.

Bibliography

NOTE: This Bibliography is a listing of materials consulted in the preparation of the book. It does not contain all of the sources cited in the footnotes. The latter also are designed to serve a bibliographical purpose and a great deal of commentary on various sources will be found there. This formal Bibliography has been divided into three sections. Section I includes a wide variety of primary sources which, generally speaking, are official in nature—state papers, including reports from all levels of the tsarist administration, projects, memoranda, police observations, surveys of industry and transport, budgets, laws, regulations, and statistics on population, commerce, industry, education, and cities. University records and materials relating to the history of education have also been placed in this section, together with documents published from the archives of the Academy of Sciences, its publications and technically oriented periodicals of the early nineteenth century. Section II consists of primary sources of a more personal nature—memoirs, diaries, autobiographies, journals, letters, relevant scientific, philosophical, and literary works by contemporaries, and finally, early nineteenth-century travel accounts by Russians and foreigners. Section III includes secondary sources—monographs, articles, and various types of histories. The most important types of these histories may be singled out. First, numerous histories of technical and engineering schools as well as of universities were used. Most of the larger Russian schools have both tsarist and Soviet versions of their histories. Histories of specific industries form another category of secondary sources. Soviet scholarship in recent years has filled in the picture of almost all the major industries in Russia with numerous monographs and articles. Urban histories also are available in tsarist and Soviet versions for the main Russian cities, and have been utilized for almost every Chapter in this book. Finally, the numerous official histories of government agencies published in the tsarist period have been of help in assessing state industrial policy.

I. Primary Sources of an Official Nature

Arkhiv gosudarstvennago soveta, vol. IV (St. Petersburg, 1881), "Zhurnaly po delam departamenta gosudarstvennoi ekonomii."
Arkhiv grafov Mordvinovykh (St. Petersburg, 1901-1903), 10 vols.
"M. B.," editor, "K likvidatsii possessionykh fabrik," *Istoricheskii arkhiv*, vol. I (1936).
Bakhturin, A., *Vodokhodstvo rossiiskoi imperii* (St. Petersburg, 1802).
Confino, M., editor, "Grèves dans l'Oural au XIX° siècle," *Cahiers du monde russe et soviétique*, vol. I (1960), 332-50 (translated documents).

Desiatiletie ministerstvo narodnago prosveshcheniia 1833-1843 (St. Petersburg, 1864).

Dokumenty i materialy po istorii Moskovskogo universiteta vtoroi poloviny XVIII veka (Moscow, 1960-1963), 3 vols.

Ekonomicheskoe sostoianie gorodskikh poselenii evropeiskoi Rossii v 1861-62 g. (St. Petersburg, 1863), 2 vols.

Gornii zhurnal (begins publication, 1825).

Gosudarstvennaia vneshnaia torgovlia (begins publication, 1824).

Hagemeister, Iu. A., "O finansakh Rossii," A. P. Pogrebinskii, editor, "Gosudarstvennye finansy Rossii, nakanune reformy 1861 goda," *Istoricheskii arkhiv* (1956), 100-25.

Iatsunskii, V. K., editor, "Materialy po istorii uralskoi metallurgii v pervoi polovine XIX v.," *Istoricheskii arkhiv*, vol. IX (1953), 280-327.

———, "Materialy o sostoianii sukonnoi promyshlennosti Rossii v 1845 g.," *Istoricheskii arkhiv* (1956), no. 4, 82-126.

Izvlechenie iz vsepoddanneishago otcheta ministra narodnago prosveshcheniia (1843-1846).

Kelsiev, V., *Sbornik pravitel'stvennykh svedenii o raskol'nikakh* (London, 1861-1862), 3 vols.

Krasnyi arkhiv

———, Bakareva, V., "Usad'ba nachala XIX v.," vol. 78 (1936), 254-62.

———, Krutikov, M., editor, "Pervye zheleznye dorogi v Rossii," vol. 76 (1936), 83-155.

———, ———, "Polozhenie rabochikh na postroike Peterburgo-Moskovskii zheleznoi dorogi 1843-1845 g.g.," vol. 83 (1937), 45-106.

———, Mel'nikov, P. P., "Svedenia o russkikh zheleznykh dorogakh," vol. 99 (1940), 127-79.

Krusenstern, Alexandre de, *Précis du système, des progrès et de l'état de l'instruction publique en Russie* (Warsaw, 1837).

Kusheva, E. N., "Proekt uchrezhdeniia aktsionernogo 'obshchestva uluchsheniia chastnogo sel'skogo khoziaistva' 30-kh godov XIX v.," *Istoricheskii arkhiv*, vol. VII (1951), 46-95.

Mel'nikov, P. I., editor, *Materialy dlia istorii khlystovskoi i skopicheskoi eresei* (no date or place of publication).

Miliutin, B., *Ustroistvo i sostoianie evreiskikh obshchestv v Rossii* (St. Petersburg, 1849-1850).

Miliutin, D., "Ob opasnosti prodolzheniia v 1856 g. voennykh deistvii," *Istoricheskii arkhiv* (1959), 206-08.

Modzalevskii, L. B., *Materialy dlia biografii N. I. Lobachevskii* (Moscow-Leningrad, 1948).

Mysli Moskovskago zhitelia o vozmozhnosti uchredit obshchestvo na aktsiiakh dlia sooruzheniia zheleznoi dorogi ot St. Peterburga do

Moskvy (St. Petersburg, 1838). Signed "A . . . A . . ." (probably Abaza).

Ob izdanii gornago zhurnala i uchrezhdenii uchenago komiteta po gornoi i solianoi chasti (St. Petersburg, 1825).

Obzor razlichnykh otraslei manufakturnoi promyshlennosti Rossii (St. Petersburg, 1863), 3 vols.

Odesskoe obshchestvo istorii i drevnosti, zapiski (begins publication, 1844).

Official Catalogue of the Great Exhibition of Works of all Nations, "Russia," (London, 1851), 295-300.

Pokrovskii, V. I., editor, *Sbornik svedenu po istorii i statistike vneshnei torgovli Rossii* (St. Petersburg, 1902).

Polnoe sobranie zakonov rossiiskoi imperii (St. Petersburg, 1825-1916).

Popov, N. I., "Materialy dlia istorii bespopovshchinskikh soglasii v Moskve," *Chteniia v imperatorskom obshchestve istorii i drevnostei rossiskikh,* vols. 69-70, supplement (174 pp.).

Rabochee dvizhenie v Rossii v xix veke 1800-1825, 1826-1860 (Moscow, 1955), 2 vols.

Report of George W. Whistler to His Excellency, the Count Kleinmichael on the Gauge of Russian Railways, Sept. 9, 1842. Typewritten copy from the Russian archives in the possession of the New York Public Library.

Rozhdestvenskii, S. V., editor, *S-Peterburgskii universitet v pervoe stoletie ego deiatel'nosti 1819-1919. Materialy po istorii St. Peterburgskogo universiteta, 1819-1835,* vol. I (Petrograd, 1919).

Sblizhenie srednei azii c Evropoiu ili proekt o zheleznykh dorogakh mezhdu Varshavoiu i Tiflisom i mezhdu Chernom Morem i Kaspiem (St. Petersburg, 1858), probable author, G. Liubanskii.

Sbornik Imperatorskago Russkago Istoricheskago Obshchestva (St. Petersburg, 1867-1916).

⸺, "Istoricheskoe obozrenie putei soobshcheniia i publichnikh zdanii c 1825 po 1850 god," vol. 98, 530-91.

⸺, Kulomzin, A. N., editor, "Finansovye dokumenty tsarstvovaniia Imperatora Aleksandra I," vol. 45, 1-617.

⸺, Polovtsoff, M., editor, "Le duc de Richelieu, correspondance et documents, 1766-1822," vol. 54, 1-639.

⸺, "Vedomost sostoiashchem v St. Peterburg fabrikam, manufakturam i zavodam 1794 goda," vol. 1, 352-61.

Sbornik materialov dlia istorii prosveshcheniia v Rossii izvlechennykh iz arkhiva ministerstva narodnago prosveshcheniia (St. Petersburg, 1893-1897), 3 vols.

Sivkov, V. A., "O stroitele parovykh mashin A. S. Viatkine," *Istoricheskii arkhiv* (1957), no. 2, 201-03.

Sokolov, D., editor, *Istoricheskoe i statisticheskoe opisanie Gornago Kadetskago Korpus* (St. Petersburg, 1830).

Svod zakonov rossiiskoi imperii (St. Petersburg, 1832—).

Tekhnologicheskii zhurnal (begins publication, 1804).

Titov, A. A., editor, "Dnevnye dozornye zapisi o Moskovskikh raskol'nikakh," *Chteniia v imperatorskom obshchestve istorii i drevnostei Rossiiskikh*, 1885, 1886, and 1892, supplements (443 pp.).

Trudy Imperatorskago Volnago Ekonomicheskago Obshchestva (begins publication, 1765).

Tseitlin, E. A., editor, "Iz istorii mashinago proizvodstva v Rossii: Pervonachal'noe tekhnicheskoe oborudovanie Aleksandrovskoi manufaktury," Academy of Sciences, U.S.S.R., *Trudy Instituta Istorii Nauki i Tekhniki*, 1st series, issue 3 (1934), 263-72.

Uchebnye zavedeniia vedomstva ministerstva narodnago prosvesh-cheniia (St. Petersburg, 1895).

Ushinskii, K. D., *Arkhiv* (Moscow, 1960), 4 vols.

Winans, William, *Proshenie i prilozheniia predstavlennye ego imperatorskomu velichestvu gosudariu Imperatoru Aleksandru II, amerikanskimi grazhdanami Uainans, Garrison i Uainans otnositel'no ikh iska na rossiiskoe pravitel'stvo* . . . (London, 1863).

Zhurnal ministerstva narodnago prosveshcheniia (begins publication, 1834).

II. Primary Sources of a Personal Nature

Alexander, James E., *Travels to the Seat of War in the East Through Russia and the Crimea in 1829* (London, 1830), 2 vols.

Atkinson, G. F., *Pictures from the North* (London, 1848).

Boiarkin, N., "Vzgliad na selo Ivanovo," *Moskovskii telegraf* (1826) part 11, 111-16.

Bremner, Robert, *Excursion in the Interior of Russia* (London, 1839), 2 vols.

Burianov, V., *Progulka c det'mi po S. Peterburge i ego okrestnostiam* (St. Petersburg, 1838), 3 vols.

Collignon, Edouard, *Les chemins de fer Russes de 1857 à 1862* (2nd edition, Paris, 1868).

Dallas, Susan, editor, *Diary of George Mifflin Dallas* (Philadelphia, 1892).

DeLaveau, C., *Guide du voyageur à Moscou* (Moscow, 1824).

Delvig, A. I., *Polveka russkoi zhizni. Vospominaniia A. I. Delviga 1820-1870* (Moscow-Leningrad, 1920), 2 vols.

German, E. F., "Opisanie zavodov pod vedomstvom Ekaterinburgskogo gornogo nachal'stva sostoiashchikh," *Tekhnologicheskii zhurnal*, vol. II (1805), parts 1-4; vol. III, part 1.

Gerstner, Franz Anton Ritter von, *O vygodakh postroeniia zheleznoi dorogi iz Sankt-Peterburga v Tsarskoe Selo i Pavlovsk* (St. Petersburg, 1836).

Gilbert, Linney, *Russia Illustrated* (London, no date), possibly the 1840's.

Golovin, Ivan, *Russia Under the Autocrat Nicholas I* (London, 1846).

————, *Russian Sketch Book* (London, 1848).

Gornfeld, A. G., editor, *Sobranie sochinenii S. T. Aksakova*, vol. III (St. Petersburg, 1909), "Vospominanie ob Aleksandre Semenovich Shishkove," 333-95.

Griffin, G. W., *Memoir of Colonel Charles S. Todd* (Philadelphia, 1873).

Harrison, Joseph, *The Iron Worker and King Solomon*, with an appendix containing Harrison's memoirs of Russia (2nd edition revised, Philadelphia, 1869), 49-138.

————, *Letter Books 1844-1850*, unpublished letters from Russia in the possession of the Pennsylvania Historical Society, Philadelphia, Pennsylvania.

————, *The Locomotive Engine and Philadelphia's Share in Its Early Improvements* (revised edition, Philadelphia, 1872).

Haxthausen, A. von, *The Russian Empire, Its People, Institutions and Resources* (English edition, London, 1856), 2 vols.

Herzen, Alexander, *My Past and Thoughts* (London, 1924), vol. I.

Izbrannye sotsial'no-politicheskie i filosofskie proizvedeniia dekabristov (Moscow, 1951), 3 vols.

Jerrmann, Edward, *Pictures from St. Petersburg* (New York, 1852).

Khomiakov, A. S., *Polnoe sobranie sochinenii* (Moscow, 1911-14), 3 vols.

————, *Description of the Moskva, a New Rotary Steam Machine, Invented and Patented by Alexis Khomiakoff of Moscow* (London, 1851).

Kohl, J. G., *Russia and the Russians in 1842* (London, 1843), 2 vols.

Korf, M., "Iz zapisok Barona (vposledstvii Grafa) M. A. Korfa," *Russkaia starina*, vol. 103 (1900), 33-55.

Kreeft, Christopher, *First Russian Railroad* (London, 1837).

Kupffer, A. T., *Voyage dans l'Oural entrepris en 1828* (Paris, 1833).

Lamanskii, E. I., "Iz vospominanii E. I. Lamanskago," *Russkaia starina*, vol. 162 (1915), 338-52.

Latrobe, John H., *Journal*, unpublished manuscript in the possession of the Maryland Historical Society, Baltimore, Maryland.

LeRoy-Beaulieu, Anatole, *The Empire of the Tsars and the Russians* (New York, 1896), 3 vols.

Lomonosov, M. V., *Sochineniia* (Moscow-Leningrad, 1961).

L'vov, P., "Prichina naimenovaniia Mariiskago Kanala," *Otechestvennye zapiski* (1820), part 4, 108-24.

————, "O sisteme plavaniia po Mariiskomu Kanalu," *Otechestven-nye zapiski* (1821), part 5, 278-89.

————, "Vzgliad na Mariiskoi Kanal," *Otechestvennye zapiski* (1820), part 2, 163-88.

Lyall, Robert, *The Character of the Russians and a Detailed History of Moscow* (London, 1823).

Mavrodin, V. V., editor, *Leningradskii universitet v vospominaniiakh sovremennikov*, vol. I, *Peterburgskii universitet 1819-1895* (Leningrad, 1963).

Maxwell, John S., *The Czar, His Court and People* (2nd edition, New York, 1848).

Moor, Henry, *A Visit to Russia in the Autumn of 1862* (London, 1863).

Morley, Henry, *Sketches of Russian Life Before and During the Emancipation of the Serfs* (London, 1866).

Morozov, F., editor, *N. S. Mordvinov, izbrannye proizvedeniia* (O.G.I.Z.: GIPL, 1945).

Moskovskii universitet v vospominaniiakh sovremennikov (Moscow, 1956).

Moskva, ili istoricheskii putovoditel po znamenitoi stolitse gosudarstva rossiiskago (Moscow, 1827-1831), 4 vols.

Murchison, Roderick, "A Few Observations on the Ural Mountains to Accompany a New Map of a Southern Portion of That Chain," *Royal Geographical Society, Journal*, vol. 13 (1843), 269-324.

Nekrasov, N. A., *Polnoe sobranie sochinenii* (Moscow, 1948), vol. II.

Odoevskii, V. F., *4338-i god, fantasticheskii roman* (Moscow, 1926).

Oliphant, Lawrence, *The Russian Shores of the Black Sea* (New York, 1854).

Ostrovsky, Alexander, *Plays*, translated and edited by George Rapall Noyes (New York, 1917).

Panaev, V. A., "Vospominaniia Valeriana Aleksandrovicha Panaeva," *Russkaia starina*, vol. 107 (1901), 31-66.

Pelchinski, V. S., *Système de législation, d'administration et de politique de la Russie en 1844* (Paris, 1845).

Przhetslavskii, O. A., "Vospominanie Przhetslavskago," *Russkaia starina*, vol. 11 (1874), 451-77.

Pushkin, A. S., "Puteshestvie iz Moskvy v Peterburg," *Polnoe sobranie sochinenii* (Academy of Sciences, U.S.S.R., 1949), vol. 11.

Raikes, Thomas, *A Visit to St. Petersburg in the Winter of 1829-1830* (London, 1838).

Ritchie, Leitch, *Russia and the Russians* (Philadelphia, 1836).

Rybnikov, I. N., "Rossiiskoe kupichestvo na obede u Imperatora

Nikolaia Pavlovicha (1833)," *Russkii arkhiv* (1891), vol. III, 563-69.

Shtukenberg, A. I., "Iz istorii zhelezno-dorozhnago del v Rossii, Nikolaevskaia doroga mezhdu Peterburgom i Moskvoiu 1842-1852," *Russkaia starina*, vol. 46 (1885), 309-22, vol. 48 (1885), 309-36, vol. 49 (1886), 97-128, vol. 50 (1886), 443-48.

Spottiswoode, William, *A Tarantasse Journey Through Eastern Russia in the Autumn of 1856* (London, 1857).

Storch, Heinrich, *Picture of Petersburg* (London, 1801).

Joseph Gardner Swift Manuscripts, containing letters of Major George Washington Whistler from Russia, 1843-1849, in the possession of the Manuscript Division of the New York Public Library, New York City, New York.

Taylor, Bayard, *Greece and Russia* (New York, 1859).

Tietz, M. von, *St. Petersburg, Constantinople and Napoli di Romania in 1833 and 1834* (New York, 1836).

Tooke, W., *View of the Russian Empire* (3rd edition, Dublin, 1801).

Turgenev, N., *La Russie et les russes* (Brussels, 1847), 3 vols.

Vevier, Charles, *Siberian Journey, Down the Amur to the Pacific, 1856-1857* (Madison, Wisconsin, 1962).

Vigel, F. F., *Zapiski* (Moscow, 1892).

Vistengof, P., *Ocherki Moskovskoi zhizni* (Moscow, 1842).

Vsevolojsky, N. S., *Dictionnaire géographique-historique de l'empire de Russie* (2nd edition, Moscow, 1823), 2 vols.

Vtorov, I. A., "Moskva i Kazan v nachale xix-go veka," *Russkaia starina*, vol. 70 (1891), 1-22.

Whistler, Anna, *Journal 1843-1848*, in the possession of the Manuscript Division of the New York Public Library, New York City, New York.

Papers of Thomas and William Winans, in the possession of the Maryland Historical Society, Baltimore, Maryland.

Zagoskin, M. N., *Moskva i moskvichi* (Moscow, 1848-1851), 4 vols.

III. Secondary Sources

Abramov, A., *Prichiny ekonomicheskoi otstal'nosti tsarskoi Rossii* (Leningrad, 1941).

Akademicheskii spiski imperatorskago universiteta Sv. Vladimir 1834-1884 (Kiev, 1884).

Aksakov, I., *Izsledovanie o torgovle na ukrainskikh iarmarkakh* (St. Petersburg, 1858).

Amburger, Eric, "Der fremde Unternehmer in Russland bis zur Oktoberrevolution im Jahre 1917," *Tradition, Zeitschrift für Firmengeschichte und Unternehmerbiographie*, 2nd year (1957), no. 4, 337-55.

Ames, Edward, "A Century of Russian Railroad Construction, 1837-1936," *American Slavic and East European Review*, vol. VI (1947), 57-74.

Andreev, V. V., *Raskol i ego znachenie v narodnoi russkoi istorii, istoricheskii ocherk* (St. Petersburg, 1870).

Arnold, Arthur Z., *Banks, Credit and Money in Soviet Russia* (New York, 1937).

Ashurkov, V. N., *Gorod masterov* (Tula, 1958).

Baburin, D. M., *Ocherki po istorii manufakturnoi kollegii* (Moscow, 1939).

Barsukov, I., *Graf Nikolai Nikolaevich Muraviev-Amurskii* (Moscow, 1891).

Becker, Christopher, "*Raznochintsy*: the Development of the Word and the Concept," *American Slavic and East European Review*, vol. XVIII (1959), 63-74.

Berendts, E., *Imperatorskii Aleksandrovskii universitet v Finliandii* (St. Petersburg, 1902).

Berengren, Erik, *Alfred Nobel, the Man and His Work* (London, 1962).

Berlin, P. A., *Russkaia burzhuaziia v staroe i novoe vremia* (Moscow, 1922).

————, "Russkaia kupichestvaia voina 1812 goda," Dzhivelegov, A. K., Melgunov, S. P., and Picheta, V. I., editors, *Otechestvennaia voina i russkoe obshchestvo 1812-1912* (Moscow, 1912), vol. V, 114-20.

Beskrovnyi, L. G., editor, *K voprosu pervonachal'nom nakoplenii v Rossii (XVII-XVIII v.v.), sbornik statei* (Moscow, 1958).

Best, Paul, "The Origins and Development of Insurance in Imperial and Soviet Russia" (unpublished doctoral dissertation, New York University, 1965).

Bestuzhev, I. N., *Krimskaia voina 1853-1856 g.g.* (Moscow, 1956).

————, "Krimskaia voina i revoliutsionnaia situatsiia," *Revoliutsionnaia situatsiia v Rossii v 1859-1861 g.g.* (Moscow, 1963), vol. III, 189-213.

Betetskii, *Istoricheskii obzor deiatel'nosti Vilenskago uchebnago okruga 1803 g.-1832 g.* (Vilna, 1908).

Bezrukikh, P. E., *Stoletnii gigant, istoricheskii ocherk proletarskogo zavoda, 1826-1926* (Leningrad, 1929).

Bill, Valentine, *The Forgotten Class: the Russian Bourgeoisie from the Earliest Beginnings to 1900* (New York, 1959).

Biograficheskii slovar professorov i prepodavatelei imperatorskago Kazan'skago universiteta (Kazan, 1904), 2 vols.

Biograficheskii slovar professorov i prepodavatelei imperatorskago Moskovskago universiteta za istekaiushchee stoletie, sostavlennyi trudami professorov i prepodavatelei (Moscow, 1855), 2 vols.

Biograficheskii slovar professorov i prepodavatelei imperatorskago universiteta Sv. Vladimira (1834-1884) (Kiev, 1884).

Bishop, John L., *A History of American Manufactures from 1608 to 1860* (Philadelphia, 1866), vol. II.

Black, C. E., *The Dynamics of Modernization* (New York, 1966).

————, "Mechanical Technology in Russia Before World War I," provisional draft of paper presented to the American Historical Association, 1962 meeting.

————, "The Modernization of Russian Society," *The Transformation of Russian Society* (Harvard, 1960), 661-80.

————, "Russian History in the Perspective of Comparative Modernization," provisional draft of paper presented to the American Association for the Advancement of Slavic Studies, 1964 meeting.

Bliokh, I. S., *Finansy Rossii XIX stoletiia* (St. Petersburg, 1882), vols. I and II.

————, *Vlianie zheleznykh dorog na ekonomicheskoe sostoianie Rossii* (St. Petersburg, 1878), vol. I.

Bliumin, I. G., *Ocherki ekonomicheskoi mysli v Rossii v pervoi polovine XIX veka* (Moscow-Leningrad, 1940).

Blum, Jerome, *Lord and Peasant in Russia from the Ninth to the Nineteenth Century* (Princeton, 1961).

Blum, K. L., *Eines Russischen Staatsmanns, des Grafen Jakob Johann Sievers, Denkwürdikeiten zur Geschichte Russlands* (Leipzig, 1858).

Blumenfeld, Hans, "Russian City Planning of the Eighteenth and Early Nineteenth Centuries," *Journal of the American Society of Architectural Historians*, vol. 4, no. 1 (Jan. 1944), 22-33.

Bogdanovich, M., *Istoriia tsarstvovaniia Imperatora Aleksandra I* (St. Petersburg, 1869-71), 6 vols.

Borovoi, S. Ia., "Gosudarstvennyi dolg kak istochnik pervonachal'nago nakopleniia v Rossii," *Voprosy genezisa kapitalizma v Rossii* (Leningrad, 1960), 217-28.

————, "K istorii promyshlennoi politiki Rossii v 20-50kh godakh XIX v.," *Istoricheskie zapiski*, vol. 69 (1961), 276-90.

————, *Kredit i banki Rossii seredina XVII v.-1861 g.* (Moscow, 1958).

————, "Kreditnaia politika tsarizma v usloviiakh razlozhenie krepostnichestva," *Voprosy istorii* (1954), no. 2, 129-38.

Botkin, A. P., *Pavel Mikhailovich Tretiakov v zhizni i iskusstve* (2nd edition, Moscow, 1960).

Brandt, B. F., *Inostrannye kapitaly v Rossii* (St. Petersburg, 1899).

Britkin, A. S., *Pervye tulskie stroiteli slozhnykh vododeistvuiushchikh mashin* (Moscow, 1950).

Bulich, N. N., *Iz pervykh let Kazan'skago universiteta, 1805-1819* (2nd edition, St. Petersburg, 1904), 2 vols.

Buryshkin, P. A., *Moskva kupicheskaia* (New York, 1954).

Cadot, M., "Les débuts de la navigation à vapeur et l'émigration française en Russie," *Cahiers du monde russe et soviétique*, vol. IV (1963), 382-99.

Christoff, Peter, "A. S. Khomiakov on the Agricultural and Industrial Problem in Russia," A. D. Ferguson, editor, *Essays in Russian History* (Archon: Hamden, Conn., 1964), 134-57.

Chulkov, N. P., "Moskovskoe kupichestvo XVIII i XIX vv.," *Russkii Arkhiv* (1907), vol. III, 489-502.

Clapham, J. H., *An Economic History of Modern Britain* (Cambridge, 1950-1952), 2 vols.

Clark, Victor S., *History of Manufactures in the United States* (New York, 1929), vol. I.

Confino, Michael, "Maîtres de forges et ouvriers dans les usines métallurgiques de l'Oural aux XVIIIe-XIXe siècles," *Cahiers du monde russe et soviétique*, vol. I (1960), 239-84.

————, *Domaines et seigneurs en Russie vers la fin du xviiie siècle*, Institut d'Etudes Slaves, *Collection historique*, vol. XVIII (1963).

Corti, E., *The Rise of the House of Rothschild* (New York, 1928).

Crihan, Anton, *Le capital étranger en Russie* (Paris, 1934).

Crosby, Alfred, *America, Russia, Hemp and Napoleon, American Trade with Russia and the Baltic, 1783-1812* (Ohio State University Press, 1965).

Curtiss, John S., *The Russian Army Under Nicholas I, 1825-1855* (Duke University Press: Durham, N. C., 1965).

Danilevskii, V. V., *Russkaia tekhnika* (2nd edition, Leningrad, 1948).

Dementev, A. G., Zapadov, A. V., and Cherepakhov, M. S., *Russkaia periodicheskaia pechat 1702-1894 g.g., spravochnik* (Moscow, 1959).

Dmitriev, N. N., *Pervye russkie sittsenabivnye manufaktury XVIII v.* (Moscow, 1935).

Druzhinin, N. M., *La genèse du capitalisme en Russie* (Moscow, 1955).

————, *Gosudarstvennye krest'iane i reforma P. D. Kiseleva* (Moscow, 1946-1958), 2 vols.

————, "Sotsial'no-politicheskie vzgliady P. D. Kiseleva," *Voprosy istorii* (1946), nos. 2-3, 33-55.

Ekzempliarskii, P. M., *Istoriia goroda Ivanova* (Ivanovo, 1958), vol. I.

Entner, Marvin, *Russian-Persian Commercial Relations*, University of Florida Monographs, Social Sciences, no. 28, Fall 1965.

Eventov, L. Ia., *Inostrannye kapitaly v russkoi promyshlennosti* (Moscow-Leningrad, 1931).

Evreiskaia entsiklopediia (Obshchestvo dlia Nauchnykh Evreiskikh Izdanii and Brockhaus-Efron, St. Petersburg, no date).

Falkovskii, N. I., *Moskva v istorii tekhniki* (Moscow, 1950).

Feoktistov, E., *Magnitskii, materialy dlia istorii prosveshcheniia v Rossii* (St. Petersburg, 1865).

Figurovskii, N. A., editor, *Istoriia estestvoznaniia v Rossii* (Moscow, 1957), vol. I, parts 1 and 2.

Fiziko-matematicheskii fakultet Kharkovskogo universiteta za pervye 100 let ego sushchestvovaniia, 1805-1905 (Kharkov, 1908).

Fuss, M. P. H., *Coup d'oeil historique sur le dernier quart de siècle de l'existence de l'Académie Impériale des Sciences de Saint-Pétersbourg* (St. Petersburg, 1843).

Gamel, I., *Istoricheskii ocherk elektricheskikh telegraf* (St. Petersburg, 1886).

Garelin, Ia. P., *Gorod Ivanovo-Voznesensk* (Shuia, 1884), vol. I.

Garfunkel, A., Nikulin, L., and Semanov, S., *Materialy po istorii Leningradskogo universiteta 1819-1917* (Leningrad, 1961).

Genezis kapitalizma v promyshlennosti (Moscow, 1963).

Gershenkron, Alexander, *Economic Backwardness in Historical Perspective* (New York, 1965).

Giatsintov, N., "Pravitel'stvo i chastnaia zheleznodorozhnaia promyshlennost v Rossii v tsarstvovaniia imperatorov Nikolai I i Aleksandra II," *Russkoe ekonomicheskoe obozrenie*, No. 8 (1902), 1-46.

Gnevushev, A., *Politicheskie i ekonomicheskie vzgliady Gr. N. S. Mordvinova* (Kiev, 1904).

Golovshchikov, K., *Pavel Grigorevich Demidov i istoriia osnovannago im v Iaroslave uchilishcha 1803-1886* (Iaroslav, 1887).

Gorlovskii, M. A., and Piatnitskii, A. N., *Iz istorii rabochogo dvizheniia na Urale* (Sverdlovsk, 1954).

"Gornii Institut za 150 let, kratkii istoricheskii ocherk," *Gornii zhurnal*, 99th year (1923), 668-98.

"Graf Egor Frantsevich Kankrin: ocherk ego zhizneopisaniia," *Russkii arkhiv* (1866) vol. IV, 113-26.

Grekov, B. D., "Tambovskaia imenie M. S. Lunina v pervoi chetverti XIX v.," *Izvestiia Akademii Nauk SSSR, Otdelenie Obshchestvennykh Nauk* (1932), 481-520, 623-48.

Grigorev, V. V., *Imperatorskii St. Peterburgskii universitet v techenie pervykh piatidesiati let ego sushchestvovaniia* (St. Petersburg, 1870).

Grunwald, Constantin de, *La vie de Nicolas Ier* (Paris, 1946).

Gutman, Peter, "The Serf Entrepreneur in Russia: a Comment," *Explorations in Entrepreneurial History*, vol. 7 (1954), 48-52.

Haber, Ludwig, *The Chemical Industry During the Nineteenth Century* (Oxford, 1948).

Hagen, Everett E., *On the Theory of Social Change* (Homewood, Illinois, 1962).

Halperin, Jean, *Le rôle des assurances dans les débuts du capitalisme moderne* (published thesis, University of Zurich, 1945).

Bibliography

Hans, Nicholas, *A History of Russian Educational Policy, 1701-1917* (London, 1931).

————, *The Russian Tradition in Education* (London, 1963).

Henderson, W. O., *The Industrial Revolution in Europe 1815-1914* (Chicago, 1961).

Henry, J. D., *Baku* (London, no date).

Hidy, Ralph, *The House of Baring in American Trade and Finance 1763-1861* (Harvard, 1949).

Iakovlev, A. F., *Ekonomicheskie krizisy v Rossii* (Moscow, 1955).

Iakovlev, B., "Vozniknovenie i etapy razvitiia kapitalisticheskogo uklada v Rossii," *Voprosy istorii* (1950), no. 9, 91-104.

Iakovtsevskii, V. N., *Kupicheskii kapital v feodal'no-krepostnichestkoi Rossii* (Moscow, 1953).

Iarotzkii, A., *Elektromagnitnii telegraf—velikoe Russkoe izobretenie* (Moscow, 1953).

Iatsunskii, V. K., "Geografiia rynka zheleza v doreformennoi Rossii," *Voprosy geografii*, vol. 50 (1960), 110-45.

————, "Materialy pravitel'stvennogo obsledovaniia zavodov chernoi metallurgii Rossii v pervoi polovine 50-kh godov XIX v. kak istori- cheskii istochnik," *Voprosy sotsial'no-ekonomicheskoi istorii i istochnikovedeniia perioda feodalizma v Rossii, sbornik statei k 70- letuiu A. A. Novosel'skogo* (Moscow, 1961), 357-62.

————, "Pomeshchichi sakharnye zavody v Rossii v pervoi polovine XIX v.," *Akademiku Borisu Dmitrievichu Grekovu ko dniu semi- desiatiletiia, sbornik statei* (Moscow, 1952), 343-50.

————, "Promyshlennii perevorot v Rossii," *Voprosy istorii* (1952), no. 12, 48-70.

————, "Rol otechestvennogo mashinostroieniia v snabzhenii pria- dil'nym oborudovaniem russkikh fabrik v pervoi polovine XIX v.," *Istoricheskie zapiski*, vol. 42 (1953), 276-84.

————, "Rol Peterburga v promyshlennom razvitii Rossii," *Voprosy istorii* (1954), no. 9, 95-103.

————, "Znachenie ekonomicheskikh sviazei s Rossii dlia kho- ziaistvennogo razvitiia gorodov pribaltiki v epokhu kapitalizma," *Istoricheskie zapiski*, vol. 45 (1954), 105-17.

Ikonnikov, V. S., *Graf N. S. Mordvinov* (St. Petersburg, 1873).

————, *Kiev v 1654-1855 gg., istoricheskii ocherk* (Kiev, 1904).

Ischchanian, B., *Die ausländischen Elemente in der russischen Volks- wirtschaft* (Berlin, 1913).

Istoricheskii ocherk oblozheniia torgovli i promyslov v Rossii (St. Petersburg, 1893).

Istoricheskii ocherk razvitiia zheleznykh dorog v Rossii c ikh osno- vaniia do 1897 g. vkliuchitel'no (St. Petersburg, 1898).

Istoriia Moskovskogo universiteta (Moscow, 1955), vol. I.

Istoriia Moskvy (Moscow, 1954), vol. III.

Iuditskii, A. D., "Evreiskaia burzhuaziia i evreiskii proletariat v tekstil'noi promyshlennosti pervoi poloviny XIX v.," *Istoricheskii sbornik*, vol. 4 (1935), 108-33.

Iuksimovich, Ch. M., *Manufakturnaia promyshlennost v proshlom i nastoiashchem* (Moscow, 1915), vol. I.

Iuprevich, V., *Istoricheskii ocherk piatidesiatiletiia Imperatorskago Odesskago Obshchestva Istorii i Drevnostei 1839-1889* (Odessa, 1889).

Izmailovskaia, E. I., *Russkoe sel'sko-khoziaistvennoe mashinostroenie* (Moscow, 1920).

Johnson, William H., *Russia's Educational Heritage* (Pittsburgh, 1950).

Kafengauz, B. B., *Istoriia khoziaistva Demidovykh XVIII-XIX vv.* (Moscow-Leningrad, 1949), vol. I.

————, "Voina 1812: ieie vlianie na sotsial'no-ekonomicheskuiu zhizn Rossii," *Voprosy istorii* (1962), no. 7, 69-80.

Kagan, V. F., *Lobachevskii* (Moscow-Leningrad, 1944).

————, *N. Lobachevskii and his Contribution to Science* (Moscow, 1957).

Kahan, A., "Continuity in Economic Activity and Policy During the Post-Petrine Period in Russia," *Journal of Economic History*, vol. XXV (1965), 61-85.

————, "The Costs of 'Westernization' in Russia: The Gentry and the Economy in the Eighteenth Century," *Slavic Review*, vol. XXV (1966), 40-66.

————, "Entrepreneurship in the Early Development of Iron Manufacturing in Russia," *Economic Development and Cultural Change*, vol. X (1962), 395.

Kaminka, A., *Aktsionerniia kompanii* (St. Petersburg, 1902).

Karaev, G. N., *Vosniknovenie sluzhby voennykh soobshchenii na zheleznykh dorogakh Rossii 1851-1878* (Moscow, 1949).

Karataev, N. K., *Ekonomicheskie nauki v Moskovskom universitete 1755-1955* (Moscow, 1956).

Karnovich, E., *Zamechatel'nye i zagadochnye lichnosti XVIII i XIX stoletii* (2nd edition, St. Petersburg, 1893).

Kashkarov, M., *Denezhnoe obrashchenie v Rossii* (St. Petersburg, 1898), 2 vols.

Kerner, Robert J., *The Urge to the Sea* (Berkeley, 1946).

Kharkovskii gosudarstvennyi universitet imeni A. M. Gorkogo za 150 let 1805-1955 (Kharkov, 1955).

Khodnev, A. I., *Istoriia Imperatorskago Volnago Ekonomicheskago Obshchestva* (St. Petersburg, 1865).

Khromov, P. A., *Ekonomicheskoe razvitie Rossii v XIX-XX vekakh 1800-1917* (Academy of Sciences, U.S.S.R., 1950).

————, *Ocherki ekonomiki feodalizma v Rossii* (Moscow, 1957).

Bibliography

Kiev i universitet Sv. Vladimir pri Imperator Nikolai I, 1825-1855 (Kiev, 1896).

Kislinskii, N., *Nasha zheleznodorozhnaia politika po dokumentam arkhiva komiteta ministrov* (St. Petersburg, 1902), vol. I.

Kniazev, G. A. and Koltsov, A. V., *Kratkii ocherk istorii Akademii Nauk S.S.S.R.* (2nd edition, Moscow-Leningrad, 1957).

Knyzkov, S. A. and Serbov, N. I., *Ocherki istorii narodnogo obrazovaniia v Rossii do epokhi reform Aleksandra II* (Moscow, 1910).

Kolarz, Walter, *Religion in the Soviet Union* (St. Martin's Press, 1961).

Kolman, E., *Velikii russkii myslitel N. I. Lobachevskii* (Moscow, 1956).

Kononenko, K., *Ukraine and Russia, a History of the Economic Relations Between Ukraine and Russia 1654-1917* (Marquette, 1958).

Kononkov, A. F., *Istoriia fiziki v Moskovskom universitete 1755-1859* (Moscow, 1955).

Konstantinov, N. A. and Struminskii, V. Ia., *Ocherki po istorii nachal'nogo obrazovaniia v Rossii* (Moscow, 1949).

Kopanev, A. I., *Naselenie Peterburga v pervoi polovine XIX veka* (Moscow-Leningrad, 1957).

Korbut, M. K., *Kazan'skii gosudarstvennyi universitet imeni V. I. Ulianov-Lenina za 125 let 1804/5-1929/30* (Kazan, 1930), vol. I.

Kovalevsky, Pierre, "Le Raskol et son rôle dans le développement industriel de la Russie," *Archives de sociologie des religions*, vol. 3 (1957), 37-56.

Kovbasiok, S. M., *Odessa, ocherk istorii goroda-geroia* (Odessa, 1957), vol. I.

Kratkii istoricheskii ocherk nachala i rasprostraneniia zheleznykh dorog v Rossii po 1897 vkliuchitel'no (St. Petersburg, 1898), vol. I.

Kratkii istoricheskii ocherk uchebnykh zavedenii vedomstva putei soobshcheniia (St. Petersburg, 1900).

Kulisher, Josef, "Die kapitalistischen Unternehmer in Russland (insbesondere die Bauern als Unternehmer in den Anfangsstadien des Kapitalismus)," *Archiv für Sozialwissenschaft und Sozialpolitik* (1931), vol. 65, 309-55.

———, *Ocherk po istorii russkoi torgovli* (Petrograd, 1923).

Kuznetsov, B. G., *Lomonosov, Lobachevskii, Mendeleev, ocherki zhizn i mirovozzreniia* (Moscow-Leningrad, 1945).

Kuznetsov, I. V., editor, *Liudi russkoi nauki* (Moscow, 1961).

Lalaev, M., *Istoricheskii ocherk voenno-uchebnykh zavedenii* (St. Petersburg, 1880), 2 vols.

Lapatin, P., *Moskva, ocherki po istorii velikogo goroda* (Moscow, 1959).

Lappo-Danilevskii, A., *Russkie promyshlennye i torgovye kompanii v pervoi polovine XVIII stoletiia* (St. Petersburg, 1899).

Lebed, A. and Iakovlev, B., "Transportnoe znachenie gidrotekhnicheskikh sooruzhenii S.S.S.R.," Institute for the Study of the History and Culture of the U.S.S.R., Munich, *Issledovanie i materialy,* series I, vol. 14 (1954).

LeFleming, H. M. and Price, J. H., *Russian Steam Locomotives* (London, 1960).

Levitskii, G. V., editor, *Biograficheskii slovar professorov i prepodavatelei imperatorskogo Iurevskogo, byvshogo Derptskogo universiteta za sto let ego sushchestvovaniia, 1802-1902* (Iurev, 1902), vol. I.

Lisovskii, N. M., *Bibliografiia russkoi periodicheskoi pechati 1703-1900* (Petrograd, 1915).

Litvinova, E. F., *Lobachevskii, N. I., ego zhizn i nauchnaia deiatel'nost* (St. Petersburg, 1895).

Liubomirov, P. G., *Ocherki po istorii promyshlennosti v XVIII i nachale XIX vv.* (PRIBOI, 1930).

———, *Vygovskoe obshchezhitel'stvo* (Moscow-Saratov, 1924).

Livanov, Fedor V., *Raskol'niki i ostrozhniki, ocherki i razskazy* (St. Petersburg, 1872-73), 3 vols.

Livshitz, R. S., *Razmeshchenie promyshlennosti v dorevoliutsionnoi Rossii* (Moscow, 1956).

Loone, L. A., "Iz istorii promyshlennogo perevorota v Estonii," *Voprosi istorii* (1952), no. 5, 77-96.

Loranskii, A., *Aperçu sur les institutions subsidiaires pour les ouvriers attachés aux établissements métallurgiques en Russie* (St. Petersburg, 1876).

———, *Istoricheskii ocherk Gornago Instituta* (St. Petersburg, 1873)

———, *Kratkii istoricheskii ocherk administrativnykh uchrezhdenii gornago vedomstva v Rossii 1700-1900 g.g.* (St. Petersburg, 1900).

Lukianov, P. M., *Istoriia khimicheskikh promyslov i khimicheskoi promyshlennosti Rossii* (Moscow-Leningrad, 1948), vol. I.

Maksimov, A. and Medvedev, E., "Iz istorii Kazan'skoi sukonnoi manufaktury," *Istoriia proletariata S.S.S.R.,* vol. 4 (16) (1933), 171-206.

Martinson, E. E., *Istoriia osnovaniia Tartuskogo (b. Derptskogo-Iurevskogo) universiteta* (Leningrad, 1954).

Maslov, S. A., *Istoricheskoe obozrenie deistvii i trudov Imperatorskago Moskovskago Obshchestva Sel'skago Khoziaistva so vremeni ego osnovaniia do 1846 goda* (Moscow, 1846).

Matthesius, Oscar, *Russische Eisenbahnpolitik im XIX Jahrhundert 1836-1881* (Berlin, 1903).

Materialy po izucheniiu Smolenskoi oblasti (Smolensk, 1957), vol. II.

Mavrodin, V. V., "Krepostnicheskii kharakter dvorianskogo predprinimatel'stva kontsa XVIII i nachala XIX vv.," *Problemy istorii dokapitalisticheskikh obshchestv* (1934), no. 4.

———, Sladkevich, N. G. and Shilov, L. A., *Leningradskii universitet* (Leningrad, 1957).

Maydell, B. von, "Die Stieglitz aus Arolsen," *Deutsches Familienarchiv* (1956), vol. V, 78-86, and plates.

Mayevski, N., "Mémoire sur les expériences faites à l'établissement de M. Krupp à Essen au mois de novembre 1867 pour déterminer les pressions des gaz de la poudre dans l'âme des bouches à feu," *Mémoires couronnés et autres mémoires publiés par l'Académie Royale des Lettres et des Beaux Arts de Belgique* (Bruxelles, 1870), vol. XXI, no. 4.

Mekhanicheskii zavod Liudvig Nobel 1862-1912 (no author, date or publisher).

Mel'nikov, P. I., *Polnoe sobranie sochinenii* (2nd edition, St. Petersburg, 1909), vol. VII.

Menshutkin, B., *Russia's Lomonosov* (Princeton, 1952).

Meshalin, I. V., *Tekstil'naia promyshlennost krest'ian Moskovskoi gubernii v XVIII i pervoi polovine XIX veka* (Moscow-Leningrad, 1950).

Mezhenko, Iu. A., *Russkaia tekhnicheskaia periodika, 1800-1916* (Moscow-Leningrad, 1955).

Migulin, P., *Nasha bankovaia politika 1729-1903* (Kharkov, 1904).

Mikhailovskaia Artilleriiskaia Akademiia i Uchilishche (St. Petersburg, 1889).

Ministerstvo finansov, 1802-1902 (St. Petersburg, 1902), vol. I.

Monas, Sidney, *The Third Section* (Harvard, 1961).

Moskovskoe Strakhovoe ot Ognia Obshchestvo za 50 let sushchestvovaniia 1858-1908.

Nasonov, A. N., "Iz istorii krepostnoi votchiny XIX veka v Rossii," *Izvestiia Akademii Nauk SSSR*, VI series (1926), 499-526.

———, "Khoziaistvo krupnoi votchiny nakanune osvobozhdeniia krest'ian v Rossii," *Izvestiia Akademii Nauk SSSR, Otdelenie Gumanitarnykh Nauk*, VII series (1928), 343-74.

Nebolsine, G. P., *Statisticheskoe obozrenie vneshnei torgovli Rossii* (St. Petersburg, 1850), 2 vols.

Nemirov, G., *Moskovskaia birzha 1838-1889* (Moscow, 1889).

Nevzorov, "Russkie birzhi," *Uchenye zapiski Imperatorskago Iurevskago universiteta*, vol. 5 (1897), nos. 3 and 4.

Nifontov, A. S., "Polotnianye manufaktury Rossii v 1854 g.," *Istoricheskie zapiski*, vol. 43 (1953), 222-36.

Nikitin, V. P., *Vedushchaia rol otechestvennoi nauki i tekhniki v razvitii elektricheskoi svarki metallov* (Moscow, 1953).

Nikol, C. D., *Établissement du lycée Richelieu à Odessa* (Paris, 1917).

Nikol'skii, N. M., *Istoriia Russkoi tserkvi* (Moscow-Leningrad, 1931).

Odessa 1794-1894 (Odessa, 1895).

Okun, S. B., *The Russian American Company* (Harvard, 1951).

V pamiat 75-ti letnego iubileia Pervago Rossiiskago Strakhovago Obshchestva Uchrezhdennago v 1827 godu (St. Petersburg, 1903).

Parry, Albert, *Whistler's Father* (New York, 1939).

Pashkov, A., editor, *Istoriia russkoi ekonomicheskoi mysli* (Moscow, 1958), vol. I, part 2.

———, *A History of Russian Economic Thought*, vol. I, part 1, translated by John M. Letiche (Berkeley-Los Angeles, 1964).

Pavlenko, N. I., *Istoriia metallurgii v Rossii XVIII veka* (Moscow, 1962).

———, *Razvitie metallurgicheskoi promyshlennosti Rossii v pervoi polovine XVIII veka* (Moscow, 1953).

Pazhitnov, K. A., *Ocherki istorii tekstil'noi promyshlennosti dorevoliutsionnoi Rossii, khlopchatobumazhnaia, l'no-penkovaia i shelkovaia promyshlennost* (Moscow, 1958).

———, *Ocherki istorii tekstil'noi promyshlennosti dorevoliutsionnoi Rossii, sherstianaia promyshlennost* (Moscow, 1955).

———, *Problema remeslennykh tsekhov v zakonodatel'stva russkago absolutizma* (Moscow, 1952).

———, "K voprosu o promyshlennom perevorote v Rossii," *Voprosy istorii* (1952), no. 5, 68-76.

Pecherin, Ia. I., *Istoricheskii obzor rospisei gosudarstvennykh dokhodov i raskhodov s 1803 po 1843 god vkliuchitel'no* (St. Petersburg, 1896).

———, *Istoricheskii obzor rospisei gosudarstvennykh dokhodov i raskhodov s 1844 po 1864 god vkliuchitel'no* (St. Petersburg, 1898).

Petukhov, E. V., *Imperatorskii Iurevskii byvshii Derptskii universitet za sto let ego sushchestvovaniia 1802-1902, istoricheskii ocherk* (Iurev, 1902), vol. I.

Picheta, V. I., "Fritredery i protektsionisty v Rossii v pervoi chetverti XIX veka," *Kniga dlia chteniia po istorii novogo vremeni* (St. Petersburg, 1912), vol. III, 620-51.

Pintner, Walter M., "Government and Industry During the Ministry of Count Kankrin, 1823-1844," *Slavic Review*, vol. XXIII (1964), 45-62.

———, "Inflation in Russia during the Crimean War Period," *American Slavic and East European Review*, vol. XVIII (1959), 81-87.

———, *Russian Economic Policy Under Nicholas I* (Cornell, 1967).

Platov, A. and Kirpichev, L., *Istoricheskii ocherk obrazovaniia i razvitiia artilleriiskago uchilishcha 1820-1870* (St. Petersburg, 1870).

Pogozhev, A., "Votchinye fabriki i ikh fabrichnye," *Vestnik Evropy*, vol. 138 (1889), 5-43.

Pogrebinskii, A. P., *Ocherki istorii finansov dorevoliutsionnoi Rossii* (Moscow, 1954).

Pokshishevskii, V. V., "Territorial'noe formirovanie promyshlennogo kompleksa Peterburga v XVII-XIX vekakh," *Voprosy geografii*, vol. 20 (1950), 122-62.

Poliakhov, N. N., *Ocherki po istorii Leningradskogo universiteta* (Leningrad, 1962), vol. I.

Polianskii, F. Ia., *Pervonachal'noe nakoplenie kapitala v Rossii* (Moscow, 1958).

Portal, Roger, "Origines d'une bourgeoisie industrielle en Russie," *Revue d'histoire moderne et contemporaine*, vol. VIII (1961), 35-60.

———, *L'Oural au XVIIIᵉ siècle* (Paris, 1950).

———, "Du servage à la bourgeoisie: la famille Konovalov," *Revue des études slaves*, vol. 38 (1961), 143-50.

Postroika Nikolaevskoi Zheleznoi Dorogi 1842-1851, kratkii istoricheskii ocherk (St. Petersburg, 1901).

Predtechenskii, A. V., "Bor'ba protektsionistov c fritrederami v nachale XIX veka," Leningrad State University, *Uchenye zapiski*, No. 48 (1939), 143-56.

———, and Golant, V. Ia., *Kolybel russkoi nauki* (Leningrad, 1959).

———, *Ocherki obshchestvenno-politicheskii istorii Rossii v pervoi chetverti XIX veka* (Moscow-Leningrad, 1957), 295-322.

Preobrazhenskii, A. A., "O sostave aktsionerov Rossiisko-Amerikanskoi Kompanii v nachale XIX v.," *Istoricheskie zapiski*, vol. 67 (1960), 286-98.

Puryear, Vernon, "Odessa, Its Rise and International Importance, 1815-1850," *Pacific Historical Review*, vol. III (1934), 192-215.

Raffalovich, A., *Russia: Its Trade and Commerce* (London, 1918).

Rapaport, I., *Les faits de castration rituelle, essai sur les formes pathologiques de la conscience collective* (published doctoral thesis, University of Paris, 1945).

Rashin, A. G., *Formirovanie promyshlennogo proletariata v Rossii* (Moscow, 1940).

———, *Naselenie Rossii za 100 let 1811-1913* (Moscow, 1956).

Reifer, Stanley, "The Duke de Richelieu and the Growth of Odessa 1803-1814" (unpublished master's thesis, New York University, 1964).

Riasanovskii, N., *Nicholas I and Official Nationality in Russia 1825-1855* (Berkeley, 1959).

Romanovich-Slavatinskii, A., *Dvorianstvo v Rossii* (St. Petersburg, 1870).

Rosovsky, Henry, "The Serf Entrepreneur in Russia," *Explorations in Entrepreneurial History*, vol. VI (1953-1954), 207-29.

Rostow, W. W., *The Stages of Economic Growth* (Cambridge, 1960).

Rozenfeld, S. Ia. and Klimenko, R. I., *Istoriia mashinostroeniia S.S.S.R.* (Moscow, 1961).

Rozhdestvenskii, S. V., *Istoricheskii obzor deiatel'nosti ministerstva narodnago prosveshcheniia 1802-1902* (St. Petersburg, 1902).

Rozhkov, N. A., "Prokhorovskaia manufaktura za pervye 40 let eie sushchestvovaniia," *Istorik marksist*, vol. 6 (1927), 79-110.

Rozhkova, M. K., *Ekonomicheskaia politika tsarskogo pravitel'stva na srednem vostoke vo vtoroi chetverti XIX veka i russkaia burzhuaziia* (Moscow-Leningrad, 1949).

————, editor, *Ocherki ekonomicheskoi istorii Rossii pervoi poloviny XIX veka* (Moscow, 1959).

————, "Promyshlennost Moskvy v pervoi chetverti XIX veka," *Voprosy istorii* (1946), nos. 11-12, 89-103.

————, "K voprosu znachenii iarmarok vo vnutrenei torgovle doreformennoi Rossii (pervaia polovina XIX v.)," *Istoricheskie zapiski*, vol. 54 (1955), 298-314.

Rustik, O., "Staroobriadcheskoe Preobrazhenskoe kladbishche, kak nakoplialis kapitaly v Moskve," *Bor'ba klassov* (1934), nos. 7-8, 70-79.

Ryndziunskii, P. G., *Gorodskoe grazhdanstvo doreformennoi Rossii* (Academy of Sciences, U.S.S.R., 1958).

————, "Staroobriadcheskaia organizatsiia v osloviiakh razvitiia promyshlennogo kapitalizma," *Voprosy istorii religii i ateizma*, vol. I (1950), 188-248.

Schmookler, J., *Invention and Economic Growth* (Harvard, 1966).

Schulze-Gaevernitz, G., *Volkswirtschaftliche Studien aus Russland* (Leipzig, 1899).

Seleznev, I. Ia., *Istoricheskii ocherk Imperatorskago byvshago Tsarskosel'skago nyne Aleksandrovskago Litseia za pervoe ego piatidesiatiletie c 1811 po 1861 god* (St. Petersburg, 1861).

Sellers, Colman, "An obituary notice of Mr. Joseph Harrison, Jr.," *American Philosophical Society, Proceedings*, vol. 14 (1875), 347-55.

Semmes, John E., *John H. B. Latrobe and His Times, 1803-1881* (Baltimore, 1917).

Shevyrev, S., *Istoriia Moskovskogo universiteta* (Moscow, 1855).

Shimkin, D., "The Entreprencur in Tsarist and Soviet Russia," *Explorations in Entrepreneurial History*, vol. II (1949-1950), 24-34.

Shkvarikov, V. A., *Ocherki istorii planirovki i zastroiki Russkikh gorodov* (Moscow, 1954).

Sinclair, Angus, *Development of the Locomotive Engine* (New York, 1907).

Singer, Charles *et al.*, editors, *A History of Technology* (Oxford, 1954), vol. IV.

Sinitsyn, P. V., *Preobrazhenskoe i okruzhaiushchie ego mesty, ikh proshloe i nastoiashchee* (Moscow, 1895).

Skalkovsky, C., *Les ministres des finances de la Russie 1802-1890* (Paris, 1891).

Sivkov, K. V., "Biudzhet krupnogo sobstvennika-krepostnika pervoi treti XIX v.," *Istoricheskie zapiski*, vol. 9 (1940), 125-51.

Skerpan, A., "The Russian National Economy and Emancipation," A. Ferguson and A. Levin, editors, *Essays in Russian History* (Archon: Hamden, Conn., 1964).

Sliozberg, G. B., *Baron G. O. Gintsburg, ego zhizn i deiatel'nost* (Paris, 1933).

———, *Baron Horace O. de Gunzbourg, sa vie et son oeuvre*, French translation by Prince Vladimir Bariatinsky (Paris, 1933).

Sokolovskii, E., *Piatidesiatiletie Instituta i Korpus Inzhenerov Putei Soobshcheniia* (St. Petersburg, 1859).

Solov, V. V., "Nachalo zheleznodorozhnago dela v Rossii 1836-1855," *Vestnik Evropy*, vol. 197 (1899), 117-63, 581-626.

Stasov, V., "Pavel Mikhailovich Tretiakov i ego kartinnaia gallereia," *Russkaia Starina*, vol. 80 (1893), 569-608.

Stine, Wilbur, *The Contributions of H. F. E. Lenz to Electromagnetism* (Philadelphia, 1923).

Sto let Pulkovskoi Observatorii, sbornik statei (Moscow-Leningrad, 1945).

Stoletie voennago ministerstva, 1802-1902 (St. Petersburg, 1902), vol. VII: *Glavnoe inzhenernoe upravlenie, istoricheskii ocherk.*

———, vol. IX: *Imperatorskaia Voenno-Meditsinskaia Akademiia, istoricheskii ocherk.*

———, vol. X: *Glavnoe upravlenie voenno-uchebnykh zavedenii, istoricheskii ocherk.*

Stolpianskii, P. N., *Zhizn i byt Peterburgskoi fabriki 1704-1914* (Leningrad, 1925).

Storozhev, V. N., editor, *Istoriia Moskovskago Kupicheskogo Obshchestva* (Moscow, 1914), 5 vols.

———, *Voina i moskovskoe kupichestvo* (Moscow, 1914).

Strumilin, S. G., *Chernaia metallurgiia v Rossii i v S.S.S.R.* (Moscow-Leningrad, 1935).

———, *Istoriia chernoi metallurgii v S.S.S.R.* (Moscow, 1954), vol. I.

———, *Ocherki ekonomicheskoi istorii Rossii* (Moscow, 1960).

Sukhomlinov, M. I., *Istoriia Rossiiskoi Akademii* (St. Petersburg, 1874-88), 8 vols.

Sytin, P. V., *Istoriia planirovki i zastroiki Moskvy 1762-1812* (Moscow, 1954), vol. 2.

———, *Iz istorii moskovskikh ulitz* (3rd edition, Moscow, 1958).

Tarle, E. V., "Byla li ekaterininskaia Rossiia ekonomichesku otstaloiu stranoiu?," *Sochineniia*, vol. IV (Moscow, 1958), 2 vols.

———, *Krimskaia Voina* (2nd edition, Moscow, 1950), 2 vols.

Taylor, George R., *The Transportation Revolution 1815-60* (New York, 1951).

Technischer Verein zu Riga, *Beiträge zur Geschichte der Industrie Rigas* (Riga, 1910-1912) vols. I-III.

Tengoborskii, L., *Commentaries on the Productive Forces of Russia* (English edition, London, 1855-56), 2 vols.

Terentev, P. N., *Kratkii istoricheskii ocherk deiatel'nosti Prokhorovskoi Trekhgornoi Manufaktury po tekhnicheskomu i obshchemu obrazovaniiu rabochikh 1816-1899 gody* (Moscow, 1899).

Tikhonov, B. V., "Obzor 'zapisok' mestnykh sel'skokhoziaistvennykh obshchestv 30-50kh godov XIX v.," *Problemy istochnikovedeniia*, vol. IX, 92-162.

———, "Ofitsial'nye zhurnaly vtoroi poloviny 20-kh i 50-kh godov XIX v. ('Zhurnal manufaktur i torgovli,' 'Gornii zhurnal,' 'Zhurnal ministerstva gosudarstvennykh imushchestv,' i 'Zhurnal ministerstva vnutrennikh del') kak istochnik dlia izucheniia istorii russkoi promyshlennosti," *Problemy istochnikovedeniia*, vol. VII, 150-203.

———, "Razvitie sveklosakharnoi promyshlennosti vo vtoroi polovine 40-kh i 50-kh godakh XIX v., (K istorii nachala promyshlennogo perevorota)," *Istoricheskie zapiski*, vol. 62 (1958), 126-69.

Timofeev, A. G., *Istoriia S-Peterburgskoi birzhi 1703-1903* (St. Petersburg, 1903).

———, *Istoriia S-Peterburgskago Kommercheskago Uchilishcha* (St. Petersburg, 1901), 2 vols.

Timoshenko, Stephen, "The Development of Engineering Education in Russia," *Russian Review*, vol. 15 (1956), 173-85.

Tridtsat let deiatel'nosti Tovarishchestvo Neftianogo Proizvodstva Brat'ev Nobel 1879-1909 (no date or place of publication).

Trusov, G. M., *Podvodnye lodki v russkom i sovetskom flote* (2nd edition, Leningrad, 1963).

Tugan-Baranovskii, M. I., *Russkaia fabrika v proshlom i nastoiashchem* (St. Petersburg, 1898), vol. I.

———, "Voina 1812 i promyshlennoe razvitie Rossii," *Otechestvennaia voina i russkoe obshchestvo 1812-1912* (Moscow, 1912), vol. VII, 105-12.

Tyslov, N., *Alfavitnyi ukazatel k atlasu 13-ti chastei S. Peterburga* (St. Petersburg, 1849).

Upravlenie imperatorskikh zavodov, *Imperatorskii Farfarovii Zavod 1744-1904* (St. Petersburg. 1904).

Bibliography

Urodkov, S. A., *Peterburgo-Moskovskaia Zheleznaia Doroga, istoriia stroitel'stva 1842-1851* (Leningrad, 1951).

Vainshtein, O. L., Gukovskii, M. A., and Mavrodin, V. V., *Leningradskii universitet 1819-1944* (Leningrad, 1944).

Varadinov, N. V., *Istoriia ministerstva vnutrennykh del* (St. Petersburg, 1858), vol. I, parts 1 and 2.

Varsanoveva, V. A., *Moskovskoe Obshchestvo Ispytatelei Prirody i ego znachenie v razvitii otechestvennoi nauki* (Moscow, 1955).

Vasilev, B. N., "Formirovanie promyshlennogo proletariata Ivanovskoi oblasti," *Voprosy istorii* (1952), no. 6, 99-117.

Vassilief, A., *P. L. Tchébychef et son oeuvre scientifique* (Turin, 1898).

Vavilov, S. I., *Akademik V. V. Petrov 1761-1834* (Moscow-Leningrad, 1940).

Velikin, B., *Peterburg-Moskva, iz istorii Oktiabr'skoi Zheleznoi Dorogi* (Leningrad, 1934).

Virginskii, V. S., "Bor'ba vokrug podgotovki k stroitel'stvu pervoi bol'shoi russkoi zh-d. magistrali Peterburg-Moskva," *Istoricheskie zapiski*, vol. 32 (1950), 67-96.

—————, *Russkie izobretatelei Cherapanovy—sozdateli pervoi paravoi rel'sovoi dorogi v Rossii* (Moscow, 1953).

—————, *Tvortsy novoi tekhniki v krepostnoi Rossii* (2nd edition, Moscow, 1962).

—————, *Vozniknovennye zheleznykh dorog v Rossii do nachala 40-kh godov XIX veka* (Moscow, 1949).

Vladimirskii-Budanov, M. F., *Istoriia Imperatorskago Universiteta Sv. Vladimira* (Kiev, 1884), vol. I.

Vobly, K. G., *Opyt istorii sveklo-sakharnoi promyshlennosti SSSR* (Moscow, 1928), vol. I.

Voprosy genezisa kapitalizma v Rossii (Leningrad, 1960).

Voprosy istorii narodnogo khoziaistva SSSR (Moscow, 1957).

Voronov, A. A., *Istoriia Tekhnologicheskogo Instituta 1828-1917* (Leningrad, 1928).

Vose, George L., *A Sketch of the Life and Works of George W. Whistler* (Boston, 1887).

Vsepoddanneishii otchet po vedomstvu putei soobshcheniia za 25 let c 19 fevralia 1855 do 19 fevralia 1880 goda (St. Petersburg, 1880).

Vucinich, A., *Science in Russian Culture* (Stanford, 1963).

Vvedenskii, A. A., *Dom Stroganovykh v XVI-XVII vekakh* (Moscow, 1962).

Weber, Max, *The City* (Free Press: Glencoe, Illinois, 1958).

Zablotskii-Desiatovskii, A. P., *Graf P. D. Kiselev i ego vremia* (St. Petersburg, 1882), 4 vols.

Bibliography

Zakolpskii, N., *Graf N. S. Mordvinov, ego vzgliady na sovremennye emu ekonomicheskie zadachi russkoi zhizn* (Viazinki, 1910).

Zaleskii, V., "K stoletiiu Imperatorskago Kazan'skago Universiteta (1804-1904): period goneniia na nauku (1819-1826)," *Zhurnal ministerstva narodnago prosveshcheniia*, vol. 350 (1903), 41-130.

Zaozerskaia, E. I., *Manufaktura pri Petre I* (Moscow-Leningrad).

———, *Razvitie legkoi promyshlennosti v Moskve v pervoi chetverti XVIII v.* (Moscow, 1953).

Zelnik, Reginald, "An Early Case of Labor Protest in St. Petersburg: the Aleksandrovsk Machine Works in 1860." *Slavic Review*, vol. XXIV (1965), 507-20.

Zenkovsky, S. S., "The Ideological World of the Denisov Brothers," *Harvard Slavic Studies*, vol. III (1957), 49-66.

Zhitkov, S. M., *Institut Inzhenerov Putei Soobshcheniia Imperatora Aleksandra I, istoricheskii ocherk* (St. Petersburg, 1899).

Ziablovskii, E., *Statisticheskoe opisanie Rossiiskoi imperii v nyneshnem eie sostoianii* (St. Petersburg, 1808).

Zlotnikov, M. F., *Kontinental'naia blokada i Rossiia* (Moscow-Leningrad, 1966).

———, "Ot manufaktury k fabrike," *Voprosy istorii* (1946), nos. 11-12, 31-48.

Zvorikine, A. A., "Remarques sur l'histoire des inventions et de la pensée scientifique et technique russes des XVIIIe et XIXe siècles," *Contributions à l'histoire russe, cahiers d'histoire mondiale*, special issue (1958), 183-211.

Index

Abaza, A. A., railroad promoter, St. Petersburg-Moscow railroad, 279-80, 282

Abel, Rudolph, industrialist, 18

Academy of Sciences, 35, 254, 337, 346, 361, 365, 371, 379, 407; electrical inventions and experiments, early 19th century, 347, 396, 398-400; founding, 30, 31; technology, 18th century, 32; technology and reform of 1804, 332

Admiralty College, 351

Afonin, Matvei, technologist, 32

Agricultural Gazette, 367

Agricultural Society of South Eastern Russia, 346

Agricultural Society of South Russia, 346

Akkerman School of Horticulture, 382

Aksakov, Ivan, *Izsledovanie o torgovle na ukrainskikh iarmarkakh*, 75n; on Jewish merchants of the Ukraine, 232; on Karaites sect, 76n; on Russian industry and trade, 147

Alaska, 135

Aleksandrovsk state cotton spinning factory, 46, 47, 114, 117, 251n, 345, 387; labor force, 108, 166n; machinery and inventions, 63, 396

Aleksandrovsk state locomotive works, 63, 115, 251, 279, 303, 305, 313; administration and inspection, 310; bureaucratic corruption, 309; cholera epidemic, 309; early development, 304; facilities and organization, 307; financing of operations, 306; labor force, 306; production, 1840's, 311; police, 307; today, 311; transfer to American management, 304; wages and working conditions, 308-309

Alekseev factory, 222

Alekseev family, industrialists, 210

Alexander I, 32, 90-91, 108, 115, 118, 122, 123, 125, 126-27, 132, 138, 149, 150, 151, 152, 156, 157, 164, 170, 181, 182, 187, 191, 199, 212, 214, 232, 233, 238, 241, 246, 258, 262, 328, 329, 330, 334, 335, 346, 365, 374, 376, 379, 396, 407; economic views, 127n, 172; educational reforms, 332-33; military technical schools, 383; and Old Believers, 216; political considerations, 172; river transport, 268; tariff policy, 172; on Russian industrialization, 127n

Alexander II, 187n, 284, 310, 379, 408; and committee to plan St. Petersburg-Warsaw railroad, 320; and Railroad Committee for St. Petersburg-Moscow railroad, 283; Rector of Helsinki University, 353

Amsterdam, 243, 256

aniline, 370

Anosov, P. P., technologist, 390, 398

aptekarskii prikaz, 29

Arakcheev, Aleksei, 269, 284

Archangel, 254, 267

Architecture School, 381

armaments industry, weapons and gunpowder, 17th century, 12

Armenians, 228, 228n, 229

Arolsen, 255

Arsenev, K. I., economist, 145

Arshenevskii, Senator, official, report on Russian industry, 1811, 153

Artillery Journal, 351

artisan guilds, founding, 106; legislation, 106; members, 1858, 106; organization, 107

assignat ruble, see currency

Astrakhan, cotton weaving industry, 46

Augustus Canal, 267

Austria, 172, 186, 232, 271, 276, 317, 392; organization of mines copied by Russia, 159

Awkwright, Richard, English industrialist, 241

Babst, E. F., economist, on Russian industrialization, 145-46, 147

Baburin factory, 118

Baird, Charles, Scottish machinist, 251; education, 252; factories in Russia, 62, 252; founds St. Petersburg's first machine factories, 114; steamship line, 252

Baird, Francis, industrialist, 253

Bakrushin family, merchants, 195, 197

Baku, 66; oil deposits, 62

Baldwin, foreign entrepreneur, 18

Baltic provinces, 5, 23, 68-69, 73, 89, 98, 230, 254, 353

Baltic Sea, 267, 275, 320

Baltimore, 281, 305

Baltimore and Ohio Railroad, 289, 305

Balugiansky, economist, 145

banks and banking, Berdichev banks, 90, 233; central state bank, 259-60; discount offices, 89; European bankers, 243-44; foreign loans to government 1769-1862, 243; Jews of

at, 89; development, 17th century, 12; increasing role of Russian industrial goods in trade, 74; market for European and American goods, 74; market for Urals iron, 57; outstripped by Moscow markets, 74. *See also* fairs

Nizhnii-Tagil factory, capital and plant, 1850's, 59-60; number of workers, early 19th century, 59, 108; production, 1850's, 59

Nobel family, industrialists, 249, 249n, 312; machine works, 115

Nobel, Alfred, 249; instruction in chemistry and explosives in St. Petersburg, 370

Nobel, Immanuel, 249

nobility, Iusopov budget, 101, 203-204; industrial investments of, 201; Kurakin budget, 203; poverty and debts incurred, 202; Sheremetev budget, 202-203

non-Euclidian geometry, 373

"non-postal" road, 80

Norov, A. S., official, 330, 340; and technical education, 339

Northeastern Insurance Company, 95n

Northern Ant (periodical), 351

Northern Post, 176, 350

notes of credit, *see* currency

Notes for Agricultural, Plant, and Factory Managers (periodical), 348

Notes of the Scientific Committee of the Naval Staff (periodical), 351

Novgorod, 11, 318

Novgorod province, 265

Novosiltsev, N. N., official, 330

"obligated" factories, 164, 165; at Kazan, 166-67

Obraztsov Institute of Engineers of Railroad Transportation, *see* Institute of Engineers of Ways of Communication

Obukhov, P. M., engineer, 398

October Car Repair Plant, *see* Aleksandrovsk State Locomotive Works

Odessa, 59, 95, 98, 129, 235, 255, 257, 271, 273, 275, 317, 320, 338; exchanges, 77; growth of port and city, 84-85; growth of wheat trade, 85; population growth 1797-1863, 97

Odessa Educational District, 340

Odoevskii, Prince V. F., on railroads, 270; on Russia and China in the fifth millennium, 401; on Russian

industrialization, 146; *The Year 4338*, 270

Office of Public Charity, Irkutsk woolens factory, 166

Ogarev factory, 115

Oginski Canal, 267

oil industry, 62

Oktensk munitions plant, 386

Old Believers, 90, 193, 233, 239, 407; capital accumulation, 216-18, 228-29; entrepreneurship and other religious minorities, 227-28; Haxthausen on, 221, 223; industrial enterprises in Moscow, 40, 212; and labor force, 229; Moscow communities and industry, 216-18; Moscow worsteds factory, 49; numbers by 1850, 212n, 213; Priestist sect, 212-13, 221; Priestless sect, 212, 215; proletarianization of serfs in Moscow province, 108; puritanism of, 215; recruitment of Moscow factory labor, 219-20; secularization of, 223-24; Shore Dweller sect, 214, 215, 222, 223, 226, 229; Theodosian sect, 216-18, 219, 220, 221, 222, 223, 224, 225, 229; and Vyg commune, 215; at Ukrainian fairs, 76

Old Ritualists, *see* Old Believers

Oldenburg, Prince George Paul, canals, 266

Oliphant, L., on strategic value of Russian railroads, 317

Omsk, 383

Oranienbaum, 259

Orenburg, 99

Orenburg province, 58, 163, 177, 383; gold fields, 61; industries, 1800-1853, 157

Orlov family, urban serf entrepreneurs, 209, 210

"original accumulation of capital," application to Russia, 404-405; Marx on, 404-405; and Russia, 14; Soviet historians on, 404. *See also* "preconditions for take off," preparatory period for rapid economic development

Osokin family, industrialists, Kazan woolens factory, 166-67

Ostashkov, 79, 81

Ostrogradsky, M., scientist, 347, 354, 379, 384, 385

Ostrovsky, Alexander, on mid-19th century Russian middle class, 190

Otis, American engineer, first steam shovels used in Russia, 292

otkupshchiki, and liquor industry, 56

Panaev, Valerian, engineer, 291, 294,

Index

Valuev, P. A., official, 187n
Vasilev, Theodosii, 215
Vasilevskii Island, St. Petersburg, 106; and Germans, 253
Velikin, B., Soviet historian, 300
Vereba River bridge, 292, 315
Vernadsky, I. V., economist, on Russian industrialization, 145, 147
Vienna, Polytechnical Institute, 357; University, 357
Vilna, 232, 383; "real" classes, 338, 339; Seminary, 367
Vistula River, 267
Vitebsk province, 234, 298
Vladimir province, 10, 44, 67-68, 116, 189, 209; cotton weaving industry, 46
Volga, river steamship, 268
Volga River, 266, 267, 268, 272, 275, 288, 291, 292, 320, 322; steamships, 268-69
Volhynia province, 231; Jewish woolens industry, 233
Volta, A., Italian scientist, 399
Von Derviz, railroad financier, 260, 321
Von Humboldt, W., German scientist, 352; on Nizhnii-Tagil factory, 108n
Von Liebig laboratory, Russian train at, 369
Von Meck, railroad financier, 321
Von Rosenbusch, industrialist, 18
Vorontsov, Count N. S., official, 126
Vorsina, 209
Voskresenskii, A. A., scientist, 367, 370; application of chemistry to industry and agriculture, 369-70
Voskresenskii monastery, 17th century industries of, 13
Voznesensk, *see* Ivanovo
Vronchenko, F. P., official, 142n, 175, 235
Vyg commune, commercial and industrial activities of, 215
Vyshnegradskii, Ivan A., official, 155, 178
Vyshnevolotsk Canal, 28, 31, 267
Vyshnii Volochok, 314, 318

wage labor in industry, 12, 15, 19, 37; cotton industry, 39; estate factories, 200; growth of, early 19th century, 42, 108-109; Guchkov Moscow worsteds factory, 49; iron industry, 1860, 58; and monasteries, 14; Muscovite and Kievan periods, 12; Old Believer recruitment, 219-20, 227; Petrine period, 19; silk industry, 53; Skoptsy, 238; statistics, 1804-1860, 423; wages and condi-

tions of workers, Aleksandrovsk state locomotive works, 308-309; wages, construction workers, St. Petersburg-Moscow railroad, 298-300; in Urals, 158; Volga fisheries, 14; woolens industry, 50-51
war, economic impact of Crimean War, 183-87; and Russian industrialization, 181-87, 410; and Russian state finances, 182-83
Warsaw, 66, 177, 259, 271, 317, 320, 383
Watt, James, 36
Wealth of Nations, publication in Russia, 144. *See also* Adam Smith
Weber, Max, 6, 98; on Russian religious dissenters and capital accumulation, 227-28, 228n
Westernizers, 270; on Russian industrialization, 146-47
Western Railroad of Massachusetts, 289-90
Wheatstone, Charles, English inventor, 400
Whistler, Major George W., American engineer, 8, 285, 287, 292, 293, 297, 298, 304, 309, 310, 311; career in the United States, 289-90; and construction of St. Petersburg-Moscow railroad, 290-92; gauge of St. Petersburg-Moscow railroad, 294; historical evaluation of, 289; on Count Kleinmikhel, 294; on Russian bureaucracy, 294; and Russian government, 285; on Russian transportation development, 291
White Sea, 266, 268
White Sea Company, 129
Wilkins factory, 115, 251
Wilson, General Alexander, Scottish machinist, 47, 246, 251n
Winans family, American engineers, 242, 249, 249n, 251, 306, 307, 309
Winans, Ross, 305
Winans, Thomas, 8, 305
Winans, William, 8, 305, 310, 311, 315; "cigar" boat and gunboats for Russian navy, 312; criticism of his business methods, 314; and St. Petersburg-Moscow railroad, 313
Winter Palace, reconstruction by Kleinmikhel, 284
Witte, Sergei, 155, 178
woolens industry, 39, 40; chemical technology, 50; Department of Manufactures and Domestic Trade, 164-65; dyes, 51; estate factories, 25-26, 51; export, 1850, 48; export to China, 48; growth after 1820, 48; import of fabric from King-